Low-Income Homeownership

Low-Income Homeownership

Examining the Unexamined Goal

Nicolas P. Retsinas
Eric S. Belsky
Editors

Joint Center for Housing Studies
Cambridge, Massachusetts

Brookings Institution Press
Washington, D.C.

ABOUT BROOKINGS

The Brookings Institution is a private nonprofit organization devoted to research, education, and publication on important issues of domestic and foreign policy. Its principal purpose is to bring knowledge to bear on current and emerging policy problems. The Institution maintains a position of neutrality on issues of public policy. Interpretations or conclusions in Brookings publications should be understood to be solely those of the authors.

1775 Massachusetts Avenue, N.W., Washington, D.C. 20036
www.brookings.edu

Library of Congress Cataloging-in-Publication data

Low-income homeownership : examining the unexamined goal / Nicolas P. Retsinas and Eric S. Belsky, editors.
p. cm.
Includes bibliographical references (pp.) and index.
ISBN 0-8157-0614-6 (cloth) — ISBN 0-8157-0613-8 (paper)
1. Home ownership—Social aspects—United States. 2. Low-income housing—United States. 3. Low-income housing—United States—Finance. 4. Homeowners—United States—Economic conditions. I. Retsinas, Nicolas Paul, 1946– II. Belsky, Eric S.
HD7287.82.U6 L68 2002
363.5'0973—dc21 2002008414

9 8 7 6 5 4 3 2 1

The paper used in this publication meets minimum requirements of the American National Standard for Information Sciences—Permanence of Paper for Printed Library Materials: ANSI Z39.48-1992.

Typeset in Adobe Garamond

Composition by Betsy Kulamer
Washington, D.C.

Printed by R. R. Donnelley and Sons
Harrisonburg, Virginia

Contents

Foreword

The United States is essentially a nation of homeowners and people who aspire to be homeowners. Belief in the benefits of homeownership cuts across racial, ethnic, class, and geographic lines. Homeownership builds wealth. Homeownership is a stable investment. Homeownership encourages neighborhood involvement by residents. Homeownership builds up communities. Homeownership creates positive environments for children and families.

Unfortunately, the benefits of homeownership, while widely perceived, have not been universally realized. Homeownership rates have lagged considerably for low-income and minority households. Approximately three-fourths of white, non-Hispanic households own their homes, one and one half times the homeownership rate of African American and Hispanic households. Homeownership rates for suburbs also outpace central cities. In central cities, 52 percent of households own their homes, compared to 75 percent in the suburbs.

In the past decade, however, a prosperous economy and innovative public and private sector policies combined to make homeownership a reality for millions of Americans. Mortgage lending to minority homeowners increased substantially during the 1990s—rising 98 percent for African American homebuyers and 125 percent for Hispanic homebuyers. Lending to low-income households nearly doubled, increasing 94 percent.

These were and are remarkable achievements. They did not happen by accident. The leadership of the federal government was critical on several fronts. In the early 1990s, Congress established new affordable housing goals for the secondary market entities and created the HOME program. In the mid-1990s, the Clinton administration expanded the government's enforcement of the Community Reinvestment Act and Fair Housing Act and extended fair lending efforts. Homeownership counseling and education efforts qualified more and more borrowers for home mortgages.

The private sector responded in kind. Fannie Mae and Freddie Mac rose to the challenge of new federal oversight and created new initiatives to expand homeownership. The private sector created new loan products that allow more flexible lending criteria, qualifying more borrowers for home mortgages. Extended outreach on the part of lenders has not only attracted new categories of borrowers, but has also opened up new urban markets.

Our national appetite for wider homeownership—and more favorable homeownership policies—is far from over. Consider these recent events. In May 2002 the Millennial Housing Commission submitted its report on national housing policy to Congress. The report recommended strong support for new federal initiatives on homeownership, including the homeownership tax credit proposed by the Bush administration. During the same month, the United States Conference of Mayors issued a National Housing Agenda that called for a 50 percent reduction in the difference between white and non-white homeownership rates by the end of the decade. In June 2002 President Bush set a national goal of 5.5 million new minority homeowners by the end of the decade, and Housing and Urban Development Secretary Mel Martinez proposed a "Homebuyer Bill of Rights," designed to reduce the difficulty many borrowers face when applying for a new mortgage or refinancing an existing one.

As the federal government prepares to expand our national commitment to homeownership, it is essential to step back and examine what we really know about the benefits of homeownership for low-income families. What impact does homeownership have on these households? How does homeownership affect communities in which low-income homeowners live? How do these benefits differ by neighborhoods? Do low-income families buying homes in low-income neighborhoods realize the same benefits as other homebuyers? What has been the impact of low-cost lending on low-income families? Have low-income homeowners been placed in precarious financial situations, particularly given the recent downturn in the economy? What are the research gaps?

These and other questions are explored in depth in this compendium. The editors of the book—Nicolas Retsinas and Eric Belsky—are two of the nation's foremost experts on housing and homeownership. They have assembled a formidable team of housing scholars, researchers, and practitioners that has examined the gamut of low-income housing issues.

The conclusions they reach are encouraging and should renew Americans' resolve to promote homeownership among low-income families. Their findings should also provide helpful guidance for owners, lenders, communities, and the government. Our challenge is to apply this knowledge so that homeownership can become a reality for many more Americans.

Bruce Katz
Brookings Center on Urban and Metropolitan Policy

Acknowledgments

This book is the culmination of a daylong symposium devoted to critically evaluating low-income homeownership as a business, public policy, and household wealth-building strategy. The Ford Foundation, Freddie Mac, and the Research Institute for Housing America (RIHA) provided the principal funding for the symposium and this volume. The editors are indebted to these organizations for seeing the value in an objective and rigorous examination of the goal of low-income homeownership.

We are particularly indebted to four extraordinary individuals who gave freely of their considerable intellect and experience to ensure the success of this endeavor. Frank DeGiovanni of the Ford Foundation, Edward Golding of Freddie Mac, Steven Hornburg of RIHA, and Karl E. Case of Wellesley College all deserve special recognition for their wise counsel and active contribution to shaping the research questions addressed by this collection of papers. At the Joint Center for Housing Studies, Pamela Baldwin, Mark Duda, Annette Bourne, Paola Martino, Elizabeth England, and Jackie Hernandez deserve special thanks for their hard work and dedication to the project.

Ann Schnare, formerly of Freddie Mac, Susan Wachter of the Wharton School of Business, and Thomas Stanton, a lawyer based in Washington, D.C., also contributed to the intellectual foundations of this effort when in its formative stages. Their presentations to an interdisciplinary study group at Harvard supported by the Provost's Office helped sharpen our focus. Other members of the study group who helped us develop our ideas and who were unstintingly supportive colleagues include Leland Cott of the Harvard Graduate School of Design, Kent Colton, a Joint Center for Housing Studies fellow, Edward Glaeser of the Faculty of Arts and Sciences, Paul Grogan, a Joint Center for Housing Studies fellow, Duncan Kennedy of the Harvard Law School, Gary Orfield of the Harvard Graduate School of Education, Guy Stuart of the Kennedy School of Government, Edward Robbins and James Stockard of the Harvard Graduate School of Design, and Julie Wilson of the Kennedy School of Government.

The contributors also deserve special praise for their excellent ideas, rigorous analysis, and their indulgence of the editors during the process of honing the chapters. They, along with the following people who commented on the papers at the symposium, have contributed to our collective understanding of the limits and potentials of low-income homeownership: Alan Schlottman of the University of Nevada, Bruce Katz and Karen Brown of the Brookings Institution, David Listokin of Rutgers University, Dwight Robinson of Freddie Mac, Ellen Seidman of the Office of Thrift Supervision, Francine Justa of Neighborhood Housing Services, Glen Canner of the Federal Reserve, Gordon Steinbach of the Mortgage Guarantee Insurance Corporation, Ira Goldstein of the Reinvestment Fund, Ira Jackson of the Kennedy School of Government, James M. Murphy of New England Realty Resources Inc., John Quigley of the University of California–Berkeley, John Taylor of the National Community Reinvestment Coalition, Karen Hill of the American Home Owner Education Counseling Institute, Lynn Browne of the Federal Reserve Bank of Boston, Melvin Oliver of the Ford Foundation, Michael LaCour-Little of CityMortgage Inc., Regina Lowrie of Gateway Funding Diversity, Richard Green of the University of Wisconsin, Richard Godfrey Jr. of the Rhode Island Housing and Finance Corporation, Robert Kucab of the North Carolina Housing Finance Agency, and Stuart Gabriel of the University of Southern California.

Finally, we wish to acknowledge Joan Retsinas and Cynthia Wilson for their enduring support and ever-fresh perspective and interest in our work.

Low-Income Homeownership

1

Examining the Unexamined Goal

NICOLAS P. RETSINAS AND
ERIC S. BELSKY

Anthropologists point out that the notion of ownership is a cultural construct. In some societies, land and buildings constitute community wealth; those societies would find the notion that an individual might "own" a house—and even the notion of "ownership" itself—bizarre.[1]

This construct, though, is embedded in American culture; it is oft equated with the American Dream. From its agrarian roots in medieval England, the concept of landholding as a precondition of liberty has evolved into a yearning for ownership.[2] We have the attendant rituals: the wedding checks amassed toward a down payment, the housewarming parties, the burn-the-mortgage celebrations, the "starter" home, the intense spending to give it bigger bathrooms, gourmet kitchens, more square footage. A few communitarian societies, focused on a utopian ideal, have existed, but in the history of American housing, those enclaves are footnotes. For the most part, Americans have wanted to own their patch of space—whether it is a one-acre lot in exurbia or a one-bedroom condo on a yuppified city block. And homeowning Americans have lavished attention (and money) on those spaces, considering them anchors—psychologically, physically, and economically.

1. One nomadic tribe in Northern Africa describes homes as "graves for the living."

2. In commenting on the Homestead Act of 1860, Proudfit (1924) notes: "The primary conception of the home as the only basis of State and national permanence has been kept intact."

Government has helped, using its bully pulpit to spur homeownership.[3] In 1918 the Department of Labor launched the "Own Your Own Home" campaign. Herbert Hoover, as secretary of commerce, established "Better Homes of America," a program supported by Presidents Warren Harding and Calvin Coolidge.

The government also acted. Some actions were overt: the initial land grants gave people land for homesteading; the Veterans Administration subsidized mortgages for veterans (just as the GI bill subsidized their college educations); fair housing laws attacked race-based exclusionary practices; the 1977 Community Reinvestment Act required banks to look beyond their traditional borrowers, to inner-city residents.

Other actions indirectly bolstered housing, a side effect of programs initiated to spur economic recovery. For instance, the pre–New Deal Federal Home Loan Banks, the New Deal Federal Housing Administration, and its companion, the first National Mortgage Association, aimed to restore liquidity to a Depression-era banking system in collapse. These agencies bolstered the shaky underpinnings of banks, thereby guarding against insolvency but also bolstering their ability to make mortgage loans. Similarly, in 1918 the first income tax allowed a deduction for all loan interest, not just mortgage interest. Tax architects did not foresee its impact on housing. (But in 1986 when Congress expressly retained that deduction while dropping most other deductions, Congress recognized this deduction as a homeownership incentive.)

Today politicians stand firmly behind homeownership, cheering at every incremental boost in the number of homeowning households (now up to a record high 68 percent of households in 2001). Fannie Mae and Freddie Mac, the two secondary mortgage market behemoths that bought or securitized nearly three-fifths of prime conventional conforming mortgages written last year, have a special status as "government-sponsored enterprises" because they undergird the current flux of first-time home buyers. Every state but Arizona has a Housing Finance Agency, authorized to issue bonds using a federal tax exemption to subsidize mortgages for low- and moderate-income first-time buyers. Local communities use their federal block grant moneys to spur homeownership among inner-city residents.

Today supplying credit to home buyers and owners is an enormous industry, with debt outstanding on single-family properties alone at over $5 trillion in 2001, a level that exceeds either corporate or federal government debt. The mortgage finance system has become highly specialized and regulated. Though banks and thrifts still hold some loans they originate in their portfolios, they are more apt to sell their loans into the secondary market and retain only the servicing rights and take origination fees. Increasingly, they lend through mortgage

3. Retsinas (1999).

company affiliates that, together with independent mortgage companies, originate the lion's share of mortgages. Banks and thrifts are under regulatory pressure to lend to low-income borrowers and areas (in the form of the Community Reinvestment Act), and Fannie Mae and Freddie Mac are as well (in the form of goals established annually for them by the Department of Housing and Urban Development).

Homeownership, in short, is valued and promoted by government: it is considered good for the buyers, good for their communities, and good for the country. It is not far behind motherhood and apple pie as an American symbol. At least in the abstract, nobody questions this American icon.[4]

It is time, however, for some iconoclastic scrutiny—time to examine the unexamined goal. With the industry geared up to lend to low-income borrowers in ways the nation has never seen before, the government egging them on, and cultural norms drawing renters into the market, the time is ripe to pause and take stock of what we know and do not know about low-income homeownership. Rhetoric aside, is homeownership truly good for low-income buyers, their communities, and the country? Even if homeownership was a worthy goal two generations ago, have times changed to devalue the notion that individuals should own their homes?

Supported by the Ford Foundation, Freddie Mac, and the Research Institute for Housing America, Harvard's Joint Center for Housing Studies organized the symposium "Low-Income Homeownership as an Asset-Building Strategy." The symposium asked researchers to play the role of iconoclasts, statistically probing the impact of housing on these buyers and their communities. Their findings, published herein, deserve attention. On the one hand, the authors offer reassurance to policymakers: homeownership as a national goal does merit government support. For individuals struggling to save for a down payment, it is worth the effort; for the country struggling to bolster homeownership, it is a worthwhile goal. On the other hand, America at the dawn of this century is a markedly different place from the America of 1960: the "typical" home buyers of today bear only a passing resemblance to their earlier counterparts. The benefits, the constraints, the pitfalls—all have changed within the past few decades. To sustain the current high level of homeownership, and to increase that rate, policymakers will need to reexamine their strategies.

The Home Buyers of Today

The most startling fact about homeownership today lies in the title of the symposium: "Low-Income Homeownership." A generation ago, there were not

4. Interest in the value of homeownership has increased recently; see DiPasquale and Glaeser (1999); Green and White (1997); Rohe and Stewart (1996); Rossi and Weber (1996).

enough low-income home buyers to warrant a study. Consider the typical buyer of the 1920s. Banks required a 50 percent down payment and offered a loan of three to five years. Wealthy people owned their own homes; they could bypass banks. But the nonwealthy homeowners tended to be frugal older couples with moderate-but-not-modest incomes who had saved throughout their working lives. Households with low incomes could rarely save enough for a 50 percent down payment.

The New Deal's banking subsidies lowered banks' risk, letting them lend to more borrowers, for longer periods, with lower down payments. By the 1950s the typical borrower put 20 percent down and got a fixed-rate mortgage for twenty years. That buyer had a moderate income. Still, a 20 percent down payment shut most low-income households out of the market, even in neighborhoods of modest homes. (Race and foreign accents closed the door still tighter.)

Today a buyer can put as little as nothing down, get a variable-rate mortgage, and amortize a loan for as long as thirty years. The secondary mortgage market, buttressed by statistical techniques that assign a "credit score" that correlates well with loan repayment behavior, has let lenders (which now include mortgage companies as well as traditional banks) reach out to people whom the lenders of the 1960s would have shunned. Low-income households are no longer shut out; now families with incomes of $30,000 or less can buy a house. From 1993 to 2000 the number of home-purchase loans to low-income families surged by 79 percent. Mortgage lenders recognize low-income borrowers as a profitable market. Evidence presented in the following chapters shows that, properly insured against losses, low-income loans can be every bit as profitable to lenders as others, especially now that technology has cut mortgage origination costs.

Growing recognition of the capacity to lend profitably to borrowers and in areas once thought too risky has spawned a surging industry of "subprime" lenders. Pushing the envelope even further, these lenders have been marketing mortgages to borrowers with shaky credit histories, borrowers even aggressive "prime" mortgage lenders still turn away. But that too is changing, and conventional mainstream lenders are experimenting with products that grade into the subprime market.

Minorities also are no longer shut out. From 1994 to 2000 loans to black home buyers soared 89 percent, loans to Hispanic buyers rose by 138 percent, but loans to whites grew by only 25 percent. Admittedly, a racial and ethnic gap persists: holding income constant, a higher proportion of whites own homes than do blacks and Hispanics. But most studies attempting to control for both income and wealth differences find that most of the disparities are caused by these differences, which emanate not from housing markets but from education and labor markets.[5] And, as census data demonstrate, the buyer of today may well be a Latin American, Caribbean, or Asian immigrant or a person of color native to the United States.

As for the "traditional" Beaver Cleaver family-owner of the 1960s (two parents with a stay-at-home mother watching over a few children), it no longer predominates. Homeownership rates are up sharply among single-parent families, with female-headed households nearing the 50 percent mark for homeownership in 2001. The homeownership rates of people living alone have also surged: from 50 percent in 1994 to 54 percent in 2001. And among married couples youth is no impediment to homeownership, as 62 percent of those under age 35 now own their home, up from 56 percent in 1994. Whatever the mixture of people that can constitute a "household," chances are high and growing that they will own a home.

Their homes, though, may not be the "traditional" ones: high-rise condos, suburban capes and ranches, or to-be-gentrified townhouses. For many low-income households, an "affordable" house is a "manufactured" one. In the South, 40 percent of low-income buyers bought manufactured housing in the 1990s, often on the periphery of the urban core on tracts of leased land (in the noneuphemistic vernacular, in trailer parks).

Overcoming Borrowing Constraints

Today's good news is that low-income borrowers' access to credit has improved dramatically. A decade ago, lenders did not offer loan terms and underwriting standards that would help low-income borrowers overcome their income and wealth constraints. Mortgages with low down payments were scarce, and few lenders were willing to let borrowers—many already spending well over half their incomes on rent for years on end—qualify for a loan whose payments with taxes and insurance amounted to more than 28 percent of their income. The government through the Federal Housing Administration (FHA) was willing to let them devote more of their income to these payments but did not stretch in

5. Using data from the 1989 American Housing Survey, Wachter and Megbolugbe (1992) found that variation in household (income, age, education, family type, and gender) and market (price and location) "endowment" factors explained 80 percent of the racial and ethnic gap in homeownership rates, with income and marital status being most important. They suggest that the 20 percent of the homeownership gap unexplained by their regression model may be due to discrimination, but caution that other unobserved influences (such as employment and credit histories) might account for some or all of the residual. Many others cite wealth as the key unobserved influence, including Linneman and colleagues (1997), who assess the relative importance of the income and wealth constraints, finding that while each acts to lower the rate of homeownership, wealth has a more pronounced effect. Gyourko, Linneman, and Wachter (1999) find little difference in ownership rates among households that are not wealth-constrained but that minorities are far more likely to be wealth-constrained than whites.

the ways lenders now will under some circumstances. As for low-income borrowers with less-than-stellar credit histories, banks rarely let them even get past the front desk. A strike on their credit history or problems documenting a credit history disqualified them.

Today neither low income nor flawed credit is as insurmountable a barrier to homeownership. One in six borrowers puts down 5 percent or less, and if their credit history is solid and their down payment large enough, lenders are prepared to let them qualify for loans with housing payments closer to 40 percent of monthly income. Increasingly, borrowers with minor to serious past credit problems can qualify for a loan if they are willing to pay higher than a "prime" mortgage interest rate to cover the added risk they pose for lenders. As Stuart Rosenthal points out, credit constraints may delay homeownership for some households and overall may depress ownership rates by 4 percent, but progress in better understanding the risks posed by such borrowers may reduce their depressive effect on homeownership.

Low-income borrowers, though, do face two hurdles. First, the low-income borrower must keep up payments. Each borrower is only a crisis—a pink slip, an illness, a broken car—away from delinquency or default on a loan that will impair his or her credit history and add to the mortgage borrowing costs. After low-income borrowers purchase a home, because they are a population that historically has been at greater risk of job loss, they are more likely to face difficulties staving off default. (Low-income borrowers rarely have wealthy families who can tide them over in a crisis.) Not surprisingly, home buyers with low incomes and poor credit histories fall behind on their payments more often than higher-income borrowers with unblemished credit histories.

As Abdighani Hirad and Peter Zorn point out, though, credit counseling helps. By now credit counseling is standard for many low-income borrowers: a lender gives them a home-study kit, hooks them up to telephone instructions, enrolls them in a class, or gives them one-on-one counseling. Hirad and Zorn, reviewing 40,000 mortgages, conclude that borrowers who receive classroom instruction are 23 percent less likely to be delinquent after fifty days than their noncounseled counterparts. Individual counseling works even better: a remarkable 41 percent were less likely to be delinquent. (Neither telephone counseling nor home study reduced the risk of delinquency.) As awareness of the value of credit counseling spreads, some borrowers who failed to make payments in the past may seem like better risks in the future if they are counseled.

Michael Collins, David Crowe, and Michael Carliner point out that a second hurdle for the low-income borrower is finding an inexpensive house. A family that can borrow enough for a $70,000 home needs to be able to find that $70,000 starter. Some regions of the country—indeed, some neighborhoods—have a surfeit of low-priced homes (though the bargain fixer-uppers may require thousands of dollars of cash, not just sweat equity). In other regions, few houses sell for less than $70,000, a circumstance that explains the popularity of manufactured houses on leased land, which can sell for as little as $25,000.

Profitable Business Proposition

Back in the 1960s and 1970s, lending to low-income borrowers and their communities was shrouded in mystery. Few studies examined how credit was supplied to these people and areas. Suspicion in the 1970s that lenders were "redlining" low-income communities and withholding credit from them under the untested assumption that they represented unmanageable or impossible-to-price risks gave rise to the Community Reinvestment Act (CRA) of 1977 and the Home Mortgage Disclosure Act (HMDA) of 1975.[6] CRA affirmed the obligation of banks and thrifts to lend to low-income communities and authorized federal regulators to deny or condition an application for acquisition or merger if lenders failed to meet that obligation. HMDA began as a trickle of public disclosure of information on mortgage lending that became—especially from the lenders' perspective—a flood by the early 1990s.

Slowly at first, lenders under community pressure began to step up lending in low-income areas and to experiment with more lenient underwriting standards. By the 1990s the advent of powerful new risk assessment tools and technologies converged with stepped-up regulation and enforcement of community lending laws, as well as sometimes withering media attention on fair lending, to drive low-income mortgage lending to new heights. Aided by a strong economy and automated underwriting tools, mortgage lenders were emboldened to reach out to low-income, minority, and immigrant markets in new ways.

All the while, many lenders complained that reaching out to low-income borrowers resulted in higher origination costs and higher credit losses that eroded the profitability of loans to low-income borrowers. Thus many have assumed that low-income lending is less profitable than loaning money to higher-income buyers. But investors in mortgages incur more than just credit risk: the risk that borrowers will not make their payments and that some fraction of them will ultimately default on their loans. They also incur risk that borrowers will pay off their mortgages ahead of when originally scheduled or estimated by "prepayment" models and that investors will get stuck with their cash in a lower-interest-rate environment than when they first invested. These prepayments therefore have a cost to the investor: lower returns on their invested capital. For those who service loans, prepayments can mean a complete cessation of the income stream on the loan.

According to Wayne Archer, David Ling, and Gary McGill, because low-income borrowers are more likely to have greater income constraints and are

6. See Litan and others (2000).

more likely to take out loans with small initial down payments, they are less likely than others to refinance when interest rates fall enough to make it profitable for them to do so. And although low-income loans do indeed tend to carry greater credit costs, Robert Van Order and Peter Zorn find that they tend to carry far smaller prepayment-related costs. Moreover, though the evidence available is only suggestive and limited to a sample of loans purchased in the 1990s by Freddie Mac, it does indicate that the prepayment savings associated with low-income lending may more than offset the higher credit costs. Hence the presumption that low-income loans need be less profitable demands rethinking. Indeed, as long as fewer low-income borrowers prepay, and given the prospect for lowering credit losses through better home-buyer counseling and reducing the fixed costs of mortgage origination and servicing, many forms of low-income mortgage lending could prove to be as profitable as other loans, if not more so.

Families' Financial Capital

Behind the homeownership-is-good mantra is an unexamined premise: that homeownership is an asset-building strategy for low-income buyers.

Low-income buyers typically do not hold stock portfolios. They are not likely to hold bonds. Few have 401K nest eggs, Roth IRAs, or trust funds. Often they have no pensions. Instead, they plough whatever savings they have into buying a home and, postpurchase, plough much of the money they might have saved and invested back into their homes to keep them in good repair. And most do not benefit from the deduction of mortgage interest payments and real estate taxes that makes homeownership such an attractive financial choice for wealthier home buyers. The mortgages and property taxes of low-income owners are often too small to make it pay to itemize their deductions, so they forgo itemizing them in favor of taking the standard deduction.

So the question of the financial merits of homeownership is a salient one. Do low-income buyers build housing wealth? The answer is encouraging: yes, in most cases. Although housing prices do fluctuate—leaving some regions of the country at some periods of time with housing that has lost value (such as the Southwest in the late 1980s)—most lower-income owners have benefited from house price appreciation and fared *better* than those who purchased higher-cost homes. Looking at owners of low-cost homes in four metropolitan areas, for example, Eric Belsky and Mark Duda found that between 70 and 78 percent of those who sold within just two and a half years sold them for more than their purchase price (after adjusting for inflation and transaction costs). Still, though, relatively little is known about the financial performance of low-income homeowners, and much more needs to be done to assess the chances that they will come out ahead of renting, even over short holding periods.

Also, homeownership constitutes enforced savings and, if accompanied by a fixed-rate mortgage, fixes the largest component of housing costs: capital costs. Academicians' models may posit "alternative" investment scenarios for renters that make investing in other ways look better than renting. Indeed, William Goetzmann and Mark Spiegel find that housing has a lower historical return than stocks and bonds and an even poorer risk-adjusted return, making it a more sensible investment only if it is part of a diversified portfolio. But in the world beyond the models, given today's high rents, the low-income renter is hard-pressed to save and may see a host of financial benefits in owning. The promise of fixing housing costs so that they do not rise with inflation may alone be sufficient to justify the risks. Insulation from the corroding effects of housing inflation is a powerful incentive to buy, especially among low-income families who do not intend to move and have long successfully found ways to pay the rent even in the face of adversity. And low-income borrowers are able to risk relatively little money on a home now in pursuit of potentially high leveraged returns later because down payment requirements have been loosened, but this option is not available to low-income people investing in financial instruments. Furthermore, there is a potent sense that paying rent does nothing to build equity, while paying off a mortgage does.

Families' Social Capital

Aside from financial gains, the advocates of homeownership for low-income families firmly believe that homeownership will improve families' functioning and childhood outcomes, another largely unexamined premise. Does buying a home make a family more stable, the children more successful in school, the family happier? Advocates assume yes, but that answer is more a matter of faith than of demonstrable statistical proof.

For researchers, this is murkier terrain than calculating gains in assets. After all, a family that owns a home may be, by virtue of owning the home, less mobile and hence more "stable." But is that stability desirable? Would a renter-family, able to move quickly, be able to find better jobs or better schools? Assuming that stability is good, do owner-families stay rooted in their communities longer because their desire for stability prompted them to buy homes in the first place? That same self-selection conundrum haunts research on children's success: Donald R. Haurin, Toby L. Parcel, and R. Jean Haurin find that children in owner-occupied homes do better in school. But perhaps those children's parents were more concerned about their children's progress in school, a concern that prompted them to buy homes in places with better schools and safer neighborhoods. Though researchers have tried to control for neighborhood effects, these controls have mostly been weak and aimed at levels of geography much broader than a neighborhood or the service area of an elementary school.

As for families' overall well-being or happiness, researchers would have to define happiness, holding constant expectations, social mores, and individual definitions; the terrain grows murkier. And researchers would have to consider the threat of foreclosure that haunts many low-income families. William M. Rohe, Shannon van Zandt, and George McCarthy find that there is some evidence to suggest that homeownership affords people a greater sense of control over their lives, spurs them to greater civic participation, and helps their children do better in school, but also that delinquencies and defaults can have the opposite effect.

Nevertheless, the research offers a tentative yes to the question of whether families benefit from owning a home. Apart from statistical validation, moreover, the fact that children who grow up in owner-occupied homes tend to buy homes more often than their counterparts who grew up in renter-occupied homes argues that the psychic benefits of homeownership, however hard to define, do lead successive generations to aspire toward it.

Community Capital

Mayors and city councils see homeownership as a fulcrum. It is not too much of an exaggeration to say that many of them believe that as homeownership rates in low-income neighborhoods creep up, crime rates, juvenile delinquency, vandalism, vacant properties, truancy, and even litter will plummet. Indeed, they look to homeownership to increase property values, school attendance, reading scores, even voter participation. In short, they have faith that homeownership will resurrect neighborhoods in decline. So local politicos trust.

In fact, there are few studies that look at the positive externalities of homeownership and its potential role in neighborhood revitalization. One study in this volume provides limited support for their trust. In their seminal study on the impact of homeownership on property values in New York City, Ingrid Ellen, Scott Susin, Amy Schwartz, and Michael Schill show a demonstrable positive impact. But homeownership is no panacea for neighborhood decline. It does not automatically remove other impediments to regeneration such as poor schools, crime, and a deteriorated housing stock. As a cornerstone of redevelopment efforts, renovation and rehabilitation of housing, combined with promotion of homeownership, can be a potent force.

Once again, though, the self-selection of home buyers stymies ironclad conclusions about less-quantifiable variables. If neighborhoods of low-income owners show higher indices of "good" traits and lower indices of "bad" traits, is part of the explanation the differing motivations of renters and owners? Consider front yard gardens. Homeowners, particularly new ones, plant them more often than renters. Those of us who have gone from renting to owning can attest to a change in our perception of space: the "ownership" fosters a mix of care-taking, pride, and responsibility. Hence, in a rite of spring, many of us plunk straggly perennials into the dirt. Renters rarely do this, especially if they won't be there long enough to see them come back the next year. Yet does that desire to plant a garden spur some renters to contemplate buying? Or does ownership itself foster the desire?

Whichever comes first, local officials push for homeownership, not because a study has convinced them of its merits but because they have seen enough benefits up close to believe in a redemptive power to low-income homeownership.

The End of the Socratic Exercise

Americans want to own homes. The anthropologist who studies us in the future may wonder whether, like Robertson Davies's protagonist in *What's Bred in the Bone*, our yen to claim space and buildings is "bred in the bone," whether we have an almost genetic yearning, borne from centuries of ancestral serfdom, to claim and fence and demarcate our dwellings, physically and legally, from others.

Lower-income Americans share the same yearning as upper-income families. Their home may be a triple-decker tenement, a condo, or a "manufactured" side-by-side. Indeed, for some immigrant families, the promise of America is freedom, jobs, and the chance to own a house. Is this yearning rational? Is the lower-income household that scrimps for a house better off than a renting household? Is the family? Is the neighborhood? Researchers at the symposium that resulted in this volume, after the caveats and the codicils, concluded that the answer is yes.

So the confluence of actors behind the current surge of low-income homeowners—the mortgage industry, the government, the city and town councils—should persevere. At this writing in 2001, only 52 percent of low-income households own their own homes, while 82 percent of upper-income households do. We can, and should, aim higher.

References

Archer, W., D. Ling, and G. McGill. 2001. "Prepayment Risk and Lower-Income Mortgages." Working Paper LIHO.01-9. Joint Center for Housing Studies, Harvard University.

Belsky, E. S., and M. Duda. 2001. "Asset Appreciation, Timing of Purchase and Sales, and Return to Low-Income Homeownership." Working Paper LIHO.01-6. Joint Center for Housing Studies, Harvard University.

DiPasquale, D., and E. Glaeser. 1999. "Incentives and Social Capital: Are Homeowners Better Citizens? *Journal of Urban Economics* 45: 354–84.

Ellen, I., M. Schill, S. Susin, and A. E. Schwartz. 2001. "Do Homeownership Programs Increase Property Values in Low-Income Neighborhoods?" Working Paper LIHO.01-13. Joint Center for Housing Studies, Harvard University.

Goetzmann, W. and M. Spiegel. 2001. "The Policy Implications of Portfolio Choice in Underserved Mortgage Markets." Working Paper LIHO.01-8. Joint Center for Housing Studies, Harvard University.

Green, R. K., and M. J. White. 1997. "Measuring the Benefits of Homeowning: Effects on Children." *Journal of Urban Economics* 41 (3): 441–61.

Gyourko, J., P. Linneman, and S. Wachter. 1999. "Analyzing the Relationship among Race, Wealth, and Home Ownership in America." *Journal of Housing Economics* 8: 63–89.

Haurin, D., R. J. Haurin, and T. Parcel. 2001. "The Impact of Homeownership on Child Outcomes." Working Paper LIHO.01-14. Joint Center for Housing Studies, Harvard University.

Hirad, A., and P. Zorn. 2001. "A Little Knowledge Is a Good Thing: Empirical Evidence of the Effectiveness of Pre-Purchase Homeownership Counseling." Working Paper LIHO.01-4. Joint Center for Housing Studies, Harvard University.

Linneman, P., I. F. Megbolugbe, S. M. Wachter, and M. Cho. 1997. "Do Borrowing Constraints Change U.S. Homeownership Rates?" *Journal of Housing Economics* 6: 318–33.

Litan, R., N. P. Retsinas, E. S. Belsky, and S. White Haag. 2000. "The Community Reinvestment Act after Financial Modernization: A Baseline Report." U.S. Department of the Treasury (April).

Proudfit, S. V. 1924. *Public Land System of the United States*. Government Printing Office.

Retsinas, Nicolas P. 1999. "Beyond the Bully Pulpit." *Harvard Design Magazine* (Summer).

Rohe, W. M., and L. S. Stewart. 1996. "Homeownership and Neighborhood Stability." *Housing Policy Debate* 7 (1): 37–82.

Rohe, W., G. McCarthy, and S. Van Zandt. 2001. "The Social Benefits and Costs of Homeownership." Working Paper LIHO.01-12. Joint Center for Housing Studies, Harvard University.

Rosenthal, S. 2001. "Eliminating Credit Barriers to Increase Homeownership: How Far Can We Go?" Working Paper LIHO.01-3. Joint Center for Housing Studies, Harvard University.

Rossi, P. H., and E. Weber. 1996. "The Social Benefits of Homeownership: Empirical Evidence from National Surveys." *Housing Policy Debate* 7 (1): 1–35.

Van Order, R. and P. Zorn. 2001. "Performance of Low-Income and Minority Mortgages." Working Paper LIHO.01-10. Joint Center for Housing Studies, Harvard University.

Wachter, S. M., and I. F. Megbolugbe. 1992. "Racial and Ethnic Disparities in Homeownership." *Housing Policy Debate* 3 (2): 333–70.

PART 1

Homeownership in the 1990s

2

Anatomy of the Low-Income Homeownership Boom in the 1990s

ERIC S. BELSKY AND MARK DUDA

Despite an unprecedented boom in homeownership that added 7 million net owners between 1994 and 1999 and drove the homeownership rate nearly 3 percentage points higher, to 66.8 percent, relatively little is known about where people have been buying homes and the types of homes they have been buying. Analysis of the 1990s boom has focused principally on describing who is buying—by income, racial, ethnic, and family characteristics—not on where and what homes they are buying (Bostic and Surette, 2000; Wachter, 1999; Masnick, 1998).

The concentration of the growth in homeowners among minorities has been especially striking. Though in 1993 minority households accounted for only 15 percent of owners, over the next five years they accounted for 41 percent of net growth in owners.

Although the number of low-income (those earning less than 80 percent of the area median income) non-Hispanic white owners actually declined by 225,000 over the period, the number of low-income minority owners rose by more than 800,000 and accounted for nearly 11 percent of the net growth in owners. This shift in the racial and ethnic composition of low-income homeowners reflects the faster household growth of minorities through immigration and the younger age distribution of minorities. Fewer low-income non-Hispanic whites became owners than were lost through shifts of tenure, changes in income, and death and institutionalization of elderly owners. Minorities accounted for a growing share of first-time buyers, as a larger proportion of a faster-growing population reached their first-time buying years. Indeed, minority first-time buyers as a share of all first-time buyers rose from 19.1 percent in 1993 to 30 percent in 1999.

As a consequence, homeownership rates of low-income and minority households have been rising more rapidly than for others. The share of mortgage loans made to both low-income and minority households also surged between 1993 and 1999. While the number of loans to high-income buyers (those earning 120 percent or more of the area median income) grew by 52 percent, loans to low-income home buyers surged by 94 percent. Growth in loans to white home buyers was a more modest 42 percent; much more dramatic was the 98 percent growth in loans to black buyers and the 125 percent growth in loans to Hispanic buyers.

Interest is mounting in understanding where low-income home buyers have been purchasing, as businesses strive to serve these buyers and policymakers consider the social and economic implications of the recent surge in low-income homeownership. The social and economic implications of their tenure choices are significant because owners tend to remain longer in the same home and therefore make a longer-term commitment to an area. Indeed, although half of renters move in three years or less, half of owners stay in their homes for ten years or more.[1] In addition, investment in homes can result in significant returns to owners, significant lost opportunities to invest funds in other assets, or outright losses of principal and credit reputation.

The spatial pattern of home purchases by low-income buyers is important because it determines their access to education and other public goods as well as to jobs and social networks. Access to education, jobs, and social capital is, in turn, key to economic and social mobility (Temkin and Rohe, 1998; DiPasquale and Glaeser, 1999), and evidence suggests that the children of homeowners do better on a variety of achievement indicators (Boehm and Gordon, 1999; Green and White, 1997). Location is also important because house price appreciation varies spatially and therefore plays a central role in determining the financial returns to homeownership (Goetzmann and Spiegel, 1997; Case and Mayer, 1995; Case and Marynchenko in this volume; Smith and Ho, 1996; Li and Rosenblatt, 1997).

As a result, some scholars have questioned whether moves by low-income and minority home buyers herald an improvement in their opportunity set—a move up as well as out (Stuart, 2000). Answering this question requires detailed information about the locations to which low-income and minority buyers are

1. More than 50 percent of renters and owners had been in their homes for three and ten years, respectively, according to both the 1999 and 1997 American Housing Survey (AHS) (variable = MOVED).

moving. To date, however, few studies have examined the spatial patterns of home purchases. In an effort to find gentrifying and mixed-income neighborhoods, Wyly and Hammell (1999) examined these patterns to identify central city neighborhoods that have attracted a significant share of high-income home buyers. The Joint Center for Housing Studies (2000) found that few high-income buyers have been purchasing homes in low-income neighborhoods in central cities but that large shares of minority and low-income buyers have been purchasing homes in suburbs—including middle- and higher-income suburbs. Detailed research in Boston indicates that the relocation of low-income and minority buyers to suburbs is not necessarily associated with reduced segregation. In fact, Stuart (2000) found that the suburbanization of minorities has been largely concentrated in just a handful of communities. Similarly, in Chicago, Immergluck (1998) found that almost half of all black buyers over the 1995–96 period purchased homes in predominantly minority census tracts, though just 27 percent had done so five years earlier. Several papers by Frey and colleagues examine settlement patterns by race and income for all households, not just owners; Frey and Farley (1996) report that segregation decreased for blacks, though it remains high, and increased for Hispanics and Asians over the decade of the 1980s (see also Frey and Geverdt, 1998; Frey and Speare, 1995).

Still, many questions remain unanswered. At a descriptive level, the following are the most fundamental. Where are low-income mortgage borrowers purchasing homes? How does this differ from the places where those with higher incomes are purchasing? Do these patterns vary by race and ethnicity? And to what extent do these patterns vary among metropolitan areas with different economic, social, and demographic characteristics and different patterns of access to credit? Once these questions are answered, more fundamental policy issues can also be addressed, such as the returns these buyers reap in improved access to education and other opportunities for themselves and their children.

In this chapter, we examine the where and what of the low-income homeownership boom. We also provide insight into variations in the patterns of low-income home buying in metropolitan areas by examining nine metropolitan areas that differ in size, racial and ethnic composition, the size of their central cities, regional location, and economic condition. Although many of our results are presented in terms of the standard geographic distinction between central city and suburb, our analysis of these nine areas also examines differences in the distance from the city center that low-income movers are settling when they buy homes. Because of variations in the political geography of metropolitan areas, the suburbs of large cities may begin within a mile of the central business district (in Boston, for example) or tens of miles outside (as in Phoenix and San Antonio). Consequently, more distant places that attract buyers may fall within central cities in some metropolitan statistical areas (MSAs) but be suburban in others, even though their absolute distance from the central business district

(CBD) may be equal. Put another way, the terms "city" and "suburb" do not sufficiently identify a location's distance from the CBD.

Constraints, Patterns, and Progress in Low-Income and Minority Homeownership

Much of the research relevant to the present study has been concerned with identifying the problems encountered by low-income/low-wealth buyers attempting to become homeowners and with specifying solutions to help them overcome the hurdles blocking their path to this goal. A related research stream attempts to discern if, and to what extent, minority groups face barriers to homeownership over and above the income and wealth constraints facing buyers of all racial and ethnic backgrounds. Several other studies have examined the racial and ethnic composition of the growth in homeowners and what happens when low-income and minority buyers do manage to become homeowners by describing the spatial distribution of buyers within MSA housing markets by income and race.

Constraints Faced by Low-Income/Low-Wealth Buyers and Efforts to Overcome Them

One vein of homeownership research examines the constraints on achieving homeownership posed by low incomes and wealth. Linneman and his colleagues (1997) explain that mortgage underwriting criteria present two potential borrowing constraints for low-income home buyers, both of which arise because lenders ration credit rather than price for risk. The wealth constraint results from the buyers' need to amass down payment capital and funds to cover other up-front costs necessary to initiate the transaction. Engelhardt and Mayer (1998) emphasize the centrality of wealth in home buying, showing that recipients of intergenerational wealth transfers spend less time saving for a down payment, put down a larger share of a home's value, and buy larger homes than nonrecipients. The income constraint results from maximum allowable total debt-to-income and housing debt-to-income ratios employed in mortgage underwriting. Simulations run by Linneman and colleagues indicate that relaxing both constraints could increase the homeownership rate by 3 percentage points.[2] Among others, Engelhardt (1994), Engelhardt and Mayer (1998), and

2. Linneman and colleagues raised average loan-to-value ratio from 80 to 95 percent and debt-to-income ratio from .28 to .33 simultaneously. The magnitude of the 3 percentage point boost to homeownership is underscored by the study's revelation that the homeownership rate responds with only a 1.2 percentage point drop as a result of increasing the mortgage interest rate from 7 to 13 percent.

Haurin, Hendershott, and Wachter (1996) have also stressed the importance of wealth in the decision to own a home.

Linneman and Wachter (1989) and Linneman and colleagues (1997) assess the relative importance of the two borrowing constraints and find that although each constraint acts to lower the rate of homeownership, wealth has a more pronounced effect. A comparison of results from the earlier and later studies indicates that the effect of the income constraint has weakened over time, a fact the authors attribute to the increased use of adjustable-rate mortgages (ARMs) during the 1980s, which lower monthly payments, and hence debt-to-income ratios, by reducing interest rates. The large shares of borrowers using high loan-to-value (LTV) products has likely had a similar impact on the wealth constraint over the 1990s. In either case, however, borrowers and lenders must trade one constraint off against the other, and trade off interest rate and collateral risk. Making a smaller down payment increases the monthly payment and hence the level of income necessary to qualify for a loan while increasing collateral risk for lenders. Borrowers who choose an adjustable rate loan in order to lower their monthly carrying cost increase their vulnerability to interest rate movements and raise their risk of default if rates rise higher than they can afford.

The two borrowing constraints are often viewed as policy targets. Galster, Aron, and Reeder (1999) point out that the goal of HUD's regulation of Freddie Mac and Fannie Mae (government-sponsored enterprises, or GSEs) to make loans available to underserved markets implies that today's pool of renters harbors a large subset of would-be owners, a finding supported by surveys in which two-thirds of renters indicate that they intend to buy a home. The authors compare a renter pool with owners and find on the basis of their sample that roughly 5 million renter households are at least as predisposed to homeownership as the average owner and that half of these households have low to moderate incomes. Further, these same households pose little additional default risk to lenders when compared with existing owners. In order to make homeownership available to these renters, the authors advocate targeting them in outreach efforts, encouraging primary lending to low-income and minority borrowers, enhancing civil rights enforcement, and making more low-cost housing available through urban revitalization.

Eggers and Burke (1996) attempt to gauge the potential impact of different policy interventions by examining the effect of reducing barriers to homeownership. They assume that high-income whites—those earning in excess of $80,000 annually—are fully able to exercise their tenure preferences and calculate the impact, in additional owners, of narrowing income and race-based discrepancies. Simultaneously eliminating both barriers raises overall homeownership to 85 percent, but most of this gain is achieved by removing income-based barriers, which alone increases the overall rate to 83 percent. Eliminating racial barriers without accounting for income brings overall ownership up only slightly, to 69 percent (from a base of 65 percent in each case).[3] Gyourko, Linneman, and Wachter (1999) found little difference in ownership rates among unconstrained households but that minorities are far more likely to be wealth-constrained than whites.[4] They also found that, controlling for wealth, minorities are far more likely to own in central cities than whites. In fact, wealth-constrained whites are more likely to live in suburbs than unconstrained minorities.[5]

Race/Ethnicity and Homeownership

Because pronounced and persistent gaps exist between the ownership rates of whites and minorities (Collins and Margo, 1999; Joint Center for Housing Studies, 2000), numerous studies have attempted to determine whether these gaps can be explained by other factors or whether they result from discrimination. In addition to Eggers and Burke (1996) and Gyourko, Linneman, and Wachter (1999), Rosenbaum (1996) also explored the reasons for gaps in minority and white homeownership. She found that minorities in the New York metropolitan area were less likely to own their own homes and more likely to live in lower-quality housing, even after controlling for income and family composition. She ascribes this result at least in part to the way minority home seekers were treated by housing market agents. Herbert (1997) finds that supply-side factors, especially the greater concentration of multifamily housing in the areas where blacks tend to live more than others, partially explain their lower ownership rates.

Wachter and Megbolugbe (1992), using data from the 1989 American Housing Survey (AHS), found that variation in "endowment" factors explained 80 percent of the racial and ethnic gap in homeownership rates. Of the household endowment factors (income, age, education, family type, and gender) and market endowments (price and location) they consider, income is the most important, followed by marital status and gender of the household head. Further, the likelihood that minority households will become owners is more income elastic than that of majority households. Wachter and Megbolugbe attribute the 20 percent of the homeownership gap that is unexplained by their regression model to racial or ethnic discrimination but caution that other unobserved influences may account for some of this residual.[6]

3. Although minorities of all income levels have lower homeownership rates than whites, eliminating income-based barriers has a larger impact on overall ownership because almost all households are affected by income constraints though only one-fifth of households are minority.

4. They found that half of minority households but only one-third of whites are constrained.

5. The authors note that this tendency could affect minority wealth-building through homeownership because suburban housing markets have historically outperformed urban ones.

6. Because this is a residual category, it may be pulling in the effects of employment and credit histories and cultural disposition toward homeownership, among other factors.

Focusing on changes in patterns and levels of low-income lending that have occurred amid the robust economy, dynamic lending innovation, and policy changes of the 1990s, Wachter's (1999) research using data from the 1997 AHS suggests that policies of the federal government may be lifting homeownership among low-income and minority borrowers.[7] She compares actual ownership rates by race and income in 1997 with rates for 1997 projected from 1991 ownership rates. Virtually all categories exceeded their projections, and the overall homeownership in 1997 was 2.4 percentage points above its projected rate, but the rates for the lowest income categories, under $20,000 and $20,000–40,000, exceeded their projections by a greater 2.9 and 3.2 percentage points, respectively. More strikingly, minorities in the $20,000–40,000 category exceeded their projected ownership rate by 4.2 percentage points. Bostic and Surette (2000) also conclude that public policies likely played a role in boosting homeownership in the 1990s. They report that, while homeownership is up across the board, it is only among low-income borrowers (including lower-income minorities) that it cannot be explained by socioeconomic and demographic changes. Though they note that their conclusions are not definitive, they believe that their findings indicate that housing policy has helped change the mortgage-lending environment and has led to elevated homeownership rates.

Wachter also found support for her argument that policy has had an effect on low-income and minority lending in the 1990s by examining ownership by race and age, and race and intrametropolitan location. She found that, although the ownership rate for 25-to-34-year-old minorities is barely above its projected level, for minorities in the 35–44 age group it is 5.7 percentage points above projections, nearly double the differential for all groups. For whites, the biggest differences between actual and projected rates are among those between 25 and 34 years and those under 25. Wachter attributes these patterns to the effect that policy has had on lowering down payment constraints for all buyers, an effect that reaches minorities later in life because it takes them longer to overcome wealth and income constraints. Again looking at racial differentials in projected versus actual ownership rates, Wachter found both whites and minorities exceeding projections by similar rates (1.6 and 1.9 percentage points) in central cities, but with a somewhat more noticeable difference in the suburbs (2.1 and 2.6 percentage points). Suburban households earning less than $20,000 had actual ownership rates that were 4 percentage points above their projected ownership rates, whereas in central cities this group's actual rates did not exceed expectations by any more than others'. Of all income groups, those earning

7. In particular, Wachter speculates that the superior performance of low-income homeownership rates in general, and minority rates in particular, beyond demographic expectations, is evidence of the combined impact on these rates of Community Reinvestment Act (CRA) enforcement, Justice Department fair-housing cases, and a revitalized Federal Housing Administration (FHA).

\$20,000–40,000 surpassed expectations by the largest amount: 3.6 percentage points above projections.

For Hispanics and Asians, gaps in homeownership with whites are partially explained by immigration, their younger age structure, and their higher fertility rates (Masnick, 1998). In addition, these groups are not evenly dispersed throughout the United States, and both groups (but Asians in particular) tend to live in relatively high-cost MSAs, further reducing their likelihood of homeownership (Coulson, 1999). Controlling for these differences, he found that Asians are actually more likely to be homeowners than whites, and the same factors, plus education, explain all or most of the difference between black and Hispanic rates. Controlling for immigration and housing market effects, Hispanics own at almost the rate of whites, have less crowded housing, and pay less for it (Krivo, 1995). Simply disaggregating Hispanics into foreign- and native-born categories shows the ownership rate of the former lagging that of blacks and the latter leading it. Although being an immigrant negatively affects one's probability of homeownership within racial and ethnic groups, the effect all but disappears with time (Coulson, 1999; Krivo, 1995; Masnick, 1998; Masnick, McArdle, and Belsky, 1999).

Being an immigrant can work against ownership at both the individual and aggregate levels. Individual immigrants are disadvantaged in accessing information and networks, dealing with realtors, mortgage providers, and landlords, demonstrating solid credit, and through discrimination. Further, location in immigrant enclaves reinforces attachments to these areas, which decreases motivation for integration and mobility. If Hispanic immigrants' housing searches are limited to Hispanic neighborhoods, the result can be housing that is small, inferior, and rented (Krivo, 1995).[8]

Spatial Patterns of Homeownership at the MSA Level

Few studies have looked at the spatial pattern of home buying or the implications of homeownership policies. Eggers and Burke (1996) used information on the distribution of homeowners by age, race/ethnicity, household type, income, and tenure from the 1991 AHS and household projections to 2000 by Masnick and McArdle (1993) to project the spatial results of policies aimed at eliminating income and wealth constraints to homeownership. They estimated that central cities would gain nearly 1.5 million homeowners; that the number of suburban households would increase only slightly, but that an additional 1.75 million homeowners would locate in the suburbs; and that nonmetro ownership ranks would rise by 1.25 million.

8. Ratner (1996) notes that there is significant variation in the home-buying behavior and experience of immigrants based on country of origin, and that the experiences of those from English-speaking countries more closely mirrors those of native-born citizens.

Stuart (2000) examined metropolitan patterns of home buying at the township level in the Boston primary MSA (PMSA). As Frey and Geverdt (1998) found for all households, Stuart found relatively high levels of suburbanization among minority buyers.[9] He also found, however, that half of black and Hispanic buyers moved to just seven of the 126 communities in metro-Boston (excluding the city of Boston).[10] Further, about a quarter of all blacks, Hispanics, and Asians bought homes in suburbs where they constituted an above-average share of home buyers. Looking at income, Stuart found that families with different incomes bought into different communities, and that whites with the lowest incomes were as segregated from whites in the highest income category as whites were from blacks in Boston's suburbs. Stuart also found that the likelihood of buying in the city of Boston itself decreased steadily with income in the case of Hispanics and sharply in the case of blacks.

Immergluck (1998) found a similar pattern for black home buyers in Chicago, where the proportion of blacks buying in tracts where 75 percent or more of all buyers were black increased from 27 percent in 1990–91 to 45 percent by 1995–96. Further, just 5 percent of all tracts where the share of black home buyers increased over the period accounted for 50 percent of the total increase in black buyers.[11] He noted that despite the positive side of increased black homeownership, these findings raise concern because the socioeconomic problems of blacks have been linked to segregation and spatial isolation. Specifically, he notes that other studies have linked segregation and isolation to reduced access to employment, concentration of poverty, weak local economies, lower socioeconomic status, and lower wealth accumulation through reduced house price appreciation. Immergluck concludes that government must turn toward opening up housing markets as aggressively as it has extended credit options to minority borrowers. By calling attention to the increasing segregation of black owners in Chicago, he calls into question whether homeownership rates alone are the correct metric for evaluating the impact of these policies aimed at increasing homeownership among minorities.

Stuart and Immergluck both underscore the importance of delving below the level of the metropolitan area to gauge the impact of the move to homeownership on the spatial access of new low-income and minority owners to education, employment, and social capital. Their works suggest productive veins for future research aimed at assessing the relationship of ownership gains to expanded opportunities.

9. Forty percent of African American, 60 percent of Hispanic, and 90 percent of white home buyers located outside the city of Boston.

10. The seven communities were Chelsea, Randolph, Everett, Lynn, Somerville, Milton, and Malden.

11. These tracts also accounted for 13 percent of the increase in white buyers over the period.

The "Who" and "What" of Low-Income Home Buying: Results from the 1997 AHS

The American Housing Survey provides a rich data set for comparing the demographic and housing characteristics of homes being purchased by buyers in different income and racial/ethnic groups because it contains information about both sets of characteristics. To date, the construction of the income cutoffs used to classify households relative to local area medians in the 1997 AHS make it better suited than the 1999 AHS for comparing income groups.[12]

An analysis of buyers who purchased their homes in the year leading up to the 1997 survey reveals that much larger shares of low-income recent buyers than those who remained low-income renters were married couples (see table 2-1). Given the greater propensity of married couples across all income categories, especially those with children, to buy homes, this is unsurprising. Also unsurprising is the fact that the mean household income of low-income recent buyers was one-quarter higher than that of low-income renters, while the median income of these buyers, at $20,000, was over 50 percent greater than the median income of those who continued to rent. All else equal, one would expect the incomes of low-income buyers to mass closer to the upward cutoff than the incomes of those who remained renters. Similarly, the age distribution of low-income renters who recently bought homes is skewed slightly toward younger age groups, especially those aged 35–44, the age span when first-time home-buying rates peak among minorities. The difference is balanced by a larger share of continuing low-income renters in the over-55 bracket. Finally, low-income renters who recently bought homes were nearly half as likely to buy in cities and twice as likely to buy in nonmetropolitan areas as continuing low-income renters were likely to rent in those areas.

As noted above, however, this is not an entirely appropriate comparison because recent low-income renters who bought homes are drawn more heavily from the top of the low-income band than those who remain renters. A more appropriate comparison therefore is between recent renters with household incomes between 50 and 80 percent of area median income who bought homes and those in the same income band who remained renters because about half of low-income home buyers typically fall in this income range (see table 2-1). Importantly, differences in distribution by family type remain. Recent owners who formerly rented are one-third more likely to be married with no children

12. In order to generate respondent income classes as a share of MSA median income, we merged HUD's 1997 MSA median income data file with the AHS data. After eliminating all records that were vacant or where the interviewee was not present and weighting the data to reflect the nation's housing stock, we threw out all respondents that reported both negative incomes and rent above fair market. Finally, we added income cutoffs to match the borrower categories used in the HMDA analysis presented later based on the area median income and the family size of respondents.

and even more likely—65 percent more likely—to be married with children than continuing renters. Continuing renters are also about one-third more likely to be single. Differences in the geographic distribution also remain, with those making the recent move to homeownership more concentrated in nonmetropolitan areas and less concentrated in cities. In all likelihood, these results reflect the fact that access to low-cost manufactured housing, which is more available in rural areas, plays a major role in explaining which low-income renters are able to make the move to homeownership.

There are also marked differences in the types of homes that low- and high-income households have been buying. Although a majority of all new owners purchased single-family homes, the share of high-income buyers who bought them, at 87 percent, was much greater than the share of low-income buyers who did so (see table 2-2). This is primarily because much larger shares of low-income buyers bought manufactured homes instead of conventional stick-built single-family homes. In fact, more than one-quarter of new, low-income owners purchased manufactured homes, but only 15 percent of middle-income and 5 percent of high-income recent buyers did so. In the South, fully 40 percent of low-income buyers bought manufactured homes; in the other regions, manufactured homes satisfied closer to one-fifth of low-income ownership demand. Multifamily condominiums were more important in satisfying low-income than high-income demand for ownership, but only 10 percent of low-income buyers nationwide purchased condos. In the Northeast and central cities, however, one-quarter of recent low-income buyers bought apartment condos. A larger share of low-income buyers in cities (71 percent) than in suburbs (66 percent) or nonmetropolitan areas (52 percent) bought single-family homes because manufactured homes are a more common choice in the latter areas.

Differences in housing type by racial and ethnic characteristics of home buyers are less pronounced. The share of non-Hispanic whites purchasing single-family homes is only slightly higher than for minorities. However, blacks were significantly more likely to purchase manufactured homes than non-Hispanic whites, and Hispanics and Asians were significantly more likely to purchase multifamily condos than non-Hispanic whites. In the Northeast, minorities were especially likely to purchase apartment condos. There, fully one-third of minorities and only about 20 percent of non-Hispanic whites bought apartment condos. Minorities were slightly less likely to buy manufactured homes than non-Hispanic whites in every region but the South. Minorities living in nonmetropolitan areas were much more likely to buy manufactured homes but about as likely as non-Hispanic whites to do so in the suburbs.

Differences in the characteristics of housing units purchased by recent buyers with different incomes and of different races and ethnicity are also evident. Not surprisingly, the homes of low-income buyers are more likely to lack the amenities that higher-income buyers are better able to afford. Recent low-income

Table 2-1. *Demographic Characteristics of Low-Income Recent Buyers and Low-Income Current Renters*

	<80 percent of area median income (AMI)				*50–80 percent of area median income (AMI)*			
	Recent buyers/previous renters		*Current renters*		*Recent buyers/previous renters*		*Current renters*	
	Number	*Percent*	*Number*	*Percent*	*Number*	*Percent*	*Number*	*Percent*
Age of head								
<35	352,278	44.3	8,797,774	41.6	328,316	44.5	3,033,827	46.9
35–44	224,295	28.2	4,438,234	21.0	188,654	25.6	1,445,288	22.4
45–54	89,876	11.3	2,532,002	12.0	76,701	10.4	852,023	13.2
55+	127,981	16.1	5,362,877	25.4	144,133	19.5	1,133,205	17.5
Total	794,430	100.0	21,130,87	100.0	737,804	100.0	6,464,343	100.0
Family type								
Married, no children	86,752	10.9	1,886,685	8.9	119,446	16.2	783,437	12.1
Married with children	251,045	31.6	3,458,521	16.4	255,921	34.7	1,367,704	21.2
Other with children	154,852	19.5	4,558,996	21.6	93,099	12.6	1,009,545	15.6
All other	51,198	6.4	1,561,657	7.4	32,300	4.4	520,569	8.1
Single	209,398	26.4	8,178,964	38.7	201,370	27.3	2,229,445	34.5
Nonfamily, no children	41,185	5.2	1,486,064	7.0	35,668	4.8	553,643	8.6
Total	794,430	100.0	21,130,887	100.0	737,804	100.0	6,464,343	100.0

Racial/ethnic group								
Hispanic	135,741	17.1	3,665,613	17.3	103,543	14.0	933,371	14.4
Black	141,388	17.8	4,750,551	22.5	76,258	10.3	1,153,190	17.8
Non-Hispanic white	482,042	60.7	11,559,883	54.7	520,147	70.5	4,053,541	62.7
Other	35,259	4.4	1,154,840	5.5	37,856	5.1	324,241	5.0
Total	794,430	100.0	21,130,887	100.0	737,804	100.0	6,464,343	100.0
Location								
Central city	211,489	26.6	10,178,061	48.2	169,007	22.9	2,776,403	42.9
Suburb	299,683	37.7	7,441,298	35.2	327,364	44.4	2,635,600	40.8
Nonmetro	283,258	35.7	3,511,528	16.6	241,433	32.7	1,052,340	16.3
Total	794,430	100.0	21,130,887	100.0	737,804	100.0	6,464,343	100.0
Mean income	$19,240		$14,501		$25,242		$24,873	
Median income	$20,000		$13,012		$24,800		$24,000	

Source: Joint Center for Housing Studies tabulations of the 1997 American Housing Survey.

Note: Because of rounding, not all percentages add to 100.

Table 2-2. *Structure Type and Characteristics of Housing by Income Class and Race/Ethnicity*

	Weighted sample		*Single-family units (attached and detached)*		*Multifamily units*		*Manufactured housing*	
	Number	*Percent*	*Number*	*Percent*	*Number*	*Percent*	*Number*	*Percent*
Income								
Low	1,452,000	28.5	896,675	61.8	143,377	9.9	411,948	28.4
Medium	1,041,679	20.5	845,261	81.1	64,764	6.2	131,654	12.6
High	2,599,785	51.0	2,271,167	87.4	133,462	5.1	195,156	7.5
Total	5,093,464	100.0	4,013,103	78.8	341,603	6.7	738,758	14.5
Race/ethnicity								
Non-Hispanic white	4,014,601	78.8	3,211,443	80.0	239,675	6.0	563,483	14.0
Minority total	1,078,863	21.2	801,660	74.3	101,928	9.4	175,275	16.2
Black	455,616	8.9	312,947	68.7	34,433	7.6	108,236	23.8
Hispanic	399,887	7.9	31,220	78.6	39,571	9.9	46,096	11.5
Asian	165,440	3.2	134,781	81.5	22,738	13.7	7,921	4.8
Other	57,920	1.1	39,712	68.6	5,186	9.0	13,022	22.5
Total	5,093,464	100.0	4,013,103	78.8	341,603	6.7	738,758	14.5
			High satisfaction		*At least 3 bedrooms*		*Unit has air conditioning*	
Income								
Low			1,077,117	74.2	837,722	57.7	796,939	54.9
Medium			796,243	76.4	746,417	71.7	596,807	57.3
High			2,164,054	83.2	2,062,432	79.3	1,889,776	72.7
Total			4,037,414	79.3	3,646,571	71.6	3,283,522	64.5
Race/ethnicity								
Non-Hispanic white			3,209,910	80.0	2,853,731	71.1	2,627,616	65.6
Minority total			827,504	76.7	792,840	73.5	655,906	60.8
Black			379,994	83.4	361,365	79.3	319,944	70.2
Hispanic			295,922	74.0	258,816	64.7	216,917	54.2
Asian			109,627	66.3	127,623	77.1	90,211	54.5
Other			41,961	72.4	45,036	77.8	28,834	49.8
Total			4,037,414	79.3	3,646,571	71.6	3,283,522	64.5

Source: Joint Center for Housing Studies tabulations of the 1997 American Housing Survey.

home buyers were less likely to have air conditioning or at least three bedrooms than either middle- or high-income buyers. Differences in unit characteristics and neighborhoods likely give rise to the 7 percentage point gap between the shares of low- and high-income buyers registering high levels of satisfaction with the unit they purchased.[13]

Despite their lower average incomes and wealth, however, slightly larger shares of minority home buyers bought homes with three or more bedrooms and, because of their greater concentration in the South, larger shares of black home buyers than any other group bought homes with air conditioning. When broken out by region, however, a smaller share of minority than non-Hispanic white buyers bought air-conditioned homes in each region.

We turn now to how the housing purchased by low-income buyers who previously rented compares with that of those who remained renters. Nearly two-thirds who previously rented bought single-family homes, but only a little more than one-quarter of renters lived in single family homes. Nearly one-third bought manufactured homes, but only one-twentieth of renters rented them (see table 2-3). The share of previous low-income renters who had the highest satisfaction with their homes, 75 percent, was much greater than the 54 percent registered by continuing low-income renters. This is strongly suggestive that the move to homeownership was associated with dramatic shifts in the types of homes and satisfaction levels of low-income buyers, though lack of information about their previous residence and satisfaction makes direct comparisons impossible to draw from the AHS. Similar dramatic shifts are evident among previous minority renters when compared with continuing minority renters.

The "Where" of Low-Income Home Buying: Results from the Home Mortgage Disclosure Act Data

Data reported pursuant to the Home Mortgage Disclosure Act (HMDA) permit detailed geographic analysis of the places where low-income and minority home buyers have been purchasing homes. HMDA does not provide a complete census of home buyers because not all financial institutions that originate mortgages are required to disclose information, and the quality of information from reporting mortgage companies is not as good as that from banks and thrifts; in addition, there is no information about seller-financed or all-cash home purchases.[14] Coverage outside of MSAs is limited to the activities of lenders also

13. Satisfaction is computed from AHS variable HowH2, which asks the occupant to rate the housing unit as "a place to live" on a scale from 1 (worst) to 10 (best). The discussion here and in the figures refers to the proportion of householders answering 8–10, which we label the high-satisfaction share.

14. See Berkovec and Zorn (1996) for an assessment of the completeness of HMDA coverage of the mortgage market.

Table 2-3. *Structure Type and Characteristics of Recent Buyers and Current Renters*

	Low-income previous renters (<80 percent of AMI)		*Low-income current renters (<80 percent of AMI)*		*Non-Hispanic white previous renters*		*Non-Hispanic white current renters*	
Characteristic	*Number*	*Percent*	*Number*	*Percent*	*Number*	*Percent*	*Number*	*Percent*
Single-family	484,286	61.0	6,502,407	30.8	1,324,048	78.4	7,224,161	34.8
Multifamily	75,240	9.5	13,724,683	65.0	106,546	6.2	12,494,678	60.3
Manufactured housing	234,904	29.6	903,797	4.3	263,420	15.4	1,011,514	4.9
At least three bedrooms	469,366	59.1	4,833,797	22.9	1,182,316	69.1	5,203,793	25.1
Air-conditioning	409,974	51.6	7,065,483	33.4	1,009,085	58.9	8,352,933	40.3
Occupants highly satisfied with unit								
6–10[a]	730,071	91.9	16,983,510	80.4	1,606,531	93.8	17,447,150	84.2
8–10[a]	594,967	74.9	11,748,883	55.6	1,307,678	76.4	11,742,647	56.6

Source: Joint Center for Housing Studies tabulations of the 1997 American Housing Survey.

a. Occupants' rating of units as "a place to live" on a scale from 1 (worst) to 10 (best).

active in MSAs. It is likely that these coverage issues introduce a spatial bias within MSAs because mortgage companies play a more significant role in low- and moderate-income areas than elsewhere and seller financing is arguably more common in these areas. However, the extent of the bias is difficult to quantify, and broad patterns observed in HMDA are likely accurate reflections of the pattern of purchases.

Suburban Shares of Low-Income Home Buying

National analysis of HMDA data reveals that the majority of both low-income and minority borrowers have been purchasing homes in the suburbs and outside of low-income census tracts, but also reveals considerable cross-metropolitan variation. Similarly, the data show that very small fractions of high-income buyers have been purchasing homes in low-income census tracts, especially those in the central city.

Over the 1993–99 period low-income buyers and minorities each received substantial shares of all loans. Of the loans reported in those years, over 27 percent went to low-income borrowers and just under 20 percent to minorities. Though both groups accounted for a larger share of all loans in 1999 than in 1993, minorities' share increased 1 percentage point more (6 versus 5 percentage points). Turning to the distributions by tract incomes, low-income borrowers purchased roughly equal shares of homes in low- and high-income tracts, and 59 percent bought in middle-income areas. By comparison, less than 7 percent of high-income borrowers bought homes in low-income tracts.

Combining buyer race and income shows that the composition of the change is similar for both groups. High-income whites, who received 35 percent of all loans over the 1993–99 period, had a share 5.8 percentage points lower by the end of the period than they had at the beginning, while low-income whites' share was up 3 percent. Low-income minorities' share of all loans grew by 3.2 percentage points while that of high-income minorities managed to grow half of 1 percentage point. Low-income minorities, in fact, made up a larger share of all loans recorded over the study period than high-income minorities.

Among low-income minorities, one-third of borrowers bought homes in low-income tracts, more than half chose middle-income tracts, and 13 percent moved to high-income areas. Further, less than 2 percent of low-income minorities moved to low-income, predominantly minority areas.

Loans to central cities as a share of the total were down slightly over the period, to about 30 percent of the total, as buyers continued to head to the suburbs. Central city figures are higher among low-income and minority borrowers, however: 35 percent of purchases by the former and 40 percent by the latter occurred in the central city. However, even a slight majority of low-income minority borrowers (53 percent) bought homes in the suburbs. Both high-income and white shares in the central city were somewhat below the 30 percent average figure, at 27.3 and 27.5 percent, respectively.

Explaining Geographic Home Purchasing Patterns

Both Stuart (2000) and Immergluck (1998) argue convincingly that in Boston and Chicago minorities and low-income home buyers are sharply segregated from non-Hispanic white and high-income home buyers. These studies contribute to a vast literature that underscores the segregation of residential space in metropolitan America. Their findings and those just discussed suggest that the move to homeownership for both low-income people and minorities has not necessarily resulted in significantly lower levels of segregation by race and income.

Less studied is why such large shares of low-income and minority home buyers opt to live outside central cities and why there are significant cross-MSA variations in these shares. Certainly, part of the explanation for the cross-sectional variations lies in the simple fact that in some cities significantly more of the metropolitan land area is defined as central city than in others for the purposes of federal and state data collection. But it likely lies equally in variations in the forces that tend to deter people from buying homes in the central city (push factors) and that attract people to suburbs and less densely settled patterns of development in general (pull factors).

For more than 100 years, Americans of all income levels have demonstrated a preference for decentralized living (Jackson 1985). Today the strong preference for the suburbs remains intact and is evident in the consistently faster rates of suburban than city population and housing growth (McArdle 1999; Joint Center for Housing Studies 2000). Especially over the past three decades, the decentralization of employment has further buttressed the trend toward population decentralization, drawing workers out of the city and into lower-density fringes. Suburban employment centers drive demand for housing in the suburbs and increasingly make it possible for workers to live in rural or nonurbanized parts of metropolitan regions (Garreau 1991).

To act on their preference for living in the suburbs, however, the interest of low-income people must be joined with supply-side opportunities to purchase affordable homes in the suburbs. The greater the supply of preexisting affordable housing and the fewer the restrictions on its future development, the higher the likely share of low-income buyers living outside the central city should be. The more restrictive the laws and the more fragmented the local political geography, the fewer will be the opportunities for low-income buyers to find suburban homes and the more likely that they will end up segregated in different towns from higher-income buyers. Income growth, by making relatively more expensive suburban housing affordable and by making the tax advantages of owner-occupied housing more appealing, can also pull buyers out to the suburbs.

Another likely influence on the extent to which pull factors are at work is the nexus between an MSA's variations in school quality, its age structure, and its distribution of household types. Because of the ongoing disparity between the quality of urban and suburban public schools, families with children often move to the suburbs in search of better educational opportunities. Because childbearing and -rearing occurs during specific phases of the life cycle, the suburbs should exert a stronger pull in MSAs with larger shares of residents in their childbearing years. This factor is also conditioned, however, on the distribution of household types, which measures the demand for schools among families.

On the push side, well-known urban ills such as crime, noise, and pollution collectively influence the quality of life in the central city and hence the willingness of residents of all income and racial/ethnic groups to live there. A related issue is the degree to which poverty is concentrated in the central cities; high concentrations of poverty simultaneously push out those who can afford to leave the center city and confine many of the poor to specific parts of the MSA. Similarly, the age, type, size, and quality distribution of the housing stock are important: people may head outward in pursuit of housing that is more likely to be single-family, newer, and equipped with modern conveniences. The demonstrated preference of whites for segregated living can also be considered a push factor where minorities are disproportionately concentrated in central cities.

Despite a relatively straightforward set of testable hypotheses for cross-MSA variations in the share of low-income buyers purchasing homes in the suburbs, these hypotheses have not yet been tested.

Moving beyond the Central City/Suburb Dichotomy

The conventional distinction between central city and suburb, while broadly descriptive of real distinctions between parts of metropolitan area housing markets, is limiting. The most notable body of work questioning and attempting to move beyond the city/suburb dichotomy is a series of papers by Frey, Speare, and colleagues (Speare, 1993; Frey and Speare, 1995; Frey and Farley, 1996; Frey and Geverdt, 1998).[15] They develop a "functional" typology of intra-MSA communities based on distance from central city, racial/ethnic composition, and economic performance and conclude that different processes produce different settlement patterns in each type of area.[16] Frey and Farley (1996), for instance, found that though black segregation decreased almost everywhere during the 1980s, it was lowest (and most likely to have declined) in multiethnic MSAs—places where other minorities' share grew faster than blacks' did. The authors

15. These researchers identify the six intra-MSA community types as major city; inner employment center; outer employment center; inner residential suburbs; outer residential suburbs; and low density area.

16. Los Angeles, for example, is a "multiethnic high immigration area," Atlanta a "white-black fast growing area," and Detroit a "white-black slow growing area."

attribute this to new Asian and Hispanic immigration dispersing entrenched racial minorities as well as long-term, relatively assimilated, immigrants.

In an effort to understand the distance that low-income and minority home buyers are buying from the traditional urban core, we create a distance-to-central business district[17] measure and apply it to home purchases over the 1993 to 1999 period in nine MSAs: Atlanta, Detroit, Hartford, Houston, Miami, Milwaukee, Philadelphia, Phoenix, and Portland (Oregon). These areas were selected because they are not multinucleated and because the geographic size of each city relative to the suburbs and the proportion of minorities living in them varies. We impose the monocentrism constraint to reduce the complexity arising from understanding purchasing patterns in places with multiple urban cores.

Four distance bands were drawn in concentric circles around the centroid of the central business district in each place. The first band, less than or equal to eight miles from the CBD, is intended to capture central urbanized core areas, whether they are defined as parts of central cities or as inner-ring suburbs. The next band, eight to fourteen miles, captures those places that offer easy commuting to the city but are likely to have the lower densities typically associated with suburban living. The third band, fourteen to twenty miles, represents outer suburbs, and the final band, beyond twenty miles, encompasses housing located at great distances from the center of the city.

In most MSAs the band nearest to the CBD contains the largest share of all tracts. The share typically trails off with distance, reflecting the much higher population densities at the urban core.[18] In all of the MSAs, low-income tracts are found overwhelmingly in the innermost ring while high- and middle-income tracts are spread relatively evenly throughout. Likewise, more than half of the predominantly minority tracts are located within eight miles of the CBD in all nine places.

Income segregation of home purchases by distance from the CBD varied considerably among the nine MSAs but was generally less severe than segregation by race and ethnicity (see tables 2-4a and 2-4b). For instance, home buying in the eight miles closest to the CBD accounted for about 40 percent of low-income borrowers' total in Hartford, Philadelphia, and Portland, and 59 percent in Milwaukee, but not more than 22 percent (and as little as 8 percent) in the other five MSAs. Unsurprisingly, geographically large MSAs such as Houston and Atlanta had high shares of borrowers in all income classes; in Detroit, more than 30 percent of low-income home buyers bought homes at least twenty miles from the CBD. In eight of the nine MSAs (all except Milwaukee), a majority of low-income borrowers bought homes at least eight miles from the CBD, indicating ongoing decentralization of low-income buyers in these places.

17. See Appendix 2A for central business district definitions.
18. See Appendix 2B for distance band selection methods.

Further evidence for the dispersal of low-income borrowers comes from data on the share of low-income purchases in low-income tracts. In several places (Atlanta, Phoenix, Detroit, Hartford, and Houston), these purchases are notably more spread out than the tracts themselves. The difference is most pronounced in Atlanta, where 62 percent of low-income tracts are in the inner band but only 39 percent of all *purchases* made in low-income tracts take place in this band. The disparity between the share of low-income tracts in the inner band and the share of purchases occurring in low-income tracts likely reflects buyers' continued preference to leave central cities, even if the area they choose outside of the inner band is still a low-income area.[19]

Despite the fact that more than half of the predominantly minority tracts were located within eight miles of the CBD, only 27 percent of blacks and Hispanics and only 18 percent of Asians bought homes within that closest ring. The race-by-distance data suggest that there are two types of MSAs, those where minority purchasers are heavily concentrated in central areas and those where minorities have been able to move to the middle rings. In Atlanta, Detroit, Houston, Miami, and Phoenix, black and Hispanic buyers are purchasing homes primarily in the second and third rings (see table 2-4b). In Hartford, Milwaukee, and to a lesser extent Portland and Philadelphia, however, black and Hispanic buyers remain concentrated near the urban core. In fact, from 60 to 84 percent of black and Hispanic home buyers in Hartford, Milwaukee, and Philadelphia purchased homes within eight miles of the CBD. In contrast, purchases by whites were fairly evenly dispersed across our four distance categories in these places.

In many places the share of blacks buying in predominantly minority tracts near the CBD actually exceeds the share of all tracts with these characteristics in these areas. In other words, black home buyers are to some degree concentrating in predominantly minority inner census tracts in Milwaukee, Philadelphia, Hartford, and Portland and are slightly overrepresented among them in Detroit. Only in Miami and Houston, where mostly white tracts represent the smallest shares of the total, are less than half of all white purchases made outside mostly white tracts. Where the share of mostly white tracts is high (Hartford 62 percent, Milwaukee 57 percent, Philadelphia 58 percent, Portland 63 percent), the share of whites buying in these tracts (88 percent, 91 percent, 76 percent, 74 percent) is even higher and is spread across all distance bands. This pattern is repeated in Atlanta and Phoenix, where 68 and 55 percent of whites bought in mostly white tracts, though only 35 and 33 percent of all tracts are mostly white.

19. Further evidence of the preference for suburban-style living comes from high-income tract data. Though only 25 percent of higher-income census tracts are located twenty miles or more from the CBD, 34 percent of purchases in high-income tracts occurred there.

Table 2-4a. *Share of Buyers by Borrower and Tract Income Characteristics in Nine Cities*

Distance from central business district (CBD)	*Number of buyers*	*Borrower income (percent of AMI)*			*Tract income (percent of AMI)*		
		<80	*80–119.9*	*≥120*	*<80*	*80–119.9*	*≥120*
All nine MSAs							
8 miles or less	481,540	22.1	14.5	14.3	50.7	14.8	9.7
8.01–14 miles	738,771	28.8	26.1	23.3	21.3	29.1	24.2
14.01–20 miles	700,005	21.5	25.9	25.9	7.3	21.8	32.5
20+ miles	939,317	27.7	33.6	36.5	20.7	34.3	33.5
Total	2,859,633	916,361	804,355	1,138,917	318,149	1,301,118	1,208,428
Atlanta							
8 miles or less	59,153	11.1	9.2	12.6	39.2	6.5	9.4
8.01–14 miles	78,257	18.6	13.0	12.3	17.7	17.2	12.7
14.01–20 miles	128,588	24.7	23.2	24.3	6.1	24.4	29.9
20+ miles	266,770	45.6	54.6	50.8	37.1	51.9	48.0
Total	532,768	185,887	150,556	196,325	185,887	150,556	196,325
Detroit							
8 miles or less	24,046	8.2	3.7	3.0	25.8	2.6	2.0
8.01–14 miles	118,454	35.8	24.8	13.7	38.9	33.1	9.6
14.01–20 miles	111,296	21.0	26.2	23.7	7.3	22.0	30.5
20+ miles	220,714	35.1	45.3	59.6	28.0	42.4	58.0
Total	474,510	171,695	139,487	163,328	171,695	139,487	163,328
Hartford							
8 miles or less	31,034	37.5	30.8	27.2	50.4	32.4	26.4
8.01–14 miles	32,940	31.6	31.9	38.3	31.1	28.1	46.8
14.01–20 miles	23,894	21.7	26.8	25.7	8.6	27.5	22.7
20+ miles	9,206	9.2	10.5	8.8	9.9	12.0	4.1
Total	97,074	34,322	30,324	32,428	34,322	30,324	32,428
Houston							
8 miles or less	46,320	12.9	8.6	14.5	38.6	7.1	10.1
8.01–14 miles	67,526	30.8	17.7	10.9	36.7	26.9	9.9
14.01–20 miles	105,601	25.9	33.4	28.3	4.5	26.9	35.6
20+ miles	147,198	30.4	40.2	46.3	20.1	39.1	44.4

Total	366,645	108,025	87,695	170,925	108,025	87,695	170,925
Miami							
8 miles or less	47,207	20.9	19.5	28.7	79.7	23.0	13.3
8.01–14 miles	79,142	46.2	41.7	38.0	14.4	56.5	36.9
14.01–20 miles	59,034	26.3	34.2	30.1	4.0	11.1	48.1
20+ miles	8,385	6.6	4.7	3.1	2.0	9.4	1.7
Total	193,768	41,655	56,308	95,804	41,655	56,309	95,804
Milwaukee							
8 miles or less	51,275	59.0	38.7	23.4	94.1	45.9	13.4
8.01–14 miles	30,732	16.2	21.9	29.2	4.3	16.2	37.5
14.01–20 miles	24,350	12.0	18.3	23.0	0.5	14.6	28.2
20+ miles	26,700	12.9	21.2	24.4	1.1	23.3	20.9
Total	133,057	38,209	42,893	51,955	38,209	42,893	51,955
Philadelphia							
8 miles or less	89,918	40.3	17.3	10.2	78.5	22.4	6.9
8.01–14 miles	89,423	20.4	24.0	21.8	10.1	22.8	24.1
14.01–20 miles	90,892	16.8	23.4	26.1	3.6	19.9	29.8
20+ miles	137,547	22.6	35.3	41.9	7.8	35.0	39.2
Total	407,780	135,426	108,288	164,066	135,426	108,288	164,066
Phoenix							
8 miles or less	58,972	22.1	10.1	8.6	37.1	12.7	6.7
8.01–14 miles	150,586	34.8	35.3	33.9	16.4	31.8	43.1
14.01–20 miles	127,273	24.0	31.2	32.4	18.5	24.1	37.4
20+ miles	98,146	19.0	23.4	25.1	28.0	31.4	12.8
Total	434,977	146,774	118,935	169,268	146,774	118,935	169,268
Portland, Ore.							
8 miles or less	73,615	41.6	32.0	30.2	76.0	24.4	35.4
8.01–14 miles	91,711	35.3	42.0	45.5	11.3	44.5	53.3
14.01–20 miles	29,077	11.2	13.8	14.1	0.0	18.1	9.4
20+ miles	24,651	11.9	12.3	10.1	12.7	13.0	1.8
Total	219,054	54,368	69,868	94,818	54,368	69,868	94,818

Source: Authors' tabulations of 1993–99 HMDA data.

Table 2-4b. *Share of Buyers by Race and Tract Racial Characteristics in Nine Cities*

	Race of borrowers (percent)				*Minority percentage in tract*			
Distance from CBD	*Asian*	*Black*	*Hispanic*	*White*	*<10*	*10–19.9*	*20–49.9*	*≥50*
All nine MSAs								
8 miles or less	17.7	27.0	27.0	14.3	11.3	17.8	21.3	37.5
8.01–14 miles	27.0	34.1	34.5	23.8	23.8	27.0	27.5	35.2
14.01–20 miles	31.2	25.0	27.9	23.7	22.5	30.8	27.8	23.0
20+ miles	24.1	13.8	10.6	38.2	42.4	24.4	23.4	4.3
Total	72,680	246,069	246,239	2,066,608	1,616,982	476,969	434,533	299,211
Atlanta								
8 miles or less	4.9	12.9	7.3	11.0	4.3	12.8	16.1	39.7
8.01–14 miles	19.4	32.0	21.4	10.2	6.0	20.8	31.6	40.7
14.01–20 miles	31.6	35.0	32.4	20.9	22.6	36.1	27.9	15.5
20+ miles	44.0	20.0	38.9	57.9	67.0	30.3	24.4	4.1
Total	13,998	89,672	11,862	379,133	302,592	92,921	71,105	44,643
Detroit								
8 miles or less	6.2	21.7	14.2	3.1	2.5	3.7	10.3	40.9
8.01–14 miles	15.1	51.6	30.6	22.5	23.1	20.2	34.8	51.0
14.01–20 miles	32.5	15.2	16.9	24.2	23.7	29.5	34.2	3.2
20+ miles	46.2	11.5	38.2	50.3	50.6	46.6	20.8	4.9
Total	8,812	42,530	3,527	391,971	394,480	33,013	20,637	26,019
Hartford								
8 miles or less	53.2	73.6	63.8	26.6	25.1	47.9	64.9	98.9
8.01–14 miles	31.6	20.8	26.1	35.3	35.2	38.4	24.7	0.0
14.01–20 miles	10.4	4.6	5.5	27.6	29.2	5.4	7.1	1.1
20+ miles	4.8	1.0	4.7	10.5	10.4	8.3	3.3	0.0
Total	1,495	5,973	3,826	79,089	78,447	9,796	6,190	2,623
Houston								
8 miles or less	6.9	9.2	16.2	12.7	12.3	8.8	9.3	27.0
8.01–14 miles	20.8	34.2	40.0	11.9	7.5	7.9	21.8	48.4
14.01–20 miles	51.4	40.1	25.3	26.2	5.9	33.1	42.2	20.6
20+ miles	20.9	16.5	18.5	49.2	74.3	50.1	26.6	4.0

Total	18,156	28,420	52,856	232,836	74,892	100,165	136,808	49,743
Miami								
8 miles or less	16.0	19.8	22.1	32.6	1.3	7.7	25.0	25.5
8.01–14 miles	46.2	57.7	38.3	40.1	98.7	92.3	36.8	37.4
14.01–20 miles	34.6	18.2	36.4	20.6	0.0	0.0	29.3	34.3
20+ miles	3.2	4.3	3.3	6.8	0.0	0.0	9.0	2.8
Total	2,185	19,427	112,718	41,249	2,517	10,485	55,055	124,900
Milwaukee								
8 miles or less	51.1	79.0	83.7	33.6	31.6	63.0	63.1	100.0
8.01–14 miles	33.4	19.0	8.6	23.5	22.8	31.9	33.2	0.0
14.01–20 miles	11.2	1.6	5.4	20.2	21.4	5.1	3.7	0.0
20+ miles	4.3	0.4	2.4	22.7	24.2	0.0	0.0	0.0
Total	1,835	8,676	3,111	111,253	110,295	9,010	8,214	5,471
Philadelphia								
8 miles or less	36.3	59.8	68.6	14.8	16.3	17.8	39.1	72.7
8.01–14 miles	23.0	14.5	11.6	23.3	24.5	20.0	15.1	8.1
14.01–20 miles	20.9	15.2	9.3	23.7	19.8	39.9	14.7	12.9
20+ miles	19.8	10.5	10.5	38.2	39.4	22.3	31.1	6.3
Total	9,844	41,342	12,112	309,537	279,378	68,161	34,508	25,495
Phoenix								
8 miles or less	14.1	22.8	40.6	10.3	5.0	15.0	24.6	51.5
8.01–14 miles	39.1	37.1	30.4	35.0	33.4	44.8	31.5	5.7
14.01–20 miles	31.7	25.2	18.1	30.6	32.6	35.5	15.0	26.6
20+ miles	15.1	14.9	10.9	24.2	28.9	4.8	28.9	16.2
Total	7,476	7,847	41,941	336,816	218,198	105,226	94,036	17,336
Portland, Ore.								
8 miles or less	41.0	64.6	31.5	32.9	25.2	49.5	85.5	100.0
8.01–14 miles	50.7	29.0	38.6	41.5	46.9	37.1	7.1	0.0
14.01–20 miles	6.1	5.2	16.4	13.7	15.3	10.6	0.0	0.0
20+ miles	2.2	1.3	13.6	11.9	12.6	2.8	7.4	0.0
Total	8,879	2,192	4,286	184,724	156,183	48,192	7,980	2,891

Source: Authors' tabulations of 1993–99 HMDA data.

Minorities are not necessarily settling in less-segregated communities outside the innermost ring. In fact, although 69 percent of all predominantly minority tracts are located in the innermost band across the nine metro areas, only 38 percent of purchases by minorities in predominantly minority tracts occurred in this band. Thus the majority of minority purchases in mostly minority tracts are occurring more than eight miles out from the CBD.

Whites are far more likely to buy twenty miles or more from the CBD in every area. There is evidence from each MSA that whites and minorities are not heading for the same zones of the MSA. In the nine MSAs combined, just 3 percent of whites and 9 percent of Asians bought homes in predominantly minority tracts, while 40 percent of blacks and 46 percent of Hispanics did so (see table 2-5). The differential between an MSA's share of mostly white tracts and the share of blacks purchasing homes in these tracts is generally quite large. Milwaukee is the leader in this regard with 12 percent of black purchases occurring in mostly white tracts, though these tracts represent 57 percent of the total. This is of special concern because of the possibility that the "success" of minority home buyers in moving away from urban cores is being countered by white efforts to leave these areas. If this is the case, suburban segregation of minority owners may be replacing the urban segregation of minority renters that many of these new minority owners intended to leave behind (Orfield and Yun, 1999).

Turning to the share of blacks purchasing homes in low-income areas, we find that the share increases with distance from the CBD in Atlanta, Detroit, and to some extent Houston (see table 2-6). This is also true of Hispanics in these places and in Miami. In contrast, black purchases in low-income tracts are concentrated closer to the CBD in Hartford, Milwaukee, Philadelphia, and Portland.

Blacks who bought homes in high-income areas tend to be concentrated in one distance band, though which band varies from one MSA to the next. In Detroit, for example, 68 percent of black borrowers in high-income areas bought between eight and fourteen miles out; Hartford, Miami, Philadelphia, and Milwaukee have similar concentrations of blacks in high-income tracts in either the first or second distance band.

More than any other group, Hispanics have been concentrating in middle-income areas, but the location of these tracts again varies in each place. These areas were close to the CBD in Hartford, Milwaukee, Philadelphia, and Portland, but less so elsewhere. Whites and Asians both avoided low-income tracts generally, especially near the city center, but moderate shares of them bought close to downtown in Hartford, Philadelphia, and Milwaukee.

Borrower Income, Tract Income, and Distance

Low-income borrowers in all MSAs were far more likely to buy in middle-income tracts, and about as likely to buy in high-income tracts, than they were to buy in low-income tracts. Low-income buyers were least likely to purchase homes in low-income tracts in Hartford, Atlanta, and Miami, where in each only about 15 percent did so.

Table 2-7 shows that, despite some cross-MSA similarities, low-income buyers purchasing in low-income tracts did so mostly within different distance bands in different MSAs. In Milwaukee, for instance, where 57 percent of low-income borrowers purchased homes in middle-income tracts, 58 percent of these tracts were located within eight miles of the CBD. The pattern was quite different in Atlanta, Detroit, Houston, and Phoenix, where low-income purchases in middle-income tracts were spread evenly throughout the second, third, and fourth income bands. The pattern of low-income buyers' purchases in high-income tracts also varies from one MSA to the next. Nearly half of these purchases in Atlanta and Detroit occurred more than twenty miles from the CBD, and 70 percent or more occurred at least fourteen miles from the CBD in Detroit, Houston, and Philadelphia. In contrast, low-income buyers' purchases in high-income tracts in Hartford, Phoenix, and Portland were concentrated much closer to the CBD.

Mapping

Collectively, the results of the preceding section indicate that, though all buyers are decentralizing, whites and Asians have done so to a greater extent than blacks and Hispanics. Mapping results from the study cities can demonstrate whether home buying by low-income people and minorities appears to be resulting in desegregation or resegregation. In this section, we attempt to develop an impression of settlement patterns as they unfolded over the 1990s in four MSAs with a substantial minority presence (see pages 53–56). We look at two MSAs with relatively large African-American shares, Detroit and Philadelphia, and two with large Hispanic shares, Phoenix and Houston. By and large, we find that while some of both groups are able to select homes in sectors farther out, both low-income and minority buyers are concentrated near the urban core. A comparison of low-income and minority maps shows that low-income buyers are more likely to move outward and that minorities cluster in areas where there are larger concentrations of minority borrowers than low-income buyers.

The Detroit maps show distinct clusterings of both low-income and minority buyers around the CBD. A comparison of the two maps, however, shows tracts with high shares of minority buyers to be less dispersed and more tightly clustered near the city center. Further, they are more likely to be contiguous. The pattern in Philadelphia is similar, where both minority and low-income home buyers focused on the city center. In both places there are large areas where minorities made up less than 10 percent of all home buyers yet where low-income purchasers constituted 10–20 or 20–50 percent of the total. Both Houston and Phoenix show concentrations of low-income and minority buyers close to downtown, but there are also significant shares of both types of buyers outside the core area.

Table 2-5a. *Location of Home Purchases by Race or Ethnicity of Borrowers in Nine Cities, 1993–99*

	Asian borrowers (percentage in tract)					*Black borrowers (percentage in tract)*				
Distance from CBD	*<10*	*10–19.99*	*20–49.99*	*≥50*	*Total*	*<10*	*10–19.99*	*20–49.99*	*≥50*	*Total*
All nine MSAs										
8 miles or less	6.4	4.5	4.4	2.2	17.6	3.4	2.2	4.9	16.6	27.0
8.01–14 miles	11.8	6.0	5.8	3.5	27.1	4.0	3.9	9.5	16.9	34.4
14.01–20 miles	10.0	7.9	10.7	2.8	31.4	4.7	6.1	8.4	5.9	25.2
20+ miles	15.7	4.3	3.7	0.2	24.0	7.2	2.5	2.9	0.9	13.5
Total (percent)	43.8	22.7	24.8	8.8	100.0	19.3	14.7	25.7	40.3	100.0
Total (number of borrowers)	31,743	16,453	17,858	6,369	72,423	47,168	35,968	62,800	98,449	244,385
Atlanta										
8 miles or less	1.1	1.1	1.4	1.1	4.7	0.6	0.6	1.0	10.6	12.8
8.01–14 miles	3.2	4.2	10.2	2.0	19.6	2.2	4.3	10.1	15.9	32.5
14.01–20 miles	15.3	10.0	6.4	0.3	32.0	8.0	10.2	10.8	6.4	35.4
20+ miles	34.6	8.1	0.9	0.1	43.7	13.1	3.4	2.3	0.5	19.3
Total (percent)	54.3	23.4	18.9	3.4	100.0	24.0	18.4	24.2	33.4	100.0
Total (number of borrowers)	7,514	3,235	2,620	473	13,842	21,205	16,321	21,420	29,548	88,494
Detroit										
8 miles or less	2.6	0.6	1.7	1.4	6.2	0.2	0.2	1.4	19.8	21.6
8.01–14 miles	12.6	0.8	1.3	0.4	15.1	7.9	5.8	11.3	26.7	51.7
14.01–20 miles	24.6	6.9	1.0	0.0	32.5	4.2	3.5	6.4	1.1	15.2
20+ miles	38.3	6.9	0.6	0.4	46.2	7.0	1.8	1.6	1.2	11.5
Total (percent)	78.0	15.2	4.6	2.2	100.0	19.3	11.2	20.7	48.8	100.0
Total (number of borrowers)	6,873	1,340	405	190	8,808	8,188	4,766	8,780	20,744	42,488
Hartford										
8 miles or less	34.0	10.4	6.8	1.9	53.1	11.6	11.7	25.5	24.9	73.6
8.01–14 miles	24.4	4.9	2.3	00	31.6	8.4	8.8	3.7	0.0	20.9
14.01–20 miles	9.6	0.5	0.4	0.0	10.4	3.5	0.5	0.6	0.0	4.6
20+ miles	3.7	1.1	0.0	0.0	4.8	0.6	0.2	0.1	0.0	1.0
Total (percent)	71.8	16.9	9.5	1.9	100.0	24.0	21.2	29.9	24.9	100.0
Total (number of borrowers)	1,072	252	142	28	1,494	1,433	1,268	1,783	1,487	5,971
Houston										
8 miles or less	1.7	1.3	2.5	1.2	6.7	0.3	0.4	1.2	6.7	8.7
8.01–14 miles	1.1	1.5	8.1	10.1	20.8	0.2	0.6	13.2	20.7	34.7
14.01–20 miles	0.2	9.7	34.3	7.4	51.6	0.2	5.2	22.0	13.2	40.6
20+ miles	3.9	6.3	10.4	0.3	20.9	2.9	5.1	7.3	0.8	16.0

Total (percent)	7.0	18.8	55.3	19.0	100.0	3.6	11.3	43.7	41.4	100.0
Total (number of borrowers)	1,261	3,404	9,999	3,430	18,094	1,018	3,167	12,261	11,621	28,067
Miami										
8 miles or less	0.0	0.2	5.5	10.1	15.8	0.0	0.1	1.7	17.7	19.6
8.01–14 miles	1.5	6.1	20.2	18.5	46.3	0.7	1.3	11.4	44.4	57.8
14.01–20 miles	0.0	0.0	11.2	23.4	34.7	0.0	0.0	5.1	13.1	18.3
20+ miles	0.0	0.0	2.3	0.9	3.2	0.0	0.0	1.6	2.7	4.3
Total (percent)	1.5	6.3	39.2	53.0	100.0	0.7	1.4	19.9	78.0	100.0
Total (number of borrowers)	33	137	855	1,156	2,181	141	269	3,859	15,100	19,369
Milwaukee										
8 miles or less	17.7	10.9	13.5	9.0	51.1	5.2	13.5	22.4	37.9	79.0
8.01–14 miles	24.2	4.8	4.4	0.0	33.4	4.6	5.1	9.3	0.0	19.0
14.01–20 miles	10.8	0.2	0.2	0.0	11.2	1.6	0.0	0.0	0.0	1.6
20+ miles	4.3	0.0	0.0	0.0	4.3	0.4	0.0	0.0	0.0	0.4
Total (percent)	57.0	15.9	18.1	9.0	100.0	11.8	18.6	31.7	37.9	100.0
Total (number of borrowers)	1,046	291	333	165	1,835	1,022	1,609	2,753	3,289	8,673
Philadelphia										
8 miles or less	12.0	6.6	11.9	5.9	36.3	14.4	5.2	12.4	27.8	59.8
8.01–14 miles	16.0	5.9	1.0	0.2	23.0	5.4	2.2	3.2	3.8	14.5
14.01–20 miles	12.2	7.3	0.7	0.7	20.9	3.1	5.4	1.9	4.7	15.2
20+ miles	16.3	2.1	1.2	0.3	19.8	3.9	2.2	3.7	0.7	10.5
Total (percent)	56.4	21.9	14.7	7.0	100.0	26.8	15.0	21.2	37.0	100.0
Total (number of borrowers)	5,551	2,152	1,449	687	9,839	11,075	6,194	8,742	15,286	41,297
Phoenix										
8 miles or less	1.6	4.7	6.8	1.0	14.1	1.2	3.9	9.5	8.2	22.8
8.01–14 miles	17.0	14.8	7.2	0.1	39.1	10.2	10.2	16.3	0.4	37.1
14.01–20 miles	12.6	14.7	3.4	1.0	31.7	9.9	9.1	4.3	1.9	25.2
20+ miles	8.3	0.4	6.2	0.3	15.1	8.3	0.5	5.2	0.9	14.9
Total (percent)	39.4	34.6	23.6	2.4	100.0	29.6	23.7	35.3	11.4	100.0
Total (number of borrowers)	2,944	2,589	1,763	177	7,473	2,323	1,861	2,766	891	7,841
Portland, Ore.										
8 miles or less	20.3	16.9	3.1	0.7	41.0	10.2	12.6	19.8	22.1	64.7
8.01–14 miles	34.7	16.0	0.1	0.0	50.9	19.5	9.4	0.1	0.0	29.1
14.01–20 miles	4.6	1.5	0.0	0.0	6.1	4.3	0.9	0.0	0.0	5.2
20+ miles	1.9	0.1	0.1	0.0	2.0	0.9	0.1	0.0	0.0	1.1
Total (percent)	61.5	34.5	3.3	0.7	100.0	34.9	23.0	20.0	22.1	100.0
Total (number of borrowers)	5,449	3,053	292	63	8,857	763	503	436	483	2,185

Source: Authors' tabulations of 1993–99 HMDA data.

Table 2-5b. *Location of Home Purchases by Race or Ethnicity of Borrowers in Nine Cities, 1993–99*

	Hispanic borrowers (percentage in tract)					*White borrowers (percentage in tract)*				
Distance from CBD	*<10*	*10–19.99*	*20–49.99*	*≥50*	*Total*	*<10*	*10–19.99*	*20–49.99*	*≥50*	*Total*
All nine MSAs										
8 miles or less	2.5	2.2	8.2	14.0	26.8	7.3	3.1	2.4	1.3	14.2
8.01–14 miles	3.1	3.7	11.4	16.5	34.7	16.2	4.6	2.6	0.7	24.1
14.01–20 miles	2.0	3.0	8.6	14.5	28.0	15.3	5.2	2.9	0.6	24.0
20+ miles	3.8	2.0	3.5	1.2	10.5	29.2	4.5	3.6	0.3	37.7
Total (percent)	11.5	10.8	31.7	46.1	100.0	68.1	17.4	11.6	2.9	100.0
Total (number of borrowers)	28,068	26,324	77,534	112,919	244,845	1,388,837	355,830	236,980	58,221	2,039,868
Atlanta										
8 miles or less	0.9	1.0	1.9	3.2	7.0	3.1	2.9	2.6	1.8	10.4
8.01–14 miles	3.2	5.3	10.9	2.5	21.9	3.9	3.6	2.6	0.7	10.7
14.01–20 miles	10.9	11.8	9.6	0.8	33.1	14.6	5.3	1.9	0.2	22.0
20+ miles	29.0	7.1	1.8	0.1	38.0	46.6	6.0	3.9	0.4	56.9
Total (percent)	44.0	25.1	24.3	6.6	100.0	68.3	17.7	11.0	3.0	100.0
Total (number of borrowers)	5,109	2,920	2,818	768	11,615	245,849	63,895	39,669	10,791	360,204
Detroit										
8 miles or less	2.6	1.5	7.3	2.7	14.1	2.2	0.2	0.2	0.4	3.0
8.01–14 miles	24.2	3.1	2.2	1.2	30.7	20.8	0.9	0.5	0.3	22.5
14.01–20 miles	13.7	1.6	1.4	0.2	16.9	21.4	1.7	1.0	0.1	24.2
20+ miles	27.1	4.8	4.5	1.9	38.3	46.1	3.2	0.8	0.1	50.3
Total (percent)	67.6	11.0	15.5	5.9	100.0	90.5	6.2	2.5	0.9	100.0
Total (number of borrowers)	2,380	387	547	208	3,522	354,585	24,090	9,634	3,361	391,670
Hartford										
8 miles or less	17.0	19.7	16.2	10.8	63.8	20.7	3.4	1.9	0.6	26.6
8.01–14 miles	9.4	3.9	12.8	0.0	26.1	31.1	3.4	0.9	0.0	35.3
14.01–20 miles	5.0	0.3	0.3	0.0	5.5	26.6	0.6	0.4	0.0	27.6
20+ miles	1.4	2.2	1.0	0.0	4.7	9.5	0.8	0.2	0.0	10.5
Total (percent)	32.7	26.1	30.3	10.8	100.0	87.9	8.2	3.3	0.6	100.0
Total (number of borrowers)	1,252	1,000	1,159	415	3,826	69,511	6,451	2,633	482	79,077
Houston										
8 miles or less	0.5	0.6	2.3	12.3	15.6	3.3	3.2	4.1	1.7	12.3
8.01–14 miles	0.3	2.5	19.3	18.4	40.5	2.0	2.4	5.4	2.3	12.1
14.01–20 miles	0.5	4.7	16.6	3.8	25.6	1.6	10.5	13.5	1.0	26.6
20+ miles	3.8	5.9	7.4	1.1	18.3	20.5	17.3	10.8	0.4	49.0

Total (percent)	5.0	13.7	45.6	35.6	100.0	27.4	33.4	33.7	5.5	100.0
Total (number of borrowers)	2,630	7,156	23,797	18,595	52,178	62,857	76,533	77,348	12,517	229,255
Miami										
8 miles or less	0.0	0.2	5.0	16.6	21.8	0.0	1.2	14.6	16.4	32.3
8.01–14 miles	0.8	2.8	8.0	26.8	38.4	2.8	12.2	15.5	9.7	40.2
14.01–20 miles	0.0	0.0	7.9	28.6	36.5	0.0	0.0	10.2	10.5	20.7
20+ miles	0.0	0.0	1.8	1.5	3.3	0.0	0.0	4.8	2.0	6.8
Total (percent)	0.8	2.9	22.8	73.5	100.0	2.8	13.4	45.1	38.6	100.0
Total (number of borrowers)	943	3,288	25,570	82,530	112,331	1,166	5,526	18,517	15,881	41,090
Milwaukee										
8 miles or less	24.9	21.5	24.1	13.2	83.7	27.9	2.9	1.7	1.0	33.6
8.01–14 miles	5.7	1.3	1.6	0.0	8.6	20.3	1.9	1.4	0.0	23.5
14.01–20 miles	3.9	0.5	1.0	0.0	5.4	19.6	0.4	0.2	0.0	20.2
20+ miles	2.4	0.0	0.0	0.0	2.4	22.7	0.0	0.0	0.0	22.7
Total (percent)	36.8	23.2	26.7	13.2	100.0	90.5	5.2	3.3	1.0	100.0
Total (number of borrowers)	1,145	722	831	412	3,110	100,622	5,746	3,668	1,156	111,192
Philadelphia										
8 miles or less	27.8	7.4	13.8	19.6	68.5	10.2	2.3	1.4	0.8	14.8
8.01–14 miles	8.9	1.7	0.8	0.3	11.7	18.8	3.5	1.0	0.1	23.3
14.01–20 miles	3.6	3.2	1.2	1.3	9.3	15.4	6.9	1.2	0.3	23.7
20+ miles	5.3	2.2	2.6	0.4	10.5	31.3	4.1	2.5	0.3	38.2
Total (percent)	45.6	14.5	18.3	21.6	100.0	75.7	16.7	6.1	1.5	100.0
Total (number of borrowers)	5,526	1,751	2,220	2,609	12,106	234,162	51,739	18,879	4,590	309,370
Phoenix										
8 miles or less	0.6	4.4	22.5	13.0	40.5	2.9	3.5	3.2	0.7	10.2
8.01–14 miles	6.3	7.3	16.1	0.8	30.5	18.2	11.1	5.4	0.2	35.0
14.01–20 miles	4.5	6.1	5.0	2.5	18.1	18.1	8.7	3.0	0.9	30.6
20+ miles	4.5	0.6	4.6	1.1	10.9	16.0	1.2	6.4	0.5	24.2
Total (percent)	15.9	18.5	48.2	17.4	100.0	55.2	24.6	17.9	2.2	100.0
Total (number of borrowers)	6,660	7,730	20,215	7,292	41,897	185,892	82,948	60,430	7,433	336,703
Portland, Ore.										
8 miles or less	12.9	11.5	5.1	2.1	31.6	18.3	10.8	2.9	1.1	33.1
8.01–14 miles	27.2	9.1	2.5	0.0	38.8	34.3	7.8	0.2	0.0	42.3
14.01–20 miles	6.9	9.6	0.0	0.0	16.5	11.7	2.3	0.0	0.0	14.0
20+ miles	10.0	1.9	1.2	0.0	13.1	9.7	0.6	0.3	0.0	10.6
Total (percent)	56.9	32.2	8.8	2.1	100.0	74.0	21.5	3.4	1.1	100.0
Total (number of borrowers)	2,423	1,370	377	90	4,260	134,193	38,902	6,202	2,010	181,307

Source: Authors' tabulations of 1993–99 HMDA data.

Table 2-6. *Location of Home Purchases by Borrower Race or Ethnicity and Tract Income in Nine Cities, 1993–99*

	Asian (percent of AMI)				*Black (percent of AMI)*				*Hispanic (percent of AMI)*				*White (percent of AMI)*			
Distance from CBD	*<80*	*80–119.99*	*120+*	*Total*	*<80*	*80–119.99*	*120+*	*Total*	*<80*	*80–119.99*	*120+*	*Total*	*<80*	*80–119.99*	*120+*	*Total*
All nine MSAs																
8 miles or less	7.4	6.6	3.6	17.6	4.9	15.6	8.4	28.8	0.9	18.5	10.1	29.6	5.1	1.7	15.1	21.9
8.01–14 miles	2.3	12.7	12.0	27.1	7.5	6.2	19.3	33.0	4.9	23.6	3.6	32.1	10.4	6.2	19.6	36.2
14.01–20 miles	0.6	11.7	19.0	31.4	8.7	1.0	14.0	23.7	6.3	17.3	0.8	24.5	4.5	10.6	15.8	30.9
20+ miles	0.8	8.3	15.0	24.0	6.7	1.6	6.2	14.5	3.5	9.3	1.1	13.8	3.2	1.9	5.9	11.0
Total (percent)	11.1	39.3	49.6	100.0	27.7	24.5	47.8	100.0	15.6	68.7	15.6	100.0	23.2	20.4	56.4	100.0
Total (number of borrowers)	8,046	28,458	35,919	72,423	72,423	63,983	124,761	261,167	55,614	100,597	88,634	244,945	166,638	953,102	920,128	2,039,868
Atlanta																
8 miles or less	1.5	1.3	1.9	4.7	0.8	9.3	3.8	13.9	0.7	10.1	0.4	11.3	0.8	0.9	3.7	5.4
8.01–14 miles	3.0	10.8	5.8	19.6	3.4	5.5	22.9	31.8	5.3	25.7	0.4	31.4	7.7	1.8	11.6	21.1
14.01–20 miles	0.5	14.1	17.4	32.0	5.5	1.2	27.4	34.1	7.5	28.1	0.1	35.7	11.3	5.4	17.5	34.2
20+ miles	0.8	16.2	26.6	43.7	7.5	2.4	10.3	20.3	6.1	15.3	0.2	21.6	10.0	9.1	20.1	39.2
Total (percent)	5.8	42.5	51.7	100.0	17.2	18.4	64.4	100.0	19.7	79.2	1.1	100.0	29.8	17.3	52.9	100.0
Total (number of borrowers)	803	5,881	7,158	13,842	14,757	51,723	22,014	88,494	1,256	6,558	3,801	11,615	25,289	165,619	169,296	360,204
Detroit																
8 miles or less	5.1	0.8	0.3	6.2	1.3	16.8	3.3	21.3	1.0	17.8	0.8	19.6	1.3	0.2	8.3	9.8
8.01–14 miles	2.8	9.8	2.6	15.1	3.1	18.3	27.4	48.8	4.2	42.6	0.5	47.3	12.4	1.0	18.1	31.5
14.01–20 miles	0.6	11.1	20.8	32.5	6.6	1.1	6.5	14.2	6.1	12.5	0.1	18.7	5.1	4.1	10.0	19.2
20+ miles	3.1	10.0	33.1	46.2	9.4	3.0	3.3	15.6	4.3	9.5	0.7	14.5	9.2	7.7	22.6	39.5
Total (percent)	11.6	31.7	56.7	100.0	20.4	39.1	40.5	100.0	15.5	82.4	2.1	100.0	28.0	13.0	59.0	100.0
Total (number of borrowers)	1,021	2,790	4,997	8,808	16,927	17,545	8,016	42,488	1,075	1,670	777	3,522	31,355	209,552	150,763	391,670

Hartford																
8 miles or less	6.4	33.5	13.2	53.1	11.7	16.4	45.7	73.8	2.4	53.6	10.9	66.9	23.0	2.2	39.9	65.1
8.01–14 miles	3.1	12.7	15.7	31.6	7.0	4.0	7.7	18.7	5.5	15.2	6.9	27.6	4.9	2.2	16.3	23.3
14.01–20 miles	0.4	7.3	2.7	10.4	2.3	0.5	2.8	5.6	0.6	3.3	0.2	4.1	2.7	0.5	3.4	6.7
20+ miles	0.3	3.6	0.9	4.8	1.1	0.1	0.7	1.9	0.0	0.7	0.7	1.4	1.9	0.1	2.9	4.9
Total (percent)	10.3	57.2	32.5	100.0	22.1	21.0	56.9	100.0	8.5	72.8	18.7	100.0	32.5	5.0	62.5	100.0
Total (number of borrowers)	154	854	486	1,494	1,424	3,850	697	5,971	1,531	1,989	306	3,826	3,715	49,923	25,439	79,077
Houston																
8 miles or less	1.4	1.4	3.9	6.7	3.4	5.0	0.9	9.3	0.6	4.6	12.4	17.6	1.0	0.7	9.1	10.8
8.01–14 miles	2.9	11.5	6.4	20.8	10.5	5.6	13.6	29.7	5.4	18.2	12.9	36.5	13.9	2.1	23.7	39.6
14.01–20 miles	0.4	20.4	30.8	51.6	26.0	0.5	17.4	43.9	9.3	21.3	0.7	31.4	7.4	7.2	15.0	29.5
20+ miles	0.2	6.5	14.2	20.9	10.5	1.2	5.4	17.1	4.0	8.4	2.1	14.5	4.9	4.5	10.7	20.1
Total (percent)	4.9	39.8	55.4	100.0	50.5	12.2	37.3	100.0	19.3	52.6	28.1	100.0	27.1	14.5	58.4	100.0
Total (number of borrowers)	881	7,195	10,018	18,094	4,388	13,375	10,304	28,067	15,033	24,194	12,951	52,178	16,964	68,123	144,168	229,255
Miami																
8 miles or less	5.9	4.8	5.1	15.8	2.1	14.5	6.9	23.5	0.8	10.3	25.1	36.3	4.5	2.6	11.5	18.7
8.01–14 miles	0.3	17.5	28.5	46.3	6.2	3.0	52.0	61.1	6.2	30.5	6.4	43.1	9.8	9.4	20.3	39.5
14.01–20 miles	0.6	3.0	31.1	34.7	4.6	2.0	3.5	10.1	7.2	9.7	0.8	17.7	2.6	16.5	19.3	38.4
20+ miles	0.0	2.2	1.0	3.2	0.4	0.5	4.3	5.2	0.1	2.3	0.6	3.0	1.2	0.4	1.7	3.4
Total (percent)	6.8	27.5	65.7	100.0	13.4	19.9	66.7	100.0	14.4	52.8	32.9	100.0	18.2	28.9	52.8	100.0
Total (number of borrowers)	149	599	1,433	2,181	3,240	10,850	5,279	19,369	12,060	38,745	61,526	112,331	4,496	9,668	26,926	41,090
Milwaukee																
8 miles or less	24.2	23.1	3.8	51.1	9.4	43.2	24.5	77.1	0.9	62.0	16.6	79.5	16.7	0.8	59.6	77.1
8.01–14 miles	0.8	11.3	21.3	33.4	6.1	1.4	11.8	19.4	2.9	14.9	0.1	17.9	3.4	2.6	6.1	12.0
14.01–20 miles	0.0	4.3	7.0	11.2	2.1	0.0	0.5	2.6	0.8	1.3	0.0	2.2	2.2	1.6	3.8	7.5
20+ miles	0.0	1.9	2.4	4.3	0.8	0.0	0.2	1.0	0.1	0.3	0.0	0.5	0.9	0.8	1.7	3.3
Total (percent)	25.0	40.5	34.4	100.0	18.4	44.6	37.0	100.0	4.8	78.4	16.7	100.0	23.1	5.7	71.2	100.0
Total (number of borrowers)	459	744	632	1,835	4,450	3,691	532	8,673	1,851	1,009	250	3,110	6,096	58,730	46,366	111,192

continued on next page

Table 2-6. *Location of Home Purchases by Borrower Race or Ethnicity and Tract Income in Nine Cities, 1993–99 (continued)*

	Asian (percent of AMI)				*Black (percent of AMI)*				*Hispanic (percent of AMI)*				*White (percent of AMI)*			
Distance from CBD	*<80*	*80–119.99*	*120+*	*Total*	*<80*	*80–119.99*	*120+*	*Total*	*<80*	*80–119.99*	*120+*	*Total*	*<80*	*80–119.99*	*120+*	*Total*
Philadelphia																
8 miles or less	20.3	12.3	3.7	36.3	7.9	32.1	20.4	60.3	1.5	46.6	10.6	58.7	13.9	0.8	45.7	60.3
8.01–14 miles	2.1	7.7	13.1	23.0	5.0	1.7	7.6	14.2	3.3	11.3	0.4	15.1	4.9	1.6	7.8	14.3
14.01–20 miles	0.3	6.4	14.2	20.9	4.5	1.0	8.4	13.9	3.8	11.9	0.2	15.8	3.5	2.2	6.2	11.9
20+ miles	0.2	6.8	12.8	19.8	4.3	0.8	6.4	11.5	2.0	8.2	0.2	10.4	4.5	1.9	7.0	13.4
Total (percent)	23.0	33.2	43.8	100.0	21.6	35.6	42.8	100.0	10.6	77.9	11.4	100.0	26.8	6.5	66.6	100.0
Total (number of borrowers)	2,261	3,270	4,308	9,839	16,190	19,470	5,637	41,297	6,047	4,874	1,185	12,106	17,790	143,281	148,299	309,370
Phoenix																
8 miles or less	5.5	6.7	1.9	14.1	8.4	7.4	5.8	21.6	0.5	6.8	39.0	46.3	9.2	0.7	25.0	34.8
8.01–14 miles	2.2	11.8	25.0	39.1	23.4	2.0	10.2	35.6	5.2	11.0	7.1	23.4	10.4	5.6	18.8	34.7
14.01–20 miles	2.7	8.1	21.0	31.7	19.0	2.0	5.4	26.3	4.0	7.5	7.6	19.1	4.4	3.8	11.1	19.3
20+ miles	1.1	9.6	4.4	15.1	9.1	1.5	6.0	16.6	0.9	4.4	5.9	11.2	3.8	0.6	6.7	11.1
Total (percent)	11.6	36.2	52.2	100.0	59.8	12.9	27.3	100.0	10.7	29.7	59.6	100.0	27.8	10.7	61.6	100.0
Total (number of borrowers)	864	2,705	3,904	7,473	1,615	3,413	2,813	7,841	15,728	18,889	7,280	41,897	39,280	135,410	162,013	336,703
Portland, Ore.																
8 miles or less	15.7	17.3	8.1	41.0	34.0	9.0	3.4	46.4	2.5	39.6	20.0	62.1	6.6	1.9	18.0	26.4
8.01–14 miles	0.6	26.7	23.6	50.9	42.1	0.2	3.6	45.9	6.4	17.8	5.0	29.1	15.1	4.6	22.1	41.8
14.01–20 miles	0.0	4.3	1.8	6.1	5.0	0.0	0.8	5.8	0.8	3.2	0.0	4.0	8.5	0.9	9.4	18.8
20+ miles	0.2	1.7	0.2	2.0	1.7	0.0	0.2	1.9	0.1	0.6	4.0	4.8	5.4	0.1	7.5	13.0
Total (percent)	16.4	49.9	33.7	100.0	82.8	9.3	7.9	100.0	9.8	61.3	29.0	100.0	35.6	7.5	56.9	100.0
Total (number of borrowers)	1,454	4,420	2,983	8,857	992	844	349	2,185	1,033	2,669	558	4,260	21,653	112,796	46,858	181,307

Source: Authors' tabulations of 1993–99 HMDA data.

Table 2-7. *Location of Home Purchases by Borrower Income and Tract Income in Nine Cities, 1993–99*

	Low-income borrowers (percent of AMI)				*Middle-income borrowers (percent of AMI)*				*High-income borrowers (percent of AMI)*			
Distance from CBD	*<80*	*80–119.99*	*120+*	*Total*	*<80*	*80–119.99*	*120+*	*Total*	*<80*	*80–119.99*	*120+*	*Total*
Atlanta												
8 miles or less	5.8	3.0	1.6	10.4	2.8	3.1	2.6	8.6	1.8	3.3	7.2	12.3
8.01–14 miles	3.0	12.9	4.0	19.8	1.1	8.0	4.4	13.5	0.6	4.3	7.6	12.5
14.01–20 miles	0.9	17.7	7.8	26.4	0.5	12.2	11.5	24.1	0.2	6.0	18.6	24.8
20+ miles	5.3	25.4	12.7	43.4	3.3	29.3	21.2	53.8	1.4	21.4	27.6	50.4
Total (percent)	15.0	58.9	26.1	100.0	7.7	52.6	39.7	100.0	4.1	35.0	61.0	100.0
Total (number of borrowers)	26,056	102,610	45,481	174,147	11,157	75,980	57,349	144,486	7,825	67,340	117,463	192,628
Detroit												
8 miles or less	5.9	1.9	0.2	8.1	1.7	1.3	0.6	3.6	0.8	0.8	1.4	2.9
8.01–14 miles	9.4	24.6	1.9	35.8	2.5	18.7	3.6	24.8	0.8	7.7	5.2	13.7
14.01–20 miles	1.3	13.7	6.0	21.0	0.8	13.3	12.2	26.2	0.4	7.1	16.3	23.7
20+ miles	4.9	20.5	9.7	35.1	2.5	24.3	18.5	45.3	1.8	21.1	36.7	59.6
Total (percent)	21.6	60.6	17.8	100.0	7.4	57.7	34.9	100.0	3.8	36.7	59.6	100.0
Total (number of borrowers)	36,995	103,969	30,565	171,529	10,344	80,440	48,605	139,389	6,172	59,842	97,217	163,231
Hartford												
8 miles or less	7.4	26.2	3.9	37.5	2.8	21.4	6.5	30.8	1.0	12.7	13.5	27.2
8.01–14 miles	4.5	20.6	6.6	31.6	2.0	18.9	11.1	31.9	0.5	13.0	24.8	38.3
14.01–20 miles	1.0	17.0	3.6	21.7	0.6	19.1	7.1	26.8	0.3	15.5	9.9	25.7
20+ miles	1.3	7.2	0.6	9.2	0.7	8.6	1.2	10.5	0.2	6.7	1.9	8.8
Total (percent)	14.2	71.0	14.7	100.0	6.1	68.0	25.9	100.0	2.0	47.9	50.1	100.0
Total (number of borrowers)	4,889	24,375	5,050	34,314	1,844	20,624	7,853	30,321	661	15,516	16,244	32,421
Houston												
8 miles or less	8.2	1.9	1.8	11.9	3.3	2.3	2.7	8.3	2.3	2.8	9.3	14.4
8.01–14 miles	9.2	18.0	4.3	31.5	3.3	9.6	5.0	18.0	1.3	3.4	6.4	11.0
14.01–20 miles	0.9	12.6	13.0	26.5	0.5	11.8	21.6	33.9	0.2	5.7	22.6	28.5

continued on next page

Table 2-7. *Location of Home Purchases by Borrower Income and Tract Income in Nine Cities, 1993–99 (continued)*

	Low-income borrowers (percent of AMI)				*Middle-income borrowers (percent of AMI)*				*High-income borrowers (percent of AMI)*			
Distance from CBD	*<80*	*80–119.99*	*120+*	*Total*	*<80*	*80–119.99*	*120+*	*Total*	*<80*	*80–119.99*	*120+*	*Total*
20+ miles	4.1	15.4	10.7	30.1	2.5	16.1	21.2	39.8	1.0	10.6	34.4	46.0
Total (percent)	22.3	47.9	29.8	100.0	9.6	39.9	50.5	100.0	4.8	22.5	72.7	100.0
Total (number of borrowers)	23,592	50,562	31,513	105,667	8,321	34,502	43,679	86,502	8,201	38,079	123,159	169,439
Miami												
8 miles or less	11.8	6.5	2.4	20.6	9.0	7.5	2.6	19.1	7.8	8.5	12.2	28.5
8.01–14 miles	2.8	30.0	13.6	46.4	2.0	24.5	15.3	41.9	0.9	11.2	26.0	38.1
14.01–20 miles	0.7	4.5	21.2	26.3	0.6	4.8	28.9	34.3	0.3	2.8	27.1	30.2
20+ miles	0.6	5.2	0.9	6.7	0.2	3.7	0.7	4.7	0.1	1.9	1.1	3.1
Total (percent)	15.8	46.2	38.0	100.0	11.8	40.6	47.6	100.0	9.1	24.5	66.4	100.0
Total (number of borrowers)	6,549	19,175	15,798	41,522	6,628	22,746	26,650	56,024	8,677	23,368	63,456	95,501
Milwaukee												
8 miles or less	23.4	33.1	2.4	59.0	6.8	27.8	4.1	38.7	2.4	13.0	8.0	23.3
8.01–14 miles	0.8	8.5	6.9	16.2	0.5	10.1	11.3	21.9	0.2	6.7	22.3	29.2
14.01–20 miles	0.1	5.9	5.9	12.0	0.0	8.1	10.1	18.3	0.0	8.1	14.9	23.0
20+ miles	0.1	9.5	3.3	12.9	0.1	14.7	6.3	21.2	0.1	11.5	12.9	24.5
Total (percent)	24.4	57.1	18.5	100.0	7.4	60.7	31.9	100.0	2.6	39.3	58.0	100.0
Total (number of borrowers)	9,328	21,798	7,059	38,185	3,189	26,026	13,662	42,877	1,372	20,425	30,131	51,928
Philadelphia												
8 miles or less	21.9	16.9	1.4	40.2	4.1	10.7	2.5	17.2	1.2	4.4	4.6	10.1
8.01–14 miles	2.1	13.2	5.1	20.4	1.1	13.4	9.5	24.0	0.3	6.1	15.4	21.9
14.01–20 miles	0.7	9.0	7.1	16.8	0.4	11.6	11.5	23.4	0.2	7.4	18.5	26.1
20+ miles	1.2	13.9	7.5	22.6	1.0	20.4	14.0	35.4	0.5	14.8	26.6	41.9
Total (percent)	26.0	53.0	21.1	100.0	6.6	56.0	37.4	100.0	2.2	32.7	65.1	100.0
Total (number of borrowers)	35,150	71,695	28,503	135,348	7,106	60,615	40,493	108,214	3,616	53,556	106,808	163,980

Phoenix												
8 miles or less	11.5	8.9	1.7	22.0	3.4	4.5	2.2	10.1	1.5	2.4	4.7	8.5
8.01–14 miles	4.0	18.1	12.7	34.9	2.3	14.3	18.7	35.3	1.0	7.3	25.6	33.9
14.01–20 miles	3.9	10.4	9.8	24.1	2.9	11.1	17.2	31.2	1.5	8.3	22.7	32.5
20+ miles	6.0	10.7	2.3	19.0	4.4	14.9	4.1	23.4	2.1	13.0	9.9	25.1
Total (percent)	25.3	48.1	26.6	100.0	13.1	44.8	42.1	100.0	6.1	31.0	62.9	100.0
Total (number of borrowers)	37,165	70,553	38,979	146,697	15,554	53,231	50,100	118,885	10,380	52,465	106,369	169,214
Portland, Ore.												
8 miles or less	19.0	18.4	4.7	42.0	9.9	16.3	6.0	32.2	4.2	11.9	14.2	30.4
8.01–14 miles	2.6	26.4	7.0	36.0	1.5	30.4	10.9	42.8	0.7	25.4	20.1	46.2
14.01–20 miles	0.0	9.6	1.8	11.4	0.0	11.7	2.4	14.0	0.0	11.4	2.9	14.3
20+ miles	2.3	8.0	0.2	10.5	2.1	8.5	0.3	10.9	0.9	7.5	0.8	9.1
Total (percent)	23.9	62.4	13.7	100.0	13.5	67.0	19.5	100.0	5.8	56.2	38.0	100.0
Total (number of borrowers)	12,723	33,232	7,324	53,279	9,245	45,876	13,380	68,501	5,410	52,518	35,538	93,466

Source: Authors' tabulations of 1993–99 HMDA data.

Contrasting the two sets of cities shows Phoenix and Houston relatively free of places where either low-income or minority borrowers constitute less than 10 percent of the total. Philadelphia and Detroit had many such tracts. Although we are reluctant to speculate on the reason for this discrepancy, it seems likely to be related to the mix of minorities in each place and to the stock of developable land. We suspect that it is generally easier for all groups to move out of the central city in Houston and Phoenix where undeveloped land is common, and that Hispanics in these places have been better able to escape concentration in core urban areas than have blacks in Philadelphia and Detroit.

Conclusion

Rapidly escalating homeownership in the 1990s has been associated with greater progress for low-income and especially minority households than for others. Both income and wealth constraints to obtaining a mortgage have been significantly relaxed, and the industry has expanded its outreach at a time of unusually rapid economic growth and modest interest rates. Meanwhile, public policies ranging from the Community Reinvestment Act to affordable housing goals for Fannie Mae and Freddie Mac to fair housing laws and enforcement have encouraged the private market to better serve low-income and minority markets and reduce gaps in homeownership rates. Though progress has been made, significant gaps in the homeownership between whites and minorities remain. Most research has found that these gaps are largely accounted for by the lower average wealth and incomes of minorities and the greater proportions of recent immigrants and single-person and single-parent households among them. Nonetheless, others argue that some fraction of the gap reflects ongoing discrimination in housing markets or other factors such as more weakly developed credit histories.

Manufactured housing has played a particularly important role in satisfying the demand of low-income home buyers. Nationwide, more than one-quarter of such buyers purchased manufactured homes in 1997, and in the South 40 percent did so. In the Northeast and in central cities, apartment condos also have played an important role in meeting low-income ownership demand—as much as one-quarter—but for only about 10 percent of that demand nationwide. In comparison with continuing low-income renters, low-income recent buyers who previously rented are in more spacious accommodations and report higher levels of satisfaction with their homes.

It is apparent that large shares of low-income and minority borrowers are purchasing in the suburbs and outside of low-income census tracts. It is equally clear that very few high-income borrowers are purchasing homes in low-income inner-city census tracts. The extent to which the move to low-income homeownership has been associated with a move to opportunity remains an open

Detroit: Share of All Loans Made to Low-Income Borrowers by Census Tract, 1993–99

Detroit: Share of All Loans Made to Minorities by Census Tract, 1993–99

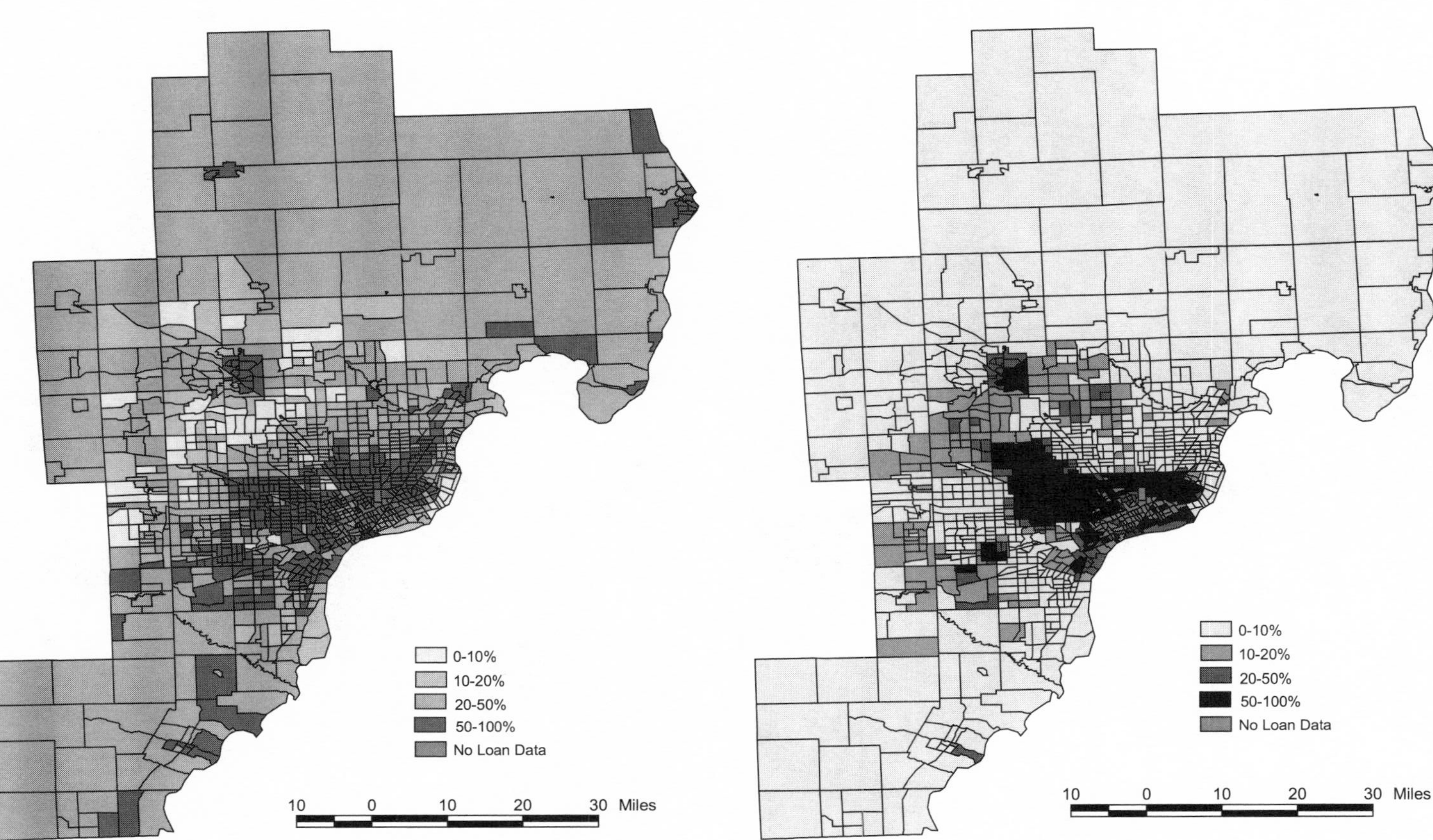

Houston: Share of All Loans Made to Low-Income Borrowers by Census Tract, 1993–99

Houston: Share of All Loans Made to Minorities by Census Tract, 1993–99

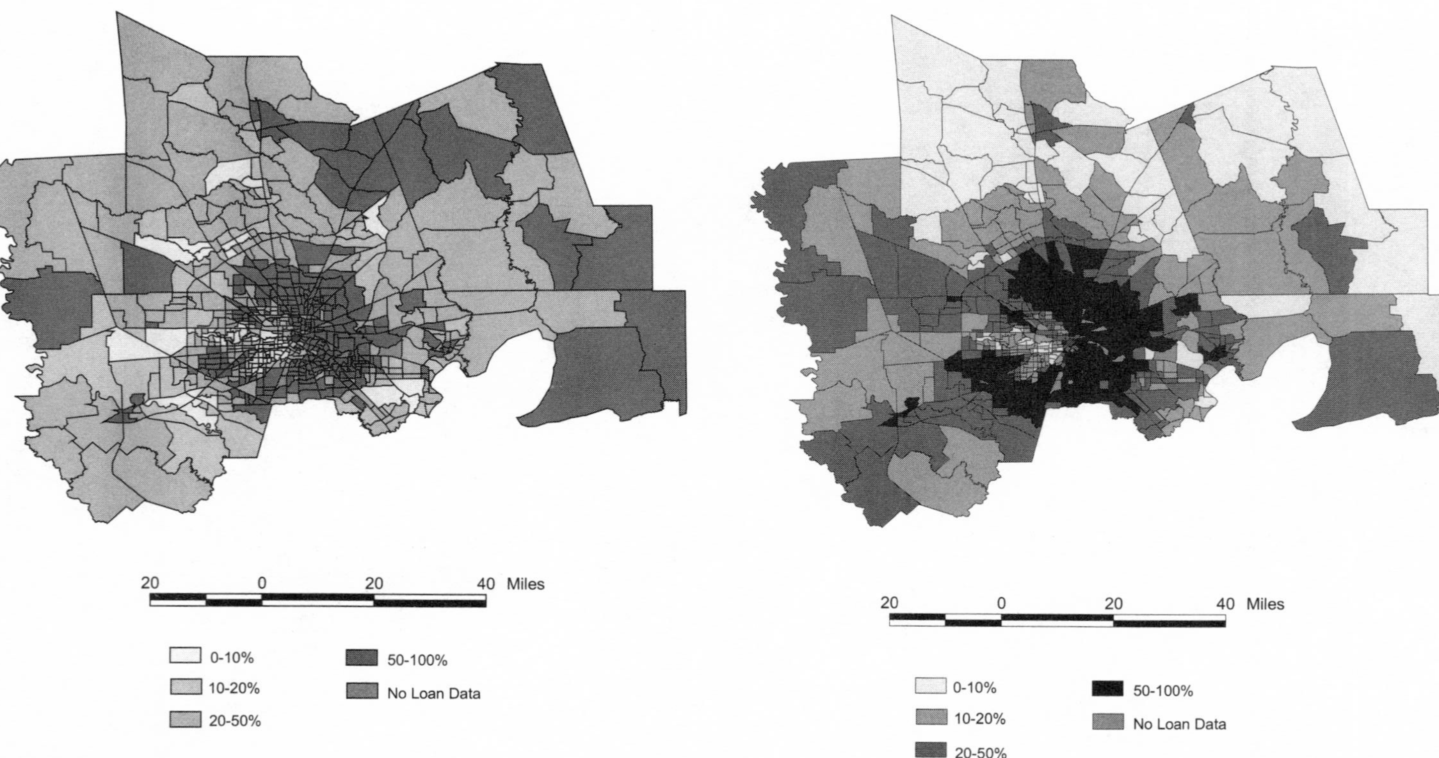

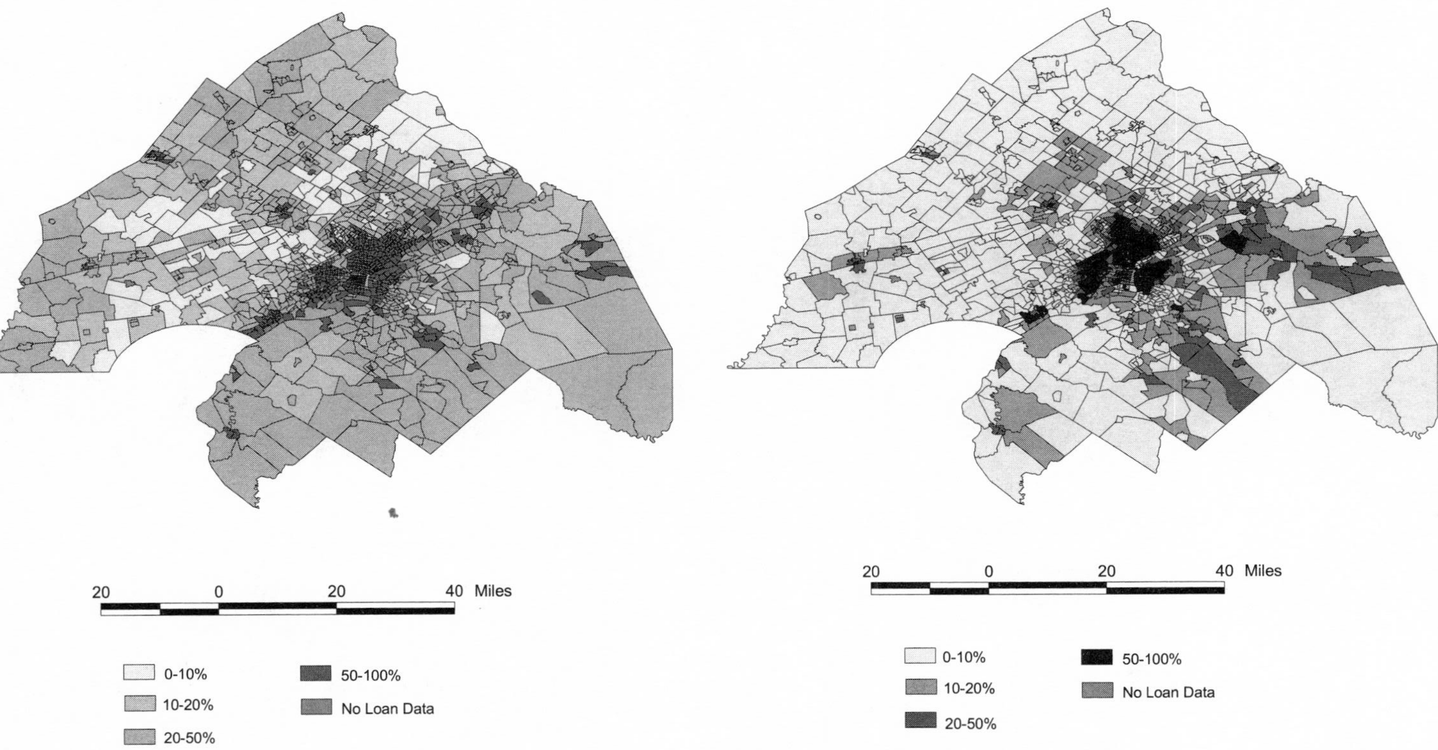
Philadelphia: Share of All Loans Made to Low-Income Borrowers by Census Tract, 1993–99
20
0
20
40
Miles
0-10%
10-20%
20-50%
50-100%
No Loan Data
Philadelphia: Share of All Loans Made to Minorities by Census Tract, 1993–99
20
0
20
40
Miles
0-10%
10-20%
20-50%
50-100%
No Loan Data

Phoenix: Share of All Loans Made to Low-Income Borrowers by Census Tract, 1993–99

Phoenix: Share of All Loans Made to Minorities by Census Tract, 1993–99

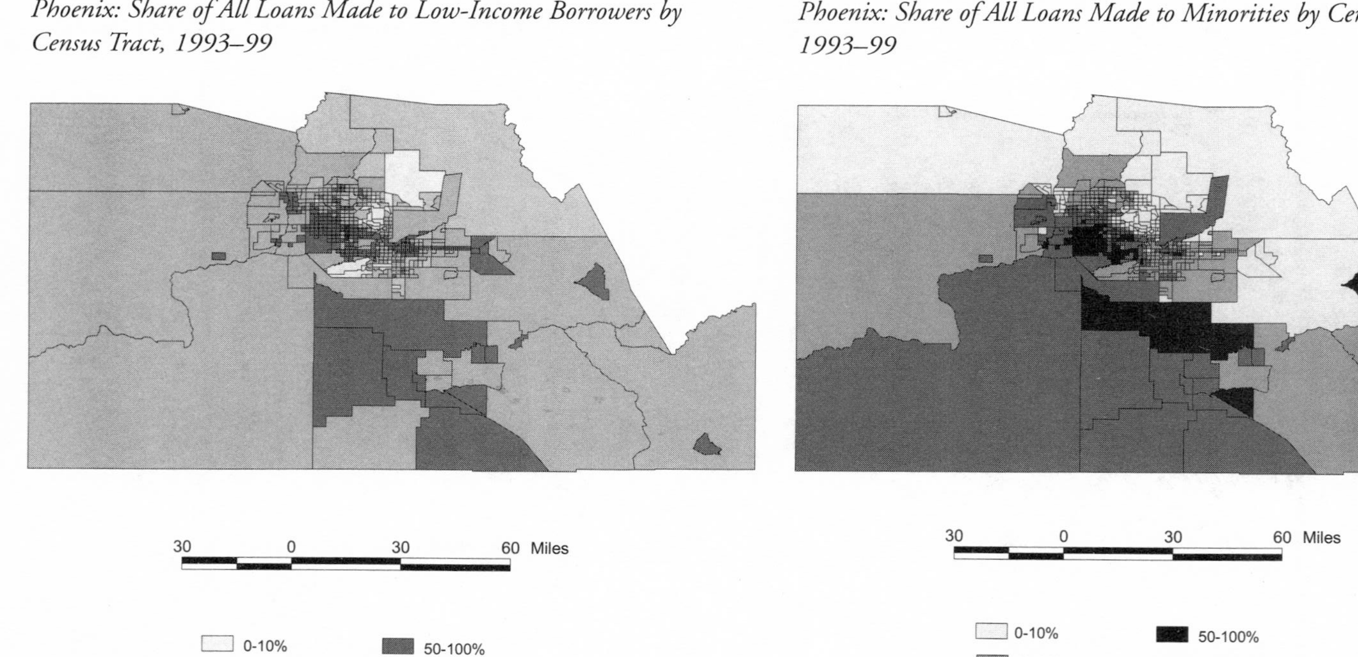

question, but it appears to have led to at least some income mixing in the suburbs. Indeed, significant portions of low-income borrowers in the suburbs have been purchasing homes in moderate- and middle-income census tracts. It also appears, however, that this change has not led to materially lower levels of segregation by race in the case of blacks, but it is less clear whether it has done so for ethnic Hispanics. Whites and Asians have largely avoided buying homes in areas where a majority of other buyers over the 1993–99 period were minorities. In both the cases of the income and the race/ethnicity of home buyers, however, clustering remains more the rule than the exception. Low-income home buyers, although less clustered near the urban core than low-income renters, nevertheless are far more likely to buy near the CBD than are high-income buyers. Minorities also tend to purchase homes closer to the CBD, but the degree to which this is the case varies widely in the nine MSAs examined, and it is truer for blacks than Hispanics. In most places, there are many census tracts where more than half of the buyers are low-income minorities, and these are typically contiguously located close to the center of the city.

In considering these results, it is important to remember that they are a preliminary step in moving beyond national-level analysis and past the traditional city-suburb metropolitan dichotomy. Though we believe that our distance-to-CBD measure has value, it obviously has less explanatory power in places with multiple employment centers.

Much work remains to be done to better describe and understand the spatial pattern of low-income home buying and its implications. First, there is a need for more studies of home buyer segregation and patterns at the metropolitan level along the lines done by Stuart (2000) and Immergluck (1998). These are the most promising of the studies for understanding the spatial expression of increasing homeownership among minorities and those with low incomes. Second, more cross-sectional comparisons of these patterns are needed to shed light on their determinants and on their regularity. Third, econometric models aimed at testing hypotheses about the role that push and pull forces play in explaining intra- and intermetropolitan differences in home-buying patterns by race, ethnicity, and income are needed. Fourth, and perhaps most important, destinations of low-income and minority home buyers need to be correlated with neighborhood and education quality, as well as economic opportunities, to determine whether the move to homeownership is resulting in benefits beyond the private pecuniary gains that at least some low-income and minority buyers reap.

Appendix 2A: Central Business District Definitions

We define the center of the metropolitan statistical area (MSA) as the centroid of the polygon formed by combining all of the tracts constituting the central business district (CBD). Using MSA census tract maps from the Census Bureau in a GIS, and the Census Bureau's CBD tract definitions, we built these polygons and calculated their center points. We then calculated the centroids of each tract in the MSA and measured the distance from these points to the center of the CBD polygon.

Our choice of distance-to-central business district (CBD) as a key characteristic in our analysis of low-income home buying assumes that it best proxies the location of the highest concentration of economic activity of an MSA.[20] According to the Alonzo-Muth model of land-rent gradients, buyers radiate out from a core area by trading off commuting time and other amenities against land costs. While this theory of MSA organization has been rendered suspect by studies documenting the migration of jobs to suburban areas such as that of Garreau (1991), it was not possible to locate all of these "edge cities" and make multiple and overlapping distance measures from each tract centroid to different points within each MSA. The fact that housing is priced by quality, which is largely a function of the age of the stock/unit, and newer stock is progressively farther out from the CBD means there is still reason to expect distance-related differences in the quality and hence desirability of the stock.

Appendix 2B: Developing Distance Bands

Clearly, there is a danger that in selecting a single set of distance bands for all MSAs we are homogenizing differences in settlement patterns of MSAs. While acknowledging this danger, we are forced to make assumptions in order to get beyond the locational concepts embodied in the terms "central city" and "suburbs," which are clearly inadequate for comparisons of the extent to which low-income buyers are purchasing homes outside the urban core in cities such as Hartford and Houston. In general, because most MSAs develop around a core urban area that is surrounded by what are now considered inner and middle-ring suburbs, we expect the greatest differences between MSAs to lie in the outer suburbs. In fact, none of the MSAs examined here had particularly large shares of loans thirty miles or more from the CBD, and more than 80 percent of all census tracts are within twenty miles of the CBD.

Table 2B-1 shows that one-quarter of all loans in these MSAs were made within ten miles of the CBD, half within sixteen miles, and more than four-fifths within twenty-five miles of the CBD. There is considerable variation in the distribution of lending by distance-to-CBD among the MSAs, with nearly 50 percent of Atlanta's purchases beyond 20 miles, against 10 percent for Hartford and Portland, and just 4.4 percent for Miami. Likewise, while the overall

20. We chose CBD rather than an alternate measure of the MSA's center because it seemed less arbitrary and more likely to be a commuter node than other options. We considered using the tract where the city hall is located but rejected it for this reason.

share of purchases within six miles was 10 percent, Detroit's share was less than 2 percent while Hartford, Milwaukee, and Portland each exceeded 20 percent.

At a finer level, opportunities to buy in a given tract are related to the population in those tracts. If, for example, most tracts near the CBD contain fewer people, then it would be unsurprising to find few borrowers of any incomes and races in these areas (see table 2B-2).

Appendix 2C: Home Mortgage Disclosure Act Data Cleaning for Nine MSAs

In building our database, we first eliminated all records that were not in the nine MSAs we chose to study, including only loans approved for the purchase of one- to four-family homes. In all cases where the MSA was part of a consolidated MSA (CMSA), which we avoided because of complications with our distance-to CBD measure, we use only the PMSA including the city we were interested in. This meant, for example, removing records of Racine from the Milwaukee CMSA to get the Milwaukee PMSA.[21] This left a total of 2,859,650 loans in our study sites during the period 1993.

We follow the conventions established in the annual FFIEC HMDA press releases in classifying applicants into income and race categories (see table 2C-1). For income this means establishing categories based on the annual metropolitan area median income (AMI) estimates supplied by HUD. These are released annually, so borrower incomes reported in the HMDA data are compared to the MSA median income estimate for the year in which the loan was made in order to classify the applicant into low-, middle-, and upper-income categories corresponding to less than 80, 80–119.99, and 120 percent or more of area median income.

The race variable is based on a combination of the applicant and coapplicant races reported in lenders' HMDA filings. If there is no coapplicant or both the applicant and coapplicant are of the same race, then the borrower is considered to be of that race. If either the applicant or coapplicant is white but the other listed party is not, then the application is considered "mixed." For the purpose of our race/ethnicity analyses we consider only Asian, black, Hispanic, and white applicants, dropping American Indian, other, and mixed borrowers.[22]

21. The following is a list of PMSAs in our study with their removed PMSAs: Detroit: Ann Arbor, Flint. Houston: Galveston, Brazoria. Miami: Ft. Lauderdale. Milwaukee: Racine. Philadelphia: Atlantic/Cape May, Vineland, Wilmington. Portland, Oregon: Salem.

22. These categories are too small to provide meaningful results once the data are separated into MSAs and divided into categories based on distance-to-CBD and tract characteristics. All told, we lose 94,336 of a total of 2,725,932 observations by omitting these groups from our race tabulations.

Table 2B-1. *Share of MSA Home Purchases by Tract Distance from CBD*

Distance	*All MSAs*	*Atlanta*	*Detroit*	*Hartford*	*Houston*	*Miami*	*Milwaukee*	*Philadelphia*	*Phoenix*	*Portland, Ore.*
≤2 miles	1.7	2.1	0.6	2.0	1.2	2.1	1.3	2.6	1.1	2.7
2.01–4 miles	3.6	3.0	0.2	7.8	2.9	6.7	7.8	3.0	2.9	8.8
4.01–6 miles	5.1	2.7	1.0	11.5	3.9	6.2	16.5	6.9	3.8	10.5
6.01–8 miles	6.5	3.2	3.2	10.6	4.6	9.4	12.9	9.5	5.8	11.7
8.01–10 miles	7.8	4.3	7.6	11.3	4.2	11.6	9.3	8.0	8.3	15.8
10.01–12 miles	9.3	5.3	8.9	12.7	7.2	14.1	9.2	6.5	13.7	14.6
12.01–14 miles	8.7	5.1	8.7	10.0	7.0	15.1	4.6	7.4	12.6	11.5
14.01–16 miles	9.5	6.9	8.0	9.6	9.1	15.7	7.4	9.8	14.5	5.4
16.01–18 miles	7.3	8.8	7.9	9.2	8.7	7.7	5.2	6.6	6.0	3.8
18.01–20 miles	7.7	8.4	7.4	5.8	11.4	7.1	5.7	5.9	8.8	4.1
20.01–25 miles	14.5	19.9	18.0	8.6	20.6	2.1	8.3	16.2	11.3	4.7
25.01–30 miles	9.1	16.0	11.8	0.9	9.2	1.4	6.0	9.9	6.7	1.8
30.01–40 miles	6.6	11.9	10.1	0.0	6.7	0.3	5.8	6.8	1.7	3.7
>40 miles	2.6	2.3	6.6	0.0	3.3	0.6	0.0	1.0	2.8	1.1
Total	100.0	100.0	100.0	100.0	100.0	100.0	100.0	100.0	100.0	100.0

Source: HMDA data, 1993–99.

Table 2B-2. *Share of Tracts in Four Distance-to-CBD Bands*

	All MSAs	*Atlanta*	*Detroit*	*Hartford*	*Houston*	*Miami*	*Milwaukee*	*Philadelphia*	*Phoenix*	*Portland, Ore.*
8 miles or less	47.4	50.7	35.3	45.2	49.4	71.8	71.1	42.2	40.0	56.0
8.01–14 miles	21.7	13.7	24.4	26.0	21.4	19.7	12.7	20.2	31.8	27.0
14.01–20 miles	13.4	12.7	17.3	19.9	11.3	5.2	7.8	14.5	17.0	7.3
20+ miles	17.5	22.8	23.0	9.0	18.0	3.3	8.4	23.1	11.1	9.7

Source: U.S. Bureau of the Census.

Table 2C-1. *Summary Characteristics of Loans in Combined Nine-City HMDA Database*

Borrower characteristics	*Number of borrowers*	*Tract characteristics*	*Number of loans*
Income (percent of AMI)		*Income (percent of AMI)*	
<80	916,361	<80	318,149
80–119.99	804,355	80–119.99	1,301,118
120 or more	1,138,917	120 or more	1,208,428
Race/ethnicity		*Minority percentage (1990)*	
Asian	72,680	<10	1,616,982
Black	246,069	10–19.99	476,969
Hispanic	246,239	20–49.99	434,533
White	2,066,608	50+	299,211

Source: HMDA data, 1993–99.

References

Berkovec, J. A., and P. Zorn. 1996. "How Complete Is HMDA? HMDA Coverage of Freddie Mac Purchases." *Journal of Real Estate Research* 11 (1): 39–55.

Boehm, T. P., and T. M. Gordon. 1999. "Does Homeownership by Parents Have an Economic Impact on Their Children?" *Journal of Housing Economics* 8: 217–32.

Bostic, R. W., and B. J. Surette. 2000. "Have the Doors Opened Wider? Trends in Homeownership Rates by Race and Income." Working Paper. Washington: Board of Governors of the Federal Reserve System (April).

Case, K., and C. Mayer. 1995. "The Housing Cycle in Eastern Massachusetts: Variations among Cities and Towns." *New England Economic Review* (March/April).

———. 1996. "Housing Price Dynamics within a Metropolitan Area." *Regional Science and Urban Economics* 26: 387–407.

Collins, W. J., and R. A. Margo. 1999. "Race and Homeownership 1900–1990." Working Paper 7277. Cambridge, Mass.: National Bureau of Economic Research.

Coulson, N. E. 1999. "Why Are Hispanic and Asian-American Homeownership Rates So Low? Immigration and Other Factors." *Journal of Urban Economics* 45: 209–27.

DiPasquale, D., and E. Glaeser. 1999. "Incentives and Social Capital: Are Homeowners Better Citizens?" *Journal of Urban Economics* 45: 354–84.

Eggers, F. J. and P. E. Burke. 1996. "Can the National Homeownership Rate Be Significantly Improved by Reaching Underserved Markets?" *Housing Policy Debate* 7 (1): 83–101.

Engelhardt, G. 1994. "House Prices and the Decision to Save for Downpayments." *Journal of Urban Economics* 36: 209–37.

Engelhardt, G., and C. Mayer. 1998. "Intergenerational Transfers, Borrowing Constraints, and Saving Behavior: Evidence from the Housing Market." *Journal of Urban Economics* 44: 135–57.

Federal Housing Finance Board. 2000. "Monthly Interest Rate Survey." Figure 1: Terms on Conventional Single Family Mortgages, Annual National Averages, All Homes.

Federal Financial Institution Examination Council (FFIEC). 2000. "Nationwide Summary Statistics for 1999 Home Mortgage Disclosure Act Data Fact Sheet" (August 2000) (www.ffiec.gov/hmcrpr/hm080800.htm [accessed 8/12/00]).

Frey, W. H., and R. Farley. 1996. "Latino, Asian, and Black Segregation in U.S. Metropolitan Areas: Are Multiethnic Metros Different." *Demography* 33 (1): 35–50.

Frey, W. H., and D. Geverdt. 1998. "Changing Suburban Demographics: Beyond the 'Black-White, City-Suburb' Typology." Paper presented at the Harvard Civil Rights Project Suburban Racial Change Conference.

Frey, W. H, and A. Speare Jr. 1995. "Metropolitan Areas as Functional Communities." In *Metropolitan and Nonmetropolitan Areas: New Approaches to the Geographic Definition*, edited by D. Dahmann and J. Fitzsimmons. Washington: Population Division, U.S. Bureau of the Census.

Galster, G. 1996. "William Grigsby and the Analysis of Housing Sub-Markets and Filtering." *Urban Studies* 33 (10): 1797–1805.

Galster, G., L. Aron, and W. Reeder. 1999. "Encouraging Mortgage Lending in 'Underserved' Areas: The Potential for Expanding Home Ownership in the U.S." *Housing Studies* 14 (6): 777–810.

Garreau, J. 1991. *Edge Cities: Life on the New Frontier*. New York: Doubleday.

Goetzmann, W. N., and M. Spiegel. 1997. "A Spatial Model of Housing Returns and Neighborhood Stability." *Journal of Real Estate Finance and Economics* 14 (1/2): 11–31.

Green, R., and M. White. 1997. "Measuring the Benefits of Homeowning: Effects on Children." *Journal of Urban Economics* 41: 441–61.

Gyourko, J., P. Linneman, and S. Wachter. 1999. "Analyzing the Relationship among Race, Wealth, and Home Ownership in America." *Journal of Housing Economics* 8: 63–89.

Herbert, C. 1997. "Limited Choices: The Effect of Residential Segregation on Homeownership among Blacks." Ph.D. dissertation, JFK School of Government, Harvard University.

Haurin, D. R., P. H. Hendershott, and S. Wachter. 1996. "Wealth Accumulation and Housing Choices of Young Households: An Exploratory Investigation." *Journal of Housing Research* 7: 35–57.

Immergluck, D. 1998. "Progress Confined: Increases in Black Homebuying and the Persistence of Racial Barriers." *Journal of Urban Affairs* 20 (4): 443–57.

Jackson, K. T. 1985. *Crabgrass Frontier*. New York: Oxford University Press.

Joint Center for Housing Studies. 2000. *The State of the Nation's Housing*. Harvard University.

Krivo, L. 1995. "Immigrant Characteristics and Hispanic-Anglo Housing Inequality." *Demography* 32 (4): 599–615.

Li, Y., and E. Rosenblatt. 1997. "Can Urban Indicators Predict Home Price Appreciation?" *Real Estate Economics* 25 (1): 81–104.

Linneman, P., and S. Wachter. 1989. "The Impacts of Borrowing Constraints on Homeownership." *AREUEA Journal* 17 (4): 389–402.

Linneman, P., I. F. Megbolugbe, S. M. Wachter, and M. Cho. 1997. "Do Borrowing Constraints Change U.S. Homeownership Rates?" *Journal of Housing Economics* 6: 318–33.

Masnick, G. 1997. "Citizenship and Homeownership among Foreign Born Residents in the U.S." Working Paper N97-1. Harvard University, Joint Center for Housing Studies.

———. 1998. "Understanding the Minority Contribution to U.S. Owner Household Growth." Working Paper W98-9. Harvard University, Joint Center for Housing Studies.

Masnick, G., and N. McArdle. 1993. "Revised U.S. Household Projections: New Methods and Assumptions." Working Paper W93-2. Joint Center for Housing Studies, Harvard University.

Masnick, G., N. McArdle, and E. Belsky. 1999. "A Critical Look at Rising Homeownership Rates in the United States Since 1994." Working Paper W99-2. Joint Center for Housing Studies, Harvard University.

McArdle, N. 1999. "Outward Bound: The Decentralization of Population and Employment." Working Paper W99-5. Joint Center for Housing Studies, Harvard University.

Orfield, G., and J. T. Yun. 1999. "Resegregation in American Schools." Harvard Civil Rights Project (June) (www.law.harvard.edu/civilrights/publications/resegreation99.html [accessed 11/3/00]).

Ratner, M. S. 1996. "Many Routes to Homeownership: A Four-Site Ethnographic Study of Minority and Immigrant Experiences." *Housing Policy Debate* 7 (1): 103–45.

Rosenbaum, E. 1996. "Racial/Ethnic Differences in Homeownership and Housing Quality, 1991." *Social Problems* 43 (4): 403–26.

Smith, L. B., and M. H. C. Ho. 1996. "The Relative Price Differential between Higher and Lower Price Homes." *Journal of Housing Economics* 5: 1–17.

Speare, A., Jr. 1993. *Changes in Urban Growth Patterns 1980–90*. Cambridge, Mass.: Lincoln Institute of Land Policy.

Stuart, G. 2000. "Segregation in the Boston Metropolitan Area at the End of the 20th Century." Harvard Civil Rights Project (January).

Temkin, K., and W. M. Rohe. 1998. "Social Capital and Neighborhood Stability: An Empirical Investigation." *Housing Policy Debate* 9 (1): 61–88.

U.S. Bureau of the Census. 1998. *State and Metropolitan Area Data Book 1997–98*. Washington.

———. 1999. "Housing Vacancies and Homeownership Annual Statistics: 1999" (www.census.gov/hhes/www/housing/hvs/annual99/ann99t12.html [accessed Aug. 10, 2000]).

———. 2000. "Housing Vacancy Survey Second Quarter 2000" (www.census.gov/hhes/www/housing/hvs/q200tab5.html [accessed Aug. 10, 2000]).

Wachter, S. 1999. "Presentation to the Joint Center for Housing Studies Interfaculty Working Group on Low-Income Homeownership." Harvard University, November.

Wachter, S. M., and I. F. Megbolugbe. 1992. "Racial and Ethnic Disparities in Homeownership." *Housing Policy Debate* 3 (2): 333–70.

Wyly, E. K., and D. J. Hammel. 1999. "Islands of Decay in a Sea of Renewal: Housing Policy and the Resurgence of Gentrification." *Housing Policy Debate* 10 (4): 711–71.

3

The Industrial Structure of Affordable Mortgage Lending

FRANK E. NOTHAFT AND
BRIAN J. SURETTE

Ensuring the widespread availability of mortgage credit for lower-income families and borrowers who reside in lower-income neighborhoods has long been a public policy concern. Legislative efforts aimed at financial institutions intensified during the 1970s with the passage of the Home Mortgage Disclosure Act (HMDA) in 1975 and the Community Reinvestment Act (CRA) in 1977 and the Federal Reserve Board's promulgation of Regulation C.[1] Other legislative efforts have sought to ensure, by authorizing targets for loan purchases, that the secondary mortgage market facilitate lending to low- and moderate-income borrowers and those living in underserved areas, the first such regulations issued by the U. S. Department of Housing and Urban Development (HUD) in 1978.[2] Because the target populations are similar across the two sets of regulations, the laws complement each other in ensuring that bor-

We appreciate Jim Follain's early, formative input; Eric Belsky and Raphael Bostic provided helpful comments; Robert Avery generously provided a file from the National Information Center database; and Marie Anderson provided valuable research assistance with the Home Mortgage Disclosure Act data.

1. See 12 CFR 203.

2. See 24 CFR 81.16(d) and 81.17 (1992 codification). The Housing and Urban Development Act of 1968 authorized HUD to establish regulations to require that a portion of Fannie Mae's purchases be related to the national goal of providing adequate housing for low- and moderate-income families. The Financial Institutions Reform, Recovery, and Enforcement Act of 1989 extended HUD's regulatory authority to Freddie Mac.

rowers from the lower end of the income distribution and those living in historically underserved neighborhoods have access to the mortgage credit they need to purchase and keep their homes.

This chapter examines trends in prime market mortgage lending to low- and moderate-income families and to families living in underserved areas, hereafter referred to as *affordable* lending. We undertake this examination in two parts: First, we identify and discuss how the mix of institutions providing affordable mortgage credit changed in the aggregate during the 1990s. In the prime market, affordable lending was increasingly done by mortgage company subsidiaries of depositories.[3] Savings institutions and independent (unaffiliated) mortgage companies provided a declining fraction of all affordable loans.

Against the backdrop of emerging trends in the mortgage market as a whole, the second part of the analysis looks at variations in affordable lending at the level of the lending organization with a special emphasis on the factors that explain that variation. Four specific hypotheses about the determinants of affordable lending are examined:

—*Economies of scale*: Is there a significant association between the size of an institution and its share of lending to low- and moderate-income families or families living in underserved areas? At issue is whether the increased size of financial institutions during the 1990s has had an appreciable impact on the provision of funds to low- and moderate-income home buyers and underserved areas. In general, we find that depositories operating in only a single metropolitan statistical area (MSA) do more affordable lending as a fraction of their origination business than other institutions. Across most institution types, we find negative relationships between origination volume and affordable lending, though there are offsetting positive relationships among very large depositories.

—*Economic conditions*: Are there significant differences in the lending patterns of financial institutions under various economic conditions, such as refinance booms or recessions? Such differences may emerge if marketing and underwriting policies vary with economic activity. The effects of economic conditions on affordable lending are somewhat mixed. Lending to low- and moderate-income families exhibits a strong procyclical trend. Lending to traditionally underserved areas exhibits a procyclical trend in some specifications, but a countercyclical trend in others.

—*Financial sector consolidation*: Does the number or concentration of lenders in an MSA affect the overall provision of credit to low- and moderate-income borrowers and underserved areas? This question is particularly relevant in light of the passage in 1999 of the financial services modernization legislation, which

3. The term "depositories" includes savings institutions and bank holding companies. As defined here, mortgage company subsidiaries of depositories include (nonbank) holding company affiliates.

is expected to lead to further consolidation in this industry.[4] Measures of concentration (Herfindahl indices) are used to test this hypothesis. Among savings institutions and both independent and depository-affiliated mortgage companies, we generally find a positive relationship. This result is consistent with the conclusion that legislative efforts have been successful at increasing the amount of affordable lending.

—*Cultural affinity*: Do minority-owned financial institutions provide a disproportionately larger share of their lending to low- and moderate-income borrowers and families living in underserved areas than other institutions? If so, then perhaps efforts to improve the diversity of the management of financial institutions should be enhanced and encouraged by regulators. We do generally find a positive relationship between affordable lending and minority ownership. However, the small number of minority-owned institutions in our data suggests caution in interpreting this result.

Many of the recent trends in mortgage lending raise concerns about the provision of prime mortgage credit to lower-income borrowers and borrowers living in traditionally underserved areas. Our analysis of trends in lending to such borrowers helps identify which concerns may be warranted. The efforts expended by all parties—regulators, lenders, and secondary market investors—to ensure a sufficient quantity of such lending, and in particular HUD's new regulation raising the affordable mortgage purchase requirements for Freddie Mac and Fannie Mae, makes our investigation of these trends, and potential explanations for them, especially important.

The chapter is structured as follows. We first discuss federal mortgage market regulations as they pertain to affordable mortgage lending. In the next sections we describe the data and methodology used and the aggregate level and aggregate patterns in the mortgage market as a whole between 1993 and 1999. Finally, we examine affordable mortgage lending patterns at the firm and MSA level.

Affordable Lending Regulation

The term *affordable mortgage* used in this chapter refers to a home purchase loan or a refinance loan that satisfies either the low- and moderate-income goal or the underserved areas goal of HUD's regulation of Freddie Mac and Fannie Mae (the government-sponsored enterprises, or GSEs) as promulgated in 1995.

4. The Gramm-Leach-Bliley Act of 1999 repeals the restrictions on banks affiliating with securities firms contained in sections 20 and 32 of the Glass-Steagall Act and creates a new "financial holding company" under section 4 of the Bank Holding Company Act. Such holding company can engage in a statutorily provided list of financial activities, including insurance and securities underwriting and agency activities, merchant banking, and insurance company portfolio investment activities.

These "housing goals" enumerate levels of affordable mortgages that the GSEs must purchase each year. For 1996, the low- and moderate-income housing goal was set at 40 percent of homes financed, and the underserved area housing goal was set at 21 percent of homes financed; for each of the years 1997 to 2000, the housing goals were set at 42 percent and 24 percent, respectively. HUD raised the housing goal levels to 50 percent and 31 percent, respectively, for the years 2001 to 2003.[5] Because GSE mortgage purchases constitute a large part of the prime market, these substantial affordable housing goals make understanding the factors that affect affordable mortgage lending particularly important.

A loan purchase can meet HUD's affordability criteria by financing a home for a *low- and moderate-income* family or by financing a home in an *underserved area*. A low- and moderate-income family is defined to be one whose income is no more than the median family income in the MSA in which the property being purchased is located. An underserved area mortgage is one extended to a family living in a census tract with a median family income no greater than 90 percent of the median MSA family income, or a census tract with a median family income no greater than 120 percent of the MSA median and where at least 30 percent of the population is nonwhite or Hispanic.[6] This chapter examines separately lending to both the low- and moderate-income segment and the underserved area segment (collectively, the affordable segment) of the prime, conventional mortgage market.

The types of borrowers targeted by the affordable housing goal regulations overlap substantially with those targeted by another prominent mortgage market regulation: the Community Reinvestment Act. The CRA encourages depositories to help meet the credit needs of qualified borrowers in the communities they serve.[7] An enumeration of the specific criteria on which banks will be judged under the CRA is beyond the scope of this chapter.[8] In general, however, one of the three main objectives of the legislation is to encourage banks to extend mortgage credit to lower-income families and those living in lower-income neighborhoods in areas in which the banks operate branch offices.[9] As such, borrowers

5. The goal definitions for 1996–2000 can be found in HUD (1995). The new regulation enumerating affordable housing goals for 2001–03 was published in HUD (2000b).

6. In nonmetropolitan areas, somewhat different definitions apply based on the county or nonmetropolitan state demographic information. We restrict our analysis to metropolitan areas, except in table 3-1, which includes nonmetropolitan lending.

7. There are no laws requiring mortgage companies (independent or subsidiaries of depositories) to lend to the affordable segment of the mortgage market, with the possible exception of the Equal Credit Opportunities Act (ECOA). ECOA requires all lenders to extend credit without prejudice based on the borrower's race or other protected characteristics.

8. For a review of the original provisions of the CRA, see Garwood and Smith (1993).

9. Families with incomes less than 80 percent of the area median income and census tracts with median incomes less than 80 percent of the area median income are considered lower-income under the CRA. The other two main objectives of the CRA are to encourage banks to invest in their communities and to provide other credit-related services, such as counseling, to their communities.

who satisfy CRA requirements often also satisfy HUD's affordable housing goal requirements for the GSEs. This complementarity partly motivates the analysis of the share of affordable mortgage lending by lender: the regulations clearly make the share of affordable loans an outcome that bank and GSE managers take into account when making underwriting and loan purchase decisions.

Data and Methodology

We undertake our examination of the industrial structure of affordable mortgage lending in two parts. First we identify and discuss how the mix of institutions originating mortgages to the affordable segment of the market changed in the aggregate during the 1990s. The second part of the analysis examines variations in affordable lending at the lender and the lender-MSA level, with a special emphasis on the factors that explain that variation. Explanatory factors include firm-specific and MSA-specific characteristics that can be used to test our hypotheses, including measures of lender size, the local unemployment rate, and industry concentration within each local market. To simplify the exposition, we analyze lending patterns for two groups of years: 1993–96 and 1997–99.

Our analysis is based primarily on HMDA origination data for owner-occupied, single-family mortgages during the years 1993 through 1999. HMDA covers an estimated 80 percent of such lending activity, providing an excellent basis for our examination of aggregate and lender-specific patterns in affordable mortgage lending.[10] To measure the influence of economic and other factors on affordable lending, we examine the lending patterns of individual *lending organizations*, defined here to be a separate entity for each lender-MSA combination.[11] Our focus is on lending organizations' *affordable shares*—the fraction of mortgages that individual lending organizations devote to the affordable segments within their MSAs. To focus the analysis on the firms that commit a de minimus level of resources to a particular MSA, we further limit the analysis to organizations that originated at least twenty loans within their MSA in each year.

Our selection of the MSA as the relevant unit of observation is admittedly a compromise.[12] On one hand, broad underwriting guidelines are typically estab-

10. Federal Reserve Board staff has estimated that HMDA covered 80 percent to 87 percent of all home purchase loans during 1993–97; see Avery and others (1999).

11. "Lender" is defined here to be the HMDA filer. Some large institutions make multiple HMDA filings in a given year and may therefore have multiple observations within a single MSA. Similarly, a lender active in more than one MSA is treated as a separate lending organization for each MSA in which it makes loans. A lending organization is considered active in an MSA even if it has no offices within that MSA. A single lending organization may have multiple offices within an MSA.

12. Other researchers have used similar data constructs to define their units of observations by geography. In their analysis of consolidation and the CRA, Avery and others (1999) define "banking organizations" at the level of the lender-county combination.

lished at the lender, not the lending-organization level. On the other hand, loan terms and pricing often vary from one market to another. By focusing on within-MSA lending while also accounting for lender-level factors that may be the same across affiliated lending organizations, our analysis accounts for both national (lender) and local determinants of affordable lending shares.

This chapter focuses on what we call "prime" conforming mortgage lending: conventional, single-family, owner-occupied, home purchase and refinance mortgages that fall below the GSE loan limit at origination. This is by far the largest segment of the (nonjumbo) mortgage market but has the lowest share of affordable loans. We omit government-insured loans and lenders who serve primarily the subprime and manufactured housing sectors.[13] In the analysis we do not distinguish between refinance and home purchase loans, primarily because the CRA and the GSE's affordable housing goals do not distinguish between the two types of loans in evaluating the affordable mortgage activities of covered institutions. We believe these regulatory mandates make it essential to document first and foremost the dynamics of the entirety of the prime affordable mortgage market—the focus of this paper. However, a reexamination of several of our hypotheses separately for home purchase and refinance loans would be interesting and potentially illuminating. We leave such an examination for future work.

The Size of the Prime, Subprime, and Government-Backed Markets

The share of mortgage originations going to the affordable segment (the affordable share) varies substantially by lender type, reflecting differences in location and product offering. Lenders who specialize in lending for the purchase of manufactured housing, for example, make a large share of loans to lower-income borrowers and in underserved areas, reflecting the relatively low price of manufactured housing and the lower-income location where most of these dwellings are sited. Lenders that focus primarily on government-backed products—such as loans insured or guaranteed by the Federal Housing Administration (FHA), the Department of Veterans Affairs (VA), and Rural Housing Service (RHS)—also serve a lower-income clientele, reflecting loan limits, low

13. In this chapter, subprime and manufactured housing lenders are those lenders whom HUD has identified as specializing in those market segments. HUD's list of subprime and manufactured housing specialty lenders is provided at www.huduser.org/datasets/manu.html. Based on estimates of the total size of the subprime market, the lenders identified as subprime by HUD provide reasonably good coverage of this market, accounting for roughly 62 percent of subprime dollar origination volume in 1999, according to Inside Mortgage Finance Publications (2001). The unaccounted-for subprime loans are those originated by "prime" lenders who do not specialize in the subprime market; such loans cannot be separately identified and thus are included in the analysis. Similarly, prime loans originated by subprime and manufactured housing lenders are excluded, though such loans probably account for a very small part of the prime market.

down payments, more lenient underwriting, and other product features that attract lower-income borrowers. More recently, the growth of conventional lending to borrowers with impaired credit histories, known as "subprime" lending, has disproportionately catered to lower-income borrowers.[14] Each of these segments of the market is dominated by mortgage companies that are independently owned—that is, they are owned by entities other than banks and savings institutions and are thus outside the purview of the federal banking regulators; these lenders tend to be specialists in lending to each of these market niches. As shown in table 3-1, in 1999 independent mortgage companies that specialized in manufactured housing or subprime lending accounted for 67 percent and 64 percent, respectively, of the lending volume in those market segments.[15]

At the other end of the spectrum is the jumbo segment of the single-family market; jumbo loans exceed the loan-size purchase limits of the GSEs. In contrast to other market segments, banks and savings institutions dominate jumbo lending: depositories accounted for 54 percent of jumbo originations in 1999, and 83 percent included mortgage company subsidiaries. This segment has the lowest share of affordable loans: only 3 percent of borrowers are low- and moderate-income, and only 12 percent live in underserved areas.

Aggregate Lending Trends in the Conventional Market

Hereafter we focus our analysis on the prime (conventional conforming) market between 1993 and 1999. Within the prime market there has been marked variation in the volume of both total and affordable mortgage lending, as well as in the mix of institutions extending those loans. To a large extent, origination volumes have cycled with interest rates and refinance activity. However, during the 1990s there was a prominent, secular increase in lending by mortgage company subsidiaries of depositories and a corresponding decline in lending by independent mortgage companies and savings institutions.

Between 1993 and 1999, overall prime, conventional conforming origination volumes in metropolitan areas varied from a low of 2.6 million loans in 1995 to a high of 6.1 million loans in 1998. The fraction of total originations going to low- and moderate-income borrowers varied from a low of 32 percent in 1993 to a high of 41 percent in 1999 (see figure 3-1). In most years other than 1993 and 1998 (both refinancing booms), the low- and moderate-income share hovered around 40 percent. The underserved area shares follow essentially the same pattern as the low- and moderate-income shares, experiencing lows of 18 per-

14. Canner, Laderman, and Passmore (1999).

15. Regulatory concerns have recently focused on predatory lending practices of some lenders in the subprime market. See *Curbing Predatory Home Mortgage Lending* (HUD 2000a), a report summarizing information gathered at five field forums by a joint HUD-Treasury Task Force on Predatory Lending.

Table 3-1. *Lender Market Shares, Aggregate Dollar Volumes, and Aggregate Affordable Shares of Residential Mortgage Originations, 1999*

	Lender market shares (percent)[a]						*Aggregate affordable shares*	
			Mortgage companies					
Loan type	*Savings institutions*	*Commercial banks*	*Subsidiaries of depository institutions*	*Independent*	*Credit unions*	*Volume (billions of dollars)*	*Low- and moderate-income share*[b] *(percent)*	*Underserved area share*[b] *(percent)*
Conventional single-family								
Subprime	13	5	18	64	0	99	58	47
Manufactured housing	4	5	23	67	0	18	69	52
Prime (conforming)	20	23	31	22	4	629	40	28
Prime (jumbo)	28	25	29	17	1	217	3	12
FHA, VA, and RHS single-family	6	6	41	46	1	134	65	38
Conventional multifamily	37	32	7	23	0	31	n.a.	59
FHA and RHS multifamily	0	1	17	82	0	1	n.a.	48
Total residential	20	20	30	28	2	1,128	44	31

Source: Federal Financial Institutions Examination Council, authors' tabulations of 1999 Home Mortgage Disclosure Act data.

a. For each institution type, reported shares reflect percentage of dollar volume of originations.

b. Low- and moderate-income and underserved area percentages reflect percent of number of loans originated for home purchase or refinance to each "affordable" segment. Low- and moderate-income percentages not available for multifamily.

Figure 3-1. *Affordable Originations as a Share of Aggregate, Prime Market Originations, 1993–99*

a. Low- or moderate-income shares under CRA and GSE definitions

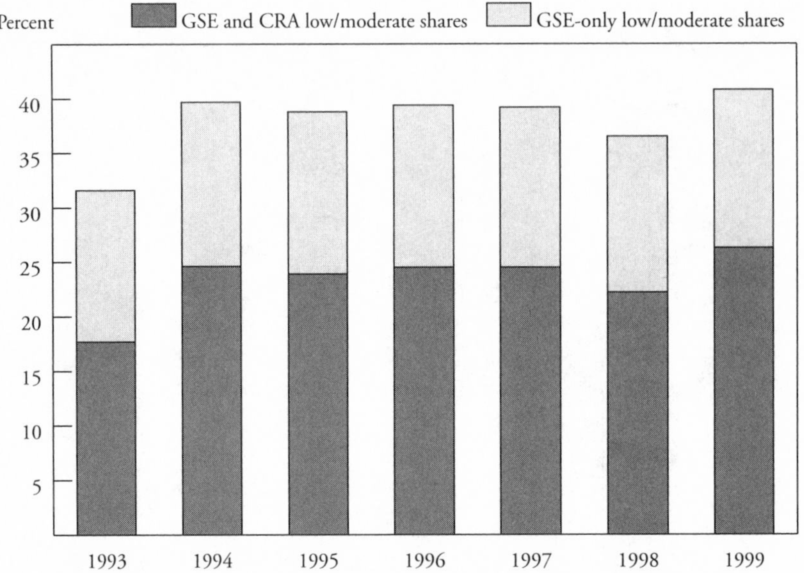

b. Underserved area shares under CRA and GSE definitions

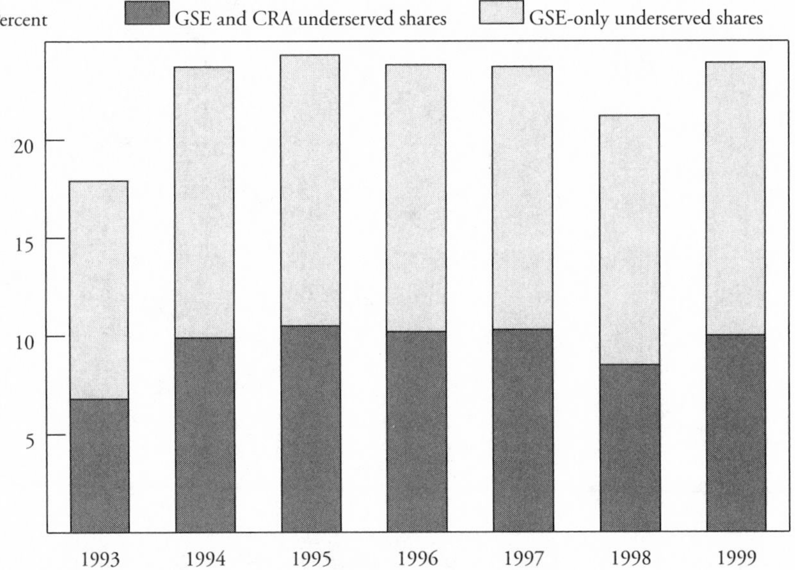

Source: Authors' calculations from 1993–99 HMDA.

cent in 1993 and 21 percent in 1998, but hovering around 24 percent in most other years.

The figures make clear that in terms of mortgage originations, the GSE housing goals cover a broader population of borrowers than the CRA. About two-thirds of borrowers designated as "low- and moderate-income" under the GSE housing goals also qualify as "lower-income" under CRA definitions. About two-fifths of borrowers designated as living in "underserved areas" would also meet the CRA's geography-based lending criteria.[16] Thus, although there is substantial overlap in the populations targeted by the CRA and the GSE housing goals, the overlap is not total. As a consequence, each of these regulations may have a distinct effect on the affordable segment of the mortgage market.

Mortgage Company Subsidiaries of Depositories Account for an Increasing Fraction of Lending

For conventional conforming originations attributable to each type of institution (market share), the trend since 1993 has been away from savings institutions and independent mortgage companies and toward mortgage company subsidiaries of depositories, most of which are subsidiaries of commercial banks (see figure 3-2). Commercial banks' market share varied notably from year to year—especially from 1998 to 1999—but showed no clear trend over the seven-year period.[17] Mortgage banking operations (independent companies and subsidiaries of depositories) garner higher market shares during refinance booms; in 1993 and 1998, mortgage companies accounted for over half of the originations.

The trend toward mortgage company subsidiaries is quite strong. Indeed, in 1993 they accounted for just 20 percent of originations but grew more or less steadily to 29 percent in 1999.[18] The trend away from independent mortgage companies is equally strong: Their share fell steadily over this period from 32 percent to 22 percent. At the same time, the market share controlled by savings institutions fell from 24 percent to 20 percent.

The relative increase in the fraction of mortgages extended by nonbank affiliates or subsidiaries of depositories raises several concerns about the provision of mortgage credit to the affordable segment. First, these affiliates are much larger and operate across larger geographic areas than depositories. They may, as a con-

16. On the other hand, the figures do not reflect banks' nonmortgage CRA obligations (service to and investment in the banks' communities).

17. The volatility in the commercial bank and subsidiary mortgage company series between 1998 and 1999 could be driven by the way these institutions report under HMDA. Several large subsidiaries and their commercial bank parent filing separately in 1998 but jointly in 1999 could explain this pattern.

18. Table 3-1 reports the dollar volume of originations. The figures chart the number of originations.

Figure 3-2. *Aggregate Prime Market Shares by Institution Type, 1993–99*

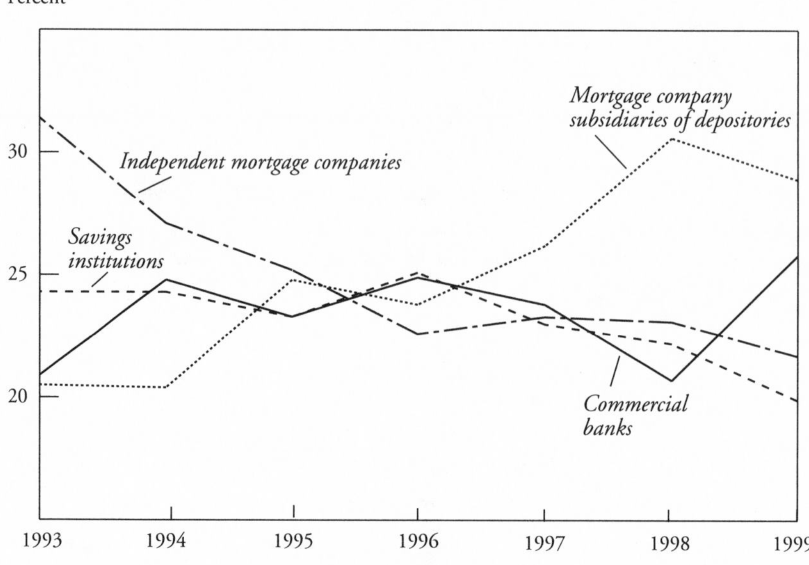

Source: Authors' calculations from 1993–99 HMDA.

sequence, have less connection to local communities than depositories and may have less incentive to serve the affordable segment. Second, to the extent that connections to the community generate local knowledge important for lending profitably to this segment, affordable lending may be lower than otherwise. Finally, such institutions are only indirectly, if at all, subject to the CRA. While these concerns may be warranted, the data do not show a substantial decline in the overall share of originations devoted to affordable lending over the 1990s. Thus, while the mix of originators changed substantially, aggregate affordable lending has continued apace.

Affordable Lending Has Increased Most among Mortgage Companies

Consistent with the considerable growth in the overall market share of mortgage company subsidiaries of depositories, these institutions accounted for an increasing fraction of mortgages to low- and moderate-income borrowers and mortgages originated in underserved areas between 1993 and 1999 (figures 3-3, 3-4). Mortgage company subsidiaries of depositories accounted for 19 percent of total low- and moderate-income originations in 1993, rising more or less steadily to 28 percent in 1999. Similarly, over the same period, mortgage company subsidiaries' share of underserved area originations rose from about 16 percent to 27 percent. Most of the subsidiaries' increases in affordable lending shares came at the expense of independent mortgage companies and savings

Figure 3-3. *Share of Aggregate, Prime Market Low- and Moderate-Income Originations, by Institution Type, 1993–99*

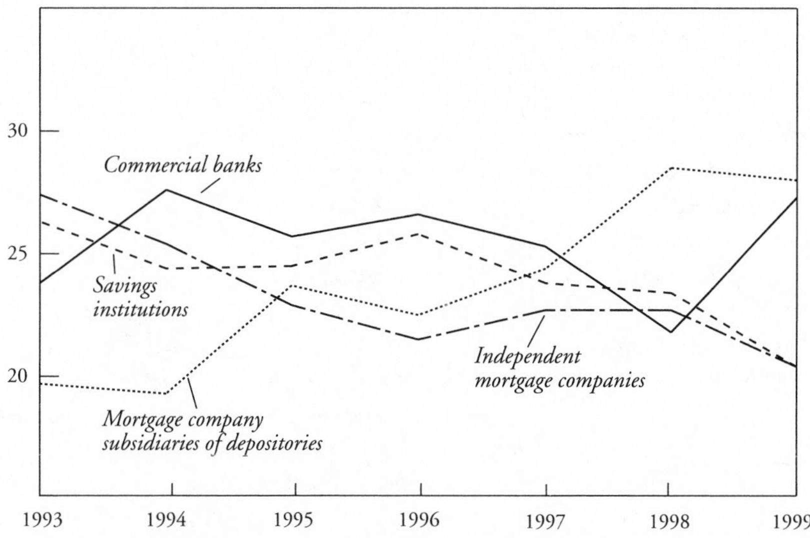

Source: Authors' calculations from 1993–99 HMDA.

Figure 3-4. *Share of Aggregate Prime Market Underserved Area Originations, by Institution Type, 1993–99*

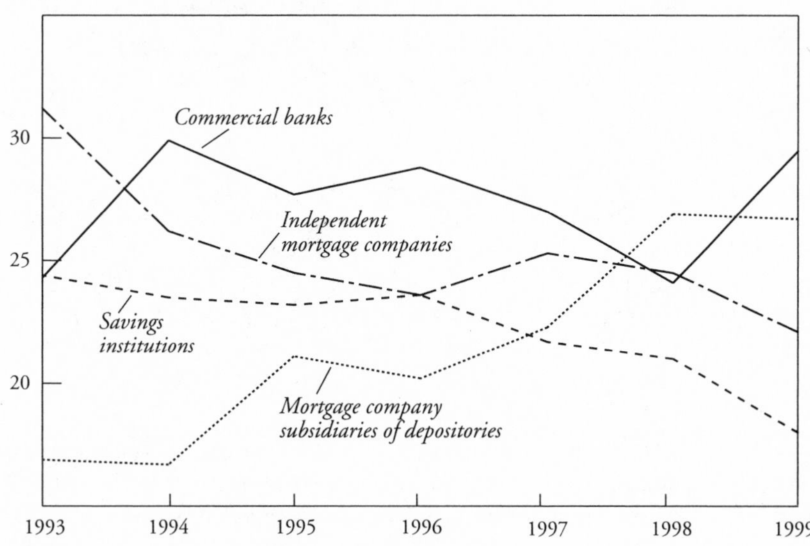

Source: Authors' calculations from 1993–99 HMDA.

institutions. Savings institutions' low- and moderate-income market share dropped from 26 percent to 20 percent, and their underserved area market share fell from 24 percent to 18 percent between 1993 and 1999. The affordable lending market shares among independent mortgage companies fell even more dramatically throughout the period.[19]

At least two possible conclusions about the structure of mortgage lending are suggested by the trends in overall and affordable mortgage lending. First, the trends are almost certainly the result of acquisition activity on the part of depositories, particularly commercial banks. As more mortgage company subsidiaries are created, either de novo or through acquisitions of independent mortgage companies, the subsidiary mortgage company share of the market should grow at the expense of independent mortgage companies.[20] A second possible conclusion follows from the first. As depositories have acquired or otherwise established mortgage company subsidiaries, they may have increasingly diverted customers seeking mortgage loans to their mortgage company subsidiaries.

Left unanswered is the question of why depositories increased their use of mortgage company subsidiaries. One view is that depositories have simply diversified across loan production channels in an effort to reduce the costs associated with originations. Branch offices are costly to operate and may not afford the opportunity to expand and contract in response to the overall level of mortgage activity. An important motivation for such diversification may therefore be the substantial year-to-year variation in the volume of originations. Mortgage company subsidiaries may afford more operational flexibility in this regard, for example, by utilizing correspondent (mortgage broker) networks at the point of origination.

The use of subsidiaries and affiliates offers depositories a further advantage with respect to how their CRA performance is measured. Depositories are permitted by examiners to either include or omit, at the depositories' discretion, the originations of nonbank affiliates and subsidiaries. Thus the increased use of nonbank affiliates and subsidiaries affords banks the opportunity to improve their measured CRA lending performance.

At the same time, there is no evidence in the aggregate data to suggest that the overall volume of affordable originations has declined as a result of the trend toward subsidiaries. As figure 3-1 shows, affordable originations as a fraction of total originations held about constant in most years, except for the refinance years 1993 and 1998. By this metric, the trend away from savings institutions

19. This trend could also be driven in part by measurement error. If improvements in the identification of lenders that specialize in manufactured housing or subprime lending led to a larger fraction of such lenders being identified as such by HUD over time, then the decline in independent mortgage companies' market shares over time would be exaggerated.

20. A congressionally mandated study of the effects of the CRA also notes that the increase in lending to low- and moderate-income borrowers and areas is partly attributable to the nonbank affiliates of depositories acquired after 1992. See Litan and others (2000).

and independent mortgage companies does not appear to have caused a decline in affordable lending.

The Subprime Market Is Dominated by Independent Mortgage Companies

It is worth noting at this point that market share trends are markedly different in the manufactured housing and subprime (MHSP) segment, a market that tends to be dominated by independent mortgage companies. Owing to the large current size of the MHSP market and its dramatic growth since 1993, independent mortgage companies have played an increasingly important role in total (prime and subprime) conventional conforming lending. Indeed, when loans originated by lenders whom HUD has identified as serving primarily the subprime and manufactured housing market are considered with the rest of the conventional conforming market, the secular market share decline of independent mortgage companies discussed above is halted or reversed. In that case, the share of all conventional conforming mortgages attributable to independent mortgage companies holds about constant over the period, and their share of the total affordable originations rises modestly over time. The increase in market share for mortgage company subsidiaries over time persists but is less dramatic, both as a fraction of all originations and as a fraction of all affordable originations. Both types of depositories' market shares and affordable lending shares decline modestly when the MHSP lenders are included in the analysis. The fraction of all originations that qualify as "affordable" rose steadily over the 1990s.

Average Affordable Lending Shares at the Lender and Lender-MSA Level

Against the backdrop of a substantial shift of aggregate, prime market origination activity out of independent mortgage companies and savings institutions and into mortgage company subsidiaries, we now examine how average affordable lending changed during the 1990s and the factors that contributed to those changes.

As noted earlier, this part of our analysis is based on individual *lenders*, defined as distinct HMDA filers, and *lending organizations*, which are defined as lender-MSA combinations. We present mean characteristics for lending organizations in two groups of years: 1993–96 and 1997–99 (see table 3-2). The groupings are a convenient way to examine changes in affordable shares and other characteristics over time.[21]

21. Ideally, we would like to have included 1996 in the second period because the GSEs' underserved area goal as defined in this chapter first took effect in 1996. However, we do not have data on one of our main variables of interest: which firms were owned by minorities or women before 1997. On the other hand, the GSE housing goals were higher for the 1997–99 period than for 1996 and earlier. Thus the selected year groupings are still economically important.

Table 3-2. *Mean Characteristics of Lending Organizations, by Institution Type and Year*[a]

					Mortgage companies			
	Commercial banks		*Savings institutions*		*Independent*		*Subsidiaries of depository institutions*	
Characteristic	*1993–96*	*1997–99*	*1993–96*	*1997–99*	*1993–96*	*1997–99*	*1993–96*	*1997–99*
Affordable lending shares								
Low- and moderate-income share	0.428	0.431	0.393	0.390	0.337	0.376	0.333	0.348
Underserved area share	0.272	0.273	0.227	0.214	0.222	0.247	0.185	0.194
Economies of scale								
MSA originations	194	218	265	285	206	202	232	307
Outside-MSA originations	1,357	9,219	7,904	22,272	19,326	26,594	19,851	45,548
Spline segments in outside-MSA originations								
0 to 1,000 (percent of observations)	0.787	0.583	0.557	0.411	0.267	0.248	0.097	0.051
1,001 to 10,000	0.175	0.245	0.232	0.255	0.350	0.372	0.383	0.230
10,001 or more	0.038	0.172	0.210	0.334	0.383	0.380	0.521	0.719
Single MSA lender	0.351	0.200	0.169	0.095	0.018	0.012	0.007	0.003
Cultural affinity								
Minority- or woman-owned	n.a.	0.010	n.a.	0.001	n.a.	0.019	n.a.	0.005

Local economic conditions[b]								
Median MSA family income ($000)	42.0	48.4	44.8	51.0	44.2	50.2	43.6	49.5
FHA loan limit ($000)	109	126	123	139	122	137	118	133
MSA fair market rent ($/month)	537	575	608	635	602	628	576	605
MSA unemployment rate (percent)	5.5	4.1	5.8	4.2	5.9	4.3	5.4	4.1
Industry concentration								
MSA Herfindahl index	0.042	0.034	0.035	0.029	0.035	0.029	0.037	0.031
Secondary market factors								
Percentage of loans sold	26.0	26.8	34.3	43.6	84.9	86.3	81.2	86.4
Portfolio lender (sold no loans)	42.3	42.9	28.7	22.7	4.8	3.6	1.8	0.6
Other firm/market characteristics								
Percentage of loans refinanced	53.4	58.5	47.4	51.3	49.1	51.7	42.6	53.0
MSA size (square miles)	2,300	2,273	2,257	2,179	2,879	2,855	2,316	2,274
Total number of lender-MSA observations	16,199	13,969	12,660	10,184	17,779	14,549	13,121	12,690

Source: Authors' calculations based on HMDA data.

a. Variables are reported here in levels only. Several of these variables enter the regression as natural logarithms, as noted in table 3-4.

b. Dollar figures are adjusted to 1999 dollars using the CPI all urban consumers series.

We define *low-mod shares* and *underserved area shares* as, respectively, the fraction of prime originations going to low- and moderate-income owner-occupants and to owner-occupants living in underserved areas. Collectively, low-mod and underserved area shares are referred to as *affordable shares*. Much like aggregate affordable origination volumes, among lending organizations the average fraction of originations going to the affordable segment (affordable shares) cycled with interest rates: during low-interest rate periods—the so-called refinance booms of 1993 and 1998—refinance activity rose and average affordable shares fell. In years other than the refinance booms, average affordable shares remain within a fairly narrow range.

At the same time, affordable shares varied along several other important economic dimensions. First, average affordable shares rose modestly for both types of mortgage companies during the 1990s, suggesting that something more than a simple composition shift occurred in affordable mortgage lending. Second, there are large differences in the average affordable shares by lender size. Finally, affordable shares vary notably according to the degree of market concentration and the state of the local economy.

Differences in Average Affordable Lending Shares by Institution Type

The average lending shares devoted to low- and moderate-income families and those living in underserved areas follow a fairly consistent pattern across time and institution type. With the exception of the refinance booms of 1993 and 1998, average affordable shares remained within a narrow range across time for each institution type (see figures 3-5 and 3-6). Particularly among depositories, average affordable shares show little in the way of a secular trend. In all years commercial banks devoted a higher share of their prime mortgage originations to the affordable segments than other institution types, while mortgage company subsidiaries of depositories lent the smallest share to the affordable segments.

Excluding 1993 and 1998, in each year commercial banks made an average of about 44 percent of their loans to low- and moderate-income families and about 28 percent of their loans to families in underserved areas. Over the same period, savings institutions made about 40 percent of their loans to low- and moderate-income families and between 21 and 25 percent of their loans to families living in underserved areas.

Both types of mortgage companies exhibited modest increases in average affordable shares over the 1993 to 1999 period. Independent mortgage companies' average low- and moderate-income shares rose (in fits and starts) from 37 percent in 1994 to 39 percent in 1999. Their average underserved area share rose from about 22 percent in 1994 to 24 percent in 1999, with a peak of 27 percent in 1997. Mortgage company subsidiaries of depositories' average low- and moderate-income shares held steady at about 35 percent from 1994 to 1997. After a dip in 1998, they rose to 38 percent in 1999. Their average under-

Figure 3-5. *Share of Low- and Moderate-Income Shares among Lending Organizations, by Lender Type, 1993–99*

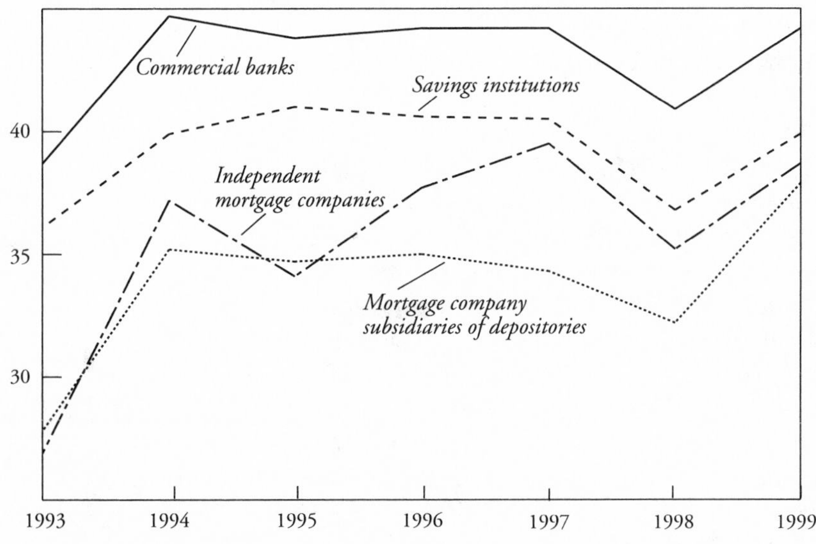

Source: Authors' calculations from 1993–99 HMDA.

Figure 3-6. *Average Underserved Area Shares among Lending Organizations, by Lender Type, 1993–99*

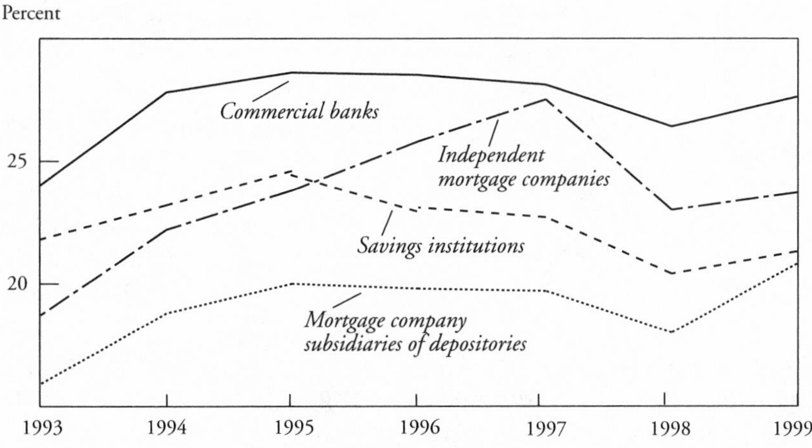

Source: Authors' calculations from 1993–99 HMDA.

served area shares followed a similar pattern, rising from 19 to 21 percent over the period.

These trends in average affordable shares indicate that the dramatic increases in total and affordable market shares attributable to mortgage company subsidiaries of depositories discussed in preceding sections partly results from changes in the average lending behavior of each lender type. These offsetting trends partly explain why, in the aggregate, affordable lending shares have not declined.

Differences in Affordable Lending by Size of Lender and Lending Organization

As a result of consolidation, economic prosperity, and other factors, financial institutions grew dramatically in size between 1993 and 1999. Because local knowledge and community ties are commonly believed to be important factors that determine the extent of affordable lending, there is a risk that larger or more geographically diverse organizations will do less of it. On the other hand, technological advances have automated much of the underwriting and origination process and may have made it less costly for lenders to originate loans to the affordable segment and to ensure consistency in underwriting. Associated with technological advances, the unbundling of various components of mortgage underwriting, origination, and servicing may have encouraged specialization in market niches previously not well served by the mortgage industry, including the affordable segment. Because both technology and the extent of geographic diversity and lender size have changed markedly over the decade, we explore here whether large organizations have higher or lower affordable shares than smaller organizations, and whether the relationship between size and affordable lending has changed over time.

Because we believe both local (MSA) and national (lender) considerations affect the provision of affordable mortgage credit, we use two distinct measures of size to test for the presence of economies of scale: (1) the number of total originations nationwide by each lender (total lender originations) and (2) the number of originations by each lending organization within its MSA (MSA originations).

We find fairly convincing evidence among depositories that affordable shares decline and then rise with total lender originations. Very small and very large depositories had higher low-mod and underserved area shares than mid-sized depositories (see figures 3-7, 3-8). These patterns are equally strong in both the 1993–96 and 1997–99 periods (not shown separately). Such patterns are consistent with the conclusion that small depositories, such as community banks, can lend to the affordable segment profitably owing in part to their more detailed knowledge of the few markets they operate in, and that technological and process innovations, such as automated underwriting, have not disproportionately favored affordable lending by larger lenders. The patterns are also consistent with the conclusion that size-based efficiencies and automation enable larger deposito-

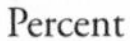

Figure 3-7. *Average Low- or Moderate-Income Shares, by Lender Type and Total Lender Originations, 1993–99*

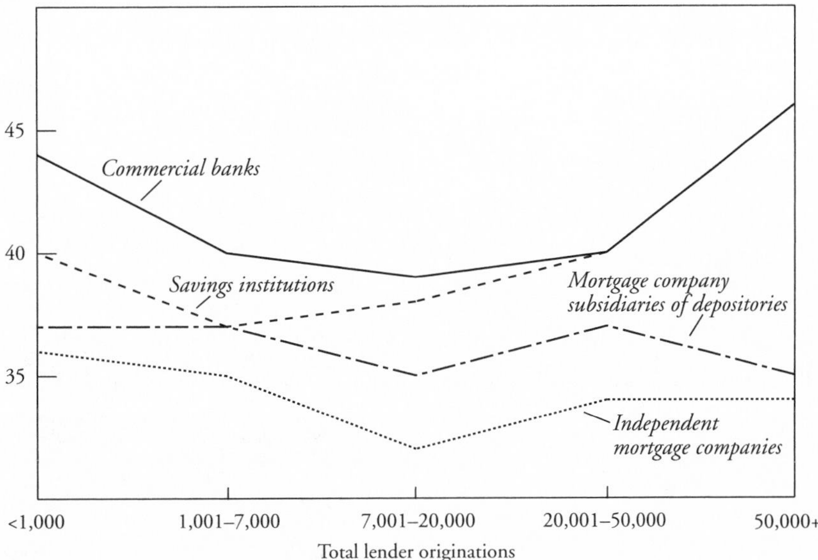

Source: Authors' calculations from 1993–99 HMDA.

ries to lend profitably to the affordable segment. Because larger lenders' affordable lending patterns may be more closely scrutinized by regulators than mid-sized or smaller depositories, the CRA may also help explain the pattern.

When we measure the size of a lending organization by the number of originations made within its MSA, commercial banks' average affordable shares exhibit a pattern similar to that observed for total lender originations. Mid-sized commercial bank organizations devote the smallest fraction of their loans to both underserved area and low- and moderate-income segments (see figures 3-9 and 3-10). For example, commercial bank organizations that originated between 250 and 1,000 mortgages in 1999 extended an average of 42 percent of their loans to low- and moderate-income families, compared to 45.1 percent for organizations that extended fewer than 50 mortgages and 43.5 percent for organizations that extended more than 1,000 mortgages. This pattern is present in most years examined.[22]

22. The patterns of affordable lending and origination volume are weaker among savings institutions. This is due partly to changes over time in the patterns of affordable shares by institution size. Savings institutions exhibit pronounced diseconomies of scale in affordable lending in some years, but negligible or positive economies in other years. In the multivariate analysis below we discuss in more detail differences over time in the relationship between size and affordable shares.

Figure 3-8. *Average Underserved Area Shares, by Lender Type and Total Lender Originations, 1993–99*

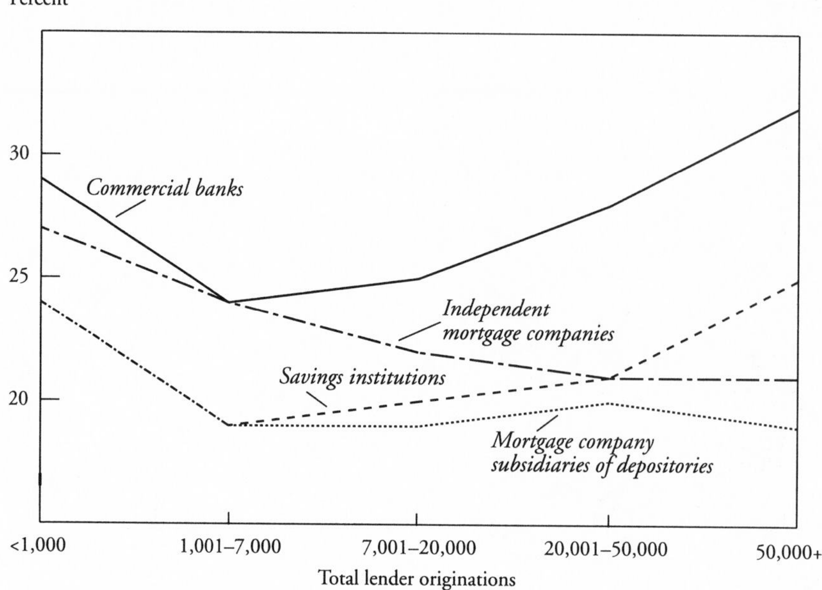

Source: Authors' calculations from 1993–99 HMDA.

Among mortgage companies, the relationship between affordable shares and size differs depending on the size measure used. Given that mortgage companies typically originate many more loans than depositories and are more likely than depositories to operate across multiple MSAs (see table 3-2), we believe the negative relationships between national volume and affordable shares shown in figures 3-7 and 3-8 are more important economically. These findings suggest that smaller mortgage companies may have a comparative advantage over larger mortgage companies in the affordable segment. Such an advantage may stem from informational advantages associated with proximity to borrowers, unbundling, or the development of technologies that may have enabled smaller mortgage companies to profitably serve niches within the affordable segment of the market.

The U-shaped pattern in scale economies among commercial banks and savings institutions at the level of both the lender and the lending organization partly explains why in the aggregate the affordable segment did not shrink as a fraction of total originations over the course of the 1990s. Despite the trend toward greater market share for mortgage company subsidiaries and the apparent diseconomies of scale in mortgage company subsidiaries' affordable shares, aggregate affordable shares remained about constant because of higher average

Figure 3-9. *Average Low- or Moderate-Income Shares, by Lender Type and Number of MSA Originations, 1993–99*

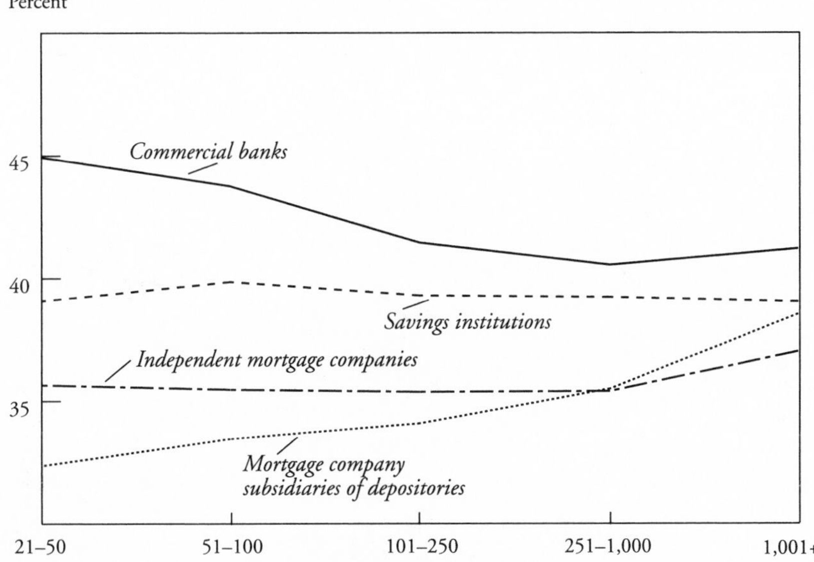

Source: Authors' calculations from 1993–99 HMDA.

affordable shares among the largest depositories and the substantial growth in the number of very large depositories. Such results suggest that consolidation among depositories that occurred during the 1990s and the growth in the average size of depositories over that period have not caused depositories to reduce the fraction of their loans going to the affordable segment.

Differences in Affordable Lending by Local Economic Conditions

Affordable lending shares are affected by a wide variety of factors other than lending organization type and size. The business focus of different institutions, the condition of the local economy, and the degree of concentration and competition within local markets all play a significant role in determining the extent to which lenders can profitably originate affordable mortgages, and hence their availability to families in the affordable segment.

Particularly important for explaining variations in affordable shares across lending organizations are the limited financial resources families in the affordable segment typically have at their disposal. Such families may be more susceptible to downturns in their local economy and pose more risk to lenders than do other borrowers. When local economic conditions are measured by the unemployment rate within each MSA, average lending shares to low- and moderate-

Figure 3-10. *Average Underserved Area Shares, by Lender Type and Number of MSA Originations, 1993–99*

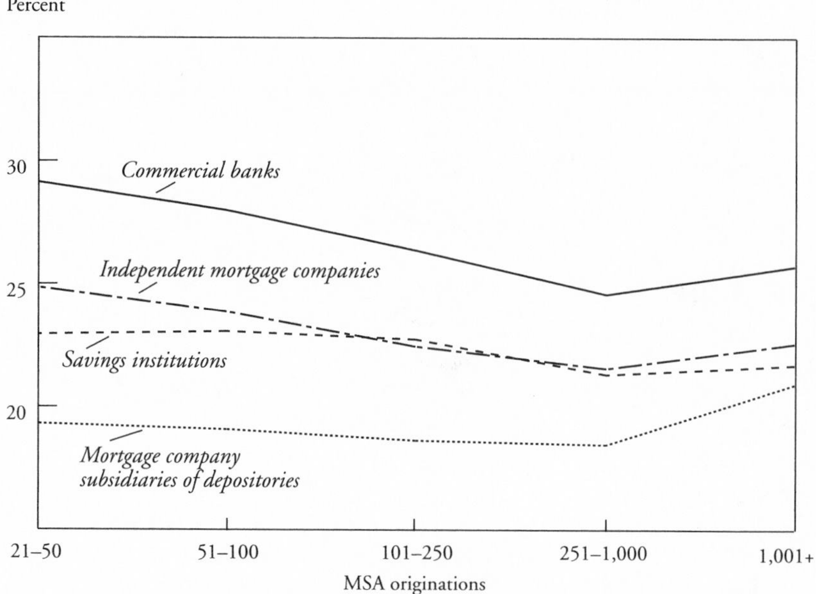

Source: Authors' calculations from 1993–99 HMDA.

income families appear to exhibit a strong procyclical pattern:[23] MSAs with very low rates of unemployment had very high low- and moderate-income shares (see table 3-3). In contrast, lending shares to underserved areas appear to have been uncorrelated with the unemployment rate in the bulk of MSAs. However, in MSAs with an unemployment rate above the 80th percentile, average underserved area shares are considerably higher compared to other MSAs. Both of these trends are quite strong in both the 1993–96 and 1997–99 periods.

Neither of these trends individually is particularly surprising. What is surprising is that the two trends go in opposite directions: strongly procyclical low- and moderate-income shares and weakly countercyclical underserved area shares. Part of the explanation for these patterns may lie in simple algebra: In the MSAs with the highest unemployment rates, the number of underserved area loans appear to be less sensitive to variations in local economic conditions than total MSA originations, while low- and moderate-income originations appear to be more sensitive to local economic conditions than total MSA originations.

23. Our use of the terms "procyclical" and "countercyclical" is somewhat nonstandard. We infer cyclicality primarily from cross-sectional variations in economic conditions, rather than from intertemporal variations, as is customary. However, because the entire economy, and virtually all regions of the country, enjoyed robust economic growth throughout the time period examined, analyses of cross-sectional variation may be the only way to gauge cyclicality.

Table 3-3. *Average Low- or Moderate-Income Shares, Underserved Area Shares, and 1990 MSA Population Living in Underserved Tracts, by MSA Unemployment Rate Quintile, 1993–96 and 1997–99*
Percent

MSA unemployment rate	*Average low- or moderate-income share*	*Average underserved area share*	*1990 MSA population living in underserved tracts*
1993–96			
Lowest quintile	38.8	20.5	37
Second quintile	37.9	21.7	40
Third quintile	37.1	21.9	38
Fourth quintile	36.3	20.4	38
Highest quintile	31.7	27.5	45
1997–99			
Lowest quintile	42.2	21.7	37
Second quintile	39.9	23.1	38
Third quintile	38.6	21.0	39
Fourth quintile	36.8	21.1	38
Highest quintile	31.9	27.8	46

Source: Authors' tabulations from 1993–99 HMDA. MSA unemployment rates published by the Bureau of Labor Statistics, based on the Current Population Survey.

Such a pattern may be a consequence of the static definitions of underserved areas, which are based on census tract and MSA characteristics in 1990. We note first that the cyclicality of both low-mod and underserved area shares is strongest when MSA unemployment is highest: the decline in low-mod shares and the rise in underserved area shares are largest going from the fourth to the fifth quintile of the MSA unemployment rate. This pattern is equally strong in both the 1993–96 and the 1997–99 periods. This suggests that there is something unusual (and persistent) about the MSAs with the highest unemployment that may explain the puzzling relationships between affordable shares and local unemployment rate.

It turns out that in the MSAs with the highest unemployment rates a substantially higher fraction of the population lives in underserved tracts than is the case in other MSAs, whereas by definition exactly 50 percent of families in any MSA are low- and moderate-income. About 45 percent of the population in those MSAs lives in underserved tracts, compared to about 38 percent in the other MSAs (see table 3-3). Thus underserved area shares may be higher in MSAs with high unemployment in part because significantly more families live in such areas than in other MSAs. The large decline in low-mod shares moving from the fourth to the fifth MSA unemployment rate quintile may also be explained by related factors.

Though tract population is a reasonable explanation for these patterns, the evidence is not conclusive. We cannot reject the hypothesis that there is something else unusual about the MSAs with high unemployment that explains this pattern. For example, regulatory incentives may play a role in explaining the relationships between affordable shares and the unemployment rate. Most lenders in the prime market have a regulatory-based incentive to make loans in low-income neighborhoods, either directly as a result of the CRA (depositories) or indirectly through the GSE housing goals (mortgage companies and depositories). If lenders target special affordable products more aggressively in underserved areas, and if such efforts are less sensitive to local economic conditions than other lending products, one might expect the ratio of underserved area originations to total originations to exhibit a countercyclical pattern. The GSEs' provision of liquidity for such products, stemming from their housing goals, may also play an affirmative role.

Multivariate Analysis of Affordable Shares

Thus far the data have shown considerable variation in the amounts of affordable lending extended by different types of originators. A wide variety of lender- and market-related factors—measures of market concentration, organization size, cultural affinity, and economic conditions—potentially explain the variation in affordable shares we observe across different types of lenders. We now test, using a multivariate regression model, the extent to which these factors explain affordable lending.

The substantial differences across institutions in the regulatory environment they operate in, along with observed differences in affordable lending shares, led us to model affordable shares separately for each institution type and for each year, 1993 through 1999. To simplify the exposition, we present only two sets of regression results for each institution type: for the pooled 1993–96 data and the pooled 1997–99 data (see table 3-4). The main results discussed here are qualitatively unaffected by the pooling.

We estimate these models using ordinary least squares (OLS), where the dependent variables are the fraction of each lending organization's MSA originations made to low- and moderate-income families and the fraction to families living in underserved areas.[24] Standard errors and hypothesis tests are based on asymptotically consistent covariance matrices.[25] As before, we limit the analysis

24. We present and discuss unweighted regression results here. Weighting the regressions by originations by the lending organization does not alter our qualitative conclusions.

25. See Huber (1967). We test and reject the hypothesis of no heteroskedasticity. However, we have such a large number of observations that the standard errors of the regressions are only marginally affected by correcting the covariance matrix.

to conventional conforming mortgages for the purchase or refinance of owner-occupied, single-family properties. The explanatory variables in these regressions include a broad array of firm- and market-related characteristics. The means and the definitions of the independent variables are presented in Appendix 3A.

Economies of Scale

With respect to affordable lending shares at the organization level, the data show fairly clear diseconomies of scale. Smaller organizations and firms that operate in only a single MSA generally extend a larger fraction of their mortgages to the affordable segment than other lenders do. Among large depositories we find some evidence of an offsetting positive relationship between lender origination volume and affordable shares.

We focus on three measures of lending volume with which we test for the presence of economies of scale in affordable lending: (1) The number of originations by each lending organization within its MSA (MSA originations), (2) the number of originations by the lender as a whole outside the lending organization's MSA (outside-MSA originations), [26] and (3) an indicator variable identifying banks and savings institutions with operations in only a single MSA.[27] To accommodate the apparent U-shape in the relationship between lender size and affordable shares observed in figures 3-7 and 3-8, outside-MSA originations enter the models as linear splines, with two kink points. The kink points (respectively 1,000 and 10,000 outside-MSA originations) were selected to ensure a sufficient number of observations to estimate the slope of each line segment. The qualitative results are not very sensitive to modest variations in the selected kink points.

The strongest trend apparent in these results is the large positive effect of having mortgage operations in only a single MSA. Depositories operating on this scale do notably more affordable lending—on the order of 1 to 5 percentage points more—than otherwise similar depositories operating in multiple MSAs. Such a result supports the conclusion that local knowledge and community ties stemming from a narrow geographic focus are keys to originating a large fraction of both low- and moderate-income and underserved areas loans. This result is also consistent with technological advances enabling smaller lenders to continue profitably originating mortgages in the affordable segments.

Among depositories, the other measures of economies of scale indicate that affordable shares decline with origination volume up to a point, and then either

26. For example, if an organization makes 500 mortgages within its MSA, and the lender that the organization is a part of makes 1,500 mortgages across all MSAs, outside-MSA originations equals 1,000 (1,500 – 500).

27. Depending on the year, between 15 and 40 percent of banks and savings institutions have operations (consisting of at least twenty originations annually) in only one MSA. The corresponding figures for mortgage companies are typically well under 5 percent.

Table 3-4a. *Low- or Moderate-Income Share OLS Regression Results, by Institution Type and Year*[a]

Dependent variable Low- and moderate-income share of originations	*Commercial banks*		*Savings institutions*		*Mortgage companies*			
					Independent		*Subsidiaries of depository institutions*	
	1993–96	*1997–99*	*1993–96*	*1997–99*	*1993–96*	*1997–99*	*1993–96*	*1997–99*
Economies of scale								
MSA originations	–0.006‡	–0.009‡	–0.010‡	0.000	0.001	0.001	0.011‡	0.011‡
Spline segments in outside-MSA originations								
0 to 1,000	0.009†	0.010‡	–0.015‡	–0.017‡	–0.005	0.000	–0.019‡	–0.008
1,001 to 10,000	0.003‡	–0.003‡	0.005‡	–0.002‡	–0.004‡	–0.006‡	–0.002‡	–0.003‡
10,001 or more (× 100)	0.007	0.024‡	0.180‡	0.086‡	0.012‡	0.022‡	0.012‡	–0.020‡
Single MSA lender	0.018‡	0.028‡	0.011‡	0.024‡	n.a.	n.a.	n.a.	n.a.
Cultural affinity								
Minority- or woman-owned	n.a.	0.004	n.a.	0.039‡	n.a.	–0.004	n.a.	0.139‡
Local economic conditions								
MSA median income[b]	0.392‡	0.418‡	0.343‡	0.354‡	0.375‡	0.419‡	0.420‡	0.347‡
FHA loan limit[b]	–0.062‡	–0.080‡	0.000	–0.070‡	–0.067‡	–0.115‡	–0.065‡	–0.099‡
MSA fair market rent[b, c]	–0.093‡	–0.199‡	–0.090‡	–0.105‡	–0.082‡	–0.170‡	–0.067‡	–0.047‡
MSA unemployment rate[b]	–0.008	–0.020‡	–0.039‡	–0.032‡	–0.024‡	–0.039‡	–0.007	–0.020‡
Industry concentration								
Herfindahl index	0.187‡	–0.146	0.658‡	0.778‡	0.191‡	0.267‡	0.313‡	0.487‡

Secondary market factors								
Percentage of loans sold	–0.120‡	–0.085‡	–0.053‡	–0.043‡	n.a.	n.a.	n.a.	n.a.
Portfolio lender only	0.013‡	0.004	0.005	–0.028‡	n.a.	n.a.	n.a.	n.a.
Other firm/market characteristics								
Percentage of loans refinanced	–0.077‡	–0.053‡	–0.105‡	–0.026‡	0.097‡	0.110‡	0.033‡	0.047‡
MSA size (square miles)[b]	0.010‡	0.005‡	0.012‡	0.001	–0.008‡	–0.012‡	–0.018‡	–0.012‡
Year dummies[c]								
1993 (or 1997)	–0.031‡	0.003	0.010†	0.019‡	–0.113‡	0.012‡	–0.079‡	–0.028‡
1994 (or 1998)	0.001	–0.019‡	0.019‡	–0.031‡	0.007	–0.051‡	0.003	–0.063‡
1995 (or omitted)	–0.004	n.a.	0.013‡	n.a.	–0.018‡	n.a.	0.008‡	n.a.
Number of MSA-lender combinations	16,199	13,969	12,660	10,184	17,779	14,549	13,121	12,690
Adjusted R-square	0.194	0.172	0.163	0.138	0.198	0.184	0.231	0.216

a. Parameter estimates designated with a ‡ (†) are statistically significant at the 99 percent (95 percent) level of confidence. Hypothesis tests performed on asymptotically consistent (Huber-White) covariance matrices.

b. These variables are included in the regression as natural logarithms.

c. The year dummies given outside (in) parentheses are used in the first (second) period models. The years 1996 and 1999 are the excluded categories.

Table 3-4b. *Underserved Area Share OLS Regression Results, by Institution Type and Year*[a]

Dependent variable Low- and moderate-income share of originations	*Commercial banks*		*Savings institutions*		*Mortgage companies: Independent*		*Mortgage companies: Subsidiaries of depository institutions*	
	1993–96	*1997–99*	*1993–96*	*1997–99*	*1993–96*	*1997–99*	*1993–96*	*1997–99*
Economies of scale								
MSA originations[b]	–0.008‡	–0.008‡	–0.011‡	–0.005‡	–0.005‡	–0.009‡	–0.002	–0.001
Spline segments in outside-MSA originations								
0 to 1,000	0.010†	0.012†	–0.008	–0.009	0.005	–0.004	–0.022‡	–0.036‡
1,001 to 10,000	0.001	–0.001‡	0.002‡	–0.001	–0.006‡	–0.006‡	–0.002‡	–0.000
10,001 or more (× 100)	0.098†	0.017‡	0.104‡	0.030‡	0.018‡	0.009‡	0.016‡	0.002
Single MSA lender	0.025‡	0.037‡	0.034‡	0.054‡	n.a.	n.a.	n.a.	n.a.
Cultural affinity								
Minority- or woman-owned	n.a.	0.110‡	n.a.	0.201‡	n.a.	0.006	n.a.	0.151‡
Local economic conditions								
MSA median income[b]	–0.231‡	–0.120‡	–0.153‡	–0.076‡	–0.146‡	–0.076‡	–0.086‡	–0.082‡
FHA loan limit[b]	–0.008	–0.031†	–0.060‡	–0.089‡	–0.049‡	–0.036‡	–0.079‡	–0.038‡
MSA fair market rent[b, c]	0.230‡	0.150‡	0.279‡	0.224‡	0.302‡	0.238‡	0.267‡	0.280‡
MSA unemployment rate[b]	–0.007	–0.002	0.018‡	0.031‡	0.043‡	0.047‡	0.037‡	0.048‡
Industry concentration								
Herfindahl index	–0.153	–0.197	0.432‡	0.739‡	0.291‡	0.434‡	0.101	0.725‡

Secondary market factors								
Percentage of loans sold	–0.094‡	–0.087‡	–0.020‡	–0.019‡	n.a.	n.a.	n.a.	n.a.
Portfolio lender only	0.013‡	0.007	0.009	–0.011†	n.a.	n.a.	n.a.	n.a.
Other firm/market characteristics								
Percentage of loans refinanced	–0.023‡	–0.001	–0.000	0.038‡	0.139‡	0.168‡	0.102‡	0.073‡
MSA size (square miles) [b]	0.043‡	0.038‡	0.038‡	0.027‡	0.008‡	0.013‡	0.008‡	0.011‡
Year dummies [c]								
1993 (or 1997)	–0.042‡	–0.009	–0.044‡	–0.004	–0.131‡	0.012‡	–0.095‡	–0.015‡
1994 (or 1998)	–0.016‡	–0.014‡	–0.014‡	–0.030‡	–0.051‡	–0.038‡	–0.028‡	–0.046‡
1995 (or omitted)	–0.007	n.a.	0.007	n.a.	–0.017‡	n.a.	0.003	n.a.
Number of MSA-lender combinations	16,199	13,969	12,660	10,184	17,779	14,549	13,121	12,690
Adjusted R-square	0.084	0.070	0.088	0.081	0.230	0.173	0.162	0.155

a. Parameter estimates designated with a ‡ (†) are statistically significant at the 99 percent (95 percent) level of confidence. Hypothesis tests performed on asymptotically consistent (Huber-White) covariance matrices.

b. These variables are included in the regression as natural logarithms.

c. The year dummies given outside (in) parentheses are used in the first (second) period models; 1996 and 1999 are the excluded categories.

level off or increase with origination volume. Among both commercial banks and savings institutions, affordable shares generally decline modestly with MSA originations.[28] For example, a lending organization that originates 200 mortgages within its MSA (about the average for MSA originations) has about half a percentage point lower low- or moderate-income share than an otherwise similar organization that originates 100 mortgages within its MSA.

At the same time, depositories that are part of lenders that originate a very large number of outside-MSA mortgages have a higher share of within-MSA affordable mortgages than other depositories. The overall pattern is more complicated than the simple U shape documented in figures 3-7 and 3-8. This offsetting positive relationship is most readily apparent in the parameters on the third spline segment, for outside-MSA origination volumes above 10,000 each year, almost all of which are positive. However, the estimates indicate that only very large depositories are able to match the higher affordable shares observed among smaller and single-MSA lenders. The positive offset among very large depositories is decidedly weaker after 1996.

Among both independent mortgage companies and mortgage company subsidiaries of depositories, the relationship between affordable shares and origination volume is generally negative. In almost all cases, the coefficients on the first and second spline segments are negative; they are also large relative to the coefficients on the third segments, swamping any potential offset among large mortgage companies. Although the coefficients on within-MSA originations in the low- and moderate-income share regressions are occasionally positive, because mortgage companies' outside-MSA originations are generally much larger than their MSA originations (see table 3-2), the negative effect of outside-MSA originations dominates.

Overall, the data show that larger lending organizations generally devote a smaller fraction of their business to the affordable segment. Very large depositories have higher affordable shares than mid-sized depositories, however. Among mortgage companies we observe a stronger, more consistently negative relationship between size and affordable share. The patterns are consistent with the conclusion that local knowledge, the development of market niches that smaller lenders can serve well, and size-based efficiencies are important for lending organizations to have high affordable shares. Because large depositories may be subject to more intense regulatory scrutiny, the positive relationship between size and affordable share among very large depositories is also consistent with an affirmative role for CRA.

28. MSA origination volumes enter the model as logs. By construction, these variables have a diminishing absolute effect on affordable shares. Using dummy variable groupings for the number of MSA originations does not alter the main inferences from table 3-4.

Market Concentration and Competition

The question of whether there are economies of scale in affordable lending feeds naturally into a discussion of the effects of industry concentration on affordable lending shares. Concentration is measured by a Herfindahl index, which is the market share of each lending organization, squared and summed for all organizations lending within each MSA.[29] Such measures are typically viewed as gauges of the intensity of competition within a market. In this view, higher values of the index imply more concentration and less competition. Somewhat surprisingly, the level of concentration within an MSA declined between 1993 and 1999 (see table 3-2).[30] On average, during 1993–96, individual lending organizations controlled a larger fraction of MSA originations than after 1996.

Higher levels of concentration were generally positively related to affordable shares for savings institutions and mortgage companies. If the Herfindahl index measures the level of competition in an MSA, the positive relationship implies that less competition is generally associated with more affordable lending. Though this result contradicts expectations, these relationships could reflect the impacts of increased affordable lending scrutiny by regulators as a result of past (or pending) consolidation. Recall that CRA ratings are an important factor in regulator approvals of bank mergers and acquisitions. In markets where a substantial amount of consolidation occurred, Herfindahl values should be higher and affordable lending may also be higher as a result of CRA considerations.

However, independent mortgage companies are not subject to the CRA, though through their loan sales they are indirectly affected by both the CRA and the GSEs' affordable housing goals. The positive relationship between affordable shares and concentration for independent mortgage companies suggests that both CRA and GSE housing goals may be an important part of the explanation for the observed positive relationships.

Local Economic Conditions and the Price of Housing

The state of the local economy and the price of housing are of particular interest in any examination of affordable mortgage lending. Borrowers in this segment tend to have limited financial resources and may be less able to meet their credit obligations in the event of an unexpected decline in income, such as would occur if the borrower were to become unemployed. As a consequence of such risks, one

29. Market share is defined as the ratio of each lending organization's number of MSA originations to the total number of MSA originations for all lending organizations within an MSA. For more background on the Herfindahl index, see Rhoades (1993).

30. Declining Herfindahl values over time appear to be a consequence of our grouping the data by MSA-lender combinations. Ungrouped, the data show a clear increase in Herfindahl values over time, indicating that the national concentration of originations increased between 1993 and 1999.

might expect affordable lending to be positively associated with measures of local economic health and inversely related to the costs of homeownership.

As it turns out, however, the relationship between local economic conditions—measured by the unemployment rate and the median MSA family income—and average affordable lending shares across lending organizations is more complicated than that. On one hand, average lending shares to low- and moderate-income families exhibit what appears to be a strong procyclical pattern: low-mod shares are higher in MSAs where unemployment is lower and in MSAs with higher median incomes.[31] On the other hand, lending shares to underserved areas generally appear to be countercyclical. These patterns hold in both the 1993–96 and the 1997–99 periods.

At first blush, these countervailing trends are a bit puzzling. If the financial well-being of borrowers in the affordable segment is more sensitive to economic conditions, procyclical low-mod shares are unsurprising. But clearly something very unusual is happening in underserved area lending. Though puzzling, these patterns may simply be artifacts of the definitions of low-mod borrowers and underserved areas, coupled with the CRA obligations of banks and the GSEs' affordable housing goals. By construction, exactly 50 percent of families in an MSA are low- and moderate-income because the definition of such borrowers is based on median MSA income. Underserved area designations under both the GSEs' affordable housing goals and the CRA are based on median census tract family income in 1990 relative to median family income for the MSA in 1990.[32] As noted earlier, MSAs with high unemployment tend to have the largest fractions of their population living in tracts designated as underserved.[33] Thus MSAs with persistently high unemployment or low median family incomes during the 1990s appear to simply be "rich" in borrowers living in underserved tracts. We might, therefore, expect high volumes of underserved area lending in MSAs with persistently high unemployment or low median family incomes.

Further, when the regression models exclude all measures of local economic conditions except median family income, both the underserved shares and the low-mod shares exhibit procyclical patterns. The inclusion of any other local economic condition reverses this pattern for underserved shares.[34] We infer from this

31. The same procyclical pattern for low- and moderate-income shares was reported in PricewaterhouseCoopers (2000).

32. This definition applies to the CRA. For the GSE housing goals, middle-income tracts with high minority concentrations also qualify as underserved.

33. Census tracts are generally intended to be homogeneous, about equal-population geographic areas. In practice, there is considerable variation in population size and income within tracts. Changes over time in the affluence and number of families living in particular tracts exacerbate this problem.

34. The problem does not appear to stem from multicollinearity. Variance inflation tests proposed by Belsley, Kuh, and Welsch (1980) suggest that the unemployment rate and median family income do not appear to be collinear.

supplemental evidence that the countercyclical relationship among the unemployment rate, MSA median family income, and underserved area lending shares is probably more an artifact of definitional factors. It seems to us that in the event of an economic downturn, aggregate underserved area shares would fall.

The price of housing almost certainly affects homeownership and mortgage originations in the affordable segment. We use two housing cost measures to control for local price effects: The MSA FHA loan limit proxies for the local price of homeownership, and HUD's MSA rent series proxies for the cost of renting.[35] Not surprisingly, FHA loan limits and affordable shares are inversely related. In high house-price areas, the share of both low- and moderate-income and underserved area loans is lower than in more modestly priced areas. Local rent has opposing effects on the share of low- and moderate-income loans and underserved area loans. However, the relative cost of homeownership (not shown), defined as the ratio of the annual payment associated with a loan at the FHA loan limit to annual local rent, is generally negatively related to affordable shares.[36] Consistent with expectations, the more expensive it is to own than to rent, the lower are the shares of both low- and moderate-income loans and underserved area loans.

Cultural Affinity

It has often been argued that discrimination partly explains why minority families tend to have higher mortgage denial rates and lower rates of homeownership than nonminority families.[37] If discrimination is widespread, then one should expect lending organizations owned and operated by minorities to extend a larger fraction of their mortgages to minorities than other lenders, ceteris paribus.[38] Indeed, this may be the case even in the absence of discrimination if minority-owned firms engage in community outreach by targeting minorities and other traditionally underserved borrowers to a greater extent than other lenders. Moreover, because minorities constitute a disproportionate fraction of lower-income families and those living in underserved areas, one would expect minority-owned lenders to have higher shares of affordable loans as defined by HUD.

To test this hypothesis, we included in the regression an indicator for whether each firm was minority- or woman-owned or -managed (MWO).

35. Median house price data for all MSAs for the period under study are not publicly available. Although it is not the median local price of single-family dwellings, the MSA FHA loan limit is widely regarded as approximating the middle of the distribution of the price of single-family dwellings in an MSA.

36. The annual payment is simply the payment associated with a thirty-year fixed-rate loan at the loan limit, with monthly payments and a 7 percent interest rate.

37. See, for example, Munnell and others (1996). For a dissenting view, see Benston (1999).

38. For a detailed discussion of the cultural-affinity hypothesis and empirical findings on that topic, see Kim and Squires (1998); Hunter and Walker (1996); and Calomaris, Kahn, and Longhofer (1994).

Before turning to the results, it is important to keep in mind that only a small fraction of lending organizations (about 1 percent) are owned by minorities or women. Thus, although the results reported here are statistically significant, they may be decidedly less robust to alternative specifications than the other results discussed in this chapter. Data on minority ownership were only available for the years 1997–99 and were included in the second period's model only.[39]

The data generally support the conclusion that minority- and women-owned lenders extend a higher fraction of originations to families living in underserved areas, the exception being independent mortgage companies. These findings are largely consistent with the findings by Kim and Squires (1998), who report a positive association between the level of black and Hispanic employment at a lender and that lender's loan approval rates.

The evidence is more mixed with respect to low- and moderate-income lending. Being a minority- or woman-owned lender raises low- and moderate-income shares only among savings institutions and mortgage company subsidiaries of depositories. The effects of cultural affinity are quite large. Affordable shares are 4 to 20 percentage points higher among minority- or woman-owned organizations than among other lenders.

The Role of Secondary Market Loan Sales and Refinance Shares

Because a large fraction of mortgages are sold on the secondary market after origination, and because the largest purchasers of prime market originations—Freddie Mac and Fannie Mae—are subject to affordable mortgage purchase regulations, it is important to examine whether the fraction of originations sold by an organization has any effect on affordable lending.[40]

It is difficult to assess the effects of mortgage sales among mortgage companies because they typically sell almost all the mortgages they originate. That is, there is very little meaningful variation in the fraction of mortgages sold by mortgage companies with which to assess the effects of sales on affordable lending. We therefore examine the effects of mortgage sales on the affordable shares of depositories only.

39. In 1999 we identified 156 MWO lenders that reported in HMDA. The following sources were used to compile the list of MWOs used in this analysis: FFIEC's NIC database, the U.S. Treasury's Minority Bank Deposit Program, and ownership information Freddie Mac collects from its loan sellers and servicers.

40. The explanatory variable is the fraction of loans sold, regardless of the purchaser. The purchaser could be a depository, a GSE, or another financial services firm such as an insurance company or pension fund. We do not distinguish among purchasers because many loans, particularly those to borrowers in the affordable segment, are sold to loan wholesalers or other third parties before they are purchased by depositories or GSEs. As a consequence, the purchaser field does not measure which institution ultimately ends up with the loan. Notwithstanding this measurement error, distinguishing among purchaser types in the regressions does not alter the pattern of results discussed here.

In general, the fraction of mortgages sold has a negative effect on affordable lending by depositories. The larger the fraction of originations sold, the lower the depositories' low- and moderate-income and underserved area shares. This relationship holds across both the 1993–96 and 1997–99 periods but is notably weaker in the second period. A large fraction of depositories sell very little or none of their originations to secondary market participants. The model includes a dummy variable to identify those "portfolio lenders" who sell none of their loans. The declining parameter value on this variable indicates that although portfolio lenders had higher affordable lending shares than other lenders during the 1993–96 period, they had about the same or lower affordable lending shares than others during the 1997–99 period. Coupled with the declining negative effect of loan sales, this pattern suggests that the secondary market for affordable loans changed in an important way over the course of the 1990s.

There are at least three plausible explanations for these patterns. First, they could have resulted from technological and financial innovations. The introduction of automated underwriting has allowed lenders and secondary market participants to identify investment-quality prime market borrowers in the affordable segment. Financial market innovations have enabled secondary market investors to more efficiently hedge credit risk. Both of these developments should have enhanced the ability of the GSEs and others to purchase prime affordable loans.[41]

Second, favorable economic conditions over the latter half of the 1990s may have enhanced the ability of secondary market participants to purchase mortgages originated in the affordable segment. The relatively low level of long-term interest rates substantially reduced the ARM share of lending in the second time period; the ARM share of conforming home purchase loans averaged 27 percent over 1993–96 but fell to 15 percent during 1997–99.[42] Because ARMs are more likely to be originated and held by depositories, the relatively low ARM share explains in part the increase in secondary market sales (as shown in table 3-2) and increases the likelihood that a representative mix of originations is sold into the secondary market.

Third, CRA reforms and higher GSE affordable housing goals may have increased sales of affordable loans. Revisions to CRA regulations permitted mortgage-backed securities that primarily contained CRA-eligible loans or served community development purposes to be counted toward the CRA investment criteria.[43] Further, the level of affordable mortgage purchases

41. On the ability of investors to hedge their credit risk, see Vetrano and Lyons (1999). Among others, Mark Zandi and Brian Nottage have argued that income gains by lower-income families, along with improved underwriting systems and risk-based pricing, have enabled borrowers who previously would have qualified only for an FHA or VA loan to qualify for a prime conventional loan; see Zandi and Nottage (2000).

42. Authors' calculations from the Federal Housing Finance Board's Monthly Interest Rate Survey.

43. See Mahoney (1998).

required by HUD rose over the course of the 1990s, which may have provided additional incentive to the GSEs to securitize affordable loans.

Summary and Conclusions

As part of the ongoing consolidation in the financial services industry, the 1993 to 1999 period saw a migration of prime mortgage originations out of independent mortgage companies and savings institutions and into the nonbank subsidiaries and affiliates of depositories. This trend raises several concerns about the provision of prime mortgage credit to lower-income and traditionally underserved families. Has the increased size of financial institutions adversely affected the provision of affordable prime mortgages? What have been the competitive effects of increased market concentration on such lending? What is the role of local economic conditions? Do minority-owned financial institutions provide a disproportionately larger share of affordable lending than other institutions? The extensive regulatory efforts aimed at ensuring an adequate supply of prime mortgage credit to the affordable segment of this market, and the efforts of depositories, secondary market participants, and others make these questions particularly important.

In the aggregate, there was a notable decline in the fraction of prime originations by savings institutions and independent mortgage companies and a prominent secular increase in prime originations by mortgage company subsidiaries of depositories. However, affordable prime mortgage lending measured as a fraction of total prime market originations held about constant over the 1993–99 period, with the exception of the two refinance booms in 1993 and 1998.

At the level of individual lenders and lending organizations, we observe a U-shaped pattern with respect to size and affordable lending. Very small and very large depositories tend to devote the largest fractions of their originations to the affordable segments of the market. We do find that larger mortgage companies tend to do less affordable lending. Although an adverse effect on total affordable lending has not been apparent to date, the trend toward originations among mortgage company subsidiaries of depositories and away from savings institutions raises the concern that consolidation has the potential to reduce overall affordable lending in the future. Attenuating such concerns are technological advances, which have automated and unbundled much of the origination process. Such developments may have further enabled lenders of all sizes to originate loans profitably in the affordable segment.

With respect to market concentration, we find that at the MSA level concentration actually declined between 1993 and 1999, even while aggregate (nationwide) concentration increased. The fraction of total origination volume controlled by a single lending organization in its MSA was on average smaller later in the period than earlier. More concentrated markets saw more affordable lending by savings institutions and both types of mortgage companies. Affordable lending among commercial banks was unaffected by market concentration. It is difficult to draw firm conclusions from these patterns. They are consistent with increased regulator scrutiny of affordable lending patterns stemming from merger and acquisition activities. Though not definitive, the results suggest an affirmative role for the CRA in encouraging lenders, particularly depositories, to extend mortgage credit to the affordable segments of the market.

The relationship between local economic conditions—measured by the unemployment rate and the median MSA family income—and average affordable lending shares across lending organizations turned out to be quite complicated. On one hand, average lending shares to low- and moderate-income families exhibit a strong procyclical pattern: low- and moderate-income shares are high in low unemployment MSAs and high median-income MSAs. On the other hand, lending shares to underserved areas appear to be uncorrelated with unemployment across MSAs except in those areas with the highest unemployment rates. Though not definitive, the weight of the evidence suggests that both underserved area shares and low- and moderate-income shares are procyclical. These patterns hold in both the 1993–96 and the 1997–99 periods.

As for the cultural-affinity hypothesis, we do generally find a positive relationship between affordable lending and minority ownership. However, the small number of minority-owned institutions in our data suggests caution in interpreting this finding.

The overall set of results reported here provides important insights into the structure of the affordable prime mortgage market. Many of the issues addressed and the trends identified and discussed in this chapter are worthy of further study. For example, it would be interesting to reexamine several of the chapter's hypotheses separately for refinance and home purchase loans. Further research should also attempt to reach more definitive conclusions about the magnitude of economies of scale, the impacts of consolidation, and the role of local economic conditions. We hope that this chapter, by addressing these and related questions, will serve as a roadmap for those future efforts.

Appendix 3A. *Variable Definitions for Lenders and Lending Organizations*

Unit of observation	*Definition*
Lender	The organization that files under HMDA. Large and organizationally complex companies may file multiple HMDA submissions, one for each line of business or business area. In the analysis, such companies are treated as distinct lenders.
Lending organization	Unique lender-MSA combination. A lending organization must originate at least twenty loans to be retained in the analysis. Lending organizations may or may not operate a branch office within their MSA.
Affordable lending shares	
Low- and moderate-income share	Fraction of prime MSA originations to owner-occupants with incomes less than the MSA median income.
Underserved area share	Fraction of prime MSA originations to owner-occupants living in neighborhoods (tracts) with median 1990 income less than 90 percent of the MSA median income in 1990. If minority population is at least 30 percent, tract income may be up to 120 percent of the MSA median income.
Economies of scale	
MSA originations	Number of originations by a lending organization in its MSA.
Outside-MSA originations	Number of originations by the lender in all MSAs other than the lending organization's MSA.
Outside-MSA spline segments	Percent of observations with outside-MSA originations in each group: 0–1,000, 1,001–10,000, and 10,001 or more.
Single MSA lender	Indicator variable for whether a lender operates in just a single MSA (1 = lender makes loans in a single MSA).
Cultural affinity	
Minority- or woman-owned	Indicator variable identifying lenders in which minorities or women have a controlling ownership interest, including institutions identified as such by the U.S. Treasury's Minority Bank Deposit Program, FFIEC's National Information Center, and Freddie Mac data.
Local economic conditions	
Median MSA family income	Median family income (in thousands of dollars) for each MSA. Published annually by HUD.
FHA loan limit	Highest FHA loan limit (in thousands of dollars) for each MSA.
MSA fair market rent	Fair market (monthly) rent series published by HUD. The series consists of the 45th percentile of the MSA rent distribution for 1993 and 1994 and is the 40th percentile for 1995–99.
MSA unemployment rate	Unemployment rate (percent) for each MSA published annually by the Bureau of Labor Statistics.

continued on next page

Appendix 3A. *Variable Definitions for Lenders and Lending Organizations (continued)*

Unit of observation	*Definition*
Industry concentration	
MSA Herfindahl index	Sum of squared market shares, where market share is the fraction of all originations in an MSA attributable to each lending organization. The index ranges from zero to one, with the latter signifying that there is only one lending organization in the MSA.
Secondary market factors	
Percentage of loans sold	Percentage of all originations sold by each lending organization to any secondary market participant, including loans sold to depositories.
Portfolio lender	Indicator variable for having sold no originations during a given year.
Other firm/market characteristics	
Percentage of loans refinanced	Percentage of all originations by each lending organization that were refinancings.
MSA size	Geographic size of an MSA, in square miles (according to the U.S. census).

References

Avery, Robert B., Raphael W. Bostic, Paul S. Calem, and Glenn B. Canner. 1999. "Trends in Home Purchase Lending: Consolidation and the Community Reinvestment Act." *Federal Reserve Bulletin* 85 (February): 81–102.

Belsley, D., E. Kuh, and R. Welsch. 1980. *Regression Diagnostics.* John Wiley and Sons.

Benston, George J. 1999. "The Community Reinvestment Act: Looking for Discrimination That Isn't There." Policy Analysis 354. Washington: Cato Institute (October 6).

Calomaris, Charles W., Charles M. Kahn, and Stanley Longhofer. 1994. "Housing Finance Intervention and Private Incentives: Helping Minorities and the Poor." *Journal of Money Credit and Banking* 26 (August): 634–74.

Canner, Glenn, Elizabeth Laderman, and Wayne Passmore. 1999. "The Role of Specialized Lenders in Extending Mortgages to Lower-Income and Minority Home Buyers." *Federal Reserve Bulletin* 85 (November): 709–31.

Federal Financial Institutions Examination Council. 2000. 1999 Home Mortgage Disclosure Act Press Release, August 8.

Garwood, Griffith L., and Dolores S. Smith. 1993. "The Community Reinvestment Act: Evolution and Current Issues." *Federal Reserve Bulletin* (April): 251–67.

Huber, P. J. 1967. "The Behavior of Maximum Likelihood Estimates under Non-Standard Conditions." In *Proceedings of the Fifth Berkeley Symposium in Mathematical Statistics and Probability*, 221–33. University of California Press.

Hunter, William C., and Mary Beth Walker. 1996. "The Cultural Affinity Hypothesis and Mortgage Lending Decisions." *Journal of Real Estate Finance and Economics* 13 (July): 57–70.

Inside Mortgage Finance Publications. 2001. *The 2001 Mortgage Market Statistical Abstract Annual.* Volume 1. Bethesda, Md.

Kim, Sunwoong, and Gregory D. Squires. 1998. "The Color of Money and the People Who Lend It." *Journal of Housing Research* 9 (2): 271–84.

Litan, R., N. Retsinas, E. Belsky, and S. White Haag. 2000. "The Community Reinvestment Act after Financial Modernization: A Baseline Report." U. S. Department of the Treasury (April).

Mahoney, Peter E. 1998. "From Command to Demand: Creating Markets for CRA Securities." *ABA Journal of Affordable Housing & Community Development Law* (Spring) 7: 254–69.

Munnell, Alicia H., Geoffrey M. B. Tootell, Lynn E. Browne, and James McEneaney. 1996. "Mortgage Lending in Boston: Interpreting HMDA Data." *American Economic Review* 86 (March): 25–53.

PricewaterhouseCoopers. 2000. "The Impact of Economic Conditions on the Size and the Composition of the Affordable Housing Market." April 5.

Rhoades, Stephen A. 1993. "The Herfindahl-Hirschman Index." *Federal Reserve Bulletin* 79 (March): 188–89.

U.S. Department of Housing and Urban Development. 1995. *The Secretary of HUD's Regulation of the Federal National Mortgage Association (Fannie Mae) and the Federal Home Loan Mortgage Corporation (Freddie Mac).* Final Rule, Federal Register (60), December 1: 61846–62005.

———. 2000a. *Curbing Predatory Home Mortgage Lending.* Washington, D. C., June 20.

———. 2000b. *HUD's Regulation of the Federal National Mortgage Association (Fannie Mae) and the Federal Home Loan Mortgage Corporation (Freddie Mac)*; Final Rule, Federal Register (65), October 31: 65044–65229.

Vetrano, Frank, and Bill Lyons. 1999. "Credit Derivatives." *Secondary Mortgage Markets* 16 (December): 1, 15–20.

Zandi, Mark M., and Brian Nottage. 2000. "The Outlook for Mortgage Credit Quality." *Regional Financial Review* (October): 21–27.

PART 2

Overcoming Borrowing Constraints

Owing to the longest economic expansion in U.S. history, the lowest mortgage interest rates in a generation, and changes in the demographic makeup of the nation's population, homeownership rates rose for six years in a row to a record level of 67.7 percent as of the third quarter of 2000.[1] The resulting increase in the homeownership rate has been broad based, spanning all racial/ethnic groups and income groups.

For example, between 1994 and 2000, the homeownership rate for individuals with incomes below the median rose from approximately 48 percent to 51 percent, an increase of 6 percent, while those with incomes at or above the median experienced a 4 percent increase in homeownership, to 82 percent.[2] Although households with higher incomes are more likely to be homeowners than those with lower incomes, the relative gap between the two income groups has narrowed since 1994.[3] One concern, however, is that the affordability of homeownership is being threatened by rising home prices.

Despite large gains in homeownership rates for African American and Hispanic families, minority homeownership levels still lag significantly behind those of whites. For example, 74 percent of non-Hispanic whites own their

1. Nothaft (2000).
2. See the chapter by Nothaft and Surette here.
3. Bostic and Surette (2001).

homes; in contrast, 47 percent of African Americans and 46 percent of Hispanics are homeowners.[4] These differences are not fully explained by differences in demographic characteristics such as age and income.[5]

Two major obstacles that inhibit the expansion of homeownership, particularly among lower-income and minority families, are credit barriers and the limited availability of affordable housing stock. The three chapters in this section address these issues. Stuart Rosenthal estimates how much homeownership rates would increase if borrowers were not constrained by lenders' underwriting criteria. Abdighani Hirad and Peter Zorn measure the effect of home-buyer counseling on the performance of home mortgages and offer evidence on how credit barriers might be reduced. Finally, Michael Collins, David Crowe, and Michael Carliner look at how the supply of affordable housing units affects homeownership rates among low-income households.

Barriers to Homeownership: Credit Markets

Advances in technology and innovations in mortgage lending, including a wider range of mortgage products, have reduced many of the costs borrowers once faced when applying for mortgages. U.S. Census Bureau estimates suggest that a reduction of $1,000 in origination costs could help an additional 116,000 renters afford homeownership, and a reduction of $2,000 in origination costs could make it possible for an additional 314,000 renters to afford a home.[6] Combining the benefits of automated underwriting systems with other technologies, such as the use of the Internet to search and apply for loans, can reduce borrowers' costs of origination by $800 to $2,100.[7] Increased accuracy in measuring credit risk due to automated underwriting has led to the development of new, more affordable mortgage products such as zero-money-down loans; loans with nontraditional documentation; and "A-minus" or subprime loans, for borrowers with prior credit problems.[8] As the costs of information continue to decline, lenders will have more ability to match loan terms with the characteristics of individual applicants. In sum, according to Harvard's Joint Center for Housing Studies, the advent of new loan products has enabled "more

4. Joint Center for Housing Studies (2000).

5. Ibid.

6. Savage (1999), table 5-3.

7. Estimates of borrower savings from Internet-based technology of between $800 and $1,800 are given in Nottage (1999), pp. 11–16. Similar estimates of borrower savings of about $2,100 are presented in Danford (1999), pp. 2–8. Of the total savings from Internet-related technology, Freddie Mac estimates that approximately $300 to $650 is directly due to the use of automated underwriting systems such as Loan Prospector®; see Freddie Mac (1996), p. 8.

8. Peterson (2001).

income-constrained and cash-strapped borrowers at the margin to qualify for mortgage loans."[9]

As a result of these developments, many argue that we are nearing the limit of homeownership rates and that the remaining nonowner segment can be explained by preferences. In his chapter, Rosenthal examines whether the mortgage industry can further expand homeownership by relaxing borrowing constraints—that is, underwriting standards such as down payment, payment-to-income limits, and debt-to-income requirements. Using data from the 1998 Survey of Consumer Finances, this chapter addresses the role of preferences for homeownership by estimating how high homeownership rates would rise if borrowing constraints (underwriting standards) were eliminated. The findings suggest that if all borrowing constraints were removed and households were limited only by their incomes, owner-occupancy rates would increase by more than 4 percentage points. In addition, the author finds that borrowing constraints particularly depress homeownership rates among low-income and minority renters.

Increasingly, lenders are offering affordable mortgage products that require borrowers to undergo home-buyer education.[10] These requirements vary but are based on the premise that borrowers who better understand how to obtain and maintain a mortgage are less likely to be delinquent or default. Many housing advocates argue that counseling and education are effective ways to reduce losses. In an innovative study, using previously unanalyzed data, Hirad and Zorn examine the effect of home-buyer education on credit risk. Many financial institutions, including Freddie Mac and Fannie Mae, offer affordable home lending initiatives that apply flexible underwriting standards. In many cases, for example, in lieu of traditional criteria, lenders often require that borrowers participate in some form of home-buyer education program. Hirad and Zorn analyze the performance of loans from one such affordable home loan program over a five-year period in order to assess the relationship between home-buyer counseling and loan delinquency. In addition, these authors evaluate the effectiveness of different educational delivery mechanisms (such as classroom teaching, home study, and individual counseling), as well as the effectiveness of different types of counseling administrators (such as a government agency, lender, or nonprofit organization). This analysis shows that borrowers who received prepurchase counseling were less likely to become sixty-day delinquent than similarly situated borrowers who did not receive prepurchase counseling. In addition, classroom and individual counseling proved to mitigate default risk, which was not the case for home study and telephone counseling approaches. One implication of these findings is that there is a positive relationship between the effectiveness

9. Joint Center for Housing Studies (1998).
10. McCarthy and Quercia (2000).

of home-buyer counseling and the costs to administer this counseling. Further research is necessary to quantify the tradeoff between investments in home-buyer counseling and the resulting reduction in credit risk.

Barriers to Homeownership: Housing Markets

Removing credit constraints will have only a limited impact on low-income and minority homeownership rates if there is an inadequate supply of housing units available for low-income households to purchase. Affordability of homes depends on incomes, house prices, the presence of single-family homes, and housing unit construction. One of the biggest challenges is making it possible for low-income families to afford homeownership. Thanks to the strong economic conditions of the past few years, both home prices and household incomes have grown faster than inflation since 1994.[11] However, a concern is that if income growth fails to keep up with house price appreciation, the supply of affordable homes may be threatened.

In their chapter, Collins, Crowe, and Carliner examine how the supply of affordable housing units affects homeownership rates for low-income households. These authors use data from the American Housing Survey (AHS) to estimate a target affordable value for each metropolitan statistical area. They use this estimate to determine the size of the available housing stock that would be affordable for a low-income family earning less than 80 percent of the local median family income. These authors find that 44 percent of existing owner-occupied units were affordable to a low-income family in 1999—down from 47 percent in 1997. Between 1997 and 1999 there were about 500,000 fewer affordable homes available. They also find that low-income home buyers are more likely to select mobile homes or condominiums, and many mobile homes do not include the ownership of land. The authors suggest that homeownership for many low-income families is constrained by the lack of adequate housing units at an affordable price, and that this outcome is due to house-price inflation and the existence of homes that become vacant but are not reoccupied.

Future Research and Policy Directions

These chapters address important barriers to homeownership opportunities in both mortgage and housing markets. More research similar to Hirad and Zorn's work is needed to improve the understanding of mortgage defaults and to identify new variables such as home-buyer counseling and other nontraditional credit enhancements that could potentially offset credit constraints. In general, the constraint on research in this area is the lack of large data sets that include

11. Joint Center for Housing Studies (1998).

both mortgage performance and nontraditional credit variables, such as rent payment history.

Technology has transformed risk assessment and underwriting in the mortgage market and in the form of the Internet is likely to fundamentally change the way people navigate housing and mortgage markets. Increasingly, home buyers use the Internet to gather information about homes for sale, to obtain credit and homeownership counseling, to shop for and apply for mortgages, and to communicate with agents and lenders. However, there are substantial differences in Internet access and use across income, racial, and ethnic groups. This disparity in Internet use, known as the digital divide, could result in informational disadvantages for lower-income and less-educated consumers. The housing and mortgage industries must consider the disparities in Internet access in their provision of information and outreach to lower-income and minority populations.

On the housing side, more research is needed to evaluate solutions to the problem of inadequate supply of affordable units for purchase. In particular, the industry would benefit from insights into efficiencies in conversion and rehabilitation of existing properties.

In addition to the challenges described in these chapters, there remain a number of other barriers to homeownership for low-income and minority home buyers. According to the Federal Reserve's Survey of Consumer Finances, in 1998 approximately 9.5 percent of households in the United States did not have any type of bank transaction account, such as checking or savings, and over 13 percent did not have a checking account.[12] A critical issue is how to extend homeownership opportunities to "unbanked" consumers, who disproportionately include low-income and minority households. Because automated underwriting models used to originate mortgages rely on records established through traditional banking relationships, potential home buyers who lack these relationships may be at a disadvantage. One solution is to collect and centralize payment data from nontraditional sources, such as rent and utilities. Another possibility is for policymakers to induce banks to enter these neighborhoods through regulation and incentives.

Taken together, these chapters point to important challenges to homeownership opportunities for low-income families in credit and housing markets. Rosenthal demonstrates that there are plenty of families who want to be homeowners but cannot meet existing mortgage underwriting requirements. Hirad and Zorn's findings suggest that prepurchase homeownership counseling may be one way to further expand mortgage lending. Finally, Carliner, Collins, and Crowe remind us that there must be houses for low-income families to purchase once credit barriers are removed.

EDWARD L. GOLDING

12. Kennickell, Starr-McCluer, and Surette (2000).

References

Bostic, Raphael, and Brian J. Surette. 2001. "Have the Doors Opened Wider? Trends in Homeownership Rates by Race and Income." *Journal of Real Estate, Finance, and Economics* (November): 411–34.

Danford, David P. 1999. "Online Mortgage Business Puts Consumers in Driver's Seat." *Secondary Mortgage Markets* (April) (www.freddiemac.com/finance/smm/apr99/pdfs/online.pdf).

Freddie Mac. 1996. *Automated Underwriting: Making Mortgage Lending Simpler and Fairer for America's Families* (September) (www.freddie mac.com/corporate/reports/#).

Joint Center for Housing Studies. 1998. "1998 State of the Nation's Housing Report." Harvard University.

———. 2000. "The State of the Nation's Housing: 2000." Harvard University.

Kennickell, Arthur B., Martha Starr-McCluer, and Brian J. Surette. 2000. "Recent Changes in U.S. Family Finances: Results from the 1998 Survey of Consumer Finances." *Federal Reserve Bulletin* (January): 1–29.

McCarthy, George W., and Roberto G. Quercia. 2000. "Bridging the Gap between Supply and Demand: The Evolution of the Homeownership Education and Counseling Industry." Institute Report 00-01. Washington: Research Institute for Housing America (May).

Nothaft, Frank E. 2000. "Trends in Homeownership and Home Equity." Report to the Consumer Federation of America's National Forum to Promote Lower-Income Household Savings (November).

Nottage, Brian. 1999. "E-Banking." *Regional Financial Review* (December): 11–16.

Peterson, Paul. 2001. "Keeping Promises." *Mortgage Banking* (March): 70–77.

Savage, Howard. 1999. "Who Can Afford to Buy a House in 1995?" Current Housing Reports H121/99-1. U.S. Census Bureau (August).

4

Eliminating Credit Barriers: How Far Can We Go?

STUART S. ROSENTHAL

Few symbols of personal economic success loom larger in the minds of Americans than owning one's own home. Norms favoring homeownership have been further buttressed by the belief that because homeownership is a site-specific investment homeowners take better care of their neighborhoods and therefore make good citizens.[1] Although evidence on whether homeowners make better neighbors is still tentative, it is certain that as a society we value homeownership for both personal and social reasons.[2] This is clear from a long

I would like to thank Anthony Pennington-Cross, Eric Belsky, Johnny Yinger, and two anonymous referees for helpful comments. Support for this project from the Joint Center for Housing Studies at Harvard University and the Research Institute for Housing America is gratefully acknowledged. Any remaining errors, of course, are my own.

1. A growing literature on social capital has examined whether homeowners invest in social capital that would serve to enhance the vitality of their neighborhoods (see, for example, Rohe, McCarthy, and Van Zandt, 2000; DiPasquale and Glaeser, 1999). For example, do homeowners vote more often than renters, do they donate more of their time to community functions, do they take better care of their homes? All such behavior benefits the neighborhood and society in general.

2. It is difficult to show that homeowners make good neighbors because of a strong simultaneity problem. Families that invest in their local neighborhoods likely expect to remain in their community for an extended time. Yet the cost of owner-occupied housing declines with length of stay because the high costs of moving to and from owner-occupied housing can be spread out over a longer period (Rosenthal, 1988). For that reason, families intending to remain stationary for a long time are more likely to own their home, ceteris paribus, and for the same reason are more likely to invest in a variety of forms of neighborhood social capital.

history of tax policies that encourage homeownership by reducing the cost of housing for owner-occupiers (Rosen, 1979; 1985). In addition, the past decade has witnessed a series of government and industry efforts designed to reduce mortgage borrowing constraints for low-income families and other disadvantaged groups. These efforts have focused primarily on relaxing wealth requirements and have culminated in the recent introduction of zero and near-zero down payment mortgages for eligible borrowers.[3]

Innovations in affordable mortgage lending—along with the dramatic economic expansion of the 1990s—have helped to raise U.S. homeownership rates to historic levels, from 64 percent in 1989 to just over 67 percent by 2000. Against that backdrop, an important question for both government and the financial industry is as follows: To what extent can further relaxation of borrowing constraints boost homeownership rates, both for the U.S. population overall and for families of different ages, races, ethnicities, and financial status? This chapter seeks to answer that question by estimating homeownership rates that would prevail for various subgroups of the population if all borrowing constraints were eliminated but households otherwise abided by their budget constraints.

Addressing these issues is difficult because of three fundamental problems that all studies on the impact of borrowing constraints face. Researchers must identify which families are credit-constrained; they must evaluate how those families would behave if borrowing constraints were relaxed, ceteris paribus; and they must control for the myriad possible constraints that lenders impose on prospective borrowers. In the context of homeownership, such constraints include down payment standards, as well as house payment–to-income and total debt payment–to-income ratios, and the various ways these standards are applied for different types of loans (such as fixed- versus variable-rate mortgages). In addition, to the extent that nonmortgage debt like auto and consumer loans can be used as substitutes for mortgage debt, borrowing constraints outside of the mortgage market potentially affect housing tenure decisions as well.

The solution to these problems offered here is to apply sample selection methods to unusually rich data from the 1998 Survey of Consumer Finances (SCF).[4] At the core of the estimation strategy is a unique set of survey questions

3. For example, Zero DownTM is an affordable mortgage product offered by Bank of America; it is available in twenty-three states and Washington, D.C. It is a conventional mortgage that requires zero down payment. In addition, closing costs can come from a gift or the seller, or can be financed (see Bank of America, 1998). These loans and other affordable mortgage products are typically issued only to individuals with low or moderate income relative to the areas in which they live. Moreover, as a broad characterization, the more relaxed the underwriting standards, the more strict the eligibility criteria with regard to credit risk that govern whether a prospective borrower would have access to the mortgage product.

4. The principal limitation of the SCF is that strict regulations designed to protect confidentiality do not allow the researcher to observe any information related to the geographic location of the

that enable one to identify a priori a group of households that almost certainly hold as much mortgage debt as they would like given prevailing market rates and the menu of existing mortgage products. These families are characterized as not credit-constrained (unconstrained) in the analysis to come, while all other households are characterized as *possibly* credit-constrained for reasons that will become apparent later in the chapter. Housing tenure preferences—to own or to rent—are then estimated for just the unconstrained families, controlling for the endogenous selection of families into the unconstrained group through a three-celled bivariate probit model. The resulting housing tenure coefficients reflect the impact of household demographic and financial characteristics on preferences for owning when families are subject to their budget constraints but not subject to binding borrowing constraints. Those coefficients are used to predict homeownership rates that would prevail for the entire population—unconstrained and possibly credit-constrained families. Comparing predicted with actual homeownership rates permits one to evaluate how much higher homeownership rates would likely rise if all borrowing constraints were eliminated, ceteris paribus.

Is there opportunity for industry and government to expand homeownership through further relaxation of borrowing constraints? Results from the analysis suggest a qualified yes. If all borrowing constraints were suddenly removed, and all households could instantly change their housing tenure if they so chose, the owner-occupancy rate among nonfarm families in the United States would increase by just over 4 percentage points. Not surprisingly, these impacts are distributed unequally across different subgroups of the population. Borrowing constraints have far more impact on homeownership rates among low-income families than any other group, roughly 10 percentage points. Opportunities to expand homeownership also exist among young and middle-aged families for whom elimination of borrowing constraints would boost homeownership rates by roughly 7 percentage points. In addition, borrowing constraints appear to have more impact on Hispanic homeownership rates than on whites, while the evidence is mixed for African Americans.

To further explore these findings, two modifications are made to the model to shed light on a different but related question: To what extent do borrowing constraints serve to delay—rather than permanently exclude—access to owner-occupied housing? To examine this question, current housing tenure status is replaced with a survey question that inquires whether families *expect* to own a home in the next five to ten years. In addition, the model is estimated only over current renters. If borrowing constraints have no effect on renter expectations of

household. However, as will become apparent, the density of development in the household's neighborhood is available, and this variable acts as an excellent proxy for central city status. Additional details on the SCF data are provided later in the chapter.

future owner-occupancy status, then families that currently rent because of borrowing constraints must expect to overcome those constraints within a decade.

Results indicate that the percentage of renters who expect to own in the next decade rises by 7.56 percentage points with the elimination of borrowing constraints. Assuming renter expectations are fully realized, that figure translates into a 2.47 percentage point increase in the share of current households (owners and renters combined) that *eventually* attain homeownership, because renters account for one-third of all families. In contrast, elimination of borrowing constraints increases owner-occupancy rates by 4 percentage points as discussed above. The comparatively small effect on renter expectations suggests that borrowing constraints depress current owner-occupancy rates at least in part by delaying access to owner-occupied housing, consistent with recent findings by Goodman and Nichols (1997). Government and industry efforts to expand homeownership, therefore, may want to focus on mortgage product designs that alleviate borrowing constraints primarily in the early years of a mortgage to encourage earlier access to owner-occupied housing.[5]

The remainder of the chapter is organized as follows. The next section reviews selected portions of the literature that bear on discussions of the impact of borrowing constraints on homeownership. That literature is placed in the context of recent policy debates that have affected the operation of the mortgage market during the 1990s. As will become apparent, those debates also influenced the direction of academic research in this area. Following sections describe the empirical model, present the data, and finally present the results from the bivariate probit analyses and simulations.

Literature Review and Policy Context: The Impact of Borrowing Constraints on Homeownership

Before proceeding further, it is useful to clarify why lenders would choose to ration credit through down payments and other underwriting criteria rather than simply using the loan rate to clear the market. Imperfect competition coupled with racial discrimination is certainly one motivation for such behavior. More generally though, Stiglitz and Weiss (1981) provide much of the theoretical foundation for why competitive lenders would choose to ration credit through terms other than the loan rate. They argue that moral hazard, adverse selection, and asymmetric information between borrowers and lenders regarding credit risk can give rise to equilibrium credit rationing in which loan rates may

5. For example, graduated payment mortgages (GPMs) and price-level-adjusted mortgages (PLAMs) reduce tilt problems by allowing for increasing nominal payments over the life of the mortgage.

be set at below-market clearing levels. Such an outcome arises because information is costly and lenders have an imperfect ability to classify borrowers according to default risk. Under such conditions, lenders price loans based on the expected return on the loan portfolio rather than the expected return on the individual loans. The expected return on the pool of loans, however, depends both on interest earnings on loan payments and on expected default costs, each of which rises with the loan rate. In the latter case, as the loan rate increases, borrowers have an incentive to invest in riskier projects (moral hazard) with higher expected returns. In addition, as loan rates rise, prospective borrowers with strong aversions to default tend to drop out of the applicant pool first (adverse selection), raising the average propensity to default of the remaining pool of borrowers. Competitive lenders respond to such effects by setting interest rates lower than they would in the absence of moral hazard and adverse selection effects. Under such conditions, Stiglitz and Weiss show that it is possible that the competitive equilibrium will occur at below-market clearing interest rates.[6]

In an extension of the initial model, Stiglitz and Weiss (1981, part IV) further describe a redlining model in which lenders vary loan rates across borrowers on the basis of observable differences in credit risk—a model that more closely fits mortgage markets in practice. That model still allows for an equilibrium in which sufficiently high-risk loan applicants may be credit-constrained because of adverse selection and moral hazard. Duca and Rosenthal (1994b) extend that model further and argue that regulatory restraints such as fair lending laws may have had the unintended effect of increasing the degree to which lenders use nonrate terms to control for perceived differences in applicant credit risk. This could arise if lenders choose to offer the same mortgage rates to borrowers of different risk attributes to reduce the likelihood of costly discrimination suits.[7] Under such conditions, lenders would have an incentive to control for perceived differences in credit risk through less visible means, such as nonprice constraints like down payment standards.

One implication of these arguments is that as information becomes increasingly plentiful and inexpensive to obtain, lenders will be increasingly able to adjust individual loans—through either interest rate or nonrate terms—to meet the characteristics of individual applicants. This suggests that with the information technology revolution we should expect the degree to which lenders rely on nonrate terms to diminish, which is what appears to have occurred in the mortgage market throughout the 1990s.

6. Duca and Rosenthal (1991) provide empirical support for these ideas.

7. Using 1983 Survey of Consumer Finances (SCF) data, Duca and Rosenthal (1994b) found no evidence that lenders vary loan rates across borrowers on the basis of observable differences in risk attributes.

The "Early" Empirical Literature on Credit Rationing

The earliest empirical work that has direct bearing on the design of the present study comes from research testing the robustness of the life-cycle permanent income hypothesis (LCPIH). That literature includes a number of important cross-sectional and panel data analyses, such as those by Hall and Mishkin (1982), Hayashi (1985), and Zeldes (1989). These papers provide evidence that the time path of consumption expenditures for households that are *not* credit-constrained differs from that of families for whom borrowing constraints *may* be binding. On the basis of these findings, authors argued that borrowing constraints were binding for many people, a violation of the LCPIH. A limitation of these studies, however, is that the data used do not directly identify credit-constrained and unconstrained families. Instead, the studies assume that families with either high wealth-to-income ratios or high savings rates are not credit-constrained. Given that the demand for debt increases with wealth and income in response to increased demand for consumer durables such as housing, high-income and high-wealth families could still be credit-constrained.[8] This concern has raised questions about whether the analyses suffered from coding errors when splitting the sample on the basis of who is not credit-constrained.

In response, several studies in the early 1990s drew on the Federal Reserve's Survey of Consumer Finances (SCF). That survey allows the researcher to directly identify families that have recently been turned down for credit, received smaller-than-desired loans, or have been dissuaded from applying for credit. Using the SCF, Jappelli (1990) investigated the characteristics of credit-constrained families, and Cox and Jappelli (1993) estimated the extent to which borrowing constraints reduced the levels of debt held by such families.[9] These two studies, however, did not control for a number of variables used by lenders in evaluating loan applications, including credit history in the case of Jappelli (1990) and both credit history and wealth in the case of Cox and Jappelli (1993).

The importance of controlling for wealth and credit history when analyzing household access to credit has been underscored by a vigorous debate over the past decade about whether racial discrimination restricts the ability of minority households to obtain credit. Although that controversy dates back at least to the 1970s, when a wave of fair lending legislation was enacted, the debate became especially sharp following the publication of several sets of studies in the late 1980s. The first of these were newspaper articles that focused attention on the fact that minority populations had much more limited access to mortgage credit than majority white loan applicants, in part because of discrimination.[10]

8. Jappelli (1990) and Duca and Rosenthal (1993) provide evidence on this point.

9. See also papers by Duca and Rosenthal (1993, 1994a).

10. In May 1988 the *Atlanta Constitution* published a four-part series, "The Color of Money"; the *Detroit Free Press* published a similar series in July 1988.

Numerous press reports shortly thereafter focused attention on data from the Home Mortgage Disclosure Act (HMDA).[11] Those data showed that mortgage application rejection rates for African Americans in 1990 were 2.4 times greater than those for white families with similar income (see Canner and Smith, 1991, for a detailed description of the HMDA data).

As noted by Rehm (1991b), evidence from HMDA prompted House Banking Committee Chairman Henry Gonzalez to ask "top regulators for an 'immediate' report on what their agencies plan to do 'to correct the lending problems revealed [by the HMDA data].'" However, the HMDA data do not include household credit history or wealth, in addition to other important variables that appear on loan application forms. As a result, many other individuals in government, the banking industry, and academia questioned whether the HMDA data implied that lenders discriminate against minority loan applicants.[12] Partly in response to that debate, the Federal Reserve Bank of Boston conducted a landmark study of mortgage application denial rates in Boston using a much wider range of loan applicant characteristics than previously analyzed (Munnell and others, 1996). An important finding of the study was that allowing for differences in loan applicant wealth and credit history reduced but did not eliminate race-related differences in mortgage denial rates. Subsequent exhaustive analyses have largely supported these claims (for example, Turner and others, 1999; Turner and Skidmore, 1999).[13]

Who Chooses to Own versus Who Has the Ability to Own?

The recent literature on the impact of borrowing constraints on homeownership appears to have split along two lines that address related but different questions: who would *choose* to own a home under different underwriting criteria, and who

11. Beginning in 1990, lenders were required by HMDA to report the location of residential loans made, along with the income, race, and gender of loan applicants and whether the loan application was withdrawn (by the applicant), approved, or denied. See Rehm (1991a, 1991b) and Munnell and others (1996) for further discussion of the HMDA data.

12. For example, Rehm (1991b) notes that although Governor LaWare of the Federal Reserve described the HMDA data as "very worrisome," he indicated that more information was needed. Similarly, Rehm (1991b) reports that "leading industry groups, such as the American Bankers Association, have maintained that the Fed data do not take into account information crucial to credit decisions, such as a loan applicant's credit history, other debts, or employment."

13. In response to these findings and related community pressure, the Federal Reserve Board approved several large bank mergers conditional on the requirement that merger applicants meet lending goals in minority neighborhoods (see for example, the description of Bank of America's merger with Security Pacific in Thomas, 1992, p. A6). In addition, Fannie Mae and Freddie Mac, the dominant players in the secondary mortgage market, established new low-down-payment loan programs designed to reduce credit barriers for underserved populations (for example, Reuters, 1991). Private industry responded to these programs by originating new mortgage products targeted at previously underserved groups, knowing that they could then sell such products to the secondary market. See Listokin and Wyly (2000) for a careful review of affordable mortgage products currently available on the market and the history of how those products came to be.

would have the *ability* to purchase a home under different underwriting criteria? Studies focusing on the former question have their beginnings with papers by Linneman and Wachter (1989) and Zorn (1989). These studies identified credit-constrained households by assuming that prospective homeowners with more than a 28 percent house payment-to-income ratio were credit-constrained.[14] However, many lenders in the 1980s had house payment-to-income limits of more than 28 percent, and families with a bad credit history were likely to face tighter-than-average credit standards (see, for example, Boyes, Hoffman, and Lowe, 1989; Trans Data Corporation, 1986).[15] Nevertheless, an important finding from Linneman and Wachter (1989) is that down payment constraints appear to restrict access to homeownership with greater frequency than income does. More recently, Quercia, McCarthy, and Wachter (1998) and Haurin, Hendershott, and Wachter (1997) have used more sophisticated methods and models to stratify the sample into constrained and unconstrained households and to examine the impact of a wide range of different possible underwriting criteria. An important finding from these studies is that borrowing constraints continue to impede homeownership for underserved groups in the population, including younger families, minorities, and low-income households.[16]

In contrast, housing "affordability" studies by Savage (1999), Listokin and others (1999), and others have focused more on the question of who has the ability to own a home.[17] As a broad characterization, these studies proceed by first specifying a reference value home for each family in the sample. The reference home is most often specified as a function of the distribution of owner-occupied house values in the household's region of the country (for example, the 10th or 25th percentile).[18] Next, data are examined to determine whether individual families have sufficient income and wealth to satisfy underwriting guidelines for a range of different prospective mortgage products. That exercise deter-

14. This assumption derives, presumably, from secondary mortgage market criteria at the time that generally prohibited the securitization of mortgages with house payment–to-income ratios of more than 28 percent.

15. Trans Data Corporation data on official credit standards for primary mortgage lenders across the United States (in 1986) indicated that many lenders had house payment–to-income limits above 28 percent.

16. Mayer and Engelhardt (1996) provide additional evidence that many new home buyers receive gifts of one sort or another in the few years before purchasing their first home, especially among families likely to be credit-constrained. See also Haurin, Hendershott, and Wachter (1996) for a related discussion.

17. The housing affordability approach is also explicit in the National Association of Home Builders (NAHB) housing opportunity index (HOI) and the National Association of Realtors (NAR) housing affordability index (HAI).

18. Listokin and others (1999) also estimate the preferred house value for individual households and then compare the application of that reference house to reference values based on a percentile of the house value distribution as described above.

mines the percentage of renters capable of buying the reference home under different underwriting criteria.[19]

The housing affordability approach has made an important contribution, and the census affordability tables are a valuable resource for housing analysts. That said, in the context of this chapter it is important to bear in mind that mortgage market constraints are but one of a number of important factors governing whether families would choose to own a home. Perhaps the most general framework in this regard is the theoretical model of Henderson and Ioannides (1983) and subsequent empirical support for the model in Ioannides and Rosenthal (1994). In that model, families have both a consumption and an investment demand for housing. Consumption demand is sensitive to the demand for shelter. Investment demand is driven by portfolio considerations. If investment demand exceeds consumption demand, the family could choose to own a home equal to investment demand and rent out the unwanted space: in this case the family is better off if it owns. Alternatively, if consumption demand exceeds investment demand, the family would not want to purchase housing up to the level of consumption demand because that would constitute a bad investment: in this case the family is better off if it satisfies its consumption demand by choosing to rent its principal residence.

The Henderson-Ioannides model, while stylized, offers considerable guidance in how we might want to think about the question of who prefers to own a home in the absence of binding borrowing constraints. It is well documented that moving from owner-occupied housing is far more expensive than moving from rental housing because of realtor fees, legal fees, and taxes (see Rosenthal, 1988). For that reason, families who do not expect to move soon are more likely to prefer to own because they can spread the high transaction costs of moving to and from owner-occupied housing over a longer time. Consider, however, that both family and financial instability increase the frequency with which a family moves, reducing the return on owner-occupied housing. In the context of the Henderson-Ioannides model, such instability lowers the investment demand for housing. For these families, owning a home could be a bad investment, and many such families may prefer to rent.

As also argued by Henderson and Ioannides (1983), there is a tendency for individuals who have a taste for maintaining their dwellings to be undercompensated for such behavior in the rental market. Thus, for families that are good at maintaining their homes, owner-occupied housing may be a better investment, causing investment demand to be high: these families may prefer to own. Finally, Fu (1991) modifies the Henderson-Ioannides model to evaluate how

19. Studies by Savage (1999) and Listokin and others (1999) and affordability tables at the Census Bureau website (www.census.gov/hhes/www/hsgaffrd.html) have all been based on data from the Survey of Income Program Participation (SIPP).

household wealth affects preferences for owning. Suppose that housing consumption is a normal good and absolute risk aversion declines with wealth. Then, because owner-occupied housing is a risky investment, housing investment demand likely increases faster with wealth than housing consumption demand. As a result, wealthy families are more likely to prefer owner-occupied housing even in a setting free of taxes and financing issues.[20]

Given that the goal of this study is to estimate the homeownership rate that would prevail if borrowing constraints were eliminated, it is essential to take into account all the determinants of whether a family would choose to own a home. The discussion above suggests that household social and financial stability—important determinants of household mobility—are factors that must be considered. In addition, the family's ability to maintain its home and the family's level of wealth—an important determinant of the level of risk the family is willing to accept—are important as well. Finally, to the extent that owning a home has become a societal norm, this suggests that households value owning a home for reasons unrelated to financial gain (in contrast to the Henderson-Ioannides, 1983, model). Thus anything that might enhance the degree to which owning a home directly affects a family's sense of well-being also belongs in models of housing tenure preferences. These principles guide the variable selection in the empirical work that follows.

Empirical Model

In the most general setting, families choose their housing tenure to maximize utility subject to two sets of constraints: their intertemporal budget constraint and borrowing constraints imposed by lenders. Although the budget constraint is binding for all families provided that savings and bequests are treated as future consumption, borrowing constraints are binding only for a subset of households, as the previous section outlined. The focus of this chapter, of course, is to determine housing tenure preferences and homeownership rates subject only to the household's budget constraint. To pursue that goal, the model below is developed in a manner that is tailored to the characteristics of the Survey of Consumer Finances (SCF), three features of which are important to emphasize here.

First, the SCF is a cross section of individual households. In that regard, all families face the same macroeconomic conditions, though access to different mortgage products varies with household demographic and financial characteristics. Second, the SCF permits one to identify a priori a group of households for whom borrowing constraints are not binding, taking into account all possi-

20. Ioannides and Rosenthal (1994) provide empirical support for the idea that housing investment demand is indeed more sensitive to wealth than consumption demand.

ble credit constraints within and outside of the mortgage market. These families are referred to as *unconstrained* for the remainder of this chapter. All other families may or may not face binding borrowing constraints, for reasons that will be clarified in the next section. These families are referred to as *possibly constrained* for the remainder of this chapter. Third, survey questions in the SCF permit one to examine two different variables that shed light on housing tenure preferences: whether families currently own or rent, and whether current renters expect to own in the next five to ten years. When analyzing current housing tenure, all households are included in the sample. When analyzing whether renters expect to own, only renters are included in the sample. Apart from those differences, as will become apparent, the structure of the analysis is identical in both cases. For that reason, the model below is developed only in the context of current housing tenure status, but the reader should keep in mind that this model is also used to estimate whether current renters expect to own as well.

Housing Tenure Preferences When Borrowing Constraints Are Not Binding

Define an unobservable index I_{own} that represents the difference in utility between owning and renting when families are subject only to their budget constraints,

$$I_{own} = xa_x + Ma_m + e_{own} . \tag{4-1}$$

This equation determines a family's preferred tenure status *in the absence of binding borrowing constraints*. Elements of x include all demographic and financial characteristics of the household that influence tenure preferences as described earlier. In addition, elements of M include characteristics of the preferred mortgage product that the household would choose if it were to own, such as fixed versus variable rate, loan rate, amortization period, and down payment ratio.

What determines a_m? Macroeconomic conditions that are identical for all households given the cross-sectional nature of the data, and household characteristics that influence a family's preferred form of financing. Accordingly, M is a choice variable that depends on x and can be expressed as $M = h(x)$, where the role of macroeconomic conditions is suppressed to simplify notation.[21] Substituting into equation 4-1,

$$I_{own} = xt + e_{own} . \tag{4-2}$$

Equation 4-2 is a reduced-form expression that captures both the direct and indirect effect of household characteristics on housing tenure preferences in the

21. Macroeconomic conditions common to all households are captured in the model's constant term.

absence of borrowing constraints. However, because I_{own} is unobserved, the analysis below focuses on the observable discrete housing tenure decisions (OWN) corresponding to equation 4-2,

(4-3) $$I_{own} > 0 \rightarrow \text{OWN} = 1, \textit{ own home}$$
$$I_{own} < 0 \rightarrow \text{OWN} = 0, \textit{ rent home,}$$

where OWN equals 1 if the family owns and 0 if the family rents.

Denote now a second unobservable index that governs whether a family belongs to the unconstrained group or the possibly constrained group, I_{NotCC},

(4-4) $$I_{NotCC} = xc + e_{NotCC} \cdot$$

The discrete observable realizations corresponding to equation 4-4 are given by

(4-5) $$I_{NotCC} > 0 \rightarrow \text{NotCC} = 1, \textit{ unconstrained}$$
$$I_{NotCC} < 0 \rightarrow \text{NotCC} = 0, \textit{ possibly constrained,}$$

where NotCC equals 1 if the family belongs to the unconstrained group and 0 if the family belongs to the possibly constrained group.

In viewing equations 4-1 through 4-5, it is important to recognize that whereas NotCC is observed regardless of whether OWN takes on a value of 1 or 0, housing tenure preferences *free of borrowing constraints* are observed only for families belonging to the unconstrained group: NotCC equal to 1. As is well established in the discrete choice literature (such as Maddala, 1983), if e_{own} and e_{NotCC} are uncorrelated, observing OWN only for NotCC equal to 1 presents few difficulties. Assuming e_{own} follows a unit normal distribution, one could obtain unbiased and consistent estimates of t—the housing tenure preferences in equation 4-2—by running a univariate probit model over just that portion of the sample for which NotCC = 1.[22] More generally, however, common omitted variables that influence both the likelihood that NotCC equals 1 and the likelihood that OWN equals 1 would cause estimates of t to suffer from sample selection bias owing to the endogenous character of the sample selection procedure. To allow for this possibility, a more general estimation procedure is needed.

The Bivariate Probit Model with Three Cells

To avoid sample selection bias, it is necessary to control for correlation between the error terms in the two latent indexes, e_{NotCC} and e_{own}. If equation 4-2 could

22. Note that when e_{NotCC} is independent of e_{own}, the expected value of Iown is xt since $E[e_{own}|e_{NotCC}] = 0$, and consistent estimates of t can be obtained by running a univariate probit model on (4-3) using only unconstrained families.

be estimated directly, a common approach would be to use well-known Heckman two-step procedures by augmenting equation 4-2 with a Mills ratio term based on first-stage probit estimates of equation 4-5. Subject to identification conditions and functional form, including the Mills ratio enables one to obtain consistent estimates of *t*. In the present context, however, I_{own} is not directly observable. Instead, the discrete variable OWN is observed. In this case, a nonlinear analogue of the Heckman procedure is to estimate a bivariate probit model over equations 4-3 and 4-5 with just three cells, where OWN is observed only for NotCC = 1 as noted above.

More formally, assume that e_{NotCC} and e_{own} follow a bivariate standard normal distribution with mean zero and covariance $\sigma_{NotCC,own}$.[23] Then the log likelihood function (*L*) for this model is given by

$$(4\text{-}6) \qquad L = \sum\{(1 - \text{NotCC}) \cdot \log[F(-xc)] + \text{NotCC} \cdot \text{OWN} \cdot \log[G(xt, xc, \sigma_{NotCC,own})] + \text{NotCC} \cdot (1 - \text{OWN}) \cdot \log[G(-xt, xc, -\sigma_{NotCC,own})]\},$$

where F(·) and G(·) are the standard unit and bivariate normal distributions, respectively, and the log-likelihood function is evaluated separately for all observations in the entire sample, $i = 1, \ldots, I$.[24] Note, however, that whereas each observation in the sample contributes to the identification of *c*, the parameters governing whether a family belongs to the unconstrained group, only those families for which NotCC is equal to 1 contribute to identification of *t*, the parameters governing housing tenure preferences. In addition, sample selection effects are controlled for because the covariance between e_{NotCC} and e_{own} appears in the last two bracketed terms of equation 4-6 and is simultaneously estimated along with *t* and *c*. Thus equation 4-6 provides unbiased and consistent estimates of *t*.[25]

Simulating Owner-Occupancy Rates in the Absence of Borrowing Constraints

Estimates of *t* obtained from equation 4-6 reflect the impact of household financial and demographic characteristics on housing tenure preferences in the

23. The variances of e_{NotCC} and e_{own} are normalized to 1 because the parameters of the bivariate probit model can be estimated only up to a scale factor. See Maddala (1983) for further discussion.

24. Boyes, Hoffman, and Low (1989) estimate a similar three-celled bivariate probit model for the credit card market.

25. An issue of identification does remain. Selection models such as the one above provide more reliable results when there are variables included in the selection equation (equation 4-5 in this case) that do not belong in the equation of interest (equation 4-3). In the work that follows, as will become apparent, there appear to be several natural exclusion restrictions, most notably a set of credit history variables that clearly belong in the credit model but that have zero coefficients in the tenure preference model. For a more detailed discussion of bivariate probit models with censoring, see Maddala (1983) or Tunali (1986).

absence of borrowing constraints. Given such estimates, it is possible to simulate the percentage of the population that would choose to own by computing the mean of F(*xt*) over the entire sample, where F(·) is the unit normal distribution function as previously noted. Comparing that estimate to the actual frequency of owner-occupiers gives an estimate of the impact of borrowing constraints on homeownership rates. Repeating the simulation exercise for various subsets of the population permits one to evaluate the impact of borrowing constraints on different subgroups by race, income, or age, for example.

Data

The data used to estimate the model are taken from the 1998 Survey of Consumer Finances (SCF), a household survey that provides unusually rich information on the financial characteristics of households. The SCF provides data on roughly 4,300 households.[26] Of these, roughly 2,800 are selected so as to be representative of the entire United States; the remaining households overrepresent wealthy families and are drawn from tax files. To protect confidentiality, the public-use version of the 1998 SCF does not allow the analyst to separately identify the representative and tax-based samples. However, sampling weights provided with the data permit one to weight the data such that results are representative of the entire United States. In the work that follows, the bivariate probit model was estimated using unweighted data to obtain the parameter estimates on the assumption that all the covariates in the model are exogenous. The simulations, in contrast, were calculated using the sampling weights to ensure that the simulation results are representative of the United States.[27]

A special feature of the SCF is that households were asked if they had had a request for credit turned down by a particular lender or creditor in the past five years or had been unable to get as much credit as they had applied for. Households were also asked if there had been any time in the past five years that a household member had *thought* about applying for credit at a particular place but changed his or her mind because the household thought it might be turned down. Based on these questions, a household was classified as possibly credit-constrained (NotCC = 0) if at least one of the following three conditions held: (1) the household had had a loan request turned down; (2) the household had had a loan request only partially granted; or (3) the household had initially considered applying for credit but then chose not to because it thought that it

26. The SCF data are imputed five times to control for missing values and also to protect the confidentiality of some respondents with unusual and highly visible characteristics (such as very high wealth). When estimating the bivariate probit models, all five implicates totaling over 21,000 records were used, and the standard errors were divided by the square root of 5 to adjust for the "true" sample size. See the 1998 SCF manual and Kennickell (1998) for details.

27. See Kennickell (1999) for a careful discussion of the SCF sampling weights.

would be turned down. If *none of the three of the conditions above* held, then the family was classified as not credit-constrained (NotCC = 1).[28]

A further strength of the 1998 SCF is the rich information included on the determinants of household wealth, credit history, and expectations. Thus, in addition to the usual battery of demographic characteristics, several household attributes not typically found in most major surveys are included in the model, such as expected income growth, inheritances, gifts and settlements, credit history attributes, and indicators of employment stability. The main limitation of the SCF is that it does not provide information on household location because of strict rules governing confidentiality. However, the SCF provides information on the density of development in the household's neighborhood, and that information serves as an excellent proxy for central city or suburban status.[29] To facilitate review, a description of the principal variables in the model is provided in the tables. Additional detail is provided in the appendix.

A final point concerns sample composition and use of the SCF relative to other data sets. The most widely cited homeownership rates are those from the U.S. Census Bureau. Those estimates are based on the Consumer Population Survey (CPS) for the entire United States, including both the farm and nonfarm sectors. However, the housing needs and opportunities of individuals living on farms—both farm owners and employees—are arguably rather different from those of the nonfarm sector. In addition, much of the policy focus with regard to the creation and marketing of affordable mortgage products has centered on urban areas. For these reasons, the analysis in this study is based just on the nonfarm portion of the 1998 SCF in order to provide a sharper picture of the nonfarm sector. Estimates in this study, therefore, could potentially differ from published Census Bureau reports for two reasons: use of the SCF data and focus on nonfarm populations. Before proceeding, it is important to clarify the possible effect of these differences.

Table 4-1 compares the racial distribution of the population using the CPS and SCF based on samples that are representative of the entire U.S. farm and nonfarm population for the years 1989, 1992, 1995, and 1998. Table 4-2 makes

28. This is a more demanding definition of who is not credit-constrained than was used by Duca and Rosenthal (1994a). In that paper, families that successfully reapplied upon having a loan application rejected or only partially accepted were considered not credit-constrained. Classifying such families as NotCC = 0 reduces the efficiency of the estimated housing tenure preferences but increases the likelihood of obtaining unbiased and consistent estimates. The reason is that the three-celled probit model outlined in the previous section requires that one identify a subset of the sample that is clearly not credit-constrained. In contrast, the model does not require that everyone in the alternative category be credit-constrained. Instead, such families *may* be credit-constrained, analogous to studies testing the LCPIH by Zeldes (1989) and others.

29. The SCF reports whether nearby buildings are less than 21 feet apart, 21 to 100 feet apart, or more than 100 feet apart.

Table 4-1. *Racial Representation in the Consumer Population Survey (CPS) and Survey of Consumer Finances (SCF), Various Years*
Percent

	Farm plus nonfarm populations								*Nonfarm only*
	1989		*1992*		*1995*		*1998*		*1998*
	CPS	*SCF*	*CPS*	*SCF*	*CPS*	*SCF*	*CPS*	*SCF*	*SCF*
White	0.785	0.746	0.776	0.752	0.774	0.777	0.750	0.773	0.777
African American	0.112	0.129	0.114	0.127	0.116	0.128	0.119	0.121	0.119
Hispanic	0.077	0.080	0.081	0.075	0.082	0.057	0.094	0.074	0.072
Other	0.026	0.046	0.029	0.046	0.028	0.039	0.036	0.032	0.031

Table 4-2. *Homeownership Rates in the Consumer Population Survey (CPS) and Survey of Consumer Finances (SCF), Various Years*
Percent

	Farm plus nonfarm populations								*Nonfarm only*
	1989		*1992*		*1995*		*1998*		*1998*
	CPS	*SCF*	*CPS*	*SCF*	*CPS*	*SCF*	*CPS*	*SCF*	*SCF*
White	0.693	0.703	0.695	0.701	0.709	0.705	0.723	0.717	0.73
African American	0.419	0.420	0.425	0.431	0.422	0.426	0.466	0.459	0.473
Hispanic	0.456	0.449	0.447	0.449	0.433	0.436	0.472	0.458	0.455
Other	0.506	0.536	0.520	0.542	0.505	0.517	0.535	0.540	0.558
Total	0.639	0.639	0.639	0.640	0.647	0.647	0.661	0.661	0.674

a similar comparison of homeownership rates by race.[30] In addition, the last column in both tables reports values for the 1998 SCF based only on the nonfarm population. Bear in mind that all the SCF data are weighted to ensure they represent their respective populations as discussed earlier.

As is apparent in the tables, differences in the reported values between the CPS and SCF data are small and likely reflect differences in the manner in which certain questions are asked regarding homeownership status and race (see Kennickell, 1999, for a discussion of this point). This indicates that the sampling weights for the SCF do an excellent job of matching the CPS and that weighted data from the SCF are representative of the United States. A more substantiative difference arises when comparing the combined farm plus nonfarm

30. The combined farm plus nonfarm values are taken from Kennickell (1999).

populations with only the nonfarm population for 1998 using just the SCF. On the one hand, the racial distribution of the population is little different in the last two columns of table 4-1. On the other hand, for each subset of the population other than Hispanic (for which there is little difference), the homeownership rate in table 4-2 is more than 1 percentage point higher for the nonfarm population than for the combined farm plus nonfarm population. Those differences boost the overall homeownership rate from 66.1 percent in 1998 for the farm plus nonfarm sector to 67.4 percent for the nonfarm sector. It is important to bear in mind, therefore, that the base homeowership rate for the study group in this paper is 1.3 percentage points higher than is commonly cited in the U.S. Census reports.

Results

Summary statistics of all the variables included in the bivariate probit regressions are provided in table 4-3 for the full sample and for various subsets of the population. As before, all values are weighted to ensure they are representative of the United States in 1998.

In the top row of the table, observe that homeownership rates vary widely not just across race, but also with income, age, and location. Among families whose total household income is in the first decile, just 34.4 percent own their homes; homeownership rises to 60.2 percent for families whose incomes fall within the 25th to 50th percentiles. Only 40.7 percent of families with household heads under age 35 own their homes. Among families living in densely developed areas (areas where the nearby buildings are within twenty-one feet of each other), only 54.4 percent own their homes.

The second row in table 4-3 reports the percentage of families that currently rent but expect to buy a home in the next five to ten years. Overall, 8.7 percent of U.S. families belong to this category. Not surprisingly, such families are disproportionately found among households under age 35: 22.1 percent of this group are renters that expect to own in the next decade. African American and Hispanic families also include a higher share of renters who expect to own in the coming decade, but this is true because of the greater frequency of renters among these populations. (Table 4-5 shows that, among renters, the frequency of families that anticipate owning in the next ten years is similar for whites, African Americans, and Hispanics.)

Interpreting Estimates from the Bivariate Probit Models

Table 4-4 presents estimates for the two versions of the bivariate probit model discussed earlier, first for both renters and owners with *current owner-occupancy status* as the housing tenure variable, and then again for just renters with *expect to own in the next five to ten years* as the tenure variable. Because of the nonlin-

Table 4-3. *Sample Means of Probit Model Variables for the Full Sample and for Selected Subgroups*

	Full sample	*White*	*African American*	*Hispanic*	*Other*	*Income in lowest decile*	*Income in 10th–25th percentile*	*Income in 25th–50th percentile*	*Age <35*	*Buildings <21 feet apart*
Dependent variables										
Own home	0.674	0.730	0.473	0.455	0.558	0.344	0.494	0.602	0.407	0.544
Rent but expect to own	0.087	0.074	0.137	0.128	0.137	0.079	0.063	0.112	0.221	0.126
"Not" credit-constrained	0.717	0.750	0.551	0.630	0.715	0.668	0.720	0.662	0.511	0.663
Independent variables										
Head's gender										
Male	0.722	0.744	0.517	0.800	0.773	0.416	0.467	0.675	0.744	0.678
Head's race										
White	0.777	1.000	. . .	. . .	. . .	0.582	0.708	0.749	0.691	0.678
African American	0.119	. . .	1.000	. . .	. . .	0.297	0.167	0.121	0.136	0.166
Hispanic	0.072	. . .	. . .	1.000	. . .	0.081	0.101	0.108	0.127	0.116
Other	0.031	. . .	. . .	. . .	1.000	0.040	0.025	0.022	0.045	0.040
Head's marital status										
Married	0.525	0.551	0.283	0.588	0.653	0.172	0.266	0.420	0.449	0.435
Divorced	0.127	0.132	0.140	0.082	0.070	0.160	0.166	0.168	0.065	0.148
Head's age										
Age	48.841	50.199	46.240	40.861	43.369	49.278	53.074	49.190	27.964	46.720
Under 35 years	0.229	0.203	0.261	0.404	0.334	0.333	0.264	0.250	1.000	0.283
35 to 55 years	0.426	0.422	0.440	0.432	0.477	0.253	0.248	0.371	-	0.423
Over 55 years	0.345	0.375	0.300	0.164	0.189	0.413	0.488	0.379	-	0.294

Size of household										
Number in household	2.589	2.475	2.639	3.475	3.183	2.100	2.243	2.389	2.822	2.526
Current employment status										
Head works full time	0.637	0.634	0.565	0.733	0.759	0.216	0.368	0.623	0.804	0.645
Spouse works full time	0.284	0.289	0.219	0.276	0.416	0.070	0.084	0.191	0.322	0.251
Spouse works part time	0.076	0.081	0.032	0.085	0.083	0.038	0.037	0.060	0.082	0.064
Current, past, expected income										
Total family income in 1997	5.29E+04	5.85E+04	2.87E+04	3.17E+04	5.49E+04	4.28E+03	1.24E+04	2.48E+04	3.64E+04	4.31E+04
Real income rose in past five years	0.203	0.208	0.184	0.189	0.182	0.095	0.063	0.140	0.293	0.207
Real income expected to rise in next five years	0.234	0.213	0.295	0.333	0.298	0.256	0.202	0.207	0.412	0.264
Stable income and employment										
Know next year's income	0.722	0.757	0.586	0.570	0.729	0.536	0.568	0.709	0.614	0.685
No. of full-time jobs held by head for at least one year	2.324	2.371	1.949	2.498	2.174	0.590	1.460	2.308	2.170	2.392
Health status										
Head in bad health	0.051	0.046	0.086	0.052	0.057	0.138	0.109	0.051	0.009	0.060
Spouse in bad health	0.021	0.025	0.008	0.018	0.000	0.020	0.032	0.027	0.010	0.025
Head's education										
Less than high school	0.187	0.149	0.270	0.474	0.161	0.445	0.373	0.206	0.162	0.187
High school	0.291	0.294	0.341	0.241	0.157	0.275	0.334	0.348	0.285	0.272
Some college	0.238	0.240	0.238	0.164	0.351	0.179	0.182	0.262	0.275	0.255
College degree	0.165	0.181	0.115	0.074	0.165	0.075	0.082	0.136	0.197	0.179
Graduate degree	0.119	0.136	0.036	0.047	0.166	0.025	0.030	0.048	0.081	0.108

continued on next page

Table 4-3. *Sample Means of Probit Model Variables for the Full Sample and for Selected Subgroups (continued)*

	Full sample	*White*	*African American*	*Hispanic*	*Other*	*Income in lowest decile*	*Income in 10th–25th percentile*	*Income in 25th–50th percentile*	*Age <35*	*Buildings <21 feet apart*
Inheritances, gifts, etc.										
Received at least one inheritance/gift since 1980	0.203	0.237	0.109	0.044	0.077	0.119	0.172	0.208	0.121	0.165
$ value of inheritance/gift since 1995	8.06E+03	9.15E+03	5.34E+03	1.87E+03	5.32E+03	2.57E+03	3.64E+03	4.79E+03	4.87E+03	5.20E+03
$ value of expected inheritance/gift	2.86E+04	3.29E+04	2.03E+03	8.46E+03	7.03E+04	4.94E+03	2.27E+04	1.35E+04	4.43E+04	2.46E+04
Central city/suburb										
Neighborhood buildings <21 feet	0.464	0.405	0.647	0.746	0.592	0.534	0.506	0.523	0.574	1.000
Neighborhood buildings 21 to 100 feet	0.380	0.411	0.298	0.205	0.321	0.322	0.362	0.340	0.332	. . .
Neighborhood buildings >100 feet	0.127	0.153	0.041	0.030	0.054	0.111	0.112	0.115	0.062	. . .
Density not known	0.029	0.032	0.014	0.019	0.033	0.033	0.020	0.023	0.032	. . .
Previous marriages										
Head previously married	0.175	0.191	0.136	0.106	0.080	0.147	0.125	0.172	0.043	0.159
Spouse previously married	0.120	0.133	0.069	0.067	0.109	0.030	0.052	0.102	0.049	0.091
Financial problems										
Head or spouse ever bankrupt	0.084	0.086	0.102	0.046	0.069	0.065	0.078	0.091	0.065	0.091
Loan paid two months late	0.060	0.051	0.121	0.049	0.071	0.059	0.080	0.088	0.091	0.070

Note: All values are calculated with sampling weights to be representative of the United States.

Table 4-4. *Three-Celled Bivariate Probit Model Estimates of Who Prefers to Own in the Absence of Borrowing Constraints*[a]

	Preferred current housing tenure (sample includes owners and renters)				*Expect to own in the next five to ten years (sample includes renters only)*			
	Not credit-constrained		*Prefer to own if not credit-constrained*		*Not credit-constrained*		*Expect to own if not credit-constrained*	
	Partial[b]	*t-ratio*	*Partial*[b]	*t-ratio*	*Partial*[b]	*t-ratio*	*Partial*[b]	*t-ratio*
Household head's gender								
Male	0.00619	0.346	0.03501	1.704	0.00476	0.163	0.05042	1.116
Household head's race								
African American	–0.09242	–4.899	–0.08034	–2.883	–0.06556	–2.147	0.05478	1.069
Hispanic	–0.00859	–0.362	–0.08830	–2.841	0.01504	0.397	–0.01226	–0.212
Other	–0.01454	–0.471	–0.11590	–3.108	0.02314	0.412	–0.02290	–0.294
Current marital status								
Married	0.06254	3.414	0.20706	8.336	0.01514	0.453	0.02782	0.553
Divorced	–0.03166	–1.555	0.06118	2.669	–0.02737	–0.761	0.07032	1.293
Household head's age								
Under 35 years	0.00766	4.698	0.00132	0.667	0.00567	1.886	–0.00915	–1.947
35 to 55 years	0.00781	7.475	0.00521	3.804	0.00559	2.842	–0.00726	–2.376
Over 55 years	0.00731	9.680	0.00468	4.676	0.00748	5.478	–0.00909	–3.868
Size of household								
Number of people in household	–0.01238	–2.589	0.02213	3.213	–0.01764	–2.001	0.00247	0.156
Current employment status								
Head works full time	–0.01839	–1.044	0.09961	4.347	–0.02714	–0.868	0.12318	2.624
Spouse works full time	–0.02766	–1.816	0.02438	1.165	–0.02736	–0.834	0.15079	3.189
Spouse works part time	–0.00189	–0.083	0.01020	0.320	–0.06885	–1.190	0.13940	1.633

continued on next page

Table 4-4. *Three-Celled Bivariate Probit Model Estimates of Who Prefers to Own in the Absence of Borrowing Constraints (continued)*[a]

	Preferred current housing tenure (sample includes owners and renters)				*Expect to own in the next five to ten years (sample includes renters only)*			
	Not credit-constrained		*Prefer to own if not credit-constrained*		*Not credit-constrained*		*Expect to own if not credit-constrained*	
	Partial[b]	*t-ratio*	*Partial*[b]	*t-ratio*	*Partial*[b]	*t-ratio*	*Partial*[b]	*t-ratio*
Current, past, and expected income								
Total household income in 1997	2.12E-08	2.128	2.78E-09	0.485	0.00000	1.771	0.00000	–0.773
Real income rose in past five years	0.02190	1.476	0.03383	1.696	0.01213	0.383	–0.00114	–0.025
Real income expected to rise in next five years	–0.01174	–0.849	–0.03966	–2.059	–0.01379	–0.535	0.07507	1.948
Stability of income and employment								
Usually know next year's income	0.02628	2.069	0.05811	3.539	0.00826	0.349	0.06148	1.649
No. of full-time jobs held by household head for at least one year	–0.00802	–4.032	–0.00839	–2.728	–0.00431	–1.169	0.00005	0.010
Health status								
Head in bad health	–0.01792	–0.543	–0.04065	–1.247	–0.06602	–1.275	–0.05565	–0.504
Spouse in bad health	–0.14029	–3.234	–0.15615	–3.029	–0.09405	–1.114	0.10787	0.832
Household head's education								
Less than high school	–0.04920	–2.501	–0.08793	–3.755	. . .	. . .	. . .	. . .
Some college	–0.03143	–1.889	0.01313	0.611	–0.00200	–0.069	0.03656	0.817
College degree	0.00822	0.450	0.04483	1.979	–0.01398	–0.393	0.13902	2.533
Graduate degree	0.03248	1.609	0.04603	1.862	0.03270	0.689	0.12635	1.834

Recent and expected inheritances, gifts, settlements								
Received at least one since 1980	–0.01092	–0.713	0.07099	3.584	–0.04535	–1.147	0.15652	2.749
$ value of inheritance/gift since 1995	9.55E-09	0.448	9.48E-08	0.709	0.00000	–0.012	0.00000	0.467
$ value of expected inheritance	3.52E-09	0.435	5.16E-08	1.330	0.00000	–0.392	0.00000	1.329
Central city/suburb status								
Neighborhood buildings 21 to 100 feet apart	0.03151	2.364	0.11531	6.649	–0.00028	–0.011	–0.03000	–0.727
Neighborhood buildings >100 feet apart	0.06530	3.208	0.12327	5.023	0.11614	1.983	0.03488	0.429
Previous marriages								
Head previously married	–0.03289	–1.910	–0.00480	–0.222	...	...	...	...
Spouse previously married	–0.02333	–1.175	–0.00959	–0.348	...	...	...	...
Financial problems								
Household head or spouse ever bankrupt	–0.20573	–10.013	0.00601	0.149	–0.22033	–4.888	...	...
Loan payments two months late	–0.21752	–8.548	–0.06431	–1.148	–0.18617	–4.548	...	...
Constant	–0.12303	–2.395	–0.36955	–4.558	–0.08667	–0.981	–0.09983	–0.512
$\sigma_{NotCC,Own}$			–0.3484	–1.807			–0.4531	–2.059
Total observations		4,142		4,142		1,189		1,189
Censored observations		0		984		0		505
Uncensored observations		4,142		3,158		1,189		684

a. Controls for sample selection are based on who is not versus who may be credit-constrained. Partial derivatives are presented to facilitate interpretation.

b. Partial derivatives were calculated by forming $t_{partial} = t \cdot [\Sigma w_i \cdot f(x_i t)] / \Sigma w_i$, where t is the probit model coefficient for the tenure equation, $f(x_i t)$ is the unit normal density function, w_i is the sampling weight for observation i, and Σw_i is the sample size (appropriately weighted). See the text for additional details.

earity of the bivariate probit model, coefficient estimates from the model can be used only to evaluate the sign of the estimated relationship. To facilitate interpretation, therefore, table 4-4 presents estimates of the partial derivatives for the covariates instead of the original model coefficients. Those derivatives are calculated as

$$\theta_{\text{partial}} = \frac{\theta \cdot \left[\Sigma w_i \cdot f(x_i\theta)\right]}{\Sigma w_i},$$

where θ is the vector of probit model coefficients for the tenure and NotCC equations ($\theta = t, c$), $f(x_i\theta)$ is the unit normal density function evaluated at $x_i\theta$, w_i is the sampling weight for observation i, and Σw_i is the sample size (appropriately weighted). Calculating θ_{partial} in this manner ensures that the partial effects are representative of the United States while permitting one to interpret the partials as for a linear probability model.[31]

The Credit-Constraint Equation

Recall that the credit-constraint equation is included in the model primarily to control for sample selection effects. In that regard, results from the NotCC equation are of secondary importance. Accordingly, discussion of the NotCC results below is brief and focuses on certain key variables that help to ensure that the NotCC equation serves the function for which it is intended.[32]

At the bottom of table 4-4, observe that neither a history of bankruptcy nor having made loan payments more than two months late in the previous year has any influence on preferences for current owner-occupancy status (column 3). Those credit variables have highly significant, large negative effects on the likelihood that a family belongs to the unconstrained group. These results indicate that lenders impose tighter underwriting standards on loan applicants with a bad credit history, but that credit history has little effect on housing tenure preferences per se. As such, the credit variables serve as strong exclusion restrictions: they belong in the credit model but do not influence tenure preferences. Such

31. As an example, the probability that a family wants to own is 3.5 percentage points higher if the household head is male, as seen in the second column and first row of table 4-4.

32. Interpreting many of the coefficients in the NotCC equation is difficult because households belong to the unconstrained group if they prefer to hold less debt than lenders are willing to allow (see, for example, Duca and Rosenthal, 1993). As such, the NotCC coefficients reflect the impact of household attributes on the maximum amount of debt lenders are willing to issue *relative* to a family's demand for debt. For example, receipt of an inheritance (gift or settlement), the dollar value of such a receipt, and the dollar value of future such receipts all have zero effect on the likelihood that a family belongs to the unconstrained group. That result is consistent with the finding of Duca and Rosenthal (1993) (based on 1983 SCF data) that wealth does not affect the likelihood of being credit-constrained. This does not, however, imply that lenders care little about loan applicant wealth. Rather, it indicates that the willingness of lenders to issue more debt as household wealth increases is roughly offset by an increase in demand for debt.

exclusion restrictions reduce collinearity problems that would otherwise limit the ability of the model to control for sample selection effects.

Current Owner-Occupancy Status

Focus now on estimates of the current owner-occupancy equation (column 3) and recall that these estimates measure the impact of household attributes on preferences for living in owner-occupied housing in the absence of binding borrowing constraints, ceteris paribus. As discussed earlier, the desire to live in owner-occupied housing is influenced by family and financial stability (which affect expected mobility), ability to care for the home, wealth (which affects risk aversion), and other attributes that contribute to a family's intrinsic taste for homeownership.

Consider first the role of family stability. Because couples invariably enter into marriage with the expectation of maintaining a stable family, one would expect married families to be more likely to own a home. Indeed, of all the demographic factors, marital status is by far the most important determinant of homeownership: married couples are 20.7 percentage points more likely to prefer to own a home than nonmarried families, ceteris paribus.[33] Similarly, it is well documented that young households are more mobile. For these families owner-occupied housing could prove more expensive than renting. Estimates from the model support that argument. Each additional year of age (for the household head) has little effect on the desire to own up until age 35. After that, however, older households are increasingly likely to prefer to own. An analogous argument can be made with respect to family size. Because it is more traumatic and expensive to move large families than to move small families, larger families tend to be less mobile and should therefore be more likely to prefer owner-occupied housing. Again, estimates support this argument. With each additional person in the household, families are 2.2 percentage points more likely to prefer to own.

Consider next financial stability. Families in which the head works full time have more secure income than those in which the head does not work full time. Of the financial variables in the model, this turns out to be the most important determinant of homeownership. Among families with a head working full time, the likelihood that the family prefers to own is 9.96 percentage points higher than if the head was not working full time. Moreover, after controlling for the employment status of the head (and spouse), total household income has no effect on preferences for owning. Similarly, if the household usually knows what its income will be next year, the family is 5.8 percentage points more likely to

33. Divorced families are also more likely to prefer owning. This may reflect the possibility that owning one's home is habit forming. In addition, capital gains tax provisions still in place in 1998 created financial incentives for individuals to remain owner-occupiers once the first home had been bought (see, for example, Hoyt and Rosenthal, 1990, 1992).

want to own. Conversely, as the number of full-time jobs the head has previously held increases—after having already controlled for age of the head—the family is less likely to want to own. The interpretation on this result is that frequent job changes reflect financial uncertainty and increase the likelihood of moving, both of which reduce the appeal of homeownership. Finally, observe that an increase in real income in the previous five years has a positive effect on preferences for owning but is only marginally significant, while expectations that real income will increase in the next five years have a *negative* and significant effect on preferences for owning. The former result may signal increased financial security as the family's income status improves. The latter result could reflect option-type effects. Because housing demand increases with income and moving from owner-occupied housing is costly, if income might increase substantially in the next few years it would make sense to wait before buying until the future income is better known.

Owner-occupied housing also requires more care from the occupant than rental housing. For that reason, one might expect that families in bad health would be less likely to want to live in owner-occupied housing. Results here are intriguing. Bad health of the household head has little effect on preferences for living in owner-occupied housing. However, if the spouse is in bad health, the likelihood that the family prefers to live in owner-occupied housing is reduced by 15.6 percentage points. More research is required to sort out exactly what this pattern reflects. One possibility, though, is that the spouse is the principal family member to maintain the home. If the spouse is in poor health and the head is occupied elsewhere (at work, for example), then the family may find rental housing more attractive.

Finally, owner-occupied housing is a risky, site-specific investment. Because risk aversion tends to diminish with wealth, one would expect wealthy individuals to be more interested in owning a home (see, for example, Henderson and Ioannides, 1983; Fu, 1991; Ioannides and Rosenthal, 1994).[34] Several variables serve as a proxy for household wealth and yield results largely supportive of that argument. Families with more highly educated heads are more likely to prefer to own: someone with a college degree or more is 4.5 percentage points more likely to own than someone with a high school degree; someone with less than a high

34. The SCF contains very detailed information on household assets and debts and permits an excellent calculation of net wealth. However, owner-occupied housing is an important asset and, as such, influences the family's portfolio and its wealth. Wealth, therefore, is endogenous and cannot be directly included in the model (see Haurin, Hendershott, and Wachter, 1997, for a careful discussion of this point). Because the primary goal of this study is to forecast homeownership rates that would prevail in the absence of borrowing constraints, we include exogenous determinants of wealth directly in the model rather than attempting to use a two-stage least squares type procedure to include wealth directly in the regression. The reduced-form approach taken here is more robust relative to the goals of the study because no restrictions are placed on the exogenous determinants of wealth.

school degree is 8.8 percentage points less likely to own than someone with a high school degree. Similarly, families that have received at least one inheritance, gift, or settlement since 1980 are 7.1 percentage points more likely to prefer to own, although interestingly, the dollar value of such receipts has no influence on preferences for ownership. Finally, families living in expensive areas must lever up further to purchase a home for any given level of family wealth. Such investment strategies are risky. In keeping with this argument, families living in neighborhoods where nearby buildings are more than twenty-one feet apart (characteristic of suburban and rural neighborhoods) are roughly 12 percentage points more likely to prefer owning than if they were living in areas where nearby buildings were within twenty-one feet of each other (characteristic of central city environments).[35]

A last set of variables requires some attention. Recall that white homeownership rates are roughly 25 percentage points higher than those of African American and Hispanic families. The model variables discussed above account for most of those differences, reducing the race effects to 8.03 and 8.83 percentage points for the African American and Hispanic categories, respectively. Nevertheless, one has to question why even these sizable race effects remain. In the case of Hispanics, one possibility is that many of the Hispanic families are recent immigrants, a variable not included in the model (see Coulson, 1999, for example). More generally, the estimated race effects likely reflect the influence of omitted determinants of financial and family stability, ability to care for the home, wealth, and discriminatory treatment, all of which are correlated with race and ethnicity.[36]

Expect to Own in the Next Five to Ten Years

Results from the bivariate probit model governing whether current renters expect to own in the next five to ten years differ substantially from the current owner-occupancy model.[37] Most striking, the race-related coefficients are all insignificant, indicating that we cannot reject the hypothesis that minority and white renters have similar expectations of future home purchase after controlling for the influence of credit barriers and demographic and financial factors. Cur-

35. Whether the head or spouse has been previously married was also included in the model because the dissolution of past marriages could reduce an individual's current wealth. Although these variables have some impact in the NotCC equation, they have no impact on housing tenure preferences.

36. The "Other" race category includes people of Asian descent, Native Americans, and other less-populous groups. Because it is not possible to separate these groups, results for the "Other" category are not discussed.

37. The model below restricts the sample to renters. This restriction greatly reduced the sample size, making it difficult for the maximum likelihood model to converge. To address that problem, we dropped the *Less than high school* and *Previous marriages* variables from both the NotCC and the "Expect to Own ..." equations. In addition, the *Financial problems* variable was also dropped from the "Expect to Own ..." equation.

rent marital status also has little influence on renter expectations, but older renters are significantly less likely to anticipate future homeownership, opposite from the impact of age on preferred current housing tenure. Presumably, this latter result reflects selection effects: older families with the strongest tendency to own would already have transited out of renting. A spouse working full time and expectations of future increase in income both have positive and significant impacts on renter expectations, whereas these variables have insignificant and negative effects in the preferred current housing tenure model. This likely indicates that the ability to accumulate future wealth positively affects renter expectations of future homeownership. Receiving an inheritance also has a sharply positive impact on renter expectations of owning, but central city or suburban status has little effect. The former result is similar to the preferred current tenure model, but the latter differs in that individuals living in less densely developed areas are more likely to prefer to own their current home. This difference could again reflect selection effects in that families with strong tastes for owning their current home may have already gravitated to the suburbs.

The Impact of Borrowing Constraints on Owner-Occupancy Rates

In table 4-5, the first two columns report the sample share for which NotCC equals 0, labeled "Possibly credit-constrained" in the table, and the sample share for which NotCC equals 0 *and* families currently rent, labeled "Possibly credit-constrained and renting." For the full sample of owners plus renters, 14.2 percent of families currently rent and are possibly credit-constrained. That estimate provides an upper bound on the impact of borrowing constraints on owner-occupancy rates.

The next three columns compare actual with predicted owner-occupancy rates that would prevail in the absence of borrowing constraints. Observe that eliminating borrowing constraints would have raised the 1998 owner-occupancy rate by 4.03 percentage points. Not surprisingly, borrowing constraints have the greatest impact on the homeownership rates of lower-income families: roughly 11 percentage points among families with total household income in the first decile, roughly 6.75 percentage points among families with income between the 10th and 50th percentiles, and little effect thereafter. Effects are also more pronounced among young (under age 35) and middle-aged families (between 35 and 55 years), raising homeownership rates for both groups by roughly 6.5 percentage points, with no effect on older families. Looking across racial and ethnic lines, homeownership rates rise most for Hispanics (6.7 percent) and least for African American families (1.3 percentage points).

An additional perspective is obtained by comparing the predicted share of current owners across race. Observe that removing the influence of borrowing con-

Table 4-5. *Actual and Predicted Owner-Occupancy Rates, 1998*[a,b]

Percent

	Upper-bound impact of credit constraints (sample includes owners and renters)		*Preferred current housing tenure (sample includes owners and renters)*			*Expect to own in the next five to ten years (sample includes renters only)*		
	Possibly credit-constrained	*Possibly credit-constrained and renting*	*Actual percent own*	*Predicted percent own*[c]	*Actual minus predicted percent own*[c]	*Actual expect to own*	*Predicted expect to own*[c]	*Actual minus predicted expect to own*[c]
Total	28.33	14.20	67.38	71.42	4.03	26.72	34.28	7.56
By race								
White	24.99	11.20	72.95	77.07	4.11	27.25	35.08	7.83
African American	44.86	27.18	47.31	48.62	1.31	26.01	32.24	6.23
Hispanic	36.96	24.26	45.49	52.22	6.72	23.48	32.99	9.51
Other	28.52	15.97	55.79	62.14	6.35	31.09	34.92	3.83
By income percentile								
0 to 10th	33.17	26.93	34.41	45.51	11.10	12.01	22.20	10.19
10th to 25th	28.02	19.08	49.43	56.55	7.13	12.36	25.52	13.16
25th to 50th	33.81	18.52	60.20	66.85	6.65	28.18	36.22	8.04
50th to 75th	32.81	13.24	74.29	77.25	2.97	46.08	46.44	0.03
75th to 90th	19.03	4.43	88.63	86.89	–1.74	52.12	51.49	-0.63
90th to 100th	14.07	1.51	93.64	91.36	–2.28	57.63	59.47	1.84
By age								
<35 years	48.85	32.23	40.72	47.07	6.35	37.28	45.93	8.65
35 to 55 years	32.62	13.72	71.47	78.00	6.53	27.74	37.45	9.71
>55 years	9.44	2.84	80.00	79.41	–0.59	4.90	5.82	1.63
By distance between buildings								
<20 feet	33.68	20.19	54.42	59.28	4.86	27.62	35.75	8.13
21 to 100 feet	25.56	10.24	77.43	80.72	3.28	25.46	32.85	7.39
>100 feet	15.85	3.30	85.68	87.15	1.47	29.00	29.76	0.76

a. All figures were weighted using the modified 1998 SCF weight x42001 to ensure that the values are representative of the United States for the respective subsample (see Kennickell, 1999, for details).

b. Sample excludes farms. Mobile home occupants are counted as owners if they own either the land or the unit, or both.

c. Coefficients from the owner-occupancy/expected owner equations in table 4-4 were used to calculate the predicted values.

straints does little to reduce the gap in owner-occupancy rates between white and nonwhite families. In contrast, in table 4-3, the difference in the frequency of married families between white and African American households is 26.8 percentage points. Multiplying that value by the marital status partial in table 4-4 for the "currently own" regression yields 0.0555. Thus if one were to raise the African American marital status rate to that of the white population, ceteris paribus, the African American owner-occupancy rate would increase by 5.55 percentage points. This suggests that policymakers and industry officials seeking to narrow the homeownership gap between African American and white households may need to look further than just the elimination of borrowing constraints.

Do credit barriers depress owner-occupancy rates by delaying access to owner-occupied housing or by permanently excluding some families from owning? The last three columns of table 4-5 shed light on this question by examining renters' expectations of future homeownership. Results indicate that the percentage of renters who expect to own in the next decade rises by 7.56 percentage points with the elimination of borrowing constraints. Assuming such expectations are realized, multiplying that figure by the current frequency of renters yields a 2.47 percentage point increase in the *eventual* attainment of owner-occupancy for the present total population of owners and renters (.0247 = .0756(1 – .6738), where .6738 is the frequency of owners and 1 – .6738 is the frequency of renters). In contrast, as noted above, the elimination of borrowing constraints would increase owner-occupancy rates by 4 percentage points. Thus the impact of borrowing constraints on renter expectations of future homeownership is small relative to the effect on the overall rate of homeownership. This suggests that eliminating borrowing constraints accelerates the realization of renter expectations of owning a home. Equivalently, borrowing constraints depress current owner-occupancy rates in part by delaying access to homeownership rather than permanently excluding families from owning a home; this result is consistent with results from Goodman and Nichols (1997).

Breaking out these last results by race yields a sharper picture. For whites, removing credit barriers increases renters' expectations of future homeownership by 7.83 percentage points. This translates into an increase in the eventual attainment of homeownership among white families of 2.12 percentage points.[38] For African American and Hispanic households, comparable calculations yield estimates of an increase in eventual attainment of homeownership of 3.28 and 5.18 percentage points, respectively. In contrast, the current housing tenure model predicts that with the removal of credit barriers, homeownership rates would increase 4.11, 1.31, and 6.72 percentage points for whites, African Americans,

38. Note that 0.212 = .0783(1 – .7295), where .0783 is the impact of borrowing constraints on white renter expectations of owning and .7295 is the actual frequency of owner-occupiers in the white population.

and Hispanics. Thus, although borrowing constraints appear to depress white and Hispanic homeownership rates at least in part by delaying renter access to homeownership (2.12 is well below 4.11), results for African Americans are more consistent with the view that credit barriers depress homeownership rates by permanently discouraging some renters from owning a home.

Conclusions

Recent dramatic innovations in affordable mortgage lending along with the economic expansion of the 1990s have helped to raise U.S. homeownership rates to historic levels, from 64 percent in 1989 to 67 percent by 2000. Against that backdrop, this chapter has sought to evaluate the extent to which the elimination of borrowing constraints would further expand opportunities for homeownership. This question is evaluated by applying discrete choice sample selection methods to rich data from the 1998 Survey of Consumer Finances. A key feature of the SCF, upon which the estimation strategy is based, is that survey questions identify a group of households for whom borrowing constraints are not binding, a priori.

Is there opportunity for industry and government to expand homeownership through further relaxation of borrowing constraints? Results from the analysis suggest a qualified yes. If all borrowing constraints were suddenly removed, ceteris paribus, and all households could instantly change their housing tenure if they so chose, the owner-occupancy rate among nonfarm families in the United States would increase by just over 4 percentage points. Not surprisingly, these effects are distributed unequally across different subgroups of the population. Borrowing constraints have far more impact on homeownership rates among low-income families than any other group. Sizable opportunities to expand homeownership also exist among young and middle-aged families.

Further analysis suggests that, for white and Hispanic households, borrowing constraints depress current owner-occupancy rates in part by delaying rather than by permanently excluding access to homeownership. That result is consistent with evidence from Goodman and Nichols (1997) and suggests that government and industry officials seeking to expand homeownership opportunities may want to consider mortgage products that alleviate borrowing constraints primarily in the early years of a mortgage. Analogous estimates for African American families are suggestive that credit barriers depress owner-occupancy rates for these families by permanently discouraging some renters from homeownership. Because the approach used to identify these effects is indirect, these findings should be viewed with some caution. Nevertheless, the results here suggest that the degree to which borrowing constraints delay access to homeownership versus permanently exclude access to owning warrants further research.

Finally, model estimates also confirm that even in an environment free of borrowing constraints, household family and financial stability are important determinants of whether families prefer to own: instability favors renting while stability favors homeownership. In addition, families that are in better health and therefore more able to care for their properties are more likely to prefer to own, as are higher-wealth families who are more capable of absorbing financial risk. As an example of the potential impact of such effects on owner-occupancy rates, African American marriage rates are roughly 25 percentage points below those of the white population. That difference alone is predicted to reduce the owner-occupancy rate of African American families by roughly 5½ percentage points relative to the white population. Estimates such as these suggest that government and industry efforts to expand access to homeownership will be more fruitful if they include broad-based initiatives designed to enhance the social and financial stability of families, in addition to ensuring that affordable mortgage products are available.

Appendix 4A

Tables 4-3 and 4-4 report the variable descriptions in each row to facilitate review. Although most descriptions are complete, some require additional clarification. Under *Household head's race*, "Other" includes people of Asian descent, Native Americans, and other less-populous groups. Because it is not possible to separate these groups into their own categories, results for the Other category are largely not discussed in this study. Under *Stable income and employment*, "Know next year's income" equals 1 if the family usually knows what its income will be one year ahead.[39] Under *Recent and expected inheritances, gifts, settlements*," "Received inheritance/gift" equals 1 if the head of household or spouse has ever received an inheritance, major gift, or settlement. "$ value of inheritance/gift" is the dollar value of all inheritances, etc., received from 1995 on. "$ value of expected inheritance/gift" is the dollar value of all inheritances, etc., that the household expects to receive in the future. Under *Central city/suburb,* "Neighborhood buildings <21 ft" equals 1 if the neighborhood buildings are within 21 feet of each other. A similar interpretation applies to the remaining variables in this category except "Density not known," for which the local density of development was not reported. That variable was included in the probit regressions, but results are not reported to conserve space. Under *Financial problems,* "Household head or spouse ever bankrupt" equals 1 if the head of household or spouse has ever filed for bankruptcy, while "Loan payments two months late" equals 1 if in the previous year the family made any loan payments more than two months late.

39. This heading has been clarified in the tables themselves.

References

Bank of America. 1998. "Bank of America Launches First Ever Widely Available Zero Down Payment Mortgage." Bank of America news release, March 2.

Boyes, W., D. Hoffman, and S. Low. 1989. "An Econometric Analysis of the Bank Credit Scoring Problem." *Journal of Econometrics* 40 (1): 3–14.

Canner, G., and D. Smith. 1991. "Home Mortgage Disclosure Act: Expanded Data on Residential Lending." *Federal Reserve Bulletin* (November): 859–81.

Coulson, E. 1999. "Why Are Hispanic- and Asian-American Homeownership Rates So Low? Immigration and Other Factors." *Journal of Urban Economics* 45 (2): 74–93.

Cox, D., and T. Jappelli. 1993. "The Effect of Borrowing Constraints on Consumer Liabilities." *Journal of Money, Credit and Banking* 25 (2): 197–213.

DiPasquale, D., and E. Glaeser. 1999. "Incentives and Social Capital: Are Homeowners Better Citizens?" *Journal of Urban Economics* 45: 354–84.

Duca, J., and S. Rosenthal. 1991. "An Empirical Test of Credit Rationing in the Mortgage Market." *Journal of Urban Economics* 29 (2): 218–34.

———. 1993. "Borrowing Constraints, Household Debt, and Racial Discrimination in Loan Markets." *Journal of Financial Intermediation* 3 (1): 77–103.

———. 1994a. "Borrowing Constraints and Access to Owner-Occupied Housing." *Regional Science and Urban Economics* 24 (3): 301–22.

———. 1994b. "Do Mortgage Rates Vary Based on Household Default Characteristics? Evidence on Rate Sorting and Credit Rationing." *Journal of Real Estate Finance and Economics* 8 (2): 99–113.

Fu, Y. 1991. "A Model of Housing Tenure Choice: Comment." *American Economic Review* 81 (1): 381–83.

Goodman, J., and J. Nichols. 1997. "Does FHA Increase Home Ownership or Just Accelerate It?" *Journal of Housing Economics* 6 (2): 184–202.

Hall, R., and F. Mishkin. 1982. "The Sensitivity of Consumption to Transitory Income: Estimates from Panel Data on Households." *Econometrica* 50 (2): 461–81.

Haurin, D., P. Hendershott, and S. Wachter. 1996. "Wealth Accumulation and Housing Choices of Young Households: An Exploratory Investigation." *Journal of Housing Research* 7 (1): 33–57.

———. 1997. "Borrowing Constraints and the Tenure Choice of Young Households." *Journal of Housing Research* 8 (2): 137–54.

Hayashi, F. 1985. "The Effect of Liquidity Constraints on Consumption: A Cross-Section Analysis." *Quarterly Journal of Economics* 10 (1): 183–206.

Henderson, V., and Y. Ioannides. 1983. "A Model of Housing Tenure Choice." *American Economic Review* 73 (1): 98–113.

Hoyt, W., and S. Rosenthal. 1990. "Capital Gains Taxation and the Demand for Owner-Occupied Housing." *Review of Economics and Statistics* 72 (1): 45–54.

———. 1992. "Owner-Occupied Housing, Capital Gains, and the Tax Reform Act of 1986." *Journal of Urban Economics* 32 (2): 119–39.

Ioannides, Y., and S. Rosenthal. 1994. "Estimating the Consumption and Investment Demands for Housing and Their Effect on Housing Tenure Status." *Review of Economics and Statistics* 76 (1): 127–41.

Jappelli, T. 1990. "Who Is Credit Constrained in the U.S.?" *Quarterly Journal of Economics* 105 (1): 219–34.

Kennickell, A. 1998. "Multiple Imputation in the Survey of Consumer Finances." Federal Reserve Board Working Paper (September).

———. 1999. "Revisions to the SCF Weighting Methodology: Accounting for Race/Ethnicity and Homeownership." Federal Reserve Board Working Paper (January).

Linneman, P., and S. Wachter. 1989. "The Impacts of Borrowing Constraints on Homeownership." *AREUEA Journal* 17 (4): 389–402.

Listokin, D. and E. Wyly. 2000. "Innovative Strategies to Expand Lending to Traditionally Underserved Populations: Approaches and Case Studies." Fannie Mae Foundation Working Paper (March).

Listokin, D., E. Wyly, B. Schmitt, and I. Voicu. 1999. "The Potential and Limitations of Mortgage Innovation in Fostering Homeownership in the United States." Fannie Mae Foundation Working Paper (December).

Maddala, G. 1983. *Limited-Dependent and Qualitative Variables in Econometrics.* New York: Cambridge University Press.

Mayer, C., and G. Engelhardt. 1996. "Gifts, Down Payments, and Housing Affordability." *Journal of Housing Research* 7 (1): 59–77.

Munnell, A., G. Tootell, L. Browne, and J. McEneaney. 1996. "Mortgage Lending in Boston: Interpreting HMDA Data." *American Economic Review* 86 (1): 25–53.

Quercia, R., G. McCarthy, and S. Wachter. 1998. "The Impacts of Lending Efforts on Homeownership Rates." University of North Carolina mimeo (May).

Rehm, B. 1991a. "ABA Rebuts Bias Charge in Fed Study on Lending. *American Banker,* October 15.

———. 1991b. "Data on Bias in Lending Sparks Demands for Action." *American Banker,* October 22.

Reuters. 1991. "Fannie Mae in $10 Billion Loan Program." *American Banker,* March 15.

Rohe, W., G. McCarthy, and S. Van Zandt. 2000. "The Social Benefits and Costs of Homeownership: A Critical Assessment of the Research." Research Institute for Housing America Working Paper 00-01 (May).

Rosen, H. 1979. "Housing Decisions and the U.S. Income Tax: An Econometric Analysis." *Journal of Public Economics* 11 (1): 1–24.

———. 1985. "Housing Subsidies: Effects on Housing Decisions, Efficiency, and Equity." In *Handbook of Public Economics,* edited by A. Auerbach and M. Feldstein. North Holland, N.Y.: Elsevier Science Publishers.

Rosenthal, S. 1988. "A Residence Time Model of Housing Markets." *Journal of Public Economics* 36 (1): 89–107.

Rosenthal, S., J. Duca, and S. Gabriel. 1991. "Credit Rationing and the Demand for Owner-Occupied Housing." *Journal of Urban Economics* 30 (1): 48–63.

Savage, H. 1999. "Who Could Afford to Buy a House in 1995." United States Census Bureau report (August).

Stiglitz, J., and A. Weiss. 1981. "Credit Rationing in Markets with Imperfect Information." *American Economic Review* 71 (3): 393–410.

Thomas, P. 1992. "Bank America, Security Pacific Merger Cleared." *Wall Street Journal,* March 24, A3 and A6.

Trans Data Corporation. 1986. *Residential Mortgages: 1986—Deposit and Credit Products Program Reference Manual.* Salisbury, Md.

Tunali, I. 1986. "A General Structure for Models of Double-Selection and an Application to a Joint Migration/Earnings Process with Remigration." *Research in Labor Economics* 8 (B): 235–82.

Turner, M. and F. Skidmore. 1999. *Mortgage Lending Discrimination: A Review of Existing Evidence.* Washington: Urban Institute.

Turner, M., J. Yinger, S. Ross, K. Temkin, D. Levey, D. Levine, R. Smith, and M. DeLair. 1999. *What We Know about Mortgage Lending Discrimination in America.* Washington:

Office of Policy Development and Research, U.S. Department of Housing and Urban Development.

U.S. Census Bureau. 2000. *Housing Affordability Tables*. www.census.gov/hhes; www./hsgaffrd.html (June).

Zeldes, S. 1989. "Consumption and Liquidity Constraints: An Empirical Investigation." *Journal of Political Economy* 97 (2): 305–46.

Zorn, P. 1989. "Mobility-Tenure Decisions and Financial Credit: Do Mortgage Qualification Requirements Constrain Home Ownership?" *AREUEA Journal* 17 (1): 1–16.

5

Prepurchase Homeownership Counseling: A Little Knowledge Is a Good Thing

ABDIGHANI HIRAD AND
PETER ZORN

For the past three decades homeownership counseling has been an integral part of affordable lending in the United States. Myriad benefits have been attributed to these programs. Its advocates believe, for example, that counseling better prepares borrowers to recognize and accept the responsibilities of owning a home. By helping to get households into homes they can afford, and afford to keep, homeownership counseling has been credited with stabilizing families and neighborhoods and reducing default risk for lenders.

This study uses data on almost 40,000 mortgages originated under Freddie Mac's Affordable Gold program to assess the claim that prepurchase homeownership counseling programs lower mortgage delinquency rates. We find statistical evidence that counseling does, in fact, mitigate credit risk. Borrowers who receive prepurchase homeownership counseling under the Affordable Gold program are, on average, 19 percent less likely to become ninety-day delinquent on their mortgages than borrowers with equivalent observable characteristics who do not receive counseling.

We are deeply indebted to Jim Carey for providing us with the opportunity to do this research and for sharing his knowledge about counseling, to Oliver Zeng for his outstanding work in developing the loan matching routine, and to Jim Berkovec for his econometric insights and consultation. The views expressed in this chapter are ours alone and do not necessarily represent those of Freddie Mac or its Board of Directors.

We also find significant variation in the effectiveness of classroom, home-study, individual, and telephone counseling. Our data clearly indicate that borrowers who receive individual counseling have the greatest mitigation in credit risk. All things equal, the ninety-day delinquency rate of borrowers who received individual counseling was reduced by 34 percent, an outcome that is superior and statistically different from that obtained by either home-study or telephone counseling. Classroom and home-study counseling reduced delinquency rates at 26 percent and 21 percent, respectively, and were superior to telephone counseling, which had no statistically significant impact on borrower delinquency.

Affordable Gold borrowers receive counseling from a variety of sources, including government agencies, lenders, mortgage insurers, and nonprofit organizations. Our basic analysis, however, offers no statistical evidence that any provider administers counseling in a manner that is either more or less effective in reducing credit risk. Borrowers who received counseling from nonprofit organizations and lenders did, on average, have lower ninety-day delinquency rates than borrowers counseled by other providers. This outcome, though, primarily appears to reflect the more effective mix of counseling these groups provide.

Our data were not collected as part of a controlled experiment. We therefore also consider the possibility that the effects we attribute to counseling are in fact due to unobserved characteristics associated with borrowers' assignment or selection into counseling programs. The results of statistical tests strongly reject the hypothesis that counseling's estimated effectiveness is entirely due to such unobserved characteristics. Moreover, our best estimate after accounting for these unobserved characteristics is that counseling is more rather than less effective. We also statistically confirm the previously identified differences in effectiveness of alternative counseling programs, as well as differences among providers. We are unable, however, to statistically confirm that individual and home-study counseling's effectiveness is not due to borrower assignment or selection.

This study is the first to provide significant empirical evidence that prepurchase homeownership counseling can effectively reduce borrowers' delinquency rates.[1] Notwithstanding some unresolved issues, any evidence that homeownership counseling effectively mitigates risk is welcome news. Affordable lending programs historically have pushed the limits of underwriting in an effort to offer the benefits of homeownership to the greatest number of families. Prepurchase counseling by no means eliminates the greater credit risk of these programs—even with counseling, affordable lending loans likely will be among the riskiest of mortgages originated by most prime lenders. The empirical evidence presented in this chapter does demonstrate, however, that prepurchase homeownership coun-

1. The empirical studies that have been conducted are twenty or more years old and are generally viewed as unconvincing. A review and critique of existing statistical studies is provided in Mallach (2001) and Quercia and Wachter (1996).

seling can increase the success of affordable lending programs by helping families keep their homes, a substantial benefit to both borrowers and lenders.

Overview of Homeownership Education and Counseling

Counseling generally is conducted as part of a broader initiative to increase homeownership opportunities. As a consequence, counseling programs are geared primarily toward first-time home buyers and specifically toward minority families, immigrants, city dwellers, and others who have yet to attain homeownership at the national average rate.[2] Homeownership education and counseling began in earnest about thirty years ago, primarily in response to the high incidence of defaults and foreclosures among HUD section 235 participants. Today homeownership education and counseling programs in the United States take an almost bewildering variety of forms. Lenders, nonprofit organizations, government agencies, and others administer separate programs. The programs themselves are delivered through many different avenues, including the classroom, home study, individual counseling, and the telephone. The content of programs also varies significantly across each of these administrative and delivery mechanisms, as does the timing of the counseling—pre- and postpurchase.

Timing is a key distinction in counseling. Prepurchase counseling and education are designed to better prepare families for the responsibilities of homeownership by explaining the home-buying and financing process, encouraging financial planning and money management, and going over home maintenance and repair issues and concerns. Postpurchase counseling shares much of this focus but generally spends more time on individual budgeting and maintenance and repair issues. This study focuses entirely on prepurchase counseling.

Another important distinction is that drawn between counseling and education. Counseling is specific and is tailored to the particular needs of the individual, while education typically is administered in a generic program. Although this distinction is independent of the format, an individual format generally implies counseling because it is a one-to-one session where borrowers can discuss their individual situations and concerns. Classroom counseling also can fall into this category because, although it is administered to a group of borrowers, it too can give borrowers personal attention, sessions can be broken into several units, and it often covers more subjects than the typical individual format. Home-study and telephone formats, however, generally are considered education, not counseling. In these formats borrowers engage in self-study by following a generic program. There sometimes is the opportunity to interact with a

2. This section relies heavily on excellent reviews of homeownership counseling programs by Mallach (2001) and McCarthy and Quercia (2000).

counselor, but generally this does not happen before the administration of an exam.

While recognizing and acknowledging this distinction, we use the terms counseling and education interchangeably. This reflects the fact that it is impossible in our data to distinguish accurately between borrowers who received homeownership counseling and those who received education.

There are manifold motivations for supporting homeownership counseling. For example, counseling can provide consumer outreach in nontraditional markets, build trust in the mortgage lending process, and provide lenders with mortgage-ready applicants. A central premise, however, is that effective counseling significantly reduces borrower delinquency rates. Despite the lack of any clear empirical evidence to support this claim, or perhaps more accurately, believing in counseling's at the time undemonstrated benefits, Freddie Mac in 1993 required all Affordable Gold borrowers to receive prepurchase homeownership counseling.

Counseling in 1993 was predominantly supplied in a classroom or one-on-one setting. Freddie Mac's policy change, and an equivalent decision by Fannie Mae, significantly increased the demand for counseling in the mid-1990s. The current prominence of home-study and telephone counseling is largely the result of this pressure on supply. Home-study and telephone counseling both have the advantage that they can be put into place relatively quickly, counseling can be accomplished with a smaller time commitment from either the borrower or the provider, and the programs are far less expensive to administer than either individual or classroom counseling. Telephone counseling is the more recently adopted of these two. Its advocates view it as an improvement over home study because it provides at least some personal contact with a third party.

Data on Freddie Mac's Affordable Gold Loans

The data used in this study are loans purchased by Freddie Mac under its Affordable Gold program. The Affordable Gold program is designed specifically to help open the doors of homeownership to borrowers who earn 100 percent or less of area median income.[3] Starting in 1993, Freddie Mac has required that for each Affordable Gold loan it purchases at least one qualifying borrower receives prepurchase homeownership counseling. Lenders are free to determine the characteristics of the counseling borrowers receive, but loans submitted for Freddie Mac's purchase must record the organization that provides the counsel-

3. A borrower's income generally can be no greater than 100 percent of area median income (120 percent in California, 170 percent in Hawaii, 165 percent in the New York City MSA, and 120 percent in the Boston MSA). Incomes, however, may be higher through specially negotiated Community Development Lending alliances or other specially negotiated programs offered through housing finance agencies, public agencies, and nonprofits.

ing (lender, nonprofit, government agency, or "other") and the type of counseling delivered (classroom, home study, individual counseling, or "other").[4]

Fortunately for the purposes of our study, a natural quasi-control group is formed by the fact that roughly 3 percent of Affordable Gold loans are exempted from Freddie Mac's homeownership counseling requirements. Mortgages qualify for this exemption on the basis of their perceived lower risk, specifically if (1) at least one co-borrower has previously owned a home, or (2) the loan-to-value ratio of the mortgage is 95 percent or less, or (3) borrowers have cash reserves after closing equal to at least two monthly mortgage payments. Not all borrowers who meet these criteria are exempted from counseling, but for those borrowers that are exempted lenders record "education not required" into the administration and delivery fields described above.

Regardless of whether Affordable Gold borrowers do or do not receive counseling, we append servicing records to each loan in our data. Servicing records are available through the second quarter of 2000, so to ensure that there is a minimum of eighteen months of performance history for every loan we only include in our analysis loans originated from the first quarter of 1993 through the fourth quarter of 1998. Borrowers are classified as experiencing repayment difficulties if, over the observation period, their servicing record shows that they have ever been ninety days or more late on scheduled mortgage payments.[5]

In addition, Freddie Mac maintains a variety of data on each loan in its portfolio. Included are many of the variables typically incorporated into standard underwriting models, such as loan-to-value ratio, FICO score, and total-debt-to-income ratio.[6] These and other variables are used in running each Affordable Gold loan through an "emulated" version of Loan Prospector®, Freddie Mac's automated underwriting service.[7]

Freddie Mac's customers use Loan Prospector to get an immediate, accurate assessment of whether applications meet Freddie Mac's "investment quality" purchase standards. Loan Prospector, consequently, delivers an "accept" message to applications that meet this standard and a "caution" message to those that appear not to. For the purposes of this study, however, we need a measure that captures more subtle variations in risk. For this reason, we use an intermediate

4. Our investigations reveal that "other" in the administration field is largely mortgage insurers. "Other" in the delivery field is largely telephone counseling for mortgage insurers, a hybrid of classroom and individual counseling for lenders, and of unknown nature for government agencies and nonprofit organizations.

5. Analyses conducted using ever-sixty-day delinquency provide qualitative results similar to those presented here.

6. FICO scores are developed by Fair, Isaac, and Co. and are used to predict the probability of being ninety days delinquent on consumer loans in the first two years.

7. We use an "emulated" version because some of the variables required by Loan Prospector are unavailable in the Freddie Mac data. The missing variables primarily are limited to borrower reserves and detailed credit variables. The emulated version generally provides a good approximation of the full Loan Prospector model but is unable to fully assess nuances in credit risk.

product from Loan Prospector, automated underwriting system (AUS) score, a variable that measures the probability that a loan will go into foreclosure. A low AUS score indicates a high probability of foreclosure (the minimum is roughly 500), a high score indicates a low probability of foreclosure (the maximum is roughly 1500), and a decrease of sixty points in the AUS score doubles the odds of foreclosure.

We include three additional sets of variables to account for observable differences that may affect the risk characteristics of borrowers. First, we include characteristics of the mortgage and the property—loan origination amount, loan purpose, number of units, and property type. Second, we include demographic variables of the borrower—borrower race/ethnicity, minority population in the census tract, family income, median income in the census tract, and whether the borrower is a first-time home buyer. Third, we include variables to account for different economic environments experienced by borrowers—whether the property is located in a metropolitan statistical area (MSA), the quarter the loan was originated, and state in which the property is located.

Methodology

This study poses three questions. Does homeownership counseling demonstrably reduce ninety-day delinquency rates? Do the different types of counseling programs vary in their effectiveness? And are any of the counseling providers more or less effective in administering their programs? We answer these questions using a logit model estimating the probability that borrowers ever become ninety days or more delinquent.[8] Specifically, we estimate the following equation:

$$P(\text{delinquent}) = \frac{\exp\left(X^1\beta^1 + X^2\beta^2 + \varepsilon\right)}{1+\exp\left(X^1\beta^1 + X^2\beta^2 + \varepsilon\right)}, \tag{5-1}$$

where X^1 is a matrix composed of columns of dummy variables, one for each type of counseling/counseling provider combination (a total of sixteen mutually exclusive columns, where borrowers exempted from counseling are the omitted category), X^2 is a matrix composed of columns of observable independent vari-

8. In addition to the logit estimation we conduct an equivalent analysis using ex-post matched pairs. Each Affordable Gold borrower in our data is matched along observable individual and loan characteristics to a non–Affordable Gold borrower from among Freddie Mac's loan purchases, few of whom, if any, receive homeownership counseling. The effectiveness of homeownership counseling is then assessed by comparing the mean delinquency rates of Affordable Gold loans (in total and grouped separately by type of counseling program) to the mean delinquency rates of the loans to which they have been matched. The matched-pair analysis provides qualitative results similar to those presented here.

ables thought to be associated with mortgage delinquency, β^1 and β^2 are column vectors of estimated coefficients, and ε is a column vector of error terms assumed to be independently and identically distributed extreme value.

The β^1 can be interpreted as estimates of the marginal impact of alternative counseling programs on ninety-day delinquency rates. We can therefore express our research questions in terms of restrictions on the β^1. Specifically, if counseling has no effect on delinquency rates then the β^1 will all be zero. This leads to a test of the null hypothesis

$$H_0^1 : \beta^1 = 0. \tag{5-2}$$

Likewise, if the different types of counseling are equally effective in reducing delinquency rates, then each provider's estimated coefficients will be the same across all counseling types. This leads to the null hypothesis

$$H_0^2 : \beta^1_{ik} = \beta^1_{jk} \forall i, j \in T, \forall k \in P, \tag{5-3}$$

where T is the set of all types of counseling and P is the set of all counseling providers. Finally, if counseling providers are equally effective in administering their programs, then each counseling type's estimated coefficients will be the same for all providers. This yields the null hypothesis

$$H_0^3 : \beta^1_{ij} = \beta^1_{ik} \forall j, k \in P, \forall i \in T. \tag{5-4}$$

In addition to this basic analysis, we attempt to address the fact that borrowers in our data are not randomly assigned to counseling programs. More specifically, counseling programs likely are endogenously assigned or selected. If the error term of the underlying counseling program assignment or selection model is correlated with ε, then estimates of β^1 in equation 5-1 will be biased and inconsistent. As an example, a disproportionate number of more "motivated" lower-risk borrowers may choose to receive the more intensive classroom and individual counseling, resulting in an overestimate of the benefits of these programs.

We address this concern with a two-stage estimation procedure designed to purge any correlation between the error terms in these two models.[9] First, we estimate a model of borrower assignment or selection into counseling programs. We then incorporate these probability estimates into an alternative version of equation 5-1. Specifically, we estimate the logit model

$$P(\text{delinquent}) = \frac{\exp\left(P(X^1)\gamma^1 + X^2\gamma^2 + \eta\right)}{1+\exp\left(P(X^1)\gamma^1 + X^2\gamma^2 + \eta\right)}, \tag{5-5}$$

9. See, for example, Judge and others (1980), chapter 18.5.1, for a brief discussion of similar procedures.

where $\hat{P}(X^1)$ is a matrix of predicted probabilities that borrowers are assigned to or select alternative counseling programs, γ^1 and γ^2 are column vectors of estimated coefficients, and η is a column vector of error terms assumed to be independently and identically distributed extreme value.[10] Finally, we retest the null hypotheses in equations 5-2 through 5-4 after first substituting γ^1 for β^1:

$$H_0^4 : \gamma^1 = 0. \tag{5-6}$$

$$H_0^5 : \gamma^1_{ik} = \gamma^1_{jk} \forall i,\ j \in T, \forall k \in P \tag{5-7}$$

$$H_0^6 : \gamma^1_{ij} = \varphi^1_{ik}\ \forall j,\ k \in P, \forall i \in T \tag{5-8}$$

Empirical Results

Table 5-1 provides the distribution of the loans used in the study across the various homeownership counseling programs. A total of 39,318 Affordable Gold loans are originated between the first quarter of 1993 and the fourth quarter of 1998. Of this number, the borrowers on 1,238 loans (roughly 3 percent of the total) were exempted from counseling.

The recipients of the 38,080 loans who received counseling are far from uniformly distributed across counseling types and providers. The distribution among types of counseling, for example, is quite skewed—43 percent of counseling was delivered through home study, 34 percent was delivered by telephone, and just 10 percent and 9 percent of borrowers received individual and classroom counseling, respectively. All told, lenders provided 50 percent of the counseling, mortgage insurers provided 44 percent of the counseling, nonprofit organizations provided 3 percent of the counseling, and government agencies administered counseling to only 2 percent of borrowers.

The uneven distribution of Affordable Gold loans in these categories is less than ideal from an experimental design perspective. In particular, ever-ninety-day delinquency rates will be measured with greatest precision for the counseling types and providers used most often and with least precision for those used least often. We are, consequently, most likely to find that counseling generates statistically significant risk-mitigating benefits when it is home study provided by lenders or telephone counseling administered by mortgage insurers. This concern notwithstanding, table 5-1 illustrates that there are sufficient data to

10. The estimates of γ^1 resulting from this two-step procedure will be consistent but inefficient, providing a conservative test for our null hypotheses.

Table 5-1. *Overview of Affordable Gold (AG) Loan Characteristics and Performance*

Type of counseling and provider	*Number of loans*	*MeanAUS score*[a]	*Ever ninety-day delinquency (percent)*
Classroom			
Government agency	427	929	7.3
Lender	2,317	909	6.1
Mortgage insurer[b]	203	869	6.4
Nonprofit organization	609	922	3.9
Home study			
Government agency	332	899	4.2
Lender	12,148	904	6.7
Mortgage insurer[c]	3,470	885	7.4
Nonprofit organization	315	877	4.4
Individual			
Government agency	98	919	7.1
Lender	3,203	908	5.0
Mortgage insurer[c]	304	895	3.0
Nonprofit organization	186	867	5.4
Telephone[c]			
Mortgage insurer	12,901	891	8.3
Other[d]			
Government agency	51	882	9.8
Lender	1,483	941	4.6
Nonprofit organization	33	884	9.1
AG loans			
With counseling	38,080	900	6.9
Without counseling	1,238	943	5.7
Used in analysis	39,318	901	6.9
Freddie Mac non-AG loans[e]	9,246,002	1,059	1.8

a. AUS = Automated underwriting system.

b. Recorded as provided by "other."

c. Recorded as "other" type of counseling.

d. Mostly a hybrid of classroom and individual counseling for lenders and unknown types of counseling for government agencies and nonprofit organizations.

e. Non–Affordable Gold loans purchased by Freddie Mac originated in the same years as the Affordable Gold loans in our data.

assess the efficacy of counseling by all types and providers, with perhaps the small exception of "other" counseling provided by government agencies and nonprofit organizations.

Delinquency rates of Affordable Gold loans also are shown in table 5-1 in the far right-hand column labeled "Percent ever ninety-day delinquent." Affordable Gold loans taken as a group clearly are higher-risk than the average non–Affordable Gold loan in Freddie Mac's portfolio—ninety-day delinquency rates of Affordable Gold loans are 6.9 percent, relative to a portfolio average of 1.8 percent.[11] And Affordable Gold borrowers who received prepurchase homeownership counseling did not outperform those who did not receive counseling—6.9 percent of Affordable Gold borrowers who received counseling went into ninety-day delinquency while only 5.7 percent of the Affordable Gold borrowers who did not receive counseling performed as poorly. There is, however, substantial variation in ninety-day delinquency rates across alternative counseling delivery mechanisms, with values ranging from a low of 3.0 percent (individual counseling administered by mortgage insurers) to a high of 9.8 percent ("other" counseling provided by government agencies).

Finally, table 5-1 shows that there are significant differences in the risk characteristics of borrowers in the various counseling programs. For example, the column labeled "Mean AUS Score" shows that average AUS score values range from as low as 867 for individual counseling provided by nonprofit organizations to as high as 941 for "other" counseling provided by lenders.

Each type of counseling, moreover, has lower mean AUS scores (that is, higher risk characteristics) than loans without counseling. As a result, Affordable Gold borrowers who received counseling have an average AUS score of 900; the average AUS score for Affordable Gold borrowers who received no counseling is 943. This offers an explanation for the observed higher ninety-day delinquency rates of borrowers who received counseling, as well as for the suggestion that counseling does indeed mitigate risk. If a sixty-point reduction in AUS score roughly doubles the odds of ninety-day delinquency in our data, borrowers who receive counseling should have $2^{43/60} = 2^{0.7} = 1.6$ times greater odds of becoming delinquent than those who do not. In fact, the odds of delinquency are $(6.9/93.1)/(5.7/94.3) = 1.2$ times greater, suggesting that, on average, counseling reduces ninety-day delinquency rates by roughly 25 percent.

Basic Analysis

Our strategy, as noted above, is to improve on this crude estimate by using a logit model to control for AUS scores and other factors that may influence ninety-day delinquency rates. Table 5-2 provides summary statistics of the inde-

11. The values for the Freddie Mac portfolio are computed for all non–Affordable Gold loans purchased by Freddie Mac that were originated in 1993 through 1998.

Table 5-2. *Summary Statistics of Independent Variables in Logit Estimation*
A. Continuous variables

Variable	*Mean*	*Standard deviation*	*Minimum*	*Maximum*
AUS score	901	104	627	1,422
Loan origination amount ($100,000)	0.94	0.42	0.07	3.98
Minority population in tract (ratio of tract total)	0.20	0.23	0.00	1.00
Family income (ratio of area median)	0.83	0.33	0.05	2.5
Median tract income (ratio of area median)	0.86	0.24	0.00	3.61

B. Categorical variables

Variable	*Number of loans*	*Percent of data*
Number of units		
One	36,903	94.3
Two or more	2,235	5.7
Property type		
Condominium	3,586	9.2
Other	3,365	8.6
Single family	32,190	82.2
Loan purpose		
Purchase	38,192	97.6
Refinance/second home	949	2.4
First-time home buyer		
No	16,763	42.8
Unknown	323	0.8
Yes	22,055	56.4
Borrower race or ethnicity		
African American	3,595	9.2
Hispanic	4,161	10.6
Other minority	2,569	6.6
Unknown	1,257	3.2
White	27,559	70.4
Metropolitan statistical area		
Metro	36,300	92.7
Non-metro	2,841	7.3

pendent variables used in this logit estimation. No characteristics of the data particularly stand out. As expected from table 5-1, there is significant variation in AUS scores across Affordable Gold borrowers—the distribution of AUS scores has a standard deviation of 104. The mean loan origination amount is $94,000. On average, Affordable Gold borrowers have family incomes that are 83 percent of area median and reside in census tracts with 20 percent minority populations and median family incomes that are 86 percent of the area median.[12] Most of the loans in our analysis are taken out for the purpose of purchasing single-family, one-unit properties. About 56 percent of Affordable Gold borrowers are first-time home buyers, and about 93 percent of them reside in an MSA. A little over 70 percent of the borrowers are white, 26.5 percent are minority, and 3.2 have unknown race/ethnicity.

Table 5-3 provides the results from our logit estimation of loans becoming ninety-day delinquent. Looking first at the estimated coefficients on the counseling variables, we see clear evidence that prepurchase homeownership counseling can significantly reduce ninety-day delinquency rates. Of the sixteen estimated coefficients, seven are statistically significant at the 10 percent level—classroom counseling by lenders and nonprofit organizations, home-study counseling by government agencies and lenders, individual counseling by lenders and mortgage insurers, and "other" counseling by lenders. All seven of these coefficients are negative in value, implying that borrowers who receive these types of counseling have significantly lower delinquency rates than borrowers with similar observable characteristics who receive no counseling.

Not surprisingly, it is the counseling types with the greatest number of observations that generally are statistically significant. An interesting exception to this trend is telephone counseling by mortgage insurers; received by over one-third of Affordable Gold borrowers, telephone counseling has no statistically significant effect on ninety-day delinquency rates. Before we explore these coefficients in greater detail, however, we briefly turn to the other variables in the model.

Most of the estimated coefficients on the control variables have the expected signs and are statistically significant. The estimated coefficients on the AUS score groupings, for instance, decrease monotonically as the risk of the loan decreases (that is, as AUS scores increase), and almost all are statistically significant. They do suggest, however, that a sixty-point AUS score reduction less than doubles the odds of ninety-day delinquency—on average, estimated coefficients increase by 0.44 with each fifty-point reduction in AUS score, implying that the

12. Family income in our data is recorded as monthly income. Less than 5 percent of the time, however, annual rather than monthly income appears to be recorded (that is, reported Affordable Gold borrower income is as high as twelve times the area median). To address this inconsistency we impose an edit screen that borrower income recorded as greater than 2.5 times area median is assumed to be annual, not monthly. This edit has no impact on our logit estimations other than to increase the size and statistical significance of the estimated coefficient on family income.

Table 5-3. *Logit Estimation of Loans Ever Becoming 90-Day Delinquent*

Variable	*Coefficient estimate*	*Standard error*	*p-value*
Intercept	–5.639	1.109	0.0001
Classroom counseling			
Government	0.032	0.239	0.8941
Lender	–0.318	0.162	0.0495
Mortgage insurer	–0.498	0.327	0.1271
Nonprofit	–0.592	0.261	0.0231
Home study counseling			
Government	–0.531	0.318	0.095
Lender	–0.279	0.139	0.045
Mortgage insurer	–0.129	0.151	0.3925
Nonprofit	–0.475	0.316	0.1326
Individual counseling			
Government	0.147	0.434	0.7345
Lender	–0.446	0.158	0.0046
Mortgage insurer	–0.843	0.372	0.0236
Nonprofit	–0.470	0.370	0.2031
Telephone counseling/other counseling			
Mortgage insurer	–0.086	0.138	0.5343
Government	–0.129	0.513	0.8009
Lender	–0.475	0.189	0.0118
Nonprofit	–0.095	0.657	0.8846
No counseling	0.000	0.000	.
AUS score			
Unknown	2.975	0.297	0.0001
700 or less	4.642	0.351	0.0001
701 to 750	3.985	0.304	0.0001
750 to 800	3.468	0.297	0.0001
801 to 850	2.833	0.296	0.0001
850 to 900	2.212	0.297	0.0001
901 to 950	1.762	0.301	0.0001
950 to 1000	1.111	0.311	0.0004
1000 to 1050	0.705	0.334	0.0349
1050 to 1100	0.491	0.385	0.2022
1101 and up	0.000	0.000	. . .
Loan origination amount ($100,000)	–0.247	0.084	0.0031
Number of units			
One	0.574	0.117	0.0001
Two or more	0.000	0.000	. . .

continued on next page

Table 5-3. *Logit Estimation of Loans Ever Becoming 90-Day Delinquent (continued)*

Variable	*Coefficient estimate*	*Standard error*	*p-value*
Property type			
Condominium	–0.639	0.087	0.0001
Other	–0.041	0.087	0.6415
Single family	0.000	0.000	. . .
Loan purpose			
Purchase	–0.720	0.163	0.0001
Refinance/second home	0.000	0.000	. . .
First–time home buyer			
No	0.039	0.046	0.4051
Unknown	–0.522	0.330	0.1137
Yes	0.000	0.000	. . .
Borrower race or ethnicity			
African American	0.503	0.068	0.0001
Hispanic	–0.071	0.073	0.3314
Other minority	–0.083	0.094	0.3780
Unknown	0.198	0.117	0.0908
White	0.000	0.000	. . .
Minority population in tract (ratio of tract total)	0.460	0.109	0.0001
Family income (ratio of area median)	–0.157	0.087	0.0726
Median tract income (ratio of area median)	–0.155	0.110	0.1589
Metropolitan statistical area			
Metro	–0.289	0.085	0.0007
Non-metro	0.000	0.000	. . .
Loan origination date[a]	. . .	. . .	. . .
State[b]	. . .	. . .	. . .
Number of observations	39,141		

a. Fixed effects for the year and quarter that the loan was originated.

b. Fixed effects for the state in which the property is located.

odds of delinquency increase by exp(0.44) = 1.5, somewhat less than the assumed $2^{50/60} = 2^{0.8} = 1.8$ increase required to double the odds.[13]

We also find that delinquency rates decrease as loan origination amounts increase and, somewhat surprisingly, for borrowers who take out mortgages on condominiums (relative to those who borrow to purchase single-family units). Purchase money mortgages, as usually is the case, are less likely to be ever ninety-day delinquent. First-time home buyers are no more or less likely than repeat home buyers to become delinquent. As is typically found in these types of estimations, African American borrowers are more likely to experience repayment difficulties than nonminority borrowers, and the higher the ratio of minority population in the census tract the more likely borrowers are to become delinquent. We find no statistically significant association between delinquency and median tract income, although borrowers living in an MSA are more likely to become delinquent, as are borrowers with lower family income. Finally, we include loan origination data and state fixed effects, neither of which is reported here but both of which are statistically significant as a group.

Figure 5-1 provides goodness-of-fit measures for the logit estimation. The graph in the top panel of the exhibit depicts the distribution of delinquent loans across predicted probability deciles. If our model perfectly fit the data, 100 percent of the delinquent loans would be distributed into the (high-risk) tenth-probability decile. Our estimation obviously does not achieve this standard. Nonetheless, the graph illustrates that our model does a reasonably good job of distinguishing between loans that will and will not become ninety-day delinquent. For example, only 1 percent of delinquent loans are found in the (low-risk) first-probability decile, while 37 percent of delinquent loans are in the (high-risk) tenth-probability decile.

The lower panel of figure 5-1 provides three additional measures of fit—the Hosmer-Lemeshow test statistic, mean predictions of the dependent variable, and the Kolmogrorov-Smirov (K-S) test statistic. All three measures show that the model does a good job of distinguishing loans that become ninety-day delinquent. The Hosmer-Lemeshow test statistic shows that we cannot reject the null hypothesis that the model provides a good fit to the data.[14] Mean delin-

13. Using these empirical estimates to repeat the analysis from table 5-1 suggests that Affordable Gold borrowers who receive counseling should have $1.5^{43/50} = 1.45$ higher odds of delinquency, implying an average of an 18 percent reduction in delinquency rates from counseling.

14. For the Hosmer-Lemeshow goodness-of-fit statistic, the borrowers are grouped into "deciles of risk" by first using the logistic model to calculate each borrower's predicted probability of ninety-day delinquency and then ranking the borrowers according to this risk probability. The borrowers are then divided into ten groups, with each group containing approximately 10 percent of the total number of borrowers. Comparing the observed and predicted outcomes for each group then creates a test statistic. A well-fitting model will have a small test statistic (that is, observed and predicted outcomes will be similar), while a poorly fitting model will have a large test statistic. Simulations have shown that the test statistic is distributed approximately chi-squared with degrees of freedom equal to g-2, where g denotes the number of groups. Our test statistic of 6.51 with eight

Figure 5-1. *Goodness-of-Fit Measures for Logit Estimation*

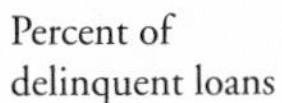

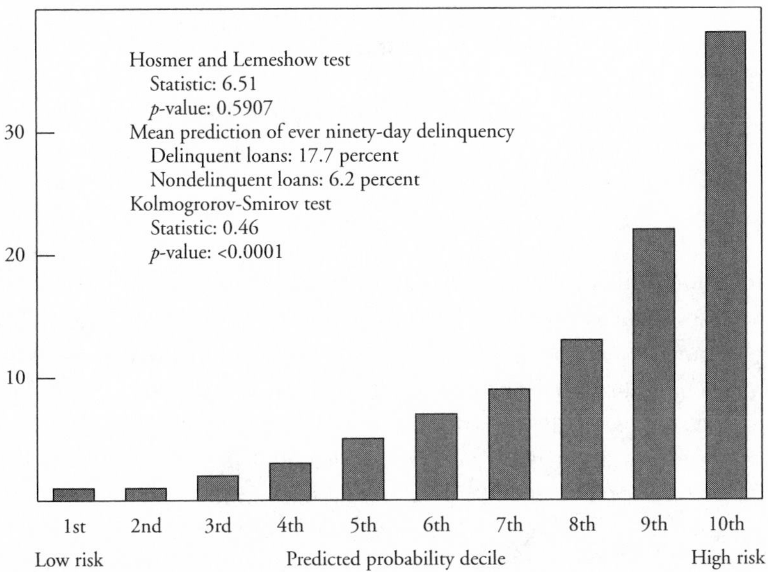

quency predictions also vary appreciably for loans that have and have not been ninety-day delinquent; mean predictions are 17.7 percent for delinquent loans and 6.2 percent for loans that never become delinquent. Finally, the K-S test statistic strongly rejects the null hypothesis that our model cannot distinguish between loans that will and will not become ninety-day delinquent.[15]

We turn now to our specific research questions and tests of the associated null hypotheses. Our first research question is whether counseling has a statistically significant impact on ninety-day delinquency rates. Our discussion of the logit results clearly suggests that it does, and this is confirmed by our strong rejection of H_0^1.[16] Similarly, we reject H_0^2, providing evidence that different types of coun-

degrees of freedom yields a *p*-value of 0.5907. We therefore are unable to reject the null hypothesis that the model fits the data.

15. The K-S statistic is a measure of the difference in the predicted probability cumulative density functions (CDFs) for delinquent and nondelinquent loans. A well-fitting model will assign high delinquency probabilities to delinquent loans and low delinquency probabilities to nondelinquent loans, yielding quite distinct CDFs. We strongly reject the hypothesis that the two groups have identical CDFs. In the scoring industry, K-S statistics of 0.30 traditionally are thought to indicate acceptable fit, while values of 0.50 or more indicate an excellent fit. The test statistic of 0.46 suggests that our model fits reasonably well.

16. We use likelihood ratio statistics to test our null hypotheses. In this instance, the restricted model has a log likelihood of –8233.32, while the unrestricted model has a log likelihood of –8211.84. The likelihood ratio statistic is calculated as twice the difference in these log likelihoods, giving a value of 42.96 that is distributed chi-squared with sixteen degrees of freedom. We therefore are able to reject the null hypothesis with a *p*-value of 0.0003.

seling vary significantly in their effectiveness at reducing delinquency rates.[17] We are, however, unable to reject H_0^3, finding no evidence of counseling providers' differential effectiveness in administering their programs.[18]

We explore these research questions more fully using simulation results designed to estimate the reduction in ninety-day delinquency rates provided by each of the counseling types. Reductions in delinquency rates are displayed in figure 5-2 in matrix format, where the rows represent the type of counseling borrowers receive and the columns represent the counseling provider. The far right column of the first five rows shows the marginal effect of each type of counseling, the first four columns of the last row show the marginal effect of each counseling provider, and the fifth column of the last row shows the average effect of counseling across all types and providers.

To construct each estimate in figure 5-2, we simulate the outcome of conceptual experiments that first create perfect matched pairs for each of the 39,318 Affordable Gold loans in our data and then randomly assign one pair-member to a "treatment" group and the other pair-member to a "control" group. We create a "control" group by using our logit estimates to predict ninety-day delinquency rates for each of the 39,318 Affordable Gold loans in the data, while assigning each loan the impact of receiving no counseling (that is, setting $\beta^1 = 0$). We create each "treatment" group by using our logit estimates to predict ninety-day delinquency rates for each of the loans in the data, while assigning them the impact of receiving one of the counseling type or provider combinations (setting $\beta^1 = \beta^1_{ij}$). The treatment effect from counseling is then estimated separately for each loan by calculating the ratio of "treatment"-predicted delinquency rate to "control"-predicted delinquency rate and converting this to a percentage reduction. The values presented in figure 5-2 are the means of these percentage reductions for all 39,318 Affordable Gold loans in our data.[19]

The main portion of figure 5-2 (columns one through four and rows one through five) clearly shows that counseling can successfully decrease ninety-day delinquency rates. All but two of the simulation point estimates are positive, and some imply quite substantial risk-mitigating effects. The simulations also show,

17. The restricted and unrestricted models have log likelihoods of –8221.80 and –8211.84, respectively, resulting in a test statistic of 19.92 that is distributed chi-squared with twelve degrees of freedom. We therefore are able to reject the null hypothesis with a p-value of 0.069.

18. The restricted and unrestricted models have log likelihoods of –8218.83 and –8211.84, respectively, resulting in a test statistic of 13.98 that is distributed chi-squared with eleven degrees of freedom. This gives us a p-value of 0.23, meaning that we are unable to reject the null hypothesis.

19. Predictions of the marginal effects are computed with auxiliary estimations that impose the appropriate restrictions on the β^1. For example, to estimate the marginal impact of classroom we impose the restriction that $\beta^1_{ij} = \beta^1_{ik}$ for $\forall j, k \in T$ and $i = classroom$. Note that this implicitly implies an unchanged distribution of providers when computing the marginal effect of counseling type, and an unchanged distribution of counseling type when computing the marginal impacts of providers. We test the null hypotheses that the marginal effects are zero by testing the significance of each "marginal" coefficient in each auxiliary estimation.

Figure 5-2. *Estimated Reduction in Ninety-Day Delinquency Rates from Counseling*[a]

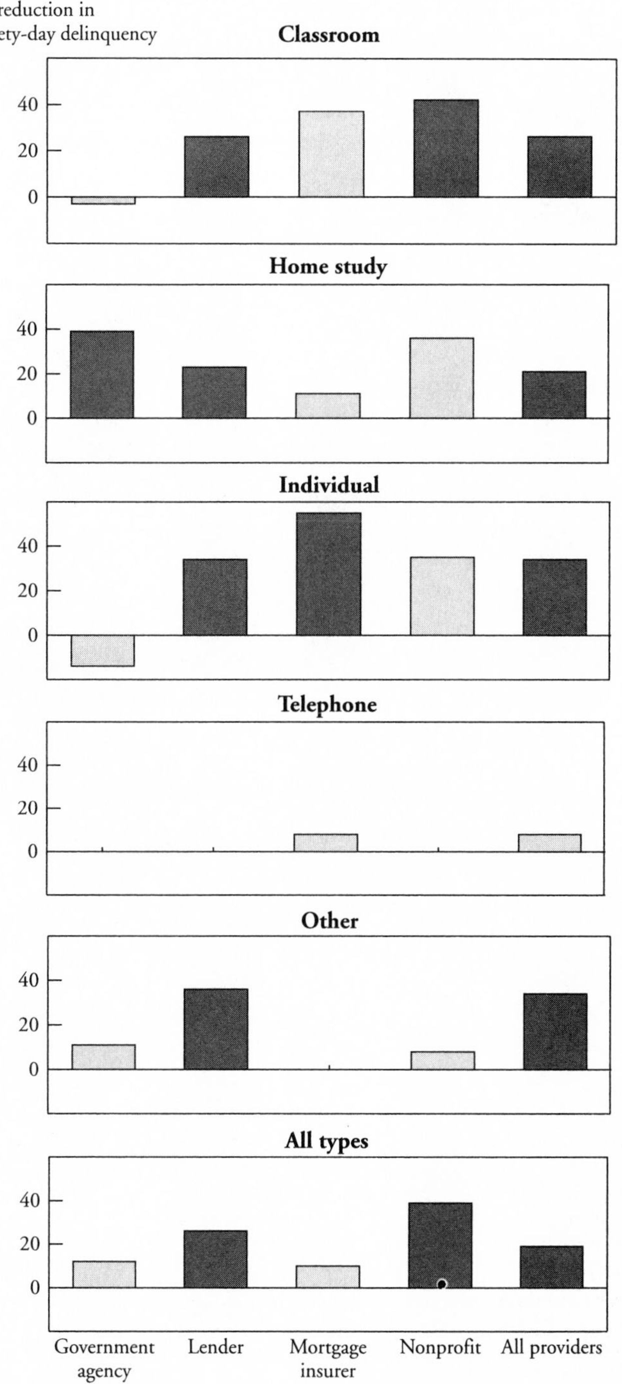

a. Dark-shaded bars indicate reductions that are statistically significant at the 10 percent level.

however, that all counseling is not equally effective. Statistically significant reductions from prepurchase homeownership counseling range from a low of 23 percent (home-study counseling by lenders) to a high of 55 percent (individual counseling by mortgage insurers). Not all estimates, moreover, are statistically significant.

Perhaps the simplest way to assess the differential impact of alternative types of counseling is by considering their marginal effects. The far-right column of figure 5-2 shows simulation results calculating the marginal effect of each counseling type. These marginal estimates confirm that there is a rank ordering in counseling's effectiveness. Individual counseling is the most effective and provides an estimated 34 percent reduction in ninety-day delinquency rates. This is followed by classroom and home study, which provide, respectively, 26 and 21 percent risk mitigation. Telephone counseling provides an estimated 8 percent reduction in delinquency rates, but this result is not statistically differentiable from zero.[20] Tests show, moreover, that individual counseling's superiority to both home study and telephone counseling is statistically significant, as are both classroom and home-study counseling's superiority to telephone.[21]

Looking at the marginal effects of counseling provider (the last row of figure 5-2), we also see a clear rank ordering. As noted earlier, however, we find no statistical difference in the effectiveness of providers in administering counseling programs. The differentials we see in the marginal effects, therefore, come from the mix of counseling administered by each provider, not from statistically significant differences in administering any given type of counseling.

Finally, the overall effect of counseling is shown in the lower right-hand corner of figure 5-2 in the cell labeled "All Types" and "All Providers." We find that borrowers who receive prepurchase homeownership counseling are, on average, 19 percent less likely to become ninety-day delinquent on their mortgages than borrowers with equivalent observable characteristics who do not receive counseling.

Analysis of Assignment and Selection

We now briefly turn to the results of our two-stage procedure for addressing potential endogeneity in counseling assignment and selection. Our first stage

20. "Other" counseling delivered by lenders is primarily a hybrid of classroom and individual counseling and appears to be as effective as individual counseling alone.

21. We use log likelihood ratio test statistics to assess whether differences in the point estimates of the marginal effects are statistically significant. The null hypothesis that individual counseling's effect is the same as that of home study and telephone counseling is rejected with p-values of 0.0212 (test statistic of 5.31 distributed chi-squared with one degree of freedom) and <0.0001 (test statistic of 17.14 distributed chi-squared with one degree of freedom), respectively. The null hypothesis that the effect of classroom and home-study counseling is the same as the effect of telephone counseling is rejected with p-values of .0064 (test statistic of 7.44 distributed chi-squared with one degree of freedom) and 0.0014 (test statistic of 10.14 distributed chi-squared with one degree of freedom), respectively. We are unable to reject the null hypothesis that individual and classroom counseling have identical effects; we are also unable to reject the null hypothesis that classroom and home-study counseling have identical effects.

estimates a nested logit model of borrower assignment or selection into counseling programs. Estimated coefficients from this model are applied to each Affordable Gold borrower to predict the probabilities of receiving each type of counseling from each counseling provider, as well as being exempted entirely from counseling. Our second stage estimates the delinquency model of equation 5-5.

Details of these procedures are provided in the appendix. We note here, however, that our nested logit model is not particularly well fitting and that our second-stage estimation of ninety-day delinquency rates suffers from symptoms of multicollinearity. Not withstanding these problems, the results of these and auxiliary estimations allow us to test the null hypotheses H_0^4, H_0^5, and H_0^6.

Our first null hypothesis assesses whether, after controlling for the endogeneity of assignment and selection, counseling has a statistically significant impact on ninety-day delinquency rates. Once again we confirm that it does—we strongly reject the null hypothesis that the γ^1 in equation 5-5 all are equal to zero.[22] Counseling's estimated effectiveness, therefore, clearly is not due entirely to unobserved differences in borrower characteristics.

Despite rejection of H_0^4, however, our individual point estimates of counseling types and programs are estimated quite imprecisely, and only the coefficients on classroom counseling are found to be statistically significant. This imprecision affects our estimate of counseling's average impact, and it too is not statistically significant. Nonetheless, we note that an estimated 37 percent average reduction in ninety-day delinquency rates from counseling suggests, albeit weakly, that accounting for endogeneity of assignment and selection tends to increase rather than decrease counseling's predictive effectiveness.

We also are able to reject H_0^5, finding that, even after accounting for borrower assignment and selection, there are statistically significant differences across types of counseling in their effectiveness at reducing ninety-day delinquency rates.[23] The marginal impacts for each type of counseling suggest roughly the same rank ordering of effectiveness as our basic analysis, although the point estimates generally are much larger than previously and classroom is not found to be more efficient than individual counseling. The standard errors also are quite large, however, and only classroom counseling shows statistical significance on average in reducing delinquency rates. Surprisingly, we also reject

22. The restricted and unrestricted models have log likelihoods of –8233.80 and –8213.92, respectively, resulting in a likelihood ratio test statistic of 39.76 that is distributed chi-squared with sixteen degrees of freedom. We therefore are able to reject the null hypothesis with a *p*-value of 0.00084.

23. The restricted and unrestricted models have log likelihoods of –8225.42 and –8213.92, respectively, resulting in a likelihood ratio test statistic of 23.00 that is distributed chi-squared with twelve degrees of freedom. We therefore are able to reject the null hypothesis with a *p*-value of 0.028.

H_0^6, finding that providers do show differential effectiveness in administering counseling programs.[24] This last result is inconsistent with our earlier analysis.

In summary, our analysis of assignment and selection provides mixed results. On one hand it supports the conclusion from our basic analysis that counseling can significantly reduce ninety-day delinquency rates and that different types of counseling vary in their effectiveness. Moreover, we are able to confirm classroom counseling's effectiveness at risk mitigation. On the other hand, however, our relatively poor success in predicting borrower assignment or selection prevents us from reliably demonstrating that the effectiveness of individual counseling and home study is not due to borrower assignment or selection. Moreover, our point estimates suggest that, after accounting for assignment or selection, classroom counseling may be more effective than individual counseling.

Implications and Caveats

The results presented in this study provide the first empirical evidence of the past twenty years that prepurchase homeownership counseling can significantly reduce the delinquency rates of borrowers. Our results also demonstrate, however, that not all counseling programs are equally successful. In particular, we find that borrowers who receive individual counseling have the lowest delinquency rates. Classroom counseling and home study also are associated with lower borrower delinquency rates, but telephone counseling is found to have no statistically significant impact.

These empirical results are not unexpected; many in the counseling industry have argued for years that individual and classroom counseling are by far the more effective tools. There is value to validating this claim, however. If nothing else, doing so confirms the crucial role that counseling can play in expanding affordable homeownership opportunities for America's families.

It also raises implications for whether and how counseling should be provided. Over one-third of the borrowers in Freddie Mac's Affordable Gold program, for example, receive telephone counseling, a delivery mechanism with no demonstrable effectiveness in reducing delinquency rates. That this is the case is not surprising: classroom and individual counseling are much more expensive to provide and in many locations are available only in limited quantity. These results however, raise questions about the necessity of requiring all borrowers in affordable lending programs to receive counseling. A more effective strategy, at least from the point of view of risk mitigation, might be to require counseling only for the highest-risk borrowers in affordable lending programs, but to

24. The restricted and unrestricted models have log likelihoods of –8223.86 and –8213.92, respectively, resulting in a likelihood ratio test statistic of 19.89 that is distributed chi-squared with eleven degrees of freedom. We are therefore able to reject the null hypothesis with a p-value of 0.047.

require that it be provided in either an individual, a classroom, or a home-study format.

Finally, although we are confident in our conclusions, our results are not definitive, and it is important to close with a few caveats. First, the data used in this study do not come from a true experiment. We attempt to control for differences in the risk characteristics of borrowers but are unlikely to have been entirely successful, and omitted variables may bias our results. Borrower assignment or selection, moreover, may account for some of the benefits attributed to homeownership counseling. Our attempt at addressing this endogeneity confirms the effectiveness of classroom counseling but is unable to do so for either individual or home-study counseling.

Second, the data for this study come from 1993 through 1998 loan originations. Our conclusions, consequently, pertain only to counseling conducted during that period. Since then the counseling industry has matured, becoming more consistent in counseling efforts and course content. It is likely that these changes have improved counseling's effectiveness, and therefore our analysis likely underestimates the benefits of current counseling programs.

Third, our data provide no information on postpurchase counseling or course content, so we can say nothing about their risk-mitigating effectiveness. Fourth and finally, our focus on ninety-day delinquency ignores any of counseling's possible beneficial impacts on the timing of delinquency or the severity of any ultimately occurring loss.

Appendix 5A: Details of Borrower Assignment and Selection Analysis

In this section, we briefly describe our borrower assignment and selection analysis. The first step in our analysis is to estimate a four-stage nested logit model. In the first stage, borrowers are assigned or selected to receive counseling or are determined not to need it. In the second stage, borrowers to receive counseling are assigned to or select either counseling service providers or industry participants. In the third stage, borrowers who were assigned to or selected counseling service providers are allocated between government agencies and nonprofit organizations, and borrowers who were assigned to or selected industry participants are allocated between lenders and mortgage insurers. In the fourth stage, borrowers are assigned or selected into the four types of counseling (classroom, home study, individual, or "other") available from each counseling provider. Estimation of the model is accomplished separately by stage, starting with the fourth. Appropriate inclusionary terms are incorporated into the estimation of stages three, two, and one. Results of the eight separate logit estimations that make up the nested logit model are not presented in an effort to save space and preserve the reader's patience.

Identification of the assignment or selection model is ensured by inclusion of variables not in the delinquency model (seller type, borrower age, borrower gender, loan-to-value ratio, and MSA population) and functional form. There are many unobserved factors, however, that likely are important in explaining counseling assignment or selection (such as when in the process borrowers apply for or receive counseling and the available supply of counseling providers). As a result, the nested logit estimation yields an adequately but not especially well-fitting model. This is illustrated in table 5A-1, which shows the mean predicted probabilities of each counseling type or provider combination (converted to percentages) for each subgroup of actual counseling type and provider outcome. The first row of table 5A-1, for example, shows the predicted probabilities for borrowers actually receiving classroom counseling from lenders. If the nested logit model is particularly well fitting then the mean predicted probability will be highest for classroom counseling by lenders. This is not the case here: both home study by lenders and telephone counseling by mortgage insurers have higher mean probabilities. This result, however, is not particularly surprising because both home study by lenders and telephone counseling by mortgage insurers occur with high frequency in the data. A less stringent fit criterion is to compare down each column of table 5A-1 rather than across each row. In this instance, the assessment involves comparing across borrower subsets of actual assignment and selection to see if the model assigns the highest mean probability to the type of counseling borrowers actually receive (that is, are the diagonal elements of the table 5A-1 matrix the largest probability in each column?). The nested logit model does far better by this measure; there are only three columns where this criterion is not met: individual counseling by non-profit organizations and "other" counseling by nonprofit organizations and government agencies.

Our next step is to use the predicted probabilities of borrower selection and assignment to estimate the probability of loans becoming ninety-day delinquent. The result of this estimation is shown in table 5A-2. The coefficients for the control variables in the borrower selection and assignment model are very similar to those in table 5-3. The coefficients for counseling type or provider, however, generally are quite a bit larger in absolute value. The standard errors are larger also, and only classroom counseling provided by lenders has a statistically significant effect in this estimation. Finally, as in table 5-3, most counseling type and provider coefficients are negative, other than home study counseling provided by government agencies and mortgage insurers and individual counseling provided by government agencies.

Figure 5A-1 provides goodness-of-fit measures for the logit estimation of the borrower selection and assignment model. Despite the high standard errors on the counseling type and provider coefficients, the nested logit model fits roughly as well as the basic model. The model presented in table 5A-2, however, is not entirely robust to alternative specifications. The far less than perfect fit of the

Figure 5A-1. *Goodness-of Fit for Nested Logit Selection or Assignment Estimation*

Actual selection or assignment	*Mean predicted probabilities of selection or assignment*																
	Classroom				*Home study*				*Individual*				*Phone*	*Other*			
Type of counseling and provider	*Lender*	*Non-profit*	*Govern-ment*	*Mortgage insurer*	*Lender*	*Non-profit*	*Govern-ment*	*Mortgage insurer*	*Lender*	*Non-profit*	*Govern-ment*	*Mortgage insurer*	*Mortgage insurer*	*Lender*	*Non-profit*	*Govern-ment*	*None*
Classroom																	
Lender	**10.4**	1.4	1.5	0.5	31.6	0.8	0.7	9.2	8.7	0.4	0.3	0.9	24.3	5.2	0.1	0.1	3.9
Nonprofit	7.3	**31.8**	2.4	0.3	24.4	2.6	1.5	5.5	5.3	1.8	0.2	0.4	12.3	1.8	0.4	0.2	1.9
Government	6.8	2.7	**3.2**	0.7	34.0	0.8	1.5	8.2	8.5	0.5	0.4	0.9	25.9	2.4	0.1	0.3	3.1
Mortgage insurer	6.2	1.4	1.4	**1.6**	33.4	2.8	1.0	7.7	6.1	1.2	0.4	0.8	29.9	3.3	0.2	0.2	2.1
Home study																	
Lender	6.1	1.0	1.3	0.5	**43.3**	0.6	0.8	7.7	8.5	0.4	0.2	0.7	23.4	2.7	0.1	0.1	2.6
Nonprofit	4.7	2.5	1.6	1.6	22.2	**4.9**	2.0	9.2	8.4	2.5	0.4	1.2	32.0	3.2	0.3	0.2	3.2
Government	5.3	2.1	3.1	0.8	28.8	2.0	**6.7**	7.3	8.3	1.7	0.8	0.7	26.5	1.8	0.2	0.5	3.3
Mortgage insurer	6.3	1.4	1.4	0.5	27.4	1.0	1.0	**14.9**	9.1	0.6	0.3	1.0	27.5	4.4	0.1	0.2	3.1
Individual																	
Lender	6.4	1.3	1.2	0.4	32.3	1.0	0.8	8.1	**12.8**	0.5	0.3	0.8	26.8	3.4	0.1	0.1	3.6
Nonprofit	4.6	1.5	1.1	1.4	34.6	2.2	1.1	10.8	6.1	**2.1**	0.3	1.6	24.0	4.9	0.1	0.1	3.4
Government	6.8	1.3	2.0	0.8	28.4	1.4	1.6	7.5	10.2	1.2	**1.4**	1.0	31.8	2.1	0.2	0.3	2.1
Mortgage insurer	6.3	1.5	1.6	0.6	30.6	1.3	1.1	10.7	9.9	0.7	0.3	**2.2**	26.4	3.0	0.1	0.1	3.4
Phone																	
Mortgage insurer	4.4	0.7	0.7	0.6	21.3	0.8	0.5	8.4	6.4	0.3	0.2	0.7	**49.1**	2.9	0.1	0.1	2.8
Other																	
Lender	7.9	0.7	0.7	0.4	22.9	0.7	0.4	11.2	7.3	0.4	0.1	0.7	23.3	**18.1**	0.1	0.1	5.0
Nonprofit	6.1	1.6	0.7	0.7	20.2	1.7	1.0	8.9	6.0	0.9	0.3	1.1	42.1	4.9	**0.2**	0.1	3.6
Government	4.5	0.8	1.7	0.7	28.5	0.8	1.2	9.3	7.3	0.6	0.3	1.0	36.2	3.7	0.1	**0.3**	3.0
None	6.6	1.0	1.2	0.4	26.6	0.7	0.8	9.9	9.1	0.4	0.2	1.2	28.6	4.6	0.1	0.1	**8.5**

Table 5A-2. *Logit Estimation of Loans Ever Becoming 90-Day Delinquent of Borrower Selection or Assignment*

Variable	*Coefficient estimate*	*Standard error*	*p-value*
Intercept	–5.123	1.666	0.0021
Classroom counseling[a]			
Government	–4.157	2.921	0.1548
Lender	–3.587	1.662	0.0310
Mortgage insurer	–5.443	3.512	0.1212
Nonprofit	–1.088	1.413	0.4411
Home study counseling			
Government	1.849	3.606	0.6082
Lender	–0.924	1.287	0.4726
Mortgage insurer	1.045	1.497	0.4852
Nonprofit	–0.365	2.338	0.8760
Individual counseling			
Government	0.799	6.012	0.8943
Lender	–1.306	1.655	0.4299
Mortgage insurer	–1.711	3.086	0.5794
Nonprofit	–1.555	3.574	0.6634
Telephone counseling/ other counseling			
Mortgage insurer	–0.635	1.281	0.6199
Government	–2.032	14.739	0.8903
Lender	–0.796	1.515	0.5996
Nonprofit	–6.650	16.577	0.6883
No counseling	0.000	0.000	. . .
AUS Score			
Unknown	2.929	0.309	0.0001
700 or less	4.559	0.364	0.0001
701 to 750	3.873	0.319	0.0001
751 to 800	3.361	0.312	0.0001
801 to 850	2.772	0.311	0.0001
851 to 900	2.153	0.312	0.0001
901 to 950	1.712	0.311	0.0001
951 to 1000	1.047	0.321	0.0011
1001 to 1050	0.678	0.339	0.0453
1051 to 1100	0.473	0.389	0.2234
1101 and up	0.000	0.000	. . .
Loan origination amount ($100,000)	–0.330	0.099	0.0009
Number of units			
One	0.793	0.143	0.0001
Two or more	0.000	0.000	. . .

continued on next page

Table 5A-2. *Logit Estimation of Loans Ever Becoming 90-Day Delinquent of Borrower Selection or Assignment (continued)*

Variable	*Coefficient estimate*	*Standard error*	*p-value*
Property type			
Condominium	–0.630	0.092	0.0001
Other	0.046	0.093	0.6195
Single family	0.000	0.000	. . .
Loan purpose			
Purchase	–0.594	0.168	0.0004
Refinance/second home	0.000	0.000	. . .
First-time home buyer			
No	–0.096	0.062	0.1232
Unknown	–0.498	0.334	0.1359
Yes	0.000	0.000	. . .
Borrower race or ethnicity			
African American	0.513	0.071	0.0001
Hispanic	–0.076	0.074	0.3037
Other minority	–0.042	0.097	0.6635
Unknown	0.192	0.122	0.1154
White	0.000	0.000	. . .
Minority population in tract (ratio of tract total)	0.378	0.117	0.0012
Family income (ratio of area median)	–0.118	0.092	0.1984
Median tract income (ratio of area median)	–0.205	0.116	0.0766
MSA			
Metro	–0.198	0.091	0.0297
Non-metro	0.000	0.000	. . .
Loan origination date	. . .	. . .	. . .
State	. . .	. . .	. . .
Number of observations	39,141		

a. Predicted probability of borrower selection and assignment.

Figure 5A-1. *Goodness-of-Fit Measures for Selection or Assignment Logit Estimation*

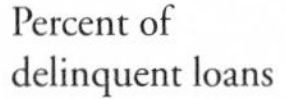

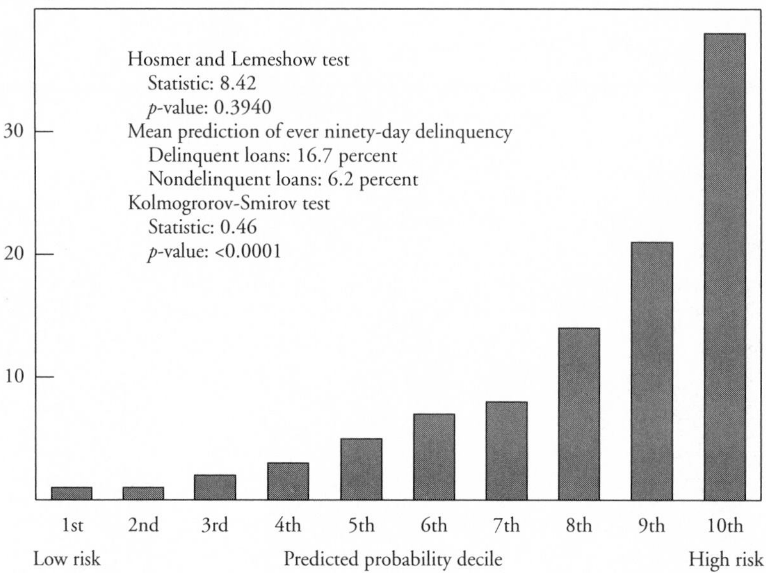

assignment and selection nested logit model provides relatively small variation in the predicted values for many counseling type and provider alternatives, as well as relatively high correlations across predictions of alternative counseling types and providers. As a result, the estimated counseling type and provider coefficients display many symptoms of multicollinearity. We crudely address this problem through a series of auxiliary estimations, each of which reduces the dimensionality of the 1 X column vector. For example, we estimate separate classroom counseling coefficients for each of the four providers while constraining providers' coefficients to be identical across all other types of counseling (that is, $\gamma^1_{ij} = \gamma^1_{ik}\ \forall j, k \in T, \forall i \neq classroom$). This approach yields no significant reduction in log likelihood but does substantially change the point estimates for some coefficients. In particular, we find that the estimated coefficients for classroom counseling are negative and significant for all providers. Because the results of these auxiliary estimations appear more robust, we rely on them and use them to conduct our simulations.

Figure 5A-2 is the equivalent of figure 5-2, and shows the results of simulations designed to estimate the reductions in ninety-day delinquency rates provided by each counseling type and provider. The overall pattern is not dissimilar to that of the basic model, although the point estimates are far larger in absolute value. From a statistical standpoint, only classroom counseling is found to have a significant impact in reducing ninety-day delinquency rates.

Figure 5A-2. *Estimated Reduction in Ninety-Day Delinquency Rates from Counseling for Selection or Assignment Logit Estimation*[a]

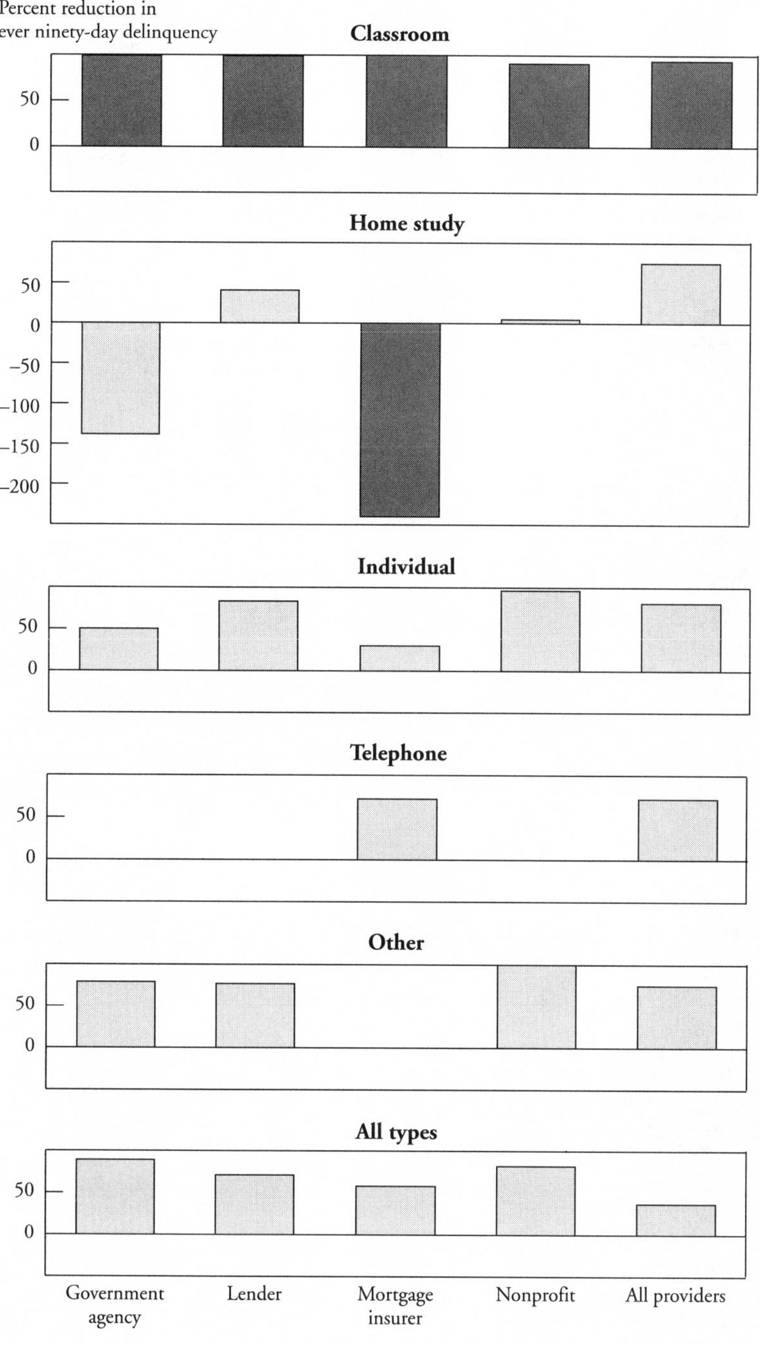

a. Dark-shaded bars indicate reductions that are statistically significant at the 10 percent level.

References

Judge, George G., and others. 1980. *The Theory and Practice of Econometrics*. New York: John Wiley and Sons.

Mallach, Allan. 2001. "Home Ownership Education and Counseling: Issues in Research and Definition." Discussion Paper. Federal Reserve Bank of Philadelphia.

McCarthy, George, and Roberto Quercia. 2000. "Bridging the Gap between Supply and Demand: The Evolution of the Homeownership Education and Counseling Industry." Institute Report Number 00-01. Washington: The Research Institute for Housing America (May).

Quercia, Roberto, and Susan Wachter. 1996. "Homeownership Counseling Performance: How Can It Be Measured?" *Housing Policy Debate* 7 (1): 175–99.

6

Supply-Side Constraints on Low-Income Homeownership

MICHAEL COLLINS, DAVID CROWE,
AND MICHAEL CARLINER

Homeownership is increasingly being utilized as a social policy believed to promote neighborhood health and stability, while also offering opportunities for low-income families to build financial assets through home equity. Between 1993 and 1997, mortgage lending overall grew by 20 percent; but in low-income census tracts in metropolitan areas it grew by over 30 percent (Can, Bogdon, and Tong, 1999). The surge in home buying among low-income households in the 1990s raises questions about the sustainability of this boom. Because the rate of house price appreciation proceeded at twice the rate of inflation in the late 1990s, one question often raised is whether the existing supply of affordably priced owner-occupied housing would be adequate to meet the added demand represented by these first-time home buyers. The decision of low-income renter households (defined as those earning less than 80 percent of the area median income as defined by the U.S. Department of Housing and Urban Development) to buy a home is contingent upon household financial status, the relative costs of owning and renting, as well as the availability of adequate and affordable housing units that are located in a place they desire to live. Given existing subsidies and affordable mortgage products, many low-income renter households may be in a position to overcome the wealth and income constraints on buying a

We are grateful to Allegra Calder of the Lincoln Institute of Land Policy and Mark Duda of the Joint Center for Housing Studies of Harvard University for research assistance.

home. However, households may still be constrained by a lack of adequate housing units at an appropriate sales price in a desirable location.

This chapter focuses on three questions: (1) What are the characteristics of owner-occupied units affordable to a household earning less than 80 percent of area median income, and how do they compare with higher-value units? (2) How does the affordable owner-occupied stock change over time? (3) How does the availability and supply of affordable units affect the homeownership rate of low-income households?

In this chapter, we first review the existing literature about supply-side constraints on low-income homeownership and potential data sources available for studying affordable owner-occupied units. Using the national American Housing Surveys (1997 and 1999) we then present a snapshot of the affordable owner-occupied stock in each year and examine changes in the affordable owner-occupied stock from 1997 to 1999. Using the metropolitan American Housing Surveys (1995, 1996, and 1998) we create a submetropolitan-level specification (using 348 neighborhood-like zones) in order to examine how the supply of affordably valued units affects homeownership rates among low-income households aged 40 to 65, controlling for household, neighborhood, and stock characteristics.

Review of Literature and Available Data

The relatively strong housing markets that characterized the 1990s in much of the nation have highlighted the issue of increasing prices and limited housing choices in many markets (Stegman, Quercia, and McCarthy, 2000). According to one newspaper article, "With housing prices rising 25 percent from May 1999 to May 2000, the Galinskys are afraid if they don't get a house now, they may never get one. They're worried they will wind up raising their baby in a studio apartment without a backyard" (*San Francisco Chronicle*, July 10, 2000). However, there has been relatively little study of the supply of housing units available for low-income households to purchase, as noted by past reviews of housing supply topics (Mayer and Somerville, 1996; Mayer, 1999; Gyourko and Tracy, 1999).

Much of the theory of housing supply dynamics is based on the work of Grigsby (1963), who subdivided housing markets into a matrix of unit and household characteristics and described the process of older units filtering down to lower-income households over time. More recently, Galster (1996) and Downs (1994) have expanded on Grigsby's theoretical work to hypothesize that filtering down of units only works in areas where net housing unit construction exceeds net household formation—areas where new housing units outnumber new households. Markets with a constrained housing supply will result in fewer units filtering down to lower-income households. Clay (1992) argued that the filtering-down process no longer works effectively because new housing construction has not produced enough affordable units to keep up since the 1980s. Malpezzi and Green (1996), however, use metropolitan American Housing Surveys (AHS) from the 1970s and 1980s to compare the change in lower-cost, substandard rental units (using the methodology refined by Thibodeau, 1991) to the additions to the supply, measured by building permits. Malpezzi and Green show that an increase in the existing rental stock of 1.4 percent, due to new construction, will increase the number of lower-priced, substandard units by 2.5 percent because of the filtering effect new units have on the value distribution. Malpezzi and Green conclude that any new rental unit that is added to the housing stock, regardless of its value, will enhance the affordability of the existing rental stock by promoting downward filtering. How this might operate in the owner-occupied stock, which experiences lower turnover rates and higher transaction costs, however, remains unexplored.

Somerville and Holmes (2000) also examine filtering in rental units using the metropolitan American Housing Survey over four-year periods, finding that 52 percent of affordable units remain affordable, 26 percent realize rent increases beyond affordable levels, 4 percent become owner-occupied, and 7 percent are demolished (the authors find that the remaining 10 percent receive a government subsidy to maintain affordability). Somerville and Holmes find that changes in neighborhood quality are most predictive of a unit increasing in relative value, but that unit characteristics are most predictive of demolition and removal from the stock. Their analysis shows the filtering process is more sensitive to neighborhood and unit characteristics than short-term changes in market rents.

Galbraith (1996) examined filtering using the metropolitan American Housing Surveys, finding that depreciation of homes to affordable levels is slower than previously thought. Malpezzi and Green (1996) conclude that the supply of low-cost rental units has fallen in recent decades, but not as much as expected. Stegman, Quercia, and McCarthy (2000) and Pare (1993) assert that the supply of affordable quality housing is restricted because the filtering process is skewed by an increasingly expensive new stock. Pare cites the work of nonprofit housing developers, such as Nehemiah in New York City and Bridge Housing in San Francisco, as strategies to overcome the fixed costs of regulations and land-use controls that often prevent for-profit developers from creating new affordable units.

Several researchers, examining the spatial mismatch between the affordable housing stock and employment opportunities, have examined constraints on housing supply in central cities. Kain and Quigley (1972) hypothesized that a "supply restriction" due to racial discrimination against African Americans limits their housing choices in the central city and suburbs. Bullard (1984) makes a case that minority home-buying is hampered by limited neighborhood options. In a revision of his previous work, Kain (1992) emphasizes that there is a shortage of affordable housing for low-income and minority households. Herbert (1997) used 1990 census data for fifty metropolitan areas to further examine the supply restriction imposed upon African Americans, finding that these restrictions were particularly evident in the Northeast and Midwest and that the availability of detached single-family homes is a strong supply-side predictor of minority homeownership rates.

Gyourko and Linneman (1993) examined the AHS and census data from 1960 to 1990, finding that the predicted demographic boom in homeownership may not be realized because lower-skilled workers have experienced decreasing real wages and increasing housing costs simultaneously. Gyourko and Linneman initially found that the quality of affordable units significantly declined as real prices increased. The authors note that as real household incomes of low-skilled workers decline, occupants may defer or neglect the cost of major housing maintenance. However, Gyourko and Tracy (1999) revised this earlier finding, concluding that the quality of the low end of the housing market has declined less than previously suggested. Yet the authors continued to find that virtually no new housing in an affordable price range is being produced. Using 1998 metropolitan American Housing Surveys, Stegman, Quercia, and McCarthy (2000) found a severe shortage of units priced so that working families can afford them in seventeen metropolitan areas. This analysis, however, only looked at vacant units for sale at the time of the survey.

Several researchers have examined the supply-side constraints placed on new construction by strict building codes, approval delays, low-density zoning laws, and impact fees (Gyourko and Linneman, 1993; Wachter and Schill, 1995; Obrinsky, 1989). The Advisory Committee on Regulatory Barriers to Affordable Housing (1991) found that code regulation and enforcement prevents housing units from filtering to more affordable levels by enforcing a minimum level of housing quality and truncating the filtering process. Malpezzi and Green (1996) explore excessive regulation as a possible reason that the supply of units at the bottom of the U.S. housing market is constricted. The authors do not find evidence that regulation directly affects tenure choice, but they do find that an increase in the number of housing regulations increases homeownership costs relative to renting. Overall Malpezzi and Green conclude that movement from a lightly regulated environment to a heavily regulated one decreases homeownership rates by 10 percent. Vandell (1994) created an index of regulatory barriers for selected metropolitan areas, one of several efforts well documented by Malpezzi (1996).[1]

Eggers and Burke (1996) simulate demand for homeownership, projecting that central cities in the United States would require 1.4 million owner-occupied units in the 1990s. The authors also found that 3.7 million single family rental units in these same areas could be converted to homeownership, however,

1. Malpezzi has posted a similar index at www.wiscinfo.doit.wisc.edu/realestate/realres1.htm.

and concluded there would not be a supply constraint limiting central city homeownership if units are allowed to change tenure.

Available Data Sources

Although there are several data sources available for an analysis of the housing supply by market value, no data set is sufficiently recent and detailed. Decennial census public use microsample (PUMS) data provide an estimate of owner-occupied housing units with owner-estimated market values and basic housing unit and occupant household characteristics by PUMAs (public use microsample areas, a collection of census tracts of approximately 100,000 people). However, as micro data, the census has less-detailed unit and household characteristics than the AHS. Moreover, 1990 census data were also ten years old at the time of this analysis. Local real estate agent associations' multiple listing services (MLS) of homes for sale and local government data on recorded real estate transactions are available from several vendors nationally. These data often have information on a unit's location and structural characteristics, such as the number of bedrooms, year built, and square footage. These data are also much more up to date than census data. However, these databases frequently only cover units involved in a transaction during a given period; they do not estimate the entire supply, and they lack any detail about occupant characteristics. MLS data are further restricted to listings and sales involving real estate brokers and do not include all home transactions.

Home Mortgage Disclosure Act (HMDA) data collected by the Federal Financial Institutions Examination Council (FFIEC) provide information about many home mortgage loans nationally, including applicant race, income, and the census tract of the property being financed. Issued annually, these data are also timely. However, HMDA data do not capture the full universe of home mortgage loans, do not provide information on home value, and are at best an approximation of demand for mortgages rather than the supply of owner-occupied housing units.

The American Housing Survey is published by the U.S. Bureau of the Census in conjunction with the Department of Housing and Urban Development every two years. The AHS tracks a panel of housing units over time, collecting over 500 data points on each unit and its current occupants. A problem with the national AHS, however, is that sample sizes are too small at the metropolitan level, and no smaller areas are available for analysis. Although the AHS data lack specific geographic locations, because they allow units to be tracked over time and provide rich detail from recent time periods, they are most useful for this analysis.

The 1995, 1996, and 1998 metropolitan AHS contain most of the variables in the national AHS, but also identifies smaller submarket areas, called "zones," of approximately 100,000 people each, depending on the city. Combined, the 1995–98 data contain thirty-three metropolitan areas and 378 zones. A list of

Table 6-1. *SMSAs and Zones Covered in American Housing Survey Data Analysis*

SMSA name	*No. of zones*	*SMSA name*	*No. of zones*	*SMSA name*	*No. of zones*
Atlanta	17	Indianapolis	9	Providence	8
Baltimore	17	Kansas City	10	Rochester	6
Birmingham	6	Memphis	7	Sacramento	10
Boston	26	Miami	14	Saint Louis	17
Charlotte	9	Minneapolis	14	Salt Lake City	5
Cincinnati	12	New Orleans	9	San Antonio	10
Cleveland	17	Norfolk/Newport News	6	San Francisco	12
Columbus	9	Oakland	10	San Jose	10
Denver	8	Oklahoma City	6	Seattle	13
Hartford	7	Pittsburgh	15	Tampa	12
Houston	15	Portland, Ore.	8	Washington, D.C.	24
				Total	378

Source: 1995, 1996, and 1998 Metropolitan American Housing Surveys.

the areas included in the sample and the number of zones for each is provided in table 6-1.

The AHS asks owner-occupants to estimate the market value of their home or, in the case of vacant units, uses the asking price for the unit. Previous analyses show that market value estimates by occupants are generally unbiased (Kain and Quigley, 1972; Thibodeau, 1982, cited in Gyourko and Linneman, 1993) or may slightly overvalue homes. However, research shows little correlation in this overestimation with unit or household characteristics (Goodman and Ittner 1992, cited in Gyourko and Linneman 1993). The U.S. Census Bureau conducted a thorough analysis of owner-estimated home values, finding that households tend to underestimate values, but, again, without systematic bias (Walters and Waltman, 1974). Kiel and Zabel (1999) study the 1978 to 1991 American Housing Surveys to find that the average owner overvalues his or her home by 5 percent. Although Kiel and Zabel found that owners who had purchased a home in the previous twelve months inflated its value more than longer-term owners, the difference between actual and reported values is not related to particular characteristics of the house, its occupants, or the neighborhood. Because the bias is not systematic, AHS occupant estimates of value are reasonable to use in this analysis.

Profile of the Affordable Owner-Occupied Housing Stock

An initial picture of the characteristics of the owner-occupied housing stock can be viewed by breaking down all units into quartiles (see table 6-2). Each quartile can be examined for occupant household, unit, and neighborhood descriptive

Table 6-2. *1999 American Housing Survey Profile of Owner-Occupied Housing Stock by Market-Value Quartile*

	Median market value									
	1st quartile: $40,000		*2d quartile: $80,000*		*3d quartile: $125,000*		*4th quartile: $230,000*		*All owner-occupied units: $110,000*	
Variable	*Mean*	*Standard error*	*Mean*	*Standard error*	*Mean*	*Standard error*	*Mean*	*Standard error*	*Mean*	*Standard error*
Householder characteristics										
Age	53.0	0.221	52.6	0.204	51.7	0.167	51.4	0.157	52.1	0.093
Percent white	83.8	0.005	85.9	0.004	89.3	0.003	89.4	0.003	87.3	0.002
Percent high school graduates	71.4	0.006	83.3	0.005	87.7	0.003	93.0	0.003	84.2	0.002
Percent college graduates	9.3	0.004	18.6	0.005	30.0	0.005	48.4	0.005	27.3	0.003
Percent median income	82.4	0.010	107.0	0.011	138.1	0.013	206.5	0.020	135.5	0.008
Unit characteristics										
Percent first-time homeowners	55.1	0.006	51.6	0.006	41.0	0.005	29.3	0.005	43.7	0.003
First occupant	11.0	0.004	7.0	0.003	12.4	0.003	18.4	0.004	12.4	0.002
Cost of annual maintenance	$331	9.171	$422	10.032	$493	9.177	$760	14.051	$508	5.583
Percent inadequate	9.0	0.004	3.7	0.002	2.8	0.002	2.0	0.002	4.3	0.001
Median decade built	1960s		1960s		1970s		1970s		1960s	
Percent mobile	32.5	0.006	2.0	0.002	0.3	0.001	0.2	0.000	8.2	0.002
Percent single-family (includes mobile)	94.3	0.003	94.1	0.003	96.2	0.002	96.7	0.002	95.4	0.001
Percent detached single-family	57.5	0.006	86.0	0.004	90.5	0.003	91.7	0.003	82.1	0.002
Unit square feet	1,479	15.156	1,785	16.112	2,067	14.915	2,760	20.666	2,049	9.028
Neighborhood characteristics										
Rating of unit	8.0	0.023	8.3	0.019	8.5	0.015	8.8	0.014	8.4	0.009
Percent in central city	22.5	0.005	25.9	0.005	21.1	0.004	21.2	0.005	30.3	0.002
Percent citing anything bothersome in neighborhood	15.4	0.004	15.3	0.004	14.4	0.004	14.6	0.004	14.9	0.002
Percent moved in past two years	16.6	0.005	13.7	0.004	14.4	0.004	18.0	0.004	15.7	0.002

Source: 1999 American Housing Survey.

Note: Standard error is the standard deviation of the sampling distribution of the mean, or $\sigma_M = \sigma / \sqrt{N}$, where σ is the standard deviation of the original distribution and N is the sample size.

Table 6-3. *Descriptive Statistics and Percent First-Time Buyers, 1999*[a]

	All first-time buyers		*First-time buyers with incomes below 80 percent of area median*	
Characteristic	*Mean*	*Standard error*	*Mean*	*Standard error*
Median value	$90,000	. . .	$65,000	. . .
Median decade built	1970s	. . .	1960s	. . .
Percent inadequate	5.6	0.007	8.3	0.014
Percent mobile	14.2	0.011	20.6	0.020
Percent single-family	90.5	0.009	89.7	0.015
Unit square feet	1,729	45.269	1,493	72.948
Rating of unit	8.4	0.047	8.2	0.085
Percent in central city	27.6	0.014	30.3	0.023
Percent citing anything bothersome in neighborhood	15.6	0.011	14.0	0.017

Source: 1999 American Housing Survey.
a. "First-time buyers" refers to those who bought in the previous two years.

statistics. The distribution of house values in the 1999 AHS shows a predictable pattern of lower-valued homes more likely to be occupied by lower-income households, with mean owner income equal to 82 percent of the area median income, compared to 107 percent in the second quartile. It is also skewed toward minorities (84 percent white, in comparison with 86 and 89 percent in higher quartiles), as well as older and less-educated householders. Lower-valued units are also more likely to be of lower quality, older in age, and smaller in size. The data also show that lower-quartile units are more likely to be part of multi-unit properties, rather than single-family properties. These units are more likely to be in central city areas and to have problems noted by residents. Table 6-2 also shows that turnover rates may be slightly higher than would be expected given the older mean age of occupants; yet because these units are also likely to be entry-level units for younger households, such turnover may be consistent.

Table 6-2 describes all homeowners, but the current market for potential low-income buyers may be better approximated by recent first-time home buyers. Table 6-3 shows all first-time buyers who recently purchased homes, as well as low-income first-time buyers from the 1999 AHS. Low-income buyers tend to purchase lower-cost homes that are older, smaller, more urban, and in poorer condition. Low-income buyers are also more likely to purchase mobile homes than other first-time buyers.[2]

Although lower-income homeowners are most likely to occupy mobile units, the share of homeowner units that are mobile varies by region. Table 6-4 shows

2. The AHS and census use the term *mobile home* to describe a unit built in a factory to national HUD code and placed on site. These units are also called *manufactured homes*.

Table 6-4. *Owner-Occupied Units by Region and Income, 1997 and 1999*

	1997			*1999*		
Region[a]	*Owner-occupied units (000)*	*Home-ownership rate (percent)*	*Mobile homes (percent)*	*Owner-occupied units (000)*	*Home ownership rate (percent)*	*Mobile homes (percent)*
All regions						
<50 percent	16,622	47	8.4	15,517	48	8.7
50–80 percent	10,753	60	8.1	11,338	59	7.2
80–120 percent	13,142	74	7.0	12,791	72	7.6
120 percent or more	24,958	88	3.1	29,134	88	3.6
Northeast						
<50 percent	3,190	44	4.2	2,911	44	4.3
50–80 percent	1,904	56	3.7	1,872	53	3.2
80–120 percent	2,429	72	3.1	2,361	71	2.4
120 percent or more	4,716	87	1.0	5,497	86	1.4
Midwest (North Central)						
<50 percent	3,956	50	5.9	3,854	52	6.9
50–80 percent	3,056	65	7.5	3,039	65	5.4
80–120 percent	3,658	80	4.2	3,413	79	5.7
120 percent or more	6,229	92	2.1	7,259	92	2.1
South						
<50 percent	6,599	53	12.6	5,953	52	12.8
50–80 percent	3,747	62	11.4	4,246	62	11.1
80–120 percent	4,431	73	11.9	4,588	72	12.5
120 percent or more	8,868	88	4.7	10,400	88	6.2
West						
<50 percent	2,877	38	8.1	2,799	39	8.1
50–80 percent	2,046	54	7.3	2,181	52	6.3
80–120 percent	2,623	70	6.2	2,430	65	6.4
120 percent or more	5,145	84	3.1	5,991	85	3.1

Source: 1997 and 1999 American Housing Surveys.

a. Figures represent percent of area median income.

both 1997 and 1999 owner-occupied units by region, including homeownership rates and the share of mobile homes. Overall, the share of mobile homes occupied by low-income homeowners is increasing, particularly in the South. Low-income homeownership rates appear to be dropping, especially in the higher-cost Northeast and Midwest.

Methodology for Calculating Target Affordable House Values

Although a distribution of market values allows a gross analysis of homes that might be affordable to lower-income families, because of the large variance in regional household incomes and home prices, the lower quartile of values nationally includes some homes that are priced well above affordable levels in lower-cost housing markets. A more refined approach is to define a target affordable price for each metropolitan housing market based on the local median income. In addition, local median property taxes and hazard insurance rates also vary dramatically across the nation's metropolitan housing markets. In order to estimate which homes are truly affordable to low-income families, a better approach is to estimate tax and insurance rates for each metropolitan area.

This analysis uses the AHS to determine a target affordable owner-occupied home price for each metropolitan statistical area (MSA) and then categorizes each owner-occupied unit in the survey as being affordable to a family earning 80 percent or less of the area median income. In general, mortgage underwriters allow a maximum ratio of housing payment to income, including the mortgage principal and interest, property taxes, and hazard insurance (referred to as PITI). This chapter uses a conventional, conforming loan underwriting "front-end" ratio of 28 percent. It also assumes a modestly aggressive loan-to-value ratio of 90 percent; it is assumed that the buyer contributes a 10 percent down payment in addition to closing costs. No mortgage insurance is assumed in this analysis, although this assumption is analyzed and discussed later in the chapter. This analysis uses a thirty-year fixed-rate mortgage and the effective mortgage rate at of the time of the survey.

The target affordable price for each market is based on the amount of monthly mortgage debt service 80 percent of the area median income will support (based on U.S. Department of Housing and Urban Development estimated area median incomes for the relevant year). The monthly payment, of course, also includes property taxes and insurance, which are calculated as a percentage of the target affordable house price. In order to solve an equation involving an estimate of house prices simultaneously with ratios involving price, a formula must be used to calculate the ratio of mortgage principal and interest to income for each metropolitan area, while still preserving a 28 percent maximum total front-end ratio. The share of income allocated to the mortgage principal and interest payment was calculated for each metropolitan area. In nonmetro or suppressed metro areas, regional values were substituted, broken down by central city, suburb, or nonmetropolitan area. Median property tax and hazard insurance rates for each area were also calculated using this same method.

The formula used to derive the ratio of mortgage principal and interest payment to income is as follows:

X = Principal and interest payment-to-income ratio (variable because of local income, taxes, and insurance)

L = Loan-to-value ratio

K = Mortgage constant (annual for 360-payment, thirty-year fixed-rate loan

P = Area median property tax as a percent of median property value (calculated by MSA as median AMTX / median VALUE)

H = Area median property hazard insurance as a percent of median property value (calculated by MSA as median AMTI / median VALUE)

I = Low-income cutoff, as provided by HUD as 80 percent of area median income adjusted for family size

R = Maximum housing-to-income ratio (assumed to be 28 percent = principal, interest, taxes, and insurance / income)

RI = Total payment

$$RI = \frac{P(XI)}{LK} + \frac{H(XI)}{LK} + XI \rightarrow$$

$$LKR = PX + HX + XLK \rightarrow$$

$$LKR = X(P + H + LK) \rightarrow$$

$$X = \frac{LKR}{(P + H + LK)}$$

The mortgage constant is calculated using a monthly payment for a thirty-year fixed-rate mortgage in the year of each survey using effective contract interest rates published by the Federal Home Loan Mortgage Corporation. The effective interest rates and mortgage constants used in this analysis are as follows:

Year	*Total effective rate (percent)*	*Annual mortgage constant*
1995	8.19	0.0897
1996	8.06	0.0889
1997	7.86	0.0872
1998	7.09	0.0806
1999	7.58	0.0847

Source: Freddie Mac Primary Mortgage Market Survey.

Note: Mortgage constant = *monthly interest rate* / [1 – (1 / (1 + *monthly interest rate*)^{360}] for a thirty-year mortgage.

Examination of Affordable Stock Given Metropolitan Median Income, Taxes, and Insurance

Table 6-5 compares the affordable owner stock, including and excluding mobile units, with the universe of all owner-occupied units and unaffordable units. Nationally, 47.3 percent of existing owner-occupied units were affordable to a

Table 6-5. *Descriptive Statistics: All Units and Affordable Units, 1997 and 1999*

		All owner-occupied units		*Affordable units*		*Affordable units (excluding mobiles)*		*Above affordable*	
	Year	*Mean*	*Standard error*	*Mean*	*Standard error*	*Mean*	*Standard error*	*Mean*	*Standard error*
Occupant characteristics									
As percentage of all owner units	1997	100	. . .	47.3	. . .	43.3	. . .	52.7	. . .
	1999	100	. . .	44.2	. . .	39.4	. . .	55.8	. . .
Mean householder age	1997	52.0	0.100	52.6	0.156	53.2	0.167	51.5	0.128
	1999	52.1	0.093	52.8	0.153	53.6	0.165	51.6	0.114
Percent white	1997	88.2	0.002	85.4	0.003	84.5	0.004	90.8	0.002
	1999	87.3	0.002	83.9	0.003	82.8	0.004	89.9	0.002
Percent high school graduates	1997	83.7	0.002	76.8	0.004	78.0	0.004	89.9	0.003
	1999	84.2	0.002	77.0	0.004	78.4	0.004	89.9	0.002
Percent median income	1997	113.2	0.005	82.5	0.006	84.4	0.006	140.8	0.008
	1999	135.5	0.008	91.4	0.007	93.3	0.008	170.4	0.012
Percent first-time homeowners	1997	46.6	0.003	56.5	0.004	58.8	0.005	37.7	0.004
	1999	43.7	0.003	54.3	0.004	56.8	0.005	35.3	0.004
Unit and neighborhood characteristics									
Percent in central city	1997	22.8	0.003	26.1	0.004	30.2	0.004	19.8	0.003
	1999	22.5	0.002	25.5	0.004	30.2	0.004	20.2	0.003
Percent citing neighborhood problems	1997	15.0	0.002	16.1	0.003	16.3	0.004	14.1	0.003
	1999	14.9	0.002	15.7	0.003	15.7	0.003	14.2	0.003
Median time to work (average for all workers in household)	1997	20		17		15		20	
	1999	20		19		18		20	

Median decade built	1997	1960s		1960s		1950s		1970s	
	1999	1960s		1960s		1950s		1970s	
Percent inadequate	1997	4.4	0.001	6.5	0.002	6.6	0.002	2.6	0.001
	1999	4.3	0.001	6.4	0.002	6.5	0.002	2.6	0.001
Rating of neighborhood	1997	8.1	0.012	7.9	0.018	7.8	0.02	8.4	0.014
	1999	8.2	0.010	7.9	0.017	7.9	0.018	8.4	0.012
Unit square feet	1997	1,966	6.374	1,605	8.097	1,708	8.951	2,268	8.62
	1999	2,049	9.028	1,608	11.183	1,709	12.84	2,383	12.68
Percent detached single-family	1997	82.1	0.002	71.5	0.004	85.1	0.003	91.6	0.002
	1999	82.1	0.002	69.6	0.004	85.1	0.003	92.0	0.002
Percent mobile homes	1997	8.0	0.002	15.9	0.003	0.0	0	0.9	0.001
	1999	8.2	0.002	18.2	0.003	0.0	0	0.3	0
Percent built in past two years	1997	3.1	0.001	2.2	0.001	0.8	0.001	4.0	0.002
	1999	2.7	0.001	1.8	0.001	0.7	0.001	3.4	0.001
Percent moved in past two years	1997	20.2	0.002	19.1	0.004	16.7	0.004	21.2	0.003
	1999	20.6	0.002	19.3	0.003	16.6	0.004	21.5	0.003

Source: 1997 and 1999 American Housing Surveys.

Table 6-6. *Share of Affordable Units by Income of Occupant, 1997 and 1999*
Percent

	Share affordable, including mobile		*Share affordable, excluding mobile*	
Household income	*1997*	*1999*	*1997*	*1999*
<50 percent of area median	65.3	62.3	60.9	56.3
50–80 percent of area median	61.8	59.1	57.9	54.7
80–120 percent of area median	51.0	50.1	47.1	45.3
120 percent or more of area median	27.1	26.1	25.0	23.3
All owner-occupied housing	47.3	44.2	43.3	39.4

Source: 1997 and 1999 American Housing Surveys.

low-income family in 1997. The affordable share decreased to 44.2 percent in 1999. In comparison with the owners of the rest of the owner-occupied housing stock, occupants of affordable units are more likely to be first-time buyers, older, nonwhite, and low-income, and are less likely to be high school graduates. Affordable units are more likely to be in central cities, lesser-quality neighborhoods, and closer to their occupants' employment. Affordable units are also older, more likely to be severely or moderately inadequate, smaller in size, less likely to be single-family detached units, and more likely to be mobile homes.

Though house values and incomes are closely correlated, people also obtain homes without tapping into income or purchase homes at earlier points in their income life cycle. As a result, many affordable units are not occupied by low-income households. Likewise, because of house price inflation and lower incomes in retirement, lower-income households might also own high-value homes. Table 6-6 presents the share of units that are affordable to households with incomes below 80 percent of the area median, by the income group of the occupant. Although lower-income households are most likely to live in housing units that are valued affordably, one-quarter to one-third of high-income households also live in homes that they value in an affordable range. A larger share of homes occupied by lower-income households are actually valued at levels that could be deemed unaffordable to them in the current period.

Table 6-7 shows the regional share of homes that are affordable given local market conditions. The West, where fewer than one in four nonmobile homes are affordable, had a dramatic decline in affordable share from 1997 to 1999. The share of homes locally affordable is highest in the South and Midwest, although much of the South's affordable stock appears to be concentrated in mobile units.

The calculations used in this analysis assume a 10 percent down payment and a 28 percent "front-end" ratio of housing cost to income. It is also assumed all closing costs are not to be financed but instead paid for out of borrower assets. Although 90 percent loan-to-value ratio mortgages may require mortgage insur-

Table 6-7. *Share of Affordable Units by Region, 1997 and 1999*
Percent

	Share affordable, including mobile		*Share affordable, excluding mobile*	
Region	*1997*	*1999*	*1997*	*1999*
Northeast	40.9	37.8	38.9	35.4
Midwest (North Central)	54.8	50.2	52.2	47.3
South	53.8	52.2	48.5	45.7
West	31.4	27.2	26.0	21.3
All owner-occupied housing	47.3	44.2	43.3	39.4

Source: 1997 and 1999 American Housing Surveys.

ance until the equity in the home increases to 20 to 30 percent of the house value, this analysis does not include mortgage insurance costs. This is reasonable because, given the ratios used, in recent years many such loans have not required mortgage insurance. However, underwriting ratios and interest rate assumptions clearly have an impact on affordability estimates. To examine the impacts of the assumptions used in this chapter, the following three scenarios are modeled. First, an 80 percent loan-to-value (LTV) ratio with a 28 percent front-end ratio and a 7.6 percent effective interest rate (the average rate at the time of the survey). Second is the scenario used throughout the rest of this chapter, a 90 percent LTV with 28 percent front-end ratio and no mortgage insurance. A third, more aggressive approach uses a 97 percent LTV with a 33 percent front-end ratio and mortgage insurance providing 30 percent coverage, estimated to cost 50 basis points and resulting in a total effective interest rate of 8.1 percent.[2]

As shown in table 6-8, the more aggressive the model, the higher the share of units that are affordable to low-income households. The impacts are generally scalar, however. Other than shifts in relative magnitudes, the trends concluded using the Model 2 approach (a 90 percent LTV and 28 percent front-end ratio) will remain relevant regardless of the assumption used. Of course, as more aggressive approaches categorize more of the stock as affordable, this subgroup will more resemble the entire population of units, muting differences between homes valued at affordable and unaffordable levels.

Units Added to Affordable Stock

Simplistically, there are three modes through which additional affordably valued units may be added to the housing stock:

2. This is similar to Fannie Mae affordable lending products. Underwriting scenarios are based on *2001 MGIC Mortgage Underwriting Guidelines*; see www.mgic.com. The cost of mortgage insurance varies by state and coverage level.

Table 6-8. *Sensitivity of Affordability Estimates to Underwriting Criteria*

	Share of affordable units by region (percent)				
Underwriting criteria	*All*	*Northeast*	*Midwest*	*South*	*West*
Model 1: 80 percent loan-to-value (LTV) ratio, 28 percent front-end ratio, 7.6 percent interest rate	43	36	49	51	26
Model 2: 90 percent LTV ratio, 28 percent front-end ratio, 7.6 percent interest rate	44	38	50	52	27
Model 3: 97 percent LTV ratio, 33 front-end ratio, 8.1 percent interest rate (with mortgage insurance)	52	46	59	61	34

Source: 1999 American Housing Survey.

—New units are built at affordable price levels (with or without subsidy), mobile units are placed, existing ownership units are subdivided into lower-priced ownership units (such as condominiums or cooperatives), or vacant units are converted into affordable ownership units.

—Units decline in value ("filter down") because of deteriorating unit or neighborhood conditions, as well as the dynamics of marketwide supply and demand for housing.

—Rental units are converted to homeownership units at affordable price levels.

New Units 1997 to 99

Table 6-9 shows that approximately 30 percent of new units (built from 1997 through 1999) were valued in the AHS at a level that would be affordable to a household earning 80 percent or less of area median income. More than a half-million units were added to the affordable stock. Most of these new units (69 percent), however, are mobile homes, of which two-thirds do not include ownership of land. Given the importance placed on homeownership as an asset-building mechanism, these units without land are of concern. It is not clear that this nonconventional form of unit ownership without land ownership is consistent with the social and financial benefits ascribed to homeownership policies.

Transition and Filtering of Affordable Units, 1997 to 1999

The panel nature of the AHS allows matching affordable units from the 1997 survey to the 1999 survey. Table 6-10 shows that nearly four out of five of the units affordable to low-income households in 1997 remained affordable in 1999. Meanwhile, 13 percent of units valued above affordable levels in 1997 became affordable by 1999. More existing units are filtering up than down; 1.4 units increase in value for every 1 that decreases in value. On net, 1.7 million units that were affordable in 1997 became unaffordable by 1999 because of changes in value.

Table 6-9. *Owner-Occupied Units in 1999 AHS by Year Built and Mobile Home Type*
Thousands

	Units two or more years old			*Units built in previous two years*			*Total*		
	All	*All mobile*	*Mobile, no lot*	*All*	*All mobile*	*Mobile, no lot*	*All*	*All mobile*	*Mobile, no lot*
Above affordable value	37,110	99	11	1,290	14	5	38,400	113	95
Affordable value	29,840	5,160	2,548	540	375	251	30,381	5,535	2,721
Total units	66,950	5,259	2,559	1,830	390	257	68,780	5,648	2,816
Affordable as percentage of total	44.6	98.1	99.6	29.5	96.3	97.9	44.2	98.0	97

Source: 1999 American Housing Survey.
Note: Approximately 1.1 million mobile units are defined as rental units and excluded from this table.

Table 6-10. *Change in Number of Affordable Owner-Occupied Units, 1997 to 1999*

Shift	*Units (000)*
From 1997 affordable owner to 1999 not affordable owner	5,675
From 1997 not affordable owner to 1999 affordable owner	3,987
Net filtering	(1,689)
From 1997 affordable owner to 1999 rental	1,247
From 1997 rental to 1999 affordable owner	1,400
Net conversion from rental	153
From 1997 affordable owner to 1999 vacant	1,152
From 1997 vacant to 1999 affordable owner	995
Net conversion from vacant	(157)
Grand totals	
From 1997 affordable owner to 1999 affordable owner	20,650
1999 new units added at affordable values	540
Net filtering	(1,689)
Net conversion from rental	153
Net conversion from vacant	(157)
Total 1999 matched affordable owner-occupied	19,498

Source: 1997 and 1999 American Housing Surveys.

Note: Affordable categories include only valid interviews where respondents provide estimates of property values in both 1997 and 1999.

Approximately 1.4 million units were converted from rentals to affordable owner-occupied units in 1999. However, 1.25 million owner-occupied units in 1997 were converted to rentals by 1999. As a result, a net of only 153,000 units were added to the affordable stock from tenure conversions. Approximately 1.2 million affordable units in 1997 became vacant by 1999. Fewer vacant units from 1997 were reoccupied as affordable units by 1999. On net, 157,000 units were lost from the affordable stock because of vacancies.

Overall, units are only being added to the affordable owner-occupied supply via a small number of rental unit conversions and new construction, most of which are mobile homes.

Conversion of Rental Units to Affordable Units 1997 to 1999

Units converted from rental to ownership are of particular interest because these units are an obvious source of supply for increased low-income ownership. Table 6-11 shows that only 56 percent of these converted units were detached single-family units in 1997. Units converted to affordable ownership units were also much smaller in size than units converted to higher-value owner-occupied units. A surprisingly large two-thirds share of rental units was converted to higher-priced homeownership units, unaffordable to low-income families.

Table 6-11. *Shift in Unit Tenure and Affordability, 1997–99*

Transition	*Units (000)*	*Percent single-family detached*	*Mean square footage*
From 1997 rental to 1999 affordable ownership	1,400	56	1,350
From 1997 rental to 1999 not-affordable ownership	993	75	1,964
From 1997 affordable ownership to 1999 rental	1,247	58	1,406
From 1997 not-affordable ownership to 1999 rental	601	74	1,857

Source: 1997 and 1999 American Housing Surveys.
Note: Table uses 1997 weights.

Stock Effects on Submarket Homeownership Rates

Homeownership rates are affected by a variety of household, unit, neighborhood, and market characteristics. This analysis focuses on mean homeownership rates among households aged 40 to 65 earning 50 to 80 percent of the area median income in each zone in the 1995 to 1998 metropolitan American Housing Surveys (378 zones). Homeownership rates for this low-income population of peak homeowning age can be modeled using aggregated household characteristics for this population at the neighborhood (zone) level, as well as housing stock and location characteristics. An MSA level variable can be used to control for larger-market influences on homeownership.

Using a regression with Huber-White robust estimations of variance (to account for heteroskedastic MSA-zone relationships) with zone homeownership rates for low-income 40- to 65-year-old households, this model seeks to provide evidence of supply characteristics that have a statistically significant impact on homeownership rates.

Household factors include the percentage of low-income 40- to 65-year-old households in the zone that are white, as a measure of cultural or racial effects, and the percentage of this subpopulation that are high school graduates, as a crude measure of permanent income. Unit characteristics include the property and unit size, the percentage of single and multifamily units built in the previous two years, resident satisfaction ratings, unit adequacy (moderately or severely inadequate), and the share of single-family, multifamily, and condominium units. Neighborhood characteristics include the zone's central city status and mean resident ratings.

Market characteristics, such as house price appreciation, regulations, and interest rates, are captured by MSA dichotomous variables. Of the thirty-three MSAs in the 1995 to 1998 surveys, thirty-two are included in the specification. (Norfolk/Newport News is left to the residual.) Table 6-12 provides descriptive labels and statistics for the variables used (the MSA dummies are omitted; see table 6-1 for a list of MSAs and zones).

Table 6-12. *Descriptive Statistics for 1995–98 Metropolitan American Housing Survey Zone–Level Data Set*

Variable definition	*Obser-vations*	*Mean*	*Standard deviation*	*Mini-mum*	*Maxi-mum*
Homeownership rate for low-income homeowners age 40–65	363	0.57	0.18	0.0	0.9
Share of owner-occupied units in zone at affordable values	378	0.37	0.25	0.0	1.0
Percent white for low-income homeowners age 40–65	372	0.76	0.29	0.0	1.0
Percent high school graduates for low-income homeowners age 40–65	372	0.81	0.19	0.0	1.0
Percent units inadequate (moderately or severely) for owner-occupied units in zone	378	0.05	0.05	0.0	0.4
Median unit size (000) for owner-occupied in zone	378	1.73	0.37	0.1	3.5
Median lot size (000) for owner-occupied in zone	378	57.98	193.27	2.5	1,000.0
Percent single-family units built in previous two years in zone	378	0.02	0.02	0.0	0.1
Percent multifamily units built in previous two years in zone	378	0.01	0.01	0.0	0.0
Single-family units as a share of rental stock in zone	378	0.40	0.18	0.0	1.0
Single-family units as a share of owner-occupied, nonmobile stock in zone	378	0.82	0.16	0.2	1.0
Condominiums as a share of multifamily stock in zone	378	0.10	0.09	0.0	0.6
Central city status of zone	378	0.32	0.47	0.0	1.0
Mean rating of neighborhood as place to live in zone	378	7.86	0.58	5.9	8.9
Percentage of incomes <80 percent of MSA median in zone	378	0.43	0.14	0.2	0.8

Source: Authors' calculations using the zone-level data from the Metropolitan American Housing Surveys.

Table 6-13 shows the results of this specification. Ceteris paribus, movement from a neighborhood that has a lower share of homes that are affordable to lower-income households to one with a larger share of affordable homes is associated with higher homeownership rates for lower-income households of peak home-buying years. Housing stock variables explain much of the variation in homeownership rates for 40- to 65-year-old low-income households. Single-family units, in both the owner-occupied (nonmobile) and rental stock, are most significant. Also, a greater share of units built in the previous two years is also a statistically significant factor in low-income homeownership rates.

Malpezzi's regulatory index is shown in parentheses next to each MSA vari-

Table 6-13. *The Impact of Supply Characteristics on Homeownership Rates*

Dependent variable				
Homeownership rate for low-income (50–80 percent of AMI) homeowners aged 40–65	*Coefficient*	*Robust standard error*	*T*	*P > |t|*
Share of owner-occupied units in zone at affordable values	0.20*	0.10*	2.01*	0.05*
Percent white for low-income homeowners age 40–65	0.00	0.04	–0.09	0.93
Percent high school graduates for low-income homeowners age 40–65	0.08	0.06	1.29	0.20
Percent units inadequate (moderately or severely) for owner-occupied units in zone	0.01	0.31	0.04	0.97
Median unit size (000) for owner-occupied in zone	–0.06	0.04	–1.35	0.18
Median lot size (000) for owner-occupied in zone	0.00	0.00	0.97	0.33
Percent single-family units built in previous two years in zone	0.88*	0.38*	2.34*	0.02*
Percent multifamily units built in previous two years in zone	0.87	1.04	0.83	0.41
Single-family units as a share of rental stock in zone	0.18*	0.07*	2.64*	0.01*
Single-family units as a share of owner-occupied, nonmobile stock in zone	0.29*	0.10*	2.82*	0.01*
Condominiums as a share of multifamily stock in zone	–0.01	0.14	–0.08	0.94
Central city status of zone	–0.06*	0.02*	–2.60*	0.01*
Mean rating of neighborhood as place to live in zone	0.04	0.03	1.54	0.13
Percent incomes <80 percent of MSA median in zone	–0.24	0.15	–1.53	0.13
Salt Lake City (19)[a]	0.30*	0.05*	5.59*	0.00*
Minneapolis (.)[b]	0.23	0.07	3.14	0.00
Boston (26)	0.20	0.07	3.04	0.00
Providence (.)	0.17	0.07	2.33	0.02
Seattle (.)	0.14	0.07	2.09	0.04
Rochester (20)	0.14	0.08	1.78	0.08
Oakland (.)	0.11*	0.06*	2.04*	0.04*
Tampa (17)	0.11	0.06	1.86	0.06
Denver (17)	0.09	0.06	1.36	0.18
Washington, D.C. (.)	0.09	0.06	1.46	0.15
Indianapolis (21)	0.08	0.06	1.24	0.22
San Jose (25)	0.08	0.06	1.24	0.22
Columbus (.)	0.07	0.07	1.07	0.29
Kansas City (19)	0.07	0.08	0.86	0.39
Cleveland (21)	0.07	0.07	1.02	0.31
Hartford (19)	0.07	0.06	1.18	0.24

continued on next page

Table 6-13. *The Impact of Supply Characteristics on Homeownership Rates (continued)*

Dependent variable *Homeownership rate for low-income (50–80 percent of AMI) homeowners aged 40–65*	*Coefficient*	*Robust standard error*	*T*	*P > |t|*
Pittsburgh (23)	0.06	0.08	0.74	0.46
Baltimore (20)	0.06	0.06	1.07	0.29
Birmingham (20)	0.06	0.06	0.96	0.34
Cincinnati (22)	0.06	0.06	1.03	0.31
Oklahoma City (18)	0.05	0.08	0.56	0.57
Saint Louis (16)	0.05	0.07	0.79	0.43
New Orleans (17)	0.03	0.08	0.36	0.72
Portland, Ore. (19)	0.03	0.07	0.47	0.64
Sacramento (26)	0.03	0.07	0.47	0.64
Charlotte (.)	0.02	0.07	0.33	0.74
Memphis (21)	0.02	0.07	0.31	0.76
San Francisco (.)	0.01	0.07	0.15	0.88
Miami (24)	0.00	0.08	–0.02	0.98
Atlanta (20)	0.00	0.07	0.01	1.00
Houston (18)	–0.01	0.07	–0.16	0.87
Houston (21)	–0.03	0.10	–0.30	0.77
Constant residual	–0.10	0.30	–0.33	0.74
Number of observations: 363	$F(46, 316)$ 10.44	Prob $>F_0$	R-squared 0.441	Root MSE 0.14135

Source: Author's calculations using the zone-level data from the 1995, 1996, and 1998 Metropolitan American Housing Surveys.

*Significant at the 90 percent level.

a. Malpezzi's regulatory index, when available, is in parentheses next to each MSA.

b. No regulatory index available.

able, although the index does not cover all of the MSAs listed. Although several of the MSA-level variables are significant, there is little correlation between markets considered to be highly regulated and constricted low-income homeownership rates.

This model remains a preliminary approach. Future research could be refined using an instrumental variable and two-stage regression approach with a larger number of zones from more surveys and richer data on local market conditions. Issues of constraints introduced by regulation could be better explored by integrating zone-level data on regulatory conditions. However, this prefatory analysis provides evidence that controlling for market, household, and housing stock characteristics, areas with a constrained supply of affordable owner-occupied units are more likely to have limited low-income homeownership rates. While perhaps an obvious conclusion, these results do indicate more emphasis needs to be placed on building and preserving affordable units for low-income buyers.

Conclusions

Many low-income renter households may be in a position to overcome the wealth and income constraints on buying a home but will still be constrained by a lack of adequate housing units at an appropriate price in a desirable location. Supply-side constraints on homeownership deserve greater attention from researchers and policymakers.

Consistent with their means, low-income homeowners and home buyers live in and purchase less-expensive homes, smaller homes, more mobile homes, more condos, and homes with more problems. The share of homes locally affordable is highest in the South and Midwest and lowest in the West. Much of the South's affordable stock appears to be concentrated in mobile homes. It is important to remember that the correlation between house prices and incomes is far from perfect. A large share of affordably valued units are occupied by households with moderate and high incomes.

Affordable homes for ownership are being lost to house price inflation and vacancies. A net 1.7 million homes became unaffordable because of changes in value, a net 153,000 became affordable because of tenure switching, and a net 157,000 were lost to the affordable stock because of vacancies. On net there were about a half-million fewer affordable owner-occupied homes in 1999 than in 1997. The result, based on one set of underwriting assumptions, is that the share of owner-occupied homes affordable to low-income households fell from 47 percent to 44 percent of the stock from 1997 to 1999. The homeownership rate for households with incomes between 50 and 80 percent of local area median fell in several regions, but overall rates increased. This pattern of homeownership rates being suppressed by a lack of affordable units is consistent with multivariate analysis of neighborhood-level data.

Mobile homes make up a majority of the affordable units added to the stock. The share of affordable units that were mobile homes increased from 15.9 percent to 18.2 percent. Two-thirds of mobile homes do not include the ownership of land, a fact that challenges conventional notions of homeownership. More research into the costs and benefits of owning a mobile home on owned and rented land is needed.

When adjustments for variables that usually affect homeownership are made, the stock of homes plays a significant role in determining homeownership for low-income households. The presence of single-family and new homes contributes to higher homeownership by low-income households. Yet very few nonmobile units are being added to the stock at affordable levels. Policymakers need to recognize the failure of filtering as a mechanism to expand the supply of affordable homes. New programs and policies that encourage conversion of vacant and rental units into affordable homes available for purchase, as well the production of new units, may deserve consideration. Further research may also be useful into the role of regulation in constraining production of units affordable to low-income first-time buyers.

References

Advisory Committee on Regulatory Barriers to Affordable Housing. 1991. *Not in My Backyard: Removing Barriers to Affordable Housing.* Washington: U.S. Department of Housing and Urban Development (July).

Bullard, Robert O. 1984. "The Black Family: Housing Alternatives in the 80s." *Journal of Black Studies* 14 (3): 347–51.

Can, Ayse, Amy S. Bogdon, and Zhong Yi Tong. 1999. "Spatial Equity in Mortgage Lending: A Closer Look at HMDA Data." Working Paper. Washington: Fannie Mae Foundation.

Clay, Philip L. 1992. "New Directions in Housing Policy for African Americans." In *The Metropolis in Black and White: Place, Power and Polarization,* edited by George C. Galster. New Brunswick, N.J.: Center for Urban Policy Research.

Downs, Anthony. 1994. *New Visions for Metropolitan America.* Brookings.

Eggers, Frederick, and Paul E. Burke. 1996. "Can the National Homeownership Rate Be Significantly Improved by Reaching Underserved Markets?" *Housing Policy Debate* 7 (1): 83–102.

Eisenberg, Elliot, and Jack Keil. 2000. "Changes in Permits and Housing Prices. Teaser: Few Permits, Big Prices." Washington: National Association of Home Builders (NAHB) research note.

Galbraith, Christopher Zigmund. 1996. "Old Houses Never Die: Assessing the Effectiveness of Filtering as a Low-Income Housing Policy." White Paper. Department of Philosophy, University of Texas, Austin.

Galster, George. 1996. "William Grigsby and the Analysis of Housing Sub-Markets and Filtering." *Urban Studies* 33 (10): 1797–1805.

Grigsby, William. 1963. *Housing Markets and Public Policy.* University of Pennsylvania Press.

Gyourko, Joseph, and Peter Linneman.1993. "The Affordability of the American Dream." *Journal of Housing Research* 4 (1): 39–72.

Gyourko, Joseph, and Joseph Tracy. 1999. "A Look at Real Housing Prices and Incomes: Some Implications for Housing Affordability and Quality." *Economic Policy Review* (Federal Reserve Bank of New York) 5 (3): 63–77.

Herbert, Christopher E. 1997. "Limited Choices: The Effect of Residential Segregation on Homeownership Among Blacks." Ph.D. dissertation, Kennedy School of Government, Harvard University.

Kain, John F. 1992. "The Spatial Mismatch Hypothesis: Three Decades Later." *Housing Policy Debate* 3 (2): 371–460.

Kain, John F., and John M. Quigley. 1972. "Housing Market Discrimination, Homeownership, and Savings Behavior." *American Economic Review* 62 (3): 263–77.

———. 1974. "Housing Market Discrimination, Homeownership, and Savings Behavior Reply." *American Economic Review* 64 (1): 230–31.

Kiel, Katherine A., and Jeffery E. Zabel. 1999. "The Accuracy of Owner-Provided House Values: The 1978–1991 American Housing Survey." *Real Estate Economics* 27 (2): 263–98.

Malpezzi, Stephen, 1996. "Housing Prices, Externalities and Regulation in U.S. Metropolitan Areas." *Journal of Housing Research* 7 (2): 209–43.

Malpezzi, Stephen, and Richard K. Green 1996. "What Has Happened to the Bottom of the Housing Market?" *Urban Studies* 33 (10): 1807–20.

Mayer, Christopher J. 1999. "Commentary." *Economic Policy Review* (Federal Reserve Bank of New York) 5 (3): 79–83.

Mayer, Christopher J., and C. Tsuriel Somerville. 1996. "Regional Housing Supply and Credit Constraints." *New England Economic Review* (November/December): 39–54.

McDonald, John F. 1974. "Housing Market Discrimination, Homeownership, and Savings Behavior Comment." *American Economic Review* 64 (1): 225–31.

Obrinsky, Mark. 1989. "Cutting Building Costs Can Boost the Housing Stock." *America's Community Banker* 110 (1): 26–28.

Pare, Terence P. 1993. "Buy a Home Downtown." *Fortune* 5 (128): 93–96.

Quercia, Robert G., George McCarthy, and Susan Wachter. 1998. "Impacts of Affordable Housing Lending Efforts on Homeownership Rates." Working Paper 304. Samuel S. Zell and Robert Lurie Real Estate Center, Wharton School, University of Pennsylvania.

Savage, Howard A. 1999. "Who Can Afford to Buy a House in 1995?" *Current Housing Reports*, U.S. Bureau of the Census (August).

Somerville, C. Tsuriel, and Cynthia Holmes. 2000. "Dynamics Market Low-Income Housing Stock: Micro-analysis of Filtering." Working Paper. Portage, Mich.: American Real Estate and Urban Economics Association (AREUEA).

Stegman, Michael, Roberto Quercia, and George McCarthy. 2000. "Housing America's Working Families." *New Century Housing*, vol. 1, issue 1. Center for Housing Policy.

Thibodeau, Thomas G. 1992. *Residential Real Estate Prices: 1974–1983*. Mt. Pleasant, Mich.: Blackstone.

Vandell, Kerry D. 1994. "Where Do We Go from Here?" *Mortgage Banking* 58 (1): 38–45.

Wachter, Susan M., and Michael H. Schill. 1995. "Housing Market Constraints and Spatial Stratification by Income and Race." *Housing Policy Debate* 6 (1): 141–69.

Walters, Charles, and Henry Waltman, 1974. "1970 Census: Special Study on Value of Home." U.S. Census Bureau (October 2).

PART 3

Returns to Homeownership

Equity in a home represents the single largest asset held by most Americans. Among owners with household incomes below $20,000, home equity accounts for approximately 72 percent of net household wealth; for those with incomes between $20,000 and $49,999, the accumulated equity in their homes constitutes 55 percent of their total wealth.

Partly out of recognition of the contribution of homeownership to wealth formation and partly for ideological reasons, a number of public and private sector efforts have been undertaken in the past ten years to assist low- and moderate-income households in becoming homeowners. These include development of innovative financial products by private financial institutions and the secondary mortgage market, development of subsidized loan products by state and local governments, and creation of a homeownership option within the federal Section 8 program.

Despite the great faith in homeownership as a vehicle for wealth creation and the many efforts to facilitate the purchase of homes by low- and moderate-income families, we know surprisingly little about whether homeownership has been an effective vehicle for building wealth among low-income households. The potential of homeownership as an asset-building strategy depends on a variety of factors that facilitate or hinder a household's ability to purchase a home and a set of factors that affect the value of the home after purchase.

The former factors include availability and cost of financing, tax policy, and an adequate supply of appropriately priced homes, among other things. The second set of factors includes *market forces,* such as trends in housing prices, real estate taxes, insurance rates, and home maintenance costs; *individual household behavior*, such as the timing of home purchase, length of time before resale, and ability to make the mortgage payment and maintain the quality of the dwelling; and the *opportunity cost of homeownership*, the risk-adjusted rate of return on investment in a particular house relative to returns on available alternative investments.

The optimal way to determine whether low-income households are able to accumulate wealth through homeownership is to conduct a longitudinal analysis of three panels of households: low-income families who purchase a home, higher-income families who purchase, and comparable renters, comparing their outcomes with alternative investment options. At this writing, such an analysis is under way in a project supported by the Ford Foundation in conjunction with a ten-year demonstration of alternative mortgage products being conducted by the Center for Self-Help in North Carolina and Fannie Mae, but it will not be completed for some time.

In the interim, the three chapters in this section attempt to fill in the gaps in our knowledge about the experience of low-income homeowners in building wealth. Through the use of careful and inventive analysis of existing data sets, they examine changes in aggregate house prices over time and the influence of some of the factors, described above, in affecting the value of homeownership by low-income homeowners. Karl E. Case and Maryna Marynchenko examine whether owner-occupied homes in low- and moderate-income areas appreciated in value during the 1980s and 1990s. Mark Duda and Eric S. Belsky analyze how the timing of purchase and resale of housing affect the financial return to homeownership experienced by low-income homeowners. Finally, William Goetzmann and Matthew Spiegel investigate the risks and returns to homeowners over the past twenty years to determine whether homeownership for low-income families has been a good investment.

Case and Marynchenko's examination of home price appreciation for low-income homeowners uses the Case-Shiller repeat sales index, operationalized as zip code–level indexes of average sale prices, to analyze patterns of price movement across neighborhoods and income groups in three cities during the fifteen-year period between 1983 and 1998. The analysis included only arm's-length sales controlling, to the extent possible, for changes in property characteristics during this period. The three cities—Boston, Chicago, and Los Angeles—were chosen because of their different housing market trends during this time period.

During the fifteen-year study period, house prices, on average, increased in real terms for the United States as a whole (137.8 percent nominal increase versus 105.9 percent increase in the consumer price index) and in eight of the nine

U.S. census regions. The pace of increase, in real terms, accelerated during the last five years of this period, more than doubling the rate of inflation. Prices increased in real terms in two of the three study cities—Boston (3 percent) and Chicago (2.3 percent)—but remained relatively flat during this period in Los Angeles (an increase of .3 percent).

An examination of the trends reveals a complex pattern of changes in house prices across the cities and, within cities, across income groups that makes it difficult to draw sound generalizations. Nonetheless, four major findings emerge. First, the three city housing markets are characterized by cyclical fluctuations in sales prices, although the nature and severity of the cycles differed. Boston experienced pronounced cycles of boom, bust, and recovery. Los Angeles also experienced pronounced periods of boom and bust, followed by a period of relative price stagnation. Chicago's housing market, in contrast, was only mildly cyclical, with prices increasing throughout the study period. Not surprisingly, the changes appear to reflect differing conditions in both the regional economies and local supply and demand dynamics.

Second, homes in lower-income areas, defined as either the lowest quintile or lowest decile in median income from the 1990 census, generally performed well in terms of real price appreciation. For example, home prices in the lowest decile increased in real terms by 3 percent in Boston, 5.1 percent in Chicago, and .1 percent in Los Angeles between 1983 and 1998. Furthermore, in Chicago prices appreciated more in low-income areas than in high-income areas for the entire study period, and in Boston and Los Angeles for parts of the housing cycle.

Third, low-income areas in each city also experienced increases in home equity for the median home buyer during the study period, although the amount and rate of equity buildup varied substantially among the cities. (Equity is estimated by assuming that homes were purchased with an 80 percent mortgage.) The largest estimated increase in equity in low-income areas is observed in Chicago, where equity grew by 20 percent annually; in comparison, equity in Boston increased by only 1 percent.

Fourth, the timing of home purchase and resale exert a major influence in value and equity appreciation for all income groups in each city. This is most pronounced in Boston and Los Angeles, with their boom and bust housing cycles. For example, households that purchased a home in Boston in the early 1980s and resold by 1988 experienced major gains in home equity, but those that purchased and resold between 1988 and 1992 saw their equity erode. Purchasers in Los Angeles experienced negative equity during the bust period of the cycle, while the equity of owners in Chicago increased throughout the entire period.

The pattern of results across the cities suggests that homeownership may be a good strategy for building wealth for low-income households under certain conditions, because low-income areas in each city experienced gains in home equity during specific periods of time between 1983 and 1998. But it is important to recognize that both low-income and high-income areas also experienced decreases in home equity during market downturns. Thus the timing of purchase within specific housing markets appears to be a key factor in determining whether homeownership is an effective way to assist low-income families to accumulate wealth. This theme is the focus of the second chapter in this section.

The chapter by Mark Duda and Eric Belsky represents a major contribution to our understanding of the price dynamics of the affordable housing stock, a proxy for housing owned by low-income households. Their study is important for two reasons. First, they focus on identifying the impact that the timing of home purchase and resale by individual owners may have on the returns achieved by the owners of low-cost housing. The chapter both examines the absolute level of appreciation for low-cost properties and compares these changes to those for mid- and high-cost homes. Second, Duda and Belsky are the first to analyze the house price appreciation of individual owners. Previous studies, such as that by Case and Marynchenko summarized above, examine aggregate rates of appreciation in low-income areas or at the bottom range of the price distribution. The authors analyze matched pairs of transactions—purchases and resales between 1982 and 1999—in four metropolitan areas chosen to represent different types of housing cycles: Boston, Chicago, Denver, and Philadelphia.

Although these are significant advances, the authors recognize that the study's analysis is limited in a number of ways. Two of these are especially important. First, they are forced to use changes observed among low-cost homes as a surrogate for changes experienced by low-income homeowners, their real interest. Low-cost homes are defined as homes that are affordable to households earning less than 80 percent of area median income using conventional underwriting criteria and the average effective interest rate in the year of purchase. Obviously, not all owners of low-cost homes are likely to be low-income. Second, use of matched pairs of sales over an eighteen-year period means that the analysis is unable to examine the gains or losses to homeowners across their life cycle. In other words, this study analyzes the returns from one period of homeownership rather than the entire time that a household owns a home. As a consequence, house price appreciation may be underestimated.

Analysis of changes in sales prices indicates quite clearly that purchase of a home, especially when measured on a one-time basis, can be a risky investment. In real terms, the percentage of owners experiencing a loss upon sale ranged from 41 percent in Denver to 57 percent in Philadelphia. Substantial year-to-year variation also exists in the incidence of real losses within each metropolitan area. For example, whereas in 1987 only 8.1 percent of the sellers in Philadelphia experienced a real loss, in 1998, 78.1 percent of sellers did so.

A comparison of the performance of low-cost homes with mid- and high-cost homes reveals a number of interesting findings. First, the market for low-cost homes within metropolitan areas is more volatile than for other classes of homes. This volatility, however, reflects greater variation in rates of price appreciation rather than a greater risk of price decline. Although at least 21 percent of all low-cost home sales resulted in real losses in each metropolitan area, a far smaller proportion of these homes than other classes of homes lost value upon sale, and a significantly greater share of these homes gained in value. For example, in Boston, overall, 24 percent of the low-cost homes and 51.1 percent of the high-cost homes were sold for a loss, while 37 percent of the low-cost homes and only 15 percent of the high-cost homes experienced more than a 50 percent real gain in price.

This superior performance of low-cost homes can be attributed to two factors: segmentation of the metropolitan housing market into classes characterized by different patterns of price movement, and differences among the classes in the timing of purchase and sale within the housing cycle. Although the study states that the evidence regarding the first factor is inconclusive, it relies on other studies, including that by Case and Marynchenko, and the finding here that low-cost homes are substantially less likely than others to be sold for a real loss during market downturns, to conclude that market segmentation contributes to the stronger performance of low-cost homes.

The most important factor, though, appears to be the markedly different pattern of home purchase and resale that characterize the different market segments. Not surprisingly, sales of homes for real losses were less likely for owners who purchased in the trough of a cycle than for those who bought at the peak of the market. In each of the cities studied, low-cost homes were more likely to be purchased during the market trough than at its peak, while high-cost homes exhibited the opposite pattern. For example, in Boston, the most cyclical of the markets examined, low-cost homes represented 12 percent of all homes purchased in the 1982–83 trough and 2.5 percent of all purchases at the market peak; the overall market share of low-cost home purchases was 8.2 percent. In contrast, high-cost homes, which had an overall market share of 72 percent of sales, accounted for 57 percent of all homes purchased during the downturn and 88 percent of all homes bought at the market peak.

Duda and Belsky identify several implications of these findings. Both the overall incidence of loss and the crucial role played by the timing of purchase within the housing market cycle point to the need for greater education of low-income consumers and housing providers regarding the financial risk of homeownership and the impact of housing market cycles on rates of return. The findings also raise an important concern that the number of low-income homeowners vulnerable to loss could be greater than in previous cycles. Low-income families represented a growing share of new home buyers during the housing boom of the 1990s because of rising incomes, moderate interest rates, development of affordable mortgage products, and more aggressive outreach to these families. Thus a greater percentage of low-income families may have purchased homes at or near the peak of the housing cycle than in previous years. As a result, attention should be paid to helping these households respond to possible future downturns.

The authors also suggest a research agenda to overcome some of the limitations of the study. Prime among these is comparison of the relative risks and returns of owning versus renting for low-income households. Despite their findings that many owners of low-cost homes experienced real rates of appreciation between 1982 and 1999, and that this segment of the market outperformed high-cost homes, Duda and Belsky conclude that, in the absence of this knowledge, "it is difficult to judge whether efforts to boost low-income homeownership are likely to be effective asset-building strategies."

The third chapter in this section is far less sanguine than the previous two about the potential of homeownership as a strategy to build assets for low-income households. William N. Goetzmann and Matthew Spiegel seek to assess the wisdom of increased mortgage lending in underserved mortgage markets by examining the risks and returns of housing and whether the current tax treatment of homeownership encourages low-income families to purchase a home.

To measure whether the homes of households that purchased between 1980 and March 2000 appreciated in value, the authors used a repeat-sales index developed by the Office of Federal Housing Enterprise Oversight (OFHEO).This index is based on nearly 12.5 million repeat sales derived from Fannie Mae and Freddie Mac mortgage purchases for all fifty states, the District of Columbia, and 328 metropolitan statistical areas (MSAs). This index is similar in concept to the index employed by Case and Marynchenko.

Goetzmann and Spiegel's analysis of house price appreciation produces findings similar to those observed in the first chapter in this section. Single-family homes appreciated by 138 percent between 1980 and March 2000, an annualized rate of 4.2 percent. During the same time period, inflation, measured by the consumer price index, increased by 3.7 percent per year, indicating a modest real rate of growth for housing overall. An analysis of real rates of appreciation for twelve MSAs revealed substantial variation across these areas, with annual real rates of returns ranging from –1.9 percent in Houston to 3.3 percent in New York City.

Goetzmann and Spiegel, though, conclude that housing is a relatively poor asset in which to invest the bulk of a household's wealth. Single-family homes did not perform as well during this period as other investments, such as U.S. stocks, bonds, and mortgage-backed securities. For example, the annualized real rate of return for thirty-year U.S. Treasury bills was 6.6 percent. A low rate of return relative to other investments would not necessarily signal a poor investment choice if it is associated with a low risk of loss. However, as indicated in the previous two chapters, many homeowners suffered a loss in the value of their homes when they sold their properties. Goetzmann and Spiegel's analysis yields a similar finding. In 30 percent of the states, in at least one five-year holding period, an average household that purchased a home with a 10 percent down payment would have lost its equity because of price declines by the end of the period. When real estate transaction costs of 6 percent are included, households in forty-one states would have seen their equity erode in at least one five-year holding period.

On the basis of these findings the authors conclude that it is "irresponsible" to use aggressive low down payment mortgage products to encourage homeownership among low-income households because their home would become the single largest asset in a portfolio that lacks diversity in level of risk and rate of return. But they also acknowledge that there may be other reasons—such as nonfinancial value to the owner and positive neighborhood externalities—to promote homeownership for low-income people.

In this case, Goetzmann and Spiegel propose three policies to benefit prospective low-income homeowners. The first, similar to a recommendation suggested by Duda and Belsky, is to help educate low-income homeowners about the relative risks and returns of homeownership. The second is to develop market instruments that could help owners manage some of the risk of negative appreciation. An example of such an instrument identified by the authors is home equity insurance derived from housing indices formed for this purpose.

The final proposal calls for reform of the tax benefits provided for home ownership to provide a tax credit that would directly subsidize mortgage interest for low-income households. According to the authors, such a policy would eliminate an incentive for low-income families to rent rather than purchase a home.

In conclusion, each of the chapters provides important new information about the potential of homeownership to build assets for low-income households. Homeownership emerges as a potentially risky strategy, because many homeowners experienced real losses when they sold their homes during the 1980s and 1990s. Nonetheless, many owners saw their homes appreciate in value, and low-income homeowners often fared better than their higher-income counterparts. Whether an owner's home gained or lost in value depended, to a large degree, on where and when they purchased and when they sold their home. Finally, the chapters by Duda and Belsky and by Goetzmann and Spiegel provide helpful recommendations that could mitigate the risk of loss faced by low-income households considering the purchase of a home.

FRANK DEGIOVANNI

7

Asset Appreciation, Timing of Purchases and Sales, and Returns to Low-Income Homeownership

ERIC S. BELSKY AND MARK DUDA

Because home equity is low-income households' dominant form of wealth, an understanding of the price dynamics of the housing stock held by these owners and the timing of their purchases and sales is important for understanding the risk-return tradeoffs associated with their decision to buy homes. In an ideal world, such an understanding would precede and inform efforts to lift the homeownership rates of low-income people. In reality, however, our understanding of price dynamics and how they intersect with the timing of purchase and sales decisions of low-income owners is limited. Only a handful of studies to date have aimed at developing this understanding, and these studies have been lopsidedly focused on understanding price dynamics, not the intersection of these with timing of buying and selling. In particular, the study of price dynamics has focused on *average* appreciation rates of homes located either in low-cost or low-income neighborhoods or at the bottom of the price distribution (Pollakowski, Stegman, and Rohe, 1992; Seward, Delaney, and Smith, 1992; Li and Rosenblatt, 1997; Case and Shiller, 1994; Case and Marynchenko, this volume).

In fact, however, the asset appreciation enjoyed or depreciation suffered by individual owners depends not only on price movements in the lower range of the house price distribution or in low-income neighborhoods. It depends also and importantly on the market timing of low-income purchases and sales and on the willingness and ability of low-income homebuyers to weather declines in home prices and the broader economic downturns that often accompany them. The only way to evaluate the shares of low-income homebuyers that sell at an inflation-adjusted price greater or less than the price they paid is to analyze linked purchase and sales information for individual low-income owners. Ideally, these purchase and sales decisions would be examined using a panel so that the influence of repeated purchase and sales decisions on lifetime wealth accumulation could be observed. The importance of taking this approach is underscored by the fact that well over half of low-income mortgage borrowers are purchasing homes outside low-income census tracts, making evaluations of house price appreciation in these tracts ill-suited to capturing the actual experience of the majority of low-income borrowers (Duda and Belsky, this volume). In addition, a large share of owners who sell homes repurchase another.

In this chapter, we build upon and advance earlier efforts by using matched pairs of housing transactions in four metropolitan statistical areas (MSAs) for homes both purchased and sold between 1982 and 1999. We compare the returns (defined restrictively throughout as change in asset value net of transaction costs) earned by buyers of low-cost housing with those of other buyers. The impact of loan amortization on equity buildup is not examined. Low-cost homes are defined as homes affordable to those earning 80 percent or less of the area median income under assumptions about mortgage terms and costs in the year of purchase.

Contrary to the general public perception that low-cost homeowners are more likely to experience real losses when they resell, findings reported here suggest that losses are generally less common and less severe among those who purchased homes that would have been affordable to low-income households at the time of purchase. Nevertheless, for all groups, real losses are remarkably common.

Although these results are compelling, it is important to note that they do not represent the eventual distribution of returns among all buyers in a given year because our data only capture owners who purchased their homes in 1982 or later *and* sold by 1999. Thus we examine no owners with holding periods longer than eighteen years, and the number of observations declines sharply as holding periods rise. Because longer holding periods, which we cannot observe, are generally associated with more favorable financial outcomes, our truncated sample overstates the proportion of all owners who sell their homes for less than they paid for them. However, the results are an accurate reflection of these proportions among those with holding periods of less than nine years over the study period. Among these shorter-term holders, in three metropolitan areas the shortest-term holders (less than 2.5 years) incurred losses at an even lower frequency than medium-term holders (2.5 to 8.5 years).

We also consider the market timing of sales decisions by looking at returns to low-, middle-, and high-cost homes in each area over different phases of the housing cycle. In almost all cases we find that low-cost owners are substantially more likely to sell at a profit during market upswings than owners of mid- and high-cost units. Owners of low-cost homes are also noticeably less likely to suffer losses when selling during market downturns. Finally, we examine how the home-price composition of purchases varies over different phases of the housing cycle in all four markets. During the 1980s and the early 1990s, low-cost homes constituted a larger share of purchases near the trough than during the peak, and high-cost owners accounted for a larger share of purchases near the peak and on the downslide. We present evidence that low-income buyers have been accounting for a growing proportion of all buyers at what now may be approaching peak prices in many areas, an observation that raises questions about the consequences of the recent surge in low-income homeownership on the distribution of returns.

Though this study advances the literature by being the first to examine house price appreciation of individual owners, it has several limitations that render its conclusions and policy implications incomplete. As noted above, the most important of these is that we are looking only at relatively short holding periods and are unable to track a panel of low-income homeowners across their life cycle. Because our data begin in 1982 and we can only track sales through 1999, we do not capture returns reaped by many long-term holders or by those who sell one home but buy and sell one or more others over their life cycle. In addition, since we restrict our analysis to the distribution of sales net of purchase prices for single turns at homeownership, the data used do not contain information on owners after they sold their homes. Some significant fraction of these sellers undoubtedly bought other homes and therefore ended up back in a home price cycle in the same MSA or somewhere else. In fact, one study finds that most home sellers over the age of 25 subsequently return to ownership (Berkovec and Zorn, n.d.). To the extent that many short-term holders of a single home repurchase, their returns are likely to more closely resemble those of long-term owners, although they incur additional transaction costs on their multiple moves.

The other principal limitation of the study is that it narrowly focuses on differences in purchase and resale prices. An ideal calculation of owners' returns would compare these returns to renting on an opportunity cost basis. Such a comparison would evaluate the costs of owning or renting under assumptions about how the initial equity investment in the home might have been otherwise invested (Pozdena, 1988; Goodman, 1998; Brueckner, 1997; Gill and Haurin, 1991).[1] We also do not consider an owner's likely net equity at the time of sale

1. The user-cost-of-capital equation for homeowners relates homeowners' after-tax expenditures on mortgage interest, property taxes, maintenance, insurance, transactions costs, and the opportunity cost of invested capital to gains made through house price appreciation and forced savings through equity paydown. Among other things, it depends crucially on the rate of return on an alternative investment for the down payment and other equity capital that a comparable renter would have invested, which determines the opportunity cost of invested capital for owners.

because we lack specific information on initial down payments and amortization schedules. Because forced savings are a significant potential benefit of homeownership and because they increase with the length of the holding period, including them would reduce the share of losses reported here, especially among those with longer holding periods.

Several other key caveats apply. First, we do not know owners' incomes so we must group units into affordability brackets based on loan terms and interest rates on typical mortgage instruments in each year. This leaves open the possibility that owners of low-cost housing are not low-income people and could, in fact, be absentee landlords and/or real estate speculators. Second, our data are net of defaulted loans. Because defaults are more common on high LTV loans, which are used disproportionately by low-income borrowers, our analysis will likely understate the differences in outcomes between low- and middle-to-upper-income buyers.[2] Third, because we have data for only four MSAs, the extent to which our results can be generalized to all U.S. housing markets is limited. Fourth, we do not know the actual loan terms and types and therefore assume all borrowers use the same fixed-rate instrument, though we know that LTV, debt-to-income ratios, and other loan characteristics vary systematically by income and over time. Fifth, by focusing solely on financial returns to owners we ignore the noninvestment benefits of housing, which may be quite substantial (DiPasquale and Glaeser, 1999; Temkin and Rohe, 1998). Sixth, we were unable to obtain detailed geography on the repeat sales, so we are unable to draw conclusions about whether purchasers of low-cost homes in low-income areas fare better or worse than those purchasing low-cost homes in moderate- and middle-income areas.

Previous Studies of Appreciation by Income and Price Range

Only a small number of studies have analyzed patterns of appreciation of houses at different points in the price spectrum. Pollakowski, Stegman, and Rohe (1992), employing a hedonic model to study five MSAs, found that low and moderately priced (those in the bottom two quintiles) single-family units fared as well as homes in the upper three-fifths of the value distribution over the 1979–83 period.

Seward, Delaney, and Smith (1992) studied price changes for low-, medium-, and high-priced properties in St. Petersburg, Florida, and found that between 1973 and 1987 high-cost homes appreciated more quickly than others during expansions but that all three price classes depreciated at similar rates during the

2. Results from the 1998 GSE public use database show that while 14 percent of borrowers earning their area's median income or less had LTV ratios above 90 percent, only 11 percent of borrowers earning more than the area median had LTVs as large.

subsequent contraction. In contrast, Kiel and Carson (1990) found that homes at the low and high end of the distribution at the beginning of their study period (1974–83) experienced higher rates of appreciation than those in the middle. Li and Rosenblatt (1997) found that local median home values were positively correlated with house price appreciation in two of the three California MSAs that they studied (Anaheim–Santa Ana and Los Angeles–Long Beach) between 1986 and 1990, but negatively correlated with it for the period 1990–94.

Case and Marynchenko (this volume) examine the performance of housing submarkets in Boston, Chicago, and Los Angeles. After ranking zip codes into quintiles based on house price levels, they found that performance between the top and bottom quintile varied over different phases of the cycle and did not follow a consistent pattern from one market to the next. In Boston, indexes constructed for the lowest-income quintiles gained most during the 1980s expansion but also lost the most in the subsequent contraction. After the market began to rise again, high-cost areas appreciated more quickly.[3] The story in Chicago was simpler, as the lowest quintile outperformed the highest over the entire period the authors examined there (1987–99). In Los Angeles, indexes across all income quintiles appreciated at the same rate during the expansion. The high end was hit hardest during the following contraction but, as in Boston, also led the eventual recovery.

Smith and Ho (1996) attempted to reconcile seemingly conflicting results by relating the price differentials between high- and low-cost homes to monetary shocks (which widen price differentials) and fiscal shocks (which narrow differentials) that affect market segments asymmetrically in the short run. Prices for high-cost homes are more sensitive to changes in inflation, working through expected house price changes and real user costs of housing, while lower-cost homes are more sensitive to changes in interest rates, income, and employment, all of which affect low-income buyers' ability to overcome income and wealth constraints to homeownership. Depending on which variables are ascendant during cycles contained in the period examined and the number of cycles in the period, different cost segments of the market will behave differently, causing the differences such as the ones observed by authors of the other studies.

Li and Rosenblatt (1997) note that if low-income buyers cannot afford high-cost homes and high-income buyers will not consider low-cost homes, distinct markets exist that can be subject, for example, to supply-side shocks that do not spill over to the other cost segment of the market. Further evidence for the

3. Case and Mayer (1995) attribute the relatively weak performance of higher-income markets during the run-up of the 1980s to a softening of demand for these homes as they were quickly priced out of the reach of all but the wealthiest buyers, and as the access to good schools in these places was devalued from buyers' perspective as enrollments declined over the period. Recoveries in enrollments combined with changes in the spatial distribution of employment in Boston combined to make higher-cost areas more attractive in the post-boom period.

Table 7-1. *Share of New Owners in 1984–85 Who Moved Every Two Years*

	Low-income	*Middle-income*	*High-income*	*Total*
Moved by 1987	12.8	12.8	12.4	12.6
Moved by 1989	20.0	23.1	25.6	23.9
Moved by 1991	27.2	30.3	34.1	31.9
Moved by 1993	30.1	35.4	41.6	38.1
Moved by 1995	35.1	42.9	47.0	43.9

Source: American Housing Surveys 1985, 1987, 1989, 1991, 1993, and 1995.

notion of distinct markets comes from Case and Shiller (1994), who suspect that demand for low-cost housing by immigrants may have attenuated price declines in low-cost areas of Los Angeles when markets dropped in the early 1990s.

In sum, differences in the rates of appreciation and depreciation of low- and high-cost homes across metropolitan areas should not be a surprise. This is because there are good reasons to believe these markets are segmented *and* because supply and demand conditions in each segment can vary by metro area.

Data Sources

The data set used in this research contains information on the month, year, and price at purchase and sale for single-family homes bought in 1982 or later and sold by the end of 1999 in Boston, Chicago, Denver, and Philadelphia. These data are the same raw inputs that are used to construct the Case, Shiller, and Weiss repeat sales indexes in these MSAs (Case and Shiller, 1987, 1989). Because only repeat sales are contained in the data set, any home bought during the study period but not also sold during it is excluded.

As a consequence, results reported on a year-of-sale basis do not include homes bought before 1982, and results reported on a year-of-purchase basis do not include homes sold after 1999 or purchased before 1982. Results therefore mostly focus on repeat sales with relatively short holding periods of less than nine years. Panel data from the American Housing Survey suggest that over the period 1985 to 1995, 35 percent of low-income homeowners who bought homes in 1984 or 1985, 43 percent of middle-income homeowners, and 47 percent of high-income homeowners moved within nine years (see table 7-1). Although relatively large shares of homeowners apparently move within nine years, low-income owners are more likely to stay longer in their homes. However, a larger proportion of low-income than higher-income owners who sold within nine years in the four MSAs studied sold within the first few years.

Several data edits have been applied to eliminate suspect transaction pairs in which differences between the purchase and selling price seem likely to reflect things other than market-driven appreciation or depreciation of the unit. Bank sales, non-arm's-length transactions, and pairs where the home's characteristics are known to have changed were all eliminated. The effect of eliminating bank sales likely overstates the proportion of low-cost homes that are sold above their initial value because the low down payments more often associated with such homes probably lead to larger proportions of foreclosure sales. The effect of eliminating non-arm's-length transactions probably introduces no appreciable bias, while eliminating homes with known changes in characteristics may introduce a bias because homes most likely to have major additions and alterations may be spatially correlated with areas of more rapid price appreciation.

Records where losses exceeded 80 percent of the purchase price in real, transaction-cost-adjusted terms, and homes that appreciated more than six times were dropped on the assumption that changes of this magnitude were unlikely to be driven by market movements alone.[4] Records of property purchased for less than \$10,000 or purchased for less than \$30,000 and then sold for more than four times the purchase price were also eliminated in an effort to delete records that reflected insurance purchases and work on homes affected by natural or human-caused disasters. After establishing a distribution of apparently market-driven transactions, we eliminated observations lying more than three standard deviations above and below the mean for their affordability class in each MSA. The screens for maximum appreciation, as well as the minimum purchase value, resulted in a heavy concentration of deletions among low-cost homes with rapid appreciation. On net, the filters employed likely attenuate the upward performance of low-cost housing, which in any case performs quite well relative to other housing types in the analysis presented here.

In order to classify properties in each MSA as affordable to borrowers at different income levels, conventional underwriting rules were applied. The maximum affordable home was determined by setting the maximum price at one that a family at 80 and 120 percent of median income could afford at 28 percent of their income and with a 10 percent down payment. Wealth constraints were considered nonbinding on all buyers up to a 10 percent down payment. Monthly payments were based on the average effective interest rate in the year of purchase,[5] property tax and insurance rates in effect in 1990 as measured by the 1990 census, and mortgage insurance rates on a loan with a loan-to-value ratio of 90 percent. Annual house price cutoffs therefore float to reflect changes in median income and interest rates in the year of purchase. Results are mostly reported for the difference between the real purchase and resale prices net of

4. The largest cyclical marketwide increase in prices experienced by any MSA in our study was in Boston in 1983–88, where prices slightly more than doubled according to Freddie Mac's Conventional Mortgage House Price Index (CMHPI).

5. We use the annual thirty-year effective fixed rate calculated from the commitment rate and points reported in Freddie Mac's Primary Mortgage Market Survey.

Table 7-2. *Selected Characteristics of Study Cases*

	Boston	*Chicago*	*Denver*	*Philadelphia*
Median income	$65.5	$67.9	$62.1	$57.8
Median sales price in 2000:2	$215	$179	$180	$125
Share of homes affordable to median earner (percent)	44.5	56.3	51.3	66.9
PMSA population (millions)	3.30	8.01	1.98	4.95
Land area (thousands of square miles)	16.7	13.1	9.7	10.0

Sources: Median income, median sales price, and share affordable to median earner are from National Association of Homebuilders' Housing Opportunity Index. PMSA population is from Census Bureau July 1, 1999, estimate (as of October 20, 2000). Land area is from the Census Bureau's *1998 Annual Metro, City and County Data Book.*

transaction costs. These transaction costs are conservatively set at 6 percent to reflect the customary real estate brokerage charges. They are therefore net of closing costs the owner paid when purchasing the home or any part of real estate and transfer taxes or buyer's closing costs that are sometimes paid by the seller. For a more detailed description of the affordability calculation methodology and annual MSA cutoffs, see Appendix 7-A.

The share of units in each MSA classified as low-cost is a function of the affordability of homes for sale relative to local incomes. In high-cost Boston, only 12 percent of the repeat sales analyzed were classified as low-cost. In Chicago and Philadelphia, 18 and 22 percent were classified as low-cost, respectively. And in Denver, the most affordable of the MSAs, 30 percent were classified as low-cost.

As noted above, the sample examined for this study is heavily weighted toward short-term holders. Long-term holders (those who own for more than 8.5 years) ranged from a low of 16 percent in Denver to a high of 23 percent in Chicago. In all four areas, the share of long-term holders was greater among purchasers of high-cost than low-cost homes.

House Price Volatility in the Case Metropolitan Areas

The four metropolitan areas are a diverse set (table 7-2) selected because they represent different types of house price cycles. Boston was selected because house prices were especially volatile there over the study period. It is broadly representative of several metropolitan areas, especially in the Northeast and West, that had rather wide price swings during the 1980s and through the mid-1990s. Chicago was selected because it had mostly steadily increasing prices with periods of slower and faster growth. Philadelphia was selected because it had a tamer cycle than Boston but nonetheless had a strong upturn and a weaker downturn. Finally, Denver was selected because, though it had a strong

Figure 7-1. *Annual Percentage Change in Real Home Prices, 1982–89*

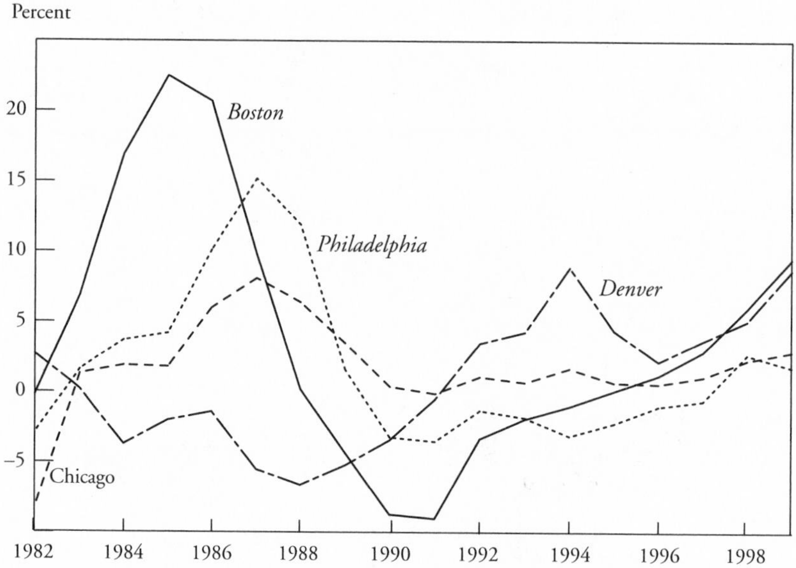

Source: Freddie Mac Conventional House Price Index.

downturn and a weaker upturn, it was out of phase with the other markets for much of the study period.

To recap, Boston was the most cyclical of the four markets studied, followed by moderately cyclical Denver and Philadelphia, and then by Chicago, which experienced slow but steady growth over the study period (see figure 7-1). Descriptive statistics on real returns upon resale as a share of real purchase price in each place confirm that the distributions of low-, mid-, and high-cost homes in Boston have larger standard deviations than those in the other markets (table 7-3).

The standard deviations of low-cost homes and middle-cost homes are strikingly similar in each market except Boston. And whereas average returns upon resale of high-cost homes in Boston mirror those in the other markets (though the standard deviation is higher), average resale returns on Boston's low- and mid-cost homes far exceed those earned in the other three markets.

A comparison of low-, middle-, and high-cost categories *within* metropolitan areas reveals that the market for low-cost homes is more volatile than that for units in other affordability classes, but also is more prone to real price appreciation. The contrast is most extreme in Boston, where the average low-cost resale resulted in a doubling in value, while the average high-cost repeat sale barely sold above the purchase price net of transaction costs. It is important to remember when interpreting the standard deviations that even after the edits to remove extreme outliers, the higher standard deviations on low-cost homes are mostly

Table 7-3. *Real Transaction-Cost-Adjusted Returns*

	Mean	Standard deviation		Mean	Standard deviation
Philadelphia			*Chicago*		
Low-cost	0.23	0.58	Low-cost	0.26	0.50
Mid-cost	0.01	0.25	Mid-cost	0.04	0.18
High-cost	–0.02	0.25	High-cost	0.01	0.19
Boston			*Denver*		
Low-cost	0.54	0.79	Low-cost	0.28	0.49
Mid-cost	0.19	0.42	Mid-cost	0.06	0.22
High-cost	–0.01	0.34	High-cost	–0.05	0.22

driven by positive, not negative, outliers. Put another way, higher return volatility among low-cost homes was the result of greater variation in rates of house price appreciation at time of sale, not greater risk of downside declines.

Returns by Housing Affordability Class

The vast majority of sellers in the edited data set sold their homes for higher prices, in nominal terms, than they bought them for. But even without netting out transaction costs or deflating sales prices to account for general price inflation between the time of purchase and sale, not insubstantial shares of owners lost money. In other words, a significant share of home resellers had to come to the settlement table with a check in hand. In highly cyclical Boston, nearly 23 percent of repeat sales resulted in nominal losses, while in steady Chicago, less than 7 percent resulted in nominal losses (see table 7-4). Adjusting for inflation and backing out transaction costs reveals that the timing of purchases and resales, combined with anemic real house price appreciation in many periods, produces a bleak picture. Indeed, the share of repeat sales culminating in lower real sales than purchase prices net of transaction costs ranges from a high of nearly 57 percent in Philadelphia to a low of about 41 percent in Denver.

It is important to underscore, however, that these findings refer mostly to those who sell within 8.5 years and are weighted especially to those who sold in less than 5.5 years. If it were possible to observe all holding periods and with equal weight, it is possible that rates of loss for all repeat sellers could be as much as half as great as those reported here. Nonetheless, the results do reflect the experiences of large proportions of borrowers on at least a single turn of ownership because short holding periods are so common.

This bird's-eye view of the distribution of losses and gains in home prices with and without inflation and transaction cost adjustments speaks volumes. Purchasing a home, especially on a single term of homeownership, is risky. The

Table 7-4. *Share of All Units Sold at a Loss by Year of Sale, 1982–99*

Percent

	In nominal terms				*In real transaction-cost-adjusted terms*			
Year of sale	*Philadelphia*	*Boston*	*Chicago*	*Denver*	*Philadelphia*	*Boston*	*Chicago*	*Denver*
1982	*	*	*	*	*	*	*	*
1983	*	*	*	*	*	*	*	*
1984	*	8.1	*	*	*	24.9	*	*
1985	6.6	3.0	*	*	33.1	6.9	*	*
1986	3.4	1.5	3.6	38.8	12.8	2.6	28.9	78.2
1987	2.5	1.8	1.6	53.5	8.1	6.5	19.0	89.0
1988	2.6	4.1	1.6	69.0	8.2	17.3	17.7	92.9
1989	3.7	10.1	1.3	69.2	13.7	34.2	20.1	92.5
1990	8.0	25.5	1.8	58.1	27.1	52.5	24.3	89.6
1991	14.2	41.5	0.0	46.4	43.3	66.2	43.4	87.4
1992	18.6	45.2	8.3	26.1	53.9	70.5		78.7
1993	22.6	45.1	8.0	14.6	62.1	75.4	44.2	61.7
1994	22.7	40.7	8.0	7.0	65.9	74.6	46.9	39.1
1995	27.3	39.1	9.3	2.9	70.9	75.2	52.4	32.5
1996	29.0	31.5	6.4	2.9	76.8	74.2	57.3	32.5
1997	30.3	23.5	7.2	2.9	77.6	67.7	59.5	30.9
1998	27.3	13.3	6.2	1.8	78.1	49.7	55.9	22.5
1999	22.6	7.5	5.1	1.0	74.7	33.7	50.0	9.8
All years	19.7	22.5	6.5	12.7	56.5	51.1	51.4	40.8
Maximum	30.3	45.2	9.3	69.2	78.1	75.4	59.5	92.9
Minimum	2.5	1.5	0.0	1.0	8.1	2.6	17.7	9.8
Range	27.8	43.7	9.3	68.2	69.9	72.8	41.8	83.1

Note: Years with small numbers of observations are suppressed.

Table 7-5. *Real Transaction-Cost-Adjusted Returns as a Share of Real Purchase Price by Affordability Class*

	Loss		Gain				
	>10 percent	*<10 percent*	*.01–10 percent*	*10.01–25 percent*	*25.01–50 percent*	*Gain > 50 percent*	*Total*
Philadelphia							
Low-cost	27.8	13.8	11.1	12.7	12.8	21.8	22.2
Mid-cost	37.6	19.3	12.8	14.1	11.6	4.6	26.1
High-cost	44.6	18.2	10.5	11.4	11.0	4.4	51.7
Total	39.0	17.5	11.2	12.4	11.5	8.3	100%
Boston							
Low-cost	12.2	11.8	12.2	13.7	13.5	36.5	12.0
Mid-cost	22.0	17.9	14.1	12.8	12.1	21.2	21.6
High-cost	45.8	13.8	10.7	10.2	10.0	9.5	66.4
Total	36.6	14.5	11.7	11.2	10.8	15.3	100%
Chicago							
Low-cost	8.7	24.6	18.7	15.3	13.8	18.8	18.4
Mid-cost	13.6	38.5	22.6	14.9	7.7	2.8	32.6
High-cost	23.0	34.8	18.6	13.9	7.7	2.1	49.0
Total	17.3	34.1	19.9	14.5	8.8	5.4	100%
Denver							
Low-cost	13.0	7.6	14.3	23.2	22.3	19.5	30.3
Mid-cost	18.8	18.8	24.3	23.5	11.5	3.1	33.7
High-cost	38.1	22.6	18.1	13.8	5.8	1.6	35.9
Total	24.0	16.8	19.1	19.9	12.7	7.6	100%

American Dream of homeownership may turn out to be just that for millions of owners, but for large shares it is not a fruitful investment unless sellers reenter the market and are able to ride one or more waves of appreciation over their lifetimes. Ex post information on the importance of home equity to net wealth among middle-aged and older owners suggests that indeed many who lose money once on homeownership offset that loss by buying again under more favorable circumstances (Joint Center for Housing Studies, 2000). But for those who are unable to buy again or whose timing once again triggers a loss, homeownership can turn out to be less than its idealized billing.

The concern of this chapter is with both the level *and* the relative performance of the low-cost home proxy for purchases by low-income homebuyers. At the most aggregate level, far smaller proportions of low-cost than other home purchases in all four metropolitan areas resulted in losses upon sale, and significantly larger proportions resulted in gains (see table 7-5). Despite the fact that relatively small absolute declines in home values could push real losses on low-cost homes beyond 10 percent of the purchase price, losses of this magnitude were *less* common for these owners than they were for owners of middle- and high-cost homes. In terms of price gains at the time of sale, low-cost units were more likely to be sold for a large real gain (greater than 50 percent of purchase price) than less-affordable homes. Furthermore, buyers of homes bought at a price that those with incomes from 80 to 120 percent of median could afford in the year of purchase also consistently outperformed buyers of homes bought at prices that only those with over 120 percent of median could afford.

Results for Boston are especially dramatic, but it is important to keep in mind that, although low-cost affordability classes accounted for between 18 and 30 percent of repeat sales in the other three areas, in Boston they represented only 12 percent. Similarly, although mid-cost affordability classes accounted for between 26 and 34 percent of all repeat sales in the other three cities, they accounted for only about 22 percent in Boston. Thus findings on the performance of low- and mid-cost classes in Boston reflect only a relatively small component of the total market.

Buyers of low-cost homes in Boston fared extremely well; less than one-quarter incurred real losses, and more than one-third sold homes at real sales prices net of transaction costs in excess of 50 percent of the purchase price. The share of low-cost owners who suffered real losses in Denver, where these owners made up more than 30 percent of repeat sellers over the study period, was well below the share of high-cost owners selling at a real loss, and even slightly lower than in Boston. In fact, the gap between the share of low-cost owners in Denver selling at a real loss and the share of high-cost owners doing so was 40 percentage points, and the gap was nearly as wide in Chicago. In Philadelphia, the market where this measure was *closest*, 21 percentage points still separated the two groups. On the positive side, though low-cost owners everywhere were not able to match Boston's 37 percent share who reaped real returns of 50 percent or more, about 20 percent did so in each of the other three markets.

Still, significant fractions of low-cost homeowners in all four markets were unable to sell their homes in real dollars for enough to cover even their transaction costs. Therefore, though low-cost buyers did better than high-cost buyers, fully 42 percent of their repeat sales resulted in real losses in Philadelphia, 33 percent in Chicago, 24 percent in Boston, and 21 percent in Denver. And an unknown number resulted in foreclosure sales. From the perspective of lenders, purchasers of low-cost homes exposed the lenders to lower collateral risk, but from the perspective of the owners themselves, the risks of earning a negative return on their homes were substantial.

Market Timing and Returns

The superior performance of repeat sales of homes affordable to low-income people is striking. Two mechanisms could produce these results. One relates to market segmentation that leads to consistently superior asset inflation in low- versus high-cost homes and to the other persistent differences in the timing of purchases and resales of low-cost and high-cost housing. Evidence suggests that both mechanisms played a role in each of the cases examined here.

With respect to the first mechanism, low-cost homes would have to consistently appreciate faster than other homes during upswings and/or decline less in slack markets to contribute to superior repeat sale returns for shorter-term low-income buyers. Looking at the distribution of house prices at the zip code level, Case and Marynchenko (this volume) did find that homes in Boston located in zip codes with house values in the bottom quintile appreciated more rapidly during the expansion of the 1980s. However, these submarkets also lost value most rapidly when the overall market declined. Appreciation was greatest in Boston's higher-priced markets during the recovery that followed. In Chicago, the authors found that low-cost homes did best over a long expansion. No findings on differences in price movements by cost ranges have been published for Philadelphia or Denver. All told, the available evidence is inconclusive about the role played by differences in house price appreciation in the four study cities. The low end did perhaps better in Boston than the mean-reverting house price process in that end would have suggested it should, and the low end unambiguously benefited from persistently higher appreciation in Chicago.

Indeed, there is strong evidence that local markets are segmented by neighborhood characteristics and by home price range (Rothenberg and others, 1991; Smith and Ho, 1996; Li and Rosenblatt, 1997). More rapid appreciation of low-cost homes could reflect persistent supply constraints or demand growth in low-cost and low-income markets. Either factor would cause prices to rise faster in these markets as rising prices become the principal mechanism to bring markets into equilibrium. Less-severe declines could reflect weaker demand contraction or more rapid supply contraction on the downside.

Another possible explanation for the superior performance of repeat sales of low-cost homes is that low-cost buyers are more likely than others to purchase at or near the bottom of house price cycles and to sell at or near the top, or before significant downturns in home prices. It is not just general price changes in low-cost markets that drive individual returns in the market, in fact, but the specific timing of purchases and sales decisions made by low-cost homebuyers that makes a difference. Thus both market timing and holding period could also play an important part in explaining the difference in returns to repeat sales. It is to these possible explanations that we now turn.

Many factors could lead to differences in timing of purchases and sales by buyers of low-cost homes. Those most likely to purchase low-cost homes (those with low incomes and low wealth), for example, could get priced out of the market when it crests and rush into the market when it bottoms out, especially if the bottom and upturn are associated with generally lower interest rates. All

Table 7-6. *Low-, Mid-, and High-Cost Home Purchases as a Share of Total Purchases by Stage of Housing Cycle*
Percent

Stage in cycle	*Low-cost*	*Mid-cost*	*High-cost*	*Total*
Philadelphia				
Trough 1982–84	23.1	26.9	50.0	100
Runup 1985–88	20.2	26.8	53.0	100
Peak 1989–91	18.3	20.8	60.9	100
Decline 1992–96	25.8	29.1	45.2	100
Total 1982–96	21.6	26.1	52.3	100
Boston				
Trough 1982–83	12.0	31.1	56.9	100
Runup 1984–87	4.6	13.9	81.5	100
Peak 1988–89	2.5	9.0	88.4	100
Decline 1990–93	16.7	31.5	51.8	100
Total 1982–93	8.2	19.8	72.0	100
Denver				
Trough 1990–92	38.4	35.5	26.1	100
Runup 1993–95	39.2	34.0	26.8	100
Peak 1983–85	3.9	17.4	78.7	100
Decline 1986–89	23.0	39.6	37.4	100
Total 1983–95	29.1	33.3	37.6	100
Chicago				
Trough 1983–85	8.4	27.6	64.0	100
Brisk growth 1986–89	14.3	31.3	54.4	100
Pause 1990–91	15.2	30.2	54.6	100
Slow growth 1992–97	25.0	36.5	38.5	100
Total 1983–97	18.3	32.9	48.9	100

Note: The data in this table are for purchasers who bought after 1982 and sold by 1999 only.

else equal, these buyers are the most marginal and should thus enter markets when soft prices and lower interest rates allow them to do so. Those most likely to be able to bid prices higher as the market peaks are those with greater incomes and wealth; they are thus more apt to be overrepresented among those buying at the top of cycles. Owners of higher-cost homes may also be more likely to sell in a downturn for a variety of other reasons. For example, they may be better able to sustain a loss because they have a more diversified investment portfolio and more willing to do so in order to move in search of employment in a downturn.

Evidence from the four case metropolitan areas reveals that timing of *purchase* is also a significant factor in the superior repeat sales performance of low-cost homes recorded in the mid-1980s through mid-1990s (see table 7-6). In all four places, low-cost purchases by those who sold by 1999 were a smaller share of purchases at market peaks than their average share for the entire study period.[6] Regardless of when the peak occurred during the study period, these results hold. In fact, especially in Philadelphia, Boston, and Denver, high-cost purchases tended to mass around peaks. Low-cost shares of purchases accounted for larger shares at the trough in all but Chicago.

The low-cost share of purchases by those who sold by 1999 during declines appears to have been related to the timing of the cycle in each city, however. In Boston and Philadelphia, where the period of decline coincided with the 1990s, low-cost purchase shares were higher during the decline. During Chicago's slower growth period of the 1990s, the same holds true. In Denver, however, where the period of decline coincided with the late 1980s, low-cost purchase shares were lower during it, suggesting something different about the low-cost market itself in Denver or the timing of the MSA's declining phase of the housing cycle.

The fact that market timing is so important and generally worked more to the advantage of buyers of low-cost than high-cost homes in the areas studied in the 1980s and 1990s raises important questions about how low-cost homebuyers will fare relative to high-cost home buyers in the next cycle. A hallmark of the 1990s is that low- and moderate-income home purchase loans, as a share of all home purchase loans, have been on the rise (Litan and others 2000). Through a combination of better outreach, rising incomes, moderate interest rates, and mortgage product innovations, the economy and mortgage finance industry have succeeded in producing more low-income homebuyers later in the cycle. This has been trumpeted as a major accomplishment, and it is; but its implications in the years ahead are uncertain. If home prices soften markedly at the end of the current boom, the proportion of low-income borrowers who resell their homes for more than they paid for them could fall relative to earlier periods.

Returns and Resale Timing

Although the golden rule of real estate is often cited as location, location, location, an equally golden rule is timing, timing, timing. Indeed, the most serious losses incurred by mortgage lenders and insurers have been triggered by widespread defaults during price declines rather than the credit rating of the borrower. Table 7-4, presented earlier, makes plain that an owner's likelihood of turning a profit is heavily dependent on the *year of sale*. In fact, the range

6. Phases are defined for each market simply as consecutive years of appreciation or depreciation, with the exception of Chicago, where we consider the entire 1983–99 period to be a long expansion, despite a slight drop (one-tenth of 1 percent) in 1991.

Table 7-7. *Share Selling for a Loss by Real Transaction-Cost-Adjusted Affordability Class and Housing Cycle Phase*
Percent

	Philadelphia	*Boston*	*Denver*	*Chicago*
Upswing	*1983–89*	*1983–88*		
Low-cost	15.7	2.9		
Mid-cost	11.5	3.6		
High-cost	13.7	12.4		
All homes	13.6	9.2		
Downturn	*1990–97*	*1989–94*	*1984–91*	
Low-cost	43.6	20.5	72.1	
Mid-cost	61.3	41.4	91.6	
High-cost	71.4	71.6	95.5	
All homes	63.1	64.3	88.6	
Upswing	*1998–99*	*1995–99*	*1992–99*	
Low-cost	58.6	29.3	13.3	
Mid-cost	83.3	52.5	30.5	
High-cost	81.0	68.3	51.9	
All homes	76.4	57.9	32.3	
Entire period	*1982–99*	*1982–99*	*1982–99*	*1982–99*
Low-cost	41.5	24.0	20.6	33.3
Mid-cost	56.9	39.8	37.6	52.1
High-cost	62.8	59.6	60.7	57.8
All homes	56.5	51.1	40.8	51.4

Note: Market conditions determined using Freddie Mac's CMHPI, annual percentage change. Chicago had a downturn of one-tenth of 1 percent in 1991, but we consider the entire period an expansion. Though the Chicago market declined substantially in 1982, there are no sales recorded in our database that year.

between the largest and smallest shares of sellers losing money in real terms annually averaged 67 percentage points in the four MSAs and was as high as 83 percentage points in Denver. Furthermore, the timing of purchase and sales decisions, as discussed above, is likely not independent of economic conditions.

Focusing on the time of sale rather than purchase, in Boston, the most volatile market, few homes sold at a real loss over the first upswing[7] (as rapid price appreciation quickly offset the transaction costs at resale) or at a real gain during the subsequent downturn (see table 7-7). Resellers of low-cost homes fared much better than others regardless of the timing of their resale. Largely as a result of poor returns to high-cost homes, a majority of all units that sold in Boston over the study period sold for real, transaction-cost-adjusted losses, including 58 percent that sold at losses during the ongoing recovery.

7. Defined simply as consecutive years of house price growth.

The distribution of real returns is skewed heavily in favor of low-cost units over virtually all housing cycle phases and markets. Even when prices decline, low-cost homes are substantially less likely to be sold at a real loss across all markets. This pattern is most pronounced in highly volatile Boston where, despite a compounded price decline of 25 percent between 1989 and 1994, only one in five low-cost home sellers suffered real losses, against more than two-thirds of those who sold high-cost homes. Further, when the Boston housing market recovered during the mid- to late 1990s, two-thirds of high-cost homes were still being sold at a loss, though only 29 percent of low-cost units sold between 1995 and 1999 failed to turn a real profit.

Returns and Matched Market Timing of Purchases and Resales

Delving more deeply into the influence of market timing on the difference in real resale and purchase price, it is possible, using the data set constructed for this study, to examine how those purchasing at peaks and at troughs fared if they resold over the study period.

Tables 7-8 and 7-9 show the distributions of years held for buyers at the peak and trough of housing market cycles.[8] Because more than half of owners move within seven years (Goodman, 1998) and our series lasts at least eleven years, we are likely capturing the outcomes for a majority of buyers in each case, though our results surely apply least well to very long term holders. In interpreting these figures, it should also be noted that losses are high for one-year holders on the "trough" figures for two reasons.[9] First, owners have had little time to experience enough appreciation to offset transaction costs. Second, because of the way that the trough is defined, it can include one or two years when prices were flat or still falling slightly at the end of the previous decline. Likewise, losses are lower for one-year holders at the "peak" because they may have caught the tail end of the preceding upswing. In short, the results for one-year holders are caused by factors different from those driving the rest of the series, and caution should be exercised in interpreting them.

Overall, the share of buyers experiencing real asset inflation in excess of transaction costs depends heavily on the housing cycle, though this effect is less pronounced where the cycle itself is mildest. Therefore, in the most cyclical market, Boston, buyers who purchased homes at the trough of the cycle and held them through at least one year of the upswing were unlikely *ever* to sell at a real loss, even when the market declined in the early 1990s. Real losses as a share of those

8. For Chicago, we define the trough as the three years of slow growth following 1982's 8.3 percent decline in home prices. Chicago's "peak" is defined as the years 1991 and 1992, when prices dropped 0.1 percent and rose 1.1 percent, respectively.

9. Holding periods are rounded to the nearest year, and all holds less than 1.5 years are considered one year. In addition, the final year really represents only six months.

who purchased homes in the trough were also relatively infrequent, regardless of holding period, in steadily appreciating Chicago, but did not shrink as much as they did in Boston, where rapid increases immediately put those who bought just before the trough was reached back into the black. The fact that the share of Philadelphia's owners that bought in the trough and suffered real losses was notably higher than in Boston for sellers holding beyond ten years reflects the fact that price increases there were not as substantial during the 1980s run-up, even though the Philadelphia market did not fall as far as Boston in the 1990s. Denver enjoyed an expansion throughout the 1990s. This lengthy period of price increases, coming on the heels of the energy industry–induced regional recession of the 1980s, virtually eliminated real losses for trough purchasers who resold in the latter part of the 1990s.

Outcomes are reversed for buyers at the peak, as real losses mount and persist for those who enter homeownership at the top of the cycle (table 7-9). This is particularly true in Boston, which suffered a severe price decline, as well as in Denver and Philadelphia. As might be expected, those who bought near the end of Chicago's period of most rapid growth, which was not followed by a real decline in house values, did not fare as badly as peak buyers in the other markets. The trend in Denver, the only market where the peak occurs early enough for us to follow what happened to past-peak sellers for more than a decade, was for the share that endured losses to climb and subsequently abate. The abatement did not happen, however, until well over a decade after the end of the peak, further indicating the persistence of real losses in cyclical markets for those who get in near the top of the cycle.

For the most part, disaggregating by affordability class produces results similar to those presented elsewhere in this chapter. Losses in Boston, for example, were less common throughout the holding period distribution for low-cost than for high-cost home purchases during both trough and peak. The differences are much more striking following the peak, however. More than 95 percent of high-cost homes bought at the top of the market that were subsequently sold were sold at a real loss; in contrast, the share that lost money on low-cost homes was only one-third and barely reached 50 percent in the worst years. In steady Chicago, the share that lost money was similar across affordability classes for homes bought in the trough but much lower for low- than for high-cost owners who purchased near the peak. Interestingly, though, overall results showed Chicago's post-peak performance besting that of Boston; this result appears to have been driven by mid- and high-cost homes (which make up a large share of all homes purchased during the peak in each place).

In Denver, real losses following both the trough and the peak are much less common on low-cost than on high-cost homes. The same is true in Philadelphia following the peak, but after the trough, smaller shares of high-cost homes were sold at a real loss in every year for which we have data. One possible explanation

Table 7-8. *Buyers Who Purchased Homes at the Trough of Local Housing Markets and Sold at a Real Loss, by Holding Period*

	Philadelphia 1982–84		*Boston 1982–83*		*Denver 1983–85*		*Chicago 1983–85*	
Years held	*Percent of purchasers*	*Percent selling at a real loss*	*Percent of purchasers*	*Percent selling at a real loss*	*Percent of purchasers*	*Percent selling at a real loss*	*Percent of purchasers*	*Percent selling at a real loss*
Low-cost home purchases								
1	6.0	22.0	6.6	12.1	12.6	17.6	3.6	16.2
2	9.5	22.0	8.7	5.9	5.1	29.7	4.0	19.0
3	10.7	15.0	14.8	1.3	6.5	42.6	4.1	18.6
4	11.8	16.0	15.2	1.3	6.3	57.8	5.1	20.8
5	9.8	14.0	9.7	0.4	6.1	54.5	4.8	18.0
6	7.5	17.1	7.9	0.0	6.0	44.2	3.1	12.5
7	6.0	19.8	4.4	0.9	5.1	75.7	3.1	6.3
8	4.9	20.5	3.3	4.9	5.3	73.7	4.7	22.4
9	4.6	22.6	3.5	4.6	6.5	51.1	5.1	24.5
10	4.6	35.8	3.3	7.1	8.2	57.6	5.3	20.0
11	5.0	31.4	4.1	11.5	7.5	46.3	9.3	9.3
11	5.0	31.4	4.1	11.5	7.2	30.8	9.3	9.3
12	4.4	31.3	4.2	17.1	6.4	23.9	13.4	18.6
13	3.8	42.7	3.3	15.9	5.7	19.5	16.0	12.6
14	4.5	47.9	3.2	7.5	3.6	0.0	9.3	10.3
15	3.9	45.5	3.6	9.9	1.8	7.7	6.7	12.9
16	2.0	45.2	3.3	4.8			2.3	12.5
17	0.9	17.4	1.0	8.0				
Total	100.0	24.0	100.0	4.9	100.0	40.4	100.0	15.5
Mid-cost home purchases								
1	3.1	46.8	3.9	28.0	4.5	54.9	1.7	43.1
2	7.7	25.3	8.1	9.1	4.6	68.7	3.4	33.6
3	12.0	14.3	15.2	0.8	5.5	86.5	6.0	29.3
4	12.7	5.9	14.2	0.3	5.7	91.3	5.9	24.8

continued on next page

Table 7-8. *Buyers Who Purchased Homes at the Trough of Local Housing Markets and Sold at a Real Loss, by Holding Period (continued)*

	Philadelphia 1982–84		*Boston 1982–83*		*Denver 1983–85*		*Chicago 1983–85*	
Years held	*Percent of purchasers*	*Percent selling at a real loss*	*Percent of purchasers*	*Percent selling at a real loss*	*Percent of purchasers*	*Percent selling at a real loss*	*Percent of purchasers*	*Percent selling at a real loss*
5	11.1	4.3	9.8	1.3	6.1	93.9	5.7	18.4
6	9.0	3.1	7.4	0.2	6.2	96.0	3.4	30.8
7	6.5	5.5	5.3	1.4	7.4	97.9	3.3	23.7
8	5.5	6.0	4.7	3.3	7.6	95.1	5.0	14.1
9	4.9	11.1	4.5	6.5	7.7	91.1	6.3	23.6
10	5.0	19.2	4.4	12.2	8.3	86.9	6.0	20.8
11	4.6	24.0	4.8	16.1	8.8	76.7	9.3	17.6
12	4.2	25.2	3.7	19.1	8.7	67.5	11.3	17.3
13	3.9	32.4	3.6	19.8	6.7	54.0	14.3	16.3
14	3.5	44.6	3.2	17.3	6.5	34.1	10.2	16.9
15	3.7	47.1	3.7	13.6	4.3	34.1	6.0	16.4
16	1.9	49.1	2.5	6.8	1.7	14.8	2.2	21.6
17	0.6	64.9	1.1	7.1				
Total	100.0	16.9	100.0	6.7	100.0	76.0	100.0	20.5
High-cost home purchases								
1	3.7	51.7	3.0	41.6	1.6	75.4	2.6	48.8
2	9.0	25.9	6.4	12.1	3.8	90.9	4.7	26.5
3	12.6	13.5	12.0	2.9	6.4	95.8	7.3	19.2
4	12.1	4.7	11.4	1.0	7.0	98.9	6.9	8.1
5	10.8	3.6	8.9	1.0	7.3	97.9	6.7	5.1
6	7.6	4.2	7.5	1.5	7.4	98.4	4.0	6.9
7	6.1	5.2	5.8	2.3	8.0	98.0	3.5	7.2
8	6.2	6.4	5.6	5.7	8.3	96.9	4.1	10.8
9	5.4	11.0	6.1	7.0	9.1	92.2	5.4	7.9

10	4.8	14.1	5.9	9.1	8.5	87.2	4.9	9.7
11	4.1	19.3	5.9	10.4	8.1	85.6	7.8	14.0
12	4.1	23.6	5.0	14.7	7.1	77.6	10.4	15.5
13	4.0	27.8	4.3	15.8	6.4	68.6	12.5	19.0
14	3.7	27.4	4.2	12.8	5.5	59.0	10.9	13.9
15	3.4	27.3	3.9	10.4	3.8	52.0	6.0	14.7
16	1.8	19.5	3.1	9.4	1.6	44.7	2.4	17.0
17	0.7	16.9	1.0	6.6				
Total	100.0	14.5	100.0	7.4	100.0	86.7	100.0	14.5
All home purchases								
1	4.0	40.5	3.7	30.8	2.5	57.8	2.4	43.7
2	8.8	24.8	7.2	10.2	4.0	83.4	4.3	27.5
3	12.0	14.0	13.3	1.9	6.2	92.2	6.7	21.7
4	12.2	7.6	12.7	0.8	6.8	96.3	6.4	13.1
5	10.7	6.0	9.3	1.0	7.1	95.9	6.3	9.2
6	7.9	6.7	7.5	0.9	7.2	96.3	3.8	13.2
7	6.2	8.6	5.5	1.9	7.8	97.4	3.4	11.6
8	5.7	9.1	5.0	4.9	8.1	96.0	4.4	12.9
9	5.1	13.5	5.3	6.7	8.8	90.8	5.6	14.1
10	4.8	20.3	5.1	9.7	8.4	86.0	5.3	14.1
11	4.4	23.8	5.3	12.0	8.2	82.5	8.3	14.6
12	4.2	25.9	4.5	16.0	7.4	73.8	10.9	16.3
13	3.9	32.4	4.0	16.9	6.5	64.2	13.3	17.5
14	3.8	37.2	3.8	13.3	5.7	52.6	10.6	14.5
15	3.6	37.3	3.8	11.4	3.9	46.7	6.1	15.0
16	1.9	33.9	2.9	7.9	1.6	37.6	2.3	17.8
17	0.7	28.1	1.0	7.0				
Total	100.0	17.3	100.0	6.9	100.0	82.9	100.0	16.3

Note: Holding periods are rounded to the nearest year, so a three-year hold is actually 2.5–3.49 years; a one-year hold is actually 0–1.49 years.

Table 7-9. *Buyers Who Purchased Homes at the Peak of Local Housing Markets and Sold at a Real Loss, by Holding Period*

	Philadelphia 1989–91		*Boston 1988–89*		*Denver 1990–92*		*Chicago 1990–91*	
Years held	*Percent of purchasers*	*Percent selling at a real loss*	*Percent of purchasers*	*Percent selling at a real loss*	*Percent of purchasers*	*Percent selling at a real loss*	*Percent of purchasers*	*Percent selling at a real loss*
Low-cost home purchases								
1	12.0	18.0	25.3	12.3	17.7	49.8	2.9	15.7
2	9.0	34.7	9.0	20.4	10.8	22.1	6.2	23.6
3	9.5	48.4	5.5	23.3	13.1	10.1	10.5	17.1
4	10.4	55.6	8.3	28.9	14.7	5.5	13.5	27.5
5	12.1	59.3	7.5	36.6	13.6	3.5	15.3	31.6
6	11.9	64.1	8.8	52.1	11.8	2.2	17.5	31.7
7	12.3	69.4	6.4	48.6	10.5	1.3	17.4	32.3
8	11.4	72.8	9.0	44.9	5.5	0.8	12.3	27.9
9	7.7	70.4	7.0	52.6	2.3	0.3	4.4	34.2
10	3.7	69.3	6.6	52.8				
11			6.6	47.2				
Total	100.0	55.3	100.0	33.4	100.0	14.2	100.0	28.4
Mid-cost home purchases								
1	3.7	64.0	7.5	37.0	9.5	64.4	1.4	35.3
2	7.0	80.3	6.4	65.1	11.1	25.1	6.4	47.6
3	9.7	86.8	6.4	84.9	14.7	11.9	10.5	50.4
4	11.3	89.6	7.4	85.4	16.4	8.2	10.6	49.6
5	13.4	91.6	10.0	90.3	14.7	4.5	15.4	58.5
6	13.3	92.5	10.7	94.3	12.8	3.1	19.0	64.3
7	14.9	93.3	10.3	93.1	11.6	1.9	17.3	65.1
8	13.2	93.6	11.9	95.3	6.4	0.8	13.2	61.2
9	9.5	92.9	11.5	92.4	2.8	0.3	6.3	57.8
10	4.0	92.5	12.3	92.1				
11			5.4	87.7				
Total	100.0	89.9	100.0	85.6	100.0	13.3	100.0	58.2

High-cost home purchases								
1	4.4	85.7	4.2	76.5	10.2	76.1	1.1	65.7
2	8.4	92.1	6.5	93.9	11.1	41.4	5.9	71.3
3	11.1	93.5	8.1	97.7	14.1	26.0	9.2	74.1
4	11.9	94.0	10.0	97.8	15.3	21.8	9.8	67.2
5	12.0	95.7	11.8	98.1	15.4	19.2	13.4	75.4
6	12.0	97.1	11.6	98.2	13.3	15.4	18.6	81.0
7	13.8	95.6	11.4	97.6	11.0	8.0	18.5	79.7
8	13.4	95.7	11.3	97.7	6.5	7.0	15.5	67.4
9	9.1	96.2	11.1	96.1	3.0	2.3	8.0	61.8
10	3.8	97.1	9.5	90.9				
11			4.4	91.3				
Total	100.0	94.8	100.0	95.5	100.0	25.8	100.0	73.6
All home purchases								
1	5.6	56.4	5.0	63.3	12.8	59.1	1.5	41.9
2	8.3	78.5	6.5	88.5	11.0	28.3	6.1	56.4
3	10.5	84.8	7.9	95.2	13.9	15.0	9.8	57.2
4	11.5	86.7	9.7	95.5	15.5	10.7	10.6	54.3
5	12.3	88.2	11.5	96.5	14.4	8.2	14.3	62.8
6	12.3	90.2	11.5	96.9	12.6	6.2	18.5	68.8
7	13.8	90.8	11.2	96.5	11.0	3.3	18.0	68.5
8	13.0	91.6	11.3	96.4	6.1	2.5	14.3	60.5
9	8.9	91.4	11.1	95.0	2.7	0.9	6.9	58.0
10	3.8	91.2	9.7	90.3				
11			4.5	89.2				
12								
Total	100.00	86.5	100.0	93.0	100.0	16.9	100.0	62.0

Note: Holding periods are rounded to the nearest year, so a three-year hold is actually 2.5–3.49 years; a one-year hold is actually 0–1.49 years.

is that prices rose more rapidly in both places for low-cost homes during the upturn and contracted less during the downturns.

Conclusion

The findings presented in this chapter illustrate that homeowners frequently sell homes for less than they paid for them in nominal terms and that especially large shares of them resell after experiencing real house price appreciation insufficient to cover even transaction costs. This perspective dramatically underscores the risks associated with purchasing a home. Equally important, people purchasing homes that were initially in the price ranges that low-income households could afford experienced significantly greater price appreciation and significantly lower risk of losses upon resale in the four metropolitan areas studied. Thus, though homeownership is risky for all, it was relatively less so for at least those who bought low-cost homes after 1982 and sold them by 1999 in each of the places studied.

The superior performance upon resale of purchasers of low-cost homes in the cities studied was attributable both to different house price cycles for their homes and to the timing of their purchases and sales. Price appreciation at the low end of the market was generally sharper in the upturns, and it appears that deflation was more modest in the downturns in at least some of the cities studied. In addition, in all of the cities, owners of low-cost homes were less likely to purchase at the top of the market, and owners of high-cost homes were more likely to do so. Perhaps this reflects the fact that as prices and interest rates rise toward the cyclical peaks, low-income owners are priced out of the market. In addition, at least in the places studied, purchasers of low-cost homes selling within 8.5 years or less were more apt to buy toward the bottom of cycles and then sell on the upside of the same cycle.

These findings have important policy implications. First, more work needs to be done to help low-income home buyers and providers better understand the risks associated with homeownership. Second, recent improvements to mortgage finance systems and the strength of the economy, which have enabled the proportion of loans to low-income borrowers for home purchase to rise more or less continuously over this homeownership boom, may leave more of these borrowers vulnerable to downturns than in previous cycles. Third, and related to the second implication, timing of purchases and sales is essential to the returns realized or the losses suffered by low-income and other owners. Housing providers especially need to educate potential borrowers of the risks of buying late in an expansion. Fourth, because a significant fraction of those purchasing low-cost properties resell their homes at real prices below the purchase price, it is important to help owners who might suffer a loss to either weather downturns

Table 7-10. *Percent of Homeowners Who Sold for Less Than the Purchase Price in Real Dollars Net of Transaction Costs*

Holding period	*Low-cost*	*Mid-cost*	*High-cost*
Philadelphia			
Less than 2.5 years	26.9	50.5	58.6
2.5–5.49 years	41.4	55.4	61.7
5.5–8.49 years	51.7	62.5	69.6
Boston			
Less than 2.5 years	22.7	35.6	44.2
2.5–5.49 years	24.8	38.0	53.6
5.5–8.49 years	27.6	46.6	72.6
Chicago			
Less than 2.5 years	32.0	63.1	66.2
2.5–5.49 years	40.6	61.8	63.4
5.5–8.49 years	31.2	48.3	63.6
Denver			
Less than 2.5 years	30.7	50.6	65.6
2.5–5.49 years	11.7	30.2	55.9
5.5–8.49 years	13.1	31.7	57.7

or jump immediately back into homeownership so they can ride subsequent waves of appreciation.

Having reached these conclusions, it is important to reiterate that the data sets and methods used to reach them have limitations. Among the most important of these limitations, these findings are derived from repeat sales of mostly short-term owners (less than 8.5 and especially less than 5.5 years) and in only four metropolitan areas. As such, they likely greatly exaggerate the proportion of all owners who experience real losses on a single turn of homeownership, although over these shorter holding periods those holding longer term did not necessarily do better than those selling even within 2.5 years (see table 7-10). In addition, they are based on price (and associated estimated mortgage costs) as a proxy for borrower incomes. They are also net of defaulted loans, and these may vary systematically with purchase price ranges. Furthermore, they examine real price appreciation net of transaction costs only and hence do not compare the cost of owning to the alternative of renting. To the extent that renters are faced with the possibility of repeated rent increases but owners are better able to stabilize their housing expenditures, owning may still prove to be the more attractive option (especially for those who put little or no money down so as not to forgo other investment opportunities). Finally, they examine only single turns of homeownership, but we know that large shares of resellers purchase a home immediately or shortly after selling their previous home.

These limitations suggest at least the need for the following future research:

—studies that follow complete cohorts of purchasers rather than truncating them so that they contain only shorter-term holders;

—studies of the lifetime chances of earning positive returns from homeownership;

—comparative studies of the ex-post cost of owning and renting;

—studies of other metropolitan areas;

—studies based on known low-income buyers rather than price-based proxies for them; and

—studies that take into account the actual mortgage terms and products of low-income buyers as well as some of their demographic characteristics.

Until more is known about the relative risks and rewards of owning, rather than renting, for low-income homeowners, it is difficult to judge whether efforts to boost low-income homeownership are likely to be effective asset-building strategies. Certainly, forced savings in the form of amortization over the life of the loan is likely to lead to asset accumulation for low-income owners who hold their loans to term or pay them off. However, it is equally clear that if the past is prologue many low-income homeowners will sell for a loss at least once in their lives, and that other investments have more attractive risk-return profiles than housing. Efforts to support low-income homeownership, however, might equally be justified for the greater control it affords those who want to own a home over their housing conditions and its potential to insulate families from rent inflation.

Appendix 7A: Calculating Affordability Limits

In order to subdivide our data into homes that were affordable to low-, middle-, and high-income buyers, we calculated the highest-cost home that would be affordable to buyers earning 80 and 120 percent of the area median income in each MSA in each year. Because the limits are a function of the terms of the loan itself, assumptions about the specific financing instrument had to be made. We chose a thirty-year fixed-rate loan because it is the closest thing to a "standard" loan over the entire period.

In order to calculate the maximum affordable unit, we assume that buyers put 10 percent down and can devote no more than 28 percent of their income to housing expenses (property taxes, insurance, and mortgage payment). Because everything else is known, we use the following formula to calculate the share available for principal and interest after paying property taxes and hazard insurance.

$$RI = \frac{P(XI)}{LK} + \frac{H(XI)}{LK} + XI \,, \qquad \text{(7A-1)}$$

where

L = loan-to-value ratio (90 percent by assumption);

K = mortgage constant[10] (annual for 360-payment, fixed-rate loan);

R = maximum housing expense-to-income ratio (28 percent by assumption);

P = median property tax as share of house value (by MSA according to the 1990 census);

H = median property hazard insurance as share of house value (by MSA according to the 1990 census);

I = annual area median income;[11] and

X = principal and interest payment-to-income ratio.

Solving for X yields

$$X = \frac{LKR}{P + H + LK}. \tag{7A-2}$$

The maximum affordable unit for low- and middle-income borrowers can then be calculated as

$$\text{Limit}_{LI} = \frac{0.8I * X}{K} \tag{7A-3}$$

and

$$\text{Limit}_{MI} = \frac{1.2I * X}{K}. \tag{7A-4}$$

Table 7A-1 shows these limits in each MSA for each year.

10. The mortgage constant is calculated on a thirty-year fixed-rate loan at the effective interest rate for that year from Freddie Mac's Primary Mortgage Market Survey (PMMS). The effective rate calculation has a ten-year refinance assumption built in, so that points are spread over ten years rather than the thirty-year life of the loan. The mortgage constant is calculated by $K = \{i/[1 - (1/(1 = I)n)]\}$, where i is the interest rate and n is the number of payment periods (here 360).

11. HUD estimates for 1984, 1986–89, 1991–1999; census figure (1992 MSA definitions) for 1990; 1982–83 are 1984 HUD estimates deflated by CPI-UX; 1985 is 1986 HUD estimate deflated by CPI-UX.

Table 7A-1. *Maximum Price of Homes Affordable to Low- and Middle-Income Buyers, 1982–99*

Dollars

	Philadelphia		*Boston*		*Chicago*		*Denver*	
Year	*Low-income maximum*	*Middle-income maximum*	*Low-income maximum*	*Middle-income maximum*	*Low-income maximum*	*Middle-income maximum*	*Low-income maximum*	*Middle-income maximum*
1982	31,160	46,739	37,035	55,552	35,999	53,998	78,242	117,363
1983	38,065	57,097	45,493	68,239	42,315	63,473	43,738	65,606
1984	38,034	57,051	45,385	68,078	42,151	63,227	43,676	65,514
1985	44,547	66,821	51,604	77,407	48,066	72,098	48,486	72,729
1986	52,974	79,461	61,768	92,651	59,267	88,901	57,803	86,705
1987	55,848	83,772	67,844	101,766	60,367	90,550	63,369	95,053
1988	59,704	89,556	73,934	110,901	63,690	95,535	69,158	103,736
1989	62,028	93,041	81,069	121,603	68,633	102,950	69,257	103,885
1990	73,271	109,906	84,589	126,883	73,254	109,881	71,491	107,237
1991	76,766	115,150	98,164	147,246	78,279	117,418	79,560	119,339
1992	82,593	123,890	107,365	161,047	94,206	141,309	87,946	131,920
1993	101,344	152,016	117,832	176,748	106,044	159,066	103,162	154,744
1994	92,932	139,398	107,741	161,612	95,575	143,363	98,901	148,352
1995	97,273	145,910	115,712	173,567	106,698	160,047	102,497	153,746
1996	102,902	154,353	124,506	186,759	107,843	161,765	113,207	169,810
1997	128,219	192,328	133,560	200,340	115,564	173,346	118,960	178,440
1998	140,527	210,790	143,417	215,126	126,744	190,116	128,454	192,680
1999	142,001	213,001	143,754	215,630	129,896	194,843	129,812	194,718

References

Ambrose, B. W., and W. N. Goetzmann. 1996. "Risks and Incentives in Underserved Mortgage Markets." Yale University/University of Pennsylvania.

Archer, W. R., D. H. Gratzlaff, and D. C. Ling. 1996. "Measuring the Importance of Location in House Price Appreciation." *Journal of Urban Economics* 40: 334–53.

Berkovec, J., and P. Zorn. 1999. "Households That Never Own: An Empirical Analysis Using the American Housing Survey." Freddie Mac.

Boehm, T. P., H. W. Herzog Jr., and A. M. Schlottmann. 1991. "Intra-Urban Mobility, Migration, and Tenure Choice." *Review of Economics and Statistics* 73 (1): 50–58.

Brueckner, J. K. 1997. "Consumption and Investment Motives and the Portfolio Choices of Homeowners." *Journal of Real Estate Finance and Economics* 15 (2): 159–80.

Case, K., and C. Mayer. 1995. "The Housing Cycle in Eastern Massachusetts: Variations among Cities and Towns." *New England Economic Review* (March/April): 24–40.

———. 1996. "Housing Price Dynamics within a Metropolitan Area." *Regional Science and Urban Economics* 26: 387–407.

Case, K., and R. Shiller. 1987. "Prices of Single Family Homes since 1970: New Indexes for Four Cities." *New England Economic Review* (September/October): 45–56.

———. 1989. "The Efficiency of the Market for Single Family Homes." *American Economic Review* 79 (1): 125–37.

———. 1994. "A Decade of Boom and Bust in the Prices of Single Family Homes: Boston and Los Angeles: 1983–1993." *New England Economic Review* (March/April): 40–51.

Crone, T. M., and R. P. Voith. 1999. "Risk and Return within the Single-Family Housing Market. *Real Estate Economics* 27 (1): 63–78.

Crowe, D. 1994. "Household Changes and Mobility." *Housing Economics* (January): 11–13.

DiPasquale, D., and E. Glaeser. 1999. "Incentives and Social Capital: Are Homeowners Better Citizens?" *Journal of Urban Economics* 45: 354–84.

Engelhardt, G. V. 1998. "House Prices, Equity, and Household Mobility. Dartmouth College.

Gill, H. L., and D. R. Haurin. 1991. "User Cost and the Demand for Housing Attributes." *ARUEA Journal* 19 (3): 383–95.

Goodman, J. 1998. "The Costs of Owning and Renting Housing: 1985–1995." National Multi-Housing Council.

Gyourko, J., and R. Voith. 1992. "Local and National Component in House Price Appreciation." *Journal of Urban Economics* 32: 52–69.

Horne, D., Li, Y, and D. Rosenblatt. 1996. "Segregation and Returns to Housing." FDIC/Fannie Mae.

Joint Center for Housing Studies. 2000. *The State of the Nation's Housing 2000.* Harvard University.

Kiel, K. A., and R. T. Carson. 1990. "An Examination of Systematic Differences in the Appreciation of Individual Housing Units." *Journal of Real Estate Research* 5 (3): 301–17.

Kiel, K. A., and J. E. Zabel. 1996. "House Price Differentials in U.S. Cities: Household and Neighborhood Racial Effects." *Journal of Housing Economics* 5: 143–65.

Li, Y., and E. Rosenblatt. 1997. "Can Urban Indicators Predict Home Price Appreciation?" *Real Estate Economics* 25 (1): 81–104.

Litan, R., N. Retsinas, E. Belsky, and S. White-Haag. 2000. *The Community Reinvestment Act after Financial Modernization: A Baseline Report.* U.S. Department of the Treasury.

Malpezzi, S., G. H. Chun, and R. K. Green. 1998. *Real Estate Economics* 26 (2): 235–74.

Nadler, J., G. Raab, K. Rosenberg, and J. Forde. 1993. "Mapping Default Zones. *Mortgage Banking* (October): 127–35.

Ozanne, L., and T. Thibodeau. 1983. "Explaining Metropolitan House Price Differences." *Journal of Urban Economics* 13: 51–66.

Pollakowski, H. O., M. A. Stegman, and W. Rohe. 1992. "Rates of Return on Housing of Low- and Moderate-Income Owners." Working Paper 92-4. Joint Center for Housing Studies, Harvard University.

Pozdena, R. J. 1988. *The Modern Economics of Housing.* New York: Quorum Books.

Rothenberg, J., G. C. Galster, R. V. Butler, and J. R. Pitkin. 1991. *The Maze of Urban Housing Markets.* University of Chicago Press.

Scanlon, E. 1996. "Homeownership and Its Impacts: Implications for Housing Policy for Low-Income Families." Working Paper 96-2. Center for Social Development, Washington University.

Seward, J. A., C. J. Delaney, and M. T. Smith. 1992. "An Empirical Analysis of Housing Price Appreciation in a Market Stratified by Size and Value of the Housing Stock." *Journal of Real Estate Research* 7 (2): 195–205.

Simons, R. A, R. G. Quercia, and I. Maric. 1998."The Value Impact of New Residential Construction and Disinvestment on Residential Sales Price." *Journal of Real Estate Research* 15 (1/2): 147–61.

Smith, L. B., and M. H. C. Ho. 1996. "The Relative Price Differential between Higher and Lower Priced Homes." *Journal of Housing Economics* 5: 1–17.

Temkin, K., and W. M. Rohe. 1998. "Social Capital and Neighborhood Stability: An Empirical Investigation." *Housing Policy Debate* 9 (1): 61–88.

8

Home Price Appreciation in Low- and Moderate-Income Markets

KARL E. CASE AND MARYNA MARYNCHENKO

At the turn of the millennium, fully two-thirds of American households were owner-occupants. In addition, through the middle of the year 2000, real home prices were rising in all but a handful of major metropolitan areas in the United States. In such a climate, the benefits of homeownership seem obvious. Owners whose property appreciates accumulate wealth, and most are protected from rising out-of-pocket housing costs by fixed or slowly adjusting mortgage rates. Renter households, in contrast, are hurt by rising real rents, and they see the dream of homeownership becoming ever more elusive.

But is homeownership the solution for all? Clearly, there are periods of time and locations where owning a home has been a liability. Examples of substantial decreases in home values have occurred in Texas, New England, California, Alaska, and Hawaii in recent years. Homeowners are also leveraged, and a home purchase is the biggest investment that most households ever make. A household that puts 10 percent down to purchase a home doubles its money if the home appreciates 10 percent. That same household sees its investment wiped out if home prices fall 10 percent.

Clearly, home price appreciation is only part of the return to an investment in an owner-occupied unit. The bulk of the return to owning accrues to the owner household in the form of valuable housing services. In addition, there are costs to be considered. The physical structure must be maintained, and even with maintenance, systems become obsolete; property taxes must be paid; mortgage interest rates and origination fees vary with time and by borrower; heating bills and insurance costs can be substantial; and of course there may or may not be income tax advantages to owning. Nonetheless, whether home prices rise or fall over time will determine to a large extent whether the investment was a good one.

This chapter begins with a broad-brush look at state and metropolitan area housing markets over the past quarter-century. The available state and metropolitan area data reveal substantial differences in the pattern of price appreciation across time and space. While some areas have experienced dramatic boom and bust cycles, other areas have experienced relatively low variance or strong trend appreciation. The second part of the chapter looks in detail at zip code–level price changes over a period of seventeen years in three major metropolitan areas: Boston, Chicago, and Los Angeles. Although the experiences in three metropolitan areas cannot be generalized to the nation as a whole, we believe that much can be learned from studying patterns of price movement across neighborhoods within cities.

Methodology

The patterns of change in home value described here are estimated with repeat sales price indexes. Case-Shiller (CS) weighted repeat sales indexes were used where available (see Case and Shiller 1987, 1989). In addition, the Office of Federal Housing Enterprise Oversight (OFHEO) makes available state-level repeat value indexes produced using Fannie Mae and Freddie Mac data. OFHEO uses a similar index construction methodology (the WRS method of Case and Shiller, 1987), but its indexes are in part based on appraisals rather than exclusively on arm's-length transactions. CS indexes are estimated only with arm's-length transactions and use controls, to the extent possible, for changes in property characteristics. Nonetheless, to capture broad movements over long time periods, the indexes tend to track each other quite well.

Changes in aggregate OFHEO indexes are presented in table 8-1, along with changes in the consumer price index (CPI) for the same time periods. On average, house prices in the United States have risen 137.8 percent since 1980, while prices in general increased 105.9 percent. In addition, price increases have exceeded inflation in eight of the nine census regions. Over twenty years, the largest increases have been in New England, the Mid-Atlantic, and the Pacific regions. Only in the West South Central region have prices fallen in real terms since 1980.

Real rates of increase accelerated during the five-year period from 1996 to 2001. For the United States as a whole, prices are up 27.3 percent versus 12.4 percent for the CPI. During 2000, home price increases were 6.5 percent, while

Table 8-1. *Percentage Change in House Prices for the Period Ending March 31, 2000*

Division	*Division ranking*	*One-year change*	*Five-year change*	*Since 1980*
New England	1	10.2	33.4	242.8
West North Central	2	7.8	31.1	110.0
Pacific	3	7.1	28.5	166.8
Middle Atlantic	4	6.5	21.3	186.1
East North Central	5	6.3	30.8	139.1
Mountain	6	5.9	30.3	123.4
South Atlantic	7	5.7	25.1	129.4
West South Central	8	5.3	23.4	60.2
East South Central	9	3.9	26.2	117.2
United States[a]	. . .	6.5	27.3	137.8
CPI-U	. . .	3.2	12.4	105.9

Source: Office of Federal Housing Enterprise Oversight, House Price Index, First Quarter 2000; Bureau of Labor Statistics, All Urban Consumers.

a. U.S. figures based on weighted division average.

the CPI was up only 3.2 percent. During 2000 and the period 1996–2001, real prices increased in all nine census regions.

Zip Code–Level Indexes

To explore intracity variations in the pattern of appreciation over time, we used zip code–level indexes produced by Case Shiller Weiss Inc. CSW produces an index for an area only when the number of paired sales is sufficient to produce reasonable confidence intervals on the coefficient estimates. A total of 428 indexes were available from the three metropolitan areas chosen. The Boston data are made up of 235 zip code indexes with observations between the first quarter of 1983 and the second quarter of 1998. The Chicago data represent eighty-four zip codes with observations between the first quarter of 1987 and second quarter of 1998. The Los Angeles data contain information on 109 zip codes between the first quarter of 1983 and the second quarter of 1998.

It is important to reiterate that the three metropolitan areas being examined here do not represent a random sample of the U.S. housing market. In some ways they were chosen not to be representative, but rather because their housing markets have behaved very differently over time.

Table 8-2 presents the characteristics of the zip code samples for each of the three metropolitan areas. The figure breaks the zip codes into quintiles based on income and shows data for the highest and lowest deciles. The data are from the 1990 census.

Median income figures show the same pattern for all three cities. Boston had higher median income than either Los Angeles or Chicago, and income was

Table 8-2. *Characteristics of Census Tract Groups by Quintile/Decile: Income, Rent, and Housing Value*

Decile or quintile	*Median income ($)*	*Median monthly rent ($)*	*Median housing value ($)*	*Annual rent housing value*	*Income housing value*
Los Angeles					
Top 10 percent	69,997.27	931.27	418,445.91	0.0280656	0.167279
Top 1/5	61,228.10	879.00	386,186.00	0.0291087	0.158546
2d 1/5	44,747.59	740.73	259,618.18	0.0364042	0.172359
3d 1/5	38,676.36	671.41	255,422.77	0.0347135	0.151421
4th 1/5	33,182.00	631.77	215,968.18	0.0363928	0.153643
Bottom 1/5	25,756.00	566.09	179,036.36	0.0402097	0.143863
Bottom 10 percent	23,502.64	546.46	185,127.27	0.0394882	0.126954
Total	40,529.84	696.14	258,081.72	0.0354232	0.157043
Chicago					
Top 10 percent	62,871.63	702.75	213,687.50	0.0691433	0.294222
Top 1/5	57,561.94	641.69	184,806.25	0.0570721	0.311472
2d 1/5	47,638.59	658.71	132,723.53	0.061004	0.358931
3d 1/5	43,098.18	600.24	123,270.59	0.0615719	0.349623
4th 1/5	36,970.00	532.88	99,558.82	0.0683252	0.371338
Bottom 1/5	27,972.59	455.35	92,235.29	0.0619974	0.303274
Bottom 10 percent	24,796.00	435.63	83,187.50	0.0662436	0.298074
Total	42,470.71	577.01	125,825.00	0.0620527	0.337538
Boston					
Top 10 percent	73,576.58	805.88	302,129.21	0.0327019	0.243527
Top 1/5	65,931.17	750.68	258,083.00	0.0361367	0.255465
2d 1/5	49,873.94	686.91	183,300.00	0.0462082	0.272089
3d 1/5	43,330.81	640.83	162,302.13	0.0478546	0.266976
4th 1/5	38,122.87	592.38	149,931.92	0.0478222	0.254268
Bottom 1/5	29,269.64	519.32	134,212.77	0.0470045	0.218084
Bottom 10 percent	26,142.38	485.92	129,166.67	0.0453193	0.202393
Total	45,305.69	638.03	177,566	0.0450053	0.255148

Source: Authors' tabulations using 1990 U.S. census public use data.

higher in every quintile. Chicago had a slightly more even distribution of income than either Boston or Los Angeles. The ratio of income in the wealthiest 10 percent of zip codes to income in the poorest 10 percent of zip codes was 3.0 in Los Angeles, 2.8 in Boston, and 2.5 in Chicago.

Los Angeles was the most expensive of the three housing markets, for both rental and owner-occupied units. Median monthly rent in Los Angeles was nearly $700, while median rent in Boston was $638 and in Chicago $577. The ratio of rent in the highest decile to rent in the lowest decile was between 1.6 and 1.7 in all three cities. The median price of owner-occupied units in Los Angeles was more than twice the median value of owner-occupied units in Chicago and nearly 1.5 times the median value of owner-occupied units in Boston.

The two right-hand columns of tables 8-2 and 8-3 show interesting ratios for the three metropolitan areas in 1990. Column 4 shows the ratio of median monthly rent to owner-occupied house value for each quintile/decile. The ratio was substantially higher in Chicago in all subgroupings than in the other two cities and was lowest in Los Angeles. Not surprisingly, the ratio of income to house value, a crude measure of affordability, was more than twice as high in Chicago as in Los Angeles. In addition, the ratio of income-to-house value was the lowest in the poor areas of Los Angeles and the highest in the middle-income areas of Chicago.

Although its housing market was the most expensive among the three, Los Angeles had the highest percentage of households in poverty: 11.1 percent; the figure was 5.6 percent for Chicago and 5.5 percent for Boston. In all three cities there was a larger percentage of African Americans in the lower-income zip codes, with substantially more concentration apparent in the low-income zip codes of Chicago.

Finally, Los Angeles had a substantially larger percentage of recent immigrants. Although immigrants were scattered across all income quintiles, the largest proportion in all three cities was in the lowest income decile.

Appreciation in High- and Low-Income Areas

This section describes patterns of appreciation and depreciation in low- and high-income neighborhoods. The last section of the chapter presents some possible explanations for the observed patterns.

Tables 8-4 and 8-5 and figure 8-1 present the main results. Table 8-4 presents annualized increases in value for Boston's 235 zip codes between the beginning of 1983 and 1988. The Boston market experienced a dramatic boom between 1983 and 1988, with home prices rising at a nominal rate of 18 percent annually and at a real rate of 13.8 percent over the five-year period.

During the Boston boom, the low-income portion of the market experienced the highest rates of appreciation. The bottom decile increased at a nominal annual rate of over 20 percent, while the top decile increased at a rate of 17.4 percent. What was remarkable and telling about the price increases in Boston was how uniform and widespread the phenomenon was. Over the period, the average house in eastern Massachusetts appreciated nearly 140 percent, while housing in the poorest 10 percent of zip codes increased more than 165 percent. As a result, over $100 billion was added to household net worth over the five-year period (see Case, 1991).

Over the next four years, however, Massachusetts and New England as a whole experienced a severe recession. Homeowners who bought near the peak in late 1988 experienced substantial declines in value. While nominal values fell at a rate of 3.8 percent on average, real declines approached 8 percent annually. In nominal terms, the total decline was about 16 percent on average, while in real

Table 8-3. *Characteristics of Census Tract Groups by Quintile/Decile: Race, Poverty, Size and Age of Household, Foreign-Born Owners, Tenure, Owner-Occupied Units*

Decile or quintile	*Percent African American*	*Percent in poverty*	*Percent one-person household*	*Percent over age 65*	*Percent foreign-born who entered after 1982*	*Percent who lived in same house in 1985*	*Percent owner-occupied housing units*
Los Angeles							
Top 10 percent	7.3	3.8	18.9	14.7	24.2	51.5	78.4
Top 1/5	7.9	4.3	20.9	15.2	27.5	52.6	73.6
2d 1/5	5.2	6.7	22.3	16.8	32.1	53.2	65.8
3d 1/5	9.4	9.1	26.4	15.7	34.3	49.9	56.1
4th 1/5	7.3	13.3	23.0	13.1	38.2	46.5	45.9
Bottom 1/5	21.3	21.6	23.1	10.6	42.9	43.4	32.6
Bottom 10 percent	15.6	24.5	22.9	11.2	43.6	43.4	29.1
Total	10.2	11.1	23.2	14.3	35.1	49.1	54.6
Chicago							
Top 10 percent	1.5	1.9	16.7	13.2	24.4	53.1	84.7
Top 1/5	1.4	2.1	17.7	12.9	22.8	53.4	82.0
2d 1/5	2.3	2.4	20.8	11.2	27.8	49.8	74.7
3d 1/5	5.4	3.7	21.7	15.1	24.4	56.3	75.0
4th 1/5	11.1	4.5	25.2	19.9	19.1	60.7	72.0
Bottom 1/5	27.7	15.1	29.5	17.6	28.3	53.6	46.4
Bottom 10 percent	37.7	19.5	29.1	14.5	31.1	51.6	37.1
Total	9.7	5.6	23.0	15.4	24.5	54.7	69.9
Boston							
Top 10 percent	1.1	2.1	14.9	14.4	21.0	66.3	86.0
Top 1/5	1.0	2.3	15.5	13.9	20.2	66.2	84.4
2d 1/5	0.8	3.1	16.9	13.1	14.0	61.9	80.2
3d 1/5	1.1	4.1	20.8	15.3	18.2	61.3	72.4
4th 1/5	3.2	5.7	22.4	17.3	18.8	61.4	68.8
Bottom 1/5	4.8	12.4	27.7	17.8	27.8	54.5	46.1
Bottom 10 percent	6.1	15.5	28.3	18.3	27.3	54.7	40.9
Total	2.2	5.5	20.7	15.5	19.8	61.1	70.4

Source: Authors' tabulations using 1990 U.S. census public use data.

Table 8-4. *Annualized Increases in Value (Nominal and Real) in Boston, 1983–98*

Decile or quintile	*Number of zip codes*	*Annual percentage change in aggregate Case-Shiller index between periods (CPI-adjusted in parentheses)*			
		1983:1–1988:2	*1988:2–1992:2*	*1992:2–1998:2*	*1983:1–1998:2*
Top 10 percent	24	17.4	−2.7	5.9	7.5
		(13.3)	(−6.7)	(3.4)	(4.0)
Top 1/5	47	17.2	−3.0	5.6	7.2
		(13.1)	(−7.0)	(3.0)	(3.7)
2d 1/5	47	17.0	−3.8	4.5	6.4
		(12.9)	(−7.8)	(1.9)	(3.0)
3d 1/5	47	17.5	−3.8	4.4	6.6
		(13.4)	(−7.8)	(1.9)	(3.1)
4th 1/5	47	18.5	−3.8	4.0	6.8
		(14.4)	(−7.7)	(1.5)	(3.3)
Bottom 1/5	47	19.4	−4.3	3.1	6.5
		(15.2)	(−8.3)	(0.6)	(3.0)
Bottom 10 percent	24	20.4	−4.3	2.0	6.4
		(16.2)	(−8.2)	(−0.5)	(3.0)
Total	235	17.9	−3.8	4.3	6.7
		(13.8)	(−7.7)	(1.8)	(3.2)

Source: Authors' tabulations using Case, Shiller, and Weiss data.

Table 8-5. *Annualized Increases in Value (Nominal and Real) in Chicago, 1983–98*

Decile or quintile	*Number of zip codes*	*Annual percentage change in aggregate Case-Shiller index between periods (CPI-adjusted in parentheses)*		
		1987:1–1992:1	*1992:1–1998:2*	*1987:1–1998:2*
Top 10 percent	8	5.8	3.8	4.8
		(1.5)	(1.3)	(1.4)
Top 1/5	16	5.9	3.6	4.7
		(1.5)	(1.1)	(1.3)
2d 1/5	17	5.9	3.5	4.7
		(1.6)	(1.0)	(1.3)
3d 1/5	17	6.8	3.9	5.3
		(2.5)	(1.4)	(1.9)
4th 1/5	17	8.0	4.4	6.1
		(3.5)	(1.9)	(2.7)
Bottom 1/5	17	9.8	6.1	7.8
		(5.3)	(3.5)	(4.4)
Bottom 10 percent	8	10.6	6.7	8.5
		(6.1)	(4.1)	(5.1)
Total	84	7.3	4.3	5.7
		(2.9)	(1.8)	(2.3)

Source: Authors' tabulations using Case, Shiller, and Weiss data.

Figure 8-1. *Boston: CSW Index (nominal values, 1983: 1 = 100)*

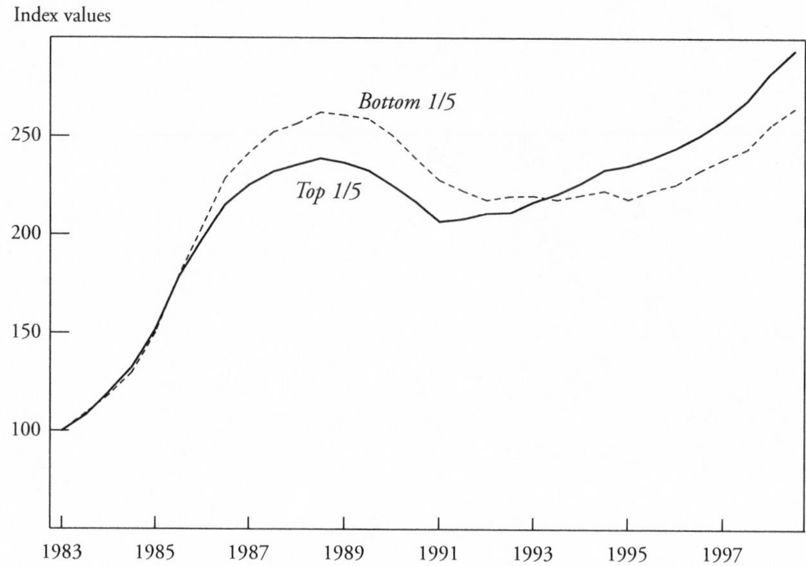

terms it was closer to one-third. The biggest declines occurred in the lowest-income zip codes. Real declines exceeded 8 percent in the bottom quintile but were only 6.7 percent in the highest decile.

Finally, prices turned around early in 1992 and rose steadily through the end of the observation period in 1998. During this period, the high end of the market substantially outperformed the low end. Nominal price increases in the highest-income group of zip codes were three times greater than price increases in the lowest-income group of zip codes. In fact, in the bottom decile, real prices actually declined at a rate of 0.5 percent annually over the six-year period.

Figure 8-1 shows the pattern for the entire period for the top and bottom quintiles. Over the entire boom-bust-recovery cycle, the high-end market did somewhat better than the low-end market, but the differences were relatively minor. The highest quintile appreciated in real terms at a rate of 3.7 percent annually; the lowest quintile appreciated in real terms at a rate of 3.0 percent annually.

As shown in Table 8-5, the pattern was completely different in Chicago. Real rates of appreciation were steady with only modest signs of cyclicality. Between 1987 and 1992, housing appreciated at an average annual rate of 7.3 percent in nominal terms, or 2.9 percent in real terms. As in Boston, the top end of the distribution lagged the bottom, with the bottom decile appreciating nominally at nearly twice the rate of the top decile.

The same pattern continued, although at a somewhat slower rate, between 1992 and 1998. Nominal increases averaged 6.7 percent annually in the lowest-

Figure 8-2. *Chicago: CSW Index (nominal values, 1987: 1 = 100)*

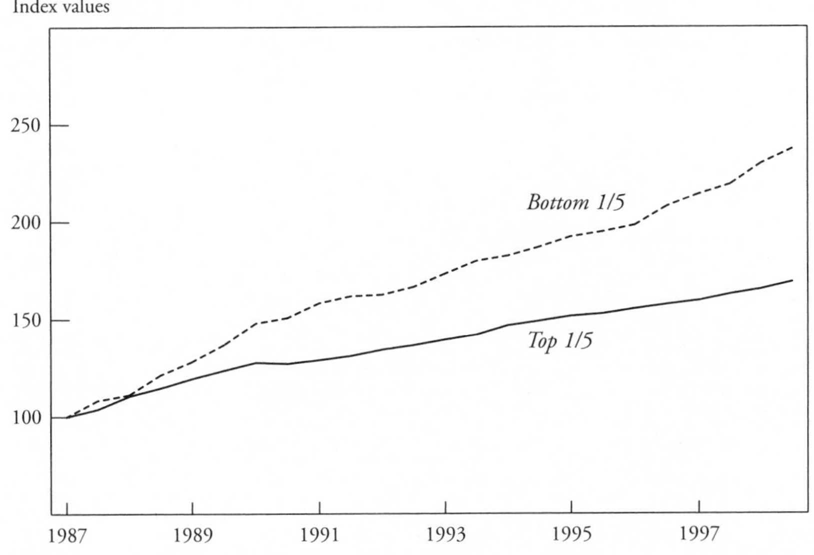

income decile while nominal increases averaged just 3.8 percent in the highest-income decile.

Figure 8-2 shows indexes for the top and bottom quintiles over the eleven-year period. Overall, between 1987 and 1998, the poorest neighborhoods did substantially better than the more wealthy neighborhoods. Real appreciation averaged 5.1 percent annually in the bottom decile and 4.4 percent annually in the bottom quintile while averaging only 1.4 percent annually in the top decile and 1.3 percent in the top quintile.

Table 8-6 presents the results of tabulations for Los Angeles. Los Angeles experienced a substantial boom between 1983 and 1990, with annual appreciation rates averaging over 10 percent in nominal terms and nearly 6 percent in real terms. The pattern was remarkably uniform with no statistically significant difference between increases in any of the quintiles. Home prices in virtually all of the 109 zip codes appreciated at approximately the same rate. Between 1990 and 1993, real home prices declined by more than a third in Los Angeles, with the largest drop occurring at the high end of the distribution. In nominal terms, the top 10 percent of zip codes fell at an annual rate of 9.1 percent, while the bottom 10 percent of zip codes fell at an annual rate of 7.5 percent.

Between 1993 and 1998 in Los Angeles, home prices in all but the top quintile stagnated in real terms. In the top quintile and the top decile, nominal appreciation was just over 4 percent, while real appreciation was about 1 percent annually. The bottom quintile and the bottom decile experienced virtually no nominal appreciation, with real values falling at a rate of about 2.5 percent.

Table 8-6. *Annualized Increases in Value (Nominal and Real) in Los Angeles, 1983–98*

		Annual percentage change in aggregate Case-Shiller index between periods (CPI-adjusted in parentheses)			
Decile or quintile	*Number of zip codes*	*1983:1–1990:2*	*1990:2–1993:2*	*1993:2–1998:2*	*1983:1–1998:2*
Top 10 percent	11	10.6	–9.1	4.0	4.4
		(6.3)	(–11.8)	(1.6)	(1.0)
Top 1/5	21	10.4	–8.5	3.4	4.2
		(6.1)	(–11.2)	(0.9)	(0.8)
2d 1/5	22	9.9	–7.3	1.5	3.6
		(5.6)	(–10.0)	(–0.9)	(0.3)
3d 1/5	22	10.3	–8.2	1.8	3.7
		(6.0)	(–10.9)	(–0.6)	(0.4)
4th 1/5	22	10.4	–8.0	1.5	3.7
		(6.0)	(–10.7)	(–0.9)	(0.4)
Bottom 1/5	22	10.3	–7.1	–0.4	3.2
		(6.0)	(–9.9)	(–2.7)	(–0.1)
Bottom 10 percent	11	10.7	–7.5	–0.1	3.4
		(6.4)	(–10.2)	(–2.5)	(0.1)
Total	109	10.2	–7.8	1.6	3.7
		(5. 9)	(–10.5)	(–0.8)	(0.3)

Source: Authors' tabulations using Case, Shiller, and Weiss data.

Figure 8-3 shows the pattern in Los Angeles for the top quintile and bottom quintile over the fifteen years. During the first seven years of the cycle, top and bottom quintiles experienced similar booms; during the bust, the low end fell the least; over the last five years of the observation period, the high end did somewhat better than the low end.

To summarize, while substantial differences in the patterns of home price appreciation and depreciation can be observed over time and across the three metropolitan areas, by and large lower-income neighborhoods have done reasonably well in comparison with higher-income areas of the same cities.

Equity Accumulation from Homeownership

Tables 8-7, 8-8, and 8-9 present the results of an exercise designed to estimate the potential wealth accumulation of ownership during different time periods in the three metropolitan areas. First, median home value was estimated for each zip code grouping from the American Housing Survey. The American Housing Survey (AHS) contains cross-tabulations of income and house value that were smoothed into continuous cumulative distributions by fitting spline functions to the data. The most recent releases of AHS data were for 1993 in Boston and

Figure 8-3. *Los Angeles: CSW Index (nominal values, 1983: 1 = 100)*

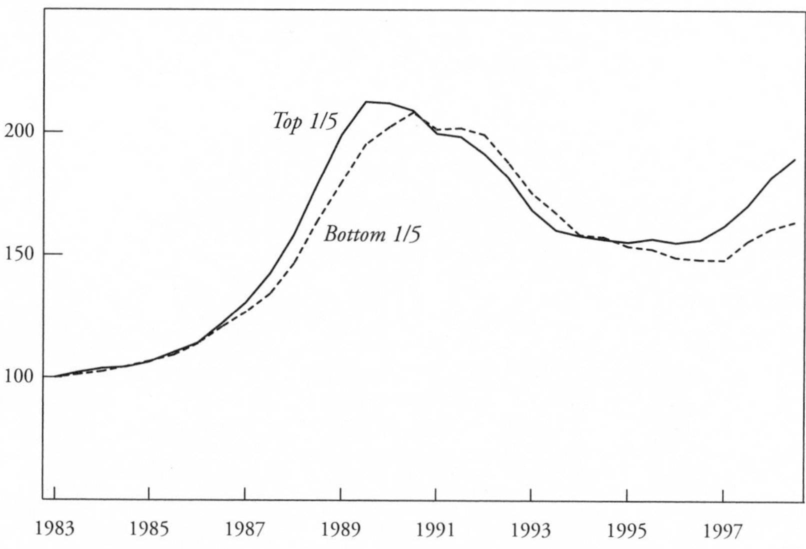

1995 in Los Angeles and Chicago. Figures for 1993 and 1995 were then inflated/deflated with CSW zip code indexes back to 1987 and forward to 1998.

Table 8-7 shows equity buildup for the median home buyer in each of the zip code groupings, assuming a home buyer purchased in 1987 with an 80 percent mortgage. For example, the median value of houses in the top decile in Boston was estimated to be $390,642 in 1987. A household purchasing that house in 1987 would begin with equity of $78,128. By 1991 that equity would have fallen by nearly 40 percent to $48,889. By 1995, however, the household equity would have risen to over $100,000, and by 1998 to nearly $200,000.

At the other end of the income distribution, the median value of houses in the bottom decile in Boston was estimated to be $59,426 in 1987. A household that purchased that house in 1987 would have begun with equity of $11,885. By 1991 that equity would have eroded to $9,630, and by 1995 it would stand at just $7,322. Finally, by 1998, the investment would have increased to $13,323, producing a nominal leveraged rate of return of just 1 percent. Recall that in 1987 Boston was approaching a cyclical peak in home prices.

In Chicago, rates of appreciation have been more steady, and lower-income neighborhoods have consistently outperformed higher-income neighborhoods. In Chicago, a home buyer in the top decile in 1987 would have begun with equity of $49,817, which would have grown to $120,342 by 1991, to $179,000 by 1995, and to $215,000 by 1998. Equity would have grown at 14.2 percent

Table 8-7. *Increase in Equity: Hypothetical Home Purchase, 1987–98*

Dollars

Distribution of households	*Median house value, 1987*	*Equity in house, 1987 (20 percent down payment)*	*Equity in house, 1991*	*Equity in house, 1995*	*Equity in house, 1998*
Boston					
Top 10 percent	390,642	78,128	48,889	130,734	194,752
Top 1/5	299,822	59,964	35,119	93,145	136,131
2d 1/5	212,006	42,401	21,807	51,226	71,415
3d 1/5	171,824	34,365	18,930	40,491	55,863
4th 1/5	130,908	26,182	17,238	27,293	41,957
Bottom 1/5	82,511	16,502	11,781	12,281	21,393
Bottom 10 percent	59,426	11,885	9,630	7,322	13,323
Chicago					
Top 10 percent	249,083	49,817	120,342	178,974	215,374
Top 1/5	184,068	36,814	90,209	131,815	157,154
2d 1/5	119,312	23,862	59,813	85,898	101,377
3d 1/5	84,473	16,895	46,293	68,162	81,613
4th 1/5	57,692	11,538	36,532	53,513	66,200
Bottom 1/5	31,332	6,266	24,540	35,176	46,948
Bottom 10 percent	20,800	4,160	17,978	25,582	34,915
Los Angeles					
Top 10 percent	372,103	74,421	286,407	151,541	238,306
Top 1/5	333,757	66,751	243,212	130,403	197,791
2d 1/5	207,409	41,482	148,260	79,763	101,843
3d 1/5	163,956	32,791	122,132	61,692	81,194
4th 1/5	132,152	26,430	98,237	52,292	67,598
Bottom 1/5	85,640	17,128	67,554	35,380	40,261
Bottom 10 percent	60,987	12,197	49,241	26,410	30,260

Source: Authors' tabulations using Case, Shiller, and Weiss data.

Table 8-8. *Increase in Equity: Hypothetical Home Purchase, 1991–98*
Dollars

Distribution of households	*Median house value, 1991*	*Equity in house, 1991 (20 percent down payment)*	*Equity in house, 1995*	*Equity in house, 1998*
Boston				
Top 10 percent	361,402	72,280	130,734	218,144
Top 1/5	274,977	54,995	93,145	156,007
2d 1/5	191,411	38,282	51,226	87,890
3d 1/5	156,390	31,278	40,491	68,210
4th 1/5	121,964	24,393	27,293	49,112
Bottom 1/5	77,789	15,558	12,281	25,171
Bottom 10 percent	57,170	11,434	7,322	15,128
Chicago				
Top 10 percent	319,608	63,922	122,553	169,858
Top 1/5	237,464	47,493	89,099	121,263
2d 1/5	155,262	31,052	57,137	77,478
3d 1/5	113,872	22,774	44,643	61,739
4th 1/5	82,685	16,537	33,518	47,468
Bottom 1/5	49,605	9,921	20,557	34,652
Bottom 10 percent	34,618	6,924	14,528	25,626
Los Angeles				
Top 10 percent	584,089	116,818	–18,048	68,717
Top 1/5	510,218	102,044	–10,765	56,622
2d 1/5	314,187	62,837	–5,659	16,421
3d 1/5	253,297	50,659	–9,781	9,721
4th 1/5	203,958	40,792	–5,153	10,153
Bottom 1/5	136,066	27,213	–4,961	–79
Bottom 10 percent	98,030	19,606	–3,224	626

Source: Authors' tabulations using Case, Shiller, and Weiss data.

annually. But the leveraged appreciation in equity is even greater at the low end. A home buyer in the bottom decile in 1987 would have seen equity grow from $4,160 in 1987 to $18,000 in 1991, to $25,600 in 1995, and to nearly $35,000 by 1998. Equity growth in the lowest decile averaged over 20 percent annually.

During the same period a 1987 Los Angeles home buyer with an 80 percent mortgage would have experienced quite a ride. In the top decile between 1987 and 1991, equity would have increased from $74,421 to $286,407; in the bottom decile equity would have increased from $12,197 to $49,241, a fourfold increase. For the same home buyers, the gains from the boom were roughly cut in half by the bust in Los Angeles. Equity in the highest decile eroded from $286,407 in 1991 to just $151,541 by 1995; equity in the lowest decile eroded from $49,241 in 1991 to $26,410 in 1995. Gains in equity over the last three years of the observation period in Los Angeles were largely concentrated in the upper-income brackets.

Table 8-9. *Increase in Equity: Hypothetical Home Purchase, 1995–98*
Dollars

Distribution of households	*Median house value, 1995*	*Equity in house 1995 (20 percent down payment)*	*Equity in house, 1998*
Boston			
Top 10 percent	419,855	83,971	171,381
Top 1/5	313,127	62,625	125,487
2d 1/5	204,355	40,871	77,536
3d 1/5	165,603	33,121	60,840
4th 1/5	124,864	24,973	46,792
Bottom 1/5	74,513	14,903	27,792
Bottom 10 percent	53,059	10,612	18,417
Chicago			
Top 10 percent	378,240	75,648	112,048
Top 1/5	279,070	55,814	81,153
2d 1/5	181,347	36,269	51,749
3d 1/5	135,740	27,148	40,599
4th 1/5	99,667	19,933	32,620
Bottom 1/5	60,241	12,048	23,821
Bottom 10 percent	42,222	8,444	17,777
Los Angeles			
Top 10 percent	449,223	89,845	176,610
Top 1/5	397,409	79,482	146,869
2d 1/5	245,690	49,138	71,218
3d 1/5	192,857	38,571	58,073
4th 1/5	158,014	31,603	46,909
Bottom 1/5	103,892	20,778	25,660
Bottom 10 percent	75,200	15,040	18,890

Source: Authors' tabulations using Case, Shiller, and Weiss data.

Table 8-8 shows the experience of hypothetical home buyers who purchased in 1991. High-end home buyers in Boston would have seen their equity grow by more than 80 percent between 1991 and 1995, while those who purchased in the lower-income zip code groups would have lost more than a third of theirs.

Households who purchased houses in Los Angeles in 1991 had negative equity by 1995 in both higher-income and lower-income neighborhoods. A home buyer in the top 10 percent of neighborhoods by income would have had to put down over $100,000; by 1995 that buyer would have –$18,048 in equity. Similarly, a household buying in the lower-income zip code grouping in Los Angeles in 1991 would have seen equity decline from $19,606 to –$3,224 by 1995.

In Chicago, the same period of time, 1991 to 1995, was very good for building equity through homeownership at both ends of the income distribution.

Equity more than doubled for home buyers in lower-income zip codes and nearly doubled for home buyers in the higher-income zip codes.

The same figure shows the equity buildup or loss of equity for 1991 home buyers by 1998. Once again, low-income home buyers in Chicago and high-income home buyers in Boston built substantial equity over the seven-year period; low-income home buyers in Boston built modest equity over the seven-year period; and home buyers in Los Angeles, particularly in lower-income zip code groupings, saw equity substantially eroded.

Finally, the same exercise is shown in table 8-9 for home buyers who purchased property in 1995. Since house prices have been rising in real terms in all three cities, homeownership was an unambiguously good strategy for accumulating wealth. For home buyers in lower-income neighborhoods, the buildup was the greatest in Chicago, where equity more than doubled over the three years, and least in Los Angeles, where equity increased by 25.6 percent.

There is no question that in some areas and during some periods of time leveraged investment in homeownership is a good strategy for building equity for low-income households. It is also true, however, that leveraged investment in homeownership can lead to serious losses.

The Causes of Changes in House Prices

An extensive literature exists on the causes of changes in house prices. A few studies compare the performance of low- and high-end markets. Case and Shiller (1994) focus attention on the pattern of price appreciation and depreciation in Los Angeles and Boston between 1982 and 1985. They conclude that prices of property at the low end of the distribution in Boston did better than prices at the high end in part because the economic growth of the 1980s reached farther down into the income distribution than it did in California. Unemployment fell much more sharply in Boston than it did in Los Angeles in the mid-1980s. As a result, first-time home buyers entered the market, driving up ownership rates among lower-income households in Boston substantially faster than was true in Los Angeles. In addition, housing prices on average in Los Angeles were 70 percent above the U.S. median at the beginning of the boom, while housing prices in Boston were only 17 percent above the U.S. median. Thus economic expansion led initially to a substantial increase in affordability at the low end of the distribution in Boston, but the gap remained large at the low end in Los Angeles.

Although the overall decline in the early 1990s in Los Angeles was deeper and longer than the corresponding decline in Boston, the low end of the distribution in Los Angeles declined less than the high end, and the opposite was true in Boston. Case and Shiller conclude that the explanation lies in the relative expansion of low-income demand in Los Angeles due to immigration and the relative expansion of low-income supply in Boston due to massive conversions of rental property to condominium units, many in low-income areas.

Other studies that compare price movements in upper and lower price tiers include Poterba (1991) and Mayer (1993). Using data from 1970–86 for four cities (Atlanta, Chicago, Dallas, and Oakland), Poterba shows that properties in the upper tier appreciated faster than properties in the lower tier. He attributes the pattern to high marginal tax rates and expectations of rising inflation.

Mayer, using the same data, argues that Poterba's focus is too narrow and looks at several alternative explanations for the observed patterns. Finding that prices in the upper tier in the four cities are more volatile than prices in the lower tier, he focuses on changes in user cost and other cyclical factors.

Smith and Tesarek (1991) show that the patterns of decline in Houston during the 1985 through 1987 bust were similar to the declines in California in the early 1990s. In Houston, "high-quality" houses lost nearly 30 percent of their value. Houses in the middle-quality tier lost 24 percent of their value, and houses in the lower tier lost only 18 percent of their value. Smith and Tesarek suggest several reasons for the pattern in Houston. First, the upper end of the market experienced the greatest appreciation during the boom. Second, building was concentrated on the upper end of the quality range, glutting the market. Third, sharp reductions in "entrepreneurial and professional income" led to steeper declines in demand in the top markets.

A major concern in looking at appreciation in low-income neighborhoods is that increases may be driven by large changes in value in neighborhoods that are gentrifying. First it should be noted that, to the extent possible, CS repeat sales indexes are quality controlled. That is, when a significant portion of the stock in a neighborhood is upgraded, either the upgraded properties are excluded from the sample or the index will not compute because of high standard errors on the coefficients.

In order to determine whether gentrification is a problem in our sample of zip codes, we did two things. First, we looked specifically at the most rapidly appreciating individual zip codes in the bottom quintile of the bottom decile of each of the three cities. Second, we looked at the variance in home price changes across our quintiles and deciles. If home price changes in the bottom decile were driven by only a few neighborhoods, the variance would be high.

Because there are no current time series data on demographics or income at the zip code level for our cities, we had to rely on "local knowledge" and press reports to identify gentrifying neighborhoods. Although we found examples of neighborhoods in which the housing stock had been upgraded and where significant displacement was likely to have occurred in our lower-income zip code clusters (Roslindale in Boston, Pasadena in Los Angeles, and Logan Square in Chicago), appreciation and depreciation of property values took place at roughly the same rates across the bulk of zip codes in our lowest-income quintile.

Exploratory Regressions

Although a structural model of price adjustment across neighborhoods is beyond the scope of this chapter, we conducted three preliminary and exploratory regressions to see if there is any systematic variation in the pattern of price appreciation across the zip code groupings and cities. The dependent variable is the annualized rate of appreciation in home value over the entire sample period, and the unit of observation is the zip code. (The tables presenting the full results of these regressions are available from the authors.)

Not surprisingly, the regressions seem to reflect some of the patterns observed in the discussion above. For example, neighborhoods with higher median home prices and lower levels of poverty in Boston did better over the entire period, ceteris paribus, while neighborhoods with concentrations of poverty in Chicago seem to have done somewhat better, ceteris paribus. No variables were statistically significant in the Los Angeles regression. Clearly, no consistent pattern emerged for the three cities.

Conclusion

The results of the tabulations presented here reveal a complex pattern of house price changes from which generalization is difficult. Several things can be concluded, however. First, whether homeownership is a good or bad investment clearly depends on the time of purchase, conditions in the regional economy, and the dynamics of supply and demand at the local level. Second, since home purchase is almost always leveraged, particularly among low-income households, effects of price changes on equity accumulation over particular periods of time can be dramatic.

Among low-income households, homeownership has been an excellent vehicle for asset accumulation since 1987 in Chicago. The same can be said for low-income home buyers who purchased in the early 1980s in Boston and for home buyers who purchased in 1995 in any of the three cities. However, significant periods of decline have led to substantial losses for low-income households in Boston and to periods of substantial negative equity for low-income households in Los Angeles.

Clearly, from these data one cannot conclude that homeownership for low-income households is in general a good or bad strategy for accumulating wealth. As we argued above, home appreciation is but one component of the overall return to an investment in housing. But appreciation is an important component, and the results presented here are at least somewhat encouraging.

References

Browne, Lynn, and Karl Case. 1992. "How the Commercial Real Estate Boom Undid the Banks." In *Real Estate and the Credit Crunch,* edited by Lynn E. Browne and Eric S. Rosengren, pp. 57–97. Federal Reserve Bank of Boston, Conference Series 36 (September).

Case, Karl. 1991. "The Real Estate Cycle and the Regional Economy: The Consequences of the Massachusetts Boom of 1984–1987." *New England Economic Review* (September–October): 37–46; revised version in *Urban Studies* (Spring 1992): 171–83.

———. 1994. "Housing and Land Prices in the United States: 1950–1990." In *The Economics of Housing in the United States and Japan,* edited by James Poterba. Chicago: University of Chicago Press.

Case, Karl, and Leah Cook. 1989. "The Distributional Effects of Housing Price Booms: Winners and Losers in Boston, 1980–89." *New England Economic Review* (March–April): 3–12.

Case, Karl, and Christopher Mayer. 1996. "Housing Price Dynamics within a Metropolitan Area." *Regional Science and Urban Economics* 26 (3–4): 387–407.

———. 1995. "The Housing Cycle in Eastern Massachusetts: Variations among Cities and Towns." *New England Economic Review* (March–April): 24–40.

Case, Karl, and Robert Shiller. 1987. "Prices of Single-Family Homes since 1970: New Indexes for four Cities." *New England Economic Review* (September–October): 46–56.

———. 1988. "The Behavior of Home Buyers in Boom and Post Boom Markets." *New England Economic Review* (November–December): 29–46.

———. 1989. "The Efficiency of the Market for Single Family Homes." *American Economic Review* (March): 125–37.

———. 1990. "Forecasting Prices and Excess Returns in the Housing Market." *Journal of the American Real Estate and Urban Economics Association* 18 (4): 253–73.

———. 1994. "A Decade of Boom and Bust in the Prices of Single-Family Homes: Boston and Los Angeles: 1983–1993." *New England Economic Review* (March): 40–51.

———. 1996. "Default Risk and Real Estate Prices: The Use of Index-Based Futures and Options in Real Estate." *Journal of Housing Research* 7 (2): 243–58.

Case, Karl, Robert Shiller, and Allen N. Weiss. 1993. "Index-Based Futures and Options Markets in Real Estate." *Journal of Portfolio Management* (January): 83–92.

Mayer, Christopher. 1993. "Taxes, Income Distribution, and the Real Estate Cycle." *New England Economic Review* (May–June): 39–50.

Miles, Mike, and Nancy Tolleson. 1997. "A Revised Look at How Real Estate Compares with Other Major Components of Domestic Investment Universe." *Real Estate Finance* (Spring): 1–21.

Office of Federal Housing Enterprise Oversight. 1999. "1999 Report to Congress." Washington.

Poterba, James M. 1991. "House Price Dynamics: the Role of Taxes and Demography." *Brookings Papers on Economic Activity* (2): 110–26.

Smith, B. A., and W. P. Tesarek. 1991. "House Prices and Regional Real Estate Cycles: Market Adjustment in Houston." *AREUEA Journal* 79 (1): 12–37.

9

Policy Implications of Portfolio Choice in Underserved Mortgage Markets

WILLIAM N. GOETZMANN AND MATTHEW SPIEGEL

> *Expanding homeownership will strengthen our nation's families and communities, strengthen our economy, and expand this country's great middle class. Rekindling the dream of homeownership for America's working families can prepare our nation to embrace the rich possibilities of the twenty-first century.*
>
> —President Bill Clinton, 1995

Homeownership in low-income neighborhoods has positive personal and social benefits. It provides residents with an incentive to maintain both their own property and the local neighborhood. Recent research also suggests that homeownership is associated with "life satisfaction" (Scanlon, 1999). Still, these externalities and "internalities" are not costless. A house is not only a dwelling; it is an investment asset. As such it has risk and return characteristics that should affect the purchase decision. This chapter examines the investment value of U.S. housing over the past twenty years. The results suggest that the capital appreciation of housing over the twenty-year period from 1980 through 1999 was substantially less than the return to U.S. stocks, bonds, and mortgage-backed securities over the same period. Although the comparison with stocks and bonds over the past two decades is somewhat unfair, given how well financial assets performed relative to historical norms, housing did not even fair well when compared with inflation. Returns to home investment exceeded inflation in most states, but only by modest amounts over the period. Not only have returns been historically low, but, when price dynamics are properly accounted for, the risk is significant. Many homeowners in the United States over the past twenty years experienced extended periods in which their home equity was negative. This evidence alone is a compelling reason to reconsider the stated fundamental goal of expanding homeownership.

Despite its relatively poor performance as an investment vehicle, housing has a private consumption value that may induce people to hold it, and the positive externalities of owner-occupied housing are a strong inducement to encourage it. Thus there are clear policy implications of the evidence we present in this chapter. First, the government should be cautious about encouraging wholesale home purchases, especially by the most financially vulnerable in society. It should provide information about risk and return beyond simply helpful guidelines for accessing mortgage credit. Second, it should develop institutions and markets that allow homeowners to insure against local areawide housing price risk. Proposals for a housing futures market by Case, Shiller, and Weiss (1993) would appear quite beneficial, given the long-term risks of homeownership. Finally, the government should reconsider a tax policy that economically favors renting rather than buying by low-income families.

The role of government-sponsored agencies (GSEs) in encouraging low-income homeownership has been much debated, particularly with respect to their role in fulfilling the mandate of the Community Reinvestment Act. Of particular concern is the development of special programs to encourage higher loan-to-value (LTV) ratios in lower-income neighborhoods. Although increasing LTV ratios relax the wealth constraints affecting tenure choice, they also add substantially to the risk of default (see Gyourko, Linneman, and Wachter, 1998; Gyourko and Linneman, 1996; Haurin, Hendershott, and Wachter, 1996). In addition, higher LTV ratios create conditions for increasing the volatility of housing prices (see Stein, 1995; Lamont and Stein, 1999) and regional recessions (see Caplin, Freeman, and Tracy, 1997).

Besides household and macroeconomic risks associated with increased leverage in low-income neighborhoods, we argue that increasing LTVs in underserved mortgage markets may encourage gentrification. Higher LTV ratios substitute down payments for higher interest rates. However, the mortgage interest deduction provides a greater benefit to higher-income families. Thus allowing high LTV ratio loans in low-income areas may simply encourage higher-income individuals to purchase housing in underserved markets. Even if gentrification issues can be resolved, it is still not clear if increasing the acceptable LTV ratio will do much good. By renting from higher-income individuals, low-income families can capture part of the tax benefits from mortgage interest and property tax payments. Both of these benefits are lost upon purchase, and neither benefit is affected by the set of available low-income loan programs. The alternative to increasing LTV ratios is a direct subsidy of home purchase in low-income neighborhoods. Ambrose and Goetzmann (1998) estimate that the necessary subsidy may be as much as 6 percent per year of the homeowner equity investment.

Housing as an Investment

The Office of Federal Housing Enterprise Oversight (OFHEO) was formed in 1992 as an independent agency within the Department of Housing and Urban Development. OFHEO has developed excellent housing price indices in a broad number of metropolitan statistical areas (MSAs) throughout the country. The quarterly indices cover all fifty states plus the District of Columbia and 328 MSAs, extending back to 1975. Calhoun (1996) describes their composition and method of construction. As of 2000, nearly 12.5 million repeat sales derived from Fannie Mae or Freddie Mac mortgage origination or purchase files were used in a weighted-repeat-sales estimation procedure based on Case and Shiller (1987) with the Goetzmann (1992) correction. These indices provide a rich source of information about the time-series behavior of U.S. housing as an investment over the past quarter-century. This information should be regarded as essential knowledge for every homeowner or potential homeowner.

Housing Returns

Treating housing as a pure investment vehicle implies that gains are realized through price appreciation, less taxes, upkeep, and transaction costs. Goetzmann and Spiegel (1997) show that the variation in the market value of the house over time is largely explained by local indices that track the capital appreciation of a home at the zip code level. If a home is maintained at the same quality level as other homes in its neighborhood, a neighborhood-level price index will typically explain 80 to 90 percent of the change in any one home's value. Thus even though an individual homeowner is not diversified across a number of homes in his region (as are Fannie Mae and Freddie Mac as residual claimants on homes on which they guarantee mortgages), the regional indices provided by OFHEO are useful measures of the return to individual home investment. However, because they are regional averages they understate the volatility of the return to investing in a single home in the area.

OFHEO reports that the value of a single-family home in the United States grew by 138 percent over the period from 1980 to March 2000. This represents an annualized rate of 4.2 percent over the past twenty-one years. Given that the consumer price index (CPI) rose at a 3.7 percent annual rate over the same time period, this suggests a relatively modest rate of long-term asset growth. Similar results can be found in Goetzmann (1993). That paper uses index data from 1971 to 1985 (created by Case and Shiller, 1987) to estimate the risk and return of investment in a single-family home. During that fifteen-year interval, average annual real returns in Atlanta, Chicago, Dallas, and San Francisco ranged between 5.8 and 8 percent per year. This pattern continues today. Summary statistics for a selection of U.S. cities over the twenty-year period ending in March 1999 are provided in table 9-1. The annual real returns for this larger collection of cities range from –1.9 percent to 3.3 percent.

Perhaps more troublesome is the difference between housing investment and the return on investment in mortgage-backed securities. The mortgage-backed securities comprising the Salomon Brothers and Lehman indices reported in the table are, for the most part, liabilities of homeowners. On a before-tax basis it appears that on average the cost of money to purchase a home far exceeds the growth in that same home's value. From table 9-2 the 10 percent nominal annual income return to the Lehman mortgage index exceeds the Houston market nominal return by 8 percent per year and the San Francisco market nominal return by 2.4 percent per year. Assuming that the highest marginal tax rate over this period was 40 percent, it appears that the nominal after-tax mortgage income return exceeded home price appreciation in nine of the twelve cities.

Although price indices give some idea of the growth in housing values, calculating the investor's return on the sale of a home requires the consideration of a number of other factors. Hendershott and Hu (1981), Case and Shiller (1990), and Goetzmann (1993) use rents, expenses, and tax variables to estimate after-tax returns to housing investment. These factors are extremely important because both maintenance and property taxes are costs unique to housing investments. Thus price indices may in general overstate the relative return a family can expect from their house, as opposed to assets such as stocks and bonds for which the rate of return is easy to calculate.

In sum, examining the most current measures of capital appreciation of homes in a number of U.S. cities over the past twenty years suggests that they are dominated as an investment asset. Nearly all markets displayed negative risk-adjusted returns over the period. Treasury bills would in general have been an attractive investment alternative. Given the poor performance of housing as an investment, it is thus surprising that housing continues to represent a significant proportion of American household portfolios. It also implies that the government should weigh housing policies in light of the dramatic trade-off between wealth accumulation by low-income families and the positive social externalities of owner-occupied housing in low-income neighborhoods. In light of this, the government has a responsibility to share this striking information about long-term housing returns with potential homeowners.

Housing Risk

Even with low expected returns, housing may still remain a somewhat attractive investment if it is a sufficiently "safe" vehicle. In our research, we have found it useful to break housing risk down into temporal and nontemporal components;

Table 9-1. *Summary Statistics for Housing and Other Assets in Real Terms, March 1980–March 1999*[a]

City	*Quarters*	*Geometric mean (percent)*	*Arithmetic mean (percent)*	*Standard deviation (percent)*	*Serial correlation (percent)*	*Sharpe ratio*
Atlanta	80	0.747	0.964	6.699	–0.391	–0.269
Chicago	80	0.716	0.764	3.139	0.532	–0.638
Dallas	80	–1.105	–1.001	4.495	–0.228	–0.838
San Francisco	80	2.500	2.607	4.731	0.600	–0.034
Detroit	80	0.914	1.031	4.836	0.118	–0.359
Houston	80	–1.971	–1.890	4.028	0.263	–1.156
New York City	80	3.264	3.458	6.488	0.370	0.107
Newark	80	1.904	2.011	4.717	0.691	–0.160
Oakland	80	1.643	1.711	3.752	0.619	–0.281
Philadelphia	80	1.102	1.166	3.632	0.415	–0.441
St. Louis	80	–0.207	–0.154	3.269	0.157	–0.893
Washington, D.C.	80	0.483	0.535	3.247	0.419	–0.687
S&P 500 total return (TR)	80	13.330	14.633	17.211	–0.008	0.690
U.S. long-term government bond TR	80	6.417	7.378	14.569	–0.043	0.317
U.S. thirty-day Treasury bill TR	80	2.766	2.775	1.332	0.417	0.006
Salomon Brothers thirty-year GNMA TR[b]	80	6.122	6.617	10.417	–0.131	0.370
Salomon Brothers thirty-year FHLMC TR[c]	80	6.480	6.972	10.372	–0.065	0.406
Lehman Brothers mortgage index income return	80	9.891	9.898	1.262	0.971	5.650
Lehman Brothers mortgage index TR	80	6.127	6.602	10.192	–0.030	0.376
Lehman Brothers mortgage index capital appreciation	80	–3.260	–2.819	9.306	–0.041	–0.600

Source: Measurements are per year, annualized from quarterly housing MSA returns available from the Office of Federal Housing Enterprise Oversight (OFHEO). All financial asset returns from Ibbotson Associates, Chicago. The serial correlation is measured on quarterly returns.

a. All housing returns are in nominal terms.

b. GNMA = Government National Mortgage Association (Ginnie Mae).

c. FHLMC = Federal Home Loan Mortgage Association (Freddie Mac).

Table 9-2. *Summary Statistics for Housing and Other Assets in Nominal Terms: March 1980–March 1999*

City	*Quarters*	*Geometric mean (percent)*	*Arithmetic mean (percent)*	*Standard deviation (percent)*	*Serial correlation (percent)*	*Sharpe ratio*
Atlanta	80	4.787	4.994	6.642	0.576	–0.287
Chicago	80	4.755	4.795	2.917	0.255	–0.721
Dallas	80	2.861	2.963	4.542	0.753	–0.866
San Francisco	80	6.611	6.718	4.833	0.627	–0.037
Detroit	80	4.962	5.064	4.595	0.088	–0.399
Houston	80	1.960	2.045	4.181	0.611	–1.161
New York City	80	7.406	7.604	6.692	0.516	0.106
Newark	80	5.991	6.101	4.873	0.715	–0.164
Oakland	80	5.719	5.795	4.051	0.596	–0.272
Philadelphia	80	5.157	5.217	3.608	0.654	–0.466
St. Louis	80	3.796	3.837	2.998	0.275	–1.021
Washington, D.C.	80	4.513	4.559	3.112	0.681	–0.752
S&P 500 total return (TR)	80	17.875	19.163	17.430	–0.316	0.704
U.S. long-term government bond TR	80	10.685	11.606	14.619	–0.317	0.322
U.S. thirty-day Treasury bill TR	80	6.888	6.898	1.493	0.825	0.000
U.S. inflation	80	4.011	4.023	1.620	0.824	–1.774
Salomon Brothers thirty-year GNMA TR[a]	80	10.378	10.848	10.443	–0.077	0.378
Salomon Brothers thirty-year FHLMC TR[b]	80	10.751	11.212	10.342	–0.065	0.417
Lehman Brothers mortgage index income return	80	10.000	10.007	1.295	0.867	2.401
Lehman Brothers mortgage index TR	80	10.383	10.831	10.188	–0.037	0.386
Lehman Brothers mortgage index capital appreciation	80	0.620	1.027	9.206	–0.148	–0.638

Sources: Measurements are per year, annualized from quarterly housing MSA returns available from the Office of Federal Housing Enterprise Oversight (OFHEO). All financial asset returns from Ibbotson Associates, Chicago.

Note: All housing returns are in nominal terms. The serial correlation is measured on quarterly returns.

a. GNMA = Government National Mortgage Association (Ginnie Mae).

b. FHLMC = Federal Home Loan Mortgage Corporation (Freddie Mac).

the temporal components grow with time and the nontemporal components are associated only with transactions. The nontemporal transactions-based risk is due to the illiquidity of housing and is most important when the holding period is short. Although housing markets are competitive, we find the transactions risk to be quite significant: as much as 6 to 8 percent in our studies of the San Francisco Bay Area (Goetzmann and Spiegel, 1995, 1997). Thus it has considerable impact on buyers who may need to move soon.

The temporal components are the risk of the citywide index, deviations of local neighborhoods around the index, and the idiosyncratic risk of the house—that is, the variation in the home price around the local neighborhood index. In our 1997 study of Bay Area housing we found that neighborhood effects were strong. Using zip code–level indices, we were able to fairly accurately predict the sales prices of homes. In our sample, only 8 percent of transactions deviated by more than 10 percent from our local indices. But over the five-year period from 1989 to 1994, we found dramatic variation across neighborhoods. The lowest-priced quartile of Bay Area housing experienced no price appreciation, while the highest-priced quartile experienced price appreciation of 23 to 36 percent. Thus even a well-constructed citywide index is likely to be averaging across dramatically different neighborhood growth rates. It is of some comfort that the returns to lower-income neighborhoods were relatively higher than returns to high-income neighborhoods and that, controlling for income, race was an insignificant factor in capital appreciation rates.

An important consideration in assessing the impact of the temporal components of residential real estate risk is the strong auto-correlation in the time-series of returns. Notice that annual standard deviation figures found in both tables 9-1 and 9-2 make it appear that housing returns are not particularly volatile. However, the high positive auto-correlations indicate that housing returns follow distinct trends, with current increases foretelling future increases and current declines foretelling future declines. This means that negative shocks to housing values persist; once prices in a region begin to decline they continue to decline. Figure 9-1 plots the price indices over the period. It is clear that housing returns do not follow a random walk.[1] Once a local housing market starts to drift lower it may be a long time before it recovers. Goetzmann (1993) shows that once idiosyncratic risk, nontemporal risk, and the trends in the index are accounted for, the annualized standard deviation of investing in a single home over a five-year period is roughly double the annual standard deviation of the city-level index.

1. See Spiegel and Strange (1992) and Spiegel (2001) for theoretical models that explain why economic forces naturally lead to predictably above or below normal expected housing returns. Thus there is no theoretical reason to believe that the serial correlation exhibited by the data is either due to a statistical artifact or likely to disappear if this information becomes more widespread in the market.

Figure 9-1. *Housing and Financial Markets*

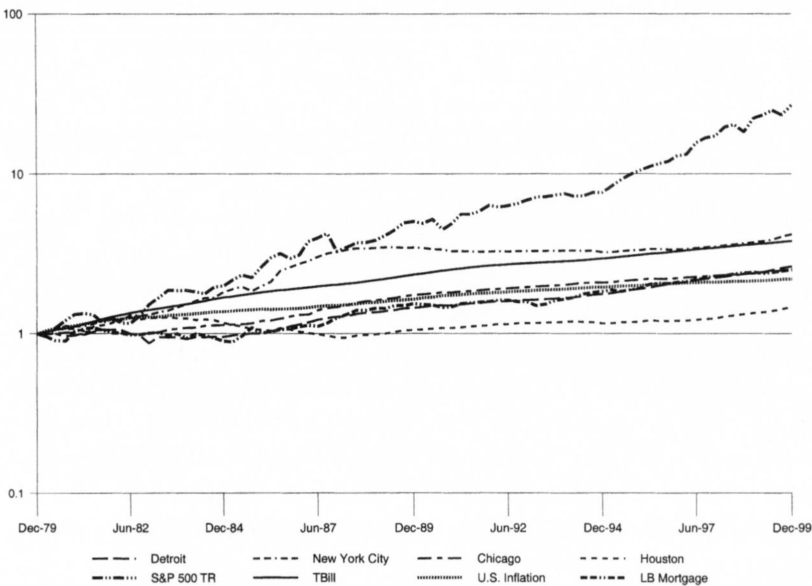

The Sharpe ratio is a common performance measure used to risk-adjust the return that an asset class provides in excess of Treasury bills. It is certainly relevant to the home purchase decision in cases for which most of an investor's wealth will be invested in that asset class. Even if we ignore the extra risk to long-term investors resulting from nontemporal components, idiosyncratic risk, and auto-correlation in the housing markets, both tables 9-1 and 9-2 show that the Sharpe ratio is negative for every city other than New York. Thus, in very general terms, over the past twenty years most homeowners across the country could have achieved greater wealth accumulation by investing in Treasury bills than in a home. The one bright spot is that housing is correlated with changes in the CPI. Thus homeownership partially hedges out an important component of inflation.

Standard asset pricing models use diversification arguments to justify low expected returns if an asset has a low or negative correlation to the market portfolio. Negative beta assets could have expected returns below T-bills and still be a part of a diversified portfolio, since the asset returns move countercyclically. The betas of most housing markets are near zero, even when four lagged quarters on S&P 500 excess returns are used as regressors. Thus we do not argue that housing is mispriced from an asset-pricing model framework. Nevertheless, the low returns suggest that, at best, houses are being priced as if investors were completely diversified, something we know is not true given the large percentage the home typically represents in a portfolio. Caplin (1999) cites evidence from the

1995 survey of consumer finances indicating that the average fraction of assets represented by the house in a homeowner's portfolio is 50 to 70 percent.

Mortgages add another level of risk because they facilitate financial leverage. Though government agencies do not advertise default risks to the general public, they are clearly aware of them. OFHEO's primary mission consists of "ensuring the capital adequacy and financial safety and soundness of two government-sponsored enterprises (GSEs) the Federal National Mortgage Association (Fannie Mae) and the Federal Home Loan Mortgage Corporation (Freddie Mac)."[2] In fact, the motivation for the indices is particularly telling. According to the OFHEO website:

> OFHEO is required by its enabling statute—The Federal Housing Enterprises Financial Safety and Soundness Act of 1992 (Title XIII of PL. 102-550)—to develop and administer a quarterly risk-based capital stress test to measure the capital adequacy of Fannie Mae and Freddie Mac. In the stress test, the statute requires OFHEO to use a house price index to account for changes in the loan-to-value (LTV) ratios of mortgages held or guaranteed by Fannie Mae or Freddie Mac.[3]

In other words, the indices are designed to allow regulators to quantify the risk that homeowner LTV ratios will become negative and thus leave the two agencies with inadequate collateral to cover the mortgages they have guaranteed. By the same token, however, the risk of increasing Fannie Mae and Freddie Mac LTV ratios is also the risk to homeowner equity.[4] The very existence of OFHEO suggests that our own government recognizes that this risk is not trivial for the agencies.

Naturally, if the value of a home represents a relatively small portion of a household's investment portfolio, then the volatility of the index and LTV ratio is of minor concern. However, for most homeowners in the United States, and particularly those in underserved mortgage markets, a house will consume most of their savings. Thus a nontrivial chance of negative equity over a five-year investment horizon poses a serious concern.

What do the OFHEO data tell us about the historical variation in LTV ratios? Using quarterly housing return indices for each of the fifty states and the District of Columbia, we examined the minimum five-year holding period return.[5] For 30 percent of the states there exists at least one five-year holding

2. See OFHEO's website: www.ofheo.gov/about.

3. See www.ofheo.gov/house/faq.html.

4. Let L equal the loan value and E equal the homeowner equity value. Then $L/(L+E)$ is the loan-to-value ratio. The homeowner's equity proportion is $E/(L+E)$ which equals $1 - L/(L+E)$.

5. For expositional simplicity the following discussion treats the District of Columbia as a state. Thus there are fifty-one indices.

period in the last twenty years for which LTV ratios increased by more than 10 percent. Thus an average family buying a home at the beginning of such a period would have seen its value drop far enough to wipe out a 10 percent down payment by the end of the period.

In fact, the 30 percent figure understates the risk. Real estate transaction costs are typically on the order of 6 percent or more once commissions, title insurance, legal fees, and title transfer taxes are taken into account. Using 6 percent as a benchmark, forty-one of these states exhibited price declines large enough to eliminate a homeowner's initial capital. Considering the increase in equity due to amortization over five years makes little difference. Assuming that the typical mortgage during this period had a thirty-year life and an 8 percent interest rate, after five years approximately 5 percent of the loan would have been paid off. Using these criteria, families in thirty-two states would have seen the value of their home decline enough not only to eliminate their initial savings, but also to eliminate the fraction of the loan they would have paid off to date. This has potentially serious consequences. If a low-income family with an out-of-area job opportunity cannot sell their home for more than the current mortgage, they may face the choice of either not moving or declaring bankruptcy. What about the simple question of whether a family might have a negative return on their investment? Ignoring transaction costs, thirty-three states had five-year periods in which a family would have lost money on their house in a given period. If one includes a 6 percent transactions cost, this figure becomes true for forty-four states!

A number of authors have explored the risk of housing and the possibility of mortgage default. Berkovec and Fullerton (1992); Brueckner (1997); Wieand (1999); Meyer and Wieand (1996); Rosenthal, Duca, and Gabriel (1991); and Voith and Crone (1999) all develop models that show the effect of systematic and unsystematic housing risk on the purchase or mortgage decision. Fratatoni (1998) and Ling and McGill (1998) provide empirical support for the importance of considering housing risk by showing that the housing and mortgage decision affects household preference for other risky assets. In particular, Ling and McGill find that, controlling for the price of the home, lower-income households are more likely to choose low mortgage debt.

Although positive externalities of homeownership are taken as given, there are potentially serious negative externalities associated with increased mortgage leverage as well. Lamont and Stein (1999) use housing data from several cities to explore the effect of leverage on the volatility of the housing price series. They find strong evidence that higher mortgage ratios in a city are associated with higher risk. Caplin, Freeman, and Tracy (1997) observe that refinancing is difficult when loan-to-value ratios have increased, and thus homeowners may not be able to take advantage of the refinancing option. They link regional recessions to the inability to finance and the constraint on labor mobility.

Policy Issues and Implications of Risk and Return Measures

Even if homeownership yields positive externalities to the community, it is irresponsible to simply encourage homeownership among modest-income groups via more aggressive lending. A home mortgage simply allows people to lever up their exposure to housing market risk. In addition, the opportunity cost of capital for a low-income household is severe. There are more attractive and liquid investments, and there are great benefits to diversifying an investment portfolio. U.S. housing policy does not effectively compensate low-income homeowners for these opportunity costs.

We suggest that HUD and other government agencies have a responsibility to disclose the historical facts to potential homeowners. The public should know about the low returns and high volatilities associated with housing. A perusal of the HUD website yields ample information about how to buy a home, indeed how to buy a HUD-owned home, but little information about how to consider the pros and cons of housing as an investment. Whereas one government agency has been established to collect information to carefully monitor the risks of housing as an asset, the other actively seeks to encourage homeownership among citizens of modest income. Homeownership may be the American Dream, but the government should not be overzealous in pushing mortgages and housing on those who cannot afford to invest in a low-returning and potentially risky asset. Otherwise it seems likely that sometime in the next twenty years a substantial number of the "beneficiaries" of this policy may find their meager savings severely diminished, or even totally depleted.

Another important step is to encourage the development of markets and instruments that can help homeowners avoid the risk of their home investment. Case, Shiller, and Weiss (1993) advocate the development of housing indices that can be used to develop home equity insurance products. Perhaps the government, through OFHEO, can provide the local index data to allow this to take place. In addition, government agencies should take the lead in developing these contracts. Of course, one problem with the creation of home equity insurance contracts is that they partially remove incentives for maintenance and upkeep, and they encourage gaming of prices by contract owners. Nevertheless, the potential exists to overcome these drawbacks and initiate programs that will make household asset portfolios safer rather than more risky.

Tax Policy, Government Policy, and Housing Choice

Poterba (1992) provides a simple model that describes how the tax code interacts with the housing market. His analysis focuses on the amount of housing families may wish to purchase but also contains a brief analysis of how it impacts the balance between rental and purchase markets. However, in the current setting we are interested in a slightly different question. Given the current tax code, how will allowing higher LTV ratios impact low-income families? In particular, will it improve their ability to compete for owner-occupied housing and will it motivate them to buy rather than rent?

How Taxes Can Undermine Other Housing Policies

Housing markets are competitive. Thus low-income prospective homeowners compete with higher-income families for the same property. In fact, they potentially compete with higher-income families seeking the property for rental income. Will looser financing allow a low-income family to outbid a high-income family? A fairly straightforward analysis suggests not.

At the margin, higher-income families pay income taxes at higher rates than low-income families. This means that the mortgage interest deduction provides more value as a family's income increases. Thus decreasing the down payment levels (and thereby increasing the interest paid) may make it even less likely a low-income family will purchase a home. To see why, imagine that a house produces a consumption dividend of C_l to a low-income family and C_h to a high-income family. Absent taxes, the low-income family will try to outbid the higher-income family so long as C_l is greater than C_h. However, the mortgage interest deduction distorts this. An interest-only mortgage (and in the initial years the payments on a thirty-year mortgage are essentially interest only) provides a family with a tax benefit equal to $trDP$. Here, t equals the family's tax rate, r the mortgage rate, P the price of the house, and D the fraction of the price financed via the mortgage (a 10 percent down payment corresponds to setting D to 0.9). Thus the total benefit to a family equals $C + trP$. This implies that, with taxes, the low-income family will only outbid the high-income family if $C_l - C_h > (t_h - t_l)rDP$, with subscripts l and h denoting low- and high-income, respectively. Clearly, as D increases (that is, as the down payment declines), the more difficult it will be for the low-income family to win a bidding war. Ultimately, then, a loosening of lending requirements in low-income areas may actually produce gentrification rather than low-income homeownership. This is clearly not the impact envisioned by policymakers wishing to encourage high LTV loans in poor neighborhoods. Housing policy that targets regions for looser credit suffers from this fundamental limitation. To help lower-income buyers, it is necessary to provide them a relative advantage.

Even if a policy of encouraging high LTV loans in underserved neighborhoods does not encourage the displacement of low-income families, there is still the question of whether it will actually increase ownership rates among the poor. All families must weigh the choice of buying versus renting when making their housing decision. For better or worse, the current tax code encourages high-income families to purchase and low-income families to rent. Consider a city in which a residence sells for P, and the mortgage interest rate equals r. In this city lives a family that faces a tax rate of t_f. If they purchase a house it will cost them

$(1 - t_f)P$ in after-tax interest and an additional EP in maintenance expenses, but they will then earn g in capital gains. For housing, capital gains are effectively tax free, so the owner will keep the entire amount. Thus the total after-tax cost of ownership comes to $(1 - t_f)rP + EP - gP$. Alternatively, the family can rent an identical home at a cost of n from another individual who pays taxes at a rate of t_0. Because the property is rented, the federal government allows the landlord to deduct interest and maintenance expenses as well as depreciation (δP) on the building before calculating the tax bill. In equilibrium, a competitive rental market should imply that landlords earn a zero economic rent and thus n must solve:

$$n(1 - t_0) = (rP + \alpha EP)(1 - t_0) - t_0 \delta P - (1 - t_g)gP, \tag{9-1}$$

where t_g equals the capital gains tax rate on landlords and α a measure of the inefficiency of third-party maintenance (so $\alpha \geq 1$). As Shiller and Weiss (2000) discuss, third-party maintenance is far less efficient than owner-occupied maintenance, and this should be accounted for in the cost calculations. So,

$$n = rP + \alpha EP - \frac{t_0 \delta P + (1 - t_g)gP}{1 - t_0}. \tag{9-2}$$

Therefore it will only pay for a family to buy rather than rent, if:

$$t_f r + g > (1 - \alpha)E + \frac{t_0 \delta + (1 - t_g)g}{1 - t_0}. \tag{9-3}$$

Notice that the result is independent of the down payment required to obtain the mortgage. This results from the fact that the equation properly accounts for the opportunity cost of tying up money in real estate rather than other investments of similar risk. A higher down payment simply means a higher lost opportunity cost in exchange for an equal reduction in the expected cost of the mortgage. The only impact the down payment requirement has is on whether purchasing is a feasible option.

Note from equation 9-3 that if a family pays taxes at a rate of zero (not unlikely for those with low incomes) and if the capital gains tax rate is less than or equal to the ordinary income tax rate (which it is), then under no circumstances will it pay for them to buy. This is irrespective of what LTV ratios the government may or may not persuade banks to use. By renting, a low-income family can at least capture part of the tax benefit via competition among landlords.

To get a feel for the point at which a family will actually purchase, consider the following scenario. Imagine the landlord pays taxes at a combined federal and state rate of 39.6 percent.[6] Further assume depreciation can be taken on a straight-line basis over thirty years. At first one might suppose that this implies that δ equals .033 (1/30). However, once the building is sold, the depreciation taken until that date will then result in a capital gains tax to be paid on the difference between the sale price and the building's book value. Thus the full depreciation allowance overstates by a considerable amount the benefit of the deduction. The current long-term capital gains tax rate equals 20 percent. If the landlord holds the building for ten years, then on average the government will recapture taxes equal to about 13 percent of the depreciation, and this figure is therefore the effective capital gains tax rate (t_g). Using these adjustments, the t_o term in front of δ in equation 9-3 becomes .396 – .13. Currently the annual percentage rate for a thirty-year, zero points mortgage equals approximately 8.509 percent. From tables 9-1 and 9-2 it would appear that annual capital gains on housing come to about 4 percent in the current inflationary environment. Assume maintenance runs about 2 percent of a home's value per year. Further assume that third-party maintenance only runs 20 percent higher than owner-occupied maintenance. Plugging all these figures into the inequality implies that a family will only purchase a home if its marginal tax exceeds 32.1 percent. To reach this marginal tax rate, a family of four in a state with a 5 percent income tax would need to earn over $43,000 per year! Based on this, it seems that tax issues may be playing a far more important role than mortgage down payment issues in discouraging low-income families from purchasing their homes. The natural conclusion is that targeting underserved communities for high LTV loans is unlikely to encourage homeownership.

One word of caution is in order about the above calculations. The marginal tax rate that causes a family to switch from renting to buying depends critically on the marginal tax rate of the marginal landlord. Table 9-3 presents figures for the cutoff point given varying tax rates on the marginal landlord. For example, if the marginal landlord faces a tax rate of 25 percent, then families with a marginal tax rate of more than 9 percent would likely prefer to purchase their residence. This would certainly include most families.

Policy Proposals and Their Potential Impact on Low-Income Homeownership

In addition to the government's proposal to relax LTV ratios to encourage low-income homeownership in underserved areas, there are currently two other proposals (that we know about) put forward by academics. The most recent is by

6. The 39.6 percent tax rate assumes that the landlord pays taxes at the top federal rate and lives in a state without an income tax (see www.quicken.com/taxes/articles/917555291_21562). While the assumption that the landlord does not pay state income taxes may seem to imply that a higher tax rate is in order, it should be remembered that it is the marginal landlord that sets rents in the market. Thus, if anything, the tax rate one should use is probably somewhat lower. Figure 9-1 provides a breakdown of how the results vary with the tax rate on the marginal landlord.

Table 9-3. *Tax Rate at Which Families Are Indifferent between Renting and Buying*

Landlord's tax rate	*Tax rate at which the family is indifferent*
.2	.03
.25	.09
.3	.158
.35	.237
.4	.329

Source: Authors' calculations.

Caplin (1999), who proposes the issuance of equity sharing contracts. Under this proposal, families would own half of their house and investors the other half. At first glance this is an appealing proposal because it helps to ameliorate the price risk faced by families due to fluctuations in the price of their home. Simultaneously, it frees them to invest in a better diversified portfolio and offers the potential for increased liquidity via investment in publicly traded securities. However, though this policy looks good from the perspective of portfolio diversification, it may suffer from a severe moral hazard problem. As Shiller and Weiss (2000) explain, it is very difficult to write enforceable contracts on home maintenance. Given this constraint, it seems likely that an equity-sharing contract for *X* percent of the home would effectively reduce a family's incentive to modernize, improve, and maintain the home by *X* percent. The arguments in both Shiller and Weiss (2000) and Spiegel (2001) suggest that reducing the maintenance incentive in this manner would likely result in a greater fraction of dilapidated homes in targeted neighborhoods. The resulting blight would then destroy the positive externalities policymakers hope to induce through homeownership.

The other academic proposal for reducing homeownership risk was put forth by Case, Shiller, and Weiss (1993). They would have a service produce a local area real estate price index. Homeowners could then short the index when they purchased their home, thereby immunizing their portfolio from fluctuations in housing prices that are beyond their control. On purely theoretical grounds this is a very appealing solution. Unlike equity sharing contracts, it does not raise moral hazard concerns. A family that ignores the maintenance requirements to their own house will see it fall in value relative to the index and thus feel the full brunt of the home's decline in value. Thus this proposal provides all the benefits of diversification without reducing the likely production of externalities families create when they look after their home. Of course, the fact that this proposal has not been implemented implies that it too is flawed. Here, however, the flaws may be psychological more than economic in nature. Many families may feel "cheated" if upon the sale of their home they lose all of the gain to the holder of their futures contract and may thus be unwilling to enter into an agreement like this in the first place. In addition, there remains the pricing of such a contract. If the index has gone up in value but the home in question down, it is likely that the family will simply declare bankruptcy and the contract will go unpaid. Before a liquid market in housing futures can arise, questions such as these will need to be resolved.

However, no policy proposal is likely to change homeownership rates in underserved areas so long as the current tax code remains in place. Poor people do not rent simply because they are poor. After all, poor people typically purchase cars and high-income people frequently rent via a lease. The difference lies in the tax treatment. Unlike the interest on a house, the interest on a car loan is not tax-deductible.[7] Thus allowing higher LTV ratios, equity-sharing mortgages, or the emergence of a local area futures contract will not have any impact so long as the government continues to "pay" low-income families to rent via the tax code. Until that is changed, all other proposals are likely to be ineffective.

Conclusion

U.S. housing policy has long encouraged homeownership, and there are a number of arguably good reasons to do so. When held in a diversified portfolio, housing provides a hedge against a major component of inflation and has a low correlation with financial assets. Nevertheless, it is dangerous for homeowners to devote too much of their wealth to an asset that has low historical return and a serious risk of loss over multiple-year horizons. We argue that if the government chooses to actively encourage homeownership, it has the responsibility to inform potential homeowners of the risks. Beyond providing information, the government should also seek new ways of helping homeowners to lay off unwanted local housing risk, perhaps by facilitating insurance contracts as suggested by Case and Shiller. We see policies that encourage overinvestment in housing and higher leverage as potentially dangerous. Overinvestment in housing by families with modest savings means underinvestment in financial assets that will grow and provide income for retirement. In fact, encouraging homeownership among low-income families will only increase the wealth gap in the United States.

Another policy problem relates to the way the tax code may interact with any attempts to encourage low-income homeownership. Because of the progressivity of the tax code, the interest deduction on a mortgage is worth more to higher-income families than to lower-income families. Since raising the LTV ratio effectively raises the interest payments, the tax code will in fact encourage higher-income families to move into underserved areas in order to take advan-

7. For the wealthy, leasing also offers some tax benefits if the lessee can claim the car as a business expense.

tage of the program targeting such areas. The result may thus be gentrification, rather than making it possible for low-income families to own their own homes.

Even if higher-income families can be prevented from accessing any new loan programs, there is still the issue of whether encouraging high LTV loans will persuade low-income families to buy rather than rent. Again a model of the tax code is instructive here. By renting, low-income families can capture some of the mortgage tax deduction via competition among high-income landlords. Unless the tax code changes, low-income families will find themselves financially better off, on average, by renting rather than buying.

Given the above issues, what should the government do? The neighborhood externalities homeowners provide should not be dismissed. Furthermore, since these externalities are a public good it is clear that the government has a role to play in their creation. However, changing LTV requirements within poor neighborhoods does not seem to be the answer. Instead, we would suggest a direct mortgage interest subsidy. Such a subsidy would make housing financially more attractive to low-income residents and have the added benefit of making ownership a financially sensible alternative to renting.

References

Ambrose, Brent W., and William N. Goetzmann. 1998. "Risk and Incentives in Underserved Mortgage Markets." *Journal of Housing Economics* 7 (3): 274–85.

Berkovec, James, and Don Fullerton. 1992. "A General Equilibrium Model of Housing, Taxes and Portfolio Choice. *Journal of Political Economy* 100 (2): 390–429.

Brueckner, Jan K. 1997. "Consumption and Investment Motives and the Portfolio Choice of Homeowners." *Journal of Real Estate Finance and Economics* 15 (2): 159–80.

Calhoun, Charles A. 1996. "OFHEO House Price Indexes: HPI Technical Description." Working Paper. Washington: Office of Federal Housing Enterprise and Oversight.

Caplin, Andrew. 1999. "Housing Asset Portfolios and the Reform of the Housing Finance Market." *TIAA-CREF Research Dialogues* 59 (February).

Caplin, Andrew, Charles Freeman, and Joseph Tracy. 1997. "Collateral Damage: Refinancing Constraints and Regional Recessions." *Journal of Money, Credit and Banking* 29 (4): 496–516.

Case, Karl, and Robert Shiller. 1987. "Prices of Single-Family Homes since 1970: New Indexes for Four Cities." *New England Economic Review* (September–October): 45–56.

———. 1990. "Forecasting Prices and Excess Returns in the Housing Market." *American Real Estate and Urban Economics Association Journal* 18 (3): 253–73.

Case, Karl, Robert Shiller, and Allan Weiss. 1993. "Index-Based Futures and Options Markets in Real Estate." *Journal of Portfolio Management* (January): 83–92.

Fratantoni, M. C. 1998. "Homeownership and Investment in Risky Assets." *Journal of Urban Economics* 44 (1): 27-42.

Goetzmann, William N. 1992. "The Accuracy of Real Estate Indices: Repeat-Sales Estimators." *Journal of Real Estate Finance and Economics* 5 (1): 5–53.

———. 1993. "The Single-Family Home in the Investment Portfolio." *Journal of Real Estate Finance and Economics* 6 (3): 201–22.

Goetzmann, William N., and Matthew Spiegel. 1995. "Non-Temporal Components of Residential Real Estate Appreciation." *Review of Economics and Statistics* 77 (1): 199–206.

———. 1997. "A Spatial Model of Housing Returns and Neighborhood Substitutability." *Journal of Real Estate Finance and Economics* 14 (1–2): 11–31.

Gyourko, Joseph, and Peter Linneman. 1996. "Analysis of the Changing Influences on Traditional Households' Ownership Patterns." *Journal of Urban Economics* 39 (3): 318–41.

Gyourko, Joseph, Peter Linneman, and Susan M. Wachter. 1998. "Analyzing the Relationships among Race, Wealth and Homeownership in America." *Journal of Housing Economics* 8: 63–89.

Haurin, Donald, Patric Hendershott, and Susan M. Wachter. 1996. "Borrowing Constraints and the Tenure Choice of Young Households." Working Paper W5630. Cambridge, Mass.: National Bureau of Economic Research.

Hendershott, Patric, and Sheng Cheng Hu. 1981. "Inflation and Extraordinary Returns on Owner-Occupied Housing: Some Implications for Capital Allocation and Productivity Growth." *Journal of Macroeconomics* 3 (2): 177–203.

Lamont, Owen, and Jeremy C. Stein. 1999. "Leverage and House-Price Dynamics in U.S. Cities." *Rand Journal* 30 (3): 498–514.

Ling, David C., and Garry A. McGill. 1998. "Evidence on the Demand for Mortgage Debt by Owner-Occupants." *Journal of Urban Economics* 44 (3): 391–414.

Meyer, Richard, and Kenneth Wieand. 1996. "Risk and Return to Housing, Tenure Choice and the Value of Housing in an Asset Pricing Context." *Real Estate Economics* 24 (1): 113–51.

Poterba, James. 1992. "Taxation and Housing: Old Questions, New Answers." *American Economic Review* 82 (2): 237–42.

———. 1994. "Tax Subsidies to Owner-Occupied Housing: An Asset Market Approach." *Quarterly Journal of Economics* 99 (4): 729–52.

Rosenthal, Stuart, John Duca, and Stuart Gabriel. 1991. "Credit Rationing and the Demand for Owner-Occupied Housing." *Journal of Urban Economics* 30 (1): 48–63.

Scanlon, Edward. 1999. "The Impact of Homeownership on the Life Satisfaction of African Americans." Working Paper. Center for Social Development, Washington University.

Shiller, Robert J., and Karl E. Case. 1996. "Mortgage Default Risk and Real Estate Prices: The Use of Index-Based Futures and Options in Real Estate." *Journal of Housing Research* 7 (2): 243–58.

Shiller, Robert J., and Allan N. Weiss. 2000. "Moral Hazard in Home Equity Conversion." *Real Estate Economics* 28 (1): 1–32.

Spiegel, Matthew. 2001. "Housing and Construction Cycles." *Real Estate Economics* 29 (4): 521–51.

Spiegel, Matthew, and William Strange. 1992. "A Theory of Predictable Excess Returns in Real Estate." *Journal of Real Estate Finance and Economics* 5 (4): 375–92.

Stein, Jeremy. 1995. "Prices and Trading Volume in the Housing Market: A Model with Down-Payment Effects." *Quarterly Journal of Economics* 110 (2): 379–406.

Voith, Richard P., and Theodore M. Crone. 1999. "Risk and Return within the Single-Family Housing Market." *Real Estate Economics* 27 (1): 63–78.

Wieand, Kenneth. 1999. "The Urban Homeowner's Residential Location Decision in an Asset-Pricing Context." *Real Estate Economics* 27 (4): 649–67.

PART 4

Low-Income Loan Performance

This section contributes to our understanding of the asset-building potential of homeownership for low-income households by taking a careful look at the repayment performance of low-income and minority borrowers from a lender's perspective. The results of the three studies have direct bearing on the evaluation of lending risks of low-income and minority borrowers and the pricing of mortgages in these markets.

Mortgage lending in recent years, driven in part by enforcement of the Community Reinvestment Act (CRA) and the imposition of Affordable Lending Goals on government-sponsored enterprises (GSEs) such as Fannie Mae and Freddie Mac, has expanded significantly in traditionally underserved markets. Borrowers in these markets, often low-income and minority (LIM) families, present an underwriting challenge because traditional evaluation tools could not be used to estimate their risk profiles. Lenders' limited experience in these markets offered little guidance on how to evaluate borrowers' creditworthiness and how to evaluate collateral risk in these markets.

Many LIM borrowers, often called subprime borrowers because their risk profiles differ markedly from prime lending candidates, have poorly established credit or banking histories. Their employment histories do not conform with the characteristic single-employer histories of prime borrowers. Lenders rely on the assistance of local, community-based organizations to help evaluate, or improve, borrower risk profiles using alternative methods. These methods include verification of regular payment of monthly bills, verification of continuous employment with multiple employers, and risk mitigation through homeownership education and credit counseling. Though most regulated lenders were coerced to serve these markets, lending in these markets has proven to be profitable.

Establishing that lending could be profitable in these markets led to an expansion of subprime lending by both regulated and unregulated lenders. The flow of subprime lending was maintained by borrower demand unmet by prime lenders. Credit at the best rates was rationed by lenders who met their minimum regulatory obligations. Other borrowers were left to do business in unregulated subprime markets. Subprime lenders offered loans with higher rates of interest and higher fees than those offered to prime candidates. The justification for this "risk-based" pricing structure was the alleged higher risk of subprime borrowers.

Accurately pricing mortgages is a daunting task. This is because the price of a mortgage depends critically on the repayment performance of the borrower and the life span of the mortgage—neither of which can be known at the time of sale. The true value of a mortgage—essentially the discounted present value of a stream of monthly payments for up to thirty years—is not known until the mortgage is terminated. Delinquency, default, and early termination of mortgages directly influence the value of the mortgage. However, the likely incidence of any of these events can only be estimated at the time of origination. Thus lenders rely on statistical methods to help price mortgages.

Expanding lending into historically underserved markets has provided lenders and GSEs with information to help them more accurately price mortgages for these markets. The three chapters that follow present some of the latest knowledge regarding the performance of LIM mortgages. The chapters focus on mortgage termination.

Conventional wisdom suggests that LIM borrowers are more likely to default because their capacity to service their mortgages is more likely to be interrupted during the life of the mortgage. Lower incomes, higher likelihood of involuntary unemployment, and more frequent reliance on multiple incomes to service their debt make subprime borrowers higher default risks. In theory, increased default risk is offset, at least in part, by a lower likelihood of prepayment. LIM homeowners are less mobile than wealthier owners and are less likely to prepay their mortgages through a sale and move. LIM homeowners are also less likely to refinance their mortgages when this option is in-the-money because they are faced with income and asset constraints that make exercising these options unaffordable. The following chapters test and evaluate conventional wisdom using data that capture the experience of LIM borrowers over the past decade.

Roberto Quercia, Michael Stegman, Walter Davis, and Eric Stein take a first look at the default and delinquency performance of a small sample of loans in a national program with what is arguably the most aggressive expansion of lending into LIM markets. The Self-Help Community Advantage Program

(SHCAP) reaches a population with the worst risk profile of any national lender. Early repayment performance of these loans has been remarkable, especially when one considers the profile of the borrowers: more than 40 percent minority (compared to 17 percent for Fannie Mae, 14 percent for Freddie Mac, and 34 percent for FHA); more than 40 percent female-headed households (16 percent Fannie, 15 percent Freddie); and more than 40 percent rural (13 percent Fannie, 15 percent Freddie); half of the borrowers have incomes below 60 percent of area median income (10 percent Fannie, 8 percent Freddie, 20 percent FHA); and more than half have loans with loan-to-value ratios (LTVs) greater than 95 percent (2 percent Fannie, 1 percent Freddie).

The authors find that fewer than 5 percent of the borrowers experienced ninety-day delinquencies in the first two years of mortgage repayment. Fewer than one-third of these loans ended in foreclosure, and an equal number were brought current. A quarter of the loans remain more than ninety days delinquent. In their behavioral analysis, the authors find that credit scores are the best predictor of loan performance. It is noteworthy that layering of risk factors (high LTV and high payment-to-income ratios) for the SHCAP borrowers does not seem to affect repayment performance.

Wayne Archer, David Ling, and Gary McGill use a set of longitudinal samples constructed from the American Housing Surveys to test and explain alleged lower prepayment rates of LIM borrowers. The authors find that LIM borrowers are just as sensitive to interest rate changes as wealthier borrowers. However, they find that income and collateral constraints impede the ability of LIM borrowers to prepay and refinance mortgages. Thus LIM borrowers prepay at significantly lower rates out of necessity rather than choice. Higher LTVs and higher payment-to-income ratios constrain low- and moderate-income borrowers from refinancing in-the-money options. Ironically, layering risks in underwriting LIM mortgages, which leads, in theory, to higher default risks, also results in less frequent exercise of prepayment options.

Robert Van Order and Peter Zorn use huge samples of loans (1.4 million loans in the default analysis and 2.8 million loans in the prepayment analysis) culled from the Freddie Mac portfolio to compare the overall performance of affordable mortgages with that of prime mortgages. They determine that the value of overall repayment behavior of low-income borrowers is about the same as for prime borrowers. Specifically, they find that LIM households default more frequently, and with higher average losses, than prime borrowers. The higher default costs are offset by lower prepayment costs estimated to be as large as, or larger than, the higher default costs.

Several important questions emerge from these chapters:

—Are the LIM borrowers who participate in these lending programs representative of all potential borrowers in these markets, or have they been selected as lower-risk candidates?

—Does LIM borrowers' overall repayment performance relative to that of prime borrowers suggest that these borrowers should be getting similarly priced mortgages?

—To what extent is repayment performance on loans related to loan terms?

—Are subprime lenders who offer alleged "risk-based" mortgages at interest rates above prime mortgages accurately pricing the loans?

—To what extent are overpriced subprime loans extracting wealth from LIM communities?

I turn my attention to the last three questions.

In theory, mortgage terms can have a direct impact on repayment performance. Higher-priced mortgages reach deeper into borrowers' income streams to maintain current repayment. With more of household income directed toward mortgage payments, less is available for other expenses or for setting aside precautionary cash reserves. Thus LIM homeowners who get mortgages at higher prices have a diminished ability to deal with repayment stress resulting from negative "trigger" events such as job loss, health problems, and marital dissolution.

Mortgage pricing models use the option-based theory of mortgage termination to evaluate risk. In these models, borrowers are expected to exercise in-the-money options to terminate mortgages through default or refinance. The short history of LIM lending analyzed in the following chapters suggests these models inaccurately represent repayment behavior of LIM borrowers. LIM borrowers default more frequently than prime borrowers, although it is not clear that default occurs when the option is in the money. LIM borrowers prepay less frequently than prime borrowers, even when the prepayment option is in the money. The cost of more frequent default is more than offset by savings from the less frequent exercise of in-the-money prepayment options.

Misspecified risks estimated using these models result in risk-based pricing that will systematically overcharge LIM households for lending services.[1] Poorer repayment performance will feed back upon itself and "predict" higher lending risks in these markets and lead to even poorer performance. The long-term result of this vicious circle, predicated on faulty evaluation tools, would be higher-priced lending and credit rationing to LIM markets.

Though one might expect that market forces should drive subprime loan rates to more accurately reflect the risk of LIM borrowers, this will occur only if proper models are deployed to evaluate risk. It is difficult to determine the contribution of mortgage terms to mortgage performance, but the results of the chapters in this section suggest that it is incumbent on lenders to evaluate carefully the tools with which mortgage risk is estimated.

GEORGE McCARTHY

1. This applies, of course, only to the cases where mortgages were actually offered to these households. Credit rationing based on bad information would likely truncate flows of lending to these households as well.

10

Prepayment Risk and Lower-Income Mortgage Borrowers

WAYNE R. ARCHER, DAVID C. LING,
AND GARY A. McGILL

Over the 1990s the U.S. housing finance system increased its attention to issues of affordable housing. The government-sponsored enterprises (GSEs), notably Freddie Mac and Fannie Mae, introduced multiple special lending programs targeted to first-time home buyers and to households with income below 80 percent of area median. At the same time, regulators for the related issue of "redlining" have carefully scrutinized banks and other depository institutions seeking merger authorization.

When loans are targeted to "affordable housing" needs, it is common to ask whether they engender differential default risk, and extensive investigation of this issue has occurred.[1] It has been less common to ask whether "affordable housing" loans incur differential prepayment risk. This is despite the fact that the residual default risk premium on home loans originated to GSE or FHA standards may be much smaller than the companion prepayment risk premium.[2] Further, although default risk appears to have been managed and

We thank Eric Belsky and Michael LaCour-Little for detailed comments on an earlier draft.

1. For evidence concerning GSE research on home mortgage default prediction, see, for example, Freddie Mac (1996) and HUD's 1996 study on mortgage foreclosures (U.S. Department of Housing and Urban Development, 1996).

2. See Hilliard, Kau, and Slawson (1998) for simulated comparisons of default and prepayment premiums. Also, note that the relative size of default and prepayment premiums is suggested by their relative frequency of occurrence. While home mortgage foreclosure rates seldom have exceeded 0.35 percent of outstanding loans (Mortgage Bankers Association, 2000), refinancings

mitigated very significantly by credit scoring and automated underwriting systems, and perhaps by better housing market information, the more systematic risk of prepayment actually may have increased because of greater homeowner financial awareness and lowered costs of refinancing.

Because the prepayment risk premium is a significant and intractable cost of home mortgage lending, it is valuable to ask whether that premium should differ for loans directed to affordable housing needs. Investigators have found that exercise of the prepayment option is dampened by income and collateral constraints (Archer, Ling, and McGill, 1996; LaCour-Little, 1999). In addition, exercise of the prepayment option may be less likely by households that are less financially endowed or less financially sophisticated. Thus there is some reason to believe that prepayment risk may be lower for loans to affordable housing borrowers, especially those that are first-time homeowners. If so, investor recognition of this advantage should facilitate greater willingness to acquire portfolios of affordable housing loans and encourage more competitive pricing.[3]

This chapter examines the differential home mortgage termination experience of "affordable housing" households in the United States from 1985 to 1995. Using five two-year panels of data from the American Housing Survey (AHS), we test for differential mortgage termination behavior by households with income at or below approximately 80 percent of median for the household's metropolitan area. Mortgage termination rates of "affordable housing" households are compared to those of other homeowners, and differentials in factors influencing the termination rate are examined. In a separate set of logistic regressions we redefine the test group to include only those low-to-moderate-income households that are first-time homeowners.

This study offers three important departures from the existing literature. First, it is the first effort known to examine differential termination behavior for affordable housing mortgage loans. Second, it relies on a data base that is thought to be the most representative of American housing experience that exists, and third, it spans an important time of mortgage termination behavior that has not yet been broadly examined, the early 1990s.

In section 2 we set out the logical framework of our analysis and review related studies. Section 3 describes the data and the empirical method used to test the model's predictions. Results and interpretations appear in section 4, and the last section offers some concluding remarks.

accounted for an average of 38 percent of new loans during the 1990s and exceeded 50 percent in three different years ("Mortgage Market Trends," 1999, table A2). Researchers recognize that heterogeneity among subpopulations of borrowers must be addressed in determining default and prepayment premiums; see, for example, Deng and Quigley (2000).

3. Nothaft and Perry (1996) have found evidence that varying risk premiums are present in conforming fixed-rate loans. Conversations by the authors with Freddie Mac staff indicate that both default risk and differential prepayment propensity are accounted for in the pricing of loans purchased.

Logical Foundations and Related Work

This section presents a general framework for the analysis of mortgage terminations. Relevant literature also is reviewed.

A General Framework for Mortgage Terminations

This study focuses on the termination of fixed-rate residential mortgages and proceeds from the following general framework (Archer, Ling, and McGill, 1997). The probability of mortgage termination for all reasons at time *t*, λ_{Tt}, may be stated as

$$\lambda_{Tt} = \lambda_{Dt} + (1 - \lambda_{Dt})\lambda_{M.NDt} + (1 - \lambda_{Dt})(1 - \lambda_{M.NDt})\lambda_{P.NDMt}, \quad (10\text{-}1)$$

where λ_{Dt} is the probability of default at time *t*,

$\lambda_{M.NDt}$ is the probability of moving and terminating, but not defaulting, at time *t*, and

$\lambda_{P.NDMt}$ is the probability of terminating (prepaying) the mortgage, conditional upon not defaulting or moving.

Note that equation 10-1 is consistent with a hierarchy of choices. The borrower can terminate and neither default nor move. Choosing this "package" of options is referred to as refinancing. A second package of options available to the borrower is to move and, therefore, prepay, but not default. Default is the third available package and involves both moving and prepaying. The total probability of terminating is equal to the sum of these three interdependent probabilities.

The probability of defaulting, λ_{Dt}, can be stated in general terms as

$$\lambda_{Dt} = \lambda_{Dt}(\mathbf{x}_t, \mathbf{s}_t, T_{DMt}, C_t), \quad (10\text{-}2)$$

where $\mathbf{x}_t$ is a vector of household and property characteristics,

$\mathbf{s}_t$ is a vector of household shocks such as divorce, loss of employment, etc.,

T_{DMt} is a vector of transaction costs due to defaulting and, therefore, moving, and

C_t is the value of the option to prepay an in-the-money call or to preserve the mortgage if interest rates have risen since origination.

The probability of moving, conditional on not defaulting, $\lambda_{M.NDt}$, can be stated as

$$\lambda_{M.NDt} = \lambda_{M.NDt}(\mathbf{x}_t, \mathbf{y}_t, T_{Mt}, C_t), \quad (10\text{-}3)$$

where $\mathbf{x}_t$ and C_t are as defined above, $\mathbf{y}_t$ is a vector of income opportunities related to potential moves, and $\mathbf{T}_{Mt}$ is a vector of transaction costs due to moving. Finally, the probability of prepayment conditional on not defaulting or moving, $\lambda_{P.NDMt}$, can be stated as

$$\lambda_{P.NDMt} = \lambda_{P.NDMt}(C_t, \mathbf{x}_t), \tag{10-4}$$

where $\mathbf{x}_t$ and C_t are as defined above. In general terms:

$$C_t = C(\mathbf{x}_t, PVIS_t, \mathbf{P}, \lambda_{M.NDt}, \lambda_{Dt}), \tag{10-5}$$

where $\mathbf{x}_t$ is the same as above,

$PVIS_t$ is the present value of the interest savings from a refinancing at time t,

$\mathbf{P}$ is a vector of parameters governing interest rate movements,

$\lambda_{M.NDt}$ is the vector of pure move probabilities from time t to the end of the mortgage term, and

λ_{Dt} is a corresponding vector of default probabilities.

Note that λ_{Dt} and $\lambda_{M.NDt}$ are interdependent with C_t. That is, the value of the interest rate call option is partially determined by current and future move probabilities, while these latter probabilities are simultaneously affected by the value of the call option. Because of this interdependency, λ_{Dt}, $\lambda_{M.NDt}$, and C_t cannot be separately estimated; estimation inherently involves simultaneous equations. To avoid this simultaneity problem, we use the present value of interest savings (PVIS), and other exogenous variables, to proxy for the influence of C_t. This allows us to estimate the probability of terminating for any reason with a single reduced-form equation. The remainder of this section discusses the three components of residential mortgage termination probabilities: interest-rate-driven calls (refinancings), moves, and defaults.

The Probability of Refinance

One option continuously available to mortgage borrowers is to simply refinance—and neither default nor move. Endogenous or "rational" prepayment models "predict" that borrowers with similar contract terms will react similarly to changes in market interest rates. However, many borrowers fail to exercise well-into-the-money call options, while others prepay when the call option is out-of-the-money. Archer, Ling, and McGill (1996) provide evidence that the refinancing behavior of households that are income- or collateral-constrained differs markedly from that of unconstrained households. A borrower considering refinancing must first qualify for a new mortgage. Current qualification standards are such that a fall in household income or the value of the home used as collateral may make qualification for a new loan difficult. In fact, Archer and colleagues conclude that household demographic characteristics are only important to the extent that they predict whether a household will be income- or collateral-constrained. In any case, interest rate influences on prepayment are conditioned upon non–interest rate factors, including the household's propensity to move.

Several previous studies have used individual loan data to analyze mortgage terminations. These studies generally have found that borrower income and housing equity are significant determinants of mortgage terminations. However, the data employed in these studies typically are measured as of the mortgage origination date rather than the termination date. Postorigination income and property values for individual observations are either proxied for by using their values at origination or estimated with aggregate adjustments. For example, the house value at origination may be inflated by the average amount of appreciation that has occurred in the surrounding market (usually metropolitan) area.[4] The measurement of postorigination income and equity in these studies is therefore hindered by data that are insufficient to capture the idiosyncratic nature of borrower incomes and house prices.[5] In contrast to the data sources of these earlier studies, the AHS data used here offer a more comprehensive set of households, more household-level detail, and actual postorigination data. Hence the AHS data offer an exceptional opportunity to study the effects of micro influences, including household income, on termination probabilities.

The Probability of Relocation

The second "package" of options includes relocation. The probability of relocating (equation 10-3) depends on household and property characteristics, $\mathbf{x}_t$, income opportunities, $\mathbf{y}_t$, transaction costs of moving, T_{Mt}, and the value of preserving any below-market mortgage debt, C_t. By selling the home and relocating, the borrower is jointly deciding to move and refinance in that moving generally precipitates the termination of the mortgage. Thus the advantages of relocating may be enhanced or diminished by simultaneously extinguishing an existing loan. For this reason, many of the same factors that determine the probability of a "pure" interest rate–driven refinancing also exert influence on relocation decisions.

From the extensive literature investigating household mobility, Archer, Ling, and McGill (1997) review and discuss variables that potentially influence mortgage termination decisions. What emerges from their analysis is that the household-level factors affecting mobility are far from simple. Rather, they appear to have considerable interaction, such as with life cycle, education, income, and employment longevity. Further, there does not appear to be any one data source

4. See, for example, Foster and Van Order (1985), Quigley and Van Order (1990), Cunningham and Capone (1990), Capone and Cunningham (1992), Caplin, Freeman, and Tracy (1993), and Peristiani and others (1996).

5. A notable recent exception is LaCour-Little (1999).

that has supported a joint analysis of all the factors that have been identified. Moreover, until Quigley's (1987) work, little had been done to incorporate financial or investment portfolio considerations into the empirical analysis of mobility. In fact, the association between investment return (appreciation) and mobility is theoretically ambiguous (Kiel, 1994). In short, a comprehensive, integrated theory of household mobility does not exist. Unfortunately, this creates an uncertain foundation for specifying the functional form of equation 10-3. Further, to the extent that the equation has been improperly specified, the error is likely to affect the estimation of $\lambda_{PNDMt}(C_t, \mathbf{x}_t)$ and $\lambda_{Dt}(\mathbf{x}_t, \mathbf{s}_t, T_{DMt}, C_t)$. In this case, it is likely to be unproductive to attempt to estimate the three equations separately and to sort out the separate effect of common variables. This leads us to rely on a reduced-form model for this study.

The Probability of Default

A third package of options available to mortgage borrowers is default. Note that the decision to default is executed simultaneously with the decision to both move and prepay. For this reason, the advantages of default may be enhanced or diminished by the simultaneous decisions to move and prepay. However, the extensive literature investigating borrower default suggests prominent roles for two factors: cash flow deficiency (high payment burden) and "negative equity." In addition, recent attention has focused on the role of transaction costs as a barrier to default even when equity is negative, and upon the importance of "trigger events" or "shocks" such as unemployment, divorce, and death (Vandell, 1995; Deng, Quigley, and Van Order, 2000). Although the theory of default behavior is perhaps more integrated than mobility theory, it still is very incomplete.

Method

This section describes the data and periods used in the analysis. The logistic regression models and associated variables are also presented and defined.

Data and Periods

The analysis employs data from the 1985, 1987, 1989, 1991, 1993, and 1995 AHSs conducted by the U.S. Bureau of the Census (U.S. Department of Commerce, various years). The AHS, conducted biennially, contains extensive micro-level data on household and property characteristics, including number, age, and marital status of occupants, income type and level, tenure status, original and current home values, home acquisition date, property tax payments, geographic location, and more. The AHS also includes detailed mortgage information for owners, including the number and amount of mortgages, mortgage interest rates and payments, origination dates, and original and remaining loan terms.

Table 10-1. *Sample Construction*

	Two-year data windows				
	1985–87	*1987–89*	*1989–91*	*1991–93*	*1993–95*
Usable owner-occupied households in window end year	27,490	27,975	28,091	29,925	28,182
Less households not in base year or end year	(6,894)	(6,868)	(6,854)	(8,262)	(6,567)
Total owner-occupied households in AHS matched by control number	20,596	21,107	21,237	21,663	21,615
Less:					
Households with no mortgage	(9,946)	(10,391)	(10,420)	(10,105)	(9,854)
Households headed by person >age 65	(354)	(293)	(365)	(367)	(360)
Mortgage older than fifteen years	(689)	(673)	(748)	(865)	(919)
Excluded for other reasons[a]	(4,553)	(4,661)	(4,749)	(4,948)	(5,849)
Sample used in analysis	5,054	5,089	4,955	5,378	4,633

a. Households had other than a fixed-rate primary mortgage, very small mortgage balances (less than 10 percent of house value), or lacked information necessary to determine whether the primary mortgage was terminated (in the case of nonmovers).

Information on the construction of our five samples is provided in table 10-1. Consider the 1985–87 sample. There were 27,490 usable owner households in the 1987 AHS. These households were first matched by unit control numbers with the 1985 sample of owner households. This matching procedure yielded 20,596 owner households. Of these 20,596 observations, 9,946 did not have a mortgage in 1985. Households headed by persons over age 65 (354 observations) and households with mortgages older than fifteen years (689 observations) were excluded. An additional 4,553 were excluded because they had other than a fixed-rate primary mortgage, very small mortgage balances (less than 10 percent of house value), or lacked information necessary to determine whether the primary mortgage was terminated (in the case of nonmovers). The final 1985–87 sample contains 5,054 households. The four remaining samples were created in the same manner and contain 5,089, 4,955, 5,378, and 4,633 households, respectively. Table 10-1 summarizes the sample construction information. Selected summary statistics are presented in table 10-2.

All explanatory variables used in the analysis are measured at the beginning of each two-year window. The dependent variable—whether the household terminated its primary mortgage—is based on a comparison of its mortgage char-

Table 10-2. *Sample Descriptive Statistics*

	Mortgage age group								
	Non-low-income			*Low-income*			*Low-income first-time owner*		
	0–4 years	*5–10 years*	*11–15 years*	*0–4 years*	*5–10 years*	*11–15 years*	*0–4 years*	*5–10 years*	*11–15 years*
1985–87 data window									
Total households	1,122	1,384	459	818	885	386	434	459	226
Households that terminated mortgages (percent)	56	35	25	52	35	33	53	33	36
Current fair market value of residence ($000s)									
Median	79.50	80.00	80.00	46.50	55.00	55.00	45.00	48.00	50.00
Mean	86.75	88.84	90.76	50.43	62.04	62.81	46.06	55.13	58.16
Standard deviation	41.87	43.45	42.85	32.01	36.76	37.10	28.78	34.26	34.76
Number of years mortgage outstanding									
Median	2.00	7.00	13.00	2.00	7.00	13.00	1.50	7.00	13.00
Mean	1.73	7.21	12.75	1.65	7.26	12.81	1.59	7.33	12.85
Standard deviation	1.38	1.57	1.34	1.34	1.59	1.43	1.31	1.60	1.43
Present value of interest savings from prepayment[a] (PVIS) ($000s)									
Median	10.00	0.58	–1.01	4.31	0.32	–0.49	4.59	0.28	–0.43
Mean	11.42	2.23	–1.08	6.20	1.38	–0.49	6.46	1.25	–0.32
Standard deviation	9.90	5.75	2.36	7.31	4.06	2.95	7.23	3.94	3.12
Mortgage call options in-the-money[b] (percent)	91	59	17	89	60	31	92	59	34
Book loan-to-value ratio (LTV)									
Median	0.71	0.45	0.25	0.71	0.47	0.27	0.75	0.50	0.27
Mean	0.69	0.46	0.28	0.69	0.48	0.30	0.72	0.50	0.30
Standard deviation	0.21	0.19	0.16	0.25	0.22	0.18	0.25	0.23	0.17
Annual payment-to-income ratio (PAYINC)									
Median	0.14	0.09	0.06	0.18	0.16	0.12	0.18	0.15	0.11
Mean	0.14	0.10	0.07	0.35	0.27	0.23	0.22	0.21	0.24
Standard deviation	0.07	0.05	0.05	3.14	0.55	0.47	0.28	0.32	0.58

Variable									
More than one mortgage (yes = 1) (SECMORT) (percent)	8	13	18	7	12	13	6	10	15
First-time homeowner (yes = 1) (FIRSTTIME) (percent)	39	39	50	53	52	59	100	100	100
Potential wasted interest as a percentage of residence fair market value (TAX)[c]									
Median	0.00	0.00	0.00	0.02	0.02	0.02	0.02	0.02	0.02
Mean	0.00	0.00	0.00	0.05	0.03	0.03	0.06	0.04	0.03
Standard deviation	0.01	0.01	0.01	0.10	0.07	0.04	0.10	0.09	0.04
Total income (INC)									
Median	43.00	45.00	45.00	21.00	21.00	20.00	21.55	21.00	20.00
Mean	48.48	50.53	49.66	19.99	19.42	18.45	20.39	19.86	18.69
Standard deviation	19.03	19.82	17.74	7.57	8.44	8.36	7.45	7.92	8.31
Two wage earners (yes = 1) (JOINTINC) (percent)	67	68	67	37	30	31	41	34	31
Age of household head (AGE)									
Median	35.00	39.00	44.00	33.00	38.00	45.00	30.00	35.00	42.50
Mean	36.19	41.01	45.80	35.99	41.23	46.54	31.65	37.49	43.94
Standard deviation	8.44	8.36	7.77	10.76	9.91	9.13	8.52	8.48	8.35
Head with two or more years of college (yes = 1) (COLLEGE) (percent)	60	59	57	35	32	24	37	32	21
Family size (FAMSIZE)									
Median	3.00	4.00	4.00	3.00	3.00	3.00	3.00	3.00	4.00
Mean	3.10	3.46	3.57	2.80	3.25	3.24	2.68	3.35	3.50
Standard deviation	1.29	1.31	1.41	1.44	1.58	1.49	1.42	1.59	1.48
African American head (yes = 1) (BLACK) (percent)	5	5	6	7	8	13	10	11	19
Hispanic head (yes = 1) (HISP) (percent)	3	4	4	4	6	6	5	7	9
Rural location (yes = 1) (RURAL) (percent)	7	7	6	18	11	13	13	9	13
1987-89 data window									
Total households	1,646	1,091	569	900	568	315	472	295	182
Households that terminated mortgages (percent)	32	33	26	37	37	32	38	38	31
Current fair market value of residence ($000s)									
Median	90.00	85.00	80.00	55.00	52.50	55.00	50.00	47.00	50.00
Mean	102.04	97.17	96.71	60.75	63.46	66.68	56.08	55.66	59.50
Standard deviation	49.82	50.53	52.08	40.50	42.77	42.59	37.73	38.97	40.38

continued on next page

Table 10-2. *Sample Descriptive Statistics (continued)*

	Mortgage age group								
	Non-low-income			*Low-income*			*Low-income first-time owner*		
	0–4 years	*5–10 years*	*11–15 years*	*0–4 years*	*5–10 years*	*11–15 years*	*0–4 years*	*5–10 years*	*11–15 years*
Number of years mortgage outstanding									
Median	2.00	8.00	12.00	1.00	8.00	12.00	1.00	8.00	12.00
Mean	1.73	7.73	12.67	1.66	7.83	12.77	1.67	7.82	12.78
Standard deviation	1.32	1.65	1.42	1.34	1.62	1.53	1.36	1.61	1.51
Present value of interest savings from prepayment[a] (PVIS) ($000s)									
Median	0.32	–0.36	–1.66	0.29	0.00	–1.06	0.36	0.06	–0.80
Mean	0.48	0.17	–1.72	0.60	0.21	–1.14	0.52	0.60	–0.93
Standard deviation	6.07	4.29	2.02	4.37	3.68	2.21	4.09	3.79	1.95
Mortgage call options in-the-money[b] (percent)	55	44	13	64	51	25	67	56	26
Book loan-to-value ratio (LTV)									
Median	0.72	0.49	0.30	0.74	0.51	0.32	0.80	0.52	0.32
Mean	0.69	0.50	0.33	0.72	0.53	0.36	0.75	0.54	0.36
Standard deviation	0.22	0.22	0.19	0.26	0.25	0.22	0.25	0.25	0.23
Annual payment-to-income ratio (PAYINC)									
Median	0.16	0.10	0.07	0.21	0.18	0.14	0.21	0.16	0.13
Mean	0.16	0.11	0.08	0.35	0.37	0.27	0.31	0.41	0.24
Standard deviation	0.07	0.06	0.05	0.97	2.21	0.49	0.59	3.02	0.46
More than one mortgage (yes = 1) (SECMORT) (percent)	5	16	18	4	12	13	3	10	12
First-time homeowner (yes = 1) (FIRSTTIME) (percent)	39	41	48	52	52	58	100	100	100
Potential wasted interest as a percentage of residence fair market value (TAX)[c]									
Median	0.00	0.00	0.00	0.03	0.03	0.03	0.03	0.04	0.04
Mean	0.01	0.01	0.01	0.07	0.06	0.05	0.07	0.07	0.05
Standard deviation	0.02	0.02	0.01	0.13	0.11	0.06	0.13	0.11	0.06

Total income (INC)									
Median	47.00	47.00	47.30	21.50	21.00	20.00	22.10	20.40	20.00
Mean	53.47	54.78	54.35	20.58	19.86	18.78	21.35	19.94	18.78
Standard deviation	22.54	25.09	22.76	7.99	8.49	8.92	7.57	8.19	8.47
Two wage earners (yes = 1) (JOINTINC) (percent)	69	67	70	31	31	29	33	34	31
Age of household head (AGE)									
Median	35.00	40.00	44.00	34.00	40.00	45.00	29.00	36.00	42.00
Mean	36.68	41.43	45.61	36.47	41.95	46.79	31.62	37.78	43.35
Standard deviation	8.40	8.30	7.24	10.97	9.96	9.37	8.27	8.30	8.29
Head with two or more years of college (yes = 1) (COLLEGE) (percent)	62	61	59	36	32	32	36	30	32
Family size (FAMSIZE)									
Median	3.00	4.00	4.00	3.00	3.00	3.00	2.00	4.00	3.00
Mean	3.06	3.37	3.45	2.70	3.14	3.05	2.57	3.38	3.35
Standard deviation	1.26	1.35	1.44	1.47	1.60	1.49	1.45	1.63	1.52
African American head (yes = 1) (BLACK) (percent)	5	5	6	7	12	13	8	17	17
Hispanic head (yes = 1) (HISP) (percent)	4	4	4	5	5	6	6	6	9
Rural location (yes = 1) (RURAL) (percent)	7	8	7	16	17	12	14	14	12
1989-91 data window									
Total households	1,778	955	629	849	435	309	459	216	174
Households that terminated mortgages (percent)	25	39	24	31	39	25	29	35	26
Current fair market value of residence ($000s)									
Median	95.00	90.00	90.00	55.00	55.00	65.00	52.00	53.00	54.50
Mean	115.68	106.43	109.41	66.70	70.48	81.60	63.39	66.52	71.17
Standard deviation	65.00	61.60	65.75	48.57	52.89	59.17	46.81	51.22	53.53
Number of years mortgage outstanding									
Median	2.00	7.00	13.00	2.00	7.00	12.00	2.00	7.00	12.00
Mean	2.00	7.38	12.69	1.76	7.51	12.50	1.72	7.32	12.43
Standard deviation	1.32	1.86	1.34	1.37	1.94	1.33	1.35	1.93	1.27

continued on next page

Table 10-2. *Sample Descriptive Statistics (continued)*

	Mortgage age group								
	Non-low-income			*Low-income*			*Low-income first-time owner*		
	0–4 years	*5–10 years*	*11–15 years*	*0–4 years*	*5–10 years*	*11–15 years*	*0–4 years*	*5–10 years*	*11–15 years*
Present value of interest savings from prepayment[a] (PVIS) ($000s)									
Median	3.19	2.16	–0.38	1.62	1.16	0.01	1.50	1.51	0.02
Mean	3.78	3.59	–0.34	2.38	2.48	–0.02	2.27	2.69	0.34
Standard deviation	6.01	5.35	2.15	4.16	4.24	2.51	4.39	4.40	2.45
Mortgage call options in-the-money[b] (percent)	80	84	40	83	80	53	82	81	57
Book loan-to-value ratio (LTV)									
Median	0.71	0.53	0.32	0.72	0.51	0.36	0.75	0.56	0.36
Mean	0.69	0.54	0.35	0.70	0.54	0.39	0.73	0.57	0.40
Standard deviation	0.21	0.24	0.19	0.24	0.28	0.24	0.23	0.27	0.25
Annual Payment-to-Income Ratio (PAYINC)									
Median	0.15	0.11	0.07	0.21	0.18	0.15	0.22	0.17	0.14
Mean	0.16	0.11	0.08	0.36	0.61	0.40	0.30	0.29	0.40
Standard deviation	0.07	0.06	0.05	1.26	6.21	1.07	0.59	0.54	1.08
More than one mortgage (yes = 1) (SECMORT) (percent)	9	16	27	3	12	13	3	11	14
First-time homeowner (yes = 1) (FIRSTTIME) (percent)	39	43	44	54	50	56	100	100	100
Potential wasted interest as a percentage of residence fair market value (TAX)[c]									
Median	0.00	0.00	0.00	0.06	0.06	0.06	0.06	0.06	0.06
Mean	0.02	0.02	0.02	0.10	0.11	0.07	0.11	0.10	0.08
Standard deviation	0.04	0.05	0.03	0.16	0.27	0.07	0.17	0.15	0.09
Total income (INC)									
Median	50.00	52.00	52.00	22.10	22.00	21.00	22.92	23.00	21.55
Mean	57.44	58.88	58.45	20.81	19.73	19.44	21.42	20.84	19.15
Standard deviation	25.15	25.98	24.73	8.19	8.86	9.35	7.97	8.36	9.72

Two wage earners (yes = 1) (JOINTINC) (percent)	68	69	69	30	28	25	30	29	25
Age of household head (AGE)									
Median	36.00	41.00	44.00	34.00	40.00	46.00	31.00	36.00	43.00
Mean	37.18	41.64	45.43	37.22	42.04	47.44	32.89	37.57	44.44
Standard deviation	8.54	8.24	7.22	10.65	9.84	9.69	8.30	8.24	9.02
Head with two or more years of college (yes = 1) (COLLEGE) (percent)	62	59	58	35	31	32	34	34	23
Family size (FAMSIZE)									
Median	3.00	3.00	4.00	3.00	3.00	3.00	2.00	3.00	3.00
Mean	3.06	3.29	3.51	2.75	2.91	2.83	2.69	3.03	3.00
Standard deviation	1.32	1.35	1.40	1.50	1.59	1.44	1.52	1.59	1.52
African American head (yes = 1) (BLACK) (percent)	4	6	5	8	10	12	11	15	16
Hispanic head (yes = 1) (HISP) (percent)	4	5	3	8	6	4	9	7	5
Rural location (yes = 1) (RURAL) (percent)	6	8	8	14	18	14	12	15	16
1991–93 data window									
Total households	1,925	1,162	700	808	443	340	443	222	181
Households that terminated mortgages (percent)	51	59	43	42	50	39	38	45	39
Current fair market value of residence ($000s)									
Median	100.00	100.00	90.00	58.00	60.00	66.50	55.00	55.00	60.00
Mean	117.79	116.58	111.03	68.27	74.16	79.73	63.67	69.12	73.07
Standard deviation	63.16	65.04	65.35	45.67	51.55	53.66	41.03	48.41	51.23
Number of years mortgage outstanding									
Median	2.00	6.00	13.00	2.00	6.00	13.00	2.00	6.00	13.00
Mean	2.00	6.68	12.93	1.94	6.76	13.00	1.95	6.68	13.07
Standard deviation	1.38	1.66	1.38	1.36	1.66	1.33	1.37	1.63	1.31
Present value of interest savings from prepayment[a] (PVIS) ($000s)									
Median	17.03	11.02	4.10	8.88	6.83	3.32	8.86	7.18	2.64
Mean	19.45	13.05	5.94	11.01	9.11	4.26	10.92	9.35	3.81
Standard deviation	13.06	9.69	5.92	9.80	8.55	4.37	9.52	8.21	4.54

continued on next page

Table 10-2. *Sample Descriptive Statistics (continued)*

	Mortgage age group								
	Non-low-income			*Low-income*			*Low-income first-time owner*		
	0–4 years	*5–10 years*	*11–15 years*	*0–4 years*	*5–10 years*	*11–15 years*	*0–4 years*	*5–10 years*	*11–15 years*
Mortgage call options in-the-money[b] (percent)	100	99	97	99	99	97	99	99	96
Book loan-to-value ratio (LTV)									
Median	0.75	0.57	0.38	0.74	0.57	0.38	0.78	0.61	0.41
Mean	0.73	0.57	0.41	0.72	0.58	0.40	0.75	0.62	0.42
Standard deviation	0.20	0.23	0.22	0.24	0.28	0.23	0.23	0.28	0.24
Annual payment-to-income ratio (PAYINC)									
Median	0.14	0.10	0.07	0.19	0.16	0.14	0.19	0.16	0.13
Mean	0.14	0.11	0.08	0.49	0.30	0.23	0.58	0.25	0.24
Standard deviation	0.07	0.06	0.06	4.94	0.56	0.26	6.60	0.40	0.30
More than one mortgage (yes = 1) (SECMORT) (percent)	8	18	28	5	13	17	3	14	17
First-time homeowner (yes = 1) (FIRSTTIME) (percent)	41	41	44	55	50	53	100	100	100
Potential wasted interest as a percentage of residence fair market value (TAX)[c]									
Median	0.00	0.00	0.01	0.06	0.06	0.05	0.07	0.07	0.06
Mean	0.02	0.02	0.02	0.10	0.10	0.08	0.11	0.11	0.09
Standard deviation	0.04	0.05	0.05	0.14	0.17	0.11	0.15	0.17	0.13
Total income (INC)									
Median	52.30	55.85	54.00	23.45	24.00	21.80	23.00	24.90	22.26
Mean	60.51	63.29	60.47	21.57	21.61	20.02	21.67	22.45	19.82
Standard deviation	26.63	28.58	26.58	8.34	8.87	9.53	8.03	8.02	10.07
Two wage earners (yes = 1) (JOINTINC) (percent)	67	68	70	33	29	24	33	32	22
Age of Household Head (AGE)									
Median	35.00	40.00	44.00	34.50	40.00	46.00	31.00	36.00	43.00
Mean	37.18	41.20	45.58	37.36	42.27	47.02	33.21	37.66	44.62
Standard deviation	8.58	8.13	7.55	10.80	10.02	8.81	8.87	8.41	8.58

Head with two or more years of college (yes = 1) (COLLEGE) (percent)	63	61	58	37	35	30	37	36	28
Family size (FAMSIZE)									
Median	3.00	3.00	3.00	2.00	3.00	2.50	2.00	3.00	3.00
Mean	3.05	3.26	3.28	2.69	2.86	2.78	2.60	3.03	2.92
Standard deviation	1.31	1.34	1.37	1.52	1.52	1.47	1.53	1.62	1.55
African American head (yes = 1) (BLACK) (percent)	5	5	6	7	9	12	10	11	17
Hispanic head (yes = 1) (HISP) (percent)	4	3	4	8	7	5	9	11	7
Rural location (yes = 1) (RURAL) (percent)	8	7	9	14	19	15	11	18	15
1993–95 data window									
Total households	1,633	1,168	457	715	453	207	403	237	105
Households that terminated mortgages (percent)	36	48	46	40	44	49	39	41	51
Current fair market value of residence ($000s)									
Median	103.00	100.00	92.00	60.00	60.00	75.00	55.00	55.00	70.00
Mean	117.37	120.11	109.89	74.54	75.97	82.71	66.49	65.05	87.32
Standard deviation	59.54	65.19	57.95	53.90	54.91	48.30	46.12	40.89	57.66
Number of years mortgage outstanding									
Median	2.00	7.00	14.00	2.00	7.00	13.00	2.00	7.00	14.00
Mean	1.98	7.00	13.37	1.92	6.92	13.19	1.89	6.86	13.37
Standard deviation	1.35	1.63	1.39	1.36	1.64	1.36	1.37	1.61	1.38
Present value of interest savings from prepayment[a] (PVIS) ($000s)									
Median	9.43	7.53	4.46	6.19	6.71	4.74	6.04	6.90	4.43
Mean	11.51	10.28	6.62	8.32	8.48	6.47	8.09	8.32	5.87
Standard deviation	10.23	10.30	7.75	9.04	8.37	6.15	8.21	7.73	5.66
Mortgage call options in-the-money[b] (percent)	96	96	97	97	98	100	97	98	99
Book Loan-to-Value Ratio (LTV)									
Median	0.77	0.61	0.43	0.76	0.63	0.46	0.81	0.65	0.45
Mean	0.75	0.60	0.45	0.73	0.61	0.47	0.76	0.63	0.45
Standard deviation	0.19	0.23	0.22	0.24	0.26	0.24	0.24	0.25	0.24

continued on next page

Table 10-2. *Sample Descriptive Statistics (continued)*

	Mortgage age group								
	Non-low-income			*Low-income*			*Low-income first-time owner*		
	0–4 years	*5–10 years*	*11–15 years*	*0–4 years*	*5–10 years*	*11–15 years*	*0–4 years*	*5–10 years*	*11–15 years*
Annual Payment-to-Income Ratio (PAYINC)									
Median	0.13	0.10	0.07	0.20	0.17	0.17	0.20	0.16	0.17
Mean	0.14	0.11	0.08	0.48	0.98	0.56	0.36	0.36	0.81
Standard deviation	0.06	0.06	0.06	2.32	12.30	2.99	0.90	1.09	4.17
More than one mortgage (yes = 1) (SECMORT) (percent)	4	13	18	3	10	15	2	11	14
First-time homeowner (yes = 1) (FIRSTTIME) (percent)	41	40	42	56	52	51	100	100	100
Potential wasted interest as a percentage of residence fair market value (TAX)[c]									
Median	0.00	0.00	0.00	0.06	0.07	0.05	0.07	0.07	0.05
Mean	0.02	0.02	0.02	0.11	0.10	0.08	0.13	0.09	0.07
Standard deviation	0.04	0.04	0.07	0.19	0.13	0.09	0.22	0.09	0.07
Total income (INC)									
Median	55.00	58.43	56.50	23.52	24.90	21.00	23.50	25.00	22.50
Mean	62.29	66.60	64.82	21.38	22.00	20.28	21.35	22.22	20.74
Standard deviation	26.41	30.74	29.15	8.95	9.41	10.24	8.94	9.52	10.35
Two wage earners (yes=1) (JOINTINC) (percent)	69	65	71	27	25	30	29	25	31
Age of household head (AGE)									
Median	36.00	40.00	45.00	35.00	40.00	45.00	32.00	36.00	43.00
Mean	37.52	41.46	45.95	37.73	41.71	47.23	34.28	38.15	45.42
Standard deviation	8.52	8.00	7.15	10.39	9.69	8.81	9.31	8.25	8.56

Head with two or more years of college (yes = 1) (COLLEGE) (percent)	63	60	60	35	35	33	33	33	30
Family size (FAMSIZE)									
Median	3.00	3.00	3.00	2.00	3.00	3.00	3.00	3.00	3.00
Mean	3.03	3.32	3.19	2.75	2.79	2.91	2.74	2.75	3.07
Standard deviation	1.33	1.43	1.38	1.58	1.45	1.53	1.62	1.41	1.68
African American head (yes = 1) (BLACK) (percent)	4	6	5	7	10	14	9	16	18
Hispanic head (yes = 1) (HISP) (percent)	5	4	4	10	8	7	12	9	9
Rural location[d] (yes = 1) (RURAL) (percent)	8	9	9	14	17	14	13	16	10

Source: Authors' tabulations and estimates from the American Housing Survey, 1985, 1987, 1989, 1991, 1993, and 1995 National Files supplemented with nonhousing expense estimates based on data from Internal Revenue Service Individual Tax Model File. Reported values are either raw percentages or sample medians, means, and standard deviations.

a. The present value of interest savings from prepayment is the market value of first mortgage debt less the book value of first mortgage debt. Market value of first mortgage debt is the present value of the remaining payments discounted over the remaining loan period using Freddie Mac's monthly commitment rate on thirty-year fixed-rate mortgages (the lowest rate for the period between the two AHS surveys is used for each window).

b. If the market value minus the book value of the primary mortgage is greater than zero, then the call option is "in the money."

c. Potential "wasted" interest as a percentage of house value is used as a proxy for the mean weighted-average tax rate at which mortgage interest is deducted. Potential wasted interest represents the maximum amount of mortgage interest that will produce no tax savings due to the difference between the household's standard deduction and other itemized personal deductions, including property taxes. The potential wasted interest dollar amount is scaled by the fair market value of the residence.

d. Ten binary variables indicating whether the home is located in one of the top ten most represented MSAs in the combined 1985–95 samples are included in the logistic regression models but not reported here.

acteristics, including date obtained and type of mortgage, at the beginning and end of each two-year window. [6]

In part, this chapter examines the variation in mortgage termination across households in response to changes in mortgage interest rates. Therefore it is important that the study include periods during which a significant number of households might consider the exercise of their call options, and, if possible, one or more in which they would not. Figure 10-1 displays Freddie Mac's monthly commitment rate on thirty-year fixed-rate mortgages from January of 1984 to December 1996. The AHS is conducted during the last four months of the survey year. Mortgage interest rates averaged 12.19 percent in September 1985, the beginning of the 1985–87 window, after steadily declining from a record high of 18.45 percent in October 1981. Rates continued to fall during the 1985–87 window, reaching a low of 9.04 percent in March 1987. The 1987–89 window complements the previous period because rates, though volatile, had little trend during that period, ranging from 9.88 to 11.05 percent. The 1989–91 rates ranged from 9.24 to 11.05 percent, with rates generally falling over the period. The 1991–93 rates ranged from 7.11 to 9.01 percent in a declining rate environment. Finally, the 1993–95 rates ranged from 6.83 to 9.17 percent, with a steep rise in the middle of the period.

Logistic regression models

A series of logistic regression models are estimated where

$$\text{TERM}_i = \mathbf{b}'\mathbf{x}_i + \mu_i \,. \qquad (10\text{-}6)$$

TERM_i is a binary variable indicating whether the *i*th household has terminated, for any reason, its primary mortgage; **b** is a row vector of coefficients, $\mathbf{x}_i$ is a vector of variables that explains the household's decision to terminate a mort-

6. The AHS follows housing units rather than housing occupants. Accordingly, several criteria were used to identify households that moved and therefore terminated their fixed-rate mortgages. First, sample observations were considered movers if the AHS survey did not indicate that at least some of the same household members lived in the unit in both the beginning and ending window years. Observations also were classified as movers if respondents reported that a move had occurred within the year before the end of the two-year window. Second, to classify remaining households as nonmovers, observations from each pair of years (1985–87, 1987–89, 1989–91, 1991–93, and 1993–95) were matched on several criteria to ensure that the sample unit contained the same household in both the beginning and ending window years. Several checks were conducted to compare household characteristics across the two sample years within each window for stability or expected change. For example, the age of the household head should increase by approximately two years between surveys. Observations that failed one or more of these checks were classified as movers, with remaining observations classified as nonmovers. The effects of default are present in the data of this study, but they are not distinguished explicitly. Rather, they are part of the total of terminations. This is unavoidable since the data do not permit identification of default terminations. However, to distinguish default cases would be unproductive in any case in a national sample of the size used here because the occurrence of default is so limited (see note 2).

Figure 10-1. *Residential Mortgage Interest Rates, 1984–96*

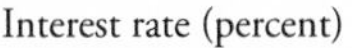

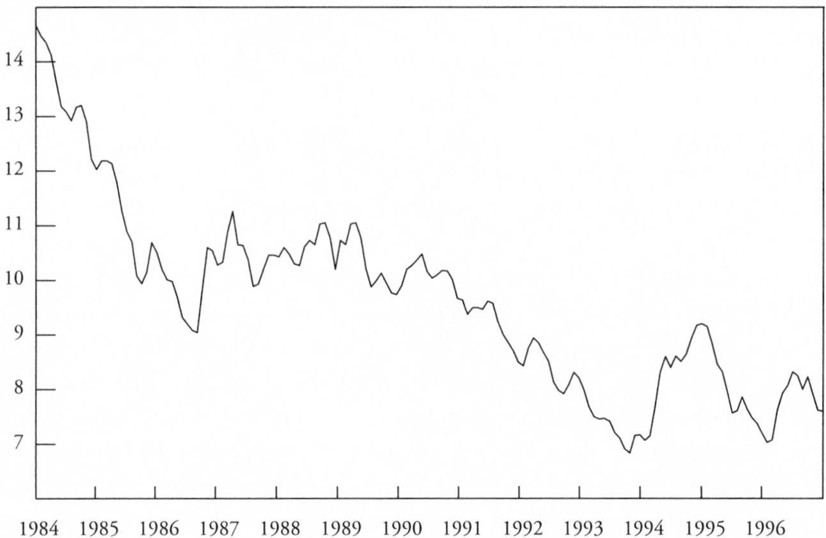

Source: Freddie Mac's monthly commitment rate on thirty-year fixed-rate residential mortgages.

gage, and μ_i is the random error term. The vector **x** contains mortgage-related variables, household characteristic variables, location variables, and interaction terms for each of these variables (see below). Our inclusion of variables is motivated by their demonstrated importance in prior theoretical and empirical studies of default, mobility, and refinancing behavior.

We first examine how low-to-moderate-income households differ from higher-income households in their propensity to terminate fixed-rate mortgages. This is accomplished by creating a binary variable (LOWINC) that takes on a value of one if the household's total income is less than 80 percent of the median income of the metropolitan statistical area (MSA) in which they reside, and a value of zero otherwise.[7] All of the explanatory variables are then interacted with LOWINC to examine the incremental intercept and slope effects of households being classified as low-to-moderate-income. We also identify the portion of the sample that is both low-to-moderate-income and a first-time homeowner (FIRSTLOW). In a separate set of logistic regressions, we interact all explanatory variables with FIRSTLOW.

Both the low-to-moderate-income interaction regressions and the first-time homeowner interaction regressions are disaggregated by mortgage age. More

7. Median income for the MSA of the housing unit from the 1990 U.S. census is scaled to the window year using the ratio of state-level median income in the window year to 1990 census state-level median income.

specifically, we partition mortgages into three categories: those that were originated less than five years earlier; those that have been outstanding for five to ten years; and those outstanding for eleven to fifteen years. Mortgages originated more than fifteen years before the analysis period are dropped from the analysis.

Mortgage-Related Variables

The mortgage variables in $\mathbf{x}_i$ include the age of the mortgage in years, the present value of the interest savings from refinancing (PVIS), book loan-to-value ratio (LTV), and the prospective payment-to-income ratio (PAYINC). In the empirical model, PVIS (the intrinsic benefit of refinancing) is set equal to the market value less the book value of the primary mortgage debt. The book value of the existing primary mortgage is based on the household's actual mortgage interest rate, term, and original amortization period. The market value of the primary mortgage is calculated as the present value of the remaining mortgage payments, discounted using the lowest Freddie Mac monthly commitment rate on thirty-year fixed-rate mortgages during the respective AHS window.[8] A household's mortgage prepayment option is considered "in-the-money" if PVIS exceeds zero. PVIS is negative for a household if market interest rates have risen since mortgage origination. This negative intrinsic benefit from refinancing may result in a "lock-in" effect where to move or refinance results in a higher cost of fixed-rate mortgage debt. The magnitude of PVIS varies significantly among mortgage age groups and across sample windows.

Book LTV is the book value of total outstanding mortgage debt (primary, plus any other mortgages) divided by the current fair market value of the residence.[9] A binary variable indicates whether the household has more than one mortgage (SECMORT). The "prospective" payment-to-income ratio (PAYINC) is calculated by assuming the current book value of the primary mortgage is refinanced as a fixed-rate, thirty-year mortgage at the prevailing rate. The denominator of this ratio is the household's total income, including earned and investment

8. The discount rate used to estimate market values of mortgages was 9.04 percent for the 1985–87 window, 9.88 percent for the 1987–89 window, 9.24 percent for the 1989–91 window, 7.11 percent for the 1991–93 window, and 6.83 percent for the 1993–95 window. Use of the lowest mortgage rate during each two-year period to calculate the present value of the remaining payments may overstate the intrinsic benefit from refinancing because many terminating households in our sample may have prepaid at a rate that is well above the lowest rate during the two-year interval. To the extent that our calculation of PVIS is upwardly biased, our estimated effect of PVIS on mortgage terminations is understated. The empirical model does not include proxies for the current mortgage interest rate (or interest rate process) because these factors do not vary cross-sectionally.

9. Market value estimates by households have been shown to be accurate on average (see, for example, Goodman and Ittner, 1992; Follain and Malpezzi, 1981; Kain and Quigley, 1972; Robins and West, 1977; and Kiel and Zabel, 1999). Kiel and Zabel found that the average U.S. owner overstates house value by 5.1 percent and that this error generally is uncorrelated with particular characteristics of the house, occupant, or neighborhood.

income.[10] Because higher current loan-to-value ratios and payment-to-income ratios indicate greater collateral and liquidity constraints, LTV and PAYINC are expected to have a negative effect on the probability of an interest rate–driven termination (Archer, Ling, and McGill, 1996). However, if equity in the house is negative (LTV > 1), or the payment burden increases substantially, a default-driven termination is more likely. Because default occurs much less frequently than interest rate–driven refinancing, the latter effect is expected to dominate the former. However, the net effect of these offsetting influences on termination must be determined empirically.

Household Characteristic Variables

A binary variable indicates whether the household is a first-time homeowner (FIRSTTIME). Potential "wasted" interest as a percentage of house value is used as a proxy for the mean weighted-average tax rate at which mortgage interest is deducted (TAX). Potential wasted interest represents the maximum amount of mortgage interest that will produce no tax savings due to the difference between the household's standard deduction and other itemized personal deductions, including property taxes (Ling and McGill, 1992). The sign of potential wasted interest is reversed in the logistic regressions because higher wasted interest represents a lower weighted-average tax rate. TAX should be negatively related to the probability of termination because higher levels of TAX represent a lower after-tax cost of mortgage debt.

Giliberto and Thibodeau (1989) and Dickinson and Heuson (1993) find that increases in household income has a positive effect on interest rate–driven terminations. However, the direction of the total household income variable (INC) in our specification is unclear because INC captures the influence of total household income after controlling for whether the household income could support a new mortgage (PAYINC). Consequently, INC could proxy for features such as the financial sophistication of the household or the cost of nonpecuniary transaction costs such as the opportunity cost of time involved in refinancing. INC also may be negatively related to termination probability from moving (see Krumm, 1984).

The binary variable JOINTINC takes on a value of one if household income is produced by two wage earners. JOINTINC is related to total income and its influence on liquidity constraints because two wage earners within a household might improve creditworthiness. However, the existence of two wage earners may signal households with greater income constraints and a reduced option to generate additional income. From the mobility literature, JOINTINC, as a signal of a married household, may proxy for higher propensity to terminate.

10. This payment burden ratio is less than a lender's front-end ratio because property taxes and insurance are excluded from the numerator and investment income is included in the denominator.

Again, both theory and prior empirical studies provide little guidance for predicting the sign of JOINTINC in our estimation.

Quigley (1987) found that the probability of termination is negatively related to the age of the household head (AGE) and positively related to family size (FAMSIZE). If AGE or FAMSIZE has an effect it should be as a proxy for life-cycle differences across households. AGE may signal a decreased benefit of moving, hence lower propensity to terminate, though the empirical mobility literature reports contradictory evidence. FAMSIZE has been reported in the mobility literature to be associated with higher mobility, implying a positive coefficient in explaining termination (Gronberg and Reed, 1992). A binary variable (COLLEGE) is created that indicates whether the household head attended two or more years of college. COLLEGE may proxy for characteristics such as financial sophistication and willingness to change. If so, COLLEGE should be positively related to termination probabilities (Quigley, 1987). COLLEGE also should have a positive effect on termination through its positive effect on mobility, perhaps again due to greater economic sophistication (Gronberg and Reed, 1992; Henderson and Ioannides, 1989).

Binary variables indicating whether the household head is an African American (BLACK) or Hispanic (HISP) are also included in the regression specification. The effects of race and ethnicity are indeterminate, except for some empirical indication from the mobility literature that nonwhites are more mobile.

Shocks (sudden or unexpected changes) can be a factor in household mobility (Quigley and Weinberg, 1977). These events could include divorce, unemployment, events that change household size or household income, or significant change in neighborhood (Boehm and Ihlanfeldt, 1986). A limitation of the AHS data is that it cannot account for such events because the survey is based on housing units rather than households. Thus it loses the household at the time of relocation and is unable to record the change in household characteristics that would signal the precipitating event.

Location variables include a binary variable indicating whether the property is located in a rural area (RURAL), and ten binary variables indicating whether the home is located in one of the top ten most represented MSAs in the combined 1985–95 samples. These location variables are included to control for variations across MSAs in house price inflation, income growth rates, and general demographic trends.

Variation across households in the cost of terminating a mortgage may also help explain cross-sectional differences in termination rates (Archer and Ling, 1993; Stanton, 1995). Besides direct financial transaction costs, any factor that creates resistance to the borrower who would prepay is, in effect, a transaction cost. A wide range of other barriers may have this effect, including lack of creditworthiness, lack of comfort with financial affairs, opportunity cost of the time required for finding and arranging new financing, and perhaps other "psychological" barriers. Transaction costs associated with refinancing are captured by LTV, representing a collateral constraint; PAYINC, representing a liquidity constraint; with SECMORT, FIRSTTIME, TAX, INC, JOINTINC, AGE, COLLEGE, FAMSIZE, BLACK, HISP, RURAL, and the MSA indicator variables controlling for the heterogeneous nature of borrowers.

Empirical Results

Tables 10-3 through 10-8 contain logistic regressions, with parameter estimates, *p*-values of the associated Wald chi-square statistics (in parentheses), and measures of goodness-of-fit, including two model classification rates. The first group of tables (10-3 through 10-5) reports results from estimating equation 10-6 with the sample partitioned by income level alone. Included is a complete set of low-to-moderate-income interaction variables. Table 10-3 contains the results for mortgages less than five years old. Tables 10-4 and 10-5 contain the corresponding results for mortgages five through ten and eleven through fifteen years old, respectively. In tables 10-6 through 10-8, the control group is again all non-low-to-moderate-income households. However, the test group consists of households that are both low-to-moderate-income households and first-time homeowners.

Results for the 1985–87 window are reported in the first column of each table, followed by the results for the remaining four windows. The –2 log likelihood statistics are significant for all models, indicating that the independent variables provide explanatory power, and the classification rates are superior to a naive model based on every household's being classified as a nonterminator. The base case (non-low-to-moderate-income) coefficients are discussed first, followed by an analysis of the low-to-moderate-income interactions in tables 10-3 through 10-5. The results for the more restrictive test group, low-to-moderate-income and first-time homeowners, are then discussed.

Results for the Higher-Income Control Group

The coefficient on mortgage age for the zero-through-four mortgage age group (table 10-3) is generally positive and significant. Thus, even within the zero-through-four age group, mortgages that have been outstanding longer are more likely to be terminated. The coefficients on PVIS in table 10-3 are positive and strongly significant in all but the 1987–89 window. This indicates that larger interest savings from refinancing have a direct and positive effect on the termination probabilities of higher-income households and is consistent with option-based explanations of mortgage prepayments. The coefficient on book LTV is consistently negative, suggesting that increased collateral constraints reduce the probability of termination for higher-income households, as would be expected given the empirical findings of Archer, Ling, and McGill (1996) and Hurst and Stafford (1996). However, this result is statistically significant only in the

1985–87 window. A potential explanation is that higher-income households generally use less mortgage debt than low-to-moderate-income households. Thus they are less likely to find themselves collaterally constrained if house values decline subsequent to origination. The estimated coefficients on LTV^2 are generally insignificant, suggesting that the effects of collateral constraints are not highly nonlinear.

Except for the 1989–91 window, the coefficients on PAYINC are negative and statistically significant. This is not surprising because households considering an interest rate–driven prepayment are likely to find loan qualification more difficult as the prospective payment burden increases. The estimated coefficients on $PAYINC^2$ suggest that the effects of payment constraints are not highly nonlinear. Taken together, the results for the mortgage variables suggest that higher-income borrowers are more likely to be liquidity- or income-constrained than to be constrained by the value of their housing collateral.

For mortgages that have been outstanding for five to ten years (table 10-4), the effects of mortgage age are much less clear than for less-seasoned mortgages. In two windows the estimated coefficient is negative and significant; in two subsequent windows the coefficient is positive and significant. Similar to the results for less-seasoned mortgages, termination rates for mortgages five to ten years of age are positively and significantly related to PVIS, generally unaffected by contemporaneous LTVs, and negatively related to contemporaneous payment burdens.

Mortgages eleven to fifteen years of age display some variations in termination rates within this age category. Most important, PVIS continues to have a positive and highly significant effect on termination rates. Thus we find no evidence among higher-income households that borrowers are less likely to respond to attractive prepayment opportunities as their mortgage age increases. The coefficients on both LTV and PAYINC are negative and significant in two of five windows for these more seasoned mortgages. Finally, there is limited evidence in tables 10-3 through 10-5 that the existence of a second mortgage is associated with higher first mortgage termination probabilities among higher-income households, all else equal.

Turning to the household characteristic variables, we find that first-time homeowners who obtained their first mortgage less than five years earlier are somewhat less frequent terminators than non-first-time owners. For more seasoned mortgages (tables 10-4 and 10-5), the first-time owners shift variable is not significant. The coefficient on TAX is generally negative and marginally significant as expected; the probability of termination decreases as TAX increases because higher levels of TAX represent lower after-tax costs of mortgage debt.

There is little evidence in tables 10-3 through 10-5 that the termination behavior of higher-income households is affected by the level of household income, after controlling for the effect of PAYINC. This is not consistent with the notion that higher income proxies for increased financial sophistication and awareness, which in turn produces larger responses to in-the-money refinancing options. There is limited evidence in tables 10-3 through 10-5 that if household income is produced by two wage earners, the probability of termination is decreased. This is clearly not consistent with the hypothesis that, for a given level of income, two wage earners within a household improves creditworthiness. It also is not consistent with evidence from the mobility literature that married households are more mobile, all else equal. This result is consistent with the notion that households with two income earners may be relatively more income-constrained.

The negative and statistically significant coefficients on AGE in tables 10-3 and 10-4 indicate that the probability of termination decreases with age. However, the positive coefficient on AGE^2 suggests that the effect of age is nonlinear. An explanation consistent with this result is that households generally become less mobile as the head ages; hence the lower probability of termination. However, as the head approaches retirement age and any children have left the house (and have not returned), the probability of downsizing or relocation may increase. In addition, older households are more likely to have accumulated enough wealth to allow them to simply pay off the remaining balance on their mortgage loan.

The coefficient on COLLEGE is consistently positive and occasionally significant. This result provides some support for Quigley's (1987) contention that COLLEGE should be positively related to termination probability. The signs and magnitudes of the coefficients on FAMSIZE provide no clear picture of the effect of family size on terminations. This contrasts with the mobility studies that have found greater household size to increase the likelihood of relocating. Similarly, the coefficients on BLACK and HISP provide no clear evidence that the termination behavior of these two groups can be distinguished from observationally equivalent nonblack or non-Hispanic households. In sum, many of the household-level variables are significant and thus make the explanatory power of the termination model greater than that of a model with mortgage and option characteristics only.

Location indicator variables for the ten MSAs that contribute the largest number of observations to our analysis were also included in the estimations in an attempt to control for differences in past market conditions, including average house price appreciation. These location variables also may proxy for cross-sectional differences in expectations about future price appreciation. Although the coefficients on these location dummies are occasionally significant, no clear geographic pattern emerges. Thus, to conserve space, these estimates are not reported.[11]

11. The ten MSAs that contribute the largest number of usable observations are Chicago, Detroit, Los Angeles, Philadelphia, Washington, D.C., Minneapolis–St. Paul, New York Metro, Nassau and Suffolk County, Houston, and Phoenix. These coefficient estimates are available from the authors upon request.

Table 10-3. *Logistic Regressions Explaining Termination of Primary Mortgage with Low-to-Moderate-Income Interactions: Mortgage Age Less than Five Years*

	Two-year data windows				
	1985–87	*1987–89*	*1989–91*	*1991–93*	*1993–95*
Intercept	2.634 (0.042)	1.831 (0.094)	1.668 (0.146)	2.847 (0.006)	4.239 (0.000)
Mortgage-related variables					
Number of years mortgage outstanding (MTGAGE)	0.117 (0.017)	0.229 (0.000)	0.067 (0.141)	0.120 (0.002)	0.287 (0.000)
Present value of interest savings (PVIS)	6.4E-05 (0.000)	0.6E-05 (0.501)	1.8E-05 (0.071)	5.1E-05 (0.000)	1.4E-05 (0.019)
Book loan-to-value ratio (LTV)	–3.376 (0.019)	–1.648 (0.115)	–1.597 (0.178)	–1.900 (0.152)	–1.421 (0.283)
Book loan-to-value ratio squared (LTV^2)	1.503 (0.140)	1.390 (0.062)	0.948 (0.265)	–0.516 (0.584)	0.425 (0.641)
Annual payment-to-income ratio (PAYINC)	–6.202 (0.037)	–9.953 (0.001)	–1.439 (0.582)	–6.100 (0.026)	–7.692 (0.019)
Annual payment-to-income ratio squared (PAYINC^2)	4.775 (0.448)	22.320 (0.001)	2.206 (0.689)	4.421 (0.483)	14.334 (0.089)
More than one mortgage (yes = 1) (SECMORT)	0.609 (0.020)	0.155 (0.531)	0.344 (0.079)	0.108 (0.584)	–0.036 (0.892)
Household characteristic variables					
First-time homeowner (yes = 1) (FIRSTTIME)	–0.038 (0.806)	–0.018 (0.896)	–0.143 (0.303)	–0.351 (0.003)	–0.434 (0.001)
Potential wasted interest as a percentage of residence fair market value (TAX)	–6.995 (0.311)	–5.598 (0.133)	–1.975 (0.300)	–0.932 (0.491)	–1.144 (0.531)
Total income (INC)	–0.004 (0.387)	0.003 (0.289)	0.004 (0.207)	–0.005 (0.052)	–0.003 (0.271)
Two wage earners (yes=1) (JOINTINC)	0.149 (0.293)	–0.348 (0.005)	–0.230 (0.068)	–0.064 (0.572)	–0.219 (0.082)
Age of household head (AGE)	–0.031 (0.612)	–0.090 (0.086)	–0.113 (0.031)	–0.051 (0.280)	–0.176 (0.001)
Age of household head squared (AGE^2)	19.5E-05 (0.795)	0.001 (0.099)	0.001 (0.043)	32.4E-05 (0.566)	0.002 (0.002)
Household head with two or more years of college (yes = 1) (COLLEGE)	0.136 (0.320)	0.036 (0.766)	–0.013 (0.915)	0.500 (0.000)	0.259 (0.028)
Family size (FAMSIZE)	–0.051 (0.334)	0.030 (0.520)	0.035 (0.448)	0.013 (0.763)	0.041 (0.363)
African American head (yes = 1) (BLACK)	–0.685 (0.030)	0.326 (0.204)	0.475 (0.073)	–1.198 (0.000)	0.050 (0.854)
Hispanic head (yes = 1) (HISP)	–0.200 (0.589)	0.032 (0.906)	0.349 (0.193)	–0.079 (0.757)	–0.145 (0.570)
Location variables					
Rural location (yes = 1) (RURAL)	–0.008 (0.960)	0.195 (0.180)	0.168 (0.299)	0.272 (0.061)	–0.284 (0.071)
Low-to-moderate-income interactions					
Income <80 percent of MSA median income (yes = 1) (LOWINC)	–0.842 (0.621)	–0.262 (0.865)	1.600 (0.349)	–1.026 (0.514)	–0.476 (0.787)

continued on next page

Table 10-3. *Logistic Regressions Explaining Termination of Primary Mortgage with Low-to-Moderate-Income Interactions: Mortgage Age Less than Five Years (continued)*

	Two-year data windows				
	1985–87	*1987–89*	*1989–91*	*1991–93*	*1993–95*
MTGAGE × LOWINC	0.013	–0.146	0.036	–0.069	–0.127
	(0.864)	(0.048)	(0.632)	(0.318)	(0.106)
PVIS × LOWINC	–2.0E-05	2.2E-05	3.0E-05	-0.8E-05	1.8E-05
	(0.261)	(0.278)	(0.179)	(0.481)	(0.134)
LTV × LOWINC	–1.387	–2.762	–3.260	–1.609	–5.477
	(0.471)	(0.068)	(0.063)	(0.405)	(0.007)
LTV^2 × LOWINC	0.551	1.348	1.712	2.213	3.371
	(0.684)	(0.211)	(0.174)	(0.107)	(0.016)
PAYINC × LOWINC	6.216	10.083	1.543	6.307	7.739
	(0.037)	(0.000)	(0.556)	(0.021)	(0.018)
$PAYINC^2$ × LOWINC	–4.774	–22.318	–2.211	–4.423	–14.338
	(0.448)	(0.001)	(0.688)	(0.483)	(0.089)
SECMORT × LOWINC	–0.840	–0.026	–0.266	0.441	0.223
	(0.039)	(0.954)	(0.617)	(0.261)	(0.694)
FIRSTTIME × LOWINC	0.045	0.084	–0.154	–0.021	0.267
	(0.845)	(0.700)	(0.508)	(0.922)	(0.245)
TAX × LOWINC	2.090	2.878	–2.055	–1.791	–2.874
	(0.766)	(0.450)	(0.314)	(0.243)	(0.152)
INC × LOWINC	0.008	–0.006	–0.007	0.015	–0.013
	(0.571)	(0.611)	(0.601)	(0.200)	(0.274)
JOINTINC × LOWINC	–0.269	0.259	–0.259	0.093	0.072
	(0.231)	(0.222)	(0.268)	(0.664)	(0.767)
AGE × LOWINC	0.033	0.045	–0.014	–0.015	0.086
	(0.678)	(0.532)	(0.857)	(0.831)	(0.276)
AGE^2 × LOWINC	–44.0E–05	-56.0E–05	17.1E–05	37.9E–05	-91.0E–05
	(0.655)	(0.517)	(0.853)	(0.656)	(0.332)
COLLEGE × LOWINC	–0.274	–0.178	–0.040	–0.712	–0.090
	(0.202)	(0.373)	(0.850)	(0.000)	(0.678)
FAMSIZE × LOWINC	0.053	–0.005	–0.036	–0.040	–0.039
	(0.510)	(0.948)	(0.632)	(0.573)	(0.597)
BLACK × LOWINC	0.161	–0.078	0.108	0.913	–0.616
	(0.711)	(0.839)	(0.782)	(0.029)	(0.165)
HISPANIC × LOWINC	0.622	0.308	–0.485	–0.017	–0.104
	(0.234)	(0.458)	(0.235)	(0.965)	(0.794)
Number of observations	1,940	2,546	2,627	2,733	2,348
–2 log-likelihood statistic	2470.634	3090.045	2905.846	3416.553	2872.250
(p-value of chi-squared statistic)	(0.000)	(0.000)	(0.000)	(0.000)	(0.000)
Within-sample classification rate	60.0	67.1	74.3	61.4	63.7
Paired rank correlation ("c" statistic)	0.683	0.647	0.637	0.701	0.682

Note: Reported values are parameter estimates from logistic regressions with p-values of Wald chi-square statistics in parentheses. See table 10-2 and the text for variable definitions. Ten binary variables indicating whether the home is located in one of the top ten most represented MSAs in the combined 1985–95 samples are included in the logistic regression models as location control variables, but these results are not reported here. Tables including these variables are available from the authors on request.

Table 10-4. *Logistic Regressions Explaining Termination of Primary Mortgage with Low-to-Moderate-Income Interactions: Mortgage Age Five to Ten Years*

	Two-year data windows				
	1985–87	*1987–89*	*1989–91*	*1991–93*	*1993–95*
Intercept	4.096	5.050	1.732	3.483	3.675
	(0.007)	(0.003)	(0.327)	(0.035)	(0.021)
Mortgage-related variables					
Number of years mortgage outstanding (MTGAGE)	–0.045	–0.140	–0.111	0.159	0.077
	(0.349)	(0.002)	(0.006)	(0.000)	(0.051)
Present value of interest savings (PVIS)	12.9E–05	0.9E–05	5.5E–05	4.0E–05	2.9E–05
	(0.000)	(0.588)	(0.000)	(0.000)	(0.000)
Book loan-to-value ratio (LTV)	–2.180	–2.959	–0.786	–1.362	–1.197
	(0.108)	(0.011)	(0.512)	(0.264)	(0.274)
Book loan-to-value ratio squared (LTV^2)	1.459	2.357	–0.199	–0.143	0.247
	(0.245)	(0.014)	(0.837)	(0.880)	(0.763)
Annual payment-to-income ratio (PAYINC)	–19.528	–2.436	–10.113	–3.864	–5.738
	(0.000)	(0.531)	(0.012)	(0.304)	(0.081)
Annual payment-to-income ratio squared ($PAYINC^2$)	46.681	2.343	25.775	10.661	9.148
	(0.001)	(0.839)	(0.029)	(0.297)	(0.298)
More than one mortgage (yes = 1) (SECMORT)	0.585	–0.004	–0.035	0.108	0.014
	(0.006)	(0.986)	(0.871)	(0.569)	(0.943)
Household characteristic variables					
First-time homeowner (yes = 1) (FIRSTTIME)	0.031	–0.157	–0.009	–0.075	–0.226
	(0.834)	(0.319)	(0.958)	(0.622)	(0.126)
Potential wasted interest as a percentage of residence fair market value (TAX)	–1.983	–7.495	–3.474	–2.097	–3.563
	(0.843)	(0.084)	(0.084)	(0.239)	(0.067)
Total income (INC)	–0.010	0.005	0.005	0.003	0.005
	(0.008)	(0.150)	(0.143)	(0.301)	(0.079)
Two wage earners (yes = 1) (JOINTINC)	–0.057	–0.216	–0.126	–0.085	–0.068
	(0.669)	(0.153)	(0.421)	(0.559)	(0.616)
Age of household head (AGE)	–0.102	–0.150	–0.024	–0.164	–0.148
	(0.140)	(0.046)	(0.761)	(0.024)	(0.040)
Age of household head squared (AGE^2)	98.1E–05	0.002	15.2E–05	0.002	0.001
	(0.210)	(0.070)	(0.865)	(0.041)	(0.081)
Household head with two or more years of college (yes = 1) (COLLEGE)	0.162	–0.059	0.141	0.375	0.119
	(0.217)	(0.683)	(0.352)	(0.006)	(0.363)
Family size (FAMSIZE)	0.018	–0.080	–0.005	–0.040	–0.050
	(0.724)	(0.145)	(0.933)	(0.444)	(0.289)
African American head (yes = 1) (BLACK)	–0.009	0.083	–0.375	–0.711	–0.174
	(0.976)	(0.793)	(0.259)	(0.022)	(0.529)
Hispanic Head (yes = 1) (HISP)	0.248	0.266	0.072	–1.733	–0.158
	(0.407)	(0.445)	(0.830)	(0.000)	(0.616)
Location variables					
Rural location (yes = 1) (RURAL)	–0.094	0.143	0.306	0.292	–0.153
	(0.589)	(0.428)	(0.104)	(0.124)	(0.377)
Low-to-moderate-income interactions					
Income <80 percent of MSA median income (yes = 1) (LOWINC)	–2.831	–1.338	–0.762	1.462	1.493
	(0.196)	(0.599)	(0.788)	(0.592)	(0.568)

continued on next page

Table 10-4. *Logistic Regressions Explaining Termination of Primary Mortgage with Low-to-Moderate-Income Interactions: Mortgage Age Five to Ten Years (continued)*

	Two-year data windows				
	1985–87	*1987–89*	*1989–91*	*1991–93*	*1993–95*
MTGAGE × LOWINC	–0.065	–0.176	68.3E–05	–0.058	0.006
	(0.377)	(0.032)	(0.993)	(0.453)	(0.931)
PVIS × LOWINC	0.4E–05	7.9E–05	0.2E–05	–0.1E–05	–1.0E–05
	(0.871)	(0.022)	(0.943)	(0.972)	(0.444)
LTV × LOWINC	–1.168	–0.311	–1.848	–3.178	–1.575
	(0.509)	(0.860)	(0.318)	(0.090)	(0.372)
LTV^2 × LOWINC	–0.481	–0.986	1.447	2.599	1.095
	(0.765)	(0.495)	(0.326)	(0.066)	(0.402)
PAYINC × LOWINC	20.186	2.126	9.691	3.671	5.500
	(0.000)	(0.588)	(0.017)	(0.334)	(0.096)
$PAYINC^2$ × LOWINC	–46.798	–2.342	–25.773	–10.634	–9.145
	(0.001)	(0.840)	(0.029)	(0.298)	(0.299)
SECMORT × LOWINC	–0.362	–0.294	–0.382	0.211	–0.139
	(0.266)	(0.448)	(0.386)	(0.567)	(0.720)
FIRSTTIME × LOWINC	–0.352	0.318	–0.208	–0.347	–0.107
	(0.120)	(0.243)	(0.486)	(0.222)	(0.698)
TAX × LOWINC	–10.178	4.975	–0.209	–0.872	1.371
	(0.324)	(0.267)	(0.929)	(0.675)	(0.537)
INC × LOWINC	0.024	–0.039	–0.018	–0.020	–0.023
	(0.123)	(0.025)	(0.284)	(0.242)	(0.123)
JOINTINC × LOWINC	–0.025	0.167	0.081	–0.009	0.353
	(0.911)	(0.540)	(0.787)	(0.976)	(0.213)
AGE × LOWINC	0.095	0.150	0.035	–0.068	–0.053
	(0.342)	(0.188)	(0.788)	(0.568)	(0.649)
AGE^2 × LOWINC	–0.001	–0.001	–26.0E–05	99.0E–05	57.4E–05
	(0.329)	(0.256)	(0.853)	(0.452)	(0.656)
COLLEGE × LOWINC	–0.420	–0.026	–0.227	0.416	–0.128
	(0.055)	(0.920)	(0.431)	(0.122)	(0.615)
FAMSIZE × LOWINC	–0.020	0.027	0.072	0.186	0.070
	(0.787)	(0.754)	(0.448)	(0.044)	(0.446)
BLACK × LOWINC	–0.041	–0.054	–0.603	0.089	0.248
	(0.921)	(0.900)	(0.264)	(0.857)	(0.587)
HISPANIC × LOWINC	–0.628	–0.816	0.261	1.982	0.584
	(0.172)	(0.154)	(0.637)	(0.001)	(0.237)
Number of observations	2,269	1,659	1,390	1,605	1,621
–2 log-likelihood statistic	2654.643	1988.540	1731.936	2014.221	2137.069
(*p*-value of chi-squared statistic)	(0.000)	(0.000)	(0.000)	(0.000)	(0.000)
Within-sample classification rate	68.6	66.7	62.1	62.7	56.6
Paired rank correlation ("c" statistic)	0.696	0.668	0.660	0.686	0.642

Note: Reported values are parameter estimates from logistic regressions with *p*-values of Wald chi-square statistics in parentheses. See Table 10-2 and the text for variable definitions. Ten binary variables indicating whether the home is located in one of the top ten most represented MSAs in the combined 1985–95 samples are included in the logistic regression models as location control variables, but these results are not reported here. Tables including these variables are available from the authors on request.

Table 10-5. *Logistic Regressions Explaining Termination of Primary Mortgage with Low-to-Moderate-Income Interactions: Mortgage Age Eleven to Fifteen Years*

	Two-year data windows				
	1985–87	*1987–89*	*1989–91*	*1991–93*	*1993–95*
Intercept	1.007	1.709	−1.942	4.063	7.817
	(0.788)	(0.656)	(0.609)	(0.199)	(0.054)
Mortgage-related variables					
Number of years mortgage outstanding (MTGAGE)	−0.002	0.210	0.033	−0.268	−0.169
	(0.981)	(0.007)	(0.675)	(0.000)	(0.023)
Present value of interest savings (PVIS)	27.2E–05	19.2E–05	19.6E–05	7.0E–05	4.5E–05
	(0.000)	(0.001)	(0.000)	(0.000)	(0.008)
Book loan-to-value ratio (LTV)	4.340	−0.760	−2.282	−2.356	−3.335
	(0.111)	(0.679)	(0.221)	(0.090)	(0.060)
Book loan-to-value ratio squared (LTV^2)	−0.935	1.674	2.456	1.635	1.704
	(0.753)	(0.345)	(0.192)	(0.179)	(0.254)
Annual payment-to-income ratio (PAYINC)	−18.861	1.142	−11.778	−8.021	−1.226
	(0.035)	(0.874)	(0.050)	(0.140)	(0.846)
Annual payment-to-income ratio squared ($PAYINC^2$)	42.041	15.108	32.519	23.566	6.876
	(0.146)	(0.564)	(0.050)	(0.172)	(0.736)
More than one mortgage (yes = 1) (SECMORT)	0.554	−0.687	−0.235	0.365	0.714
	(0.167)	(0.043)	(0.440)	(0.111)	(0.016)
Household characteristic variables					
First-time homeowner (yes = 1) (FIRSTTIME)	0.399	−0.187	−0.223	−0.044	−0.339
	(0.146)	(0.417)	(0.329)	(0.820)	(0.141)
Potential wasted interest as a percentage of residence fair market value (TAX)	−1.817	−11.961	−1.874	−0.916	−4.629
	(0.940)	(0.193)	(0.618)	(0.653)	(0.138)
Total income (INC)	0.008	0.016	−0.001	0.003	0.003
	(0.310)	(0.004)	(0.816)	(0.446)	(0.566)
Two wage earners (yes = 1) (JOINTINC)	0.190	0.125	−0.392	−0.142	0.017
	(0.494)	(0.599)	(0.091)	(0.464)	(0.947)
Age of household head (AGE)	−0.092	−0.213	0.047	−0.002	−0.229
	(0.571)	(0.194)	(0.765)	(0.990)	(0.161)
Age of household head squared (AGE^2)	0.001	0.002	−40.0E–05	−18.0E–05	0.002
	(0.554)	(0.275)	(0.806)	(0.895)	(0.179)
Household head with two or more years of college (yes = 1) (COLLEGE)	−0.030	−0.006	−0.054	0.082	0.632
	(0.908)	(0.978)	(0.797)	(0.640)	(0.005)
Family size (FAMSIZE)	−0.252	−0.158	0.148	0.007	0.011
	(0.018)	(0.060)	(0.072)	(0.914)	(0.898)
African American head (yes = 1) (BLACK)	−0.501	0.325	1.249	−0.438	0.280
	(0.341)	(0.436)	(0.004)	(0.232)	(0.574)
Hispanic head (yes = 1) (HISP)	0.422	0.606	−0.052	−0.207	−0.503
	(0.480)	(0.248)	(0.938)	(0.650)	(0.368)
Location variables					
Rural location (yes = 1) (RURAL)	0.411	0.141	0.146	0.019	0.080
	(0.158)	(0.617)	(0.593)	(0.934)	(0.785)
Low-to-moderate-income interactions					
Income <80 percent of MSA median income (yes = 1) (LOWINC)	6.965	1.666	2.107	−2.604	−5.807
	(0.191)	(0.757)	(0.707)	(0.590)	(0.370)

continued on next page

Table 10-5. *Logistic Regressions Explaining Termination of Primary Mortgage with Low-to-Moderate-Income Interactions: Mortgage Age Eleven to Fifteen Years (continued)*

	Two-year data windows				
	1985–87	*1987–89*	*1989–91*	*1991–93*	*1993–95*
MTGAGE × LOWINC	–0.025	–0.319	0.138	0.247	0.065
	(0.853)	(0.009)	(0.320)	(0.039)	(0.663)
PVIS × LOWINC	13.6E–05	29.5E–05	3.4E–05	2.6E–05	1.9E–05
	(0.213)	(0.017)	(0.682)	(0.535)	(0.610)
LTV × LOWINC	–7.775	–0.439	–0.726	–2.072	0.029
	(0.025)	(0.859)	(0.789)	(0.339)	(0.992)
LTV^2 × LOWINC	2.746	–1.040	–1.925	–0.387	–1.860
	(0.478)	(0.650)	(0.471)	(0.849)	(0.467)
PAYINC × LOWINC	19.578	–1.061	13.414	8.851	1.257
	(0.030)	(0.884)	(0.032)	(0.127)	(0.842)
$PAYINC^2$ × LOWINC	–42.503	–15.047	–33.428	–24.476	–6.874
	(0.142)	(0.566)	(0.044)	(0.158)	(0.736)
SECMORT × LOWINC	–0.075	0.120	–0.342	0.472	–0.275
	(0.894)	(0.834)	(0.590)	(0.269)	(0.629)
FIRSTTIME × LOWINC	–0.358	–0.301	0.026	0.301	0.538
	(0.372)	(0.446)	(0.950)	(0.358)	(0.181)
TAX × LOWINC	–13.490	6.109	–5.338	–2.951	–3.862
	(0.588)	(0.532)	(0.266)	(0.292)	(0.354)
INC × LOWINC	–0.013	–0.003	–0.024	–0.005	0.003
	(0.650)	(0.926)	(0.393)	(0.813)	(0.863)
JOINTINC × LOWINC	0.074	–0.569	0.770	–0.059	0.196
	(0.855)	(0.171)	(0.088)	(0.872)	(0.675)
AGE × LOWINC	–0.253	0.131	–0.097	–0.040	0.304
	(0.263)	(0.563)	(0.672)	(0.842)	(0.243)
AGE^2 × LOWINC	0.003	–0.001	64.4E–05	65.9E–05	–0.004
	(0.274)	(0.638)	(0.787)	(0.748)	(0.185)
COLLEGE × LOWINC	–0.493	–0.475	–0.434	–0.111	–1.251
	(0.234)	(0.226)	(0.298)	(0.730)	(0.003)
FAMSIZE × LOWINC	0.208	0.195	–0.418	–0.105	–0.271
	(0.156)	(0.165)	(0.007)	(0.377)	(0.074)
BLACK × LOWINC	1.114	–0.462	–1.164	0.098	–1.375
	(0.089)	(0.424)	(0.074)	(0.855)	(0.050)
HISPANIC × LOWINC	0.669	–0.283	–0.365	0.062	–0.054
	(0.383)	(0.709)	(0.732)	(0.931)	(0.949)
Number of observations	845	884	938	1,040	664
–2 log-likelihood statistic	827.345	936.325	923.543	1310.623	834.232
(*p*-value of chi-squared statistic)	(0.000)	(0.000)	(0.000)	(0.000)	(0.001)
Within-sample classification rate	73.8	72.3	76.7	60.6	56.5
Paired rank correlation ("c" statistic)	0.776	0.716	0.708	0.690	0.698

Notes: Reported values are parameter estimates from logistic regressions with *p*-values of Wald chi-square statistics in parentheses. See Table 10-2 and the text for variable definitions. Ten binary variables indicating whether the home is located in one of the top ten most represented MSAs in the combined 1985–95 samples are included in the logistic regression models as location control variables, but these results are not reported here. Tables including these variables are available from the authors on request.

Low-to-Moderate-Income Interactions

We now examine the incremental intercept and slope effects for households having total income less than 80 percent of area median. The intercept shift variable (LOWINC) is strikingly insignificant in all five windows and for all three mortgage age groups. Thus there appears to be no difference in the baseline rate at which low-to-moderate-income households terminate their fixed-rate mortgages. The PVIS interaction variable captures the extent to which low-to-moderate-income households differ from higher-income households in their responsiveness to interest rate changes. Recall that for higher-income households the coefficient on PVIS is positive and highly significant. Interestingly, the results reported in tables 10-3 through 10-5 provide no clear evidence that lower-income households are differentially sensitive to attractive refinancing opportunities. In particular, low-to-moderate-income households are clearly not *less* responsive than higher-income households to interest rate changes. Said differently, these results provide no evidence that the price "charged" by lenders for the embedded call option should be different for lower-income borrowers.

The LTV interaction variable captures the extent to which the current (not original) leverage ratio affects the termination probabilities of low-to-moderate-income households differently than higher-income households. Table 10-3 shows that the estimated coefficient on this interaction variable is negative in all five windows and statistically significant in three windows. This result suggests that larger amounts of mortgage debt (relative to house value) slow the terminations of low-to-moderate-income households significantly more than higher-income terminations. This may reflect the fact that low-to-moderate-income households generally have less accumulated wealth and therefore must debt-finance a larger percentage of the initial purchase price. However, if the market value of their home declines after purchase, they may not be able to qualify for a replacement mortgage as large as the outstanding balance on the existing loan. Thus even if interest rates have fallen since origination, the borrower may not choose to prepay because doing so may require the borrower to invest additional equity capital in the housing asset. Said differently, such borrowers are more likely to become constrained by the value of their mortgage collateral than borrowers who obtain lower LTVs at origination. The LTV^2 interaction term is largely insignificant.

The coefficient on PAYINC for higher-income households was negative and highly significant, as discussed earlier. The coefficients on the PAYINC interaction variable are positive and generally significant. In fact, the magnitude of the interaction coefficient effectively offsets the negative high-income coefficient in each of the five sample periods. This indicates that the termination behavior of low-to-moderate-income households is *not* responsive to changes in prospective payment burdens, all else equal. This insensitivity to changes in the payment burden is somewhat surprising. Most have posited that low-to-moderate-income households are *more* adversely affected by increases in the prospective payment burden on a new mortgage because these households generally have less wealth available to them to increase their equity down payment. However, this result may simply reflect that the lower-income test group is already significantly income-constrained. Thus further increases in the prospective payment burden have no significant effects.

Examination of tables 10-3 through 10-5 reveals that the coefficients on the remaining interaction variables are strikingly insignificant. Thus the influence of household characteristics and location variables does not appear to differ across the two income subsamples. This finding is important as a further indication that the prepayment behavior of lower-income homeowners is little different from that of other homeowners except for the influence of collateral and income constraints.

To examine the sensitivity of our results to the definition of low-to-moderate-income, we conducted tests setting LOWINC equal to one if household income was less than 60 percent of the MSA median and produced a logistic regression for each of the five sample periods. Although not reproduced here, the results were little different from the initial specification that classified as low-to-moderate-income all households with less than 80 percent of the median income in the MSA. In particular, the intercept shift variable is still insignificant in four of the five windows. Once again, the estimated coefficients on the PVIS interaction variable indicate that low-to-moderate-income households were clearly no less responsive to changes in mortgages interest rates.

Low-to-Moderate-Income and First-Time Homeowner Interactions

The interaction variables in tables 10-3 through 10-5 capture the incremental intercept and slope effects for households having total income less that 80 percent of area median. A household's status as a first-time homeowner is not separately considered. However, numerous housing policies focus on a subset of our low-to-moderate-income test group—that is, those households that are both lower-income *and* nonhomeowners. We now examine how the termination behavior of this smaller subset of households varies from the non-low-income control group. More specifically, in our second set of regressions, the control group remains the same as in tables 10-3 though 10-5—that is, all households with income above 80 percent of the area median. However, we create a new dummy variable, FIRSTLOW, that takes on a value of one if the household has income below 80 percent of the area median *and* the household head is a first-time owner. These results are reported in tables 10-6 through 10-8.

The estimated coefficients on FIRSTLOW in table 10-6 are positive but statistically significant (at the 0.079 level) only in the 1989–91 window. Largely

Table 10-6. *Logistic Regressions Explaining Termination of Primary Mortgage with Low-to-Moderate-Income and First-Time Owner Interactions: Mortgage Age Less Than Five Years*

	Two-year data windows				
	1985–87	*1987–89*	*1989–91*	*1991–93*	*1993–95*
Intercept	2.534	1.729	1.239	2.036	3.132
	(0.039)	(0.087)	(0.247)	(0.042)	(0.005)
Mortgage-related variables					
Number of years mortgage outstanding (MTGAGE)	0.116	0.225	0.059	0.103	0.269
	(0.018)	(0.000)	(0.188)	(0.006)	(0.000)
Present value of interest savings (PVIS)	6.5E–05	0.7E–05	1.7E–05	5.2E–05	1.4E–05
	(0.000)	(0.433)	(0.077)	(0.000)	(0.020)
Book loan-to-value ratio (LTV)	–3.349	–1.667	–1.608	–2.043	–1.382
	(0.020)	(0.110)	(0.175)	(0.124)	(0.297)
Book loan-to-value ratio squared (LTV^2)	1.470	1.389	0.939	–0.507	0.278
	(0.149)	(0.061)	(0.269)	(0.592)	(0.760)
Annual payment-to-income ratio (PAYINC)	–6.296	–10.015	–1.369	–5.792	–7.159
	(0.035)	(0.001)	(0.599)	(0.033)	(0.028)
Annual payment-to-income ratio squared ($PAYINC^2$)	5.049	22.438	2.013	3.567	13.416
	(0.423)	(0.001)	(0.713)	(0.567)	(0.109)
More than one mortgage (yes = 1) (SECMORT)	0.627	0.169	0.353	0.143	0.020
	(0.017)	(0.497)	(0.071)	(0.466)	(0.941)
Household characteristic variables					
Potential wasted interest as a percentage of residence fair market value (TAX)	–7.272	–5.775	–2.003	–0.976	–1.336
	(0.293)	(0.126)	(0.294)	(0.475)	(0.465)
Total income (INC)	–0.004	0.003	0.004	–0.005	–0.002
	(0.405)	(0.311)	(0.170)	(0.087)	(0.528)
Two wage earners (yes = 1) (JOINTINC)	0.144	–0.349	–0.243	–0.080	–0.247
	(0.311)	(0.005)	(0.053)	(0.476)	(0.048)
Age of household head (AGE)	–0.027	–0.083	–0.098	–0.023	–0.142
	(0.651)	(0.098)	(0.052)	(0.616)	(0.005)
Age of household head squared (AGE^2)	15.2E–05	96.9E–05	0.001	8.6E–05	0.002
	(0.836)	(0.117)	(0.067)	(0.878)	(0.008)
Household head with two or more years of college (yes = 1) (COLLEGE)	0.134	0.033	–0.011	0.	0.231
	(0.328)	(0.783)	(0.928)	495 (0.000)	(0.049)
Family size (FAMSIZE)	–0.048	0.028	0.043	0.033	0.066
	(0.355)	(0.545)	(0.347)	(0.425)	(0.136)
African American head (yes = 1) (BLACK)	–0.692	0.361	0.447	–1.215	–0.009
	(0.028)	(0.160)	(0.090)	(0.000)	(0.973)
Hispanic head (yes = 1) (HISP)	–0.190	0.051	0.329	–0.103	–0.196
	(0.609)	(0.849)	(0.221)	(0.687)	(0.439)
Location variables					
Rural location (yes = 1) (RURAL)	–0.100	0.128	0.224	0.215	–0.365
	(0.634)	(0.465)	(0.236)	(0.200)	(0.041)
Low-to-moderate income/first-time owner interactions					
Income <80 percent of MSA median income and first-time owner (yes = 1) (FIRSTLOW)	1.765	1.699	3.739	–0.803	3.143
	(0.406)	(0.375)	(0.079)	(0.672)	(0.146)

continued on next page

Table 10-6. *Logistic Regressions Explaining Termination of Primary Mortgage with Low-to-Moderate-Income and First-Time Owner Interactions: Mortgage Age Less Than Five Years (continued)*

	Two-year data windows				
	1985–87	*1987–89*	*1989–91*	*1991–93*	*1993–95*
MTGAGE × FIRSTLOW	–0.009	–0.110	0.157	–0.032	–0.109
	(0.931)	(0.249)	(0.123)	(0.727)	(0.282)
PVIS × FIRSTLOW	–3.0E–05	2.7E–05	5.4E–05	–0.5E–05	5.4E–05
	(0.127)	(0.374)	(0.089)	(0.719)	(0.004)
LTV × FIRSTLOW	–6.352	–4.540	–3.194	–1.241	–8.829
	(0.020)	(0.025)	(0.184)	(0.620)	(0.001)
LTV^2 × FIRSTLOW	3.286	2.352	1.935	2.118	5.004
	(0.067)	(0.090)	(0.261)	(0.235)	(0.004)
PAYINC × FIRSTLOW	6.940	9.341	–0.014	6.267	6.965
	(0.031)	(0.002)	(0.996)	(0.023)	(0.034)
$PAYINC^2$ × FIRSTLOW	–5.154	–21.793	–1.694	–3.571	–13.410
	(0.414)	(0.001)	(0.758)	(0.567)	(0.110)
SECMORT × FIRSTLOW	–1.297	–0.121	0.438	1.137	–0.367
	(0.017)	(0.858)	(0.499)	(0.057)	(0.698)
TAX × FIRSTLOW	–2.712	3.416	–1.238	–3.916	–2.485
	(0.714)	(0.384)	(0.570)	(0.032)	(0.241)
INC × FIRSTLOW	0.067	0.004	–0.029	0.055	–0.023
	(0.015)	(0.825)	(0.175)	(0.004)	(0.209)
JOINTINC × FIRSTLOW	–0.378	0.288	–0.042	–0.324	0.356
	(0.195)	(0.291)	(0.893)	(0.258)	(0.247)
AGE × FIRSTLOW	–0.070	–0.042	–0.125	–0.092	–0.031
	(0.497)	(0.667)	(0.217)	(0.336)	(0.757)
AGE^2 × FIRSTLOW	73.7E–05	71.7E–05	0.002	0.001	37.7E–05
	(0.576)	(0.566)	(0.212)	(0.279)	(0.760)
COLLEGE × FIRSTLOW	0.113	–0.277	0.162	–0.898	0.163
	(0.683)	(0.283)	(0.565)	(0.001)	(0.576)
FAMSIZE × FIRSTLOW	0.028	0.048	–0.047	–0.084	0.025
	(0.782)	(0.593)	(0.629)	(0.357)	(0.789)
BLACK × FIRSTLOW	0.273	–0.743	0.223	0.724	–0.265
	(0.588)	(0.120)	(0.613)	(0.134)	(0.606)
HISPANIC × FIRSTLOW	0.432	0.033	–0.443	–0.371	0.415
	(0.488)	(0.949)	(0.407)	(0.457)	(0.373)
Number of observations	1,556	2,118	2,237	2,368	2,036
–2 log-likelihood statistic	1936.272	2532.327	2439.103	2920.147	2467.967
(*p*-value of chi-squared statistic)	(0.000)	(0.000)	(0.000)	(0.000)	(0.000)
Within-sample classification rate	60.7	67.1	75.0	63.0	64.1
Paired rank correlation ("c" statistic)	0.701	0.655	0.628	0.713	0.684

Notes: Reported values are parameter estimates from logistic regressions with *p*-values of Wald chi-square statistics in parentheses. See Table 10-2 and the text for variable definitions. Ten binary variables indicating whether the home is located in one of the top ten most represented MSAs in the combined 1985–95 samples are included in the logistic regression models as location control variables, but these results are not reported here. Tables including these variables are available from the authors on request.

Table 10-7. *Logistic Regressions Explaining Termination of Primary Mortgage with Low-to-Moderate-Income and First-time Owner Interactions: Mortgage Age Five to Ten Years*

	Two-year data windows				
	1985–87	*1987–89*	*1989–91*	*1991–93*	*1993–95*
Intercept	4.160	4.499	1.684	3.332	2.842
	(0.004)	(0.005)	(0.316)	(0.035)	(0.060)
Mortgage-related variables					
Number of years mortgage outstanding (MTGAGE)	–0.046	–0.143	–0.111	0.157	0.070
	(0.325)	(0.002)	(0.005)	(0.000)	(0.073)
Present value of interest savings (PVIS)	12.8E–05	0.9E–05	5.5E–05	4.0E–05	2.9E–05
	(0.000)	(0.602)	(0.000)	(0.000)	(0.000)
Book loan-to-value ratio (LTV)	–2.047	–3.074	–0.829	–1.357	–1.312
	(0.131)	(0.008)	(0.491)	(0.266)	(0.230)
Book loan-to-value ratio squared (LTV^2)	1.358	2.436	–0.186	–0.158	0.288
	(0.280)	(0.012)	(0.848)	(0.868)	(0.725)
Annual payment-to-income ratio (PAYINC)	–19.784	–2.423	–9.987	–3.590	–5.315
	(0.000)	(0.534)	(0.014)	(0.339)	(0.105)
Annual payment-to-income ratio squared ($PAYINC^2$)	47.170	2.664	25.451	10.167	8.318
	(0.001)	(0.818)	(0.030)	(0.320)	(0.345)
More than one mortgage (yes = 1) (SECMORT)	0.572	–0.021	–0.041	0.102	0.007
	(0.007)	(0.920)	(0.848)	(0.591)	(0.970)
Household characteristic variables					
Potential wasted interest as a percentage of residence fair market value (TAX)	–2.596	–7.573	–3.610	–1.983	–4.011
	(0.795)	(0.081)	(0.073)	(0.267)	(0.044)
Total income (INC)	–0.010	0.005	0.005	0.004	0.005
	(0.007)	(0.124)	(0.133)	(0.284)	(0.041)
Two wage earners (yes = 1) (JOINTINC)	–0.053	–0.222	–0.126	–0.083	–0.087
	(0.691)	(0.141)	(0.420)	(0.566)	(0.517)
Age of household head (AGE)	–0.104	–0.130	–0.021	–0.161	–0.120
	(0.122)	(0.075)	(0.784)	(0.023)	(0.088)
Age of household head squared (AGE^2)	99.4E–05	0.001	11.9E–05	0.002	0.001
	(0.194)	(0.104)	(0.892)	(0.039)	(0.142)
Household head with two or more years of college (yes = 1) (COLLEGE)	0.160	–0.070	0.135	0.375	0.116
	(0.223)	(0.626)	(0.372)	(0.006)	(0.377)
Family size (FAMSIZE)	0.018	–0.071	–0.006	–0.038	–0.040
	(0.719)	(0.195)	(0.915)	(0.460)	(0.384)
African American head (yes = 1) (BLACK)	97.1E–05	0.072	–0.386	–0.725	–0.212
	(0.997)	(0.820)	(0.245)	(0.019)	(0.442)
Hispanic head (yes = 1) (HISP)	0.237	0.251	0.080	–1.745	–0.173
	(0.430)	(0.473)	(0.811)	(0.000)	(0.585)
Location variables					
Rural location (yes = 1) (RURAL)	–0.231	0.103	0.195	0.497	–0.222
	(0.265)	(0.624)	(0.384)	(0.026)	(0.258)
Low-to-moderate-income/first-time owner interactions:					
Income <80 percent of MSA median income and first-time owner (yes = 1) (FIRSTLOW)	–1.403	–3.008	3.363	4.160	2.098
	(0.592)	(0.334)	(0.346)	(0.242)	(0.543)

continued on next page

Table 10-7. *Logistic Regressions Explaining Termination of Primary Mortgage with Low-to-Moderate-Income and First-time Owner Interactions: Mortgage Age Five to Ten Years (continued)*

	Two-year data windows				
	1985–87	*1987–89*	*1989–91*	*1991–93*	*1993–95*
MTGAGE × FIRSTLOW	–0.160	–0.204	–0.071	–0.089	–0.030
	(0.094)	(0.056)	(0.497)	(0.422)	(0.774)
PVIS × FIRSTLOW	1.2E–05	9.9E–05	–3.0E–05	–3.0E–05	1.0E–05
	(0.746)	(0.029)	(0.498)	(0.204)	(0.704)
LTV × FIRSTLOW	–4.339	1.662	–2.646	–5.427	–1.445
	(0.048)	(0.473)	(0.344)	(0.042)	(0.554)
LTV^2 × FIRSTLOW	1.542	–2.790	1.229	4.611	1.366
	(0.434)	(0.148)	(0.579)	(0.018)	(0.436)
PAYINC × FIRSTLOW	20.527	2.025	9.033	2.152	3.021
	(0.000)	(0.607)	(0.033)	(0.607)	(0.469)
$PAYINC^2$ × FIRSTLOW	–47.361	–2.660	–25.407	–9.456	–8.332
	(0.001)	(0.818)	(0.031)	(0.356)	(0.351)
SECMORT × FIRSTLOW	–0.328	0.146	0.164	0.536	0.841
	(0.473)	(0.777)	(0.794)	(0.271)	(0.085)
TAX × FIRSTLOW	–7.835	3.815	–1.304	0.694	1.355
	(0.455)	(0.415)	(0.666)	(0.744)	(0.678)
INC × FIRSTLOW	0.010	–0.048	–0.024	–0.029	–0.071
	(0.668)	(0.035)	(0.440)	(0.340)	(0.021)
JOINTINC × FIRSTLOW	0.228	0.339	0.032	0.234	0.491
	(0.429)	(0.329)	(0.940)	(0.547)	(0.198)
AGE × FIRSTLOW	0.090	0.257	–0.139	–0.199	–0.067
	(0.473)	(0.080)	(0.424)	(0.236)	(0.684)
AGE^2 × FIRSTLOW	–0.001	–0.003	0.002	0.003	96.4E–05
	(0.486)	(0.095)	(0.379)	(0.162)	(0.619)
COLLEGE × FIRSTLOW	–0.118	–0.208	–0.021	1.162	0.365
	(0.683)	(0.538)	(0.958)	(0.004)	(0.292)
FAMSIZE × FIRSTLOW	–0.017	–0.021	0.181	0.297	0.213
	(0.859)	(0.843)	(0.151)	(0.013)	(0.118)
BLACK × FIRSTLOW	0.344	–0.174	–0.738	0.431	–0.035
	(0.456)	(0.723)	(0.254)	(0.487)	(0.946)
HISPANIC × FIRSTLOW	–0.634	–0.432	0.275	1.564	–0.058
	(0.257)	(0.521)	(0.695)	(0.020)	(0.927)
Number of observations	1,843	1,386	1,171	1,384	1,405
–2 log-likelihood statistic	2118.906	1670.058	1445.093	1714.498	1846.257
(*p*-value of chi-squared statistic)	(0.000)	(0.000)	(0.000)	(0.000)	(0.000)
Within-sample classification rate	70.1	66.2	62.9	62.9	56.6
Paired rank correlation ("c" statistic)	0.700	0.654	0.667	0.696	0.639

Notes: Reported values are parameter estimates from logistic regressions with *p*-values of Wald chi-square statistics in parentheses. See Table 10-2 and the text for variable definitions. Ten binary variables indicating whether the home is located in one of the top ten most represented MSAs in the combined 1985–95 samples are included in the logistic regression models as location control variables, but these results are not reported here. Tables including these variables are available from the authors on request.

Table 10-8. *Logistic Regressions Explaining Termination of Primary Mortgage with Low-to-Moderate Income and First-time Owner Interactions: Mortgage Age Eleven to Fifteen Years*

	Two-year data windows				
	1985–87	*1987–89*	*1989–91*	*1991–93*	*1993–95*
Intercept	2.360	0.941	−2.708	3.992	6.015
	(0.527)	(0.805)	(0.468)	(0.189)	(0.126)
Mortgage-related variables					
Number of years mortgage outstanding (MTGAGE)	0.010	0.209	0.015	−0.273	−0.170
	(0.916)	(0.007)	(0.847)	(0.000)	(0.022)
Present value of interest savings (PVIS)	27.4E–05	19.1E–05	19.3E–05	7.1E–05	4.5E–05
	(0.000)	(0.001)	(0.000)	(0.000)	(0.009)
Book loan-to-value ratio (LTV)	4.708	−0.829	−2.261	−2.438	−3.194
	(0.085)	(0.651)	(0.229)	(0.080)	(0.070)
Book loan-to-value ratio squared (LTV^2)	−1.398	1.744	2.522	1.715	1.616
	(0.636)	(0.323)	(0.184)	(0.159)	(0.279)
Annual payment-to-income ratio (PAYINC)	−18.623	1.842	−11.949	−8.411	−2.491
	(0.040)	(0.798)	(0.049)	(0.126)	(0.694)
Annual payment-to-income ratio squared ($PAYINC^2$)	41.346	13.919	33.011	24.757	11.096
	(0.160)	(0.594)	(0.048)	(0.157)	(0.591)
More than one mortgage (yes = 1) (SECMORT)	0.496	−0.714	−0.230	0.373	0.698
	(0.219)	(0.036)	(0.451)	(0.104)	(0.019)
Household characteristic variables					
Potential wasted interest as a percentage of residence fair market value (TAX)	−3.706	−11.550	−1.655	−0.956	−4.494
	(0.874)	(0.206)	(0.659)	(0.639)	(0.148)
Total income (INC)	0.010	0.017	−0.001	0.003	0.003
	(0.221)	(0.002)	(0.832)	(0.500)	(0.584)
Two wage earners (yes = 1) (JOINTINC)	0.181	0.133	−0.380	−0.149	0.052
	(0.516)	(0.572)	(0.101)	(0.444)	(0.838)
Age of household head (AGE)	−0.143	−0.190	0.078	0.001	−0.167
	(0.382)	(0.245)	(0.616)	(0.991)	(0.297)
Age of household head squared (AGE^2)	0.001	0.002	−64.0E–05	−19.0E–05	0.002
	(0.410)	(0.326)	(0.691)	(0.889)	(0.302)
Household head with two or more years of college (yes = 1) (COLLEGE)	−0.046	−0.027	−0.049	0.080	0.622
	(0.860)	(0.900)	(0.817)	(0.647)	(0.006)
Family size (FAMSIZE)	−0.262	−0.151	0.153	0.011	0.024
	(0.015)	(0.071)	(0.062)	(0.874)	(0.787)
African American head (yes = 1) (BLACK)	−0.394	0.311	1.188	−0.460	0.234
	(0.454)	(0.451)	(0.006)	(0.207)	(0.635)
Hispanic head (yes = 1) (HISP)	0.499	0.530	−0.106	−0.184	−0.525
	(0.412)	(0.313)	(0.872)	(0.685)	(0.349)
Location variables					
Rural location (yes = 1) (RURAL)	0.568	0.047	0.139	0.098	−0.120
	(0.104)	(0.884)	(0.648)	(0.699)	(0.720)
Low-to-moderate-income/first-time owner interactions					
Income <80 percent of MSA median income and first-time owner (yes = 1) (FIRSTLOW)	11.869	4.676	1.966	2.744	1.424
	(0.090)	(0.458)	(0.775)	(0.623)	(0.863)

continued on next page

Table 10-8. *Logistic Regressions Explaining Termination of Primary Mortgage with Low-to-Moderate Income and First-time Owner Interactions: Mortgage Age Eleven to Fifteen Years (continued)*

	Two-year data windows				
	1985–87	*1987–89*	*1989–91*	*1991–93*	*1993–95*
MTGAGE × FIRSTLOW	–0.110	–0.357	0.059	0.270	0.013
	(0.515)	(0.024)	(0.756)	(0.080)	(0.949)
PVIS × FIRSTLOW	56.2E–05	35.8E–05	0.8E–05	0.3E–05	–0.7E–05
	(0.003)	(0.096)	(0.933)	(0.951)	(0.896)
LTV × FIRSTLOW	–6.603	–1.029	–1.832	–1.709	–0.625
	(0.146)	(0.725)	(0.557)	(0.527)	(0.862)
LTV^2 × FIRSTLOW	1.426	–0.912	–1.356	–1.095	–0.465
	(0.795)	(0.739)	(0.642)	(0.670)	(0.886)
PAYINC × FIRSTLOW	17.854	–2.653	15.051	12.135	2.330
	(0.052)	(0.755)	(0.027)	(0.053)	(0.713)
$PAYINC^2$ × FIRSTLOW	–41.462	–15.289	–35.582	–28.450	–11.090
	(0.158)	(0.562)	(0.034)	(0.108)	(0.591)
SECMORT × FIRSTLOW	0.072	0.539	–0.275	0.277	–0.431
	(0.914)	(0.503)	(0.723)	(0.625)	(0.573)
TAX × FIRSTLOW	–6.487	5.869	–5.992	–1.857	1.605
	(0.792)	(0.578)	(0.252)	(0.499)	(0.759)
INC × FIRSTLOW	–0.037	–0.008	–0.056	–0.028	–0.039
	(0.363)	(0.859)	(0.159)	(0.348)	(0.193)
JOINTINC × FIRSTLOW	0.124	–0.742	0.769	0.010	0.878
	(0.806)	(0.133)	(0.185)	(0.984)	(0.194)
AGE × FIRSTLOW	–0.456	0.030	–0.032	–0.255	0.110
	(0.134)	(0.914)	(0.914)	(0.279)	(0.739)
AGE^2 × FIRSTLOW	0.005	–9.0E–05	4.8E–05	0.003	–0.002
	(0.104)	(0.975)	(0.988)	(0.241)	(0.647)
COLLEGE × FIRSTLOW	–0.529	–0.889	–0.111	–0.253	–1.499
	(0.348)	(0.082)	(0.853)	(0.551)	(0.008)
FAMSIZE × FIRSTLOW	0.275	0.285	–0.370	–0.098	–0.367
	(0.126)	(0.088)	(0.050)	(0.486)	(0.056)
BLACK × FIRSTLOW	1.106	–0.314	–1.635	–0.304	–0.908
	(0.116)	(0.632)	(0.036)	(0.631)	(0.266)
HISPANIC × FIRSTLOW	0.479	–0.538	–0.768	0.251	–0.944
	(0.580)	(0.521)	(0.565)	(0.753)	(0.380)
Number of observations	685	751	803	881	562
–2 log-likelihood statistic	634.039	788.432	793.526	1104.434	716.747
(*p*-value of chi-squared statistic)	(0.000)	(0.000)	(0.000)	(0.000)	(0.000)
Within-sample classification rate	74.9	71.9	75.8	60.6	55.0
Paired rank correlation ("c" statistic)	0.801	0.709	0.705	0.701	0.687

Notes: Reported values are parameter estimates from logistic regressions with *p*-values of Wald chi-square statistics in parentheses. See Table 10-2 and the text for variable definitions. Ten binary variables indicating whether the home is located in one of the top ten most represented MSAs in the combined 1985–95 samples are included in the logistic regression models as location control variables, but these results are not reported here. Tables including these variables are available from the authors on request.

insignificant results are also found for more seasoned mortgages (tables 10-7 and 10-8). Thus, relative to the control group, there appears to be little difference in the baseline rate at which lower-income, first-time owner households terminate their fixed-rate mortgages.

Recall that the results reported in tables 10-3 through 10-5 contain no clear evidence that lower-income households are more sensitive to attractive refinancing opportunities than the control group. Interestingly, the results in table 10-6 provide limited evidence that lower income, first-time owners are actually *more* sensitive than the control group to in-the-money call options because the PVIS-FIRSTLOW interaction variable is positive and statistically significant in both the 1989–91 and 1993–95 windows. Certainly, these results do not support the contention that the price charged by lenders for the embedded prepayment option should be different—that is, lower—for lower-income, first-time owners.

In table 10-3 the estimated coefficient on the LTV-LOWINC interaction variable is negative in all five windows and statistically significant in three windows. Similarly, the LTV-FIRSTLOW interaction coefficient is negative and significant in three of the five windows for the zero-through-four mortgage age group (table 10-6) and negative and significant in two of the three windows for mortgages that have been seasoned for five to ten years. Although negative, the LTV-FIRSTLOW interaction coefficient is not significant in the most seasoned (eleven to fifteen years) mortgage age group. In sum, these results suggest that larger amounts of mortgage debt (relative to house value) do slow the terminations of lower-income, first-time owners more than the control group.

Tables 10-3 through 10-5 show that the coefficients on the PAYINC-LOWINC interaction variable are positive and generally significant. These results carry over to the PAYINC-FIRSTLOW interaction results contained in tables 10-6 through 10-8. Again, the magnitude of the PAYINC-FIRSTLOW interaction coefficients effectively offsets the negative control group high-income coefficients. This indicates that the termination behavior of the test group is generally *not* responsive to changes in prospective payment burdens, all else equal.

Examination of tables 10-6 through 10-8 reveals that the coefficients on the remaining interaction variables are largely insignificant. Thus we again conclude that the influence of household characteristics and location variables on the termination behavior of the test group largely does not vary from their influence on the control group.

Summary

This study examines mortgage termination behavior at the household level with a focus on the effects of household income and first-time home purchase. Results from the estimation of a series of logistic regressions suggest that the propensity for mortgage prepayment by low-to-moderate-income households is little distinguished from that of higher-income households. In particular, low-to-moderate-income households are no less responsive to interest rate changes than higher-income households are. In fact, they appear to be slightly more responsive. The fact that lower-income households exhibit lower prepayment rates appears to be attributable to the effect of constraints. Specifically, the slope coefficients on the two underwriting variables, LTV and PAYINC, are significantly different for low-to-moderate-income households. High current LTVs do not appear to impede the terminations of higher-income households. However, high LTVs do significantly slow low-to-moderate-income terminations. On the other hand, it seems contradictory that higher prospective payment burdens significantly slow higher-income terminations but have little effect on the mortgage terminations of lower-income households. This contradiction may be explainable, however, by the fact that the lower-income groups are, by definition, universally income-constrained. None of these results change when the analysis focuses on the prepayment behavior of only lower-income first-time home buyers.

Finally, the low-to-moderate-income interaction coefficients on the household characteristic and location interaction variables are remarkably insignificant. Thus although numerous demographic and locational variables are shown to significantly affect termination behavior, their effects on low-to-moderate-income households cannot be distinguished from their effects on higher-income households. This result contributes further to the impression that differences in prepayment behavior between non-low-income and lower-income households are attributable largely to differences in income and collateral constraints.

The study further partitioned households by age of mortgage. This partitioning reveals little difference in results. The primary findings of strong interest rate sensitivity and the influence of collateral and income constraints remain consistent across mortgages from zero through four years old, mortgages five through ten years old, and mortgages eleven through fifteen years old.

There are several reasons to believe that the findings of this study are credible. First, the estimated equations have a high degree of statistical significance across five separate panels of data that cover a ten-year period. Further, the estimated coefficients show a strong pattern of consistency across the five separate two-year time intervals of data. Finally, the individual coefficients have a large measure of economic plausibility. In light of this credibility, it is significant that we find little indication that low-to-moderate-income households have lower prepayment propensity than other home borrowers. This result has significant implications for the pricing of fixed-rate mortgages at both origination and in the secondary market.

References

Archer, W. R., and D. C. Ling. 1993. "Pricing Mortgage-Backed Securities: Integrating Optimal Call and Empirical Models of Prepayment." *Journal of the American Real Estate and Urban Economics Association* 21 (4): 373–404.

Archer, W. R., D. C. Ling, and, G. A. McGill. 1996. "The Effect of Income and Collateral Constraints on Residential Mortgage Terminations." *Regional Science and Urban Economics* 26 (3–4): 235–61.

———. 1997. "Demographic versus Option-Driven Mortgage Terminations." *Journal of Housing Economics* 6 (2): 137–63.

Boehm, T., and K. R. Ihlandfeldt. 1986. "Residential Mobility and Neighborhood Change." *Journal of Regional Science* 26 (3): 411–24.

Caplin, A., C. Freeman, and J. Tracy. 1993. "Collateral Damage: How Refinancing Constraints Exacerbate Regional Recessions." Working Paper 4531. Cambridge, Mass.: National Bureau of Economic Research (November).

Capone, C. A., and D. F. Cunningham. 1992. "Estimating the Marginal Contribution of Adjustable-Rate Mortgage Selection to Termination Probabilities in a Nested Model." *Journal of Real Estate Finance and Economics* 5 (4): 333–56.

Cunningham, D. F., and C. A. Capone. 1990. "The Relative Termination Experience of Adjustable to Fixed-Rate Mortgages." *Journal of Finance* 45 (5): 1687–1703.

Deng, Y., and J. M. Quigley. 2000. "Woodhead Behavior and the Pricing of Residential Mortgages." University of Southern California; University of California, Berkeley.

Deng, Y., J. M. Quigley, and R. Van Order. 2000. "Mortgage Terminations, Heterogeneity and the Exercise of Mortgage Options." *Econometrica* 6 (2): 275–307.

Diamond, D. B., Jr., and M. J. Lea. 1995. "Sustainable Financing for Housing: A Contribution to Habitat II." Working Paper. Washington: Fannie Mae Office of Housing Research.

Dickinson, A., and A. J. Heuson. 1993. "Explaining Refinancing Decisions Using Microdata." *Journal of the American Real Estate and Urban Economics Association* 21 (3): 293–311.

Follain, J. R., and S. Malpezzi. 1981. "Are Occupants Accurate Appraisers?" *Review of Public Data Use* 9 (1): 47–55.

Foster, C., and R. Van Order. 1985. "FHA Terminations: A Prelude to Rational Mortgage Pricing." *Journal of the American Real Estate and Urban Economics Association* 13 (3): 371–91.

Freddie Mac. 1996. *Automated Underwriting: Making Mortgage Lending Simpler and Fairer for America's Families.* Washington.

Giliberto, S. M., and T. G. Thibodeau. 1989. "Modeling Conventional Mortgage Refinancings." *Journal of Real Estate Finance and Economics* 2 (4): 285–99.

Goodman, J. L., and J. B. Ittner. 1992. "The Accuracy of Homeowners' Estimates of House Value." *Journal of Housing Economics* 2 (4): 339–57.

Gronberg, T. J., and W. R. Reed. 1992. "Estimation of Duration Models Using the Annual Housing Survey." *Journal of Urban Economics* 31 (3): 311–24.

Henderson, J., and Y. Ioannides. 1989. "Dynamic Aspects of Consumer Decisions in Housing Markets." *Journal of Urban Economics* 26 (2): 212–30.

Hilliard, J. E., J. B. Kau, and V. C. Slawson Jr. 1998. "Valuing Prepayment and Default in a Fixed-Rate Mortgage: A Bivariate Options Pricing Technique." *Real Estate Economics* 26 (3): 431–68.

Hurst, E., and F. Stafford. 1996. "Collateral Constraints and Household Mortgage Refinancing:1993–1994." Working Paper. Institute for Social Research, University of Michigan.

Kain, J. F., and J. M. Quigley. 1972. "Note on Owner's Estimate of Housing Value." *Journal of the American Statistical Association* 67 (3–4): 803–06.

Kiel, K. A. 1994. "The Impact of House Price Appreciation on Household Mobility." *Journal of Housing Economics* 3 (2): 92–108.

Kiel, K. A., and J. E. Zabel. 1999. "The Accuracy of Owner-Provided House Values: The 1978–1991 American Housing Survey." *Real Estate Economics* 27 (2): 263–98.

Krumm, R. J. 1984. "Household Tenure Choice and Migration." *Journal of Urban Economics* 16 (3): 259–71.

LaCour-Little, M. 1999. "Another Look at the Role of Borrower Characteristics in Predicting Mortgage Prepayments." *Journal of Housing Research* 10 (1): 45–60.

Ling, D. C., and G. A. McGill. 1992. "Measuring the Size and Distributional Effects of Homeowner Tax Preferences." *Journal of Housing Research* 3 (2): 273–303.

Mortgage Bankers Association. 2000. *National Delinquency Survey, U.S Housing Market Conditions, 1st Quarter 2000.* Washington: U.S. Department of Housing and Urban Development, Office of Policy Development and Research.

"Mortgage Market Trends." 1999. *Freddie Mac Secondary Mortgage Markets* 16. Washington.

Nothaft, F. E., and V. G. Perry. 1996. "Do Mortgage Rates Vary By Neighborhood? Implications for Loan Pricing and Redlining." Washington: Freddie Mac.

Peristiani, S., P. Bennett, G. Monsen, R. Peach, and J. Raiff. 1996. "Effects of Household Creditworthiness on Mortgage Refinancings." Research Paper 9622. Federal Reserve Bank of New York.

Quigley, J. M. 1987. "Interest Rate Variations, Mortgage Prepayments and Household Mobility." *Review of Economics and Statistics* 69 (9): 636–43.

Quigley, J. M., and R. Van Order. 1990. "Efficiency in the Mortgage Market: The Borrower's Perspective." *Journal of the American Real Estate and Urban Economics Association* 18 (3): 237–52.

Quigley, J. M., and D. H. Weinberg. 1977. "Intra-Urban Residential Mobility: A Review and Synthesis." *International Regional Science Review* 2 (1): 41–66.

Robins, P. K., and R. W. West. 1977. "Measurement Error in the Estimation of Home Value." *Journal of the American Statistical Association* 72 (June): 290–94.

Stanton, R. H. 1995. "Rational Prepayment and the Valuation of Mortgage-backed Securities." *Review of Financial Studies* 8 (3): 677–708.

U.S. Department of Commerce, Bureau of the Census. Various years. *American Housing Survey 1985, 1987, 1989, 1991, 1993, 1995.* Computer File. Washington.

U.S. Department of Housing and Urban Development. 1996. *Providing Alternatives to Mortgage Foreclosure: A Report to Congress.* Washington.

Vandell, K. D. 1995. "How Ruthless Is Mortgage Default? A Review and Synthesis of the Evidence." *Journal of Housing Research* 6 (2): 245–64.

11

Performance of Low-Income and Minority Mortgages

ROBERT VAN ORDER AND PETER ZORN

This chapter analyzes the performance of low-income and minority mortgage loans relative to other mortgages for a large sample of fixed-rate mortgages originated in the 1990s and followed through 1999. Evaluating performance differences is complicated. For instance, it is not just a matter of credit risk. For fixed-rate mortgages it is clearly the case that prepayment risk, the risk that comes from borrowers exercising their option to refinance when mortgage rates fall (which amounts to exercising a call option), has a cost of at least the same order of magnitude as credit risk. Hence low-income and minority loans may have had higher default rates than other loans, while also having different and more favorable prepayment characteristics.

We examine differences in prepayment and default behavior across groups and their effects on loan performance, which is measured by value to mortgage investors.[1] One way of tracking performance is to look at historic returns. We do not have market prices of the individual loans over time, so we cannot do this. We do, however, have data on the main things that affect performance,

We have received valuable help from Abdigani Hirad and Adama Kah and comments from Michael Bradley and Stuart Gabriel. What follows does not necessarily reflect the opinions of Freddie Mac.

1. We mean investor in a rather broad sense. For instance, most mortgages now go into mortgage-backed securities, where the pool issuer, for example, Freddie Mac, takes the credit risk, but investors in the pools take the prepayment risk. By investor we mean a composite of all the stakeholders.

default and prepayment. Both of these can be viewed as options that impose costs on investors, and we can ask questions about the differences in borrowers' propensity to exercise these options and use a generic pricing model to estimate "shadow prices" for the differences.

We first estimate models for prepayment, and we find that low-income and minority loans (LIMLs) have a lower propensity to exercise the prepayment option. We then analyze the extent to which this is the case (1) when the option is "in the money" (that is, when mortgage rates have fallen), and (2) when the option is not in the money (for example, because of less mobility or a lack of access to other forms of raising money). From an investor's perspective it matters.

Clearly, if LIML options are exercised less when they are in the money, then LIMLs are more valuable to investors because their "optionness" is less valuable to borrowers. However, if LIMLs prepay less rapidly when the option is either "close to the money" or "out of the money," then they are less valuable. If the option is close to the money, mortgage investors prefer borrowers who pay off quickly because they get a long-term rate for a short-term loan, and because quick prepayment means that the refinancing option will be outstanding for a shorter period of time; if the option is out of the money, refinancing represents a windfall to lenders, so refinancing less rapidly lowers value to lenders.[2]

The issue of prepayment differences between LIML borrowers and others and their implications for pricing was raised in Chinloy and Megbolugbe (1994). Their argument was based on the notion that LIML borrowers are less mobile and less liquid than other borrowers, so they prepay less. That in itself does not get you to the proposition that LIML borrowers have less prepayment risk because lower mobility implies slower prepayment when the option is out of the money, which makes mortgages *less* valuable, and it has no particular implication for refinancing when the option is in the money. The liquidity problem will tend to offset this when the option is out of the money, because refinancing might be the only way for LIML borrowers to raise money, but it also suggests a propensity to exercise the option when it is in the money that is no less than anyone else's. Our contribution is the distinction between behavior when the option is in and out of the money and our use of a large data set to get an empirical handle on the problem. We do find that the basic proposition in Chinloy and Megbolugbe, that LIML borrowers have less prepayment risk, is correct.

We find in our data that, absent controls for loan characteristics, both low-income and minority borrowers are slower to prepay when the option is in the

2. Rates on shorter-term mortgages are always lower than those on longer-term ones, in part because the prepayment option allows long-term borrowers to take advantage of any downward slope in the mortgage yield curve by converting their mortgages into shorter-term ones via prepayment. This is also reinforced by the general tendency of yield curves for noncallable debt to be upward sloping.

money than is the case for base case loans (more so for blacks and Hispanics than for low-income borrowers), but they are about the same for other (close to or out of the money) prepayments. This suggests potentially important differences in value to investors not due to credit risk differences.

If we adjust for loan characteristics, particularly credit history, loan-to-value (LTV) ratio, and loan amount, the results change, and low-income and minority loans are slow both in the money and out of the money by about the same multiple. This complicates performance analysis. In situations where the option is especially valuable (for example, when rates fall, or in terms of ex ante valuation, when the yield curve is downward sloping, indicating market expectations of an interest rate decline, or when rates are especially volatile), the LIMLs will be more valuable. However, they will be less valuable when rates are rising or, ex ante, in a sharply rising yield curve or low-volatility environment.

We estimate similar models for default rates, and we also estimate determinants of differences in loss severity. Absent adjustment for loan characteristics, we find that low-income and minority loans default at significantly higher rates than base case loans. This, along with somewhat higher rates of loss severity, implies higher default costs. When we adjust for loan characteristics, especially credit history and loan-to-value ratio, we find that borrower race/ethnicity has very little effect, but we do find explanatory power for borrower income and neighborhood minority composition and income.

We have two main results:

—LIMLs in our sample performed about the same as or better than other loans when prepayment risk is taken into account. That is, the (ex ante) shadow values of the default and prepayment differences from the base cases, taken from a generic pricing model, are, in absolute value, on the same order of magnitude. If anything, the prepayment difference is more valuable, but the crudeness of our pricing calculations does not allow us to be sure.

—Most of the performance differences between LIMLs and other loans can be explained by observable characteristics like downpayment and credit history. This is especially true for credit risk.

Whether the default or prepayment results will continue to hold in the wake of recent changes in mortgage markets is a different matter. We test for past stability by estimating separate models by exposure (calendar rather than origination) year. We find that during the 1990s the income effect on prepayment fell, but the race effect changed little; and for default we find little change for race and some worsening of the income effect, but no big changes. In contrast, in the prepayment models with controls for mortgage and borrower characteristics the coefficients of race/ethnicity were quite stable over time, but the income effect declined to virtually zero. Coefficients in default models with controls were generally not statistically significant in individual exposure years.

Models

It is by now well established that prepayment and default behavior can be viewed as exercising options. Prepayment is equivalent to exercising a call option, which gives the borrower the option to buy back the mortgage at a price equal to the mortgage balance, and default is equivalent to exercising a put option to sell the house to the lender at a price equal to the value of the mortgage. But these options are not perfectly or predictably exercised in the way that, say, corporate bond options are exercised. For default, this is because exercising the put option involves significant costs to borrowers (for example, worse credit history and diminished access to future credit). The same is true for prepayment; for instance, most mortgages are not assumable (the lender has the right to demand payment if the house is sold), so they are usually prepaid when the house is sold. Hence a reason for exercising the call option is mobility. Furthermore, different borrowers have different access to other forms of credit. A borrower who has limited access to other credit opportunities and/or who lacks liquid assets might exercise an out-of-the-money call option on a mortgage in order to refinance and take out equity in order to pay for something else.

Pricing options is a growth industry that has been extended to the mortgage business (see Hendershott and Van Order, 1987; Kau and Keenan, 1995, for surveys of option type models as applied to mortgages). The methodology is simple in principle but in practice can be very complicated. The basis of all pricing models is that the value of a mortgage is the (risk-adjusted) expected present value of its cash flows, taking account of the way borrowers exercise their options. The value of the prepayment option is the difference in value between a mortgage without a prepayment option and the value with it. This can be turned into an interest rate differential by comparing the coupon rate on a par-valued mortgage without a prepayment option to the (higher) coupon rate on a comparable mortgage with a prepayment option. This same methodology can also be used to answer questions about increases or decreases in mortgage rate due to differences in the extent to which different borrowers or borrower classes exercise the prepayment option. The methodology can be used in much the same way to price the level of credit risk and differences in credit risk across borrowers. In general, it is easier to calculate up front values (for example, via expected present value calculations, using Monte Carlo techniques) than it is to calculate coupon rate differences (holding value constant), but there are rules of thumb that allow for simple conversions from one to the other (for example, for a thirty-year fixed-rate mortgage a 1 basis point increase in coupon rate generally leads to a 4 or 6 basis point increase in up-front value, depending on the duration of the mortgage).

We estimate prepayment and default probabilities with proportional hazard models of the form:

$$h(t) = \exp(Bx), \tag{11-1}$$

where $h(t)$ is the probability over some small time interval of the borrower's prepaying (or defaulting) conditional on having survived (neither prepaying nor defaulting) until time t, x is a vector of explanatory variables, and B a vector of coefficients. The x's can take on a wide variety of forms. For instance, they can represent time trends or the age of the mortgage; for example, some of the x's might be a series of dummy variables for the age of the loan or the quarter in which the loan was originated. An important property comes from the multiplicative nature of the model. For instance, if the x's are categorical variables, then there is an easy interpretation of the Bs as multipliers; $\exp(B_1)$ gives a multiplier for the effect of being in category 1, relative to some baseline.

In principle, the two hazards, default and prepayment, should be modeled and estimated jointly (see Deng, Quigley, and Van Order, 2000). We estimate them separately, but we take account of jointness implicitly by using the same explanatory variables in the two equations. To the extent that this presents problems it is likely to be in the estimates of default rather than prepayment, which is our main focus. This is because default is a very small number, typically 10 to 30 basis points per year, relative to prepayment, which fluctuates from around 10 to 40 percent per year. Hence ignoring default in modeling prepayment is not likely to be quantitatively important.

A key variable is the extent to which the option is in the money, which in the case of prepayment can be measured by the difference (or ratio) between the rate on the mortgage and the current rate on a par mortgage.[3] The coefficient of this variable measures the propensity of the borrower to exercise the option as it goes into the money. Differences in this coefficient across groups will lead to different mortgage values across groups. We test for such differences by looking at the extent to which different groups have greater or smaller propensities to exercise their options for different categories of difference between mortgage rate and current coupon rate (that is, different degrees of "in-the-moneyness").

We control for observable loan characteristics by treating them as categorical variables, which can be modeled as fixed effects. For each calendar quarter of origination we create fixed effects from "pseudo-pools" by dividing originated loans into relatively homogeneous groupings based on observed characteristics—such as contract rate (50 basis point buckets), LTV (4 buckets), credit history measured by FICO score[4] (4 buckets), and loan amount (3 buckets). For each origination quarter this results in roughly 200 pseudo-pools. Each of these

3. In the case of default it might be represented by difference between current house price and mortgage value; however, house prices are seldom observed over time, so proxies like original loan-to-value ratio along with information about house price trends are typically used.

4. This is a generic credit score developed by Fair Isaac Corporation (FICO), which has become widely used in mortgage credit scoring models.

pseudo-pools is then given a fixed effect for each quarter it is "alive" (up to twenty-seven quarters). With twelve origination quarters in the study, this amounts to a total of over 50,000 fixed effects in the model; because our data have well over 1 million loans and millions of loan quarters, this leaves plenty of degrees of freedom.

This structure is particularly good at accounting for the complex time-varying pool characteristics that plague traditional prepayment models. For instance, burnout (the notion that seasoned pools that have been exposed to one or more periods of low mortgage rates prepay at lower speeds than new pools) and seasoning effects are captured separately for each pseudo-pool by its quarter age fixed effect.

In the prepayment model we break the data down into quarters where the option is in the money (that is, when the current coupon rate on a par mortgage is less than the average coupon of the mortgage pool) and out of the money (when the current coupon is higher than the average mortgage coupon of the pool), to varying degrees. We then estimate versions of equation 11-1 with race and income and other explanatory variables for each of these samples. The coefficients of race and income tell us borrowers' propensity to exercise options when they are in the money and when they are out of the money. We have five in-the-moneyness groups, described below. We then use a generic pricing model, one that uses the expected present value methodology to price mortgages but that was estimated with a different data set, to give back-of-the-envelope estimates of how much these differences in propensity to exercise options affect mortgage rates.

We do something similar for default, although we do not have comparable data on whether the option is in or out of the money. In particular, we estimate a hazard model like equation 11-1 for default to see if LIMLs default differently, and we also estimate determinants of loss severity rates. There is no available generic pricing model for credit risk, but we do have reasonable ideas about the likely expected present value of default costs of a baseline mortgage, to which we apply multipliers from our estimated models. This gives us estimates of price and implied coupon rate differences among groups.

Data and Methodology

We use two different data sets. One consists of all thirty-year fixed-rate mortgages originated from 1993 through 1995 and purchased by Freddie Mac and for which key data are not missing. The data are used to model default; they contain about 1.4 million loans. The other data are the same except that they include loans originated from 1993 through 1997. This set contains about 2.8 million loans and is used to model prepayments. The reason the second set of data is not used for default modeling is that loans originated after 1996 have extremely low default rates; it is too soon for them to have defaulted.[5] However, loans originated in 1996 and 1997 were exposed to one major rate decline, in 1998, and have a lot of prepayments.

In general, our data are richer in prepayment experience because the loans have all been exposed to at least one period of declining rates (there were sharp mortgage rate declines in 1993, 1995, and 1998). The default modeling suffers from excessively good times in the 1990s and relatively small levels of default. Happily for us modelers, the California economy did rather poorly in the early part of the period and provides us with some significant default data. The performance of all loans was followed through the end of 1999.

Equation 11-1 is defined for a model with continuous time. We group our observations into quarters. Prentice and Gloecker (1978) show that for data observed during discrete time intervals equation 11-1 becomes the complementary log-log model:

$$\log(-\log(1-h(t))) = \mathbf{Bx}, \tag{11-2}$$

where the observations of **x** happen over discrete intervals (in our case quarters), so each $h(t)$ is the hazard rate for a particular loan during a quarter.[6] This formulation has the advantage that the estimates are not affected by size of the interval (for example, weeks versus quarters). It is this equation that we estimate in order to obtain estimates of the **B**'s.

We estimate two sorts of models: simple and complicated. The simple models are standard hazard models that have race/ethnicity and income variables as the main **x**'s, and baseline hazards that are fixed effects for loan age and in the case of default the state in which the house is located. These models give *average* or *unconditional* effects of these variables on default and prepayment. The complicated models add thousands of interactive fixed effects by creating pseudo-pools of mortgages as described above; they give *marginal* or *conditional* effects of race and income on default and prepayment.

An analogy to typical panel data analysis is useful here. We can divide x into characteristics that vary within a group (pseudo-pool) and those that vary only across groups. For the purposes of this study we are interested in estimating within group variation in behavior: how LIML behavior varies conditional on observable characteristics (that is, within a pseudo-pool). To accomplish this we partition x as follows. Let

$$y = \log(-\log(1-h(t))) = \mathbf{Bx}. \tag{11-3}$$

5. Given our estimation procedure, which we discuss below, we would throw out most of these observations anyway because they would introduce log(0) into the equations.

6. See Agresti (1990) for a discussion of complementary log-log models.

If we let y^{ij} be the value of y for the ith borrower in the jth pseudo-pool, we can partition the right-hand side into two parts, so that

(11-4) $$y^{ij} = \mathbf{B}_1\mathbf{x}_1{}^{ij} + \mathbf{B}_2\,\mathbf{x}_2{}^{j},$$

where $\mathbf{x}_1{}^{ij}$ is a vector of the individual characteristics of the ith individual in the jth pseudo-pool (the variables in which we are interested, borrower income and race/ethnicity) and $\mathbf{x}_2{}^{j}$ includes characteristics common to all borrowers in the jth pseudo pool (the fixed effect for the pseudo-pool that the loan is in).

We are interested in estimates of $\mathbf{B}_1$. Following the analogy with panel data analysis, this can be accomplished by including group (pseudo-pool) level fixed effects to capture the effects of $\mathbf{x}_2{}^{j}$.

Alternatively, this can be accomplished through the subtraction of group-level means. Subtracting pseudo-pool means from both sides, we can rewrite equation 11-4 as

(11-5) $$y^{ij} - \bar{y}^{j} = (\mathbf{x}_1{}^{ij} - \bar{\mathbf{x}}_1{}^{j})\mathbf{B}_1 + (\mathbf{x}_2{}^{j} - \bar{\mathbf{x}}_2{}^{j})\mathbf{B}_2,$$

where $\bar{y}^{j}$ is the fraction of loans in the loan's pseudo-pool that prepaid (or defaulted) in the quarter in question and $\bar{\mathbf{x}}_1{}^{j}$ and $\bar{\mathbf{x}}_2{}^{j}$ are the mean levels of $\mathbf{x}_1{}^{ij}$ and $\mathbf{x}_2{}^{j}$ in the jth pseudo-pool.

Because $\mathbf{x}_2{}^{j} = \mathbf{x}_2{}^{j}$ we have

(11-6) $$y^{ij} - \bar{y}^{j} = (\mathbf{x}_1{}^{ij} - \bar{\mathbf{x}}_1{}^{j})\mathbf{B}_1,$$

which we can rewrite as

(11-7) $$y^{ij} = (\mathbf{x}_1{}^{ij} - \bar{\mathbf{x}}_1{}^{j})\mathbf{B}_1 + \bar{y}^{j}.$$

We estimate equation 11-7 using maximum likelihood.[7] Note that creating pseudo-pools by fully interacting the control variables allows us to control for observable characteristics in a rather nonparametric way. We do not produce estimates of $\mathbf{B}_2$. The creation of the pseudo-pools allows us to control for their effects without estimating thousands of parameters. This is a very simple but also rather complete representation, which allows us to look at the effects of race, income, and other factors within pools, holding effects at the pool level constant.

Borrower income is a categorical variable, indicating whether at origination the borrower is in one of four income groups relative to area median income. Our coefficients are estimated relative to the high income (greater than 120 percent of median), so that the coefficient of the lowest income group (less than 80

7. Pseudo-pools with no prepayments or defaults are excluded from the analysis because there is no within-group variation to explain. Mathematically, this results in values of log(0) for $\bar{y}^{j}$. We use a SAS program for estimation of log-log models.

Table 11-1. *Cumulative Prepayment and Default Rates by Race and Income*

Borrower income (percent of median)	*Black*	*Hispanic*	*Other minority*	*White*	*Total*
Prepayments (percent that ever prepaid)[a]					
0–80	29	31	40	42	41
81–100	31	33	43	46	44
101–120	32	34	45	47	46
120+	34	36	45	49	48
Total	32	34	44	47	46
Default (percent that ever defaulted)					
0–80	2.8	1.6	0.9	0.7	0.8
81–100	2.2	2.3	1.1	0.6	0.8
101–120	1.9	2.5	1.1	0.6	0.7
120+	1.4	2.3	1.2	0.5	0.6
Total	1.9	2.2	1.2	0.6	0.7

Source: Freddie Mac.

a. The prepayment database included 2.8 million loans, of which 3 percent were to black borrowers, 4 percent to Hispanics, 6 percent to other minorities, and 88 percent to whites.

percent of median) represents a "multiplier," which tells us, for instance, the extent to which low-income borrowers are more or less likely to prepay when their option is in the money. Similarly, we measure race/ethnicity by four categorical variables: black, Hispanic, other minority, and white. We suppress the white variable in our estimates so that the coefficients represent multipliers relative to white.

Results

Table 11-1 presents simple cross tabs. The prepayment rates (the percentage that ever prepaid during the sample period) by race/ethnicity and income provide the basic story. Blacks and Hispanics prepay significantly more slowly than whites and other minorities, and low-income borrowers prepay more slowly than high-income borrowers. On the default side, blacks and Hispanics have higher default rates than whites. Low-income borrowers tend to default more, but the differences are not very large, and the relationship does not hold for all groups. For instance, for Hispanics and other minorities defaults increase with income. These are, of course, crude statistics. For instance, we should at a minimum correct for the fact that these rates are averages over loans that were originated at different times and exposed to risks for different periods of time. We now turn to estimates of various forms of hazard model.

Table 11-2. *Basic Prepayment Results: Hazard Model Controlling for Age*
Dependent variable: prepayment rate

Black	–0.48	–0.34
	(0.01)[a]	(0.01)
Hispanic	–0.40	–0.24
	(0.01)	(0.01)
Other minority	–0.11	–0.02
	(0.0004)	(0.004)
Inc1[b]	–0.17	–0.17
	(0.002)	(0.003)
Inc2[c]	–0.09	–0.10
	(0.003)	(0.003)
Inc3[d]	–0.04	–0.05
	(0.003)	(0.003)
Min1[e]	...	0.36
		(0.005)
Min2[f]	...	0.22
		(0.005)
Min3[g]	...	0.11
		(0.006)
TractInc1[h]	...	0.08
		(0.004)
TractInc2[i]	...	0.02
		(0.002)
TractInc3[j]	...	0.02
		(0.002)

Source: Freddie Mac and U.S. Census.
a. Standard errors in parentheses.
b. Borrower income = 0–80 percent of median.
c. Borrower income = 81–100 percent of median.
d. Borrower income = 101–120 percent of median.
e. Minority share of population = 0–10 percent.
f. Minority share of population = 11–30 percent.
g. Minority share of population = 31–50 percent.
h. Tract income = 0–80 percent of median.
i. Tract income = 81–100 percent of median.
j. Tract income = 101–120 percent of median.

Prepayment Models

AVERAGE EFFECTS. Table 11-2 presents results for estimates of complementary log-log hazard models like equation 11-4. The $\mathbf{x}_1^{ij}$ variables are the race/ethnicity and borrower income variables; the $\bar{\mathbf{x}}_2^{j}$ variable is the age of the mortgage, which is a series of dummy variables for the number of quarters since origination. The age coefficients are not shown. Not surprisingly it tells the same story as the cross tabs.

Table 11-3. *Basic Prepayment Results: Hazard Model Controlling for Loan Age by Exercise Category*

	Discount[a]	*Current*[b]	*Premium*[c]
Black	0.01	–0.28	–1.57
	(0.01)[d]	(0.01)	(0.02)
Hispanic	–0.02	–0.24	–1.18
	(0.008)	(0.01)	(0.02)
Other minority	–0.13	–0.09	–0.22
	(0.006)	(0.008)	(0.01)
Inc1[e]	0.08	–0.06	–0.60
	(0.004)	(0.005)	(0.006)
Inc2[f]	0.004	–0.06	–0.21
	(0.004)	(0.006)	(0.006)
Inc3[g]	–(0.004)	–0.04	–0.06
	(0.004)	(0.005)	(0.006)

Source: Freddie Mac and U.S. Census.

a. Let $1 - a$ = current coupon rate / coupon rate on mortgage. Then $a < -0.035$ = discount.

b. $-0.035 < a < 0.035$ = current.

c. $0.100 < a < 0.25$ = premium.

d. Standard errors in parentheses.

e. Borrower income = 0–80 percent of median.

f. Borrower income = 81–100 percent of median.

g. Borrower income = 101–120 percent of median.

The right-hand column adds two location variables: the average income of households in the loan's census tract relative to the area median, and the minority (black + Hispanic + other minority) share of households in the census tract. Including these variables affects the race/ethnic coefficients, lowering them a bit. For instance, the coefficient for black increases from –0.48 to –0.34, and the coefficient for low minority concentration (Min1 (0 to 10)) is .36, relative to high concentration (greater than 50 percent). Hence the result that minorities tend to prepay less is partly explained by the racial composition of the neighborhood as well as the race of the borrower. For income there is virtually no change in the explanatory power of individual income but a small effect of neighborhood income on prepayment.

Because it matters whether lower prepayments rates happen when the prepayment option is in or out of the money, we divided our observations into loan quarters where the option was in or out of the money to varying degrees, as described above, and ran separate versions of the model in table 11-3 for each category. We have five categories. Going from most out of the money to most in the money, they are: Discount, Current, Cusp, Premium, and Super Premium. In the interest of saving space and readers' time we do not report results for "Cusp" or "Super Premium" and focus primarily on mortgages that were Discount (option out of the money) or Premium (option in the money).

Results are depicted in tables 11-3 and 11-4. Table 11-3 redoes the first column of table 11-2, and table 11-4 redoes the second column. The results are

Table 11-4. *Basic Prepayment Results: Hazard Model Controlling for Loan Age with Census Tract Variables*

	Discount[a]	*Current*[b]	*Premium*[c]
Black	0.08	–0.22	–1.11
	(0.01)[d]	(0.01)	(0.2)
Hispanic	0.05	–0.18	–0.67
	(0.01)	(0.01)	(0.02)
Other minority	–0.08	–0.05	0.01
	(0.006)	(0.01)	(0.009)
Inc1[e]	0.05	–0.05	–0.58
	(0.004)	(0.005)	(0.006)
Inc2[f]	–0.01	–0.05	–0.21
	(0.004)	(0.006)	(0.006)
Inc3[g]	–0.02	–0.04	–0.08
	(0.004)	(0.005)	(0.006)
Min1[h]	0.22	0.16	1.11
	(0.008)	(0.01)	(0.02)
Min2[i]	0.16	0.11	0.71
	(0.008)	(0.01)	(0.02)
Min3[j]	0.07	0.05	0.42
	(0.009)	(0.01)	(0.02)
TractInc1[k]	0.20	0.04	0.05
	(0.006)	(0.008)	(0.01)
TractInc2[l]	0.11	–0.03	–0.03
	(0.004)	(0.005)	(0.005)
TractInc3[m]	0.04	–0.03	0.05
	(0.003)	(0.005)	(0.005)

Source: Freddie Mac and U.S. Census.

a. Let $1 - a$ = current coupon rate / coupon rate on mortgage. Then $a < -0.035$ = discount.

b. $-0.035 < a < 0.035$ = current.

c. $0.100 < a < 0.25$ = premium.

d. Standard errors in parentheses.

e. Borrower income = 0–80 percent of median.

f. Borrower income = 81–100 percent of median.

g. Borrower income = 101–120 percent of median.

h. Minority share of population = 0–10 percent.

i. Minority share of population = 11–30 percent.

j. Minority share of population = 31–50 percent.

k. Tract income = 0–80 percent of median.

l. Tract income = 81–100 percent of median.

m. Tract income = 101–120 percent of median.

rather striking and similar in direction for both race and income. In table 11-3 we see virtually no difference for black and Hispanic prepayment rates (and a small decline for other minority) when the option is out of the money, a small difference when the option is close to the money, but a big decline when the option is in the money. For instance the coefficient for "black" implies that for premium loans blacks are exp(–1.57) or 0.2 times as likely to prepay as whites and exp(–.28) or about 0.8 for current coupon loans. For the lowest-income groups the results are similar but not as large. For instance, for the lowest-income group prepayment speeds are exp(–0.60) or 0.5 times as likely to prepay as those with incomes more than 120 percent of median (about half the loans in the sample) with very little difference when the option is out of the money.

Table 11-4 redoes the estimates adding census tract variables to those in table 11-2. Results are very similar. They suggest, if anything, that differences are bigger, for example, for a black borrower in a minority neighborhood.

Clearly, this means that LIMLs were made more valuable by the difference in prepayment behavior. We do not have an easy way of converting our multipliers into value to investors, but we can use some back-of-the-envelope calculations to get orders of magnitude. First, we can look at some market rates. At the time of writing, current coupon (7.5 percent) Freddie Mac mortgage pools were trading at prices that corresponded to yields that were about 75 basis points greater than yields on Freddie Mac noncallable debt of comparable duration. This difference is not just due to the value of the call option on the mortgages because the debt is generally more liquid than pass-through securities and on that account can be sold with a lower yield. A reasonable guess is that around 40 to 50 basis points represent the part of mortgage rate due to the prepayment option, a rough estimate of the maximum reduction in cost that could come from low prepayment response. The coefficient of 0.2 for black mortgages would probably take away most of this cost difference.

To evaluate the effect on value a little more rigorously, we applied a pricing model from Salomon Brothers (see Hayre and Rajan [1995] for a description), which is a generic pricing model that is widely available but proprietary. It uses Monte Carlo techniques combined with empirical prepayment models to compute the value of a mortgage as the expected present value of mortgage cash flows. A disadvantage of using the model is that because it is proprietary we do not know the details (coefficients) of the model, and our ability to tweak the model is limited. However, this is offset by the fact that it is widely used and we have the ability to change some of its parameters, by multiples like the sort we estimate, so that we can compare changes in value due to changes in the propensity to exercise prepayment options. In particular, the Salomon model can be broken down into an option-exercising part and a part that takes account of other factors. To the extent that we can identify these with our in-the-money and out-of-the-money coefficients we can use the model to predict pricing and mortgage rate differences given the multipliers we estimate. This is, of course, imprecise. First, our model does not have the same functional form as the Salomon model; second, it was estimated with an entirely different data set; and third, the multipliers we apply are quite low and imply prepayment functions that are probably outside the experience of the Salomon model.

We adjusted the Salomon prepayment model so that it was 0.2 times its baseline (the multiplier for premium mortgages) when the option is in the money, slightly lower when the option is close to the money, and the same when out of the money. We did this in two ways. First (call this scenario 1), we multiplied

Figure 11-1. *Prepayment Sensitivity*

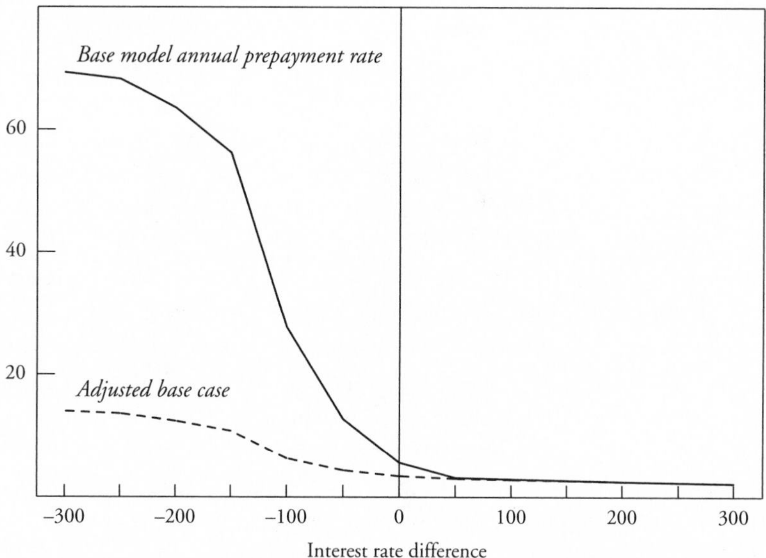

their coefficient for "prepayment incentive," which is a sort of interest elasticity of prepayment speed, by 0.2. (The Salomon refinancing incentive variable is similar to ours; in particular, it is in ratio rather than difference form.) Because we do not know the functional form of the model this may not be comparable to our multiplier, which multiplies the whole function by 0.2. Second (scenario 2), we adjusted this coefficient until the Salomon prepayment function (which we can graph) was approximately 0.2 times the baseline function for options in the money. A version of the old and new prepayment functions in this case are depicted in figure 11-1; the picture for scenario 1 is similar.

We analyze a current coupon 7.5 percent thirty-year fixed-rate mortgage. The model requires inputting the yield curve and a measure of interest rate volatility. We do not adjust the model's volatility numbers, but we do explore prices for different yield curves.

Our base case uses a historically typical yield curve, which is upward sloping with ten-year Treasuries 125 basis points above three-month Treasuries. We ask the model to give us the difference between a base case price for the mortgage and the one adjusted for the new prepayment model. We then ask the model for the difference in mortgage coupon rate between the base case and the adjusted case, assuming both are priced at par. The latter is the more interesting question; because in the Salomon model for scenario one a 1 basis point increase in coupon rate leads to a 5 basis point increase in value, the answer is approximately the price difference divided by 5 (6 for scenario 2). The answer for scenario 1 is a difference of about 25 basis points in mortgage coupon rate. We then chose a downward-sloping yield curve, like the one observed in September 2000, and a sharply upward sloping one; we got answers of about 35 basis points and 15 basis points, respectively. For scenario 2, which has a lower and flatter prepayment function, the results were close to 5 basis points greater.

For low-income borrowers the multiplier is 0.5, and the effect is smaller. Repeating the above estimates gives a base case of about 15 basis points, in mortgage rate, for scenario 1 with a range of about 10 to 20 basis points.

Our estimated hazard models had a super premium category, which had a larger multiplier, 0.8, and a "cusp" (barely into the money) category with a multiplier of 0.5, as well as "premium." Because these multipliers are both greater than the 0.2 used in the simulations our procedure overestimates the price difference somewhat. We cannot tweak the Salomon model in a way that readily allows two or three multipliers, so we cannot incorporate these differences directly. However, we suspect that they are small. For instance, at 8 percent mortgage rates, the cusp variable applies only to cases where rates are between 7.2 percent and 7.7percent—that is, where the option is not very far into the money; and the multiplier is quite low, 0.5, anyway (as we saw above, for the low-income calculations, if the multiplier is .5 across the entire range the effect is still on the order of 15 basis points).

Super premium loans have a multiplier that is closer to one. We note that the super premium category is for loans for which the current mortgage rate is less than .75 times the rate on the mortgage. At 8 percent rates this means the difference only kicks in when rates have fallen to 6 percent. In the Salomon model and in reality this has a low probability of happening, and even with a 0.2 multiplier many mortgages will have been prepaid by the time rates get to 6 percent. We simulated the model several times for prepayment functions that became very steep after a 2 percent rate decline and found very small effects. A difference of 5 basis points would be high; hence we believe that our calculations are, in a back-of-the-envelope sense, not much affected by assuming a multiplier of 0.2 throughout, but they probably do err on the high side.

MARGINAL EFFECTS. The above looks at average experience. Our data allow us to control for LTV ratio, credit history (measured by the Fair, Isaac and Company's credit scoring model, or FICO score), loan amount, and other variables as described above. Tables 11-5 and 11-6 report estimates of *B* in equation 11-7. The new coefficients are, as before, for race/ethnicity and income by extent in and out of the money as in tables 11-3 and 11-4, but now they are marginal effects, after controlling for loan characteristics listed in the table, which define our pseudo-pools.

Table 11-5 corresponds to Table 11-3. The controls have significant effects on the structure of the coefficients. In particular, for both blacks and Hispanics

Table 11-5. *Marginal Prepayment Results: Hazard Model Controlling for Origination Quarter, Coupon, Age, FICO, LTV, and Loan Amount*

	Discount[a]	*Current*[b]	*Premium*[c]
Black	–0.58	–0.56	–0.62
	(0.02)[d]	(0.02)	(0.009)
Hispanic	–0.53	–0.47	–0.59
	(0.02)	(0.02)	(0.008)
Other minority	–0.27	–0.15	–0.15
	(0.01)	(0.01)	(0.006)
Inc1[e]	–0.13	–0.07	–0.07
	(0.007)	(0.007)	(0.004)
Inc2[f]	–0.14	–0.06	0.02
	(0.007)	(0.007)	(0.004)
Inc3[g]	–0.11	–0.04	0.04
	(0.007)	(0.007)	(0.004)

Source: Freddie Mac and U.S. Census.

Notes: FICO: credit score from scoring mode of Fair, Isaac and Company. LTV is the loan-to-value ratio at origination.

a. Let $1 - a$ = current coupon rate / coupon rate on mortgage. Then $a < -0.035$ = discount.

b. $-0.035 < a < 0.035$ = current.

c. $0.100 < a < 0.25$ = premium.

d. Standard errors in parentheses.

e. Borrower income = 0–80 percent of median.

f. Borrower income = 81–100 percent of median.

g. Borrower income = 101–120 percent of median.

the coefficients when the option is in the money fall in absolute value, and the coefficients when it is close to or out of the money become negative to the point where the three sets of coefficients are essentially the same. For low-income borrowers differences become quite small and almost the same across in-the-moneyness categories.[8] Table 11-6 repeats table 11-4. The controls almost wipe out the income effects, but not the race/ethnicity effects.

These results complicate the pricing because we now have offsetting effects; for LIMLs, controlling for loan characteristics, prepayment is slower when the option is out of the money, which makes the loans less valuable and tends to offset the (now diminished) tendency to prepay less when the option is in the money. We redid the pricing exercise above, in this case multiplying the entire

8. The FICO score is doing much of the work here. Apparently low FICO score borrowers prepay more when the option is out of the money and less when it is in the money. A hypothesis is that this reflects limited financing alternatives, so that low FICO score borrowers do not have access to other non-mortgage sources of funds and sometimes have refinanced a low-rate mortgage when they need money, but they are more likely to have trouble qualifying for a new loan when the option is in the money and they want to refinance a high-rate mortgage. The correlation between FICO and race accounts for much of the change in coefficients. Loan balance is also a factor; low balance loans prepay in ways similar to low FICO loans.

Table 11-6. *Marginal Prepayment Results with Tract Variables: Hazard Model Controlling for Origination Quarters, Coupon, Age, FICO LTV, and Loan Amount*

	Discount[a]	*Current*[b]	*Premium*[c]
Black	–0.49	–0.47	–0.47
	(0.02)[d]	(0.02)	(0.01)
Hispanic	–0.43	–0.36	–0.41
	(0.02)	(0.02)	(0.01)
Other minority	–0.21	–0.08	–0.06
	(0.01)	(0.01)	(0.01)
Inc1[e]	–0.12	–0.06	–0.05
	(0.007)	(0.007)	(0.004)
Inc2[f]	–0.13	–0.06	0.03
	(0.007)	(0.007)	(0.004)
Inc3[g]	–0.10	–0.04	0.04
	(0.007)	(0.007)	(0.004)
Min1[h]	0.24	0.27	0.39
	(0.01)	(0.01)	(0.01)
Min2[i]	0.21	0.18	0.21
	(0.01)	(0.01)	(0.01)
Min3[j]	0.10	0.10	0.13
	(0.002)	(0.02)	(0.01)
TractInc1[k]	–0.03	0.03	–0.02
	(0.01)	(0.01)	(0.006)
TractInc2[l]	–0.10	–0.05	–0.03
	(0.006)	(0.007)	(0.004)
TractInc3[m]	–0.09	–0.04	0.02
	(0.005)	(0.006)	(0.003)

Source: Freddie Mac and U.S. Census.

Notes: FICO: credit score from scoring mode of Fair, Isaac and Company. LTV is the loan-to-value ratio at origination.

a. Let $1 - a$ = current coupon rate / coupon rate on mortgage. Then $a < -0.035$ = discount.

b. $-0.035 < a < 0.035$ = current.

c. $0.100 < a < 0.25$ = premium.

d. Standard errors in parentheses.

e. Borrower income = 0–80 percent of median.

f. Borrower income = 81–100 percent of median.

g. Borrower income = 101–120 percent of median.

h. Minority share of population = 0–10 percent.

i. Minority share of population = 11–30 percent.

j. Minority share of population = 31–50 percent.

k. Tract income = 0–80 percent of median.

l. Tract income = 81–100 percent of median.

m. Tract income = 101–120 percent of median.

prepayment function by exp(–0.60) or about 0.6. For the current yield curve, which is the downward-sloping (suggesting an expectation of falling rates) case, we found that the option part dominated and the difference in mortgage rates was about 10 basis points in scenario 1. However, for the more normal yield curve (ten-year Treasuries 125 basis points above three-month Treasuries), where the option part is less important, we found the results approximately canceled out. For a sharply upward-sloping yield curve the LIMLs are less valuable. For low-income borrowers the effects are in the same direction, but because the multipliers are quite small the effects are also quite small.

STABILITY OVER TIME. Mortgage markets changed rapidly in the 1990s, particularly with respect to prepayments; it has become increasingly easy to refinance, and it may well be that it has become increasingly easy for LIML borrowers to get loans. Hence the coefficients estimated above may have changed over time. Because of the large size of our data set we can test this by reestimating the above models for different exposure years (that is, calendar rather than origination year). Results from some of the estimates are reported in tables 11-7 and 11-8.

Table 11-7 presents results from the simple or *average* model, reestimated for each exposure year; it presents only the coefficients for blacks and Hispanics and the two lowest income groups. The results are comparable to those in tables 11-2 and 11-3. Part A presents results for all loans, that is, without separating the sample into in- and out-of-the-moneyness (this is comparable to column one of table 11-2). Note that results for the black and Hispanic coefficients have a similar pattern; the coefficients are especially big in 1998, about zero in 1994, and small but negative in the other years. The years with big effects, 1993 and 1998, were years of sharp interest rate declines and big refinancing waves; 1994 was a very small refinancing year because it was a year when interest rates went up; and the other years were in between; 1995 saw rates drop, but many of the loans alive then were originated in 1993 and were out of the money (we need to control for age and in-the-moneyness). This is a pattern consistent with previous results: less exercise in years when the option is valuable and no difference when it is not.

Part B gives results for the premium loans. This corresponds to column three of table 11-3. The central result is that although coefficients do change from year to year there is little apparent pattern. Aside from 1994, when there were few premium loans and the results are insignificant, the year with the biggest coefficient is 1998.[9] The only hint of a trend is one point; the lowest year is 1999. Hence the lower rate of option exercise by blacks and Hispanics when the

9. The 1998 result is consistent with the notion that the differences are biggest in heavy refinancing years (the second biggest multiplier was in 1995, which was also a year when mortgage rates dropped and refinancing increased), which suggests that the effect is not proportional and that by underweighting the heavy refinancing years we are underestimating the shadow price difference. Note, however, that this pattern does not hold up when we add our controls in table 11-9.

Table 11-7. *Average Prepayment Results over Time by Exposure Year, 1993–99*

	1993	*1994*	*1995*	*1996*	*1997*	*1998*	*1999*
A. All loans							
Black	–1.43	0.04	–0.13	–0.23	–0.27	–1.24	–0.45
	(0.2)[a]	(0.03)	(0.02)	(0.01)	(0.01)	(0.02)	(0.01)
Hispanic	–1.03	–0.06	–0.18	–0.24	–0.24	–0.97	–0.29
	(0.1)	(0.03)	(0.02)	(0.01)	(0.01)	(0.01)	(0.01)
Inc1[b]	–1.57	0.05	–0.06	–0.03	–0.04	–0.44	–0.16
	(0.1)	(0.01)	(0.01)	(0.01)	(0.01)	(0.01)	(0.01)
Inc2[c]	–0.78	–0.01	–0.06	–0.04	–0.04	–0.18	–0.08
	(0.05)	(0.01)	(0.01)	(0.01)	(0.01)	(0.01)	(0.01)
B. Premium loans							
Black	–1.49	–4.84	–2.39	–1.46	–0.96	–2.95	–0.72
	(0.71)	(11.31)	(0.15)	(0.07)	(0.04)	(0.05)	(0.03)
Hispanic	–30.16	–4.61	–1.95	–1.51	–0.72	–1.92	–0.44
	(2.42)	(9.8)	(0.12)	(0.07)	(0.03)	(0.03)	(0.02)
Inc1	–1.56	–0.11	–1.65	–0.76	–0.37	–0.69	–0.33
	(0.30)	(0.8)	(0.04)	(0.02)	(0.02)	(0.01)	(0.01)
Inc2	–0.41	–0.70	–0.52	–0.23	–0.15	–0.22	–0.12
	(0.18)	(1.08)	(0.03)	(0.02)	(0.02)	(0.01)	(0.1)

Source: Freddie Mac and U.S. Census.

a. Standard errors in parenthesis.

b. Borrower income = 0–80 percent of median.

c. Borrower income = 81–100 percent of median.

option is in the money appears not to be changing much. The effect of income does appear to be declining, however. For the lowest income group the multiplier was about 0.7 in 1999; it was about 0.5 for the sample as a whole.

Table 11-8 depicts the results with control variables added, as in table 11-5. Part A presents results for premium loans. The coefficients for black and Hispanic are quite stable across exposure years, but with a small decline in 1999. The coefficients for low-income borrowers go to close to zero. We have estimated exposure year variants of all the models in tables 11-5 and 11-6, which are not shown here. We found that minority census tract concentration has the same sort of effect as before, but no surprising trends were found.

In summary, we found some tendency for prepayment behavior of low-income borrowers to converge with that of high-income borrowers; there is little or no tendency for that to be the case for black and Hispanic borrowers; and the equations with the controls added are rather stable over time and are similar to those reported for the sample as a whole.

Default Models

AVERAGE EFFECTS. To analyze performance with respect to default we go through similar exercises. Table 11-9 presents a model similar to that in table

Table 11-8. *Marginal Prepayment Results over Time by Exposure Year, 1993–99*

	1993	*1994*[a]	*1995*	*1996*	*1997*	*1998*	*1999*
A. Premium loans							
Black	–0.47	. . .	–0.77	–0.72	–0.73	–0.63	–0.51
	(0.37)[b]		(0.05)	(0.04)	(0.03)	(0.01)	(0.02)
Hispanic	–1.17	. . .	–0.76	–0.75	–0.62	–0.63	–0.43
	(0.38)		(0.04)	(0.03)	(0.03)	(0.01)	(0.01)
Inc1[c]	–0.18	. . .	–0.17	–0.12	–0.05	–0.07	–0.04
	(0.17)		(0.02)	(0.02)	(0.01)	(0.01)	(0.01)
Inc2[d]	0.07	. . .	0.00	0.02	0.03	0.02	0.03
	(0.44)		(0.02)	(0.01)	(0.01)	(0.01)	(0.01)
B. Discount loans							
Black	0.32	–0.50	–0.60	–0.64	–0.59	–0.63	–0.51
	(0.71)	(0.07)	(0.05)	(0.04)	(0.04)	(0.07)	(0.03)
Hispanic	0.51	–0.55	–0.62	–0.59	–0.59	–0.51	–0.40
	(0.59)	(0.06)	(0.05)	(0.04)	(0.03)	(0.07)	(0.03)
Inc1	–0.48	–0.30	–0.24	–0.17	–0.12	–0.09	–0.01
	(0.34)	(0.02)	(0.02)	(0.01)	(0.01)	(0.037)	(0.01)
Inc2	–0.42	–0.21	–0.22	–0.17	–0.14	–0.11	–0.05
	(0.34)	(0.02)	(0.02)	(0.01)	(0.01)	(0.03)	(0.01)

Source: Freddie Mac and U.S. Census.

a. Not enough premium loans to estimate the model.

b. Standard errors in parenthesis.

c. Borrower income = 0–80 percent of median.

d. Borrower income = 81–100 percent of median.

11-2 except that it explains defaults, controlling for age of loan and state. Again, not surprisingly, it tells the same story as the simple cross tabs in table 11-1. In the left-hand column the model implies a multiplier for black of exp(1.01), or about 3, and for low-income borrowers of exp(.25), or about 1.3. The right-hand column adds census tract variables. Note that the right-hand column implies a rather large effect for neighborhood income rather than individual borrower income. This result is similar to that in Van Order and Zorn (2000).

To analyze default cost we need to model loss severity rates as well. We do this in tables 11-11 and 11-12. These tables present OLS results from regressing log of loss severity (including all sorts of transaction and opportunity costs) divided by mortgage balance on the same variables as in table 11-9. It suggests small differences by race but bigger differences by income. Table 11-12 controls for LTV, FICO, etc. and adds census tract variables. It suggests that the major explanatory factor is census tract income.

We do not have a generic pricing model to use to assess the extra cost of the higher default and severity rates; there is not much of a market for trading credit risk. But from recent Freddie Mac history we can approximate a baseline level of default to which we can apply our estimated multipliers. In this sample the

Table 11-9. *Basic Average Default Results: Hazard Model Controlling for State and Age*

Black	1.01	0.77
	(0.04)[a]	(0.04)
Hispanic	0.77	0.53
	(0.03)	(0.04)
Other minority	0.34	0.24
	(0.03)	(0.03)
Inc1[b]	0.25	0.06
	(0.03)	(0.03)
Inc2[c]	0.20	0.08
	(0.03)	(0.03)
Inc3[d]	0.16	0.08
	(0.03)	(0.03)
Min1[e]	. . .	–0.26
		(0.04)
Min2[f]	. . .	–0.18
		(0.04)
Min3[g]	. . .	0.02
		(0.04)
TractInc1[h]	. . .	0.77
		(0.03)
TractInc2[i]	. . .	0.56
		(0.03)
TractInc3[j]	. . .	0.33
		(0.03)

Source: Freddie Mac and U.S. Census.
a. Standard errors in parentheses.
b. Borrower income = 0–80 percent of median.
c. Borrower income = 81–100 percent of median.
d. Borrower income = 101–120 percent of median.
e. Minority share of population = 0–10 percent.
f. Minority share of population = 11–30 percent.
g. Minority share of population = 31–50 percent.
h. Tract income = 0–80 percent of median.
i. Tract income = 81–100 percent of median.
j. Tract income = 101–120 percent of median.

median loan has an LTV just under 80 percent. History suggests that these loans have about a 2 percent chance of ever defaulting; this was higher in the early 1990s during the recession and was quite small in the late 1990s. Average loss severity rates on these have been about 30 percent. This suggests average losses of about 0.6 percent, which discounted to the present implies an expected present value of about 0.5 percent of loan balance. Using a "divide by 5" rule of thumb, this implies an annual charge of about 10 basis points. A reasonable range around this is probably 5 to15 basis points (at the lower end at the end of the period). For loans to blacks the overall multiplier (including severity rates) is

Table 11-10. *Marginal Default Results: Hazard Model Controlling for Origination Quarter, State, Age, FICO, LTV, Debt Ratio, Loan Amount, and Purpose*

Black	0.06	–0.08
	(0.04)[a]	(0.04)
Hispanic	0.13	–0.02
	(0.04)	(0.04)
Other minority	0.15	0.08
	(0.04)	(0.04)
Inc1[b]	0.32	0.24
	(0.03)	(0.03)
Inc2[c]	0.16	0.11
	(0.03)	(0.03)
Inc3[d]	0.08	0.05
	(0.03)	(0.03)
Min1[e]	. . .	–0.25
		(0.04)
Min2[f]	. . .	–0.23
		(0.04)
Min3[g]	. . .	–0.07
		(0.04)
TractInc1[h]	. . .	0.40
		(0.04)
TractInc2[i]	. . .	0.26
		(0.03)
TractInc3[j]	. . .	0.13
		(0.03)

Source: Freddie Mac and U.S. Census.
a. Standard errors in parentheses.
b. Borrower income = 0–80 percent of median.
c. Borrower income = 81–100 percent of median.
d. Borrower income = 101–120 percent of median.
e. Minority share of population = 0–10 percent.
f. Minority share of population = 11–30 percent.
g. Minority share of population = 31–50 percent.
h. Tract income = 0–80 percent of median.
i. Tract income = 81–100 percent of median.
j. Tract income = 101–120 percent of median.

around 3.2, suggesting a range of cost of 16 to 48 basis points and a difference from the baseline of roughly 11 to 33 basis points. For low-income borrowers the multiplier, including severity rate differences, is about 1.7, which suggests a mean of 17 basis points and a range of default costs of 11 to 26 basis points with a differential of 6 to 11 basis points.[10]

10. A factor not included is capital costs. To the extent that riskier loans require more capital, this can increase costs. Note that capital cost might increase cost differences for both credit risk and prepayment risk.

Table 11-11. *Loss Severity: OLS estimates for Log of Loss/Loan Balance*

Black	0.14
	(3.51)[a]
Hispanic	0.06
	(1.69)
Other minority	–0.03
	(–0.90)
Inc1[b]	0.38
	(13.31)
Inc2[c]	0.20
	(6.42)
Inc3[d]	0.11
	(3.56)

Source: Freddie Mac and U.S. Census.
a. *t* ratios in parenthesis.
b. Borrower income = 0–80 percent of median.
c. Borrower income = 81–100 percent of median.
d. Borrower income = 101–120 percent of median.

An implication of this is that although LIMLs do indeed have higher default costs, the lower costs from exercising the prepayment option have at least offset these for our loan sample.

MARGINAL EFFECTS. As with prepayment, we want to control for other determinants of default. We do not have the ability to measure in-the-moneyness at the loan level as we did with the prepayment model, so we must create proxies. We created pseudo-pools to control for LTV, FICO, age, the ratio of borrower debt payments to borrower income, loan amount, loan purpose (refinance or purchase), and state in which the property is located. Again, we have pseudo-pools for every combination of these, and we report the new coefficients for race/ethnicity and other factors (comparable to table 11-5) in table 11-10. The outstanding characteristic of table 11-10 is how little is left for the race variables to explain after controlling for the other variables. In the first column the coefficients for black and Hispanic drop precipitously from those in table 11-9. In the second column the sign for black turns negative, although there is a significant effect for minority composition of the neighborhood. It is, however, also the case that the controls do not lower the income effect.

Redoing the pricing reveals almost no effect for race and a smaller (because of the new severity rate coefficients) effect for income. Of some interest is the effect of neighborhood (census tract) variables. Our data set does not allow us to say much about why we might see these effects. Two possibilities are that they capture information about property values (for example, volatility might differ across neighborhoods) or they are a proxy for some better measure of (permanent) income.

Table 11-12. *Marginal Loss Severity: OLS Estimates of Log of Severity Rate, Controlling for LTV, Origination Amount, Units, FICO and State*

Black	0.04	–0.03
	(0.98)[a]	(0.7)
Hispanic	0.02	–0.04
	(0.65)	(–1.01)
Other minority	–0.06	–.09
	(–1.63)	(–2.52)
Inc1[b]	0.05	0.00
	(1.49)	(0.08)
Inc2[c]	–0.03	–0.06
	(–0.87)	(–1.72)
Inc3[d]	–0.02	–0.04
	(–0.49)	(–1.12)
Min1[e]	. . .	–0.08
		(–1.83)
Min2[f]	. . .	–0.08
		(–2.07)
Min3[g]	. . .	–0.1
		(–0.29)
TractInc1[h]	. . .	0.32
		(7.92)
TractInc2[i]	. . .	0.13
		(4.16)
TractInc3[j]	. . .	0.08
		(2.64)

Source: Freddie Mac and U.S. Census.
a. *t* ratios in parentheses.
b. Borrower income = 0–80 percent of median.
c. Borrower income = 81–100 percent of median.
d. Borrower income = 101–120 percent of median.
e. Minority share of population = 0–10 percent.
f. Minority share of population = 11–30 percent.
g. Minority share of population = 31–50 percent.
h. Tract income = 0–80 percent of median.
i. Tract income = 81–100 percent of median.
j. Tract income = 101–120 percent of median.

STABILITY OVER TIME. As in the prepayment section, we reran our models by exposure year to see if default behavior had changed over time. This yields less information. First, the sample is smaller because in the default sample we look only at loans originated from 1993 through1995; and second, the exposure years 1993 and 1994 have very few defaults (the loans are too new to default, especially in a growing economy). Because of the thinness of the results we present a broad summary of the results, rather than tables. Our basic results for 1995 through 1999 are as follows:

—Coefficients for black and Hispanic in the simple, average model (corresponding to table 11-9) were somewhat below average in 1995 and 1996 and were stable at about their sample-wide levels from 1997 through 1999. Hence there was little change; if anything, there was a slight increase.

—The effect of borrower income (that is, the tendency of low-income borrowers to default more) increases over time, and the coefficient for the lowest income group was 0.34 in 1999 (vs. 0.25 for the period as a whole; see table 11-9).

—Tract income had a stable positive effect of about the same size as in table 11-9.

—Minority tract composition had a slightly increasing effect over time.

—When we added controls as in table 11-8, black and Hispanic coefficients fell dramatically, as before, but we could not discern a pattern across time because the coefficients in individual years were not significant.

—After controls, the income effect showed some sign of declining. Minority tract composition effects increase slightly over time.

Overall there is little reason to believe there have been significant changes in default behavior during the period.

Comments

Our major results are:

—The data imply that LIMLs generally performed the same as or better than other loans. This is because they were significantly less likely to refinance when mortgage rates dropped. The crudeness of our pricing calculations does not allow us to be confident about the extent to which the prepayment effect is larger.

—Much of this can be explained by loan characteristics like credit history and LTV.

A question is whether these results can be projected into the future. A major change in mortgage markets over the past decade has been the increased quickness with which borrowers refinance and the increased ability of riskier borrowers to get loans. Given this change, it seems unlikely that, to the extent the low prepayment multiplier is due to lack of sophistication or market opportunity, it will continue to be so low. But much of the gap in prepayment behavior can be explained by variables like FICO. If those variables are "fundamental," then we might project long-run prepayment differences to come from projections that eliminate the race and income effects in tables 11-5 and 11-6, but this might be mitigated by increased ability of low FICO borrowers to get loans causing the FICO effects to decline over time.

When reestimated by exposure year we found evidence that income effects on prepayment have fallen over time and after adding controls have about vanished, but we found very little reason to believe there have been changes in prepayment coefficients for black and Hispanic borrowers. Changes in default behavior over time are more difficult to be sure of, but our estimates by exposure year suggest little change over time for black or Hispanic borrowers with ambiguous (and small) results with and without the controls for the income effect.

References

Agresti, A. 1990. *Categorical Data Analysis.* Wiley.

Chinloy, P., and I. Megbolugbe. 1994. "Hedonic Mortgages." *Journal of Housing Research* (Fannie Mae) 5 (1): 1–21.

Deng Y. H., J. Quigley, and R. Van Order. 2000. "Mortgage Terminations, Heterogeneity and the Exercise of Mortgage Options." *Econometrica* 68 (2): 275–307.

Hayre, L., and A. Rajan. 1995. "Anatomy of Prepayments: The Salomon Brothers Prepayment Model." New York: Salomon Brothers.

Hendershott, P., and R. Van Order. 1987. "Pricing Mortgages: An Interpretation of Models and Results." *Journal of Financial Services Research* 1 (1): 77–111.

Kau, James, and Donald Keenan. 1995. "An Overview of Option-Theoretic Pricing of Mortgages," *Journal of Housing* 6 (2): 217–44.

Prentice, R., and L. A. Gloeckner. 1978. "Regression Analysis of Grouped Survival Data with Application to Breast Cancer Data." *Biometrics* 34 (1): 57–67.

Van Order, R., and P. Zorn. 2000. "Income, Location and Default: Implications for Community Lending." *Real Estate Economics* 28 (3): 385–404.

12

Performance of Community Reinvestment Loans: Implications for Secondary Market Purchases

ROBERTO G. QUERCIA, MICHAEL A. STEGMAN,
WALTER R. DAVIS, AND ERIC STEIN

The government-sponsored enterprises (GSEs) have been very successful in extending credit to nontraditional borrowers using technology, homeownership education, and outreach. For instance, between 1993 and 1999 the Federal National Mortgage Association (Fannie Mae) and the Federal Home Loan Mortgage Corporation (Freddie Mac) increased their combined total purchases of home loans by 22 percent. Their purchases of home loans originated to very low- and low-income borrowers increased at much higher rates (Bunce, 2000).

In all likelihood, if the GSE affordable market is to continue to grow, the GSEs will need to expand their guidelines for affordable loan purchases. This requires the development and mainstreaming of new affordable and more flexible products. These products must offer a different mix of underwriting requirements than is currently available, and the GSEs are pilot-testing several such products. Unfortunately, these are limited in number and not as aggressive as many community lending portfolio products.

Alternatively, the GSEs could purchase aggressively underwritten community lending portfolio products. In general, they have been reluctant to do so because these products may allow for low borrower credit scores, low or no down pay-

The authors would like to thank Spencer Cowan for his assistance on an earlier version of this chapter.

ment, high debt-to-income ratios, and no mortgage insurance. Moreover, the GSEs have little knowledge about the performance of these loans over time. Thus a central question is whether community lending products that feature such flexible guidelines are prudent targets for GSE purchase.

This chapter begins filling this void by undertaking an analysis of the performance of a sample of portfolio loans within twenty-four months of purchase by Self-Help Ventures as part of its Community Advantage™ (SHCA) Home Loan Secondary Market Program. SHCA is the result of a partnership of the Ford Foundation; the Center for Community Self-Help, a North Carolina community-based organization; and Fannie Mae. Under the program, lenders can sell their nonstandard community reinvestment loans in the secondary market. By demonstrating that these community lending products perform at acceptable levels of risk, the Ford Foundation hopes to encourage mainstream lenders, secondary market institutions, and housing policymakers to incorporate loan products that feature more flexible underwriting into their core lending business, federal regulations, and national housing policies.

This study is an early evaluation within the larger and longer-term evaluation of SHCA. As such, the investigation is designed to identify baseline patterns and raise questions, not definitively test hypotheses. Models that clarify patterns of causation are not developed. Rather the goal is to examine what is the early performance of a relatively small sample of geographically concentrated community reinvestment loans that meet SHCA's purchasing guidelines. Despite the limited generalizability of the findings, the insights gained in this study will constitute the basis for future modeling efforts that will ultimately serve as guideposts to market participants and policymakers alike.

The remainder of this chapter is divided into six sections. First, barriers to homeownership, especially among underserved populations, are identified. Next is a description of how mortgage industry participants are attempting to address these barriers by developing mortgage products characterized by increasingly flexible underwriting guidelines. The authors' current knowledge of the risks in community lending and other affordable products is briefly discussed, and the need for further research is emphasized. This is followed by a description of the methodology and data used in the study to assess the early loan performance of community lending products. Empirical findings are presented next in three parts. First there is a comparison of the underwriting flexibility in selected SHCA community lending products and the GSEs' affordable products. Next is a description of the characteristics of SHCA loans with regard to demographic and other characteristics of the borrowers, as well as four risk factors: credit scores, loan-to-value ratios, back-end ratios, and reserve requirements. Third, the results of a multivariate proportional hazard model used to assess the impacts of underwriting flexibility on loan performance (the incidence of ninety-day delinquencies) are presented. In the final section, findings are summarized and future research directions are identified.

Barriers to Homeownership

For many Americans, especially low- and moderate-income households, the equity in a home represents an important form of accumulated wealth. Homeownership represents a unique opportunity for families to build economic security. Unfortunately, homeownership is an unfulfilled dream for many Americans. The national homeownership rate in 2000 reached an all-time high of 67.7 percent, surpassing the end-of-administration goal set by President Clinton in 1995. There are now 71.6 million homeowners in the United States. Yet although 72 percent of white households own their homes, only 48.2 percent of minority households and 51.9 percent of central city residents do so. Similarly, only 53.3 percent of households headed by females, 52.2 percent of households earning less than the median family income, and 61.0 percent of young married couples (35 years of age or younger) own a home (U.S. Department of Housing and Urban Development, 2000).

Reasons for these differences are complex, including household, financial, and supply considerations. Many underserved renters lack a relationship with mainstream financial and other institutions. For instance, 44 percent of all black renters with incomes below $40,000 in 1998 had no relationship with a financial institution (were unbanked).[1] Without this relationship, it is difficult for many underserved borrowers to even consider purchasing a home. In addition, many renter households may feel apprehensive and/or may lack information about the possibility of owning a home (Ratner, 1996). Apprehension and lack of knowledge may even discourage renters with the financial resources from believing that they can purchase a home. To make matters worse, many low-income and minority loan applicants are unable to meet standard mortgage underwriting guidelines. The inability to meet underwriting guidelines may be the result of blemished or no credit; insufficient cash for a down payment, closing costs, reserves, and other fees; or high housing- and debt-burden ratios due to a low income.

Data from the 1999 Home Mortgage Disclosure Act (HMDA) support this last contention. HMDA indicates that the conventional home purchase loan denial rate among white loan applicants (15.1 percent) was less than half that of African American applicants (37.1 percent) and about 60 percent that of Hispanic applicants (24.9 percent). Key reasons for loan denial are consistent across groups. High debt-to-income burdens and blemished credit histories are the two most important reasons for mortgage application denials. However, the inci-

1. Authors' calculations using data from the 1998 Survey of Consumer Finances (Board of Governors of the Federal Reserve System, 1998).

dence of these reasons differed greatly across groups. Among conventional loan applicants, only 5.2 percent of rejected white applicants were rejected because of credit problems, whereas almost half of all rejected African American applicants were rejected for such problems (46.0 percent) (Federal Financial Institutions Examination Council, 2000).

There is also evidence that a lack of appropriately priced homes prevents many renter households that could qualify for a loan from purchasing a home (Stegman, Quercia, and McCarthy, 2000). For instance, in seventeen metropolitan areas, Stegman, Quercia, and McCarthy estimate that 200,000 working renter families could afford to purchase a three-plus-bedroom house priced between $50,000 and $75,000, yet only 30,000 homes in that price range were available in the market in 1997–98.[2] As expected, the lack of adequately priced supply varies greatly from place to place. In San Francisco, about 2,500 working renter families could purchase a $75,000–$100,000 home, but when the 1998 American Housing Survey was conducted in that city, there were no houses for sale in this price range. In Boston, this potential demand was more than thirteen times larger than the number of houses that were available for sale in early 1998. Thus many face the prospect of a lifetime of renting because there are no affordable homes to buy. Unfortunately, typical efforts to expand homeownership opportunities to underserved populations have focused on addressing household and financial barriers almost exclusively.

Addressing Barriers to Homeownership

To expand lending to minority, low-income, and other nontraditional borrowers, mortgage industry participants have put in place a number of strategies. These include special marketing activities, requiring homeownership education and counseling, and the use of flexible underwriting guidelines. Special marketing activities commonly include outreach to community and religious organizations that are active in targeted markets and home buyer education fairs or seminars to reach targeted groups (Quercia, 1999).

As a rule, homeownership education and counseling (HEC) is required for all affordable products. HEC is believed to fulfill several roles in the promotion of affordable homeownership. First, although little empirical evidence is available to date, HEC is believed to compensate for the potentially higher risk inherent in the use of nontraditional or flexible underwriting guidelines (Hirad and Zorn, this volume). Before purchase, lenders require borrowers to complete a home buyer education program and to undergo individualized credit counseling (prepurchase counseling). After purchase, lenders may also use enhanced servicing

2. These families were assumed to qualify under an affordable mortgage product such as Fannie Mae's Alt 97 or Freddie Mac's Flex 97.

Table 12-1. *Standard and Affordable Underwriting Guidelines (sample)*

Guideline	*Standard*	*Affordable*
Down payment	20 percent	3 percent
Back-end ratio (ratio of mortgage principal and interest payment, property taxes, insurance, and other nonhousing debt to household income)	33 percent	Greater than 38 percent
Credit history	High credit scores (unlikely to allow less than 620)	Low or no credit scores
Cash reserves	Two months	Waived or reduced
Mortgage insurance	Required if down payment less than 20 percent	Waived or reduced
Layering of risk factors	Not allowed	Allowed

Source: Quercia (1999).

techniques, such as phone contact with delinquent borrowers, to determine the cause of the delinquency and to establish a plan to rectify the situation. Finally, the lenders may establish default prevention targeted to borrowers with serious delinquency problems (postpurchase counseling) (Quercia, 1999).

The most distinguishing characteristic of affordable lending efforts is the use of nontraditional flexible underwriting guidelines (see table 12-1). Affordable lending products allow higher loan-to-value ratios, higher debt burden limits, little or no cash reserves, low credit scores, and alternative evidence of creditworthiness. Flexible underwriting guidelines are important because they help address barriers to homeownership among nontraditional borrowers. For instance, high loan-to-value (LTV) products allow cash-poor borrowers to meet underwriting guidelines without the need for a large down payment or mortgage insurance.

Initially, institutions made marginal changes to one or more of their standard underwriting guidelines to offer somewhat more flexible and affordable loans. For instance, in the early 1990s, the GSEs started offering mortgage products that required lower down payments (higher LTV ratios) than previous products. These new mortgage products became standardized and replaced the earlier (pre-early 1990s), less-flexible products. Currently, these products are referred to as GSE standard mortgages. Over time, industry participants have introduced a number of even more flexible and affordable products than the now standard mortgages (Listokin and others, 2000). These mortgages are often referred to as affordable lending products (Quercia, 1999). They include Fannie Mae's widely available Community Home Buyers Program (CHBP).

In addition to expanding standard underwriting guidelines, institutions have developed a number of unique programs that are specifically designed for nontraditional borrowers. These more experimental products offer the most flexible

Table 12-2. *Selected Fannie Mae Affordable Lending Guidelines: Community Home Buyer's Program (CHBP) and Other Similar Products*

	CHBP	*CHBP 3/2*	*Fannie 97*	*Community 100*
Minimum down payment from borrower's own funds	5 percent	3 percent	3 percent	0 percent, but 3 percent closing costs required from borrower or other sources
Maximum LTV[a]	95 percent	95 percent	97 percent	100 percent
Maximum CLTV[b]	105 percent	105 percent	105 percent	105 percent
Minimum credit score	None	None	None	660
Reserves	None	None	One month	Two months
Ratios	33/38	33/38	28/36	28/36
Geographic	National	National	National	Pilot program

Source: Self-Help Ventures Fund Second Annual Summit Meeting, Atlanta, Georgia, September 12, 2000.

a. LTV = loan-to-value ratio.

b. CLTV = combined LTV.

guidelines but have limited availability. For instance, they may allow borrowers to make no down payment (100 percent LTV) but are being tested only in the Chicago market. The GSEs have introduced a number of such pilot products. Fannie Mae's Community 100 Program offers loans with no down payment, with 3 percent closing costs required from the borrowers or other sources (the maximum allowed combined LTV, or CLTV, is 105 percent). Additional requirements include a minimum borrower credit score of 660, a two-month reserve requirement, and 28/36 percent front-end and back-end ratios. Pilot products, such as the Community 100, are referred to as GSE emerging affordable mortgages.[3] The expectation is that the GSEs will bring these pilot products into mainstream lending efforts once the risk of the products is known. A description of the underwriting guidelines in selected Fannie Mae affordable products is presented in table 12-2.

It should be noted that none of the GSEs' affordable products permit lenders to liberalize all the applicable underwriting criteria at the same time. A loan product may allow for higher debt-to-income ratios, but it is likely to require standard credit scores. Thus the extent to which affordable loan products allow the layering of risk factors is a distinguishing characteristic. As a rule, the GSEs are more reluctant than portfolio lenders to allow for layering of risk factors (Temkin, Quercia, and Galster, 2000). This is due to the belief that loans underwritten using multiple nontraditional guidelines are at significantly greater risk of delinquency and default (Quercia, 1999).

3. These pilot products are not sold in capital markets as part of mortgage-related mortgages.

Primary lenders also have developed a number of experimental products to reach nontraditional borrowers. Frequently, these loans are held in portfolio because they contain features that fall outside of the GSEs' purchasing guidelines. These products may allow for lower down payments (with no mortgage insurance) and higher front- and back-end ratios than do the GSEs' affordable guidelines. In addition, many of these affordable portfolio products allow underwriters to qualify borrowers who would not meet the GSEs' guidelines defining an acceptable credit history (Temkin, Quercia, and Galster, 2000). In many instances, the inability to sell these portfolio products in capital markets limits the amount of community lending that primary institutions offer. A description of the underwriting guidelines in selected portfolio products is presented in table 12-3.

A word on the use of credit scores is warranted. Because of its predictive power, the industry has embraced the use of credit scores, such as the one developed by Fair, Isaac and Company (FICO), as a powerful underwriting tool. Unfortunately, the use of credit scores in underwriting has been the subject of intense debate. Credit scores evaluate previous credit performance, current level of indebtedness, the length of credit history, the types of credit in use, and the pursuit of new credit (Roche, 2000). Credit scoring can assess risks without considering age, race/ethnicity, or marital status of the loan applicant. Credit scoring is a very important part of computer-based or automated underwriting. Automated underwriting is considered by some to be fairer and faster than manual underwriting and to provide a more precise evaluation of risk (Roche, 2000), thus providing greater access to mortgage credit for minority and other underserved mortgage applicants.

In contrast, critics contend that although credit scoring is able to predict the percentage of applicants at or below any score who are likely to go into default, it is not able to precisely identify which individuals will default (Bradford, 2000). For instance, even if 100 percent of loans predicted to default have credit scores below, say, 620, not all loans with scores below 620 will default. In fact, most will not. If minorities are more likely to have lower scores, as evidence suggests they do, then rejecting low-credit-scoring applications will result in rejecting a disproportionately greater share of low-scoring minority applicants who are in fact a good risk. Thus a higher rejection of low-scoring loan applicants is likely to have a differential impact on minorities. Unfortunately, data to empirically test these contentions are proprietary and have not been made available to researchers.[4]

4. Both Fannie Mae and Freddie Mac have stated that loan applications should not be denied only on the basis of low credit scores. Despite these statements, there is a perception among some portfolio lenders that the GSEs will not purchase loans with credit scores below 620 (Temkin, Quercia, and Galster, 2000). See Berry (2000) for perspectives on potential differential impacts that may result from undue reliance on credit scores.

Table 12-3. *Selected Community Lending Guidelines*

	Lender 1	*Lender 2*	*Lender 3*	*Lender 4*	*Lender 5*
Minimum down payment from borrower's own funds	The greater of 1 percent or $500	$500	1 percent	$0	$500
Maximum LTV[a]	97 percent	97 percent	97 percent	100 percent	100 percent
Maximum CLTV[b]	103 percent for half of deliveries; 100 percent for others	100 percent; 103 percent on case-by-case basis	105 percent	105 percent	103 percent
Minimum credit score	600	580 unless there is no layering of risk	580	640	None
Reserves	None	None	None	Two months	One month
Ratios	33/42	33/42	30/45	40/40	38/38, but up to 45/45 with offsets
Geographic coverage	National	National	National	National	North Carolina flood counties

Source: Self-Help Ventures Fund 2d Annual Summit Meeting, Atlanta, Ga., September 12, 2000.

a. LTV = loan-to-value ratio.

b. CLTV = combined LTV.

Evidence on the Default Risk of Community Lending Products

Ideally, the use of flexible underwriting guidelines need not pose greater risks than the use of traditional or standard guidelines if risk-mitigating mechanisms (such as HEC) are also used. Unfortunately, nothing is known conclusively about the performance of affordable loans in general or the effectiveness of HEC as a risk-mitigating mechanism in particular.

With regard to the overall performance of affordable lending products, the evidence is mixed at best. Several studies have reported positive experiences, others have reported negative experiences, while some studies have reported both positive and negative experience, depending on the institution examined.[5] There may be several reasons for the conflicting evidence, including differences across institutions in composition and management of both affordable and standard portfolios as well as differences in the way risks are assessed and managed (Board of Governors of the Federal Reserve System, 1993). On this basis alone, it would be reasonable to expect differences in risks associated with the affordable and standard products serviced, held, insured, or purchased by different institutions. To make matters more difficult, the data needed to assess the riskiness of affordable loans are proprietary and thus not generally available to researchers. In general, researchers have been forced to rely on qualitative information, proxy measures, and/or statistical techniques to fill the data void.

With regard to determinants of risk, there seems to be some consensus, especially among secondary market institutions, that four factors are important. These include borrower credit scores, size of down payment (loan-to-value ratio), indebtedness (back-end ratio), and availability of cash reserves. The layering of these four factors is important as well.

Methodology and Data

In this study, the data limitations of prior work are addressed and an analysis undertaken of the early performance of affordable community lending products using longitudinal loan-level data from mortgage loans purchased by Self-Help Ventures as part of the Community Advantage demonstration. The performance of these loans is examined by risk factors and the extent to which layering of risks affects payment performance. Given the current industry practices, particular attention is paid to the role that credit scores play in predicting payment performance by minority borrowers. The preliminary nature of the study and the fact that the data are from a very small number of lenders operating in targeted geographic areas (urban/rural) must be stressed. For these reasons, the study is designed to identify baseline patterns and raise questions, not definitively test hypotheses.

5. See Quercia (1999) for a review of the literature and evidence, and Board of Governors of the Federal Reserve System (2000) on the performance and profitability of CRA lending.

Under SHCA, Self-Help Ventures purchases nonconforming, Community Reinvestment Act (CRA)–type mortgages from selected mortgage lenders and then securitizes these loans with Fannie Mae.[6] Because Self-Help retains full recourse for any credit losses, Fannie Mae can purchase loans that are outside its standard guidelines. Fannie Mae and Self-Help have committed to purchase and securitize $2 billion of such loans over a five-year period (1998–2003). The Ford Foundation provided capital to support Self-Help's recourse obligations. In addition to generating an expected 35,000 loans to underserved borrowers, this effort will enable Fannie Mae to measure and better understand the risks associated with nontraditional mortgages. In the long term, this could increase the liquidity of nonstandard community lending loans by permanently expanding the secondary mortgage market.

Self-Help has established partnerships with more than two dozen lending institutions. Through these partnerships, Self-Help has already purchased more than $635 million in loans. A summary of the partnerships is presented in table 12-4.

Underwriting Flexibility in Community Lending Products

SHCA enables Fannie Mae to measure and better understand the risks in mortgages underwritten with guidelines that are more flexible and aggressive than those used in its affordable products (see tables 12-2 and 12-3).[7] Consistently, the SHCA product guidelines meet or exceed those of Fannie Mae's affordable products.[8] SHCA products allow for higher LTV, CLTV, and front-end and back-end ratios, and less-stringent or alternative evidence of creditworthiness, such as a good rent payment record for twelve months before mortgage application. Moreover, they also allow for the layering of risk factors. For instance, Fannie Mae's emerging products, such as Community 100, are clearly the most aggressive GSE products. These products may require no borrower cash for

6. The SHCA demonstration relies on the participating lenders to design loan programs and to market, originate, underwrite, and service the loans. Self-Help acquires seasoned portfolios of loans (portfolio products) as well as newly originated mortgages on a "flow" basis (flow products). When a lender sells a portfolio of previously originated loans to Self-Help, the lender commits to relend the same amount to similar borrowers under similar loan programs. When Self-Help acquires seasoned loans, the loans must have a record of on-time payments for the prior nine months (or twelve months depending on CLTV). Similarly, when selling new originations to Self-Help on a flow basis, the lenders indemnify Self-Help against any defaults occurring in the first nine (or twelve) months. Other than the early term defaults, Self-Help bears the full risk of loss for ten years.

7. Table 12-3 shows only selected SHCA flow products. SHCA flow products are the central focus of the program and will eventually constitute the bulk of transactions. However, the descriptions and comparisons are based on information on both flow and portfolio products to date.

8. Both SHCA products and Fannie Mae affordable products require borrowers to receive homeownership counseling. Also, both have in place an enhanced servicing component. Finally, both product types also allow for the consideration of factors to compensate for deficiencies in one or more underwriting criteria.

Table 12-4. *Self-Help Community Advantage ACTIVE Partnerships*
Millions of dollars

Lender	*Commitment*	*Actual*
Bank of America	500 (100/year)	102.0
Bank One	250 (50/year)	11.6
BB&T	n.c.	102.2
Cambridgeport	20 (10/year)	0
Centura	50/year	71.6
Chase	250 (50/year)	7.7
Citizens Bank	15 (5/year)	0
Countrywide	250	0
First Citizens	n.c.	45.3
First South	5	0.2
FirstMerit	75 (25/year)	4.6
Flagstar Bank	24 (12/year)	0
GMAC	200 (67/year)	9.2
Huntington Bank	24 (8/year)	0
Local Government Employees FCU	n.a.	0.9
National City Bank	500 (100/year)	16.3
Sky Financial Group	n.c.	1.2
State Employees' Credit Union	n.c.	212.4
Union Planters	n.c.	50.1
Total		635.6

Source: Self-Help Community Advantage (SHCA) as of Dec. 31, 2000.
Note: n.a., not available; n.c., no commitment

down payment or closing. However, the credit scores required generally are higher (660) than those required for other affordable products.

In contrast, several SHCA products allow for less-stringent requirements in all the criteria. They may combine high LTV and high front-end/back-end ratios with low up-front buyer cash and less-stringent credit and employment histories. In addition, they do not often require mortgage insurance. For instance, one such product has a maximum LTV of 100 percent, CLTV of 105 percent, and front-end/back-end ratios of 45 percent/45 percent and requires only one month's reserves from the borrower. It also allows a soft second mortgage and has relatively lenient credit and employment history requirements.

Underwriting Flexibility and the Promotion of Homeownership

As a result of underwriting flexibility, SHCA loans are able to reach underserved populations more effectively than the GSEs. As of December 31, 2000, Self-Help had purchased more than 5,500 loans with a combined principal of $637 million under the SHCA program. A large portion of these loans were made to traditionally underserved borrowers. About 42 percent of the loans went to minority borrowers, including almost 27 percent to blacks and 11 percent to Hispanics (see table 12-5). Almost 42 percent of the loans were made to female borrowers and about 41 percent to rural borrowers. The typical borrower was relatively young—about three in every four borrowers were under 40 years of age. The median gross income for all borrowers was just $2,245 per month or about $26,940 a year. About half had incomes at or below 60 percent of area median income (AMI). Most of the remaining borrowers had incomes between 60 percent and 100 percent of AMI.

Borrower credit scores appear to be evenly distributed across credit score ranges.[9] About one in five borrowers have credit scores below 620 (20.1 percent), and another one in four have scores between 621 and 660 (23.5 percent). Fewer than three in every four borrowers were first-time home buyers. Slightly more than half the SHCA borrowers had a down payment of less than 5 percent (in comparison, 2.2 percent of Fannie Mae and 0.6 percent of Freddie Mac borrowers had a down payment of less than 5 percent).

As indicated earlier, credit scores are key criteria in mortgage underwriting. Borrower characteristics by credit score are presented in table 12-6. Race and ethnicity exhibit the strongest relationship with credit scores. White and black borrowers are about equally represented among loans with scores less than or equal to 620 (43.0 and 44.8 percent, respectively). As scores go up, whites become increasingly more represented in the population. More than three out of four white borrowers, but only one in ten black borrowers, had scores above 720. About 29 percent of all white borrowers, but only 10 percent of blacks, had credit scores of 720 or higher (see table 12-7). Conversely, whereas 5 percent of white borrowers had credit scores below 620, this was true for one-third of all black borrowers.

There is also a relationship (though weaker) between borrower income (as a percentage of AMI) and urban/rural location. Lower-income and rural borrowers are more likely to have lower scores. Finally, there is no substantively important relationship between credit scores and gender, age of borrower, or whether the borrower is a first-time home buyer.[10]

9. Borrower credit scores were available from either the time of loan origination, time of loan purchase by Self-Help, or the time of securitization (often three months after purchase). In this sample, 67.3 percent of credit scores come from the time of securitization, 21.5 percent come from the time of purchase, and 11.2 percent from the loan origination. Analyses (not presented here) indicate that the findings are consistent regardless of when the borrower credit scores were obtained. Credit scores adjusted for the age of the loan at the time the credit score was obtained were calculated, and it was found that these adjusted credit scores had a correlation of .99 with the unadjusted credit scores.

10. Most of these and other differences reported elsewhere are statistically significant in bivariate tests of association because of the relatively large sample size and the power of the chi-square and similar tests. Thus this presentation focuses on substantively important differences.

Table 12-5. *Characteristics of SHCA Borrowers*

Percent

Characteristic	*Self-Help's Community Advantage (N = 5,566)*	*Fannie Mae (1997 N = 945,181)*	*Freddie Mac (1997 N = 603,383)*	*Federal Housing Administration*	*Conforming market*
Race/ethnicity					
White	58.2	83.0	86.6	—	—
Black	26.9	3.4	3.5	14.6	5.4
Hispanic	10.9	5.0	3.9	19.3	7.1
Other	4.0	7.9	6.8	—	—
Gender					
Women	41.5	15.7	14.6		
Age					
Under 30	40.5	13.8	13.4		
30–39	31.4	35.4	35.6		
40 and over	28.1	50.8	51.0		
Income					
≤60 percent of area median income (AMI)	49.0	10.1	7.5	20.1	16.4
61–100 percent of AMI	47.9	27.2	26.1	47.0	39.0
>100 of AMI	3.1	62.7	66.4	32.9	44.6

Other characteristics			
Urban borrower	58.8	—	—
Metro (vs. nonmetro)	—	87.3	85.1
First-time home buyer	70.6	34.5	28.4
Loan-to-value (LTV) ratio			
LTV over 95 percent	56.8	2.2	0.6
LTV 80–95 percent	37.2	28.9	29.2
LTV <80 percent	6.0	68.9	70.2
Borrower credit score			
No score available	5.7		
≤620	20.1	NA	NA
621–660	23.5	NA	NA
661–720	28.8	NA	NA
>=720	22.0	NA	NA

Source: Except for race/ethnicity figures, Fannie Mae and Freddie Mac data are from Paul B. Manchester, 1998 (tables 5 and 6B). Race and ethnicity figures for Fannie Mae, Freddie Mac, FHA, and the conforming market are from Harold Bunce, 2000 (table 1). Age and LTV are reported for home purchase and refinance loans combined; other variables are for home purchase loans only. The Fannie Mae and Freddie Mac data report loans to "women only," so the entry for Self-Help is the percentage of loans to women with no co-borrower. FHA and conforming market data are from Harold Bunce and Randall M. Scheessele, 1998 (table 2). The conforming market consists of loans below the 1997 conforming loan limit of $214,600.

Note: AMI = area median income. SHCA data are as of Dec. 31, 2000.

Table 12-6. *Borrower Characteristics by Credit Score*

Characteristic	*≤620*		*621–660*		*661–720*		*>720*		*Missing score*		*Total*	
Race/ethnicity												
White	478	(43.0)	649	(49.8)	1,046	(65.4)	940	(77.2)	118	(37.3)	3,231	(58.2)
Black	498	(44.8)	482	(37.0)	319	(19.9)	146	(12.0)	45	(14.2)	1,490	(26.9)
Hispanic	98	(8.8)	114	(8.8)	168	(10.5)	92	(7.5)	132	(41.8)	604	(10.9)
Other	38	(3.4)	58	(4.4)	67	(4.2)	40	(3.3)	21	(6.7)	224	(4.0)
Total	1,112	(100)	1,303	(100)	1,600	(100)	1,218	(100)	316	(100)	5,549	(100)
Gender												
Men	555	(50.2)	684	(53.1)	926	(58.2)	671	(55.2)	211	(67.0)	3,047	(55.2)
Women	551	(49.8)	605	(46.9)	665	(41.8)	545	(44.8)	104	(33.0)	2,470	(44.8)
Total	1,106	(100)	1,289	(100)	1,591	(100)	1,216	(100)	315	(100)	5,517	(100)
Age												
Under 30	399	(37.8)	464	(37.8)	650	(45.5)	414	(42.6)	100	(31.9)	2,027	(40.5)
30–39	353	(33.5)	419	(34.1)	416	(29.1)	278	(28.6)	104	(33.1)	1,570	(31.4)
40 and over	303	(28.7)	346	(28.1)	364	(25.4)	280	(28.8)	110	(35.0)	1,403	(28.1)
Total	1,055	(100)	1,229	(100)	1,430	(100)	972	(100)	314	(100)	5,000	(100)
Income												
≤60 percent of area median income (AMI)	577	(53.2)	662	(52.0)	722	(46.2)	523	(43.9)	173	(56.2)	2,657	(49.0)
61–100 percent of AMI	481	(44.3)	571	(44.9)	797	(51.0)	612	(51.4)	134	(43.5)	2,595	(47.9)
>100 percent of AMI	27	(2.5)	39	(3.1)	44	(2.8)	56	(4.7)	1	(0.3)	167	(3.1)
Total	1,085	(100)	1,272	(100)	1,563	(100)	1,191	(100)	308	(100)	5,419	(100)
Urban/rural												
Urban	673	(61.7)	774	(60.6)	860	(54.8)	645	(54.0)	249	(79.6)	3,201	(58.8)
Rural	417	(38.3)	503	(39.4)	709	(45.2)	550	(46.0)	64	(20.4)	2,243	(41.2)
Total	1,090	(100)	1,277	(100)	1,569	(100)	1,195	(100)	313	(100)	5,444	(100)
First-time home buyer												
Yes	706	(68.4)	823	(69.5)	957	(68.6)	727	(75.3)	243	(77.4)	3,456	(70.6)
No	326	(31.6)	362	(30.5)	438	(31.4)	239	(24.7)	71	(22.6)	1,436	(29.4)
Total	1,032	(100)	1,185	(100)	1,395	(100)	966	(100)	314	(100)	4,892	(100)

Source: SHCA data and authors' calculations.

Note: Numbers in parentheses are column percentages. All characteristics are statistically significantly different across credit score categories ($p < .05$).

Table 12-7. *Race/Ethnicity by Credit Score*

Characteristic	*≤620*	*621–660*	*661–720*	*> 720*	*Missing score*	*Total*
Race/ethnicity						
White	478	649	1,046	940	118	3,231
	(14.8)	(20.1)	(32.4)	(29.1)	(3.6)	(100)
Black	498	482	319	146	45	1,490
	(33.4)	(32.4)	(21.4)	(9.8)	(3.0)	(100)
Hispanic	98	114	168	92	132	604
	(16.2)	(18.9)	(27.8)	(15.2)	(21.9)	(100)
Other	38	58	67	40	21	224
	(17.0)	(25.9)	(29.9)	(17.8)	(9.4)	(100)
Total	1,112	1,303	1,600	1,218	316	5,549
	(20.0)	(23.5)	(28.8)	(22.0)	(5.7)	(100)

Note: Numbers in parentheses are row percentages.
Source: SHCA data and authors' calculations.

Borrower characteristics by loan-to-value ratio are presented in table 12-8. Although not strong, there are relationships between some demographic characteristics and low LTV loans (≤ 89 percent). A higher presence of minority, women, older, and lower-income borrowers is found among low LTV loans than among higher LTV loans. Also, a higher presence of higher-income and non-first-time home buyers are found among high LTV loans (≥ 100 percent) than among low LTV loans. It is interesting to note that less than one of three high LTV loans was made to first-time home buyers.

Borrower characteristics by total debt burden (back-end ratio) are presented in table 12-9. There is no clear relationship between most borrower characteristics and whether a loan had a high back-end ratio (≥ 39 percent).[11] There is a weak relationship between back-end ratios and two characteristics: urban/rural location and first-time home buyers. Urban borrowers are more likely to have high ratios. About 64 percent of all loans with back-end ratios equal to or greater than 39 percent were made to urban borrowers. About three of four loans with ratios less than 39 percent were made to first-time home buyers (73.3 percent).

Borrower characteristics by cash reserves requirement are presented in table 12-10. A strong relationship can be found between two borrower characteristics and whether cash reserves are required. Urban borrowers and first-time home buyers were more likely to be required to have at least one-month reserves at closing than other borrowers. About 68 percent of all loans made with at least one-month reserves were made to urban borrowers. Similarly, more than four in five loans that required at least one-month reserves were made to first-time home buyers (82.9 percent). Alternatively, more than half of all first-time home buyers (1,151 of 2,239) were required to have cash reserves at closing.

11. The cutoff for back-end ratios was chosen based on guidelines for GSE affordable products. The highest allowable back-end ratio in a GSE affordable product is 38 percent.

Table 12-8. *Borrower Characteristics by Loan-to-Value Ratio*

Characteristic	*≤89*	*90–95*	*96–97*	*98–99*	*100+*	*Total*
Race/ethnicity						
White	321 (47.1)	1,029 (60.0)	1,207 (58.0)	412 (61.1)	262 (66.4)	3,231 (58.2)
Black	303 (44.4)	431 (25.1)	402 (19.3)	241 (35.8)	113 (28.6)	1,490 (26.9)
Hispanic	41 (6.0)	178 (10.4)	364 (17.5)	13 (1.9)	8 (2.0)	604 (10.9)
Other	17 (2.5)	77 (4.5)	109 (5.2)	8 (1.2)	12 (3.0)	223 (4.0)
Total	682 (100)	1,715 (100)	2,082 (100)	674 (100)	395 (100)	5,548 (100)
Gender						
Men	290 (42.5)	940 (55.1)	1,208 (58.5)	393 (58.4)	216 (55.5)	3,047 (55.2)
Women	393 (57.5)	767 (44.9)	856 (41.5)	280 (41.6)	173 (44.5)	2,469 (44.8)
Total	683 (100)	1,707 (100)	2,064 (100)	673 (100)	389 (100)	5,516 (100)
Age						
Under 30	171 (29.2)	595 (40.4)	869 (41.8)	305 (46.7)	87 (41.2)	2,027 (40.5)
30–39	209 (35.7)	451 (30.7)	648 (31.2)	199 (30.4)	63 (29.9)	1,570 (31.4)
40 and over	206 (35.1)	426 (28.9)	560 (27.0)	150 (22.9)	61 (28.9)	1,403 (28.1)
Total	586 (100)	1,472 (100)	2,077 (100)	654 (100)	211 (100)	5,000 (100)
Income						
≤60 percent of AMI	429 (63.6)	809 (48.1)	997 (49.9)	294 (44.0)	128 (32.5)	2,657 (49.0)
61–100 percent of AMI	209 (30.9)	803 (47.7)	993 (49.7)	357 (53.4)	233 (59.1)	2,595 (47.9)
>100 percent of AMI	37 (5.5)	70 (4.2)	10 (0.5)	17 (2.5)	33 (8.4)	167 (3.1)
Total	675 (100)	1,682 (100)	2,000 (100)	668 (100)	394 (100)	5,419 (100)
Urban/rural						
Urban	394 (59.6)	1,012 (59.5)	1,373 (68.1)	277 (40.9)	145 (37.3)	3,201 (58.8)
Rural	267 (40.4)	688 (40.5)	642 (31.9)	401 (59.1)	244 (62.7)	2,242 (41.2)
Total	661 (100)	1,700 (100)	2,015 (100)	678 (100)	389 (100)	5,443 (100)
First-time home buyer						
Yes	392 (68.1)	1,047 (76.4)	1,377 (66.2)	574 (87.6)	66 (31.3)	3,456 (70.6)
No	184 (31.9)	324 (23.6)	702 (33.8)	81 (12.4)	145 (68.7)	1,436 (29.4)
Total	576 (100)	1,371 (100)	2,079 (100)	655 (100)	211 (100)	4,892 (100)

Source: SHCA data and authors' calculations.

Note: Numbers in parentheses are column percentages. All characteristics are statistically significantly different across LTV categories ($p < .05$).

Table 12-9. *Borrower Characteristics by Back-End Ratios*

Characteristic	*<39*		*≥39*		*Total*	
Race/ethnicity						
White	2,099	(61.0)	1,121	(53.5)	3, 220	(58.2)
Black	898	(26.1)	591	(28.2)	1,489	(26.9)
Hispanic	315	(9.2)	289	(13.8)	604	(10.9)
Other	128	(3.7)	94	(4.5)	222	(4.0)
Total	3,440	(100)	2,095	(100)	5,535	(100)
Gender						
Men	1,937	(56.7)	1,098	(52.7)	3,035	(55.2)
Women	1,478	(43.3)	984	(47.3)	2,462	(44.8)
Total	3,415	(100)	2,082	(100)	5,497	(100)
Age						
Under 30	1,240	(41.5)	786	(39.1)	2,026	(40.5)
30–39	905	(30.3)	664	(33.1)	1,569	(31.4)
40 and over	844	(28.2)	558	(27.8)	1,402	(28.1)
Total	2,989	(100)	2,008	(100)	4,997	(100)
Income						
≤60 percent of area median income (AMI)	1,580	(46.8)	1,069	(52.5)	2,649	(49.0)
61–100 percent AMI	1,648	(48.9)	944	(46.4)	2,592	(47.9)
>100 percent of AMI	144	(4.3)	23	(1.1)	167	(3.1)
Total	3,372	(100)	2,036	(100)	5,408	(100)
Urban/Rural						
Urban	1,888	(56.1)	1,303	(63.6)	3,191	(58.9)
Rural	1,477	(43.9)	746	(36.4)	2,223	(41.1)
Total	3,365	(100)	2,049	(100)	5,414	(100)
First-time home buyer						
Yes	2,160	(73.3)	1,290	(66.6)	3,450	(70.6)
No	786	(26.7)	648	(33.4)	1,434	(29.4)
Total	2.946	(100)	1,938	(100)	4,884	(100)

Source: SHCA data and authors' calculations.

Note: Numbers in parentheses are column percentages. All characteristics, except age, are statistically significantly different across back-end ratio categories ($p < .05$).

Table 12-10. *Borrower Characteristics by Reserve Requirement*

Characteristic	*At least one month's mortgage in reserve*		*No reserves*		*Total*	
Race/ethnicity						
White	1,545	(57.2)	1,535	(59.0)	3, 080	(58.1)
Black	600	(22.2)	858	(33.0)	1,458	(27.5)
Hispanic	436	(16.2)	146	(5.6)	582	(11.0)
Other	118	(4.4)	64	(2.4)	182	(3.4)
Total	2,699	(100)	2,603	(100)	5,302	(100)
Gender						
Men	1,512	(55.9)	1,401	(54.1)	2,913	(55.0)
Women	1,193	(44.1)	1,187	(45.9)	2,380	(45.0)
Total	2,705	(100)	2,588	(100)	5,293	(100)
Age						
Under 30	1,067	(39.6)	861	(41.9)	1,928	(40.6)
30–39	817	(30.3)	663	(32.2)	1,480	(31.1)
40 and over	813	(30.1)	533	(25.9)	1,346	(28.3)
Total	2,697	(100)	2,057	(100)	4,754	(100)
Income						
≤60 percent of area median income (AMI)	1,393	(52.7)	1,114	(43.9)	2,507	(48.4)
61–100 percent of AMI	1,246	(47.1)	1,264	(49.8)	2,510	(48.4)
>100 percent of AMI	5	(0.2)	159	(6.3)	164	(3.2)
Total	2,644	(100)	2,537	(100)	5,181	(100)
Urban/rural						
Urban	1,831	(67.9)	1,194	(47.0)	3,025	(57.8)
Rural	865	(32.1)	1,344	(53.0)	2,209	(42.2)
Total	2,696	(100)	2,538	(100)	5,234	(100)
First-time home buyer						
Yes	2,239	(82.9)	1,151	(59.1)	3,390	(73.0)
No	459	(17.0)	796	(40.9)	1,255	(27.0)
Total	2.698	(100)	1,947	(100)	4,645	(100)

Source: SHCA data and authors' calculations.

Note: Numbers in parentheses are column percentages. All characteristics are statistically significantly different across reserve categories ($p < .05$).

Underwriting Flexibility and Loan Performance

As stated earlier, the lack of data has been a key reason for the conflicting findings in the literature on the performance of affordable community lending loans. This section presents the results of an analysis of the incidence of ninety-day delinquencies in affordable loans in SHCA over the first twenty-four months after purchase by Self-Help by three risk factors: credit score, LTV, and back-end ratio.

The data for the performance analysis consist of a subsample of 1,017 loans purchased by Self-Help in September 1998 with available payment histories beginning that month.[12] Borrower and other characteristics of these loans are displayed in table 12-11. In contrast to the borrowers in the full loan database, the borrowers included in this analysis are more likely to be African American and less likely to be Hispanic, slightly younger, less urban, and more likely to be first-time home buyers. These loans are all from North Carolina or Virginia and limited to two lenders.

Of the 1,017 loans, 48 (4.7 percent) experienced a ninety-day delinquency, 114 (11.2 percent) were terminated without a ninety-day delinquency but before twenty-four months (the house was probably sold), and 855 (84.1 percent) went the full twenty-four months without termination or a ninety-day delinquency.

Delinquency rates for different risk factors are shown in table 12-12.[13] Delinquency rates differ dramatically across credit score categories, with 10.6 percent of loans made to borrowers with credit scores of 620 or lower experiencing a ninety-day delinquency; only 0.5 percent of loans made to borrowers with credit scores higher than 720 experienced delinquency. Somewhat surprisingly, the other risk factors do not show much of a relationship to ninety-day delinquency.

A Cox proportional hazard regression was performed to assess the independent impact of various loan and borrower characteristics on the risk of default.[14]

12. Since loans were not delinquent at the time of purchase, the earliest that a loan purchased in September 1998 could be ninety days delinquent was in November 1998. Therefore the analysis covers the twenty-four months of payments from November 1998 through October 2000. It should be noted that there were sixteen other loans for which no credit score was available (as opposed to just missing). Given the small number of loans and that none of the sixteen experienced a delinquency, these loans have not been included in these analyses.

13. None of the loans in this data set required reserves.

14. Time is modeled until first ninety-day delinquency and the explanatory variables are from origination or the time of purchase, which means that there are no time-varying covariates. Each loan contributes a single "spell" to the data, with each spell ending when the loan goes ninety days delinquent, leaves the database before experiencing a ninety-day delinquency, or reaches 24 months of payments without a ninety-day delinquency. Since there are no time-varying covariates, parametric hazard/survival models could also have been used. To check the results, models were run under different distributional assumptions. Results were always very similar to the results presented here, and tests among the different distributional assumptions were not significant. The Cox proportional hazard regressions were estimated using SAS® PROC PHREG, with the TIES=DISCRETE option.

Table 12-11. *Ninety-Day Delinquency Analysis: Borrower and Loan Characteristics*
Percent

Characteristic	*Self-Help's Community Advantage (N = 1,017)*
Race/ethnicity	
White	57.8
Black	38.7
Hispanic	2.2
Other	1.3
Gender	
Women	44.0
Age	
Under 30	45.1
30–39	30.0
40 and over	24.9
Income	
≤60 percent of area median income (AMI)	49.2
61–100 percent of AMI	49.0
>100 percent of AMI	1.8
Other characteristics	
Urban borrower	43.2
First-time home buyer	83.8
Loan-to-value (LTV) ratio	
LTV over 95 percent	78.2
LTV 80–95 percent	17.0
LTV <80 percent	4.8
Borrower credit score	
≤620	18.0
621–660	29.7
661–720	33.1
>720	19.3

Source: SHCA data and authors' calculations.

Note: To make this table consistent with our earlier table comparing SHCA loans with Fannie Mae and others, "women borrowers" are defined women borrowers with no co-borrowers. In the risk models, we look at women principal borrowers regardless of whether there was a co-borrower.

Table 12-12. *Ninety-Day Delinquency Rates for Different Risk Factors*

Risk actor	*Number of loans*	*Ever ninety-day delinquent (percent)*
Credit score		
≤620	180	10.6
621–660	297	5.1
661–720	331	3.9
>720	193	0.5
Loan-to-value ratio		
<98 percent	363	5.0
≥98 percent	654	4.6
Back-end ratio		
<39 percent	635	4.4
≥39 percent	371	5.4

Source: SHCA data and authors' calculations.

Note: None of the loans eligible for the delinquency analysis required reserves. The relationship between credit scores and delinquency categories was significant at the .05 level (chi-square = 21.4, df = 3), but LTV and back-end ratios showed no significant association.

Four models are presented in table 12-13: credit scores only (Model 1); all risk factors (Model 2); layered risk, that is, interactions (Model 3); and risk factors with borrower characteristics; all controlling for the age of the loan at the time of purchase (Model 4).

Model 1 shows that credit scores are a strong predictor of performance. Loans to borrowers with credit scores of 620 or less were more than twenty-four times more likely to experience a ninety-day delinquency than those with credit scores over 720 (the comparison group). Loans to borrowers with credit scores between 621 and 660 were almost ten times more likely to experience a ninety-day delinquency than the comparison group.[15]

Model 2 adds indicator variables for an LTV greater than 97 and a back-end ratio greater than 38. These additional variables do not significantly improve the model, and the estimates for the credit score groups are only slightly different. Model 3 adds interaction terms between the lowest credit score group and the additional risk factors. These additional parameters are not statistically significant.[16] Additional models were estimated, including interactions between the

15. The parameter estimate for the group with credit scores between 621 and 660 and the parameter estimate for the group with credit scores between 661 and 720 are very close, with the first being statistically significant and the second being on the borderline. The equality of these parameters was tested using a Wald chi-square test (.484, 1 df, p = .49). This leads to the conclusion that there is no significant difference between the groups within the sample. A model combining those two groups showed a statistically significant relative risk of eight times the risk for the >720 group. The results are similar if this is done with the other models.

16. Testing the joint significance of the additional risk factors and the interactions (that is, comparing Model 3 with Model 1) gives a chi-square of 1.12 with 4 df (p = .89).

Table 12-13. *Cox Proportional Hazard Models for First-Time Ninety-Day Delinquency within Twenty-four Months of Loan Purchase*

Characteristic	*Model 1 (N = 1,001)*	*Model 2 (N = 990)*	*Model 3 (N = 990)*	*Model 4 (N = 948)*
Credit score				
≤620	3.181**	3.185**	3.474**	3.075**
	(24.07)	(24.17)	(32.26)	(21.65)
621–660	2.248*	2.244*	2.251*	2.214*
	(9.47)	(9.43)	(9.50)	(9.15)
661–720	1.984	1.985	2.003	1.967
	(7.27)	(7.28)	(7.41)	(7.15)
Other risk factors				
Loan-to-value ratio over 97 percent		.102	.382	.109
		(1.11)	(1.47)	(1.12)
Back-end ratio over 37		.017	–.052	–.012
		(1.02)	(0.95)	(0.99)
Interactions				
Credit 620*high LTV			–.630	
			(0.53)	
Credit 620*high ratio			.171	
			(1.19)	
Borrower characteristics				
Female				–.874**
				(0.42)
African American				.145
				(1.16)
Income (percent of area median income)				–.008
				(0.99)
Age				–.017
				(0.98)
First-time home buyer				–.449
				(0.64)
Loan age	–.015	–.012	–.010	–.008
	(0.98)	(0.99)	(0.99)	(0.99)
Model chi-square	23.8**	23.7**	24.7**	32.4**
Df	4	6	8	11

Source: SHCA data and authors' calculations.

Note: Numbers in parentheses are relative risk ratios. The comparison groups are credit scores >720, LTV of 97 percent or less, back-end ratios of 38 or less, males, whites, and borrowers who are not first-time home buyers. Model 4 includes data only for white and African American borrowers because of the small number of loans to borrowers of Hispanic origin and other ethnic groups.

** $p < .01$; * $p < .05$.

Table 12-14. *Current Payment Status for Loans Ever Ninety-Day Delinquent within Twenty-four Months after Loan Purchase*

	No longer delinquent	*Delinquent less than ninety days*	*Delinquent more than ninety days*	*Loan terminated*
Overall (48 loans)	14 (29 percent)	8 (17 percent)	12 (25 percent)	14 (29 percent)
Credit score				
≤620 (19 loans)	5 (26 percent)	5 (26 percent)	6 (32 percent)	3 (16 percent)
621–660 (15 loans)	4 (27 percent)	1 (6 percent)	3 (20 percent)	7 (47 percent)
661–720 (13 loans)	4 (31 percent)	2 (15 percent)	3 (23 percent)	4 (31 percent)
>720 (1 loan)	1 (100 percent)	0 (0 percent)	0 (0 percent)	0 (0 percent)

Source: SHCA data and authors' calculations.

other risk factors with the middle credit score groups (not presented), and similarly insignificant results were obtained. Consequently, no evidence could be found that layering of risk factors added to the risk of extended delinquencies in this sample.

Finally, Model 4 adds some basic demographic characteristics of the borrower.[17] The findings with regard to significance of credit scores and the lack of significance of other risk factors and the layering of risks is consistent with those in other models. After controlling for other characteristics, no borrower characteristics other than gender show a significant difference. The ninety-day delinquency risk for women is approximately 40 percent that of men.

It is important to note that even when affordable loans become ninety days delinquent, many are cured (see table 12-14). Overall, fourteen of the forty-eight loans (29.2 percent) that went ninety days delinquent within the first twenty-four months brought their payments up to date. Another eight (16.7 percent) reduced their delinquency to less than ninety days. Twelve (25.0 percent) remained ninety days delinquent or worse, but seven of those are loans that went ninety days delinquent in the last two months of observation, so some cures and improvements here could probably be expected. Finally, fourteen of the forty-eight delinquent loans (29.2 percent) were terminated after becoming more than ninety days delinquent. Table 12-13 shows that borrowers with the lowest credit scores (≤ 620) have a recovery rate as good as borrowers with credit scores between 621 and 660. However, the data are too sparse to draw any definitive conclusions about the incidence of cure rates.

17. Because so few loans were made to Hispanics or members of other ethnic groups, this analysis is limited to black and white borrowers (948 loans).

Summary and Future Directions

In this study, the data limitations of prior work were addressed, and an analysis of the early performance of affordable community lending products using longitudinal loan-level data was undertaken. Data were used from mortgage loans purchased by Self-Help Ventures as part of the Community Advantage demonstration (a joint effort between Self-Help, the Ford Foundation, and Fannie Mae), which aims at providing a secondary market outlet for CRA products. Loan performance was examined by risk factors and the extent to which layering of risks affects payment performance. Given the current industry practices, particular attention was paid to the role that credit scores play in predicted payment performance by minority borrowers. This section summarizes key findings and suggests future research directions to assess the extent to which community lending can be used by secondary market institutions to expand homeownership opportunities to underserved populations.

These results show that among the CRA-type loans purchased by SHCA, credit scores are the only risk factor that significantly affects ninety-day delinquency rates. In relative terms, this impact is quite large. Interestingly, neither loans with extremely high LTV, loans with high back-end ratios, nor the layering of factors displays any greater risk after controlling for credit scores. This may be due to the fact that, as with most affordable loans, loans in the sample have little variation in loan-to-value and back-end ratios (the values are predominantly very high). The lack of variation may explain the lack of significance. Gender is the only borrower characteristic that significantly affects delinquency risk, with male borrowers approximately 2.5 times more likely to experience an extended delinquency than female borrowers. Finally, the cure rate for loans with extended delinquencies is quite high, even among loans with the lowest borrower credit scores.

A word is warranted about findings relative to credit scores and minority status. There is a significant relationship between minority status and credit scores, but no relationship between minority status and loan performance. This indicates that a white borrower with a credit score of 620 has the same likelihood of being ninety days delinquent as a black borrower with a similar credit score. It may be tempting to see these findings as supporting views critical of the use of credit scores in underwriting. Concerns could be raised if low-scoring loan applicants are more likely to be rejected because this would result in rejecting more minority loan applicants when, in fact, minority status by itself has no impact on performance.

The reader should be cautioned against using the results in this manner. This is an early analysis of information from a data collection effort that will not be completed for a few more years. The sample is relatively small and with little geographic diversity. Thus it is too early in the evaluation to conduct a definitive analysis.

More important, it should be noted that the loans purchased by Self-Help as part of its Community Advantage demonstration are not a random sample of all affordable loans made by portfolio lenders. Loans must meet certain requirements to qualify for purchase (for example, on-time payments for nine months before purchase). This limits the generalizability of the findings. The generalizability of the analysis will be augmented when performance information from a control group is added in the future and loans with greater geographic diversity are added to the sample.

To sum up, community lending products have the potential to help the GSEs in their continued expansion of homeownership opportunities to underserved populations. These products are more flexible than the GSE affordable offerings, and they are more likely to reach women, minorities, and rural borrowers. Future research needs to address this issue of loan performance with a more representative sample, data from a survey of mortgage borrowers, and case studies of servicers, lenders, and others. This will help to explain the true costs of delinquencies and defaults.

References

Berry, Michael V. 2000. "Perspective on Credit Scoring and Fair Mortgage Lending." *Profitwise* 10 (3): 1–7.

Board of Governors of the Federal Reserve System. 1993. *Report to the Congress on Community Development Lending by Depository Institutions.* Government Printing Office.

———. 1998. *Survey of Consumer Finances.* Washington.

———. 2000. "The Performance and Profitability of CRA-Related Lending." Washington.

Bradford, Calvin. 2000. Statement of Calvin Bradford, President, Calvin Bradford and Associates, LTD. In "Perspective on Credit Scoring and Fair Mortgage Lending." *Profitwise* 10 (3): 10–14.

Bunce, Harold. 2000. "The GSEs' Funding of Affordable Loans: A 1999 Update." Housing Finance Working Paper HF-012. Washington: U.S. Department of Housing and Urban Development.

Bunce, Harold L., and Randall M. Scheessele. 1998. "The GSE's Funding of Affordable Loans: 1996 Update." Housing Finance Working Paper HF-005. Washington: U.S. Department of Housing and Urban Development.

Federal Financial Institutions Examination Council (FFIC). 2000. Aggregate Table 8-2: Reasons for Denial of Applications for Conventional Home Purchase Loans, 1 to 4 Family Homes, by Race, Gender, and Income of Applicant, 1999. www.ffiec.gov/cgi-bin/pbisa60.dll/hmda_rpt/u_aggnat_rpt/ of_main_retrieve?&as_page=1&as_part=1> (last modified July 3).

Listokin, David, Elvin Wyly, Larry Keating, Khristopher M. Rengert, and Barbara Listokin. 2000. "Innovative Strategies to Expand Lending to Traditionally Underserved Populations: Approaches and Case Studies." Center for Urban Policy Research, Rutgers University.

Litan, Robert E., Nicolas P. Retsinas, Eric S. Belsky, and Susan White Haag. 2000. "The Community Reinvestment Act after Financial Modernization: A Baseline Report." Mimeo.

Manchester, Paul B. 1998. "Characteristics of Mortgages Purchased by Fannie Mae and Freddie Mac: 1996–1997 Update." Housing Finance Working Paper HF-006. Washington: U.S. Department of Housing and Urban Development.

McCarthy, George W., and Roberto G. Quercia. 2000. "Bridging the Gap Between Supply and Demand: The Evolution of the Homeownership Counseling Industry." Institute Report 00-01. Washington: Research Institute for Housing America.

Quercia, Roberto G. 1999. "Assessing the Performance of Affordable Loans: Implications for Research and Policy." *Journal of Planning Literature* 14 (1): 16–26.

Ratner, Mitchell S. 1996. "Many Routes to Homeownership: A Four-Site Ethnographic Study of Minority and Immigrant Experience." *Housing Policy Debate* 7 (1): 103–45

Roche, Ellen P. 2000. Statement of Ellen P. Roche, Director of Corporate Relations, Freddie Mac. In "Perspective on Credit Scoring and Fair Mortgage Lending." *Profitwise* 10 (3): 8–9.

Smith, Paul. 2000. Statement of Paul Smith, Senior Counsel, American Bankers Association. In "Perspective on Credit Scoring and Fair Mortgage Lending." *Profitwise* 10 (3): 9–10.

Stegman, Michael A., Roberto G. Quercia, and George W. McCarthy. 2000. "Housing America's Working Families." *New Century Housing* (Center for Housing Policy, Washington) 1 (1): 1-48.

Stein, Eric, and Martin Eakes. 2000. *Achieving the American Dream: Increasing Homeownership through a No-Interest Second Mortgage Tax Credit.* Backgrounder, Progressive Policy Institute. www.ppionline.org/ppi_ci.cfm?contentid=1346&knlgAreaID=114&subsecid =236 (last modified April 1)

Temkin, Kenneth, Roberto G. Quercia, and George C. Galster. 2000. "The Impacts of Secondary Mortgage Market Guidelines on Affordable and Fair Lending: A Reconnaissance from the Front Lines." *Review of Black Political Economy* 28 (2): 29–49.

U.S. Department of Housing and Urban Development. 2000. Press Release. www.hud.gov/pressrel/pr00-311.html_(last modified October 31).

PART 5

Socioeconomic Impacts of Homeownership

Owning a home and a piece of land to call your own is central to the American dream. Dictated by a unique American cultural imperative and relentlessly promoted by a complex web of public and private institutions built around housing and housing finance, homeownership enjoys a pivotal role in American culture.

Historically, homeowners needed to enter the middle class before they could afford a house. In recent years, the growth of low down payment and flexible underwriting standards combined with explicit public policy goals, regulatory pressure, and an excellent economy to extend the mortgage market. Consequently, homeownership has reached into new segments of the population.

The Clinton administration played an important role in this development by publicizing and setting high goals for homeownership rates. These goals explicitly assumed that homeowners do better in terms of financial and social outcomes than renters. Many also think of homeownership as a strategy to stabilize deteriorating or dangerous neighborhoods.

How much of this drive for higher homeownership rates draws on evidence from solid research? This section examines the base of scholarly knowledge on how homeownership affects people, families, and communities. In addition, it presents provocative new looks at some of the more specific (and controversial) claims about what changes homeownership can bring about.

The Social Benefits and Costs of Homeownership: A Critical Assessment of the Research

A very thin research literature supports the many claims made for the social benefits of homeownership. William M. Rohe, Shannon Van Zandt, and George McCarthy assess the literature to see what we do and do not know about the social costs and benefits of homeownership. They show in their chapter that studies do support positive social effects associated with homeownership. Researchers have found that homeowners are more satisfied, more likely to participate in voluntary and political activities, and more committed to their neighborhoods than those who do not own their homes.

However, the evidence for the social benefits of homeownership is not as conclusive as is often presented in public dialogue and debate. Much of the evidence supporting these findings does not carefully separate the effects of owning a home from the impact of earning more or having more education. Not controlling for these two influences may overstate the social benefits of homeownership.

Rohe, Van Zandt, and McCarthy also argue that we have also paid insufficient attention to potential social costs associated with homeownership, particularly for lower-income households. Researchers have shown that homeowners are less mobile than renters. Reduced mobility makes it more difficult for a household to move in search of better employment opportunities. Furthermore, households that experience long-term job loss or unexpected medical costs may not be able to pay the bills. Although breaking a lease on a rental unit is problematic, defaulting on a mortgage is much more serious and thus more stressful and traumatic.

Despite the relative lack of knowledge about the downside of homeownership, federal policy clearly and substantially favors homeownership over renting. Defenders of this policy tilt often justify their position with arguments that homeownership creates a better class of people and citizens. The next two chapters present new findings addressing the controversial question of whether a household's tenure, by itself, can have an independent effect on people's social and economic achievements and behavior.

This argument is problematic to many low-income housing advocates. They believe that, in the decremental budgetary environment that has dominated national policy for the past twenty-five years, the overwhelming emphasis placed on federal support for homeownership has short-changed affordable rental housing programs. To many, such claims have an impact on distribution of the government's investment in housing, and they also often implicitly stigmatize people who rent.

These are legitimate strategic and political concerns, but a fundamental question remains: what if these claims are true? As Rohe, Van Zandt, and McCarthy point out, there is very little literature on these questions, and what research exists is often unable to disentangle cause and effect. For instance, does homeownership encourage behavior that creates wealth, or do people with better chances at building wealth, ceteris paribus, tend to own homes? Does homeownership have an independent effect on children's educational and behavioral outcomes, or do families attracted to homeownership also coincidentally have attributes that produce better outcomes in children?

Housing and Wealth Accumulation: Intergenerational Impacts

Thomas Boehm and Alan Schlottmann tackle the first question in their chapter, examining whether parental tenure choice affects their children's likelihood of homeownership and wealth accumulation.

Boehm and Schlottmann's analysis suggests that parental homeownership directly increases the likelihood that their children will own a home and accelerates their children's first decision to buy a home. They also find a connection between parental homeownership and higher levels of education among their children (particularly among low-income homeowners), which leads to higher income. Not surprisingly, these effects (increased education and income) contribute to greater accumulation of both home equity and nonhousing wealth for children of owners. Thus Boehm and Schlottmann's research appears, on its face, to support the existence of a wealth-inducing effect of parental homeownership on their children.

Some of the connections Boehm and Schlottmann find make intuitive sense. Growing up in a "homeownership" environment could easily imprint children with a predisposition to homeownership. If, because of this preference, children of homeowners buy earlier than children of nonhomeowners, then they would have more time to accumulate home equity through price appreciation and loan amortization, a timing issue recognized by the authors.

The exact mechanism that produces higher levels of education among children of homeowners is murkier. The authors rightly point out that further research is necessary to disentangle the influence of homeownership from, say, location on these types of outcomes. Although homeownership may indeed be the culprit behind higher educational attainment, location, for instance, may play a far more significant role. With a more active constituency, most students of local politics would consider neighborhoods with high homeownership rates to have far more political influence in garnering public investment in educational facilities and programs. This could easily be a more compelling explanation of higher educational attainment than simply the fact that one's parents were homeowners.

The Impact of Homeownership on Child Outcomes

Donald Haurin, Toby L. Parcel, and R. Jean Haurin tread onto even more provocative and controversial ground in their chapter. They seek to isolate the independent impact of homeownership on children's cognitive and behavioral outcomes. They argue that homeowners' greater investment in their immediate surroundings can lead to better outcomes for children. In addition, they assert that the stability associated with homeownership can create a better chance for greater youth achievement and better behavior.

Haurin, Parcel, and Haurin find that homeownership leads to a higher-quality home environment. Children in owned homes also do better on math and reading achievement tests and have fewer behavioral problems. On the basis of existing literature, they conclude that homeownership will lead to higher educational attainment, greater future earnings, and reduced tendencies to engage in socially undesirable behaviors. This research is a very sophisticated effort to get at complex interactions and their relative importance in observed outcomes. However, even with the subtlety and rigor the authors bring to this analysis, it is not clear that Rohe, Van Zandt, and McCarthy's caution about disentangling effects and true directions of causation is sufficiently addressed.

For instance, the authors justify assessing the independent impact of homeownership on child outcomes by citing existing literature's emphasis on stability as an important factor in achievement and behavior. However, as Rohe and colleagues ask, does homeownership produce stability, or are less-mobile households more likely to own a home? Another recurrent concern is that the geography of locational opportunity may again not be sufficiently controlled for or analyzed at a sufficiently fine degree of resolution.

Do Homeownership Programs Increase Property Values in Low-Income Neighborhoods?

Location (or more specifically, proximity) plays a central role in the final offering in this section, by Ingrid Gould Ellen, Scott Susin, Amy Ellen Schwartz, and Michael H. Schill.

Anyone who has ever worked on an affordable housing project will tell you that neighborhood objections can be loud, sustained, and violently expressed. One of the biggest objections raised in community deliberations over siting is the price impact of this housing on adjacent properties and communities. Although the impact of affordable rental projects typically causes more concern, neighborhood opposition is by no means limited to rentals.

Conversely, local leaders often look to increasing homeownership opportunities as a means of revitalizing neighborhoods and communities. According to this view, homeownership brings more stability and community participation to neighborhoods, stabilizing and increasing property values and creating critically needed social capital.

Ellen and her colleagues examine the price impact on adjacent properties of two major affordable homeownership programs in New York City. The two programs—the Nehemiah Plan and the Partnership New Homes Program—develop new, affordable housing in distressed neighborhoods that is targeted to moderate-income homebuyers. The authors seek to determine whether the construction of this city-sponsored affordable homeownership has any effect on the price of buildings near the projects. Although it is difficult to conceive of New York City's housing market as representative owing to its unique size and cost, the authors' findings are heartening for affordable housing advocates.

The gap between building prices in targeted program areas and the broader community narrow by more than half after program completion. Even after controlling for price trends in the immediate neighborhoods, completion of these projects does seem to bolster the value of adjacent properties more than other comparable buildings in the same community but farther away. These programs also appear to have an impact, albeit lesser, at increased distances at completion, as well as diffusing over time to neighboring locations farther away from the target area.

Conclusion

What we learn from the research presented in this section is that, under the right circumstances, homeownership appears to have very positive social effects. Future research must clarify, however, how and when these effects are independently produced by homeownership. Studies must disentangle the effects of homeownership from the impact of income, location, and education.

Even granting the existence of independent influence, the benefits of homeownership do not accrue evenly to everyone. Research must better define the circumstances under which homeownership produces real benefits. We also need a better understanding of the downside risk of homeownership, such as the social costs of default and the loss of mobility.

Thoughtful consumers of this research will use care in interpreting and using these results in formulating social policy. With extensive economic activity riding on increasing homeownership, business interests (including the nonprofit industry) will always take heart in findings that homeownership has either palliative or curative effects on a variety of societal ills or shortcomings. However, during this period of economic retrenchment, we may see many of the recently minted homeowners struggle with their social and economic costs of their acquisition.

Even with evidence for benefits, public policy should not disproportionately promote homeownership at the expense of important investments in affordable rental housing. Rental housing remains the housing of first and last resort for many Americans. More important, rental housing is an appropriate housing choice for many, based on life cycle, employment, or just life-style preference.

All the chapters in this section have positive findings about homeownership, feeding into what we, both as housing professionals and advocates, may want to believe. They provide further fuel to the almost mythological status of homeownership in American culture. Nevertheless, we must take care not to slip into mindless boosterism and oversell homeownership to those who may be least able to cope with the downside risk. While homeownership may help to produce wealthier, more educated, and better-behaved children, we cannot simply stigmatize renters until they all become homeowners.

STEVEN HORNBURG

13

Social Benefits and Costs of Homeownership

WILLIAM M. ROHE, SHANNON VAN ZANDT, AND GEORGE McCARTHY

Homeownership is often thought to be an essential ingredient of the American Dream. Living in a single-family, owner-occupied dwelling unit is central to the American conception of a secure and successful life. Study after study has found that a large proportion of Americans would rather own than rent a home. In a recent national survey, for example, 86 percent of all respondents felt that people are better off owning than renting a home, and 74 percent said that people should purchase a home as soon as they can afford it, regardless of their marital status or whether they have children in the household. Of the renters surveyed, 67 percent said they rented because they were unable to afford to own; 26 percent said it was a matter of choice. Moreover, a full 57 percent of renters said that buying a home was a very important priority in their lives (Fannie Mae, 1994).

Recent Trends in Homeownership

Interest in homeownership among Americans has been encouraged and supported by a variety of federal programs and policies, including the federal tax code, Federal Housing Administration (FHA) programs, and the Clinton administration's National Homeownership Strategy. The federal commitment to and subsidy of homeownership has often been justified by claims that it has a variety of social and economic benefits both to individuals and to society as a whole. In this chapter, we look exclusively at arguments for the social benefits of homeownership.[1]

The introduction to the National Homeownership Strategy (1995) includes the following passages:

> Homeownership is a commitment to strengthening families and good citizenship. Homeownership enables people to have greater control and exercise more responsibility over their living environment.
>
> Homeownership is a commitment to community. Homeownership helps stabilize neighborhoods and strengthen communities. It creates important local and individual incentives for maintaining and improving private property and public spaces.

What evidence is there for these claims? Are they based on conventional wisdom or sound empirical research? How about the costs of homeownership? Is there a downside that is ignored in the rush to support homeownership? In answering these questions, we seek to accomplish several objectives:

—provide a comprehensive and critical review of the literature on the purported social impacts of homeownership;

—present a balanced view of both the potential benefits and potential costs of homeownership; and

—develop an agenda for future research on the benefits and costs of homeownership.

Individual Social Impacts

This section examines the assertions that homeownership engenders healthier and happier individuals. Personal investment in home and neighborhood are thought to lead to improved social, psychological, emotional, and financial health. However, it is not clear that these outcomes are causally related to homeownership. As will be shown, the research literature on many of these topics is sparse, and much of it leaves something to be desired methodologically. Moreover, some research suggests that, under certain circumstances, homeownership has negative impacts on psychological and physical health.

Homeownership and Satisfaction

THE THEORY. Given the social and economic benefits often attributed to it, homeownership might be expected to have a positive impact on a person's life or residential satisfaction. Life satisfaction is defined as a person's level of contentment with all aspects of his or her life (Campbell, 1976; Fernandez and Kulik,

1. For a discussion of economic costs and benefits, see McCarthy, Van Zandt, and Rohe (2001).

1981). Residential satisfaction is more narrowly defined as satisfaction with both the housing unit and the surrounding neighborhood (Rohe and Stewart, 1996).

Homeownership may contribute to life satisfaction in a number of ways. First, buying a home is an important goal for many Americans (Fannie Mae, 1998, 1999). In American society, buying a home is a rite of passage symbolizing that a person has achieved a certain economic status. Thus attaining this goal should increase an individual's satisfaction with his or her life.

Second, many homeowners find satisfaction in both maintaining and improving their homes (Saunders, 1990). Renters are less inclined to engage in these activities because they will not reap the economic benefits of improvements upon leaving their units and are less emotionally attached to their units (Austin and Baba, 1990; Galster, 1987; Saunders, 1990).

Third, homeowners have greater freedom than renters to customize units to suit their own tastes. Their living environments are likely to better support their styles of life, thus increasing their satisfaction with both the residence and life in general (Galster, 1987). Finally, homeowners are more likely to have accumulated additional wealth through a combination of mortgage amortization and home price appreciation. This, in turn, may contribute to their satisfaction with life.

These arguments, however, assume that the homeownership experience is a positive one. If the homeowner is faced with major unexpected problems with the home or the surrounding neighborhood, or the value of the home depreciates, homeownership might be expected to decrease satisfaction.

THE EVIDENCE. The limited research evidence on the relationship between homeownership and life satisfaction tends to support a positive association. Rossi and Weber (1996) report a positive relationship between homeownership and both self-satisfaction and happiness in an analysis using a National Survey of Families and Households. They found no significant relationship between homeownership and happiness, however, in an analysis of data from the General Social Survey. Control variables used in the study were confined to age and socioeconomic status, so, as the authors acknowledge, other unobserved variables could account for this association.

In a longitudinal study, Rohe and his colleagues surveyed both a group of home buyers and a comparison group of continuing renters in Baltimore. After one and a half years the home buyers were found to have experienced a statistically significant increase in their ratings of life satisfaction (Rohe and Stegman, 1994a). Moreover, in a second follow-up survey homeowners still reported higher ratings of life satisfaction three years after purchasing their homes (Rohe and Basolo, 1997). These results were found in spite of the purchased units' location in relatively less desirable neighborhoods.

Research on the determinants of residential satisfaction consistently finds that homeowners are more satisfied with their dwelling units, even after the influences of household, dwelling unit, and neighborhood characteristics are controlled for (Danes and Morris, 1986; Kinsey and Lane, 1983; Lam, 1985; Morris and Winter, 1976; and Varady, 1983). In one of the stronger studies on this topic, Lam (1985) analyzed survey data from a large national sample of adults. He constructed a housing satisfaction measure using four survey items that, based on factor analysis, seemed to measure the same underlying construct. After controlling for a host of demographic, housing unit, and neighborhood characteristics using ordinary least squares (OLS) regression procedures, he found homeowners to be substantially more satisfied with their homes than renters.

In a study of homeowners in Wooster, Ohio, and Minneapolis, Minnesota, however, Galster (1987) found the level of residential satisfaction to be determined by characteristics of the individual, the housing unit, and the surrounding neighborhood. Galster suggests that a number of homeowners "appear to translate similar residential contexts into quite different degrees of residential satisfaction." Homeowners in later stages of the life cycle, for example, tended to be more satisfied with their living situation regardless of the characteristics of the unit or neighborhood. The adequacy of interior space and plumbing facilities (measured by rooms per person and bathrooms per person) was also highly related to the level of residential satisfaction. Satisfaction levels were also found to be higher among those owning newer units. Finally, measures of the physical and socioeconomic status of the neighborhood proved to be strong predictors of neighborhood satisfaction. Other studies on this topic tend to find similar results (Danes and Morris, 1986; Kinsey and Lane, 1983; and Lane and Kinsey, 1980).

OVERALL ASSESSMENT. Future studies might delve deeper into the specific explanations for why homeowners are more satisfied. At this point, the basic relationship is well established, but we are still inferring the reasons for this relationship. A comparison of different types of ownership, such as condominium, cooperative, community land trust, and fee simple, may provide additional insights on this issue. Each of those types of ownership confers a different set of benefits, and those differences may result in differing levels of satisfaction.

Homeownership and Psychological Health

This section assesses the claims that homeownership has a variety of positive impacts on psychological health. Not unlike the mechanisms that are thought to lead to residential and life satisfaction, some have argued that the social status and personal freedom associated with homeownership leads to higher levels of self-esteem and perceived control over life. Others have argued that homeownership contributes to both psychological and physical health because homeowners have additional assets that can be used to pay for improved health care. Homeowners also have more security of tenure than renters, which may result in a less stressful life.

THE THEORY. Coopersmith (1967) defines self-esteem as an individual's personal judgment of his or her own worthiness. Using Rosenberg's (1979) principles of self-esteem, Rohe and Stegman (1994a) suggest three distinct mechanisms by which homeownership can contribute to a person's self-esteem. First, a person's self-esteem may be influenced by how he or she is viewed by others. If others hold a person in high regard, that person's self-esteem is likely to be high. Given that homeowners are afforded higher social status in American society than renters (Doling and Stafford, 1989; Dreier, 1982; Marcuse, 1975; Perin, 1977), they are likely to internalize this status in the form of higher self-esteem.

Second, self-esteem may be influenced by how individuals see themselves as compared to others. If they see themselves doing better that those around them, they are likely to have higher levels of self-esteem. Homeowners may take their housing tenure as an indication that they are doing better than many, particularly renters. This self-perception may be particularly true for lower-income persons, whose acquaintances are more likely to be renters.

Third, self-esteem may be influenced by self-assessments of their own actions and their outcomes. People who are successful in accomplishing their goals see this as evidence of their own competence. Since homeownership is a goal for an overwhelming majority of Americans (Fannie Mae, 1998, 1999; Tremblay and others, 1980), having achieved it may contribute to greater self-esteem.

Self-efficacy, sometimes referred to as perceived control, refers to an individual's belief that he or she is largely in command of important life events rather than subject to fate or the will of others. In addition to increases in self-efficacy that may result from the successful purchase of a home, homeowners may have more actual control over important aspects of everyday life than renters do. Owners are not, for example, subject to the decisions of landlords concerning rent increases or lease renewals. In addition, homeowners are better able to control who enters their units. Finally, homeowners are free to make modifications to the units to suit their needs and tastes. This greater control over their homes, the argument goes, may positively affect the more general sense of perceived control over life events, thus leading to greater psychological and physical health.

A counterargument, however, is that homeowners, particularly lower-income homeowners, do not have as much actual control as some have claimed. Financial instability puts lower-income households at risk of losing their homes owing to mortgage foreclosure. The psychological impact of homeownership could be negative for a person who is unable to pay the mortgage and is forced from his or her home. It may also be negative if the house is found to have major problems or if an owner does not have sufficient money to maintain it.

Being forced out of one's home is a particularly distressing experience. Given that owners may stand to lose their equity in a foreclosure and that foreclosure can be a psychologically traumatic experience, low-income homeowners may actually feel less in control of their living situations than do low-income renters (Doling and Stafford, 1989; Hoffmann and Heistler, 1988). Further, homeownership may tie low-income people to declining areas where the number of good jobs is dwindling, eroding their perceived control over life events (Lauria, 1976).

THE EVIDENCE. Although far from conclusive, the weight of the relatively scant empirical evidence supports the idea that homeownership may contribute to a person's self-esteem. Out of the five studies reviewed, four provided a limited amount of evidence for a positive association between homeownership and self-esteem (Rohe and Stegman, 1994a; Rohe and Basolo, 1997; Balfour and Smith, 1996; Rossi and Weber, 1996; Clark, 1997). Although several studies have found that home buyers report higher self-esteem, one of the strongest studies on this topic found that buying a home had no significant impact on self-esteem, suggesting that such a positive relationship may need to be qualified (Rohe and Stegman, 1994a).

The responses of focus groups conducted by Balfour and Smith (1996, p. 180) as part of a case study of a lease purchase program sponsored by the Cleveland Housing Network led the authors to conclude that "the opportunity to secure low-cost housing and to work toward homeownership elevates [the individual's] status in society and contributes to personal security and self-esteem." In a second qualitative study based on in-depth interviews with a nonrandom sample, Rakoff (1977, p. 93) suggests, "people spoke of the self-judging they went through, seeing evidence of their own success or failure in life in the quality or spaciousness of their houses, in their ability or inability to "move up" to better houses periodically, or even in the mere fact of owning . . . property."

In analyzing survey data from the National Survey of Families and Households, Rossi and Weber (1996) report that homeowners were more likely to agree to the statement, "I do things as well as anyone," a question meant to assess a person's self-esteem. Yet homeowners are likely to differ from renters in a variety of ways, and these variations may account for the differences found. Homeowners are likely to have higher incomes, education levels, and occupational status and are more likely to be older and married with children (Carliner, 1973). Rossi and Weber did not control for many of the variables that they acknowledge could account for the results, including household composition, housing conditions, or marital status. Further, most studies on this topic measure self-esteem with a potentially more reliable index composed of multiple questions.

Another empirical study conducted by Clark (1997) relied on a survey of 1,618 black respondents from the National Survey of Black Americans. A structural equations model was developed from these data that shows a significant but weak positive relationship between homeownership and self-esteem. Potentially confounding influences of housing type, size, and condition were not considered; nor were other potentially important social characteristics, such as the presence of children and marital status.

One of the strongest studies on this topic was conducted by Rohe and his colleagues (Rohe and Stegman, 1994a; Rohe and Basolo, 1997). They employed a panel study of 143 persons who had signed contracts to purchase newly constructed row houses on four sites in central Baltimore. The panel was interviewed three times—before move-in and then at two eighteen-month intervals. This study also surveyed members of a comparison group of Section 8 renters with comparable wage incomes at the same time intervals. Surveys included a single direct question asking respondents if they thought buying a home had a positive, a negative, or no impact on their self-esteem, as well as a five-question self-esteem index developed by Hoyle (1987).

The analysis involved a simple frequency count of the homeowners who felt that homeownership had had a positive impact on their self-esteem and the use of multiple regression models to assess the relative change in self-esteem index between the homeowners and continuing renters while controlling for potentially confounding variables. At the time of the second interview 85 percent of the home buyers said being a homeowner had made them feel better about themselves. The analysis of the self-esteem index, however, found no statistically significant differences between the self-esteem of the home buyers and continuing renters. The analysis of the third set of interviews found similar results.

Rohe and his colleagues offered three explanations for the lack of statistically significant relationships between homeownership and the self-esteem index. First, the impact of homeownership on self-esteem may have been too small to detect given the relatively small sample sizes and the relatively crude measure used. Second, buying a home may simply not be enough to alter what some believe to be a very stable self-perception (Rosenberg, 1979). Finally, the type of housing units purchased as well as the condition of the neighborhoods surrounding these units may have dampened any impacts that homeownership has on self-esteem.[2]

OVERALL ASSESSMENT. Additional research on the impacts of homeownership on self-esteem and perceived control is clearly needed. The research conducted to date suffers from a variety of methodological problems, including small sam-

2. The units purchased by the sample of homebuyers were all attached row houses with small front and/or back yards. These units do not fit the more traditional image of an owner-occupied home—a detached dwelling with an ample yard. In addition, the surrounding neighborhoods had abandoned properties as well as a relatively high level of crime and other social problems. These factors could have inhibited the positive effects that owning a home had on the buyers' self-esteem.

ple size, a lack of adequate controls for possible confounding influences, inadequately developed measures, and social expectancy bias. Assuming there really is a positive association between homeownership and psychological health, much more information about the process involved and the specific circumstances under which this relationship will hold is needed.

In addition, little, if any, research exists on the impacts of foreclosure on a person's self-esteem or any other psychological constructs. Not everyone is a successful homeowner, and given the current push to increase the homeownership rate, the number of foreclosures is likely to increase. We should have a better understanding of the impacts of these foreclosures on the persons involved.

Homeownership and Physical Health

How might homeownership affect physical health? One answer is that owner-occupied units, at least in the United States, are typically kept in better condition than rental units, so homeowners are less likely to be subject to problems related to inadequate heating and cooling systems and infestations of bugs and rodents. But the critical variable here is housing condition rather than homeownership per se. One might ask whether homeownership has an independent effect, once housing condition is taken into account.

THE THEORY. One argument is that homeownership provides individuals with additional assets that can be drawn upon in times of need. Page-Adams and Vosler (1997), for example, argue that recent economic restructuring has left many people feeling economically, socially, and psychologically vulnerable. Homeowners are in a better position to handle this vulnerability because they have an asset in the form of home equity that can be drawn on to get them through hard times. Rasmussen and his colleagues (1997) also argue that home equity can be used by the elderly to cover the increasing out-of-pocket costs of health care, suggesting that they are able to afford a higher level of care and hence remain healthy longer.

Others argue that homeownership leads to "ontological security," which might be expected to have a positive impact on physical health by promoting a general sense of well-being (Saunders, 1990). A counterargument, however, has been put forth by Nettleton and Burrows (1998). They suggest that mortgage indebtedness can lead to insecurity, anxiety, and fear, particularly for those who are at risk of losing their homes. Recent trends such as variable interest rates and less-secure employment may mean that some homeowners feel insecure about losing their homes.

THE EVIDENCE. Homeownership is a variable included in many studies of physical health, but it is seldom the main emphasis of these studies. Rather, it is often included as a control variable with little attention being paid to its independent impact on health. Although these studies tend to show that homeowners are healthier, physically as well as psychologically, they do not control for the potentially confounding influences of other characteristics of the housing units and of the surrounding neighborhoods (Baker, 1997; Greene and Ondrich, 1990; Kind and others, 1998; Lewis and others, 1998). Given that owner-occupied homes are more likely to be larger, detached units in better repair than rental properties, it is not surprising to find positive associations between homeownership and health.

Several studies have, however, been explicitly designed to assess the impacts of homeownership on health. Macintyre and others (1998) studied approximately 1,500 persons in Scotland. After controlling for age, sex, income, and self-esteem, the authors report that homeowners scored higher than renters on general health questionnaires as well as a number of more specific health indicators. In a study based on two surveys of Americans, Rossi and Weber (1996) analyzed data from the National Study of Family Health and found more positive self-assessments of physical health among homeowners, although the control variables were limited to age and socioeconomic status. Data from the General Social Survey, however, indicated no significant relationship between homeownership and health.

Page-Adams and Vosler (1997) studied 193 factory workers who were being laid off from their jobs. The results of a multivariate analysis indicate that, after controlling for income and education, homeowning workers reported significantly less economic strain, depression, and problematic alcohol use than did renters. These findings suggest that the economic and/or psychological stability engendered by homeownership may dampen stress related to job loss, although one wonders about stress associated with worrying about making mortgage payments. That issue was not addressed in the research.

Robert and House (1996) analyzed data from the Americans' Changing Lives data set, which contains interview data on 3,617 respondents 25 years or older. After controlling for education and income, they report that homeownership was associated with "functional health" (a measure of physical limitations) but not to the number of chronic conditions or to self-rated health.

Nettleton and Burrows (1998) studied the health impacts of having difficulty making mortgage payments. They analyzed data from more than 3,500 persons from the British Household Panel Survey at two time intervals: 1991 to 1992 and 1994 to 1995. Results indicate that having difficulty making mortgage payments was associated with lower scores on a general well-being scale among both men and women, and it increased the likelihood of men's visiting their general practitioners. Control variables included in this study were income changes, physical health problems (a dichotomous measure), employment changes, number of household members employed, age, residential mobility and mortgage problems.

These findings suggest that the impact of homeownership on health is contingent on whether the homeowner is able to keep up with his or her payments.

OVERALL ASSESSMENT. The weight of the limited evidence on the relationship between homeownership and health suggests that there is a positive association between homeownership and health, as long as the household is current on its mortgage payments. The existing studies, however, do not adequately control for potentially confounding variables, including socioeconomic status and housing and neighborhood conditions. Thus it seems premature to conclude that there is a causal positive relationship between homeownership and health.

Furthermore, the existing research has not identified the mechanism or mechanisms through which ownership affects health. Is it simply that homeowners tend to live in higher-quality units and thus are not exposed to health-threatening physical conditions? If so, more aggressive code enforcement or other means of improving the condition of rental properties would address this problem. Or does homeownership affect health by providing owners with greater psychological security? If that is true, the Nettleton and Burrows study suggests that the impacts of homeownership are contingent on whether a homeowner is having difficulty meeting mortgage payments.

Social Impacts

This section assesses the claims that homeownership contributes to the overall health of society by fostering social stability, social involvement, and socially desirable behaviors among both youth and adults. Homeownership is thought to lead to social stability in that homeowners move less frequently than renters. Longer tenure, along with greater economic investment in their homes, is thought to cause homeowners to take better care of their properties. Better maintenance may contribute to both the overall attractiveness of the area and local property values (Rohe and Stewart, 1996).

Homeownership is also thought to lead to higher levels of participation in local voluntary organizations and political activities as homeowners seek to protect their economic and emotional investments in their communities. Homeownership is also thought to influence behaviors such as school performance and teen parenthood among children as well as substance abuse among adults. As we will see, the research findings tend to confirm an association between homeownership and both neighborhood stability and socially or civically desirable behaviors. It is not clear, however, whether homeownership actually causes greater stability and participation or whether those who are more likely to stay put are prone to buy homes. Further, as the transaction costs associated with home buying continue to decline, we may see a decline in the stability currently associated with homeownership, along with all its putative benefits.

Homeownership and Neighborhood Stability

Neighborhood stability refers to the average length of tenure among neighborhood residents. Less turnover equals greater neighborhood stability. Neighborhood stability does not necessarily equal neighborhood health, however; nor does it necessarily imply stability in property values, although these benefits may be associated with stability.

THE THEORY. The relationship between homeownership and neighborhood stability can be seen from two perspectives: the housing tenure literature and the housing mobility literature. Thomas Boehm notes, "we have two distinct literatures; the mobility [literature] says that owners are unlikely to move, while the tenure [literature] maintains that movers are unlikely to own" (1981, p. 375). Empirical evidence from both bodies of literature bears out these relationships (Goodman, 1974; Roistacher, 1974; Rossi, 1955; Speare, 1970; Varady, 1983).

Rohe and Stewart (1996) suggest that homeownership affects stability through two mechanisms. The first mechanism involves the human capital accumulated through age, education, and income. Homeowners tend to be higher-income family households with older, more educated household heads. These households anticipate staying in a home for a longer period of time. The second process is related to the additional interests that homeowners have in their homes. Although both renters and homeowners have use interests in their homes, homeowners also have exchange interests: "This combination of interests seems to provide powerful incentives for owner-occupants to maintain their properties at a higher standard and to join organizations that protect the collective interests of homeowners in the area" (Rohe and Stewart, 1996, p. 71).

Collectively, homeownership is thought to confer benefits to the neighborhood by stabilizing property values, encouraging maintenance and upkeep of properties, and improving social conditions like high school dropout rates or crime rates (Rohe and Stewart, 1996). Economically, the individual may benefit from neighborhood stability through stable or increasing property values. Further, individuals are thought to benefit socially by becoming more invested in their communities. Rohe and Stewart suggest that, beyond homeownership, "living in a relatively stable neighborhood will further encourage participation in community organizations, local social interaction and attachment, property maintenance, neighborhood satisfaction, and positive expectations about the future of the neighborhood" (1996, pp. 54–55).

Housing policymakers interpret these theories to suggest that increasing homeownership rates will result in both economic and social benefits to residents. However, actions taken to promote neighborhood stability through increasing homeownership may be at the cost of individual mobility. The decreased mobility associated with homeownership among individuals and households living in distressed neighborhoods may perpetuate the kinds of social problems associated with these environments (see Wilson, 1987; Jargowsky, 1997; Ellen and Turner, 1997). In recent years, indices of both dissimilarity and isolation have increased, meaning that more poor households are living in areas of concentrated poverty, with less access to people different from themselves (Abramson, Mitchell, and vander Goot, 1995). Segregation and isolation impair the ability of neighborhood residents to improve neighborhood social characteristics, such as levels of employment and the number of families on public assistance, as well as physical characteristics like the number of dilapidated houses or the median value of homes (Massey and Fong, 1990).

THE EVIDENCE. Homeowners are indeed far less likely to move than renters. Whereas renters maintain their residences for a median duration of 2.1 years, homeowners stay in one residence for a median of 8.2 years. More than 70 percent of renters have lived in their current residence for fewer than four years, while more than 70 percent of owners have lived in their current residence for more than four years (Hansen, Formby, and Smith, 1998). This decreased residential mobility among homeowners confers benefits to both the neighborhood of residence and the individual household. Yet it may also have unexpected costs.

The most comprehensive and explicit examination of the relationship between homeownership and neighborhood stability was conducted by Rohe and Stewart (1996). Although most empirical studies use tenure as a control variable for examining the number and frequency of household moves, they do not examine the impact on the neighborhood. Rohe and Stewart's examination included an empirical analysis of census data for 1980 and 1990. They used these data to test the impact of homeownership rates on two measures of neighborhood stability—length of tenure and property values. Beyond the expected finding that homeowners tend to stay longer in one home than renters do, they found that an increase in neighborhood homeownership levels over time leads to an increase in the property values of single-family, owner-occupied units. Rohe and Stewart (1996, p. 66) predict that "each percentage point increase in the homeownership rate of a tract would yield about a $1,600 increase in the property value of the average single-family home over a ten-year period."

While high homeownership levels have been linked to neighborhood stability, low levels of homeownership within a neighborhood have been empirically correlated with high levels of social problems. In a study of neighborhood threshold effects, Galster, Quercia, and Cortes (2000) found that various social indicators—female headship rate, male labor force nonparticipation, overall nonemployment rate, and poverty rate—are sensitive to homeownership rates in the neighborhood. Their analysis of census and other statistical data from the nation's 100 largest metropolitan areas indicates that when renter occupancy reaches a level of 85.5 percent the census tract experiences a rapid and progressive increase in the aforementioned social indicators. These findings indirectly support the policy view that, at least in some neighborhoods, expanding levels of homeownership may counteract neighborhood decline.

Yet a growing body of empirical literature suggests that, in some instances, rather than improving the environment for residents of distressed neighborhoods, homeownership acts to trap households in those neighborhoods. In those cases, length of tenure may reflect the greater obstacles to mobility among homeowners rather than a desire to stay put. The literature identifies four groups that may be particularly susceptible to isolation within neighborhoods of poor quality: low-income households, black households, female-headed households, and older homeowners.

South and Deane (1993) use American Housing Survey data to study the relationship between race and residential mobility. After controlling for a variety of relevant variables, their analysis shows that both low-income and black households are more likely to find themselves living in distressed or declining neighborhoods. Further, these households are less likely to translate dissatisfaction into a move. As it does in the general population, homeownership consistently appears as a deterrent to mobility.

In a series of recent studies, South and Crowder use national longitudinal data from the Panel Study of Income Dynamics (PSID) to examine factors affecting the mobility of nontraditional and minority households. Though they control for a number of demographic, geographic, socioeconomic, and life-cycle characteristics, these studies do not take into account housing conditions or residential satisfaction, both important factors when evaluating residential mobility. They do report, however, that low-income households and minority households that start out in poor neighborhoods are unlikely to move to a neighborhood of better quality. Rather, they move into neighborhoods of similar or worse quality, if they move at all (South and Crowder, 1997; 1998a).

Female-headed households may also be at a disadvantage. South and Crowder (1998b) found that among female heads of household, marrying and finding employment facilitated a move from a poor neighborhood to a nonpoor one, whereas age and homeownership deterred such a move. Black single mothers are less likely than nonblack single mothers to escape distressed neighborhoods, and neither cohabitation nor public aid alleviates this result.

Noting the consistent and strong impact of age as an impediment to mobility, Burkhauser and his colleagues (1995) examined whether older homeowners are trapped in distressed neighborhoods. Using the Panel Study of Income Dynamics data set and census data, they found that older homeowners are the most likely among all groups to be living in distressed neighborhoods. Further, of those living in distressed neighborhoods, older homeowners are the least likely to move out of them, even among those with some socioeconomic means. These findings suggest that, rather than being trapped, elderly homeowners simply choose to remain in spite of the deteriorating conditions. The authors suggest that elderly homeowners stay because of the extensive attachment they have to their neighborhoods, coupled with the relatively high economic and psychological costs of moving.

OVERALL ASSESSMENT. Although the relationship between homeownership and mobility is straightforward and well documented, the impacts of decreased mobility, caused by homeownership or other structural impediments, are not so well established. The tension between individual mobility and group stability remains unresolved within housing policy. Homeownership has been shown to improve neighborhood stability, thus conferring certain benefits to the individual; at the same time, however, it restricts individual mobility, which in certain instances may stunt the individual or household's ability to escape a neighborhood of poor quality and move to a better one. Although facilitating homeownership among disadvantaged groups may enable them to escape distressed neighborhoods, it may also lead to the entrapment of such households in declining neighborhoods, thus perpetuating rather than improving the problems associated with such neighborhoods.

While the aforementioned studies clearly indicate that disadvantaged groups are less likely to move out of distressed neighborhoods and that homeownership is an obstacle to such movement, it is not clear whether recent efforts to make homeownership more widely available to underserved populations are counteracting or exacerbating the effect. Further research is needed to establish the conditions under which these outcomes occur, as well as to propose methods to facilitate the more desirable result.

Homeownership and Social Involvement

American society values participation in both voluntary associations and political organizations. In our capitalist-oriented democracy, participation in voluntary associations is needed to address some of the social issues and problems that are either beyond the influence of government or beyond our willingness to support government programs to adequately address those problems.

At the same time, our democratic form of government is based on the assumption that citizens will actively participate in the governance process. At the very least, citizens are expected to vote in local and national elections, if not become more involved by participating in political campaigns or serving on local advisory committees. Thus if homeownership encourages participation in either voluntary or political organizations, it is having a positive impact on American society.

THE THEORY. Why should homeowners participate more than renters in both voluntary organizations and political activities? Several arguments have been put forward. First, homeowners may be more likely to participate in local voluntary and political activities because they have an economic investment in their homes and they see participation in voluntary and political organizations as a means of protecting that investment (Baum and Kingston, 1984; Rohe and Stewart 1996). The equity homeowners have in their homes is affected by conditions in the surrounding neighborhood; thus homeowners work to influence these conditions by participating in both volunteer organizations and becoming active in local political affairs. Renters, in contrast, lack this strong economic incentive to get involved.

A second economic argument for why homeowners may be more civically active is that the transaction costs associated with moving are higher for owners than for renters (Cox, 1982). Owners often incur significant expenses in both selling their existing homes and buying new ones. If a deterioration in neighborhood conditions forces homeowners to move, the result may be thousands of dollars in costs. Thus there is greater economic incentive for owners to join neighborhood or community associations that work to maintain physical and social conditions in their neighborhoods.

A third explanation for why homeowners may be more actively involved in voluntary and political activities is that they tend to stay in their homes longer and may come to identify with their homes more strongly. Baum and Kingston (1984, p. 163), for example, suggest that "such feelings as pride of ownership may induce certain social psychological orientations not related to economic concerns that foster or reinforce particular social attachments." Thus a greater attachment to place may motivate homeowners to participate in voluntary and political organizations at a higher rate.

A heightened concern about property values, transaction costs, and attachments among homeowners may also have social costs, however, in the form of inappropriate discrimination against various social groups, including racial and ethnic minorities and renters. Neighborhood and other voluntary groups often engage in efforts to exclude those groups from their neighborhoods, thinking that their inclusion would threaten both their economic and social-psychological investments there. Participation at the municipal government level may also result in policies, such as exclusionary zoning, that greatly restrict the ability of lower-income families to move into communities.

THE EVIDENCE. The empirical evidence on the relationship between homeownership and participation in both voluntary organizations and local political activity is both extensive and consistent. After controlling for income, education, and other socioeconomic characteristics, homeowners are indeed more likely than renters to participate in voluntary organizations and engage in local political activity (Ahlbrandt and Cunningham, 1979; Baum and Kingston, 1984; Cox, 1982; Lyons and Lowery, 1989; Guest and Oropesa, 1986; Rohe and Stegman, 1994b; Rossi and Weber, 1996). Yet limitations in the design of most of the extant research do not fully account for the possibility of a spurious relationship between participation and homeownership. In other words, certain persons may have an underlying propensity for social involvement that leads them both to participate in voluntary and political activities and to buy a home.

DiPasquale and Glaeser (1999) analyzed data from the General Social Survey. After controlling for age, race, gender, marital status, children, income, education, and city size they found that homeownership had a strong correlation with the number of nonprofessional organizations belonged to, knowledge of local political leaders, voting, and involvement in activities designed to solve local problems. Their results indicate that, when compared to renters, homeowners are "approximately ten percent more likely to work to solve local problems or know their U.S. representatives by name. They are 13 percent more likely to know the identity of their school board head. Homeowners are 16 percent more likely to vote in local elections. On average, they are members of 0.22 more non-professional organizations than non-owners" (1999, p. 3).

Cox (1982), in a study of 400 adults in the Columbus, Ohio, metropolitan area, found that homeowners were more likely than renters to attend meetings, send letters, and engage in other political activities. Furthermore, to test whether economic incentives motivated homeowners to participate more, he investigated whether homeowners who said making a profit was an important reason for purchasing a home were more likely to participate than those who said it was not. His results show no significant differences in the participation of those with strong and weak profit orientations.

Rohe and Stegman (1994b), in a longitudinal study of a group of low-income home buyers and a comparison group of continuing renters in Baltimore, report that the home buyers were more likely to participate in neighborhood and block associations but not other types of community organizations. They also report that home buyers who perceived more neighborhood problems or who emphasized economic reasons for buying were no more likely to participate in social and political affairs.

Finally, Kingston and Fries (1994) analyzed data from the General Social Survey to see if there were differences in the social and political participation of male and female homeowners. They report that both male and female homeowners were more inclined than renters to vote in local elections, but that only female homeowners were more likely to be working to solve community problems. This is one of the few studies, however, that did not find a positive relationship between homeownership and participation in voluntary organizations.

OVERALL ASSESSMENT. The existing research on homeownership and participation in voluntary organizations and political activity supports the idea that homeowners are more actively involved than renters. The reason or reasons behind this higher participation rate, however, are still not clear. None of the studies on this topic have ruled out the possibility that the association between homeownership and social and political participation is spurious. Although unlikely, there may be a more fundamental orientation toward social involvement that predisposes people both to participate in voluntary and political activity and to purchase homes.

Moreover, the most compelling theory for why homeowners should participate more is that they seek to protect the economic investment in their homes. Yet studies that tested to see whether investment orientation influenced participation rates found no support for this proposition (Cox, 1982; DiPasquale and Glaeser, 1999; Rohe and Stegman, 1994a). DiPasquale and Glaeser (1999) suggest that the lower mobility rates among homeowners may explain the higher rates of involvement among homeowners, but their evidence is far from convincing. Thus additional research is needed to understand the mechanisms and motivations behind the higher participation rate among homeowners.

Homeownership and Socially Desirable Youth Behaviors

Neighborhood stability and social involvement reflect a commitment to producing and maintaining a quality environment. Recently, several studies have suggested that such a commitment can lead to better school performance among youth, lower school dropout rates, and lower rates of teen parenthood. Homeownership is thought to be directly or indirectly responsible for these socially desirable behaviors and outcomes among youth.

THE THEORY. Green and White (1997) offer several possible explanations for how homeownership may foster socially desirable behaviors among local youth. First, homeowners may acquire both "do-it-yourself skills" from doing their own home maintenance and financial skills from having to meet the costs of home repairs. These skills may then be transferred to the children in homeowning households. It is hard to imagine, however, that home maintenance skills translate into lower levels of adolescent crime, pregnancy, and drug use and higher levels of educational attainment and employment. Yet as Boehm and Schlottman (1999) show, children of homeowners are more likely to become homeowners themselves, suggesting that the homeowning ethic may be passed down generationally.

A second argument is that because homeowners have a greater financial stake in their neighborhoods they will be more concerned about any antisocial behaviors of local children, including their own, because those behaviors may negatively affect property values. Thus homeowners may monitor their children's behavior more closely. Haurin, Parcel, and Haurin (2000) suggest that greater investment in owned property leads to an improved home environment, one that is supportive of cognitive and emotional development in a child. The increased social capital that results from a stable home environment helps children develop stable and strong relationships with their parents and others and diminishes involvement in undesirable behavior.

Third, homeowners tend to stay longer in a neighborhood, making them more effective monitors of children in the neighborhood. This hypothesis suggests a role for the neighborhood in turning out well-behaved youngsters through, for example, collective socialization or peer influences (Jencks and Mayer, 1990; Ellen and Turner, 1997). Though most researchers acknowledge the greater influence of family and personal characteristics on youth behavior, neighborhood conditions may still play an important role. Because of the high correlation between homeownership and neighborhood quality, however, these impacts may be difficult to disentangle.

THE EVIDENCE. Four studies that addressed the relationship between homeownership and socially desirable youth behaviors were identified. Essen and his colleagues (1978) used the National Child Development Study to assess the impacts of homeownership on the school performance of 16-year-olds in Britain. After controlling for housing conditions, region, family size, gender, social class, parental education, and parental school visits, they found that children of homeowners performed better on both reading and math tests.

Green and White (1997) studied the relationships between homeownership and both staying in school and teenage parenthood. They performed separate analyses on data from the Panel Study of Income Dynamics, the Public Use Microsample from the 1980 census, and the High School and Beyond data set. In each of these analyses, they controlled for a variety of sociodemographic variables, including race, family income, parent education, family composition and size, and parent work status. They report that in all three analyses the children of homeowners were less likely than the children of renters to drop out of high school or to have children as teenagers. Both effects are largest for children of low-income households. To test for selection bias, they used a bivariate probit technique to take account of differences between parents who choose to own rather than rent. No support for selection bias was found.

Boehm and Schlottman (1999) examined the impact of homeownership on children's productivity through educational attainment and their housing choices as young adults, using data from the Panel Study of Income Dynamics. After controlling for variables that are thought to influence educational attainment, including personal characteristics, parents' educational background, parents' income, and family size, they found that homeownership is a highly significant predictor of educational attainment, even with an additional control for average house value. Based on these results, Boehm and Schlottman conclude that increased educational attainment is the primary channel by which the children of homeowners might benefit. They go on to show that children raised in owned homes translate their greater educational attainment into both increased earnings and homeownership for themselves.

Finally, Haurin, Parcel, and Haurin (2000), analyzed the impact of owning on both cognitive and behavioral child outcomes. They used panel data from the National Longitudinal Survey of Youth. Using a model that helps overcome many of the threats to causal attribution, the authors were able to explicitly credit improvements in child outcomes to an improvement in the quality of the home environment.[3] Even when controlling for a predisposition for homeowners to provide better environments (selection bias), the researchers found that homeowners offer a more stimulating and supportive home environment.

Haurin and colleagues then looked at how this improved environment influenced child outcomes. Outcomes analyzed included cognitive skills—reading recognition and math achievement—and behaviors and emotions such as having a bad temper, being argumentative, and feeling worthless, as reported by the child's mother. Although these characteristics are not necessarily "socially undesirable," they might be expected to predict delinquent behavior as the child grows into adolescence. For each of the child outcomes the researchers found that homeowning significantly and substantively raised cognitive outcomes and reduced behavioral problems. Yet, although Haurin and his colleagues found that homeowning improved the home environment by 16 to 22 percent, the improvement in child outcomes ranged from 4 to 7 percent. Such a reduction in the magnitude of the effect suggests that many other factors influence child behavior. These unidentified factors may be expected only to increase in importance as the child matures.

OVERALL ASSESSMENT. Although Green and White's (1997) findings of positive associations between homeownership and both staying in school and avoiding teenage parenthood are intriguing, other unobserved variables, such as family assets or neighborhood conditions like peer influences, may be responsible for those results. Haurin, Parcel, and Haurin's (2000) findings are indeed compelling but cannot tell us much about how these children will behave as adolescents. Although further findings from the National Longitudinal Study of Youth hold promise, there is simply not enough research on this topic to draw any firm conclusions at this time.

Future research needs to address the impacts of homeownership on a full set of possible youth behaviors, incuding youth employment, educational attainment, sexual behavior, drug use, and crime. In particular, the impact of home-

3. The quality of the home environment is measured by the Home Observation for Measurement of the Environment (HOME) scale; see Bradley and Caldwell (1984). This scale includes cognitive variables measuring how much the child is cognitively stimulated, social variables like responsiveness and warmth, and physical variables including the amount of sensory input and organization of the physical environment.

ownership on adolescent crime is a fruitful topic for research. Sampson, Raudenbush, and Earls (1997), for example, used owner-occupancy as a measure of residential stability and found that it did indeed ameliorate the rate of violent crime at the neighborhood level. Future research might look at the independent impact of homeownership on crime rates among urban and suburban youth.

Conclusion

Evidence exists for a variety of positive social impacts of homeownership for both individuals and society. This evidence, however, is stronger for certain social impacts and weaker for others. Considerable evidence suggests, for example, that homeowners are more likely than renters to be satisfied with their homes and neighborhoods, more likely to participate in voluntary and political activities, and more likely to stay in their homes for longer periods of time. Some doubt still exists, however, whether these relationships are causal, since most of the studies do not adequately account for the self-selection of households to owner and renter occupancy.

Evidence of the impacts of homeownership on other social variables is more sparse and, in some instances, less consistent. Some evidence suggests that homeownership leads to increased self-esteem except for those who buy in neighborhoods with dilapidated housing, social problems, and poor reputations. The limited amount of evidence on the relationship between homeownership and life satisfaction tends to support a positive relationship. Similarly, the limited amount of research on homeownership and health points to a positive association as long as the homeowners are current on their mortgage payments. The mechanism through which homeownership affects health, however, has not been clearly identified. Finally, the research on the impacts of homeownership on both perceived control and socially desirable youth behaviors is simply too sparse to suggest conclusions at this time.

Very little research exists on potential negative social impacts of homeownership. One British study suggests that those who are behind on mortgage payments suffer negative health consequences (Nettleton and Burrows, 1998). Some evidence also suggests that homeowners are less likely to move from high-poverty areas, although the consequences of this are not clear. No research on potentially important topics, including the impacts of mortgage payment delinquency or default on self-esteem, sense of control, life satisfaction, and other social variables, was identified.

Policy Implications

Public policy that encourages homeownership has often been justified by claims that it has a variety of benefits both to individuals and to society. Considerable, although not irrefutable, evidence exists for several of those claims. Given these benefits, there is justification for public policies that encourage and support homeownership. Whether the costs of these policies are reasonable given the anticipated benefits is a separate question beyond the scope of this chapter.

The research on the impacts of homeownership also suggests that these benefits may not accrue to all homeowners. The possibility of negative impacts suggests that those involved in promoting homeownership should be careful not to oversell homeownership, particularly among those who are less likely to be successful homeowners. Recent public policy has been focused on making homeownership available to lower-income families. Although this is clearly an important and worthy goal, not everyone is capable of becoming a successful homeowner. Homeownership counseling may help lower-income home buyers be successful homeowners, but at this point there is very little research evidence on this topic (see chapter 5 here). Caution should be exercised in encouraging homeownership among those with a relatively low probability of success. Encouraging persons to buy homes that they end up losing would do them a great disservice.

Similarly, caution should be exercised in encouraging households to purchase homes in areas that do not have a reasonable probability of stable or increasing property values and healthy social conditions. The designers of many neighborhood revitalization programs adopt homeownership as the central element of their revitalization strategy. However, efforts to increase the homeownership rate in the target area must be accompanied by investments in infrastructure and services. Otherwise the home buyers may not realize either the economic or the social benefits of homeownership. If people buy in areas characterized by depreciating property values and serious social problems, the American Dream could turn into the American Nightmare.

Future Research

Our review of the literature on the social impacts of homeownership suggests both general and specific recommendations for future research. These recommendations address methodological issues in how this research is conducted as well as specific topics in need of additional research.

Future research needs to do a better job of addressing self-selection bias. The self-selection of people into homeownership and rental occupancy represents a significant threat to the validity of most of the research done on the impacts of homeownership, making it impossible to determine the causal direction of any relationships found. Although we cannot randomly assign people to homeownership or rental occupancy, there are statistical techniques that can help account for the self-selection problem. In particular, a two-stage modeling technique developed by Heckman (1979) can be used to predict who becomes a homeowner based on known social and economic characteristics. The prediction is then used to develop an independent variable used to capture the effect of selection bias in the primary regression model. Rohe and Stewart (1996) used the technique in their study of the effects of homeownership on neighborhood stability.

Another approach to addressing the self-selection problem is through longitudinal research designs. Longitudinal designs allow for the measurement of key variables before and after the subjects become homeowners, allowing for the establishment of temporal sequences that are important in establishing causality.

Future research needs to do a better job controlling for potentially confounding variables. Much of the existing research on the impacts of homeownership fails to adequately control for alternative explanations for the relationships found. Homeownership is strongly correlated with income, education, age, stage in the life cycle, marital status, race, the presence of children, and employment tenure and security. However, many studies fail to control for one or more of these variables. Further, owner-occupied units tend to be larger, better maintained, single-family detached dwelling units located in more desirable neighborhoods. To truly isolate the impacts of owning, these variables must also be controlled.

Future research needs to better identify the mechanisms through which homeownership influences various social variables. Much of the existing research on the impacts of homeownership finds associations between homeownership and the social and economic variables under study and then goes on to infer the process or mechanism through which those impacts are produced. Future research needs to actually test them. The intermediate variables through which homeownership is thought to act need to be identified, measured, and tested.

Future research needs to better identify the circumstances under which ownership leads to both positive and negative outcomes. Most of the existing research on the impacts of homeownership does not recognize that the homeownership experience may not be the same for all types of home buyers or for those who buy in different neighborhoods or housing markets. This review of the literature suggests a bias, particularly among American researchers, toward testing for evidence of purported positive impacts of homeownership. In particular, we know very little about the social-psychological or economic impacts of mortgage payment stress or mortgage default; the role of homeownership in trapping persons in neighborhoods that they would rather leave; and the relationship between homeownership and efforts to exclude minorities, renters, and others from neighborhoods.

To develop a more balanced view of the impacts of homeownership and to better understand how to avoid the downside of homeownership these questions should be addressed in future research.

References

Abramson, A. J., M. Mitchell, and M. vander Goot. 1995. "The Changing Geography of Metropolitan Opportunity: The Segregation of the Poor in U.S. Metropolitan Areas, 1970 to 1990." *Housing Policy Debate* 6 (1): 45–72.

Ahlbrandt, R., and J. Cunningham. 1979. *A New Public Policy for Neighborhood Preservation.* Praeger.

Austin, D., and Y. Baba. 1990. "Social Determinants of Neighborhood Attachments." *Sociological Spectrum* 10: 59–78.

Baker, D. 1997. "Inequality in Health and Health Service Use for Mothers of Young Children in South West England." *Journal of Epidemiology and Community Health* 51 (1): 74–79.

Balfour, D. L., and J. L. Smith. 1996. "Transforming Lease-Purchase Housing Programs for Low Income Families: Towards Empowerment and Engagement." *Journal of Urban Affairs* 18 (2): 173–88.

Baum, T., and P. Kingston. 1984. "Homeownership and Social Attachment." *Sociological Perspectives* 27 (2): 159–80.

Boehm, T. P. 1981. "Tenure Choice and Expected Mobility—A Synthesis." *Journal of Urban Economics* 10 (3): 375–89.

Boehm, T. P., and A. Schlottmann. 1999. "Does Home Ownership by Parents Have an Economic Impact on Their Children?" Paper presented at the American Real Estate and Urban Economics Association Mid-Year Meeting, New York, N.Y.

Bradley, R. H., and B. M. Caldwell. 1984. "The HOME Inventory and Family Demographics." *Developmental Psychology* 20 (2): 315–20.

Burkhauser, R. V., and others. 1995. "Mobility Patterns of Older Homeowners: Are Older Homeowners Trapped in Distressed Neighborhoods?" *Research on Aging* 17 (4): 363–84.

Campbell, A. 1976. "Subjective Measures of Well-Being." *American Psychologist* 31 (2): 117–24.

Carliner, G. 1973. *Determinants of Home Ownership.* Institute for Research on Poverty, University of Wisconsin.

Clark, H. 1997. "A Structural Equation Model of the Effects of Homeownership on Self-Efficacy, Self-Esteem, Political Involvement and Community Involvement in African-Americans." Ph.D. dissertation, School of Social Work, University of Texas at Arlington.

Coopersmith, S. 1967. *The Antecedents of Self-Esteem.* San Francisco: W. H. Freeman.

Cox, K. 1982. "Housing Tenure and Neighborhood Activism." *Urban Affairs Quarterly* 18 (1): 107–29.

Danes, S., and E. Morris. 1986. "Housing Status, Housing Expenditures and Satisfaction." *Housing and Society* 13 (1): 32–43.

DiPasquale, D., and E. L. Glaeser. 1999. "Incentives and Social Capital: Are Homeowners Better Citizens?" *Journal of Urban Economics* 45: 354–84.

Doling, J., and B. Stafford. 1989. *Home Ownership: The Diversity of Experience.* Aldershot, England: Gower.

Downs, A. 1981. *Neighborhoods and Urban Development.* Brookings.

Dreier, P. 1982. "The Status of Renters in the United States." *Social Forces* 30 (December): 179–98.

Ellen, I. G., and M. A. Turner. 1997. "Does Neighborhood Matter? Assessing Recent Evidence." *Housing Policy Debate* 8 (4): 833–66.

Essen, J., K. Fogelman, and J. Head. 1978. "Childhood Housing Experiences and School Attainment." *Child Care, Health and Development* 4 (1): 41–58.

Fannie Mae. 1994. "Fannie Mae National Housing Survey 1994." Washington.

———. 1998. "Fannie Mae National Housing Survey 1998." Washington.

———. 1999. "Fannie Mae National Housing Survey 1999." Washington.

Fernandez, R. M., and J. C. Kulik. 1981. "A Multi-level Model of Life Satisfaction—Effects of Individual Characteristics and Neighborhood Composition." *American Sociological Review* 46 (6): 840–50.

Galster, G. C. 1987. *Homeowners and Neighborhood Reinvestment*. Duke University Press.

Galster, G. C., R. Quercia, and A. Cortes. 2000. "Identifying Neighborhood Thresholds: An Empirical Investigation." *Housing Policy Debate* 11 (3): 701–32.

Goodman, J. 1974. Local Residential Mobility and Family Housing Adjustments. In *Five Thousand American Families—Patterns of Economic Progress*, edited by J. Morgan. Institute for Survey Research, University of Michigan.

Green, R., and M. White. 1997. "Measuring the Benefits of Homeowning: Effect on Children." *Journal of Urban Economics* 41 (3): 441–61.

Greene, V. L., and J. I. Ondrich. 1990. "Risk Factors for Nursing Home Admissions and Exits: A Discrete Time-Hazard Function-Approach." *Journals of Gerontology* 45 (6): S250–S258.

Guest, A. W., and R. S. Oropesa. 1986. "Informal Social Ties and Political Activity in the Metropolis." *Urban Affairs Quarterly* 21 (4): 550–74.

Hansen, J. L., J. P. Formby, and W. J. Smith. 1998. "Estimating the Income Elasticity of Demand for Housing: A Comparison of Traditional and Lorenz-Concentration Curve Methodologies." *Journal of Housing Economics* 7 (4): 328–42.

Haurin, D. R., T. Parcel, and R. J. Haurin. 2000. "The Impact of Home Ownership on Child Outcomes." Harvard University.

Heckman, J. J. 1979. "Sample Selection Bias as a Specification Error." *Econometrica* 47: 153–61.

Hoffman, L., and B. Heistler. 1988. "Home Finance: Buying and Keeping a House in a Changing Financial Environment." In *Handbook of Housing and the Built Environment in the United States*, edited by Elizabeth Huttman and Willem van Vliet. New York: Greenwood.

Hoyle, R. 1987. *Tapping Substantive Dimensions of Self-Esteem: The Multifacted Evaluation of Self Inventory*. Department of Psychology, University of North Carolina at Chapel Hill.

Jargowsky, P. 1997. *Poverty and Place: Ghettos, Barrios, and the American City*. New York: Russell Sage.

Jencks, C., and S. Mayer. 1990. "The Social Consequences of Growing Up in a Poor Neighborhood." In *Inner-City Poverty in the United States*, edited by L. Lynn Jr. and M. McGeary. Washington: National Academy Press.

Kind, P., and others. 1998. "Variations in Population Health Status: Results from a United Kingdom National Questionnaire Survey." *British Medical Journal* 316 (7133): 736–41.

Kingston, P., and J. Fries. 1994. "Having a Stake in the System: The Sociopolitical Ramifications of Business and Home Ownership." *Social Science Quarterly* 75 (3): 679–86.

Kinsey, J., and S. Lane. 1983. "Race, Housing Attributes, and Satisfaction with Housing." *Housing and Society* 10 (3): 98–116.

Lam, J. 1985. "Type of Structure, Satisfaction and Propensity to Move." *Housing and Society* 12 (1): 32–44.

Lane, S., and J. Kinsey. 1980. "Housing Tenure Status and Housing Satisfaction." *Journal of Consumer Affairs* 14 (Winter): 341–65.

Lauria, D. 1976. "Wealth, Capital and Power: The Social Meaning of Home Ownership." *Journal of Interdisciplinary History* 7 (2): 261–82.

Lewis, G., and others. 1998. "Socioeconomic Status, Standard of Living, and Neurotic Disorder." *Lancet* 352 (9128): 605–09.

Lyons, W., and D. Lowery. 1989. "Citizen Reponses to Dissatisfaction in Urban Communities: A Partial Test of a General Model." *Journal of Politics* 15 (4): 841–68.

Macintyre, S., and others. 1998. "Do Housing Tenure and Car Access Predict Health Because They Are Simply Markers of Income or Self-Esteem?" *Journal of Epidemiology and Community Health* 52 (10): 657–64.

Marcuse, P. 1975. "Residential Alienation, Home Ownership and the Limit of Shelter Policy. *Journal of Sociology and Social Welfare* 3 (November): 181–203.

Massey, D. S., and E. Fong. 1990. "Segregation and Neighborhood Quality." *Social Forces* 69 (1): 15–32.

McCarthy, G., S. Van Zandt, and W. M. Rohe. 2001. "The Economic Costs and Benefits of Homeownership: A Critical Assessment of the Research." Working Paper 01-02. Washington: Research Institute for Housing America.

Morris, E., and M. Winter. 1976. "Housing Norms, Housing Satisfaction and the Propensity to Move." *Journal of Marriage and the Family* 38 (2): 309–20.

National Homeownership Strategy: Partners in the American Dream. 1995. Washington: U. S. Department of Housing and Urban Development.

Nettleton, S., and R. Burrows. 1998. "Mortgage Debt, Insecure Home Ownership and Health: An Exploratory Analysis." *Sociology of Health and Illness* 20 (5): 731–53.

Page-Adams, D., and N. Vosler. 1997. "Homeownership and Well-Being among Blue-Collar Workers." George Warren Brown School of Social Work, Center for Social Development, Washington University, St. Louis.

Perin, C. 1977. *Everything in Its Place*. Princeton University Press.

Rakoff, R. 1977. "Ideology in Everyday Life: The Meaning of the House." *Politics and Society* 7 (1): 85–104.

Rasmussen, D. W., and others. 1997. "The Reverse Mortgage as an Asset Management Tool." *Housing Policy Debate* 8 (1): 173–94.

Robert, S., and J. S. House. 1996. "SES Differentials in Health by Age and Alternative Indicators of SES." *Journal of Aging and Health* 8 (3): 359–88.

Rohe, W. M., and V. Basolo. 1997. "Long-Term Effects of Homeownership on the Self-Perceptions and Social Interaction of Low-Income Persons." *Environment and Behavior* 29 (6): 793–819.

Rohe, W. M., and M. Stegman. 1994a. "The Impact of Home Ownership on the Social and Political Involvement of Low-Income People." *Urban Affairs Quarterly* 30 (September): 152–72.

———. 1994b. "The Impacts of Home Ownership on the Self-Esteem, Perceived Control and Life Satisfaction of Low-Income People." *Journal of the American Planning Association* 60 (1): 173–84.

Rohe, W. M., and L. S. Stewart. 1996. "Home Ownership and Neighborhood Stability." *Housing Policy Debate* 7 (1): 37–81.

Roistacher, E. 1974. "Residential Mobility." In *Five Thousand American Families—Patterns of Economic Progress*, edited by J. Morgan. Institute for Survey Research, University of Michigan.

Rosenberg, M. 1979. *Conceiving the Self.* Malabar, Fla.: Robert E. Krieger.

Rossi, P. 1955. *Why Families Move*. Glencoe, Ill.: Free Press.

Rossi, P. H., and E. Weber. 1996. "The Social Benefits of Homeownership: Empirical Evidence from National Surveys. *Housing Policy Debate* 7 (1): 1–35.

Sampson, R. J., S. W. Raudenbush, and F. Earls. 1997. "Neighborhoods and Violent Crime: A Multilevel Study of Collective Efficacy." *Science* 277: 918–23.

Saunders, P. 1990. *A Nation of Home Owners*. London: Unwin Hyman.

South, S. J., and K. D. Crowder. 1997. "Escaping Distressed Neighborhoods: Individual, Community, and Metropolitan Influences." *American Journal of Sociology* 102 (4): 1040–84.

———. 1998a. "Avenues and Barriers to Residential Mobility among Single Mothers. *Journal of Marriage and the Family* 60 (4): 866–77.

———. 1998b. Residential Mobility between Cities and Suburbs: Race, Suburbanization and Back-to-the-City Moves. *Demography* 34 (4): 525–38.

South, S. J., and G. D. Deane. 1993. "Race and Residential Mobility: Individual Determinants and Structural Constraints." *Social Forces* 72 (1): 147–67.

Speare, A., Jr. 1970. "Home Ownership, Life Cycle Stage, and Residential Mobility." *Demography* 7 (4): 449–58.

Tremblay, K. R. and others. 1980. "An Examination of the Relationship between Housing Preferences and Community-Size Preferences. *Rural Sociology* 45 (3): 509–19.

Varady, D. 1983. "Determinants of Residential Mobility Decisions." *Journal of the American Planning Association* 49 (2): 184–99.

Wilson, W. J. 1987. *The Truly Disadvataged: The Inner-City, the Underclass, and Public Policy.* University of Chicago Press.

14

Housing and Wealth Accumulation: Intergenerational Impacts

THOMAS P. BOEHM AND ALAN M. SCHLOTTMANN

"A nation of homeowners is unconquerable."

—Franklin D. Roosevelt

As is well known, for over sixty years the federal government has promoted homeownership as a critical component of achieving the American Dream. Housing policy has formed a significant cornerstone of the nation's "poverty agenda" as well as represented a separate policy initiative. Two specific examples from the past decade illustrate this point. In 1991 *The President's National Urban Policy Report* issued by the U.S. Department of Housing and Urban Development (HUD) contained six priorities that formed the department's poverty agenda. One of these priorities was to encourage homeownership and expand affordable housing opportunities. More recently, the Clinton administration directed HUD to work with the housing industry and a number of private nonprofit organizations to develop a National Home Ownership Strategy.[1]

Recently, the analysis by Orr and Peach (1999) has reconfirmed the significant financial commitment that families are willing to bear in order to achieve

The authors would like to thank the Scholarly Research Grant Program in the College of Business Administration at the University of Tennessee and the Joint Center for Housing Studies of Harvard University for their financial support of this project.

1. For a detailed discussion of this policy initiative, see U.S. Department of Housing and Urban Development (1995).

homeownership. The financial commitment (average housing costs as a percentage of family income) associated with lower-income households is striking. As discussed by Orr and Peach (1999, p. 55–57), the percentage commitment runs from 40 percent to 60 percent. As outlined in Mayer (1999, p. 82), when the financial risks to lower-income households of homeownership are recognized, the "demand" by American families to own is quite strong.

This chapter focuses on developing a clear picture of the impact of income and wealth on the transition to homeownership. It examines specifically the process of wealth accumulation and the savings/investment dynamic for young households. These relationships are critical to the transition to homeownership and *subsequent* wealth accumulation. In particular, we stress the role of parental homeownership on the *timing* of transition to homeownership and, ultimately, wealth accumulation of their children. In this regard, we briefly discuss three recent strands of the literature in housing economics.

An extensive empirical literature was developed in the 1980s to determine the factors affecting homeownership. An interesting set of studies is referenced in Boehm (1993) and Henderson and Ioannides (1986). In general, the literature concluded that income, relative prices, and a family's life-cycle situation were the primary factors that determine the likelihood of a home purchase. The role of permanent income in the demand for housing was also established; see, for example, Goodman and Kawai (1982) and Ihlanfelt (1980).[2] However, the dynamics of wealth accumulation and intergenerational transfers were treated, in general, in fairly abstract terms, if at all.

Recent literature has tended to emphasize three general themes, all of which share a dynamic element. The first theme involves the interaction of homeownership and wealth. For example, the recent work of Gyourko, Linneman, and Wachter (1999) explores the role of wealth in the context of differential rates of homeownership by race. They find no racial differences in ownership rates among households with wealth sufficient to meet down payment and closing requirements. However, significant differences in ownership rates occur in "wealth-constrained" households.

Several studies investigate the special role of homeownership in wealth accumulation and its relationship to tenure choice. In a series of interesting studies, Haurin, Hendershott, and Wachter (1996b, 1996c) explore wealth accumulation and housing choices of young households.[3] Their empirical results confirm the joint nature of housing choice and wealth accumulation. On the one hand, homeownership is an important component of total wealth; conversely, households need a minimal level of wealth to purchase their first home given financ-

2. Specifically, in most studies estimates of permanent income elasticities are approximately twice the measured income elasticities.

3. For an interesting analysis of changing housing wealth in the United Kingdom, see Maclennan and Tu (1998).

ing requirements. Other authors have analyzed the response of savings to differential housing prices; the studies by Sheiner (1995) and Englehardt (1995) are of particular interest. Although the results of some studies contradict others, in general young households save more in cities with higher housing prices (relative to down payment requirements). These results tend to confirm the high degree of "preference" for homeownership. The role of intergenerational transfers has been addressed in several studies.[4] Not surprisingly, parental transfers can be crucial for the transition to homeownership of young households. Gifts related directly to housing markets are analyzed in Englehardt and Mayer (1994). Their results are consistent with those of Gale and Scholz (1994).

The second theme that has appeared in recent literature centers specifically on the role of down payment requirements and other borrowing constraints on tenure choice. Clearly, this issue relates to the theme of wealth accumulation and intergenerational transfers as well, but Haurin, Hendershott, and Wachter (1996a) explore mortgage borrowing constraints in detail. According to their study, even after factoring in income and wealth requirements, approximately 37 percent of young households remain constrained. This result seems consistent with recent theoretical work relating homeownership to asset allocation in the context of a household's wealth portfolio. Two studies of particular note are those by Chinloy (1999) and Flavin and Yamashita (1998).[5] All of these studies suggest that tenure choice and wealth accumulation need to be considered in a dynamic context.

The third theme has appeared recently in the literature and relates to the "social" impacts of homeownership. As Mayer (1999, p. 58) has observed, "Although the claimed benefits of homeownership are many, the empirical evidence in favor of these hypotheses is scant." Three recent studies that have appeared include Boehm and Schlottmann (1999), Glaeser and DiPasquale (1998), and Green and White (1997). Green and White (1997) and Boehm and Schlottmann (1999) pay particular attention to the benefits of parental homeownership on children. For example, children in owner-occupied homes appear to successfully complete higher levels of education. This result holds across similarly situated households by income (*including low-income households*).[6] As reviewed in Polachek and Siebert (1993), increased educational attainment is associated with higher earnings in the vast majority of studies on earnings. If that is so, then this third theme in the literature suggests a "feedback" to savings behavior and the transition to homeownership.

4. Particularly noteworthy is Gale and Scholz (1994). For a study based on Austrian intergenerational survey data, see Deutsch (1997).

5. In essence, the representative household's balance sheet consists largely of a house and a mortgage. Thus housing-market behavior underlies intertemporal wealth and consumption allocation; see Chinloy (1999).

6. See particularly Green and White (1997).

Thus the established and more recent literature in housing economics suggests a heuristic model that may be summarized as follows:

—Children of homeowners are more "successful" as measured by such factors as lower teenage pregnancy rates and higher educational attainment. Although the precise mechanisms for this success are not well documented, the result appears to be (statistically) valid for low-income households. Higher levels of educational attainment are associated with higher levels of earned income and changes in earned income. This directly affects household savings.

—Higher household savings (and permanent income) lead to quicker transitions to homeownership and thereby greater accumulation of housing wealth because of the increased length of time in which house price appreciation and loan amortization can take place.

—In addition, ownership by parents also gives rise to a preference for ownership on the part of children. If ownership is more likely to occur earlier for children of parents who own, this should also lead to an increase in housing wealth accumulation through increased appreciation and amortization over time.

Model Specification

Two primary equations must be estimated in order to calculate the expected nonhousing and housing wealth accumulation. The first equation to be estimated provides the likelihood of homeownership; the second focuses on nonhousing wealth accumulation.

It is important to point out that the empirical approach employed in this analysis allows a more appropriate means of capturing housing dynamics than heretofore has been presented in the literature. Specifically, three significant aspects of dynamic housing choice are able to be modeled. First, the sequencing of housing choice is modeled in continuous time rather than simply as the occurrence of the event. For example, homeownership is not a simple binary "event" that can occur at any time during the period of the study but rather is related to the specific year that homeownership is attained. Second, unlike traditional hazard models that measure the time until an event occurs and relate it to average measures of causal factors (such as values at the beginning or end of a period), our approach employs true time-varying covariates. For example, over a time period such as 1984–93 our independent variables (such as household income) change with each year of observation. Finally, by estimating a second set of equations over the period (that is, change in nonhousing wealth accumulation and the level of housing expenditure), predicted values are generated for these dependent variables. By combining these estimated values with the cumulative probabilities of homeownership estimated in the hazard model, a more dynamically accurate picture of wealth accumulation (and housing's role in the process) can be painted than has previously appeared anywhere in the literature.

Continuous Time Model of Homeownership

Following Heckman and Walker, let T represent the time until ownership is achieved for an individual family measured from some reference point. In this analysis, the reference point is the time at which the household head left his or her parents' home to form an independent household. In addition, let t represent calendar time measured from the same reference point. Thus the likelihood that a family is still renting at calendar time t is $P = PR(T > t)$. This probability must be determined indirectly by first estimating the hazard function h, the likelihood that $T > t$ given that the household achieves ownership in a very small time interval from t to $t + \Delta t$. This hazard rate can be made a function of a set of time-varying exogenous variables.[7]

This function can be specified more formally as

$$(14\text{-}1) \qquad h = \lim_{\Delta t \to 0} \frac{PR(T > t) \,|\, t < T < t + \Delta t)}{\Delta t}$$
$$= \exp\left[\alpha + (I \cdot \beta_I) + (PC \cdot \beta_{PC}) + (W \cdot \beta_W) + (X \cdot \beta_X)\right] \cdot t_1^{\gamma},$$

where

I = household income, which varies over time

PC = parental characteristics of the head of household

W = household's current level of nonhousing wealth, which varies over time

X = vector of independent variables describing the household and identifying the type of housing market in which the household resides, all of which are time-varying

β_I, β_{PC}, β_W, and β_X = estimated coefficients that correspond to the various independent variables.

From this estimated hazard function the probability of achieving homeownership can be calculated as

$$(14\text{-}2) \qquad P = \sum_{k=1}^{m} \int_{\alpha_{k-1}}^{\alpha_k} h(t) \exp\left[-\int_0^t h(u)du\right] dt,$$

7. The Weibull form of the hazard function employed in this analysis is a special case of the unrestricted hazard in which the hazard is a function of not only a set of time-varying independent variables but also of t, the length of time since the household entered the sample. The unrestricted hazard is specified as

$$h = \lim_{\Delta t \to 0} \frac{\Pr(t > t \,|\, t < T < t + \Delta t}{\Delta t} = \exp\left(\alpha + \beta X_t + \frac{t^{\lambda 1} - 1}{\lambda_1} \cdot \gamma_1 + \frac{t^{\lambda 2} - 1}{\lambda_2} \cdot \gamma_2\right),$$

For the Weibull hazard, $\lambda_1 = 0$ and $\gamma_2 = 0$. A number of forms were experimented with and the Weibull was selected because results derived from the other, more complex, models did not alter the results substantially. For a detailed discussion of how to select the best model see Heckman and Walker (1986).

where

m = the total number of time periods (years, months, weeks, etc.) in T

$\alpha_k = k/m$.

Nonhousing Wealth Accumulation

Continuous time duration models of the type described above provide superior insights into the intertemporal dynamics of economic relationships. To estimate the hazard function, these models make use of all the information available in a panel data set on the timing of change from one economic state of existence to another, as well as the timing and magnitude of changes in the values of the independent variable hypothesis to influence the transition from one state of existence to another.[8] As an extension of this analysis, it is also possible, in a set of secondary equations, to model and empirically estimate the changes in the independent variables included in the hazard function. In this context, one would anticipate transitory and expected income to be the primary determinants of the accumulation of nonhousing wealth and, therefore, current levels of nonhousing wealth in future time periods. More formally,

$$\text{(14-3)} \quad \Delta NHM_{t-1,t} = \beta_{\Delta Tr} \cdot \Delta Tr_{t-1,t} + \beta_I \cdot I_{t-1} + \beta_W NHW_{t-1} + \beta_{\Delta I} \Delta I_{t-1,t} , \\ + \beta_X X_{t-1} + \varepsilon$$

where

$\Delta NHW_{t-1,t}$ = change in household nonhousing wealth between one period and the next

$\Delta Tr_{t-1,t}$ = income transfers to the household between $t - 1$ and t

I_{t-1} = income of the household in the initial period

NHW_{t-1} = nonhousing wealth in period $t - 1$

$\Delta I_{t-1,t}$ = change in income between $t - 1$ and t

X_{t-1} = a vector of other control variables that could affect wealth accumulation

β_I, β_{PC}, β_W, and β_X = coefficients to be estimated that correspond to the various independent variables

ε = error term with mean = 0 and variance = 1.

Calculation of Expected Nonhousing and Housing Wealth Accumulation

Once the equations specified above have been estimated, expected nonhousing and housing wealth accumulation can be calculated as follows:

8. Perhaps the best discussion of the practical advantages of using continuous time duration models to analyze a problem rather than discrete time probability models is presented in Flinn and Heckman (1982).

(14-4) $$E(NHW)_n = NHW_0 + \left[\Delta NHW_{t-1,t} \cdot \sum_{t=1}^{n}(1+i)^n\right],$$

where

$E(NHW)_n$ = expected nonhousing wealth at time n

NHW_0 = nonhousing wealth at 0

$\Delta NHW_{t-1,t}$ = estimated change in nonhousing wealth over one time period

i = the interest rate at which savings can be invested.

(14-5a) $$C\Pr(\text{Own})_t = \sum_{t=1}^{m}\left\{\left[1-\exp^{-\exp(\beta X_t)\cdot H(\alpha_t,\gamma)}\right]-\left[1-\exp^{-\exp(\beta X_t)\cdot H(\alpha_{t-1},\gamma)}\right]\right\},$$

where

$C\Pr(\text{Own})_t$ = the cumulative probability of achieving ownership by the end of period t

βX_t = vector of coefficients estimated in equation 14-1 multiplied by the corresponding variable values in period t

$H(\alpha_t, \gamma) = \alpha_t^{\gamma+1}/(\gamma + 1)$ for the Weibull hazard

$\alpha_{t-1} = \{[-\ln(1 - C\Pr(\text{Own})_{t-1})/\exp(\beta X_t)] \cdot (\gamma + 1)\}^{1/(\gamma+1)}$

$\alpha_t = \alpha_{t-1} + 1/\text{m}$.

(14-5b) $$E(HW)_n = \sum_{t=1}^{n} w_t \cdot (AM_t + \Delta HV_t)\cdot C\Pr(\text{Own})_n,$$

where

$E(HW)_n$ = expected housing wealth in year n

$w_t = C\Pr(\text{Own})_t \,/\, \Sigma^n_{t=1} w_t\, C\Pr(\text{Own})_t$

AM_t = amount of amortization that will occur between period t and period n; for example, if n = nine years and an individual purchases in year 1, there will be eight years in which amortization can take place

ΔHV_t = the appreciation in house value that takes places between periods t and n

$C\Pr(\text{Own})_n$ = the cumulative probability of owning by period n.

In equation 14-4, changes in nonhousing wealth will be calculated based on estimates of $\Delta NHW_{t-1,t}$ using coefficients obtained from the estimation of equation 14-3. Similarly, equations 14-5a and 14-5b will be calculated using the coefficients obtained by estimating equation 14-2. These equations can be used to estimate the change in housing and nonhousing wealth accumulation that might be anticipated as the value of a variable influencing one or both of the estimated equation(s) changes. In particular, in the simulations presented subsequently, the focus is on whether the parents of the child were homeowners.

Data

This chapter employs the Panel Study of Income Dynamics (PSID) as collected by the Survey Research Center at the University of Michigan. During the period 1968 through 1992, not only did the survey continue to follow as many of the original 5,000 American families as possible, but it also followed children as they split off from their parents' households. The explicit following of children and associated new household formation is a unique feature of the survey and is central to this analysis.

In order to investigate the dynamics of wealth accumulation and homeownership, children were included who formed new households between 1980 and 1984. Each new household is subsequently followed for the next nine years in this sample. Because the number of new households (split-offs) is small, the five years of split-offs are pooled for the analysis. The total number of households available for the analysis is 878 (with complete savings data over the period available for 855 households).

Both the tenure analysis and the estimation of savings (for the period 1984 to 1989) are partitioned into two subgroups, namely those households whose real family income was above and below the median (in 1984). Of particular interest are any implications of the analysis for the lower-income households. The number of households in each income group is, of course, approximately 440 households.

Empirical Analysis

This section considers those factors affecting tenure choice, particularly the way in which the tenure choice of parents affects the tenure choice of their children. In addition, the forces that influence housing and nonhousing wealth accumulation are explored. Finally, the magnitude of the impact of parental homeownership on children's housing and nonhousing wealth accumulation is calculated.

Tenure Choice

As shown in table 14-1, variables included in the ownership equation comprised several factors. On the basis of the literature discussed above, personal characteristics such as age of the household head, marital status, gender, race, and educational attainment were included. Life-cycle factors such as family size were also included in the analysis. Wealth and estimates of permanent income were incorporated as well.[9] As discussed above, a set of parental characteristics and infor-

9. Permanent income is estimated from a set of independent variables that capture the individual's human capital, employment situation, and the region and size of the community in which the family resides. Separate equations are estimated for nonwhite households and white households in each year of the panel. The same sample is utilized that is used in the estimates of wealth accumulation. The estimation techniques closely follow the procedure in Ihlanfeldt (1980) for estimating permanent income for housing analysis using the PSID.

Table 14-1. *Parameter Estimates for Homeownership Transition*[a]

Variable	*Full sample*	*Higher-income households*[b]	*Lower-income households*[b]
Constant	–2.581***	–2.242***	–2.391***
Personal characteristics			
Age	0.029***	–0.019	0.021**
Single female	–0.913***	–0.810***	–0.967***
Single male	–0.798***	–0.624***	–0.789***
African American	–0.231*	–0.015	–0.389**
Hispanic	–0.191	–0.040	–1.107
Veteran	–0.273**	–0.199	–0.238*
Time disabled	–0.242	–0.188	–0.242
Education			
College education or more	–0.057	0.002	–0.335
Some postsecondary education	–0.216	–0.177	–0.263
High school graduate	–0.258	–0.010	–0.747*
Family size	–0.024	–0.033	0.066
Permanent income	0.075***	0.065***	0.062***
Permanent income (squared)[c]	–0.001***	–0.001***	–0.001***
Nonhousing wealth	0.001***	0.001***	0.010***
Parents' characteristics			
Homeownership	0.411***	0.555***	0.096
Nonhousing wealth	0.001	–0.000	0.001
Income	0.002	0.001	0.011**
Residence			
Large metropolitan	0.551***	0.740***	0.368
Other metro	0.744***	0.689***	0.799**
Small city	1.304***	1.267***	1.346***
Census division[d]			
Year of household formation[e]			
Time in state[f]	–0.060	–0.691	–0.053
Pseudo R^2	0.343	0.319	0.341

Source: Authors' calculations using the sample of the PSID described in the "Data" section of the chapter.

* Asymptotic *t*-test significant at the 0.10 level.

** Asymptotic *t*-test significant at the 0.05 level.

***Asymptotic *t*-test significant at the 0.01 level.

a. All variables are defined in the text; $N = 878$.

b. Based upon median income (rounded to nearest thousand dollars). The higher-income sample consists of 437 households; the lower-income sample consists of 441 households.

c. Times 10^{-1}.

d. Eight regional dummy variables were included, but their coefficient estimates are omitted here.

e. Four dummy variables representing the year of split-off from the parent household were included but are not reported here.

f. Estimate from the Weibull form of the hazard.

mation on location (such as city size and census division) was also available for the analysis. Finally, a set of (binary) variables representing the year of household formation (split-off from the parents' household) was included.

Three separate hazard functions, corresponding to equations 14-1 and 14-2, were estimated and are shown in the columns of table 14-1. The three estimated equations represent the entire sample, the higher-income households in the sample and the lower-income households. Households with higher permanent income (and changes in permanent income) have a higher likelihood of homeownership. The crucial role of the level of wealth (savings) is also clearly demonstrated. Where significant, estimates on other variables appear to be consistent with prior literature.

One result of particular interest across all three sets of households relates to the estimated parameter of "time in state" in the hazard function. Specifically, no evidence is found of (negative) duration dependence in the model when wealth and income are included.[10] As discussed earlier, the study by Orr and Peach (1999) and the commentary of Mayer (1999) tend to confirm the strong desire for homeownership among all households classified by family income. In other words, ceteris paribus, households in the sample do not lose the desire for homeownership even if they have been renting for a considerable time. If their household income and wealth position allows a transition to homeownership, these families are just as likely to make the move to homeownership, after years of renting, as they would have been earlier.

On the basis of the previous discussion of the literature, a variable was included that captures whether the parents of a household head were homeowners. The wealth equation (discussed below) already controls for gifts and inheritances and for changes in wealth from a relative joining the "new" household. In addition, the levels of parental nonhousing wealth and income are included directly in the estimation of this equation as control variables. In this context, it is particularly interesting that children raised in owner-occupied homes appear to have a "preference" for homeownership. As noted above, Green and White (1997) and Boehm and Schlottmann (1999) find that parental homeownership significantly affects children. In this analysis, the results suggest a strong preference for homeownership among those who have experienced homeownership first hand. Indeed, the results suggest, ceteris paribus, that if more families are able to achieve homeownership today, there will be a substantially higher proportion of children striving for and achieving homeownership tomorrow. The statistical insignificance of parental homeownership for the lowest-income households might reflect the fact that for the poorest of these young families the income and wealth constraints are too severe for homeownership irrespective of

10. In general, "naive" estimations, which do not incorporate a household's economic situation, can generate significant duration dependence.

Table 14-2. *Parameter Estimates for Change in Nonhousing Wealth, 1984–89*[a]

Variable	*Full sample*	*Higher-income households*[b]	*Lower-income households*[b]
Constant	–39,940**	–67,163*	234.517
Personal characteristics			
Age	997.406*	1,878.297*	199.051
Single female	–7,250	–23,651	–5,352
Single male	–2,523	–15,164	–3,725
African American	–6,271	–19,567*	–3,085
Hispanic	–548	4,408	–5,955
Family size	–757	–2,430	–895
Gifts and wealth			
Gifts and inheritances (1984–89)	1.194***	1.205***	0.888***
Nonhousing wealth[c]	–0.849***	–0.872***	–0.337***
Change in wealth from change in family composition[c]	0.001	0.001	0.274***
Income	1,339***	1,627***	–0.025
Change in family income	–0.707***	0.765***	0.257***
Parental wealth	2.887	0.953	20.582**
R^2	0.508	0.519	0.350

Source: Authors' calculations using the sample of the PSID described in the "Data" section of the chapter.

*Asymptotic *t*-test significant at the 0.10 level.

** Asymptotic *t*-test significant at the 0.05 level.

*** Asymptotic t-test significant at the 0.01 level.

a. All variables are defined in the text. The number of observations is 855, with 432 in the high-income equation and 423 in the low-income equation.

b. Based upon median income; see table 14-1.

c. All levels are measured in 1984. All change variables are defined as changes between 1984 and 1989.

preferences. This result seems consistent with the research of Haurin, Hendershott, and Wachter (1996a).

Wealth Accumulation

Table 14-2 presents parameter estimates of household change in (nonhousing) wealth over the period 1984–89 for the sample of children who left their parents' home to establish their own households between and including 1980 through 1984.[11] Changes in wealth occur not only from savings but also from income transfers. As shown in table 14-2, variables included in the analysis consist of personal characteristics of the household head and other life-cycle factors affecting savings behavior, such as family size. Except for the lower change in

11. It was necessary to estimate wealth over this period (rather than on an annual basis) because of data limitations in the PSID.

wealth for African Americans among higher-income households, personal characteristics do not explain wealth accumulation per se.

Given the primary concern of this analysis, the impact of income, gifts, and parental wealth on savings is of particular interest. These "traditional" economic variables are the key to explaining changes in nonhousing wealth over the period. In general, these variables affect wealth accumulation as expected in each of the three equations shown in table 14-2. However, the interesting questions revolve around differences in the accumulation of wealth between high-income and low-income households. Low-income households accumulate less wealth over the period per dollar of "gifts" than higher-income households.[12] This suggests that some amounts of the transfers are utilized in household consumption.[13] Among lower-income households, the insignificance of the income variable but not the variable for changes in income seems to be consistent with this observation.

In a similar manner, it is perhaps not surprising that the parameter estimate on wealth changes from new members entering the household (such as aging relatives) is significant only for lower-income households. It is particularly interesting that parental wealth is significant for low-income households, suggesting that parental assistance for these households continues even after their formal split-off in the data.

The Dynamics of Wealth Accumulation

As presented previously (see equations 14-4, 14-5a, and 14-5b), the cumulative probabilities of achieving homeownership can be calculated based upon the estimation of the entire model (equations 14-1–14-3). In addition, an accumulation of wealth composed of both a nonhousing and a housing component can be estimated from this system. Subsequently, for any variable that has an estimated impact on this system, its impact on both housing and nonhousing wealth accumulation can be calculated. The exploration of the third theme, the impact of parental homeownership on their children's (split-off households') wealth accumulation is based on an interpretation of the recent literature. Table 14-4 presents estimates of the average change in both housing and nonhousing wealth for the full sample and the high- and low-income subsamples over the nine-year period in which they were under observation for this analysis. In addition, the estimates of the components of the calculation of housing wealth accumulation (see equation 14-5b) are also presented. These components include

12. Using standard (pooled) test procedures, the estimated coefficent on "gifts and inheritances" is statistically different in the high-income equation than in the low-income equation.

13. Although gifts and inheritances appear to be particularly important in affecting savings behavior, in reality they are not, because this type of transfer occurs in so few instances (approximately 5 percent). Consequently, even though it is likely that these transfers come from parents, they are not a point of focus in the simulations conducted in the next section.

Table 14-3. *Homeownership by Parents as a Determinant of Children's Educational Attainment*

	Highest educational attainment[b]		
Sample[a]	*High school graduate*	*Some postsecondary education*	*College graduate or higher*
Full sample	0.721***	0.297	0.827***
Less upper-income quartile	0.829***	0.424	0.901***
Low-income households	1.274***	0.706***	1.260***

Source: Authors' calculations using the sample of the PSID described in the "Data" section of the chapter.

***Asymptotic *t*-test significant at the 0.01 level.

a. There were 864 observations in the full sample, 647 observations for the full sample less households in the upper-income quartile, and 435 observations for parents with household incomes below the median.

b. The omitted category is "never completed high school."

the cumulative probability of owning, the amortization of mortgage principal, and house value appreciation after a given year assuming homeownership is achieved.[14]

Table 14-5 presents calculations of the impact of parental homeownership on the wealth accumulation of the children who have split off to form their own households. Before discussing these results, the mechanisms by which parental homeownership affects children should be reviewed. First, the estimates of the likelihood of homeownership for children (table 14-1) demonstrate that parental ownership has a direct link in our calculations through this equation. In addition, the literature discussed earlier suggests that children of homeowners attain higher levels of education. This leads to higher levels of income and savings, which increase the cumulative probability of homeownership (table 14-2) and the expected level of expenditure on a home if a household chooses to purchase.

In the estimates of the impact of parental homeownership on children's wealth accumulation, the indirect channels as well as the direct are included in the calculation.

14. In order to do these calculations it was necessary to estimate a standard housing expenditure equation to generate expected house values for a given year for all the households in the sample. Once an estimate of house value was computed for a particular household or group of households, future appreciation in house values was assumed to take place at the average rate for the particular subgroup under consideration; that is, for all households in the PSID who were owner-occupants for the entire period 1984–89 the average amount of appreciation was 11 percent per year. For low-income families from this group the rate was 7 percent, and for the high-income families who achieved homeownership the appreciation rate was 13 percent. Once expected house value at the time of purchase was determined, a standard down payment (10 percent of house value) and contract interest rate (10 percent) were assumed in order to calculate the amount of amortization to expect over subsequent years.

Table 14-4. *Wealth Accumulation by Component*
Dollars, except as indicated

Year	*Cumulative nonhousing wealth*	*Cumulative housing wealth*	*Appreciation in house value*	*Loan amortization*	*Cumulative ownership probability (percent)*
Full sample					
1	5,592	1,030	44,520	3,384	6.84
2	9,427	2,893	39,487	3,010	12.82
3	13,302	5,489	34,620	2,647	18.36
4	17,093	8,796	30,094	2,307	23.61
5	20,926	12,706	24,791	1,906	28.58
6	24,759	16,976	18,509	1,427	33.10
7	29,119	21,484	12,204	943	37.37
8	34,511	26,136	6,011	466	41.47
9	41,734	31,077	0	0	45.44
High-income households					
1	10,489	2,876	79,930	4,779	12.73
2	16,387	7,596	67,184	4,074	22.96
3	22,387	13,660	56,736	3,490	31.66
4	28,183	20,861	47,954	2,990	39.27
5	34,081	28,887	38,742	2,448	45.99
6	39,979	37,175	28,334	1,813	51.79
7	46,584	45,527	18,423	1,194	57.02
8	54,600	53,744	8,928	585	61.81
9	65,201	62,034	0	0	66.21
Low-income households					
1	739	193	14,532	2,006	2.54
2	2,537	637	14,534	1,968	5.31
3	4,337	1,366	13,721	1,824	8.23
4	6,132	2,422	12,562	1,639	11.27
5	7,929	3,808	10,735	1,376	14.40
6	9,727	5,483	8,337	1,050	17.48
7	11,875	7,403	5,636	698	20.57
8	14,650	9,560	2,863	348	23.70
9	18,141	12,068	0	0	26.91

Source: Authors' calculations using the sample of the PSID described in the "Data" section of the chapter.

Table 14-5. *Effect of Homeownership by Parents on Wealth Accumulation of Children*

	Wealth accumulation (dollars)		
Sample	*Change in nonhousing wealth*	*Change in housing wealth*	*Total*
Full sample	5,073	13,069	18,142
Low-income households	538	2,065	2,603
High-income households	5,942	25,569	31,511

Source: Authors' calculations using the sample of the PSID described in the "Data" section of the chapter.

Note: Table shows the effect for the nine-year interval in which split-off households' tenure choices are observed. In terms of the amortization schedule assigned to a household (given initial homeownership and initial housing value), the assumed mortgage interest rate was 10 percent with an "average" equity down payment of 10 percent (5 percent for the lower-income households and 15 percent for the higher-income households).

In order to calculate the indirect effects, an equation similar to that presented in Boehm and Schlottmann (1999) is estimated. Table 14-3 demonstrates the impact of parental homeownership on educational attainment in this sample.[15] The impact of parental homeownership on child educational attainment is significant in all (sub)samples.

Consistent with the main results of Green and White (1997), parental homeownership significantly affects high school graduation among children from lower-income households. As noted in the earnings studies cited in Polachek and Siebert (1993), a major lifetime income break by educational attainment occurs between individuals who complete high school and those who drop out.

Table 14-4 presents both average housing and nonhousing wealth accumulation for each (sub)sample over time. The three factors presented in the fourth, fifth, and sixth columns of the table (house value appreciation, loan amortization, and the cumulative probability of ownership) are combined as set forward in equation 14-5b to produce the cumulative housing wealth amounts presented in the third column of the table. A number of insights can be gained about the dynamics of housing choice and wealth accumulation from this table. For example, considering the cumulative probabilities of homeownership, the lower-income sample never gets above a 26.91 percent chance of achieving homeownership. However, on average, the higher-income group achieves this likelihood of homeownership within the first three years of independent existence as a household. The difference in the ability of these two groups to accu-

15. The multinomial logit estimates in Boehm and Schlottmann (1999) include five major types of variables. These are grouped as personal characteristics, family background, parents' financial condition, housing values and homeownership, and parents' educational background. Full results of our estimates are available upon request.

mulate nonhousing wealth is equally clear. In addition, the value of the housing that higher-income households are likely to buy is substantially higher, as is demonstrated indirectly by the house value appreciation calculations presented in the fourth column of table 14-4.

Table 14-5 presents the impact that parental homeownership has on the wealth accumulation of children, though the precise "mechanisms" for these effects are only partially understood. As might be expected, the effects are highest among high-income households. However, given the significantly low levels of nonhousing wealth observed for low-income households ($2,618 was the average level of nonhousing wealth for the low-income portion of the sample in 1984 as compared to $17,704 for the high-income group), the figures in table 14-5 represent a substantial change in wealth accumulation for everyone. The results in table 14-5 augment the literature on housing and wealth accumulation by children. Specifically, parental homeownership not only begets future homeownership, but also a greater likelihood of ownership at an earlier time. This earlier likelihood of purchase leads to a substantial increase in housing wealth accumulation, which is clearly an important component of wealth accumulation for these households. Finally, it is worth noting that the measurement of these wealth effects was, somewhat arbitrarily, confined to the nine-year period in which these households were being analyzed. Certainly the accumulation of both housing and nonhousing wealth will continue throughout the life span of the child's family and, as the analysis demonstrates, have an impact on subsequent generations as well.

Summary, Policy Implications, and Suggestions for Future Research

This chapter examines the effect of parents' housing choices on the dynamics of homeownership and wealth accumulation of their children. The analysis employs a dynamic duration probability model of homeownership in conjunction with a secondary equation estimating intertemporal nonhousing wealth accumulation. This model demonstrates empirically not only the direct effect of factors such as parental homeownership on the likelihood of children achieving homeownership, but also the indirect effects through its impact on household income and savings. It is important to note that the probabilities stemming from this analysis are different from those of a traditional logit model or, for that matter, a duration model in which the process of wealth accumulation does not affect the likelihood of homeownership.

The results demonstrate the importance of parental homeownership on children. Homeownership provides access to housing wealth and also has indirect impacts that are crucial for low-income households. Specifically, parental homeownership indirectly affects child labor earnings through increased educational attainment that is particularly significant for lower-income households. In a similar manner, the recent literature cited here suggests that children from owner-occupied households have fewer social problems, a factor that also augments labor earnings.

This analysis also suggests that parents' housing tenure significantly affects the likelihood of a child's homeownership directly. The strong preference for homeownership exhibited by those who grew up in owner-occupied homes suggests not only that owner-occupied housing may indeed be a merit good (that is, a good that is underconsumed by individuals who, because of their lack of experience with homeownership, do not perceive its true benefits), but also that this is a relatively important factor in increasing the wealth accumulation of future generations.

Policy Implications and Suggestions for Future Research

The primary policy implication of this analysis is that programs designed to stimulate homeownership, particularly among lower-income households, have substantial benefits for wealth accumulation, not just for a given set of households but also for their children. Therefore, depending on the cost, such programs could be particularly beneficial from a societal perspective. However, before making such a general statement, one would want to conduct a comparable analysis on a broader spectrum of homeowners rather than focusing only on a group of parents and their children's first home purchase.

Though a truly general analysis of the above issue is beyond the scope of this study, we did conduct a preliminary examination of the importance of housing versus nonhousing wealth accumulation using the entire sample (of owners and renters). The sample was restricted to those households with a head under fifty years of age in order to focus on families that still had strong incentives to save. Because it seems likely that lower-value housing would not appreciate as rapidly as higher-value housing, the housing was divided into value quartiles as of 1984, the beginning of the period. The results for this more general sample make two points particularly clearly. First, regardless of value level, there is much less variation in the accumulation of housing wealth than nonhousing wealth (coefficients of variation range from 1.634 on high-value housing to 2.552 on low-value housing; alternatively, these same measures for nonhousing wealth accumulation range between 5.793 and 8.940 respectively). This difference in relative variability is likely a result of the fact that owners are locked into a kind of "forced savings" through house value appreciation and loan amortization unless they refinance at some point to draw on their equity.

Of particular interest in this additional analysis is the relative importance of housing versus nonhousing wealth accumulation across house value quartiles. For the quartile with the highest house value, though housing equity buildup is substantial, it is roughly half the average accumulation through nonhousing sources (a $56,707 change in housing equity versus a $117,932 change in nonhousing wealth during the period). However, for the quartile with the lowest house value (and the lowest-income owners), the relationship is *reversed.* Specifically, the change in housing equity is roughly twice the amount of nonhousing wealth accumulation over the period ($10,292 versus $4,970 respectively). Consequently, housing equity accumulation can be viewed as a relatively stable and substantial component of overall wealth accumulation, particularly for lower-income families (in lower-valued housing). Thus the results for children and first-time homeownership presented herein are consistent with a more "general" sample.

Future analysis should focus on modeling wealth accumulation for a more general sample and focusing on differences between various cohorts—that is, minority households versus majority households, or those households with chronically low income levels over substantial periods of time versus other income groups. In this context, a number of interesting issues could be addressed. For example, one could consider families at different life-cycle stages and document the differences in this process for those who, in all likelihood, would place a different emphasis on saving. In addition, the analysis presented in this paper does *not* explicitly consider the movement of a household through the hierarchy of housing alternatives. Conceptually, this more sophisticated estimation would be possible with the type of hazard model that has been employed in this analysis. It is easy to imagine that households that move relatively rapidly up the ownership hierarchy would accumulate more wealth than those that do not move as frequently. Also, the ability to make such moves might differ substantially across income groups. Alternatively, some households might return to renting after an initial attempt at homeownership, thus retarding their housing wealth accumulation.

Finally, returning to the primary focus of this chapter, the relationship between parental homeownership and children's success needs both further exploration and explanation. Although the analysis documents its importance, the exact mechanism by which this benefit is bestowed is not identified. However, nowhere in the literature has there been anything but speculation regarding the nature of this process. One area of exploration that might prove fruitful for understanding the mechanism at work is to compare the differences in the magnitude of this effect across owned housing with different characteristics, such as different public service packages or different neighborhood characteristics. In addition, it could prove informative to investigate how the dynamics of the parents' movement through the housing hierarchy would affect the children's ultimate success as adults. Such analysis would require a high-quality panel data set collected over a long period of time. To our knowledge, the PSID is the only data set available that comes close to having the properties required for such work, and it has its limitations. However, if effective housing policies are to be developed, which are also cost-efficient to implement, the intricacies of the process by which children raised in owner-occupied housing benefit from their environment must be better understood.

References

Boehm, Thomas P. 1993. "Income, Wealth Accumulation, and First-Time Homeownership: An Intertemporal Analysis." *Journal of Housing Economics* 3 (1): 16–30.

Boehm, Thomas P., and Alan M. Schlottmann. 1999. "Does Home Ownership by Parents Have an Economic Impact on Their Children?" *Journal of Housing Economics* 8 (3): 217–32.

Chinloy, Peter. 1999. "Housing, Illiquidity, and Wealth." *Journal of Real Estate Finance and Economics* 19 (1): 69–83.

Deutsch, Edwin. 1997. "Indicators of Housing Finance Intergenerational Wealth Transfers." *Real Estate Economics* 25 (1): 129–72.

Englehardt, Gary V. 1995. "House Prices and Home Owner Saving Behavior." Working Paper 5183. Cambridge, Mass.: National Bureau of Economic Research.

Englehardt, Gary V., and Christopher J. Mayer. 1994. "Gifts for Home Purchase and Housing Market Behavior." *New England Economic Review* (May/June): 47–58.

Flavin, Marjorie, and Takashi Yamashita. 1998. "Owner Occupied Housing and the Composition of the Household Portfolio over the Life Cycle." Working Paper. Department of Economics, University of California, San Diego.

Flinn, C. J., and J. J. Heckman. 1982. "Models for the Analysis of Labor Force Dynamics." *Advances in Econometrics* 1 (1): 35–95.

Gale, William G., and John Karl Scholz. 1994. "Intergenerational Transfers and the Accumulation of Wealth." *Journal of Economic Perspectives* 8 (4): 145–60.

Glaeser, Edward L., and Denise DiPasquale. 1998. "Incentives and Social Capital: Are Homeowners Better Citizens? Working Paper 6363. Cambridge, Mass.: National Bureau of Economic Research.

Goodman, Allen C., and Masahiro Kawai. 1982. "Permanent Income, Hedonic Prices, and Demand for Housing: New Evidence." *Journal of Urban Economics* 12 (2): 214–37.

Green, R. K., and M. J. White. 1997. "Measuring the Benefits of Homeowning: Effects on Children." *Journal of Urban Economics* 41: 441–61.

Gyourko, Joseph, Peter Linneman, and Susan Wachter. 1999. "Analyzing the Relationships among Race, Wealth, and Home Ownership in America." *Journal of Housing Economics* 8 (2): 63–89.

Haurin, Donald R., Patric H. Hendershott, and Susan M. Wachter. 1996a. "Borrowing Constraints and the Tenure Choice of Young Households." Working Paper 5530. Cambridge, Mass.: National Bureau of Economic Research.

———. 1996b. "Wealth Accumulation and Housing Choices of Young Households: An Exploratory Investigation." *Journal of Housing Research* 7 (1): 33–57.

———. 1996c. "Expected Home Ownership and Real Wealth Accumulation of Youth." Working Paper 5629. Cambridge, Mass.: National Bureau of Economic Research.

Heckman, J., and J. Walker. 1986. "Using Goodness of Fit and Other Criteria to Choose among Competing Duration Models: A Case Study of Hutterite Data." Working Paper. National Opinion Research Center, University of Chicago.

Henderson, J. V., and Y. M. Ioannides. 1986. "Tenure Choice and the Demand for Housing." *Economica* 53 (210): 231–46.

Ihlanfeldt, K. 1980. "An Intertemporal Empirical Analysis of the Renter's Decision to Purchase a Home." *Journal of the American Real Estate Urban Economic Association* 8 (2): 180–97.

Maclennan, Duncan, and Yong Tu. 1998. "Changing Housing Wealth in the UK, 1985–1993: Household Patterns and Consequences." *Scottish Journal of Political Economy* 45 (4): 447–65.

Mayer, Christopher J. 1999. "Commentary." *FRBNY Economic Policy Review* (September): 79–83.

Orr, James A., and Richard W. Peach. 1999. "Housing Outcomes: An Assessment of Long-Term Trends. *FRBNY Economic Policy Review* (September): 51–61.

Polachek, S. W., and W. S. Siebert. 1993. *The Economics of Earnings*. Cambridge, England: Cambridge University Press.

Sheiner, Louise. 1995. "Housing Prices and the Savings of Renters." *Journal of Urban Economics* 38 (1): 94–125.

U.S. Department of Housing and Urban Development. 1991. "The President's National Urban Policy Report." Washington: Office of Policy Development and Research.

———. 1995. "Homeownership and Its Benefits." Urban Policy Brief 2. Washington: Office of Policy Development and Research.

15

Impact of Homeownership on Child Outcomes

DONALD R. HAURIN, TOBY L. PARCEL, AND R. JEAN HAURIN

There are many claims that homeownership yields significant benefits for the owners, the owners' local community, and the nation, but there are relatively few studies of this assertion that fully address the complex modeling, data, and estimation issues that the claim implies. Recently, there has been substantial interest in measuring the impact of homeowning on the children of homeowners. We add to this literature by focusing on measuring the impact of homeownership on the cognitive and behavioral outcomes of young children.

Our child outcome measures include normed achievement test scores in mathematics and reading and an indicator of behavioral adjustment. Our measures of cognitive achievement have good predictive validity and are associated with contemporaneous and subsequent measures of school achievement (Baker and others, 1993), an important precursor of occupational and earnings attainment. Regarding behavioral adjustment, researchers have documented continuities between aggressive, antisocial behavior in childhood and subsequent analogous adult behaviors (see Caspi, Elder, and Bem, 1987; Forgatch, Patterson, and Skinner, 1988; Kohlberg, LaCrosse, and Ricks, 1972; Mechanic, 1980). Overcontrolled, inhibited, or fearful behaviors are associated with later learning diffi-

The authors thank the National Association of Home Builders for funding assistance. We also thank David Brasington, Nam-yll Kim, Donghui Qiu, Mikaela Dufur, and Robert Dietz for their assistance. We thank the participants of the Harvard Joint Center for Housing Studies Low-Income Homeownership Symposium for comments.

culties (Kohn, 1977). Our measure of behavior, discussed in more detail below, draws on indicators of both overly aggressive and inhibited behaviors.

We expect our findings will be important in the discussion of public subsidies for homeownership. Examples of current topics related to public intervention in the homeownership decision include the conversion of public rental housing to owned units, government subsidies to reduce down payments, and enforcement measures related to illegal discrimination in the housing market. Economists have found that one impact of a public subsidy for homeownership is to quicken the conversion from renting to owning (Bourassa and others, 1994). Finding that homeownership positively affects child outcomes strengthens the argument for early homeownership. Public subsidies of homeownership are supported if ownership reduces child behavior problems, because these behaviors are precursors of later and more significant deviant behavior. Improved child cognition not only yields increased future earnings for the child but also generates the externalities associated with a higher-achieving population.

Literature

There are few published studies about the relationship of homeownership to child outcomes. Green and White (1997) use three national data sets (Panel Study of Income Dynamics [PSID], 1980 Census PUMS, and High School and Beyond) to investigate the effect of parental homeownership on the probability that a 17-year-old will remain in school and that a 17-year-old female will give birth to a child. They find that parental homeownership reduces the probability that resident 17-year-old children will drop out or give birth.

Aaronson (2000) notes that empirical studies in the economics of education literature support the hypothesis that greater temporal stability of a household increases a child's cognitive performance (Hanushek, Kain, and Rivkin, 1999). Using the PSID, Aaronson retests Green and White's hypothesis, but he separates the mobility effect from other homeownership effects. He finds that mobility is disruptive and that the stability associated with homeownership increases the likelihood that a 19-year-old will graduate from high school. Homeownership also has a positive impact on the graduation rate other than through increased stability, but the size of the impact varies across empirical specifications.

Our approach differs from the studies by Aaronson and Green and White in many ways. We focus on cognitive and behavioral outcomes of young children, not older teenage youths; thus our approach better links the timing of homeownership with the observation of a child's outcomes. We also use multiple observations of each child's outcomes, allowing us to control for unobserved child-specific factors such as innate cognitive ability. The breadth of our control variables is much greater, including measures of household wealth and attributes of the locality. Finally, our model tests for impacts of homeownership both directly on child outcomes and through an intervening variable measuring the quality of the home environment.

Model and Research Design

Our theoretical approach draws from economics and sociology. One argument for the inclusion of home ownership in a model of child outcomes is that homeowners are willing to invest more in their home environments than renters are because they profit from the capital gain and this investment in physical and social capital positively affects child outcomes. Another argument is that homeowners tend to stay for a longer time in a dwelling than renters do and this greater stability increases the social capital of the household. Higher levels of social capital positively influence child outcomes.

Our empirical approach is to regress two indexes of the quality of the home environment on an indicator of the current homeownership status and a vector of control variables (Becker, 1965). Next, we regress two measures of a child's current cognitive outcomes and an index of behavioral problems on the indexes of the current home environment, the indicator of homeownership status, and current and past values of other explanatory variables. In these estimations, we use a random effects panel data procedure to allow for unobserved household-specific and child-specific factors. We also use an instrumental variable for the homeownership indicator to address the issue of the possible presence of an unobserved factor affecting a household's tendency to own a home and invest in a child.

Menaghan and Parcel (1991, 1995) identify control variables for the home environment estimation, including parental working conditions, family structure, and parental background characteristics. The vector of control variables in the child cognition and behavioral problems equations includes many factors that affect child outcomes. Parcel and Menaghan (1994a) suggest the importance of parental age, family size, and marital stability, as well as child characteristics such as gender, birth weight and health problems, and maternal race, education, and mental ability. We include these variables and neighborhood characteristics as controls (Haveman and Wolfe, 1995). Our featured tests are of the impact of the home environment and homeownership on child outcomes.

Data Set

Our study uses a national panel data set that links a survey of young adults, the National Longitudinal Survey of Youth (NLSY79), with the NLSY Child data (NLSY-C), this being a survey of the children of NLSY79 mothers (Center for Human Resource Research, 1994). The NLSY79 survey began in 1979 and was conducted annually through the period we study. Children in the sample are ages

Table 15-1. *Mother's Age in the Year of Birth of Her Child: Distribution in the Sample*

Age	*Distribution (percent)*
15	0.3
16	2.3
17	4.1
18	9.3
19	11.4
20	14.2
21	12.1
22	14.7
23	13.4
24	11.3
25	5.9
26	1.0

Source: National Longitudinal Survey of Youth (Washington: Center for Human Resources Research, 1994).

5 to 8 in 1988. The NLSY Child data are available for 1986, 1988, 1990, 1992, and 1994. We omit 1986 primarily because the form of the cognitive tests differs. The retention rates in both samples are excellent (90 percent of NLSY79 respondents). The NLSY79 reports the homeownership status of respondents and their geographic location. Locations are matched to households using county-level data, allowing for tests of the impact of local geographic attributes. NLSY79 mothers were ages 23 to 30 in 1988 and thus were ages 15 to 26 at the time of their children's birth. Table 15-1 lists the distribution of mothers' ages.

Dependent Variables

We estimate the determinants of two measures of a child's home environment and three measures of child outcomes.

HOME ENVIRONMENT. The NLSY-C data sets include age-appropriate sets of items derived from the Home Observation for Measurement of the Environment (HOME) scales (Bradley and Caldwell, 1984a, 1984b; Caldwell and Bradley, 1984). The HOME scales were devised to identify and describe homes of infants and young children who were at significant developmental risk (Bradley and others, 1988). They have proved useful in identifying home environments associated with impaired mental development, clinical malnutrition, abnormal growth, and poor school performance (Bradley, 1985). The scales measure cognitive variables, including language stimulation, provision of a variety of stimulating experiences and materials, and encouragement of child achievement; social variables, including responsiveness, warmth, and encouragement of maturity; and physical environmental variables, including the amount of sensory input and organization of the physical environment. The two-year test-retest reliability ranges from 0.38 to 0.56 (Yeates and others, 1983) to 0.56 to 0.57 (Ramey, Yeates, and Short, 1984). The inter-rater reliability in six studies was about 0.9 (Bradley and Caldwell, 1981).

In consultation with Bradley, the Center for Human Resource Research selected age-appropriate items to create the two HOME variables included in the NLSY-C. Each HOME scale includes both maternal report items and interviewer observations. The questions used in developing the cognitive stimulation/physical environment HOME scale (HOME-C) and the emotional support HOME scale (HOME-E) are in the appendix. HOME-C asks about the quality of the living space and the materials and time spent on children's cognitive stimulation. HOME-E asks about the nature of family members' interactions with the child. Both HOME scales are normed so the weighted average is 100 with a standard deviation of 15. A percentile score is then derived based on the assumption that the scores are normally distributed. This scoring method ensures intertemporal comparability of the HOME scales for the four surveys. A higher value on either scale implies the child lives in a more supportive home environment.

CHILD COGNITION. Our two measures of child cognition are derived from normed reading recognition and mathematical achievement scores on the Peabody Individual Achievement Test (PIAT). The reading recognition (PIAT-Reading) test begins with preschool-level items and progresses in difficulty to the high school level (Baker and others, 1993). Although the 1968 normed sample has a mean of 100, the mean normed score in the NLSY-C sample is somewhat above 100. Baker and colleagues (1993) attribute the above average mean to increases in child television viewing and preschool reading readiness programs over the past twenty-five years. These data are converted to percentile scores to ensure intertemporal comparability. A higher value indicates greater achievement on the test. One-month test-retest reliability ranged from 0.81 to 0.94 for kindergarten to third grade (Baker and others, 1993, p. 140).

The mathematics assessment (PIAT-Mathematics) measures mathematics achievement. The test begins with basic skills such as numeral recognition and progresses to geometry and trigonometry. Again, the test was normed in 1968 on a national sample of children. The NLSY-C weighted sample mean is 100. These scores are then converted into percentile scores. The correlation between PIAT mathematics and reading recognition scores is about 0.5. One-month test-retest reliability averaged 0.74 with the value increasing with grade level (Baker and others, 1993, p. 135).

CHILD BEHAVIOR PROBLEMS. The NLSY-C includes an index of child behavior problems based on twenty-eight items indicating mothers' reports. These items were included in the 1982 Child Health Supplement to the National Health Interview Survey (Zill, 1988) and were drawn primarily from the Child

Behavior Checklist (CBCL) developed by Achenbach and Edelbrock (1981, 1983). They have been used since the mid-1960s for measuring and assessing child behavior problems. Items also were drawn from Rutter (1970), Graham and Rutter (1968), and Kellam and others (1975).

Assessment items were chosen to represent relatively common behavior syndromes in children; for example, measures of "acting-out," depressed-withdrawn behavior, and anxious-distractible behavior are included, rather than rare behaviors indicative of serious pathology. Specific items include difficulties interacting with other children, difficulties concentrating, having a strong temper and being argumentative, being withdrawn, demanding attention, being too dependent/clingy, and feeling worthless or inferior. Twenty-six items were asked about for all children and an additional two items asked about only for those children attending school. The items have good test-retest reliability and discriminant validity (Baker and others, 1993, p. 107). Achenbach, McConaughy, and Howell (1987) show that parents' reports were consistent with the reports of other informants, including teachers and mental health practitioners.

Normed scores are created based on data from the 1981 National Health Interview Survey, these data having a mean of 100 and standard deviation of 15. A higher value of the index indicates a greater level of behavior problems. The weighted mean for children in the NLSY-C is 106; that is, mothers reported a greater than average amount of child behavior problems. Baker and colleagues (1993) hypothesize that this finding results from the mothers of children in the NLSY-C being younger than average and thus less experienced in child rearing. These normed scores are then converted into percentiles, with the mean being 62 for the full NLSY-C sample.

Explanatory Variables

HOMEOWNERSHIP. The parents in the NLSY79 sample are in the part of their life cycle where households frequently make the transition from renting to homeowning. In the United States, the average ownership rate is 14 percent at age 22; it rises to 42 percent by age 29 and to 60 percent by age 36. We observe the homeownership status of the children's parents each year. All households in our sample have children (an important factor in explaining the probability of homeownership); thus our sample's homeownership rates are relatively high in comparison with the age-adjusted national rates.

Control Variables: Economic

Nominal variables are deflated to a common base year, 1994, using the CPI-all item index for urban wage earners.

MOTHER'S WAGE. The NLSY79 reports the typical hourly wage rate for working women. For mothers not currently working, wages are not observed; thus potential wage earnings must be estimated. Potential wage earnings (a concept similar to permanent income) better capture the long-term potential economic contribution of the mother. We follow the human capital approach and estimate wage functions for working mothers, then apply this equation to predict wages for nonworkers. However, estimation of wages using a sample of only working mothers may result in biased coefficients because the sample may be nonrandom. Correction procedures for sample selection bias are well known (Heckman, 1979), and we use a maximum likelihood procedure to jointly estimate labor force participation and the wage equation (Greene, 1995, p. 642). Explanatory variables in the labor force participation equation include descriptors of the mother's personal and educational characteristics and descriptors of household characteristics such as the number of children. Explanatory variables in the wage equation include a measure of the mother's score on a standardized achievement test, her race/ethnicity, her education, nine regional indicators, and a dummy variable indicating whether the locality is a metropolitan statistical area (MSA). We use the estimated wage rate for all observations in the child outcome equations based on our belief that the predicted value is the best estimate of a woman's long-term wage.

FATHER'S WAGE. We calculate wage levels for fathers (or male partners) by dividing mother-reported total annual spouse earnings in the preceding calendar year by the product of usual spouse paid work hours per week and total spouse weeks worked in that year. For nonworking fathers, a wage is estimated as described above. If no father is present, the variable is set equal to zero.

NONLABOR INCOME. The NLSY79 reports calendar year income derived from returns on savings accounts, stock dividends, rents, inheritances, public transfers, and other sources. Gifts, such as from parents or grandparents, also are included. These variables are aggregated to a single nonlabor income measure.

WEALTH. Wealth is reported annually in the NLSY79, and it includes financial assets, value of owned home, other real estate, owned businesses, autos, and other durables. Debts also are reported; thus our measure is of net worth (deflated). These data have been compared to age adjusted wealth data in the Survey of Consumer Finances and found to be similar (Haurin, Hendershott, Wachter, 1996).

Control Variables: Sociodemographic

FAMILY SIZE. Blake (1989), Parcel and Menaghan (1994a), and Downey (1995) argue that the number of siblings affects the time and monetary resources available for each child. Their studies find that as the number of siblings increases, child outcomes are negatively affected.

MATERNAL MARITAL HISTORY. Mothers' marital history may influence child outcomes (Haurin, 1992; Rogers, Parcel, and Menaghan, 1991). Marital history indicates the stability of past relationships, an important input to social capital formation. We represent mothers' marital history with a series of four dummy variables. With the reference category being mothers who were married throughout the duration of the child's life, the dummy variables are: single for the duration of the child's life ("Single"); single during the birth year and married during the interview year ("Get married"); married during the birth year, divorced/separated/widowed once or more subsequently, and not remarried at the survey date ("Marital breakup"); and married during the birth year, divorced/separated/widowed once or more subsequently, and remarried at the survey date ("Remarry").

MATERNAL BACKGROUND CHARACTERISTICS. Eight mothers' background characteristics are included in the child outcome equations. They are ethnicity, age, highest grade completed (HGC), mental ability,[1] level of religiosity (Haurin and Mott, 1990),[2] the type of household in which the mother resided when she was age 14,[3] maternal mastery,[4] and the number of paid hours of work during the child's first three years of life ("Total hours mom work, yrs. 1–3") (Parcel and Menaghan, 1994b).

PATERNAL BACKGROUND CHARACTERISTICS. Father's age and highest grade completed (HGC) are included in the data set if he resides in the household. If a male partner is present in the household, we include his age and schooling.

CHILD CHARACTERISTICS. We include a child's gender, health limitations, and indicator of low birth weight (below four pounds) (Mott, 1991; Parcel and Menaghan, 1994a).

1 . The AFQT consists of the sum of scores on four subtests of the Armed Services Vocational Aptitude Battery, including word knowledge, paragraph comprehension, numeric operations, and arithmetic reasoning. Details are provided in Baker and others (1993).

2 . We include five dummy variables showing the mother's frequency of church attendance. The omitted category is no attendance, the dummy variables are "church attendance-low" (up to once per month), "church attendance-some" (two to three times per month), "church attendance-often" (once per week), and "church attendance-high" (more than once per week).

3 . We use a series of three dummy variables to define cases where the child's mother was living with both parents when she was age 14 (omitted case), was living with her mother and no other man ("Mom-alone"), was living with her mother and some other man such as a stepfather or other male relative ("Mom-pair"), and was living in some other arrangement such as with only her father (Mom-other).

4 . The Rotter scale assesses the degree to which a woman feels that she has control over the direction of her life, can follow through with the plans she makes, can get what she wants without relying on luck, and has influence over the things that happen to her. A higher value on the scale indicates a higher degree of control.

Table 15-2. *Sample Means of the Dependent Variables*

Variable	*1988*	*1990*	*1992*	*1994*
HOME: Cognitive/physical	45.8	47.4	49.9	45.5
HOME: Emotional	46.0	47.1	47.7	46.7
PIAT: Mathematics	45.7	46.8	46.5	46.1
PIAT: Reading	55.4	55.4	54.2	52.5
Behavior problems	64.8	65.6	65.9	66.8
Homeownership rate	0.35	0.38	0.42	0.45
Duration of homeownership	1.52	2.06	2.65	3.26

Source: National Longitudinal Survey of Youth (Washington: Center for Human Resources Research, 1994).

Control Variables: Community Factors

A large literature addresses the link between the quality of neighborhood and child outcomes. Jencks and Mayer (1990) review the literature and conclude that knowledge is better regarding neighborhood effects on adolescents than on children. Crane (1991a) finds evidence to support an "epidemic" model of social problems such that the incidence of problems increases nonlinearly as the quality of neighborhoods declines; in particular, the risk that both black and white adolescents will have a child and drop out of school increases sharply in the worst neighborhoods of large cities (Crane, 1991b). Brooks-Gunn and others (1993) investigate neighborhood effects on outcomes for both adolescents and children. They find that there are effects of neighborhood affluence on the IQ level of 3-year-old low-birth-weight children even when some family influences are controlled. In related work, Duncan, Brooks-Gunn, and Klebanov (1994) find positive net effects of higher concentrations of affluent neighbors on the IQ level of 5-year-old children and negative effects on externalizing behavior problems from higher concentrations of low-income neighbors net of individual-level predictors.

Our county-level measures of neighborhood variables include median household income, population density, percent black, percent Hispanic, unemployment rate, poverty rate, crime rate, and average level of education (percent high school graduates and percent with some college).

Results

We next describe the characteristics of the sample and discuss the results of testing the models of child outcomes. Means of the key variables are listed in table 15-2 by survey year. The number of observations is the same in each of the four years in the panel data set: 1,026 households, yielding 4,104 total observations.

Means of the explanatory variables are listed in table 15-3. The relatively high percentage of black children results from the NLSY-C's sample comprising relatively young mothers and the NLSY79's oversampling of black youth.

Table 15-3. *Sample Means of Explanatory Variables*

Variable	*Mean*
Male	0.50
Black	0.35
Mexican Hispanic	0.03
Other Hispanic	0.02
Health limit	0.04
Low birth weight	0.07
Mother's highest grade completed (HGC)	11.77
Mother's age	31.00
Mother's achievement test score (AFQT)	31.16
Church attendance-low	0.25
Church attendance-some	0.24
Church attendance-often	0.23
Church attendance-high	0.11
Total hours mom work, years 1–3 (000)	1.68
Crime rate index	58.61
Percent Hispanic	9.20
Percent in poverty	10.91
Median community income ($000)	19.12
Percent black	13.89
Mom-alone[a]	0.20
Mom-pair[b]	0.10
Mom-other[c]	0.09
Maternal mastery	2.27
Mother's wage	8.23
Siblings	1.67
Father's age[d]	34.83
Father's HGC[d]	12.27
Father's wage[d]	12.78
Nonlabor income ($000)	5.30
Wealth ($000)	4.70
Single	0.17
Get married	0.10
Remarry	0.26
Marital breakup	0.12
Population density (000)	16.28
Unemployment rate	7.24
Percent high school educated	49.38
Percent college educated	14.66

Source: National Longitudinal Survey of Youth (Washington: Center for Human Resources Research, 1994).

a. Mother raised by her mother.

b. Mother raised by her mother and another man.

c. Mother raised by some other combination.

d. The mean is for only fathers or partners present in the household.

Table 15-4. *Means for Households Who Were Homeowners throughout 1988–94, Renters throughout 1988–94, and Those Who Changed Tenure Status*

Variable	*Owner*	*Renter*	*Changed tenure*
HOME: Cognitive/physical	60.1	38.1	50.4
HOME: Emotional	61.3	37.3	48.8
PIAT: Mathematics	54.7	40.1	48.5
PIAT: Reading	63.3	48.2	56.1
Behavior problems	62.5	68.0	65.0

Source: National Longitudinal Survey of Youth (Washington: Center for Human Resources Research, 1994).

Table 15-4 lists the means of the dependent variables for three groups: those owning from 1988 to 1994, those renting during the same period, and those changing tenure status.[5] There are substantial differences in the means of the dependent variables for the three groups, with the children of renters scoring lower on the math and reading assessments, having more behavioral problems, and living in lower-rated home environments. The means for those households in transition are between those of continuous renters and continuous owners. The key question is whether these differences are due to differences in tenure status or differences in other influential variables.

Estimation Results

In the home environment estimation, we find that being a homeowner is highly significant and that it improves the index of the cognitive/physical environment by 23 percent, ceteris paribus. Other significant variables with positive impacts include mother's AFQT, mother's education, mother's age (with a declining marginal impact), and the church attendance variables. Significant variables with negative impacts include the child's gender being male, mother's race being black, number of siblings, and the locality's percentage of households in poverty.

In the emotional support home environment estimation we find that being a homeowner is significant and strong. It improves the index of emotional support in the home environment by 13 percent, ceteris paribus. Other significant variables with positive impacts include mother's age (declining marginal impact), father's age, and mother's education. Significant variables with negative impacts include being black, having a greater number of siblings, and the mother's marital history (being single, being remarried, or becoming divorced/separated/widowed rather than being continuously married). The negative effects of ending a marriage or remarrying upon the measure of the emotional support in the home are large.

5 . By far the most changes in tenure for this sample of young households were from renting to owning.

We conclude that homeownership affects the levels of the cognitive stimulation/physical environment and emotional support environment of the home in which a child lives. This result is quite plausible. An implication is that homeownership may affect a child's cognitive and behavior outcomes through multiple routes, including changes in the home environment and changes in household stability.

With regard to child outcomes, in the mathematics achievement equation we find that significant explanatory variables (at the 5 percent level) with positive coefficients include the cognitive/physical and emotional support home environment scales, mother's achievement test score (AFQT), mother's and father's education, a frequent or high level of church attendance, neighborhood median income, and the neighborhood poverty rate.[6] Significant variables with negative coefficients include low birth weight and a greater number of siblings.

The homeownership variable has a positive coefficient and is significant at the 10 percent level in the PIAT-Math estimation. Accepting the point estimate of the homeownership variable implies that being a homeowner directly raises PIAT-Mathematics by 3.4 points, this change representing a 7 percent increase. Further, being a homeowner raises the value of HOME-C by 10.7 points and HOME-E by 5.9 points. The calculated indirect impact of homeowning on PIAT-Mathematics through an improved home environment is 0.8 points. Combined, the total impact of homeownership on a child's mathematical cognitive outcome is to raise it about 9 percent over that of a child in a family that rents, holding constant a host of social, demographic, and economic variables.

The second set of results is for the measure of a child's reading recognition. Significant explanatory variables with positive coefficients include HOME-C, HOME-E, mother's AFQT, mother's mastery, and a high level of church attendance. Negative and significant effects occur for male children, more siblings, and a high local unemployment rate.

The homeownership indicator has a positive coefficient and is significant at the 10 percent level in the PIAT-Reading estimation. The point estimate suggests that being a homeowner raises PIAT-Reading directly by 3.2 points and indirectly by 0.7 points. These results indicate that residence in an owned home raises a child's reading score by about 7 percent over that for a child in a household that rents.

The final results are for the index of a child's behavior problems (BPI). The expected coefficient signs are the opposite of those for the models of cognition. Negative and significant coefficients occur for HOME-C, HOME-E, and mother's mastery. Significant and positive coefficients occur for male children, children with health limitations, and children whose mothers divorce and remarry.

6. The measures of the community's attributes are highly correlated; thus it is difficult to identify separate impacts.

The homeownership indicator has the expected negative coefficient, but it is not significant. According to the point estimate for a homeowner, compared with that for a similar renter, homeowning directly reduces the measure of the child's behavior problems by 1.7 points, equal to 2.6 percent of the mean value of the BPI. Homeownership also changes the cognitive/physical and emotional support home environments, this change further reducing the BPI by 0.9 points. The cumulative impact is that homeownership reduces the index of child behavior problems by about 3 percent, but the lack of statistical significance suggests that the impact could be only 1 percent.

Conclusion

In the United States, homeownership receives public sector encouragement and subsidies. The largest subsidy occurs through tax reductions such as the mortgage interest deduction, the nontaxation of capital gains, and the lack of taxation of the imputed rental income of owner-occupiers. In addition, many programs in HUD encourage homeownership, and Fannie Mae and Freddie Mac have to meet various federal regulations regarding underwriting home loans.

Although increasing the homeownership rate is a goal of the federal government, relatively little is known about the impact of homeowning on the resident households. Mentioned in support of the programs is the claim that homeowning is a good method for lower- and middle-income households to build wealth. Also mentioned are claims that homeowners are better citizens with higher levels of participation in local government, community affairs, and local schools. Another claim is that homeowners have higher levels of investment in their properties and in their neighborhood. A few studies have begun to test these claims and better estimate the impact of homeownership upon the resident households and surrounding community. We add to this literature by analyzing the impact of homeowning on the cognitive and behavioral outcomes of a household's young children.

There is a very large literature devoted to the study of child outcomes. This literature suggests that a long list of control variables is needed if one is to attempt to isolate the impact of a single variable such as homeownership status. We use four waves of a national data set to permit a panel data analysis of the relationship of owning a home to three child outcomes, including math and reading cognition and a measure of behavior problems. The wide scope of the data in the survey allows us to include as control variables social, demographic, and economic variables suggested by previous studies of child outcomes.

Our results are consistent with the following conclusions. First, we find that, when compared with renting, owning a home leads to a higher-quality home environment, where home environment is measured by indexes of the cognitive support/physical environment and the emotional support of children in that home. Second, we find that a child's cognitive outcomes are up to 9 percent higher in math achievement and 7 percent higher in reading achievement for children living in owned homes, ceteris paribus. Third, we find that the measure of a child's behavior problems is up to 3 percent lower if the child resides in an owned home. Existing literature suggests that these youths' greater cognitive abilities and fewer behavioral problems will result in higher educational attainment, greater future earnings, and a reduced tendency to engage in deviant behaviors. These results occur even when we control for numerous parental economic, demographic, and social characteristics. We also control for the child's gender and health, number of siblings, and nine characteristics of the household's locality. Thus, in a well-controlled study, we find substantial support for the hypothesis that homeownership increases child cognition and reduces behavior problems.

Policy Implications

Housing policies in support of homeownership are often targeted at particular groups or types of localities. Our finding that homeownership enhances child outcomes suggests that housing policies should be targeted at rental households that have children. In 2000, 22 percent of all married households with children are renters and 57 percent of other household types with children are renters. Quickening these groups' transitions from renting to owning would expose their children to better home environments and to homeownership for a longer period. We recommend further analysis of the impact of homeownership on children living in single-parent families to determine if there is justification for additional encouragement of homeownership among single mothers.

There continues to be illegal discrimination in the housing market, particularly regarding aspects of the search process for owner-occupied housing (Yinger, 1986) and possibly with regard to the mortgage lending process and outcomes (Berkovec and others, 1994; Ross, 2000). Our study supports the conclusion that any reduction in homeownership due to illegal discrimination also has the effect of reducing the level of cognition and increasing the behavioral problems of the children of households that are the targets of discrimination. Reducing illegal discrimination may both help solve the problem of spatial mismatch of jobs and residences and result in long-term gains of the children in these households.

A final observation about policy is that there is continuous discussion of K-through-12 educational reforms ranging from reducing class size in public schools to education vouchers. The goal of these in-school input-oriented programs is to improve child cognition. We find that significant improvement in child cognition results from homeownership and an improved home environment. In contrast to the most often suggested educational reforms, our analysis is of the out-of-school environment. Hanushek (1986, 1996) finds mixed results about the educational value of additional in-school inputs, including expenditures per pupil. Thus the general policy effort to improve the educational attainment of children should consider innovative programs that encourage homeownership of targeted households as alternatives to additional government expenditures on school inputs.

Appendix 15A: Measurement of the Home Environment

Details about the wording of the questions, coding of the questions, and creation of the indexes are in Baker and others (1993); see pp. 85–95, table 5.5.1 (p. 158), and appendix B.

The cognitive support/physical environment HOME scale for 3-to-5-year-old children includes responses to fifteen items:

QUESTION TO CHILD'S MOTHER:

1. How often do you read stories to your child?
2. How many books does your child have?
3. How many magazines does your family receive?
4. Does your child have use of a record player, tape deck, or CD player and at least five records, tapes, or CDs?
5. Have you or another adult or older sibling helped your child learn numbers at home?
6. Same as 5, but alphabet?
7. Same as 5, but colors?
8. Same as 5, but shapes and sizes?
9. How often does a family member take your child on an outing?
10. How often does a family member take your child to a museum?

INTERVIEWER OBSERVATIONS:

11. Is the child's *play environment* safe where safe is defined as no structural or health hazards (frayed wires, falling plaster, peeling paint, broken glass, rodents, poisons)?
12. Is the interior of the house dark or perceptually monotonous?
13. Are all rooms in the house/apartment visibly clean?
14. Are all rooms of the house minimally cluttered?
15. Does the *building* have potentially dangerous structural or health hazards; for example, falling plaster, peeling paint, rodents, glass, poisons and cleaning materials, flames and heat, frayed electrical wires?

The cognitive support/physical environment HOME scale for children ages 6 to 9 includes fourteen items:

QUESTION TO CHILD'S MOTHER:

1. How often do you read stories to your child?

2. How many books does your child have?

3. Is there a musical instrument that your child can play at home?

4. Does your family get a daily newspaper?

5. How often does your child read for enjoyment?

6. Does your family encourage your child to start and keep doing hobbies?

7. Does your child get lessons or belong to any organization than encourages sports, music, art, dance, drama, etc.?

8. How often has any family member taken your child to a museum within the last year?

9. How often has a family member taken your child to any type of musical or theatrical performance in the last year?

INTERVIEWER OBSERVATIONS:

10. Is the child's *play environment* safe where safe is defined as no structural or health hazards (frayed wires, falling plaster, peeling paint, broken glass, rodents, poisons)?

11. Is the interior of the house dark or perceptually monotonous?

12. Are all rooms in the house/apartment visibly clean?

13. Are all rooms of the house minimally cluttered?

14. Does the *building* have potentially dangerous structural or health hazards; for example, falling plaster, peeling paint, rodents, glass, poisons and cleaning materials, flames and heat, frayed electrical wires?

The cognitive support/physical environment HOME scale for children age 10 and above includes twelve items:

QUESTION TO CHILD'S MOTHER:

1. How many books does your child have?

2. Is there a musical instrument that your child can play at home?

3. Does your family get a daily newspaper?

4. How often does your child read for enjoyment?

5. Does your family encourage your child to start and keep doing hobbies?

6. Does your child get lessons or belong to any organization than encourages sports, music, art, dance, drama, etc.?

7. How often has any family member taken your child to a museum within the last year?

8. How often has a family member taken your child to any type of musical or theatrical performance in the last year?

INTERVIEWER OBSERVATIONS:

9. Is the child's *play environment* safe where safe is defined as no structural or health hazards (frayed wires, falling plaster, peeling paint, broken glass, rodents, poisons)?

10. Is the interior of the house dark or perceptually monotonous?

11. Are all rooms in the house/apartment visibly clean?
12. Are all rooms of the house minimally cluttered?

The emotional support HOME scale for 3-to-5-year-old children includes responses to twelve items:

QUESTION TO CHILD'S MOTHER:

1. How much choice does your child have in deciding what foods to eat?
2. How many hours per day is the TV in your home playing?
3. If your child was so angry that he/she hit you, would you hit back, send him/her to his/her room, spank him/her, talk to him/her, ignore it, give him/her a household chore, take away his/her allowance, hold the child's hands until he/she was calm?
4. Does your child ever see his or her father, stepfather, or father figure?
5. How often does your child eat a meal with both mother and father (or equivalent)?

INTERVIEWER OBSERVATIONS:

6. Did the mother spontaneously speak to the child twice or more?
7. Did the mother respond verbally to the child's speech?
8. Did the mother hug, caress, or kiss the child at least once?
9. Did the mother slap or spank the child?
10. Did the mother interfere with the child's actions or restrict him/her from exploring?
11. Did the mother provide toys or interesting activities for the child?
12. Did the mother keep the child in view?

The emotional support HOME scale for children age 6 and older includes thirteen items:

QUESTION TO CHILD'S MOTHER:

1. How often does your whole family get together with relatives or friends?
2. How many hours per weekday does your child watch TV?
3. How many hours per weekend day does your child watch TV?
4. If your child brought home a report card with grades lower than expected, how likely would you: lecture the child, talk with the child, punish the child, wait and see, tell child to spend more time on homework, help the child with homework, contact the teacher?
5. If your child was so angry that he/she said I hate you or swore at you, how would you react: grounding, spank him/her, talk to him/her, ignore it, give him/her a household chore, take away his/her allowance, take away TV or other privileges, send to his/her room for more than one hour?

4. Does your child ever see his or her father, stepfather, or father figure?
5. How often does your child eat a meal with both mother and father (or equivalent)?

6. When your family watches TV together, do you or the father discuss the program with the child?

7. How often does your child spend time with his/her father in outdoor activities?

8. How much time does your child spend with his/her father?

INTERVIEWER OBSERVATIONS:

9. Did the mother encourage the child to contribute to the conversation?

10. Did the mother answer the child's questions?

11. Did the mother converse with the child excluding scolding?

12. Did the mother introduce the interviewer to the child by name?

13. Did the mother's voice convey positive feelings about the child?

References

Aaronson, Daniel. 2000. "A Note on the Benefits of Homeownership." *Journal of Urban Economics* 47 (3): 356–369.

Achenbach, Thomas S., and Craig Edelbrock. 1981. "Behavioral Problems and Competencies Reported by Parents of Normal and Disturbed Children Aged Four through Sixteen." *Monographs of the Society for Research in Child Development* 46 (1): 1–82.

———. 1983. *Manual for the Child Behavior Checklist and Revised Child Behavior Profile.* Department of Psychiatry, University of Vermont.

Achenbach, Thomas, Stephanie H. McConaughy, and Catherine T. Howell. 1987. "Child/Adolescent Behavioral and Emotional Problems: Implications of Cross-Informant Correlations for Situational Specificity." *Psychological Bulletin* 101 (2): 213–32.

Baker, Paula C., Canada Keck, Frank L. Mott, and Steve Quinlan. 1993. *NLSY Child Handbook.* Revised edition. Center for Human Resource Research, Ohio State University.

Becker, Gary. 1965. "A Theory of the Allocation of Time." *Economic Journal* 75 (2): 493–517.

Berkovec, J. A., G. B. Canner, S. A. Gabriel, and T. H. Hannan. 1994. "Race, Redlining, and Residential Mortgage Loan Performance." *Journal of Real Estate Finance and Economics* 9 (3): 263–94.

Blake, Judith. 1989. *Family Size and Achievement.* University of California Press.

Boehm, Thomas P., and Tracy M. Gordon. 1999. "Does Homeownership by Parents Have an Economic Impact on Their Children?" *Journal of Housing Economics* 8 (3): 217–32.

Bourassa, Steven, Donald R. Haurin, R. Jean Haurin, and Patric H. Hendershott. 1994. "Independent Living and Homeownership: An Analysis of Australian Youth." *Australian Economic Review* 107 (July–Sept.): 29–45.

Bradley, Robert H. 1985. "The Home Inventory: Rationale and Research." In *Recent Research in Developmental Psychopathology, Book Supplement to the Journal of Child Psychology and Psychiatry,* edited by J. Lachenmeyer and M. Gibbs. New York: Gardner.

Bradley, Robert H., and Bettye M. Caldwell. 1981. The HOME Inventory: A Validation of the Pre-School Scale for Black Children. *Child Development* 52 (2): 708–10.

———. 1984a. "The HOME Inventory and Family Demographics." *Developmental Psychology* 20 (2): 315–20.

———. 1984b. The Relation of Infants' Home Environments to Achievement Test Performance in First Grade: A Follow-Up Study. *Child Development* 55 (3): 803–809.

Bradley, Robert H., Bettye M. Caldwell, Stephen L. Rock, Holly M. Hamrick, and Pandia Harris. 1988. "Home Observation for Measurement of the Environment: Development of a Home Inventory for Use with Families Having Children 6 to 10 Years Old." *Contemporary Educational Psychology* 13 (1): 58–71.

Brooks-Gunn, Jeanne, Greg J. Duncan, Pamela Kato Kelbanov, and Naomi Sealand. 1993. "Do Neighborhoods Influence Child and Adolescent Development?" *American Journal of Sociology* 99 (2): 353–95.

Caldwell, Bettye, and R. Bradley. 1984. "Home Observation for Measurement of the Environment." Working Paper. University of Arkansas, Little Rock.

Caspi, Avshalom, Glen H. Elder Jr., and Daryl J. Bem. 1987. "Moving against the World: Life-Course Patterns of Explosive Children. *Developmental Psychology* 23 (2): 308–13.

Center for Human Resource Research. 1994. *NLSY Child Handbook*. Columbus, Ohio.

Crane, Jonathan. 1991a. "The Epidemic Theory of Ghettos and Neighborhood Effects on Dropping Out and Teenage Childbearing." *American Journal of Sociology* 96 (5): 1226–59.

———. 1991b. "Effects of Neighborhoods on Dropping Out of School and Teenage Childbearing." In *The Urban Underclass*, edited by Christopher Jencks and Paul E. Peterson. Washington: Urban Institute.

Currie, Janet, and Aaron Yelowitz. 2000. "Are Public Housing Projects Good for Kids?" *Journal of Public Economics* 75 (1): 99–124.

Downey, Doug. 1995. "When Bigger Is Not Better: Number of Siblings, Parental Resources, and Educational Performance." *American Sociological Review* 60 (5): 746–61.

Duncan, Greg J., Jeanne Brooks-Gunn, and Pamela Kato Klebanov. 1994. "Economic Deprivation and Early Childhood Development." *Child Development* 65 (2): 296–318.

Engelhardt, Gary. 1994. "House Prices and the Decision to Save for Down Payments." *Journal of Urban Economics* 36 (2): 209–37.

Executive Office of the President. 2000. *The Fiscal Year 2001 Budget of the United States*. Government Printing Office.

Forgatch, M. S., G. R. Patterson, and M. L. Skinner. 1988. "A Mediational Model for the Effect of Divorce on Antisocial Behavior in Boys." In *Impact of Divorce, Single Parenting, and Step-Parenting on Children*, edited by E. M. Hetherington and J. D. Arestah. Hillsdale, N.J.: Erlbaum.

Graham, Philip J., and Michael Rutter. 1968. "The Reliability and Validity of the Psychiatric Assessment of the Child II: Interview with the Parent." *British Journal of Psychiatry* 114 (2): 581–92.

Green, Richard, and Michelle White. 1997. "Measuring the Benefits of Homeowning: Effects on Children." *Journal of Urban Economics* 41 (3): 441–61.

Greene, William. 1993. *Econometric Analysis*. 2d edition. Macmillan.

———. 1995. *LIMDEP, Version 7.0 User's Manual*. Bellport, N.Y.: Econometric Software.

Hanushek, E. A. 1986. "The Economics of Schooling: Production and Efficiency in Public Schools." *Journal of Economic Literature* 24 (3): 1141–77.

———. 1996. "School Resources and Student Performance." In *Does Money Matter? The Effect of School Resources on Student Achievement and Adult Success*, edited by G. Burtless. Brookings.

Hanushek, E. A., J. Kain, and S. Rivkin. 1999. "The Costs of Switching Schools." Working Paper. Rochester University.

Haurin, Donald R., Patric H. Hendershott, and Susan Wachter. 1996. "Wealth Accumulation and Housing Choices of Young Households: An Exploratory Investigation." *Journal of Housing Research* 7 (1): 33–57.

Haurin, R. Jean. 1992. "Patterns of Childhood Residence and the Relationship to Young Adult Outcomes." *Journal of Marriage and the Family* 54 (4): 846–60.

Haurin, R. Jean, and F. Mott. 1990. "Adolescent Sexual Activity in the Family Context: The Impact of Older Siblings." *Demography* 27 (4): 537–57.

Haveman, Robert, and Barbara Wolfe. 1995. "The Determinants of Children's Attainments: A Review of Methods and Findings." *Journal of Economic Literature* 33 (4): 1829–78.

Heckman, James. 1979. "Sample Selection Bias as a Specification Error." *Econometrica* 47 (1): 153–61.

Jencks, Christopher, and Susan Mayer. 1990. "The Social Consequences of Growing Up in a Poor Neighborhood." In *Inner-City Poverty in the United States*, edited by Laurence Lynn Jr. and Michael McGeary. Washington: National Academy Press.

Kellam, Sheppard G., Jeannette D. Branch, Khazan C. Agrawal, and Margaret E. Ensminger. 1975. *Mental Health and Going to School.* University of Chicago Press.

Kohlberg, Laurence, Jean LaCrosse, and David Ricks. 1972. "The Predictability of Adult Mental Health from Childhood Behavior." In *Manual of Child Psychopathology*, edited by B. B. Wolman. McGraw-Hill.

Kohn, Melvin L. 1977. *Class and Conformity, A Study in Values.* 2d edition. University of Chicago Press.

Mechanic, David. 1980. *Mental Health and Social Policy.* 2d edition. Englewood Cliffs, N.J.: Prentice-Hall.

Menaghan, Elizabeth G., and Toby L. Parcel. 1991. "Determining Children's Home Environments: The Impact of Maternal Characteristics and Current Occupational and Family Conditions." *Journal of Marriage and the Family* 53 (2): 417–31.

———. 1995. "Social Sources of Change in Children's Home Environments: The Effects of Parental Occupational Experiences and Family Conditions." *Journal of Marriage and the Family* 57 (1): 1–16.

Mott, Frank. 1991. "Developmental Effects of Infant Care: The Mediating Role of Gender and Health." *Journal of Social Issues* 47 (2): 139–58.

Office of Federal Housing Enterprise Oversight. 1998. *House Price Index.* Washington.

Parcel, Toby L., and Elizabeth G. Menaghan. 1993. "Family Social Capital and Children's Behavior Problems." *Social Psychology Quarterly* 56 (2): 120–35.

———. 1994a. *Parents' Jobs and Children's Lives.* New York: Aldine De Gruyter.

———. 1994b. "Early Parental Work, Family Social Capital and Early Childhood Outcomes." *American Journal of Sociology* 99 (4): 972–1009.

Ramey, C. T., K. Yeates, and E. Short. 1984. "The Plasticity of Intellectual Development: Insights from Preventive Intervention." *Child Development* 55 (5): 1913–25.

Rogers, Stacy, Toby L. Parcel, and Elizabeth G. Menaghan. 1991. "The Effects of Maternal Working Conditions and Mastery on Child Behavior Problems: Studying the Intergenerational Transmission of Social Control." *Journal of Health and Social Behavior* 32 (2): 145–64.

Ross, Steven L. 2000. "Mortgage Lending, Sample Selection and Default." *Real Estate Economics* 28 (4): 581–621.

Rotter, Julian B. 1966. "Generalized Expectancies for Internal vs. External Control of Reinforcements." *Psychological Monographs* 80 (1): 1–28.

Rutter, Michael. 1970. "Sex Differences in Children's Responses to Family Stress. In *The Child in His Family*, edited by E. J. Anthony and C. Koupernik. Wiley.

Yeates, K., D. MacPhee, F. Campbell, and C. Ramey. 1983. "Maternal IQ and Home Environment as Determinants of Early Childhood Intellectual Competence: A Developmental Analysis." *Developmental Psychology* 19 (5): 731–39.

Yinger, John. 1986. "Measuring Racial-Discrimination with Fair Housing Audits—Caught in the Act." *American Economic Review* 76: 881–93.

Zill, Nicholas. 1988. "Behavior, Achievement, and Health Problems among Children in Stepfamilies: Findings from a National Survey of Child Health." In *The Impact of Divorce, Single Parenting, and Step-Parenting on Children*, edited by E. M. Hetherington and J. D. Arasteh. Hillsdale, N.J.: Erlbaum.

16

Building Homes, Reviving Neighborhoods: Spillovers from Subsidized Construction of Owner-Occupied Housing in New York City

INGRID GOULD ELLEN, MICHAEL H. SCHILL,
SCOTT SUSIN, AND AMY ELLEN SCHWARTZ

Promoting homeownership has always been a central aim of housing policy in the United States. The federal tax code delivers generous tax benefits to homeowners, the Federal Housing Administration (FHA) provides insurance on high loan-to-value mortgages, a variety of other FHA and state programs have offered below-market interest rates, and the Community Reinvestment Act of 1977 provides incentives for financial institutions to make mortgage loans in low- and moderate-income communities. As cities have become more centrally involved in implementing housing policy, local officials have also begun to sponsor a large number of homeownership programs in distressed communities.

Although these efforts typically do not reach the poorest households, they are justified in large part by the positive spillovers that many argue will result from the development of new homes and by homeownership itself.[1] There is little empirical evidence, however, about the impact of home building and homeown-

The authors would like to thank the Fannie Mae Foundation for financial support and Isaac Megbolugbe and Amy Bogdon for their substantive contributions. They would also like to thank Denise DiPasquale, Frank DeGiovanni, and Eric Belsky for comments on an earlier draft, Ioan Voicu for excellent research assistance, and Jerilyn Perine, Richard Roberts, Harold Shultz, and Calvin Parker of the New York City Department of Housing Preservation and Development and Chuck Brass and Sal D'Avola of the New York City Housing Partnership for providing the data necessary to complete this research. This work was first published in the *Journal of Housing Research* 12 (2): 185–216.

1. Some cities may also support homeownership programs as an attempt to retain the middle class.

ership on local communities. In this chapter, we examine and compare the impact of two of New York City's major homeownership programs on property values in surrounding communities. Both of these programs, the Nehemiah Plan and the New Homes Program of the New York City Housing Partnership, subsidize the construction of affordable, owner-occupied homes in distressed urban neighborhoods.

Spillover Effects of Homeownership and Housing Redevelopment

There are several reasons that the Nehemiah Plan and the Partnership New Homes program might be expected to raise the value of surrounding properties. First, both replace blighted properties or land with new structures. Unlike most commodities, housing is fixed in space, and the value of a home is therefore influenced not only by its structural features and quality but also by its surroundings. The appearance of neighboring homes, the level of noise and disorder in a community, and the quality of local public services are all likely to contribute to the value of a particular home. Thus housing investments in blighted areas should, in principle, generate spillover benefits that could be capitalized into the value of surrounding properties.

Second, these housing programs may have bolstered the number of homeowners in their communities, which may in itself lead to higher property values if, for example, their greater financial stake leads homeowners to take better care of their homes than renters do.[2] Similarly, homeowners may be more involved in local organizations and activities either because of their financial stake or because they tend to stay in their homes for a longer period of time, or for both reasons. Again, these factors may improve the quality of life in a community and raise property values.[3]

These programs may also affect property values because they lead to a population change in the neighborhood. Because homeowners typically earn higher incomes than renters, the community's socioeconomic status may increase. In addition, property values may increase as a result of the population growth that occurs as vacant land is transformed into housing. This population growth may in turn lead to new commercial activity and economic growth, making the neighborhood increasingly desirable.

Finally, as Galster (1987) explains, exogenous changes to the "physical demographic character of a neighborhood" may change expectations about the future

2. Absentee landlords and homeowners have similar financial stakes in the properties they own. But the argument is that because they do not live in the property, absentee landlords are not able to control the day-to-day upkeep in the same way that homeowners can.

3. There is, in fact, little empirical evidence that homeowners do make such social and economic investments. See DiPasquale and Glaeser (1999), Rohe, Van Zandt, and McCarthy (2000), and Dietz and Haurin (2001) for evidence and discussion.

of the community and influence individual mobility decisions and investments in upkeep. As vacant and derelict land is converted into habitable housing, nearby property owners may decide to remain in the community rather than move away. They may also be more likely to invest in maintaining their own homes, thereby generating additional positive neighborhood effects.[4]

There is little work that actually examines the neighborhood spillover effects generated by the subsidized construction of owner-occupied homes. More work has focused on the relationship between investments in publicly subsidized *rental* housing and neighborhood property values. These studies offer conflicting evidence. Nourse (1963) and Rabiega, Lin, and Robinson (1984) find that newly developed public housing can have modest positive impacts on neighboring property values, while Lyons and Loveridge (1993), Goetz, Lam, and Heitlinger (1996), and Lee, Culhane, and Wachter (1999) all find small, statistically significant negative effects on property values associated with the presence of certain types of federally subsidized housing in a neighborhood. Moreover, in all of these studies, data limitations make it difficult to pinpoint the direction of causality. Are subsidized sites systematically located in weak (strong) neighborhoods, or does subsidized housing lead to neighborhood decline (improvement)? These studies typically compare price levels in neighborhoods with subsidized housing with price levels in neighborhoods without subsidized housing, but it is difficult to know whether the two groups of neighborhoods are truly comparable.

Two more recent studies of subsidized rental housing have made strides to overcome this causality problem. Briggs, Darden, and Aidala (1999) examine the early effects of seven scattered-site public housing developments on property values in neighborhoods in Yonkers, New York. Using a pre/post design with census tract fixed effects, they find little effect on the surrounding area. Santiago, Galster, and Tatian (2001) examine whether the acquisition and rehabilitation of property to create scattered-site public housing in Denver influenced the sales prices of surrounding single-family homes. The authors also use a pre/post design with localized fixed effects and find that proximity to dispersed public housing units is, if anything, typically associated with an increase in the prices of single-family homes.[5]

In short, there is no consensus about the effects of investments in subsidized rental housing on surrounding property values, although recent research suggests negligible or small positive effects. As noted, the research on the spillover

4. All of these changes are also likely to increase the flow of capital into the neighborhood by decreasing risk. An increase in the availability of bank financing for home purchase and improvement loans is likely to increase the liquidity and price of housing in the neighborhood. It will also facilitate unsubsidized rehabilitation of housing; see Galster (1987, p. 19).

5. Santiago, Galster, and Tatian (2001) also control for past *trends* in housing prices in the immediate vicinity of a project, so they test for both changes in price levels and trends after completion. This methodology is shown first in Galster, Tatian, and Smith (1999).

effects of homeownership programs is far thinner. We found only two studies that examine the impact of publicly assisted homeownership programs.[6] Lee, Culhane, and Wachter (1999) find that FHA-insured units and units developed through the Philadelphia Housing Authority's homeownership program both have positive impacts on surrounding house prices. This is the opposite of the study's overall conclusions concerning rental housing.[7] Cummings, DiPasquale, and Kahn (2000) study the effect of two Nehemiah housing developments in Philadelphia. The authors compare price trends in the census tracts that contained these developments with trends in similarly distressed tracts elsewhere in the city, using methods somewhat similar to ours.[8] They find no statistically significant spillover effects, but because they only have two developments in the city to evaluate, their confidence intervals are quite wide, and they can rule out neither large positive nor large negative effects.[9]

New York City Housing Programs

In 1986, New York City launched an unprecedented initiative to rebuild its housing stock that had been devastated in the 1970s. Between 1987 and mid-1999, the city's housing agency (the Department of Housing Preservation and Development, hereafter HPD) invested close to five billion dollars in the construction of over 22,000 homes, the gut rehabilitation of more than 43,000 units of formerly vacant housing, and the moderate rehabilitation of over 97,000 units of occupied housing.[10] Most of these efforts have focused on low- and moderate-income rental housing, but a few programs sponsor homeownership.

The Nehemiah Plan

The Nehemiah Plan was launched in the early 1980s by East Brooklyn Churches, a group of thirty-six churches in Brooklyn. The Nehemiah Plan typically built projects of 500 to 1,000 units each on large tracts of donated, city-

6. As discussed above, many argue that an increase in the proportion of homeowners should in itself bolster property values. Is the value of a property higher (or does it appreciate more rapidly) when it is located in a community with a greater share of homeowners? Few studies tackle this question, again perhaps because of concerns about endogeneity. In an analysis of 2,600 nonaffluent urban census tracts between 1980 and 1990, Rohe and Stewart (1996) found that housing prices appreciated more rapidly in neighborhoods with higher homeownership rates. But they do not analyze the root causes of this effect.

7. The section 8 New Construction Program is the only rental housing program that they find to be correlated with higher property values.

8. The key difference from our approach is that they do not control for prior trends in housing values near the developments and rely on census tract geocoding rather than measuring the actual distance of the sale from the homeownership development.

9. Their paper also provides an interesting analysis of the benefits to individual homeowners.

10. These figures, estimated by the authors, are estimates of activity beginning in fiscal year 1987 and ending in fiscal year 1998.

owned land. The units are generally quite modest, built in identical, block-long rows of single-family, eighteen-foot-wide homes. The first house was completed in 1984; nearly 3,000 homes have been built in total. About 80 percent of these homes have been built in Brooklyn. The remainder were built in the South Bronx by another group of churches (Stuart, 1997).

The high-volume, mass-production approach has allowed the Nehemiah Plan to deliver units at a very low cost. Units cost $60,000–70,000 to build, and the purchase price was lowered $10,000–15,000 through a non-interest-bearing second mortgage from the city, due only upon resale (Donovan, 1994; Orlebeke, 1997). Estimates of the average incomes of the families who moved into the Nehemiah homes range from $27,000 to $31,000, which in 1990 was somewhat higher than the average family income of census tracts in which the homes were built (under $25,000).

The Partnership New Homes Program

The New York City Housing Partnership is a not-for-profit intermediary that was organized in 1982 to help create and manage an affordable homeownership production program in the city (Wylde, 1999). Its core program—the New Homes Program—was launched soon after to develop new, affordable, owner-occupied homes in distressed communities. Partnership homes were built by private, profit-motivated developers selected by the city and the Partnership. Most Partnership projects have fewer than one hundred units, and many are located on small infill sites grouped together to make up a project (Orlebeke, 1997). The typical Partnership development contains two- and three-family homes that include an owner's unit plus one or two rental units.

According to one 1988 study of ten Partnership projects, per-unit costs during the 1980s ranged from $57,000 to $137,000 (Orlebeke, 1997). On average, the incomes of the residents moving into Partnership homes in 1990 was $32,000, again somewhat higher than the mean income of their surrounding neighborhoods. In all Partnership projects, the city has provided the land at a nominal cost ($500 per lot) and has given a $10,000 subsidy per home; the State Affordable Housing Corporation has provided an additional $15,000 subsidy per home (Donovan, 1994).

By June 1999 the Partnership New Homes program had built 12,590 new homes; like the Nehemiah Plan homes, they are primarily in Brooklyn and the Bronx. But roughly one-quarter of the homes have been built in New York's other three boroughs.

Choosing Locations

In testing the impact of new housing on surrounding areas, there is always some concern about site selection. Here, for example, the city may have tried to select "strong" sites for new housing where they believed property values were beginning to increase (or had promise in the near future). Even if the city had wanted to do so, however, there were considerable constraints on the choice of locations. First, the site had to be city-owned, which means it had been abandoned by its previous owner and vested in an *in rem* proceeding for delinquent property taxes. Because private owners were much less likely to have abandoned properties in affluent areas, the city's stock of abandoned properties was overwhelmingly concentrated in its poorest neighborhoods (Scafidi and others, 1998). Second, in the case of the Nehemiah Program, the land had to be a large, mostly vacant, contiguous parcel.

Furthermore, interviews with city officials suggest that the city did not give its best vacant sites to the Partnership and Nehemiah sponsors. In many instances, the city was also interested in realizing a high return from its land holdings and in minimizing the total subsidy required for redevelopment. As Anthony Gliedman, a former HPD commissioner, put it, "Why would we do market rate sites with the Partnership?" (Orlebeke, 1997). In other words, the process of selecting individual sites, while perhaps not fully random, was certainly far from one that sought to systematically pick winners. Rather, there is reason to believe that the city chose losers, suggesting that our spillover estimates would provide conservative estimates of the impact of randomly sited housing. Nonetheless, our research design includes various controls for systematic selection issues.

Methodology

The centerpiece of this research is a hedonic price function, in which housing is viewed as a composite good or a bundle of services. Observed house prices are the product of the quantity of housing services attached to the property and the price of these housing services, summed over all structural and locational characteristics of the property. The basic model takes the following form:

$$P_{it} = \alpha + \beta \mathbf{X}_{it} + \gamma \mathbf{Z}_{it} + \rho \mathbf{I}_t + \varepsilon_{it}, \quad (16\text{-}1)$$

where P is the sales price of the property; **X** is a vector of property-related characteristics, including age and structural characteristics; **Z** is a vector of locational attributes, such as local public services and neighborhood conditions; **I** is a vector of dummy variables indicating the year of the sale; and i indexes properties while t indexes time. As usual, α represents an intercept and β, γ, and ρ represent vectors of parameters to be estimated. ε represents an error term.[11] The

11. In principle, spatial autocorrelation in the error term, while not biasing the regression coefficients, could cause the standard errors we report to be underestimated (see, for example, Can and Megbolugbe, 1997). However, we expect that after controlling for zip code*quarter effects and also detailed building characteristics, there will be little spatial autocorrelation left. Basu and Thibodeau (1998) estimate a hedonic regression and find only modest spatial autocorrelation, even using less fine-grained geographic controls than ours.

derivative of the housing price function with respect to an individual attribute may then be interpreted as the implicit price of that attribute (Rosen, 1974). We enter housing prices as logarithms, so the coefficients may be interpreted as the percentage change in price resulting from an additional unit of the independent variable. In the case of a dummy variable, the coefficient can be interpreted as the difference in log price between properties that have the attribute and those that do not. The difference in log price closely approximates the percentage difference in price, when the difference is small enough. For the differences discussed in this chapter, which are generally smaller than 10 percent, the approximation is close, so we use this more intuitive interpretation throughout.[12]

As suggested above, because the price of housing is affected by a broad array of structural and neighborhood characteristics, estimating equation 16-1 requires a great deal of detailed data. Unfortunately, if some relevant variables cannot be included, either because they are unmeasured or because data are unavailable, the coefficients on the included variables may be biased. Thus in trying to identify the independent effect of proximity to Partnership and Nehemiah homes, our challenge is to control for a sufficient number of neighborhood attributes so that our impact estimates do not suffer from omitted variable bias.

Our basic approach is to adapt the Galster, Tatian, and Smith (1999) model, estimating the difference between prices of properties in the micro-neighborhoods (or rings) surrounding Nehemiah and Partnership sites and the prices of comparable properties that are outside the ring but still located in the same general neighborhood. Then we examine whether the magnitude of this difference has changed over time, and if so, whether the change is associated with the completion of a Partnership or Nehemiah project.[13] This approach should yield an unbiased measure of impact, if (1) we have sufficient data on the structural characteristics of the homes that sell, and (2) there are few other neighborhood influences that shaped the value of properties very near the Partnership and Nehemiah sites around the time of project completion but that do not also influence property values in the general neighborhood.

This is accomplished by supplementing the model with variables identifying properties in the ring of the housing investments (which capture the price differential between properties inside and outside the ring) and specifying those variables to allow the price differential to change over time. As always, there is no single way to implement this strategy. Instead, different ways of specifying these variables reflect different counterfactuals and offer distinct advantages.

12. The exact percentage effect of a difference in logs, b, is given by $100(eb - 1)$, although this formula is itself an approximation when b is a regression coefficient; see Halvorsen and Palmquist (1980) and Kennedy (1981).

13. Thus we form a "difference-in-difference" impact estimate. The impact of the housing investment is identified as the difference between properties inside and outside the ring, before and after the housing investment.

As described in greater detail below, our response is to estimate several alternative specifications of the model, reflecting a range of choices and alternatives. More specifically, we estimate the model for three different ring sizes—a 500-foot ring, a 1,000-foot ring, and a 2,000-foot ring—that define properties in the vicinity of Nehemiah or Partnership sites. We also investigate three alternative ways of capturing differentials in price levels and trends between properties inside and outside the ring. Our first specification includes a different ring dummy for each of the nine preceding years, with another dummy indicating ten or more prior years. There is also a similar set of ten dummies for the following years and another for the year of completion. This parameterization provides estimates of the price differential between the inside and outside of the ring in each of twenty-one years (multiyear periods in the case of the two outer dummies). Our second, more parsimonious specification generates an overall before-and-after comparison by replacing these twenty-one ring-year dummy variables with a single, "ever in the ring" dummy variable, an in-ring postcompletion dummy variable, and a postcompletion trend variable. A third specification includes controls for prior trends in the price differential inside and outside the rings before the development of the new homes (using a spline specification to allow for different trends in different time periods). Thus the third specification provides an estimate in which the counterfactual is that the price gap between the ring and the neighborhood would have continued to shrink (or grow) at the precompletion rate, if no project had been completed.

As noted, we think each of these specifications offers distinct advantages, and therefore we show the results from all three. The first is the most flexible, offering a detailed view of price changes over time, but the large number of coefficients makes it difficult to summarize the overall impact. The second is more parsimonious and straightforward, but it may be too simplistic and fail to account for trends in the ring-neighborhood price gap before the completion of the project. The third controls for these prior trends and thereby helps to mitigate concerns about selection bias, but it may be overly conservative. Since property values may begin to rise once a project is announced or started, the trends may also pick up some of the effects of the developments themselves, in anticipation of the effect the project will have on the surrounding community.[14] (According to HPD staff, community residents were involved in the planning process and often knew about these projects even years before the start of construction.) If so, then including the splines means that we simply measure the added effect that a project's completion has on property values, above and beyond the effect of its announcement or start, and that we understate its full impact.

14. Another alternative is that the construction activity generated by the new homes itself may raise property values before completion.

Unfortunately, it is impossible to know whether the prior trends in prices in the ring relative to those in the zip code would have continued at the same rate if the project had not been constructed. In our third specification we effectively assume that the trend in relative prices that occurred during the five years before the project's completion would have continued in the years after completion. In our second specification we assume that prices in the rings would have increased at the same rate as the prices in the zip code. It is likely that neither of these is fully accurate, but it is impossible to know what would have happened to prices in the rings in the absence of the newly built homes.[15]

Mathematically, our first model can be written as follows:

$$\text{(16-2)}\quad \text{Ln}P = \alpha + \beta \text{X} + \delta \textbf{Zipcode-Quarter} + \gamma \textbf{Ring\_Years\_from\_Sale} + \varepsilon,$$

where X is a vector of structural characteristics, as before, and **Zipcode-Quarter** is a vector of dummy variables indicating the neighborhood in which the property is located (measured by zip code) and the year and quarter of sale (for example, first quarter 1980, second quarter 1980, and so on).[16] These Zipcode-Quarter dummy variables enable us to control for zip code–specific levels and trends in prices, appropriately controlling for seasonality, and should therefore yield a more precise estimate of impact.[17]

As noted above, we test for differences in both price levels and trends for properties near homeownership units by including twenty-one dummy variables (denoted "Ring_Years_from_Sale"), indicating whether a sale is within a given distance of a homeownership site and the number of years between the sale and project completion (before or after).[18] As an example, for our 500-foot model, we include a dummy variable indicating if the property is located within 500 feet of a Nehemiah or Partnership site and sold during the same calendar year in which the project was completed (year 0). We also include a dummy indicating

15. It is also theoretically possible that, in the absence of the project, the gap between prices in the rings and prices in their surrounding zip codes would have closed more rapidly than it was closing before the project's completion.

16. We effectively include a dummy variable for each zip code quarter combination in the dataset; for a zip code in which properties sold in each quarter from the first quarter of 1980 through the third quarter of 1999, we therefore include seventy-nine dummy variables.

17. New York City is divided into 337 zip codes, but many of these are nonresidential. There are a total of 243 "non-unique" zip codes shared by numerous businesses and residences. (The other zip codes are assigned to post office boxes or to single organizations.) On average, the residential zip codes included slightly more than 40,000 residents in 1997. The high density of New York City makes using census tracts undesirable. In many instances, the 2,000-foot rings around developments included multiple census tracts, which would have significantly complicated the interpretation of the results.

18. In cases where a sale was within 500 feet of more than one Nehemiah or Partnership project, we use the completion date of the first project completed. Note that we do not distinguish in this specification between sales that are within a certain distance of small and large developments (see below). And we do not distinguish between sales that are within a certain distance of one development and several.

if it is within 500 feet of a site and sold in the calendar year before completion (year –1), another indicating if it is within 500 feet and sold in the calendar year immediately after the year of completion (year 1), and so on through year –10 and year 10.[19] We estimate similar models for rings defined by a 1,000-foot ring and a 2,000-foot ring.[20]

The coefficients on these dummy variables can be interpreted as the percentage difference between the prices of properties in the rings surrounding the homeownership project and the prices of properties that are outside that ring but inside the zip code. Thus we can track how prices in the ring of a project change relative to prices in the larger zip code by examining how these coefficients change over time. We can see relative price levels both before and after the completion of the homeownership project and observe whether there was any discontinuous shift after completion.

The second model (again estimated separately for the 500-, 1,000-, and 2,000-foot rings) can be written as follows:

$$\text{(16-3)}\quad \text{Ln}P = \alpha + \beta \text{X} + \delta \textbf{Zipcode-Quarter} + \gamma \textit{Ring} + \lambda \textit{Postring} + \theta \textit{Tpost} + \varepsilon.$$

Here, *Ring* indicates if a sale is within the ring of a homeownership site, whether completed or not. *Postring* represents a dummy variable indicating whether the sale is within the specified distance of a *completed* homeownership project.[21] The coefficient on the *Postring* variable is critical. It indicates the extent to which, after the completion of a homeownership development, sales prices rise in the vicinity relative to the average increase in the larger zip code.

Finally, *Tpost* is a postcompletion trend variable, a continuous variable that indicates the number of years between the date of sale in the ring and the end of the completion year. To be specific, in our 500-foot ring model, *Tpost* equals 1/365 if a sale is located within 500 feet of a homeownership project and occurs on January 1 of the year following project completion; it equals one if the sale occurs on December 31 of the year following project completion; it equals two if the sale occurs on December 31 of the subsequent year, and so on. The *Tpost* coefficient will be positive if, after completion, prices in the rings rise relative to prices in the zip code.

As noted, one drawback of this specification is that the gap between home prices in the rings and the surrounding zip codes might have been shrinking (or expanding) even before the advent of these projects, in which case a simple pre/post comparison might overstate (or understate) the magnitude of the

19. Year –10 indicates that a property is sold ten or more years before completion, and year 10 indicates that a property is sold ten or more years after completion.

20. Specifically, these include twenty-one analogous dummy variables that correspond to properties within 1,000 feet and 2,000 feet of a homeownership site, respectively.

21. Again, in cases where a sale was within the ring of more than one Nehemiah or Partnership project, we use the completion date of the first completed project.

impact. Thus we adapt the methodology of Galster, Tatian, and Smith (1999) and estimate the following model for each of our three ring specifications: [22]

$$\text{(16-4)} \qquad \text{Ln}P = \alpha + \beta \mathbf{X} + \delta \mathbf{Zipcode\text{-}Quarter} + \gamma Ring + \lambda Postring + \theta Tpost + \varphi \mathbf{Spline} + \varepsilon.$$

This equation differs from equation 16-3 only in that here we add a ring-specific time trend—**spline**—that measures the overall price trend in the ring (not simply the trend *after* completion). We measure this time trend by allowing for three separate linear segments (splines), with a knot-point at ten years before completion and another knot-point at five years before completion. Put differently, the third segment starts at five years before development and extends through the entire postcompletion period.

Because *Tpost* is included in the equation, the coefficient on this third spline variable reflects the average growth in prices for the five years before completion. Thus the coefficient on *Tpost* can be interpreted as the difference between the relative price appreciation that occurred in the ring after completion and the rate of relative appreciation that would have occurred if prices in the ring had continued to appreciate at the same rate relative to the zip code *after* completion as they did during the five years before completion.

Finally, we also explore the issue of heterogeneity in impacts. Thus far we have essentially assumed that the impacts of all homeownership developments are identical, although it seems likely that impacts will vary with the scale of a development, its type, and other factors. We explore whether the impacts differ depending on the number of homeownership units constructed, the sponsor (Nehemiah versus Partnership, which implies differences in characteristics), and the "tightness" of the housing market.

Summary of Data

We obtained detailed data from a number of unique city data sources. First, through an arrangement with the New York City Department of Finance, we

22. The key difference from Galster, Tatian, and Smith (1999) and from Santiago, Galster, and Tatian (2001) is that we include zip code quarter fixed effects, which allow for zip code–specific trends in prices. They use tract fixed effects instead, which use a finer level of geography but assume that neighborhood fixed effects are constant over time, an assumption that seems unrealistic over a time period as long as ours. As mentioned above, the high density of New York City makes using census-tract-quarter fixed effects impractical. Another difference is that we measure time relative to the time of completion. Galster and others and Santiago and others use an absolute time trend in the ring. Finally, we use a spline for the time trend, so that we extrapolate what was happening to the gap between the rings and their surrounding zip codes during the five years before completion, not the entire precompletion period. Given that only a small minority of sales in their datasets take place more than five years before occupancy, this last difference is fairly inconsequential.

obtained a confidential database that contains sales transaction prices for all apartment buildings, condominium apartments, and single-family homes over the period 1980–99.[23] Limiting the analysis to properties located within the thirty-four community districts where Nehemiah or Partnership New Homes projects were developed, our sample includes 234,591 sales spread across 137 zip codes.[24] Because of the long time span covered by the data and New York City's size, this is a large sample compared with that used by many other studies.

Second, we have supplemented these transactions data with building characteristics from an administrative dataset gathered for the purpose of assessing property taxes (the RPAD file). The RPAD data contain information about buildings but little information about the characteristics of individual units in apartment buildings (except in the case of condominiums).[25] Nonetheless, these building characteristics explain variations in prices surprisingly well. Using all transactions in 1998, a regression of the log price per unit on building age and its square, log square feet per unit, number of buildings on a lot, and dummies for the presence of a garage, abandonment, major alterations, commercial units, and location on a block corner yields an R^2 of .46. Adding a set of eighteen building classifications to the regression (for example, "single-family detached," "single-family attached," "two-family home") increases the R^2 to .68. Finally, adding zip code dummy variables increases the R^2 to 0.81.

Third, HPD provided data on the precise location (down to the block level) of all housing built through the Nehemiah and Partnership programs. We used geographic information systems (GIS) techniques to measure the distance from each sale in our database to each Nehemiah and Partnership site and create rings

23. Because sales of cooperative apartments are not considered to be sales of real property, they are not recorded and are thus not included in this analysis. This is unlikely to have a major impact on our results because cooperative apartments tend to be rare in the thirty-four community districts that have Nehemiah or Partnership New Homes developments. We should also note that most of the apartment buildings in our sample are rent-stabilized. Given that legally allowable rents are typically *above* market rents outside of affluent neighborhoods in Manhattan and Brooklyn, we do not think that their inclusion biases our results (see Pollakowski, 1997).

24. This includes three community districts in Manhattan, nine in the Bronx, twelve in Brooklyn, nine in Queens, and one in Staten Island.

25. Note that most of the RPAD data utilized in this study were collected in 1999, and it is conceivable that some of the building characteristics may have changed between the time of sale and 1999. However, most of the characteristics that we use in the hedonic regressions are fairly immutable (for example, corner location, square feet, presence of a garage). Furthermore, to examine whether the building characteristics tend to remain constant over time, we merged RPAD data from 1990 and 1999 and found that for eight of the ten variables examined the characteristic remained unchanged in 97 percent or more of the cases. "Year built" and "number of units" remained unchanged in 87 and 93 percent of the cases, respectively. We suspect that the majority of these changes are corrections rather than true changes because these characteristics change very rarely. Thus the 1999 RPAD file may actually be a better estimate of 1990 characteristics than the 1990 file. The abandonment variable was collected in 1980.

Figure 16-1. *Partnership Development on Brooklyn-Queens Border*

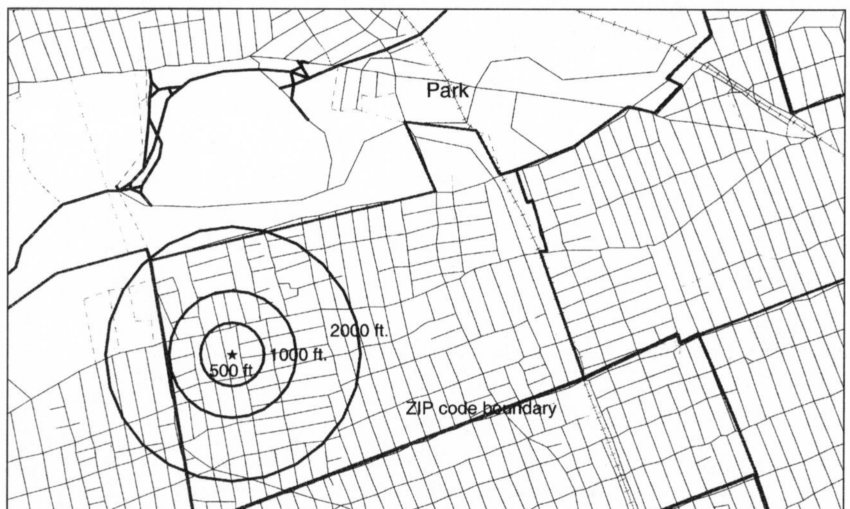

of a given distance around each project.[26] To give a sense of these rings, figure 16-1 shows an example of a Partnership development located on the Brooklyn/Queens border and its surrounding rings. The innermost ring extends 500 feet (usually one to two blocks) from the project; the second ring extends 1,000 feet (one to four blocks), and the outermost ring extends 2,000 feet (three to eight blocks).

Table 16-1 shows summary statistics from the RPAD data. The first column shows the characteristics of our full sample; the second column shows the characteristics of sales located within 500 feet of a Nehemiah or Partnership site, whether completed or not. As shown, nearly three-quarters of all buildings sold were either one- or two-family homes, and 92 percent were one-family homes, two-family homes, or small apartments. [27] Most sales were in Brooklyn and Queens, reflecting both the location of Nehemiah and Partnership develop-

26. Because all buildings in New York City have been geocoded by the New York City Department of City Planning, we used a "cross-walk" (the "geosupport file") that associates each tax lot with an x,y coordinate (that is, latitude and longitude using the U.S. State Plane 1927 projection), community district, and census tract. A tax lot is usually a building and is an identifier available to the homes sales and RPAD data. We are able to assign x,y coordinates and other geographic variables to over 98 percent of the sales using this method. For the Nehemiah and Partnership data, only the tax block on which the property is located (which corresponds to a physical block) is available. After collapsing the geosupport file to the tax block level (that is, calculating the center of each block), we were able to assign an x,y coordinate to 99.7 percent of these projects.

27. Note that we also estimated our specifications using only one-to-four-family dwellings and the results were, in general, similar to those based on all dwellings.

Table 16-1. *Characteristics of Properties Sold*[a]
Percent

	All property sales	*Sales within 500 feet of Nehemiah or Partnership site*
Borough		
Manhattan	1.5	3.3
Bronx	7.1	19.7
Brooklyn	37.2	44.1
Queens	46.4	29.1
Staten Island	7.8	3.7
Building class		
Single-family detached	25.1	14.1
Single-family attached	13.2	6.6
Two-family	34.5	35.3
Walk-up apartments	19.4	29.7
Elevator apartments	0.8	0.7
Loft buildings	0.0	0.0
Condominiums	3.6	8.3
Mixed-use, multifamily (includes store or office plus residential units)	3.5	5.2
Built before World War II	79.8	91.3
Vandalized	0.0	0.2
Other abandoned	0.2	0.5
Garage	36.1	15.8
Corner location	7.7	7.5
Major alteration before sale	1.9	3.1
In 500-foot ring	4.8	100
In 1,000-foot ring	11.4	100
In 2,000-foot ring	25.4	100
N	234,591	11,236

a. Universe = all sales in community districts with at least one Nehemiah or Partnership New Homes unit.

ments and the large share of smaller properties in these boroughs that sell more frequently than the apartment buildings more common in Manhattan and the Bronx. Over a third of the transacting properties had garages, 80 percent were built before World War II, and only a handful were vandalized or otherwise abandoned. Finally, 4.8 percent of the properties in our sample are located within 500 feet of a Partnership or Nehemiah site, 11.4 percent are located within 1,000 feet, and 25.4 percent are within 2,000 feet of a homeownership site.

The data reveal some systematic differences between properties that are located close to Nehemiah or Partnership sites and those that are not. Owing to

Table 16-2. *Characteristics of Units Built through Nehemiah and Partnership New Homes*

	Nehemiah	*Partnership New Homes*	*Total*
Borough			
Bronx	544	5,426	5,970
Manhattan	0	948	948
Brooklyn	2,394	4,104	6,498
Queens	0	1,226	1,226
Staten Island	0	886	886
Building type			
One-family	2,632	1,572	4,204
Two-family	18	7,020	7,038
Three-family	0	1,659	1,659
Condominium	288	2,112	2,300
Cooperative	0	227	227
Year completed			
1984	194	0	194
1985	170	18	188
1986	235	232	467
1987	284	263	547
1988	240	260	500
1989	317	226	543
1990	460	1,918	2,378
1991	218	867	1,134
1992	140	1,555	1,695
1993	108	1,104	1,252
1994	120	1,567	1,687
1995	138	1,183	1,321
1996	30	1,018	1,048
1997	44	1,119	1,163
1998	126	664	790
1999	114	596	710
Total	2,938	12,590	15,528

the location of these developments, properties located within the 500-foot ring are much more likely to be in Brooklyn, Manhattan, or the Bronx. They are also much older, less likely to be single-family homes, more likely to be walk-ups, and much less likely to have garages.

Turning to the Nehemiah and Partnership units themselves, table 16-2 indicates that 12,468 of the 15,528 units built (80 percent) are in Brooklyn or the Bronx and over 13,000 (85 percent) were completed during the 1990s. As for building type, 90 percent of the Nehemiah units are single-family homes, as compared with just 12 percent of the Partnership units, which are more typically two- and three-family homes.

Table 16-3. *1990 Characteristics of Census Tracts in which Partnership New Homes and Nehemiah Projects are Located*
Percent unless otherwise noted

	Tracts with Nehemiah units	*Tracts with Partnership units*	*All tracts in New York City*
Mean poverty rate	40.1	32.5	18.4
Percent of tracts with poverty rate ≥ 40 percent	48.0	37.4	12.5
Mean households on public assistance	33.0	27.3	13.8
Mean family income	$24,579	$29,342	$46,665
Mean unemployment	18.5	14.8	9.7
Mean adult residents with some college education	23.4	27.0	39.7
Mean black residents	72.0	51.5	28.9
Mean Hispanic residents	32.3	39.3	21.9
Mean homeownership	20.1	24.2	34.8
N	25	179	2,131

Table 16-3 compares the average 1990 characteristics of census tracts that include Nehemiah and Partnership units in 1998 with those that do not.[28] While 2,938 Nehemiah units were built in twenty-five census tracts, averaging 118 units per tract, Partnership units were more dispersed: 12,590 units were built in 179 tracts, averaging 70 per tract.

Table 16-3 confirms that these projects were located in distressed neighborhoods and suggests that neighborhoods in which Nehemiah units have been located are somewhat more disadvantaged. For example, the average poverty rate in a tract with Nehemiah and Partnership units was 40.1 and 32.5 percent, respectively, whereas the citywide average was 18.4 percent. Similarly, while just 12.5 percent of census tracts in New York had poverty rates of 40 percent or more, 37 percent of those with Partnership units and 48 percent of those with Nehemiah units had poverty rates this high.

Other socioeconomic variables tell the same story. Mean family income was $24,579 in Nehemiah tracts, $29,342 in Partnership tracts, and $46,665 in all tracts citywide. The unemployment rate was almost twice as high in census tracts with Nehemiah units as it was in the average city census tract. As for racial and ethnic composition, the Nehemiah and Partnership tracts housed a greater share of Hispanic residents and a much larger share of black residents than the average tract. Finally, the Partnership and Nehemiah neighborhoods have relatively low rates of homeownership. Less than one-fourth of households on average own their homes in these communities, as compared with an average of 35 percent in census tracts citywide.

28. The census tract data are taken from the 1990 census. Tracts are characterized as including Nehemiah or Partnership projects even if these projects were not built until later in the decade.

Note that our data do not identify whether a particular property received city subsidies. In order to ensure that we analyze only the sales prices of buildings neighboring Partnership and Nehemiah developments and not the developments themselves, we exclude any sales that could potentially be part of a development. Thus we excluded 2,248 sales (representing less than 1 percent of the sample) that occurred on the same block as a Nehemiah or Partnership development if the building sold was constructed after the Nehemiah or Partnership building had been completed.[29]

Results

Before presenting regression results, it is useful to show how average prices of properties that are close to homeownership sites compare with average prices in our sample. Table 16-4 shows that, in 1980, per-unit sales prices for buildings located within 500 feet of a soon-to-be-constructed Nehemiah or Partnership site were on average 43 percent lower than the prices of all buildings located in the thirty-four community districts; prices in the 1,000-foot ring were 34.9 percent lower, and prices in the 2,000-foot ring were 27.6 percent lower.

In other words, these projects were clearly located in neighborhoods with depressed housing prices.[30] Yet the table also shows that, over time, the differential has fallen. By 1999 properties sold within 500 feet of a Nehemiah or Partnership site were on average only 23.8 percent lower than the mean price in our overall sample.

The real question, of course, is whether the construction of Partnership and Nehemiah projects in these rings contributes to this relative price rise in the rings. To isolate the influence of proximity to a completed homeownership project, we estimate the regressions discussed earlier, in which the dependent variable is the log of the sales price per unit, and which control for building and local neighborhood characteristics and include a full complement of zip code and quarter interaction effects (Zipcode*Quarter fixed effects).

Table 16-5 reports the estimated regression coefficients for ring variables and their standard errors. Other variables in the regressions include age and its square; log of square footage; number of buildings on the same lot, dummy variables indicating whether the property was on the corner, had been vandalized, was of an odd-shape, or included a garage; and eighteen building classifica-

29. To provide a margin of error with respect to the recording of construction dates in RPAD, we also excluded sales of buildings on the same block as a Partnership and Nehemiah development that were built up to five years before the Partnership or Nehemiah building. These exclusions are included in the total 2,248 figure.

30. Given the evidence shown in table 16-3 that the census tracts surrounding Nehemiah and Partnership sites are notably less affluent than the city at large, it is no doubt true that prices in the rings surrounding these sites are even lower in comparison with average prices in all community districts in the city, rather than the community districts in our sample.

Table 16-4. *Difference between Average Housing Prices in Rings and Average Annual Price, by Year*[a]
Percent unless otherwise noted

	Average per unit price in 34 CDs	*Prices relative to sample mean*		
		500-foot ring	*1,000-foot ring*	*2,000-foot ring*
1980	$54,571	–43.4	–34.9	–27.6
1981	53,547	–43.1	–37.1	–29.1
1982	55,783	–35.9	–34.0	–30.3
1983	63,354	–45.8	–42.0	–33.5
1984	70,231	–50.0	–43.0	–34.9
1985	82,308	–50.5	–46.9	–39.3
1986	105,596	–53.8	–48.5	–39.9
1987	127,636	–52.0	–46.5	–39.0
1988	136,673	–48.7	–42.1	–34.8
1989	138,454	–42.6	–36.9	–29.7
1990	134,520	–42.2	–35.4	–29.8
1991	128,339	–40.5	–37.4	–30.7
1992	119,691	–36.6	–33.4	–28.9
1993	115,792	–35.0	–32.5	–27.5
1994	115.769	–28.3	–29.2	–24.3
1995	112,795	–26.0	–24.3	–21.9
1996	107,245	–32.8	–28.6	–23.1
1997	107,807	–30.3	–25.7	–21.4
1998	111,482	–26.7	–23.9	–21.5
1999	116,413	–23.8	–18.0	–17.1

a. This table is based on the coefficients of simple bivariate regressions that regress logarithm of price on year in the given geographic area and are not adjusted for other covariates. Price reports in 1999 dollars.

tion variables such as two-family home or single-family detached. Overall, the model performs well: structural variables have the expected signs and the regressions explain more than 83 percent of the variation in log prices.[31] (See Ellen and others, 2001, for the full set of parameter estimates.)

Turning to the ring dummies, recall that the coefficients can be interpreted as the percentage difference between the price of properties within the rings and

31. Briefly, results indicate that the sales price is higher if a building is larger or newer, is located on a corner, or includes a garage. Sales price is lower if the building is vandalized or abandoned. The building-class dummies are also consistent with expectations. Sales prices per unit for most of the building types are lower than those for single-family attached homes (the omitted category). Somewhat surprisingly, the coefficient on the dummy variable indicating that the building has undergone a major alteration before sale is negative, which may reflect the generally worse shape of buildings that have undergone such major alterations in ways that are not captured by our data. Statistically significant coefficients on dummy variables indicating missing values for the age or size of a building indicate that the buildings missing age data are less valuable than others (perhaps because they are older) and that buildings missing square footage data are more valuable (perhaps because they are larger). However, condominiums missing square footage data (representing 90 percent of the sales missing square feet data) are somewhat smaller. In total, just over 1 percent of property sales were missing square footage and 3 percent were missing age.

Table 16-5. *Selected Coefficients from Regressions with Full Set of Pre- and Postring Dummies (Model One)*

	500-ft. ring	*1,000-ft. ring*	*2,000-ft. ring*
≥10yr_Pre_Ring[a]	–0.1690	–0.1260	–0.0857
	(0.0077)	(0.0053)	(0.0044)
9yr_Pre_Ring	–0.2136	–0.1531	–0.1165
	(0.0145)	(0.0100)	(0.0077)
8yr_Pre_Ring	–0.1692	–0.1316	–0.1048
	(0.0142)	(0.0099)	(0.0076)
7yr_Pre_Ring	–0.1411	–0.1317	–0.1013
	(0.0144)	(0.0095)	(0.0071)
6yr_Pre_Ring	–0.1057	–0.1194	–0.0885
	(0.0136)	(0.0091)	(0.0066)
5yr_Pre_Ring	–0.1048	–0.1021	–0.0796
	(0.0137)	(0.0091)	(0.0065)
4yr_Pre_Ring	–0.1360	–0.1031	–0.0729
	(0.0139)	(0.0093)	(0.0067)
3yr_Pre_Ring	–0.0854	–0.0973	–0.0822
	(0.0140)	(0.0093)	(0.0068)
2yr_Pre_Ring	–0.0968	–0.1002	–0.0879
	(0.0142)	(0.0096)	(0.0069)
1yr_Pre_Ring	–0.0882	–0.0915	–0.0846
	(0.0135)	(0.0090)	(0.0068)
Completion_yr_Ring[b]	–0.0853	–0.0789	–0.0807
	(0.0127)	(0.0089)	(0.0070)
1yr_Post_Ring[c]	–0.0160	–0.0709	–0.0614
	(0.0140)	(0.0094)	(0.0071)
2yr_Post_Ring	–0.0476	–0.0412	–0.0586
	(0.0159)	(0.0103)	(0.0076)
3yr_Post_Ring	–0.0372	–0.0302	–0.0225
	(0.0149)	(0.0105)	(0.0077)
4yr_Post_Ring	–0.0055	–0.0428	–0.0503
	(0.0155)	(0.0104)	(0.0078)
5yr_Post_Ring	–0.0070	–0.0434	–0.0272
	(0.0160)	(0.0111)	(0.0081)
6yr_Post_Ring	–0.0673	–0.0691	–0.0462
	(0.0187)	(0.0116)	(0.0082)
7yr_Post_Ring	–0.0526	0.0723	–0.0449
	(0.0195)	(0.0126)	(0.0086)
8yr_Post_Ring	–0.0318	–0.0708	–0.0572
	(0.0226)	(0.0145)	(0.0097)
9yr_Post_Ring	–0.0346	–0.0868	–0.0491
	(0.0279)	(0.0172)	(0.0114)
=10yr_Post_Ring	–0.0909	–0.0629	–0.0349
	(0.0213)	(0.0123)	(0.0082)
Summary statistic			
Adjusted R^2	0.8380	0.8383	0.8381
N	234,591	234,591	234,591

Note: The equations are fixed-effects regressions in which the dependent variable is the logarithm of price per unit. Standard errors are in parentheses. All regressions include Zip*Quarter dummies and the full set of building controls.

a. Within the specified distance of a homeownership site, the specified number of years before completion of the project.

b. Within the specified distance of a homeownership site, during the year of completion.

c. Within the specified distance of a homeownership site, the specified number of years after completion of the project.

comparable properties located outside the rings but within the same zip code. To start, note that all the coefficients are negative and most are statistically significant. Consistent with the uncontrolled results in table 16-4, parameter estimates indicate that prices of properties located in the rings tend to be lower than the prices of comparable properties located in the zip code, both before and after project completion. Note that the estimated price differential between properties inside and outside the ring are considerably smaller than the uncontrolled price differentials shown in table 16-4. Once we control for quality, then, the price differentials diminish, suggesting that properties in the rings are of lower average quality than those outside. Second, coefficients generally get smaller over time. Thus prices in the rings rise over time relative to prices in their surrounding zip code both before and after completion. Third, the results indicate a significant reduction in the gap around the time of completion. Finally, although the gap between prices in the 500-foot ring and the zip code falls immediately after completion, it appears to take longer for the effects to be felt in the more distant rings. More specifically, the major decline in the 1,000-foot ring occurs between one and two years after project completion. In the 2,000-foot ring, the decline continues through year three. One plausible explanation is that the homeownership projects have a more immediate impact on their close surroundings, but over time they bring benefits to more distant areas as well. (This is also consistent with the apparent dissipation of the impact in the 500-foot ring, discussed below, and the greater persistence of impacts in the 2,000-foot ring.)

Figure 16-2 graphs these percentage differentials by the year relative to project completion for the 500-foot ring and indicates a decline in the gap over time. One year before the completion of a homeownership project (marked by −1 on the graph), the per unit sales price of a property within 500 feet of a future site is on average 8.8 percent lower than the price of a comparable property sold in the same year in the same zip code. After completion, the gap immediately shrinks by 7.2 percentage points to just 1.6 percent lower than the price of a comparable property in the zip code, widening somewhat several years later.

Table 16-6 shows the impact estimates from our second specification (equation 16-3).[32] For the 500-foot ring, the coefficient on the ring dummy variable indicates that before the completion of the development, properties in the ring sold, on average, for 13.3 percent less than comparable properties in the same zip code but outside the ring. The coefficient on *Postring* indicates that immediately after completion this gap shrinks by 11.4 percentage points to just 1.9 percent. In the 1,000-foot ring, our results suggest that before completion, prices of properties within 1,000 feet of an eventual site are 11.3 percentage points lower

32. Full results are available from the authors upon request.

Figure 16-2. *Price Trends in 500-Foot Ring*

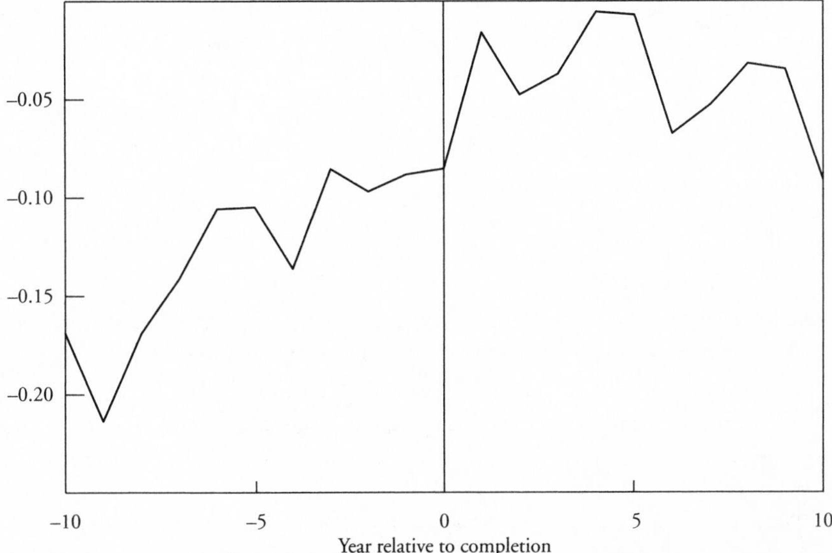

than prices for comparable properties in the same zip code but outside the ring. Immediately after completion, this gap shrinks by 6.3 percentage points. Finally, in the 2,000-foot ring, the differential between prices in the ring and prices in the zip codes shrinks by 3.5 percentage points after completion.

The coefficient estimates on *Tpost* suggest that the impact on properties within 500 and 1,000 feet of the project declines over time. For the 500-foot ring, the initial impact estimate of 11.4 percentage points declines by 0.5 percentage points per year. In the 1,000-foot ring, the estimated gap appears to widen somewhat over time, but at a slower rate of 0.2 percentage points per year. The estimated gap in the 2,000-foot ring, by contrast, continues to shrink in the years following completion by 0.14 percentage points per year.

The reasons for this decline in the inner rings are not immediately apparent. One possibility is that homes within the development may be maintained less well than other properties in the neighborhood and thus the positive externality generated by the development declines over time. Or it could be that the projects simply did not meet initial expectations (Poterba, 1984). A more optimistic explanation is that the positive externalities created by the project spread outward over time, thereby reducing the disparity between prices within 500 feet (or 1,000 feet) and those outside the 500-foot (or 1,000-foot) radius. The observation that price impacts appear more persistent in the 2,000-foot ring, possibly growing over time as indicated by the positive coefficient on *Tpost*, lends some support to this hypothesis. Finally, it might be that the larger neigh-

Table 16-6. *Selected Coefficients from Model Two Regressions*

	500-foot ring	*1,000-foot ring*	*2,000-foot ring*
In ring[a]	−0.1326**	−0.1133**	−0.0876**
	(0.0041)	(0.0029)	(0.0025)**
Postring[b]	0.1141**	0.0626**	0.0350
	(0.0105)	(0.0071)	(0.0054)
Tpost[c]	−0.0046*	−0.0019	0.0014
	(0.0019)	(0.0012)	(0.0009)
Summary statistic			
Adjusted R^2	0.8379	0.8383	0.8381
N	234,591	234,591	234,591

Note: The equations are fixed-effects regressions in which the dependent variable is the logarithm of price per unit. Standard errors are in parentheses. All regressions include Zip*Quarter dummies and the full set of building controls. * denotes significance at the 5 percent level, and ** at the 1 percent level.

a. Within the specified distance of a homeownership site, whether the development is completed or not.

b. Within the specified distance of a completed homeownership site.

c. Years since completion of a homeownership project, for sales within the specified distance of a completed project.

borhoods (zip codes) in which projects were located were also improving around the same time as a result of HPD-sponsored rental housing development or other community development efforts. If so, then the price differential between the rings and their surrounding zip codes might even begin to expand.

As noted above and as shown in figure 16-3, the average price differential between the rings and their zip codes was already declining before project completion. Even without the homeownership projects, it might have continued to decline. Our third specification provides an estimate of impact above and beyond what would have been predicted by prior trends in prices in the ring/zip code price gap (see equation 16-4). As noted, these impact estimates essentially reflect the assumption that prices in the rings would have continued to rise at the same rate relative to the zip code that they rose in the previous five years.

As shown in table 16-7, the results suggest that immediately after completion the gap between prices in the 500-foot rings and their surrounding zip codes falls by an average of 6.4 percentage points. A similar pattern obtains in the 1,000-foot and 2,000-foot rings, though changes are predictably smaller. After completion, the gap between prices in the 1,000-foot ring and prices in the larger zip code is shown to shrink by 3.3 percentage points, and the gap between the 2,000-foot ring and the zip code falls by 2.9 percentage points.[33]

Figures 16-3 and 16-4 illustrate these results in the 500-foot and 2,000-foot rings, respectively. The dashed line labeled "extended before-completion trend" indicates the change in the prices in the ring that would have occurred if predevelopment trends had continued. The continuous line plots the average change

33. Full results are available from the authors upon request.

Table 16-7. *Selected Coefficients from Model Three Regressions with Ring-Specific Time Trend*

	500-foot ring	*1,000-foot ring*	*2,000-foot ring*
In ring[a]	–0.0851**	–0.0860**	–0.0816**
	(0.0082)	(0.0057)	(0.0045)
Postring[b]	0.0642**	0.0331**	0.0288**
	(0.0138)	(0.0093)	(0.0069)
Tpost[c]	–0.0118**	–0.0077**	0.0001
	(0.0032)	(0.0021)	(0.0016)
Summary statistic			
Adjusted R^2	0.8380	0.8383	0.8381
N	234,591	234,591	234,591

Note: The equations are fixed-effects regressions in which the dependent variable is the logarithm of price per unit. Standard errors are in parentheses. All regressions include Zip*Quarter dummies and the full set of building controls. * denotes significance at the 5 percent level, and ** at the 1 percent level.

a. Within the specified distance of a homeownership site, whether the development is completed or not.

b. Within the specified distance of a completed homeownership site.

c. Years since completion of a homeownership project, for sales within the specified distance of a completed project.

in prices after homeownership units were completed, based on the estimated coefficients from the *Postring* and *Tpost* variables. The scattered "square points" show the annual ring coefficients from the specification in table 16-5, which can be interpreted as the average, quality-controlled difference between prices in the ring and prices in the zip code in each year. Once again, the impact on properties in close proximity to the homeownership units appears to decline over time, but in this specification the decline is more rapid. This is unsurprising because here the impact is estimated relative to the rate of growth that occurred during the five years before project completion, which was quite rapid. In the 500-foot ring, for example, the coefficient on *Tpost* indicates that the 6.4 percentage point differential attributable to being within the ring of a project declines by 1.2 percentage points per year. Immediately after completion, in other words, price levels in the 500-foot ring get much closer to price levels in the surrounding zip codes. Several years after completion, however, prices in the ring are *lower* relative to the zip code than they would have been in the absence of the development had prior trends continued.

Note that this estimate of the impact is likely to be a lower bound. Some of the run-up in prices in the ring relative to the zip code before completion may have been caused by the project itself. And the figure makes clear that our impact estimates are sensitive to the length of the precompletion period that we use for extrapolation. If instead of extrapolating the rate of growth that occurred during the five years before completion we instead extrapolated based upon the three years before completion, we would find a much more sustained effect.

Figure 16-3. *Price Trends in 500-Foot-Ring*

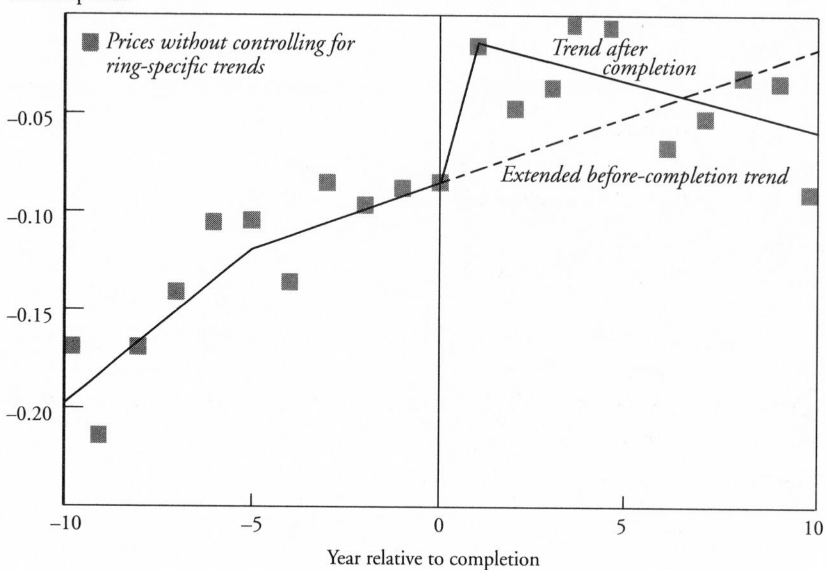

Figure 16-4. *Price Trends in 2,000-Foot-Ring*

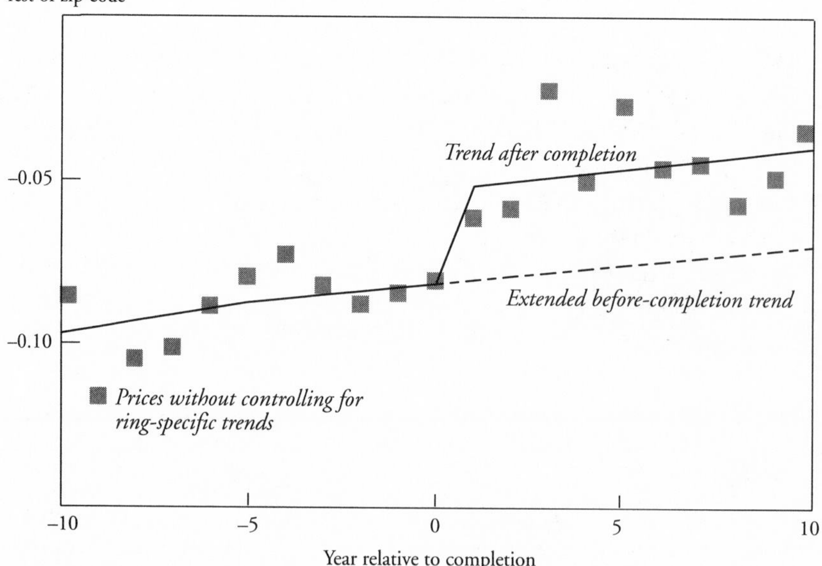

We see a similar though less dramatic story in the 1,000-foot ring, but a different pattern in the 2,000-foot ring. As shown in table 16-7, the coefficient on *Tpost* is not significantly different from zero in the 2,000-foot ring, indicating that after completion prices in the ring rise at the same rate relative to their zip codes that they did before development. As shown in figure 16-4, the initial jump in prices in the ring relative to the zip code is sustained over time. (The gap between the extended before-completion trend and the trend after completion is constant.) Again, this pattern may reflect a spread of spillover effects of the new housing units to larger areas over time.

Heterogeneity of Impacts

In this section, we explore potential differences among three sources of heterogeneity: project size (number of units); project type (Nehemiah versus Partnership); and timing (housing market conditions). We do so by supplementing the model in equation 16-4 with variables capturing size, type, and housing market conditions.

Number of Units

The notion that impacts depend on project size has broad intuitive appeal. It seems reasonable, for instance, to assume that the impact of 300 units will be greater than the impact of a single unit. In table 16-8 we examine the role of scale, testing whether there are different impacts for properties in the ring of 1–50 units; 51–100 units; 101–200 units; 201–400 units; and 401–600 units.[34] (In the 500-foot ring, these latter three categories are collapsed into one; in the 1,000-foot ring, the latter two categories are collapsed into one.)

In the 500-foot ring, larger scale indeed appears to imply significantly larger impacts. The gap between the prices of properties within the ring and properties in the zip code falls by 3.8 percentage points after fewer than fifty homeownership units are completed, by 9.5 percentage points after 50–100 units are completed, and by nearly 19 percentage points after more than 100 units are completed.

In the 1,000-foot and 2,000-foot rings, estimated impacts inside the ring of the largest developments (more than 200 units in the 1,000-foot and more than 400 units in the 2,000-foot ring) are fairly large. At the same time, the esti-

34. We experimented with several different ways to represent project size. We tested a linear model, and the coefficient on the number of units was consistently positive. A quadratic specification yielded less-consistent results, but in all rings the coefficient on the quadratic term was positive and statistically significant in the 500- and 2,000-foot rings. Note that we do not distinguish between a sale that is within a certain distance of two fifty-unit developments and another sale that is within the same distance of a single 100-unit development. Our specification simply controls for the total number of units within a certain distance.

Table 16-8. *Selected Coefficients from Regression Results with Ring-Specific Time Trend Controlling for Project Size*

	500-foot ring	*1,000-foot ring*	*2,000-foot ring*
In ring[a]	–0.0845**	–0.0870**	–0.0834**
	(0.0082)	(0.0057)	(0.0045)
Postring, 1–50 units[b]	0.0380*	0.0033**	0.0475**
	(0.0151)	(0.0104)	(0.0079)
Postring, 51–100 units	0.0953**	0.0115	0.0100
	(0.0234)	(0.0159)	(0.0114)
Postring, 101–200 units	0.1890**	0.0284	–0.0121
	(0.0319)	(0.0177)	(0.0121)
Postring, 201–400 units		0.1006**	–0.0618**
		(0.0311)	(0.0168)
Postring, 401+ units			0.0484
			(0.0263)
Tpost, 1–50 units[c]	–0.0071*	–0.0041	0.0007
	(0.0035)	(0.0023)	(0.0018)
Tpost, 51–100 units	–0.0231**	–0.0093**	0.0046*
	(0.0048)	(0.0032)	(0.0022)
Tpost, 101–200 units	–0.0218**	–0.0124**	0.0057*
	(0.0060)	(0.0035)	(0.0024)
Tpost, 201–400 units		–0.0170**	0.0045
		(0.0050)	(0.0029)
Tpost, 401+ units			–0.0078*
Summary statistic			
Adjusted R^2	0.8389	0.8392	0.8390
N	234,591	234,591	234,591

Note: The equations are fixed-effects regressions in which the dependent variable is the logarithm of price per unit. Standard errors are in parentheses. All regressions include Zip*Quarter dummies and the full set of building controls. * denotes significance at the 5 percent level, and ** at the 1 percent level.

a. Within the specified distance of a homeownership site, whether the development is completed or not.

b. Within the specified distance of a completed homeownership site of the specified size.

c. Years since completion of a homeownership project, for sales within the specified distance of a completed project of the specified size.

mated impact on properties near smaller numbers of units is typically much smaller, and in two cases negative. Interestingly, the estimated impact of proximity to 1–50 units is positive and statistically significant, while the impact of proximity to 51–200 units is negligible.

In summary, we find that larger projects typically have a larger impact on property values.[35] This pattern would be predicted by any of the mechanisms that would generate positive externalities. For example, if the city investments

35. Santiago, Galster, and Tatian (2001) also find that a larger number of projects within 1,001–2,000 feet of sale magnifies the initial positive effect. However, they do not find similar scale effects for projects that are within 1,000 feet of a sale.

raise neighborhood property values because they remove dilapidated buildings and clean up vacant lots, then larger projects should result in larger improvements. In contrast, this pattern would not be expected if the results were driven by sample selection bias—that is, the city's ability to "pick winners" by choosing sites likely to appreciate in value. If anything, this type of bias should be most important for the smallest projects because smaller tracts of land are much more readily available, giving HPD greater flexibility over site selection.

Project Type

As noted previously, the Nehemiah Plan and the Partnership New Homes programs differ in potentially important ways. Nehemiah developments typically include large numbers of identical, single-family row homes built on large, vacant tracts of city-owned land. Partnership developments include a larger variety of housing types and were often built on much smaller parcels. Nehemiah units were also considerably less costly to build and to buy, and as a result their owner-occupants have somewhat lower incomes. Thus Partnership and Nehemiah developments may well have different impacts on surrounding neighborhoods.

To explore such differences, we supplemented the models in table 16-8 with variables capturing the proportion of Nehemiah units in each of the different size categories (1–50 units, 51–100 units, more than 100 units) as well as a variable identifying whether the property sold was in the ring of a Nehemiah unit. This allowed us to investigate the extent to which the proportion of Nehemiah units within a given distance of a property has an impact on its price, after controlling for the total number of units.[36] We found that before development prices of properties within 500 feet of a future Partnership site were on average only 5.4 percent lower than those of comparable properties in their zip codes. As expected, properties located within 500 feet of future Nehemiah units were considerably more distressed, with prices on average 29.5 percent (5.4 percent plus 24.1 percent) lower than prices of comparable properties in their zip codes.

We find somewhat mixed evidence about whether the impacts differ with project sponsor or type. In the 500-foot ring, coefficients on the Postring*Share Nehemiah interaction terms are positive for the 1–50 unit and 100+ unit categories and, in the case of the 100+ unit category, statistically significant. In particular, the results suggest that being located near more than 100 completed Partnership units increases the prices in the ring relative to the zip code by 15.8 percentage points; the increase in prices caused by being near the same number of Nehemiah units is estimated at 23.6 percentage points.[37] In the 1,000-foot

36. Full results are available from the authors upon request.

37. One possible explanation is that the Nehemiah developments in the 100+ unit category actually contain a larger number of units. But this is not the case. In fact, the Partnership developments in the 100+ unit category appear to be somewhat larger on average. For sales within 500 feet

ring, by contrast, the type of unit has little effect on the magnitude of the impact. And in the 2,000-foot ring, the impact of larger shares of Nehemiah Plan units appears to be negative, at least in the case of large projects. In short, it appears that Nehemiah Plan units may have somewhat larger effects on properties that are in close proximity to the units, yet, at the same time, the geographic reach of their impact appears to be more limited. We plan to explore these differences further in future work.

Timing

The twenty-year period over which we examine housing prices covers two distinct periods in New York City's housing market. As shown in table 16-4, prices rose rapidly in our thirty-four community districts during the 1980s. Between 1982 and 1988, average housing prices rose by 145 percent, after controlling for inflation. This amounts to an average annual increase of roughly 16 percent in real terms. During the 1990s, prices fell, albeit at a much slower rate, before rising again slowly at the very end of the decade.

It is possible that we might see different impacts for these homeownership developments during these very different eras in the housing market. It may be, for example, that the private sector was willing to develop housing in our selected set of zip codes during boom times but was unwilling to do so when the housing market was less favorable. If so (and if the private sector was effectively never willing to develop housing inside the actual rings), then we might find that Nehemiah and Partnership developments had a smaller impact during the 1980s when housing prices were rising so rapidly. It might also be that the housing market cycles are somewhat different in lower-priced areas; perhaps they lag slightly behind the more affluent areas. Finally, the small positive impacts of these homeownership developments may simply be difficult to pick up in years when housing prices are rapidly rising.

To test for differences in differing housing markets, we separately examined the impact on sales during the 1980s and 1990s. In the interest of brevity, the results are not shown here, but we found few significant differences in impacts. Naturally, prices in the rings relative to the zip codes before completion were lower for properties selling in the 1980s. (Again, as shown in table 16-4, prices in the rings were lower relative to their zip codes during the 1980s.) But we see no significant differences in the immediate impact of the homeownership units. The one difference is that in the 500-foot ring the initial positive impact on prices appears to disappear almost immediately for sales in the 1980s, while for properties that sold during the 1990s, the positive effects appear to be more sustained.

of a Nehemiah development of more than 100 units, the mean number of units within 500 feet of the sale is 158. For sales within 500 feet of a Partnership development of over 100 units, the mean number of units within 500 feet of the sale is 182. More generally, the mean number of Partnership and Nehemiah units—within the given categories—is virtually identical.

Conclusion

With the benefit of more precise data than has been employed in prior studies, this chapter provides a more detailed portrait about what happens to property values following the development of affordable, owner-occupied housing. We show that prices of properties in the rings surrounding the homeownership projects have risen relative to their zip codes over the past two decades, and our results suggest that part of this rise is attributable to the affordable homeownership programs administered in New York City by the New York City Housing Partnership, South Bronx Churches, and East Brooklyn Churches. These efforts, in other words, appear to have had a positive impact on property values within their immediate neighborhoods.

The source of this positive externality is not clear. It may be due to the transformation of vacant or derelict eyesores into well-maintained, pleasant homes. It may also be caused by the inmigration of relatively higher-income residents to the neighborhoods. Finally, a higher rate of homeownership in itself may generate positive impacts for the community ranging from greater neighborhood stability to better upkeep to more community activism.

In future work we hope to shed more light on the roots of the positive effect. In particular, we will compare the effects that the city's rental housing programs have on surrounding property values with the effects of homeownership programs. To the extent that owner-occupied housing appears to have larger effects, it might suggest that owner-occupied housing yields unique benefits, above and beyond the effects of removing blight and producing pleasant and attractive homes.

As for policy implications, our results suggest that owners of properties in the relevant communities will enjoy an increase in wealth that appears to be generated by the new housing. In addition, to the extent that the city reassesses properties in these communities, additional tax revenues will be generated. Of course, higher property values may not benefit everyone financially. Rents may also increase in these areas to reflect the increase in value attributable to the homeownership programs. For low- and moderate-income households already having difficulty paying their rents, an increase in homeownership in their community may be a mixed blessing.[38] Part of this potential increase in rents would likely be ameliorated by rent regulation in many of the neighborhoods where Partnership and Nehemiah housing is located. Nevertheless, the question of whether the improvement in property values surrounding new homeownership housing units and the resulting increases in property tax revenues are greater than the costs of the program (both in actual subsidies and possible negative

38. In 1999 almost one-quarter of all renters in New York City paid more than half of their incomes in rent (New York University School of Law, Center for Real Estate and Urban Policy, 2001).

impacts on renters) requires sharper estimates and more empirical investigation. Such a cost-benefit analysis may be critical to future decision-making.

References

Basu, Sabyasachi, and Thomas G. Thibodeau. 1998. "Analysis of Spatial Autocorrelation in House Prices." *Journal of Real Estate Finance and Economics* 17 (1): 61–85.

Briggs, Xavier de Souza, Joe T. Darden, and Angela Aidala. 1999. "In the Wake of Desegregation: Early Impacts of Scattered-Site Public Housing on Neighborhoods in Yonkers, New York." *Journal of the American Planning Association* 65 (1): 27–49.

Can, Ayse, and Isaac F. Megbolugbe. 1997. "Spatial Dependence and House Price Index Construction." *Journal of Real Estate Finance and Economics* 14: 203–22.

Cummings, Jean L., Denise DiPasquale, and Matthew E. Kahn. 2000. "Inner City Homeownership Opportunities and Black Community Choice." Paper presented at the American Real Estate and Urban Economics Annual Meeting, January 2001.

Dietz, Robert, and Donald Haurin. 2001. "The Social and Private Consequences of Homeownership." Department of Economics, Ohio State University.

DiPasquale, Denise, and Edward Glaeser. 1999. "Incentives and Social Capital." *Journal of Urban Economics* 45: 354–84.

Donovan, Shaun. 1994. *Affordable Homeownership in New York City: Nehemiah Plan Homes and the New York City Partnership, A and B.* Kennedy School Case Program 1252 and 1253. Cambridge, Mass.: Kennedy School Case Program, Harvard University.

Ellen, Ingrid Gould, Michael H. Schill, Scott Susin, and Amy Ellen Schwartz. 2001. "Building Homes, Reviving Neighborhoods: Spillovers from Subsidized Construction of Owner-Occupied Housing in New York City." *Journal of Housing Research* 12 (2): 185–216.

Galster, George D. 1987. *Homeowners and Neighborhood Reinvestment.* Durham, N.C.: Duke University Press.

Galster, George C., Peter Tatian, and Robin Smith. 1999. "The Impact of Neighbors Who Use Section 8 Certificates on Property Values." *Housing Policy Debate* 10 (4): 879–917.

Goetz, Edward, Hin Kin Lam, and Anne Heitlinger. 1996. "There Goes the Neighborhood? The Impact of Subsidized Multi-Family Housing on Urban Neighborhoods." Working Paper 96-1. Minneapolis: Center for Urban and Regional Affairs.

Halvorsen, Robert, and Raymond Palmquist. 1980. "The Interpretation of Dummy Variables in Semilogarithmic Equations." *American Economic Review* 70 (3): 474–75.

Kennedy, Peter E. 1981. "Estimation with Correctly Interpreted Dummy Variables in Semilogarithmic Equations." *American Economic Review* 71 (4): 801.

Lee, Chang-Moo, Dennis P. Culhane, and Susan M. Wachter. 1999. "The Differential Impacts of Federally Assisted Housing Programs on Nearby Property Values: A Philadelphia Case Study." *Housing Policy Debate* 10 (1): 75–93.

Lyons, Robert F., and Scott Loveridge. 1993. "A Hedonic Estimation of the Effect of Federally Subsidized Housing on Nearby Residential Property Values." Staff Paper P93-6. St. Paul, Minn.: Department of Agriculture and Applied Economics, University of Minnesota.

New York University School of Law, Center for Real Estate and Urban Policy. 2001. *The State of the City's Housing and Neighborhoods.* New York.

Nourse, Hugh O. 1963. "The Effects of Public Housing on Property Values in St. Louis." *Land Economics* 39: 433–41.

Orlebeke, Charles J. 1997. *New Life at Ground Zero: New York, Homeownership, and the Future of American Cities.* Albany, N.Y.: Rockefeller Institute Press.

Pollakowski, Henry O. 1997. "The Effects of Rent Deregulation in New York City." Working Paper 67. Cambridge, Mass.: MIT Center for Real Estate.

Poterba, James M. 1984. "Tax Subsidies to Owner-Occupied Housing: An Asset Market Approach." *Quarterly Journal of Economics* 99 (4): 729–52.

Rabiega, William A., Ta-Win Lin, and Linda Robinson. 1984. "The Property Value Impacts of Public Housing Projects in Low and Moderate Density Residential Neighborhoods." *Land Economics* 60: 174–79.

Rohe, William, and Leslie Stewart. 1996. "Homeownership and Neighborhood Stability." *Housing Policy Debate* 7 (1): 37–81.

Rohe, William, Shannon Van Zandt, and George McCarthy. 2000. "The Social Benefits and Costs of Homeownership: A Critical Assessment of the Research." Working Paper 00-01. Washington: Research Institute for Housing America.

Rosen, Sherwin. 1974. "Hedonic Prices and Implicit Markets: Product Differentiation in Pure Competition." *Journal of Political Economy* 82 (1): 34–55.

Santiago, Anna M., George C. Galster, and Peter Tatian. 2001. "Assessing the Property Value Impacts of the Dispersed Subsidy Housing Program in Denver." *Journal of Policy Analysis and Management* 20 (1): 65–88.

Scafidi, Benjamin P., Michael H. Schill, Susan M. Wachter, and Dennis P. Culhane. 1998. "An Economic Analysis of Housing Abandonment." *Journal of Housing Economics* 7 (4): 287–303.

Stuart, Lee. 1997. "Come, Let Us Rebuild the Walls of Jerusalem: Broad-Based Organizing in the South Bronx." In Robert D. Carle and Louis A Decaro Jr., eds., *Signs of Hope in the City: Ministries of Community Renewal.* Valley Forge, Penn.: Judson Press.

Wylde, Kathryn. 1999. "The Contribution of Public-Private Partnerships to New York's Assisted Housing Industry." In Michael H. Schill, ed., *Housing and Community Development in New York City*, pp. 73–91. Albany: SUNY Press.

Contributors

WAYNE R. ARCHER
University of Florida

ERIC S. BELSKY
Joint Center for Housing Studies
Harvard University

THOMAS P. BOEHM
University of Tennessee

MICHAEL CARLINER
National Association of Home Builders

KARL E. CASE
Wellesley College

MICHAEL COLLINS
Neighborhood Reinvestment Corporation

DAVID CROWE
National Association of Home Builders

FRANK DEGIOVANNI
Ford Foundation

WALTER R. DAVIS
University of North Carolina–Chapel Hill

MARK DUDA
Joint Center for Housing Studies
Harvard University

INGRID GOULD ELLEN
New York University

WILLIAM N. GOETZMANN
Yale University

EDWARD L. GOLDING
Freddie Mac

DONALD R. HAURIN
Ohio State University

R. JEAN HAURIN
Ohio State University

Abdighani Hirad
Freddie Mac

Steven Hornburg
Research Institute for Housing America

David C. Ling
University of Florida

Maryna Marynchenko
Analysis Group/Economics

George McCarthy
Ford Foundation

Gary A. McGill
University of Florida

Frank E. Nothaft
Freddie Mac

Toby L. Parcel
Ohio State University

Roberto G. Quercia
University of North Carolina–Chapel Hill

Nicolas P. Retsinas
Joint Center for Housing Studies
Harvard University

William M. Rohe
University of North Carolina–Chapel Hill

Stuart S. Rosenthal
Syracuse University

Michael H. Schill
New York University

Alan M. Schlottmann
University of Nevada–Las Vegas

Amy Ellen Schwartz
New York University

Matthew Spiegel
Yale School of Management

Michael A. Stegman
University of North Carolina–Chapel Hill

Eric Stein
Self-Help

Brian J. Surette
Freddie Mac

Scott Susin
Bureau of the Census

Robert Van Order
Freddie Mac

Shannon van Zandt
University of North Carolina–Chapel Hill

Peter Zorn
Freddie Mac

Index

she wanted this. Lindsey wanted to give herself over to Camilla so completely, to trust her Mistress with every part of herself, to give her all to this woman who made her feel so many incredible things she hadn't even known she was capable of feeling.

Camilla cupped Lindsey's face and kissed her greedily. Lindsey let out a low murmur. The taste of her Mistress's lips was better than fine wine, or chocolate covered strawberries, or any of the other indulgent delights that she'd shared with Camilla.

Camilla drew her fingertips down Lindsey's cheek, down the side of her throat and between her breasts. Her Mistress's feather-light touch made goosebumps form on Lindsey's skin. Soon, Camilla's hands were all over Lindsey's body, painting invisible lines with the pads of her fingers, sculpting Lindsey's curves with her palms.

Right then and there, Lindsey forgot all about the blindfold. All her other senses were overloaded with Camilla. Her touch, her kiss, the scent of her—it flooded every cell in Lindsey's body with need.

"Oh, you like this, don't you?" Camilla traced her thumb over Lindsey's pebbled nipple. "It's not so scary after all, is it?"

"No, Mistress," Lindsey said.

Camilla slid her palm down to Lindsey's mound, skimming her middle finger between Lindsey's outspread lips with an agonizingly light touch. Lindsey pushed her hips out toward Camilla as far as she could.

"Patience." Camilla pressed herself against Lindsey. "I'll give you what you need, but only if you don't rush me, understand?"

"Yes, Mistress," Lindsey whispered.

Camilla broke away. Lindsey waited in silence. Then, she felt a puff of heat on the inside of her thigh. Camilla's breath.

Her Mistress was on her knees.

Lindsey's lips parted, a gust of air escaping them. Camilla had her tied up and at her mercy, yet she offered Lindsey this small act of submission. It paled in comparison to Lindsey's submission. But it filled Lindsey with a desire so insatiable that she felt like she was drowning.

Her Mistress kissed her way up Lindsey's thigh, grabbed onto Lindsey's ass cheeks, and drew her mouth over Lindsey's lower lips.

Camilla's lip brushed the side of Lindsey's clit, drawing a sharp hiss from her. With the blindfold keeping Lindsey in darkness, Camilla's every touch was unexpected.

"You can come whenever you want," Camilla said. "I'll be much too busy to give you permission." She swept her hand all the way up Lindsey's leg. "Just enjoy it."

Before Lindsey could say so much as a "Yes, Mistress," Camilla's mouth was between her thighs. She rolled her tongue over Lindsey's folds, from outside to inside, every stroke getting closer and closer to Lindsey's aching bud. Lindsey bit her lip, anticipation growing inside her.

Camilla ran her tongue down to Lindsey's entrance and dipped it inside. Lindsey's thighs quivered. This slow torture was too much. And the thought of her Mistress on her knees, toying with her restrained body, inflamed her even more.

Finally, Camilla slid her tongue up to Lindsey's clit. Lindsey let out a long, low moan, her muscles growing slack. If she didn't have the cross to hold her up, she would have collapsed into a puddle on the floor.

Camilla worked her mouth between Lindsey's legs, her tongue swirling and her lips sucking. A faint murmur arose from Camilla. The sound vibrated deep into Lindsey's core.

Lindsey trembled. "Mistress!"

One more stroke of Camilla's tongue was all it took to make Lindsey come apart. Her head tipped back as she let out a cry that echoed through the playroom.

When Lindsey stilled, Camilla stood up and crushed her lips against Lindsey's. She lifted the blindfold from Lindsey's eyes. Lindsey had been so lost in ecstasy that she'd forgotten she was even wearing it.

"I'm going to untie you now, okay?" Camilla said.

"Yes, Mistress."

One by one, Camilla unfastened each of the cuffs from the cross, but she didn't remove them from Lindsey's wrists and ankles. She drew Lindsey onto the bed and enveloped her with her arms.

"How are you doing?" Camilla pushed Lindsey's auburn locks out of her face. "Is there anything you need?"

"Mistress," Lindsey said. "The only thing I need right now is you."

She placed her hand on the side of her Mistress's neck and brought her lips to Camilla's. The kiss grew hungrier, more demanding. Lindsey's hands roamed Camilla's body, taking in every part of her with her fingertips. The curve of her cheekbones. The arc of her neck. The dip of her waist, and the mountain of her hip. The soft skin of her inner thighs.

Camilla's breath hitched.

"Mistress," Lindsey said. "May I?"

"Yes," Camilla said. "You can have me. Slowly."

Slowly. Lindsey withdrew her hand and shifted down Camilla's body. She dragged her lips down her Mistress's neck and along her collarbone. A gentle rumble rose from Camilla's chest. Lindsey kissed her way along her Mistress's full breasts and tongued her pebbled peak. Camilla's chest arched up from the bed, pressing herself harder into Lindsey's mouth.

Her lips still on Camilla's nipples, Lindsey snaked her hand down Camilla's stomach, all the way to where her thighs met. Camilla spread them out wide. Lindsey slid her fingers into Camilla's slit. It felt slick and warm under her fingertips.

But what Lindsey really wanted was to taste her again. She crawled all the way down her Mistress's body and parted Camilla's lips with her fingertips. She dipped her head down and licked her all over. Her petal-like folds. Her silky entrance. Her tiny, hidden bud. Lindsey got lost between her Mistress's legs, worshiping the treasure that lay within.

Camilla moaned, her hand falling down to the back of Lindsey's head gently. This wasn't like last time, when Camilla had been firmly in control. This time, Camilla yielded to Lindsey. Sure, Camilla wasn't bound and blindfolded. But Lindsey knew that for her Mistress, this was almost the same thing.

"Oh, Lindsey." Camilla threaded her fingers through Lindsey's hair, holding on tightly. "I'm so close."

Lindsey continued, using everything she could to ravish her Mistress like her Mistress had done to her moments ago. It wasn't long before Camilla let out a gasp, her body quaking as an orgasm took her.

Minutes later, the two of them lay side by side on the bed, totally spent. Lindsey closed her eyes, mumbling wordlessly. She was on another plane, one where nothing existed outside her, and Camilla, and this luxurious bed.

"Lindsey?" Camilla's voice cut through the stillness of the room.

"Mm?"

"I love you."

Something fluttered in Lindsey's chest. When she'd said those words to Camilla, she hadn't expected Camilla to say them back. Just knowing Camilla felt something for her was enough. But hearing her Mistress say those three little words made Lindsey happier than she could have ever imagined.

"I wanted to say it back to you the night of the engagement party, but I was scared."

"Why, Mistress?" Lindsey could tell that this was difficult for Camilla. Maybe it would be easier for her to talk about it as 'Lindsey's Mistress' rather than 'Camilla.'

Camilla shifted on the bed beside her. "Over the course of my life, I've become accustomed to being alone. The truth is, it's easier that way. It means that I don't ever have to worry about being a burden on anyone. I don't have to worry that those close to me will start to resent me for all my limitations."

"I would never consider you a burden," Lindsey said. "And it's obvious that you get along just fine by yourself."

"That's because I've learned to adapt every part of my life around my illness. My carefully regimented routine is a necessity, not a choice. I can't afford to stray from it, to be spontaneous and free. It's restrictive. What happens when it all becomes too much for you?"

"It won't." Lindsey reached for Camilla's hand. "Mistress, neither of us knows what the future holds. All I know is that I want to spend it with you, no matter what."

Camilla was silent. Lindsey turned to look at her. Her eyes were closed and her body was still. The only sign of life was the slow rise and fall of Camilla's chest.

Finally, she spoke. "Do you mean that? That you want to spend the future with me?"

"Yes," Lindsey said. "I do."

"Because our three months is almost up. And ever since the other night, I've been thinking about what comes next."

"So have I. I just didn't know how to bring it up." It was only days since Lindsey had told Camilla she loved her, after all. It had been clear that Camilla was still getting used to the idea. Lindsey hadn't wanted to complicate things further.

"How would you like to move into the manor permanently?" Camilla asked.

Lindsey gaped at her. "Seriously?"

"Seriously. It will be perfect. Nothing will have to change. You can spend your days in the sunroom, working on your art, without having to worry about a thing."

Lindsey let out a wistful sigh. "That does sound perfect. But I wouldn't want to be a kept woman."

Camilla laughed. "A kept woman? Is this the 1920s? Where on earth did you hear a term like that?"

"If you really want to know, it was Denise."

Camilla shook her head. "That's so like her." She placed a hand on Lindsey's shoulder. "You won't be a kept woman. You'll be my girlfriend. My partner. My submissive. So, what do you say?"

"Yes, of course. I would love to stay here with you, Mistress."

"You have no idea how happy that makes me."

Lindsey brought her lips to Camilla's. This was everything she'd ever wanted. Everything she'd ever dreamed of.

Then why did she have this unshakable sense of unease gnawing at her stomach?

CHAPTER TWENTY-ONE

Lindsey peered over her sketchpad at her Mistress. Camilla lay stretched out along a chaise lounge on her side, wearing nothing but a robe made of pale pink silk. Her straight brown hair flowed down over the arm of the couch, and the afternoon sun streamed through the window behind her, giving her a golden glow.

Lindsey looked back down at her sketchpad. For the last half hour, she'd been trying to draw Camilla. Lindsey wanted to do something nice for her, to give her a gift that was unique and personal. At first, she'd tried to draw Camilla from memory, but she couldn't get it right, so she'd asked Camilla to pose for her.

But even now, Lindsey was struggling. Maybe it was just nerves. This was the first time Lindsey had let Camilla into the sunroom she'd transformed into her studio. And just moments ago, she'd shown Camilla her art for the first time. Lindsey felt like her soul was on display.

Camilla yawned and stretched out her arms. "Christ, is this what people did before cameras were invented? I should ask June to bring me a bottle of wine."

"Hold still." When Lindsey looked up from her sketchpad again,

Camilla was giving her a frosty look. "Sorry! I mean, please hold still, Mistress."

"All right," Camilla said. "Can I talk, at least?"

"Yes, just try not to move too much."

Frowning, Lindsey attempted to fix the shading around Camilla's eyes. How was she supposed to capture the likeness of this larger-than-life woman that she knew so intimately with nothing more than a stick of charcoal and a piece of paper?

"I was thinking some more about the future," Camilla said. "About us, and you. Have you thought about making a career of your art?

"I don't know," Lindsey murmured.

"Isn't that what you always wanted to do with your life?"

"I guess." Lindsey paused, her charcoal poised above the page. "But I have all those bills to pay off."

Camilla propped herself up on one elbow. "Darling, I was always going to give you the money to cover your medical bills. That hasn't changed now that we're actually in a relationship. You don't have to worry about that anymore."

Camilla had a point. Lindsey didn't have any reason not to pursue her dreams. She felt a surge of anxiety. "I don't know if I'm ready for that yet."

"Are you really not ready? Or are you just afraid?"

Lindsey didn't answer.

"You've shown me your work, Lindsey. You have real talent. I know good art when I see it, and yours is wonderful. It would be a shame to hide it from the rest of the world."

"Maybe you're right."

"Well, if you decide you want to put yourself out there, I have a friend who owns a gallery in the city. If you put together a portfolio, I can show it to her."

"I wouldn't want to take advantage of your connections," Lindsey said.

"You wouldn't be. My friend is always looking for works by fresh talent. And she's merciless when it comes to anything that isn't to her taste. She won't hesitate to turn you down if she doesn't like your work. But I know she'll love it."

"Can I think about it?"

"Sure." Camilla settled back onto the chaise.

Lindsey stared at her sketchpad and sighed. This was all wrong. If she couldn't even draw a simple sketch of Camilla, how was she supposed to create something worthy of showing in a gallery?

"Are you okay?" Camilla asked.

"I'm just struggling with this, that's all," Lindsey said. "Maybe we should do this another time."

Camilla sat up. "Come here, Lindsey."

Lindsey placed her sketchbook on the chair and slunk over to sit next to Camilla.

Camilla draped an arm around Lindsey and pulled her close. "I'm sorry, I didn't mean to pressure you."

"It's not that. I'm just having an off day."

"You do seem tense. How about we do something else instead?" Camilla's voice dropped to a seductive whisper. "Something to help you relax."

Lindsey smiled. "Like what, Mistress?"

"Like have a little fun in the playroom together."

Lindsey glanced at the clock. It was mid-afternoon. "Don't you have to work?"

"Last time I checked, I was in charge. I can do whatever I want. And right now, what I want is you." Camilla drew Lindsey in close and kissed her, hard. "Playroom. Now."

"Relax." Camilla brushed her fingers along Lindsey's bare back. "You're still too tense."

Lindsey murmured into the pillow. She was lying naked on her stomach on the playroom bed, the cuffs around her wrists and ankles and the blindfold covering her eyes. Camilla was in the middle of giving her what could only be described as a kinky massage.

Camilla's hands were replaced by long, thin tails that swept across Lindsey's back. It had to be a flogger. She shivered, her muscles loosening. The leather strips tickled her skin.

"That's much better," Camilla said.

She flicked the flogger against Lindsey's back, first gently, then a little harder, ramping up the intensity with each strike. Lindsey moaned with bliss, letting the smacks resonate through her body. She was starting to enter that space where everything outside of her seemed to fall away.

"Are you feeling more relaxed now?" Camilla asked.

"Yes, Mistress." Lindsey's sensitized skin tingled pleasantly, and there was a faint scent of something sweet and floral in the air.

"Then it's time for the fun to really begin."

Lindsey reveled in her powerlessness. The cuffs around her ankles and wrists weren't attached to anything, so she wasn't restrained in any way. However, being blindfolded still made Lindsey feel on edge, and she found that rush almost as addictive as Camilla herself.

"Stay perfectly still," her Mistress said.

Camilla's footsteps receded from the bed. Lindsey listened carefully, but she couldn't hear a thing. She took a deep breath, and froze.

The sweet scent that had filled the room had been replaced by something else. Something smoky, like burning oil. It hung so thick in the air that Lindsey couldn't breathe. Suddenly, the cuffs around her ankles and wrists felt tight and restricting, and the darkness shrouding her seemed to swallow her up. She was trapped, unable to move, the smell of fuel and smoke from a fire she couldn't see-

"Lindsey?" Her Mistress's clear voice cut through her nightmare.

"Apple," Lindsey whispered.

At once, Camilla was on the bed with her, tearing off the blindfold. Lindsey opened her eyes to see her Mistress staring back at her.

"Are you all right?" Although Camilla tried to hide it, there was a hint of panic in her voice.

Lindsey nodded, blinking against the light. She sat up. On the nightstand next to her were two lit candles. Candles, the kind used to drip hot wax on someone's skin. That's what the smell was. Now, it smelled nothing like burning fuel. Lindsey's brain had made that part up on its own.

Camilla grabbed a thick blanket from the end of the bed and draped it around Lindsey's shoulders. Lindsey shivered and pulled it tight. Her heart was finally slowing down to normal.

"What's the matter?" Camilla asked.

"I'm sorry," Lindsey said quietly. Camilla seemed hesitant to touch her. But considering how erratically she was behaving, Lindsey didn't blame her.

"Don't be sorry. Just tell me what's going on."

"I didn't know that was going to happen. I thought I was okay with being blindfolded and all the other stuff, but I've just been feeling so off, and-" Lindsey's lip quivered. "I'm sorry."

Camilla wrapped her arms around Lindsey and pulled her in close. "Lindsey, it's fine. You used your safeword. That's a good thing. And even if you hadn't, I could tell something was wrong. Do you want to tell me what all this is about?"

Lindsey hesitated. "It was just, the darkness and the smell of smoke. It reminded me of the car accident I was in. I've been jumpy about certain things since then. Long car rides. Driving at night. Smoke, apparently, too."

"It sounds like what you went through was difficult," Camilla said.

Lindsey shrugged. "I guess."

"Have you talked to anyone about it?"

"Not really."

"Do you want to talk about it?"

"I don't know," Lindsey said. "I feel like I'm making a big deal out of nothing. Lots of people get into car accidents. I walked away from it fine in the end. Plus, it was all my fault."

"Why do you say that?" Camilla asked.

"It happened when I was driving across the country to my parents' house at the very end of senior year." Underneath the blanket, Lindsey brought her hand up to the scar on her collarbone. "I'd basically spent the whole week drinking and partying. I was sober by the time I started driving, but I was really tired. I was on this long stretch of highway, without any streetlights, and there wasn't a car in sight. I don't know what happened exactly, but the next thing I knew, my car had gone off the road and I'd hit a tree.

"I hit my head in the crash, and when I came to, the lights had gone out, and it was dark, so I couldn't see anything. And I was trapped in the car, and I couldn't move. But I could smell smoke, and all I could think about was that the car was about to burst into flames and I'd die there, all alone, trapped in the dark."

"Lindsey, that must have been awful."

"That's the thing," Lindsey said. "I wasn't really in any danger, I just thought I was. Cars don't explode like they do in movies. I looked it up afterward. It doesn't happen."

Camilla rubbed her hand along Lindsey's arm. "You didn't know that."

"That doesn't make me feel like any less of an idiot for panicking over nothing. I don't even know how long I was trapped in my car for, but it felt like forever. Eventually, a woman drove past and called 911. She stayed with me until help came. They had to cut me out of the car. I ended up with a concussion and some broken bones. Apparently, I was lucky that I wasn't injured more seriously. I had a handful of surgeries and got out of the hospital after only a couple of weeks, but I had to do physical therapy for my broken femur for months afterward. I ended up moving back across the country to live with my parents while I recovered."

Camilla stroked Lindsey's arm. "That must have been hard."

"It was," Lindsey said. "But what came next was even harder. After I recovered, it felt like the whole world had changed. I moved back here, but all my friends from art school had moved on without me. I felt so anxious, and lost, and alone, but it was more than that. I'd changed. I just wasn't the same person I used to be."

"That's not surprising," Camilla said. "What you went through sounds pretty traumatic. It would make anyone anxious. And those kinds of experiences can change you."

"But no one ever tells you how to deal with that. Once your

bones are healed, you're just thrown out into the world and expected to get on with life. But how are you supposed to do that? How are you supposed to go back to being the person you were before everything? And how do you make people understand why you feel that way?"

"Oh, Lindsey." Camilla hugged her tighter. "I understand what that's like. To have something life changing happen to you and have everyone just expect you to get on with it."

"Huh," Lindsey said. "I guess you've been through this."

"Well, it wasn't exactly the same. But when the symptoms of my illness started, I was fourteen. No one knew what was going on, and no one knew how to help me. That went on for years. And when the doctors finally figured out what was causing everything, there was very little they could do. I was basically just told to get on with things. But how could I do that when I'd been stuck with this diagnosis that was going to affect me every day for the rest of my life? How could I go back to being that carefree teenager when my future had been changed irrevocably?"

"Yes, that's exactly it." Lindsey paused. "How did you deal with that?"

"Well, eventually, I ended up seeing a new doctor who insisted I get therapy," Camilla said. "It helped. My therapist told me that it was okay to grieve for the life that I once had, for the old me. That it was okay to feel lost and hopeless sometimes. That I didn't have to pretend that everything was okay all the time. And she taught me how to deal with all those feelings. You should consider seeing someone too."

"I've never been able to afford it," Lindsey said.

"You can now. I'll pay for it. And if you don't want to talk to a stranger, you can always talk to me. Whenever you need me, I'll be right here."

"Thanks." Lindsey gave Camilla a reserved smile. "I don't know why I never thought to talk to you about it. I'm just so used to pretending it's not a problem."

Camilla kissed Lindsey on the forehead. "Well, you don't have to pretend with me. I don't want there to be anything between us that we can't talk about."

Right. Lindsey's stomach tightened. This was why she'd been feeling uneasy. Despite everything that had passed between them, Lindsey was still hiding something from Camilla. She still hadn't told Camilla that she'd never been attracted to another woman before her.

But how was she supposed to tell Camilla that their relationship began with a lie?

CHAPTER TWENTY-TWO

Lindsey lay on Camilla's bed, a book in her hand. It was Lindsey's bed now, too. She'd been sleeping in it every night since Denise came to visit, but Camilla had asked Lindsey to 'move in' after their conversation the other night. Lindsey had said yes, but she still felt like an intruder. It didn't help that Camilla was away for work again. At least it was only for a few days this time. She was due back tomorrow night.

Lindsey gazed out the window at the night sky. Here Camilla was, planning their future together, yet Lindsey was still stuck on the lie she'd told Camilla the day they'd met. Lindsey wanted to tell her. But she didn't know how. And Lindsey didn't want to hurt her.

Maybe it would be better for her to take the secret to her grave.

Lindsey put down her book and got up from the bed. Being alone in this big house, with no one but her thoughts for company, was starting to get to her. Faith was due to call for a chat when she got home from work, but that wasn't for a few hours. Lindsey left Camilla's room and made her way downstairs in search of a snack.

She entered the main kitchen. It was empty at the moment, and every surface was sparkling clean. Lindsey had only been in here a handful of times. If she wanted something to eat, she usually asked June. But what Lindsey was really looking for was a distraction.

She opened the door to the walk-in pantry and began searching the shelves. It was like a tiny grocery store in itself. She found a few shelves in the back that were full of all those sweet, indulgent snacks that Camilla liked to eat. After browsing the selection for a few minutes, Lindsey picked out a block of dark chocolate and took it over to the island in the middle of the kitchen. She sat down and broke off a few squares, munching on them idly.

"Lindsey? Do you need something?"

Lindsey turned to see June at the door, a bucket of cleaning supplies in her hand.

"I was just looking for a snack." She held up the block of chocolate.

"Do you want something more substantial? I can make you anything you want."

"No, it's fine." Lindsey hesitated. "But I could use some company."

June put down the bucket and leaned against the bench across from Lindsey. "This place feels empty without her, doesn't it? She's like the lifeblood of this house."

"She is." Lindsey held out the block of chocolate to June, who broke off a small square.

"I'm glad the two of you found each other," June said. "Lord knows Camilla could use someone to take care of her."

"Are we talking about the same person? Camilla doesn't exactly need taking care of."

"That's not what I meant." June pulled up a chair and sat down. "I have no doubt that if Camilla went bankrupt tomorrow, and if all of her friends disappeared, she'd still find a way to single-handedly claw her way back up to where she is now. She doesn't need anyone else to survive. But it's a very lonely existence when all you do is survive."

That much was true. Lindsey had been living like that ever since the accident. Sleepwalking her way through each day, lost in a fog of anxiety and listlessness.

That was, until she met Camilla.

"I guess you're right," Lindsey said. "You seem to know Camilla pretty well."

June reached over to break off another piece of chocolate. "I've known her for 20 years. Her parents hired me, but after they passed away, Camilla kept me on and promoted me to head housekeeper. I've worked for her every day since then."

"Every day?"

"Well, I take the occasional vacation. Camilla tries to make me take more, but it's hard for me to leave this place. I have a connection to it. Camilla might be the lifeblood of the house, but I'm the brain."

"Keeping this place running seems like a lot of work," Lindsey said.

"It is. But the job comes with a lot of perks. Like the pay. I'm not even fifty, and I have enough money to retire tomorrow and never work again. Plus, Camilla's been taking care of my parents. They both have health problems, so they need round the clock care. Camilla pays for them to live in a world-class care facility."

"Wow, that's generous of her."

"Are you that surprised?" June said. "I thought you'd have her figured out by now."

"What do you mean?" Lindsey asked.

"Well, we both know how prickly Camilla can be on the outside, but she's got a good heart. She shows her love by helping out others, usually in the most outrageous of ways. And not just with money. She'll march into your life, fix all your problems, and make sure all your needs are taken care of, whether you want her to or not."

Yep. That was Camilla all over.

"That's why she needs someone like you," June said. "Someone who will let her pretend that she's your rock when in reality, you're the one who will quietly be there for her without letting her know it."

Lindsey rested her chin on her hands. It was true that Camilla seemed happiest when she was making other people happy. And whenever Camilla was unwell or felt stressed, all she wanted was to hold Lindsey and smother her with affection like Lindsey was the one who needed comforting.

June stood up and tucked her chair neatly under the kitchen island. "I better get back to work. This house has to be spotless when Camilla gets back. You know how your Mistress gets when things aren't up to her standards." She reached over to take one last piece of chocolate. "At least she doesn't make me write lines."

Heat rose up Lindsey's face. As June left the room, Lindsey buried her head in her hands. She shouldn't have been surprised that June was so sharp. She'd have to be to have survived in this house with Camilla for 20 years.

Lindsey grabbed the rest of the chocolate and made her way back up the stairs. When she reached the top, she paused. Instead of going toward Camilla's rooms, Lindsey went back to her old bedroom. She felt a little more comfortable there. And she knew she wouldn't feel welcome in Camilla's rooms until she'd dealt with the problem that was causing her guilt.

She flopped down on her bed and put in her headphones, blasting some music through them. Being in a little cocoon of sound usually helped take her mind off things. Lindsey shut her eyes. Before she knew it, she was drifting off to sleep.

Lindsey woke with a start. Her phone was buzzing on her chest and the room was pitch black. She yawned. How long had she been asleep for?

Lindsey sat up and answered her phone. "Hey, Faith."

"Hi," Faith said cheerfully. "Sorry I took so long to call you. I had to stay back and have an awkward conversation with the mom I work for."

"Oh, is everything okay?"

"Yeah. My pay was late, but she assured me they'd pay me tomorrow. How are you?"

"I'm okay. A little bored. Camilla is away again."

"Is that why you wanted to talk?" Faith asked. "Feeling all lovesick because you can't bear to be apart from her for a few days?"

"It's not that." Lindsey took one of the giant cushions from her bed and hugged it to her chest. "We've been talking about the future. About me moving in with her. Permanently."

Faith let out a squeal. "That's great. You said you're in it for the long run with her, right? And that the manor feels like home now?"

"Yeah. I want this. But I can't help but feel bad about how everything between us started."

"What, because you were her sugar baby? Who cares if everything was fake at the beginning? You're not faking it anymore."

"Well, yeah," Lindsey said. "But I lied to her about being interested in women when we first met. Or at least, I led her to believe I was, which is basically the same thing."

"Right," Faith said. "So you haven't told her yet?"

"Nope. And I've had so many opportunities to tell her the truth, but I didn't. She's been so open with me about everything. I feel awful about keeping this from her."

"Then tell her."

"I don't want to hurt her," Lindsey said. "She's going to feel so betrayed. What if she can't forgive me?"

"What choice do you have?" Faith asked. "Do you really think the two of you can be happy together with this cloud hanging over your relationship?"

Lindsey sighed. "You're right. I'll tell her when she gets back." She let herself fall back down onto the pillows. "I hope she takes it well. Because if she doesn't, I don't know what I'll do. I love her so much, Faith. I never thought I'd fall for another woman, let alone one so much older than me, but here I am. Whenever I'm with her, I feel like I'm having this wonderful, impossible dream. But it's real."

"Aw, Lindsey. I'm glad you found this little slice of happiness. And for the record, I don't think your feelings for Camilla were fake at the start. You were practically swooning after that first date with her. From the outside, your feelings always seemed real, even if you didn't realize it at the time."

"I think you're right," Lindsey said. "Maybe I was falling for her all along, but I didn't understand it yet."

It was another hour before they hung up. By then, it was late. Lindsey put her phone aside and got ready for bed. She would talk to Camilla about everything tomorrow night.

She just hoped that Camilla would understand.

CHAPTER TWENTY-THREE

The next morning, Lindsey bounded out of her rooms and down the stairs. Making the decision to tell Camilla the truth had lifted a huge weight from her shoulders. Lindsey knew it would be a difficult conversation. She knew Camilla would be hurt. But she had to have faith that Camilla would forgive her.

She entered the dining room. There was no sign of June, but breakfast was laid out for Lindsey as usual. She finished it off quickly and headed back up to her rooms to brush her teeth. It was a warm, sunny day outside. Perhaps she'd go for a swim.

When she reached her rooms, she found June waiting for her by the door. The housekeeper's face wore a grave expression. A chill rolled down Lindsey's neck.

Something was wrong.

"June?" she said. "What's the matter?"

June folded her hands in front of her apron. "Camilla has requested that you leave the estate."

All warmth drained from Lindsey's body. "What are you talking about?"

"You need to pack your things. A car will be coming to take you wherever you want to go."

"This doesn't make any sense." Slowly, June's words began to sink in. "Why would Camilla do this? I need to talk to her."

"That isn't possible," June said.

"She's coming back tonight, right? Can't I wait for her?"

There was a flicker of confusion behind June's eyes. "Didn't the two of you-" she stopped short.

"June," Lindsey said. "What's going on?"

"Camilla already came back. Last night."

Lindsey's heart turned to ice. Last night, when she'd spoken to Faith about the secret she'd kept from Camilla?

"Where's Camilla now?" Lindsey asked.

"I can't tell you that," June said. "And her instructions were clear. You're to leave as soon as you've packed your things."

"You have to tell me where she is, June."

"I can't tell you where she is, because I don't *know* where she is. She left again early in the morning. I assumed she wanted space."

No. This wasn't happening.

"A car will arrive for you shortly. You better start packing. I'm also to inform you that anything Camilla bought for you is yours to take with you."

"I don't want her things!" Lindsey said. "I want to talk to her. June, please!"

"I'm sorry," June said quietly. "There's nothing I can do." Without another word, she turned and walked away.

Lindsey entered her room in a daze. This was all wrong. Lindsey needed to see her, to tell Camilla that she loved her, and she was sorry for lying.

She sank down into an armchair. Would it even make a difference? Camilla was so mad at Lindsey that she was kicking her out of the manor without even giving her a chance to explain herself.

Camilla wasn't a forgiving woman. She would never forgive Lindsey, not after this. She had trusted Lindsey, had let her in, and Lindsey had betrayed that trust.

Did Lindsey even deserve her forgiveness?

She could stay here, in this chair, and refuse to leave. She could insist on waiting for Camilla. She could cry and scream until Camilla came running.

But there was no point.

Lindsey got up and pulled her suitcase out of the closet. She looked around at all the clothes, shoes, and accessories Camilla had bought her. June had said they were hers to keep. But Lindsey didn't want any of it. Not without Camilla.

There was a knock on the door.

"Come in," Lindsey said.

June entered the room and pulled an envelope from a pocket at the front of her apron. "I forgot to give this to you. It's from Camilla."

Lindsey stared at the envelope. Was it a note? A letter? Some kind of explanation or a goodbye?

June held it out to her. "Here."

Lindsey blinked and took the envelope. "Thanks, June."

But June didn't give Lindsey her usual polite nod. She simply left the room again. Lindsey tore open the envelope, her hands trembling.

It was a check made out to Lindsey, for the exact amount Camilla had promised her before she'd moved in.

Lindsey collapsed onto her knees and started to sob.

Lindsey lay curled up on Faith's couch, tissues strewn around her. She'd called Faith in tears after leaving the manor. She had no one else to turn to, nowhere to go. Faith still had a few hours before she finished work, so Lindsey was all alone. At least she still had Faith's spare key.

The sound of the front door opening reached Lindsey's ears. She didn't bother to look. She didn't have the energy to move or do anything other than try to keep herself from bursting into tears.

"Lindsey? I'm home." Faith's footsteps approached. She sat down on the couch next to Lindsey's head. "How are you doing?"

Before Lindsey could answer her, she started sobbing into Faith's lap.

"Oh honey," Faith said. "I'm sorry."

"I messed up. I messed up so badly, and she'll never forgive me, and now it's over." Lindsey felt a wrenching in her chest. "I didn't know I could hurt this much. It's like my insides are filled with all these tiny shards of glass and it hurts to even breathe."

"I know." Faith stroked Lindsey's head. "This is what a broken heart feels like."

Lindsey sniffled. "Is it always this bad?"

"Every time."

"Then why do people do this? Why do people fall in love when this is what always happens?"

"Because when you finally find the person you're meant to be with, all of that past heartbreak is worth it. At least, I hope that's the case. For both of our sakes."

Another round of sobs racked Lindsey's body. "But *she* was the person I was meant to be with."

"It will get better," Faith said. "I promise. It'll take a while, but it'll start to hurt less. You'll be okay in the end."

"No, I won't. I'll never be okay again. Not after I hurt her so badly."

"Don't be so hard on yourself. You'll get through this. And I'll be right here with you."

Lindsey wiped her eyes. "Wait, why are you here? I thought you didn't finish work until this evening?"

"The Yangs let me go after I picked the kids up from school. There's a reason they've been paying me late. It turns out they can't afford a nanny anymore."

"I'm sorry, Faith."

Faith shrugged. "They said they'd give me a good reference. Maybe I'll find some other rich family to nanny for. On the plus side, it means I'll be around to keep you company." She sighed. "I really liked that job, though."

"I guess we can be miserable together," Lindsey said.

"Should I make some punch?"

"God, no." Still, Lindsey couldn't help but smile.

"You see?" Faith said. "Things aren't all doom and gloom. It'll be okay."

CHAPTER TWENTY-FOUR

Lindsey lay on Faith's couch, staring at the ceiling. An old sitcom was playing on the TV, but Lindsey wasn't paying attention to it. How was she supposed to do something as mundane as watch TV when she felt like her heart had been torn right out of her chest?

Ever since the accident, Lindsey had been struggling to feel anything at all. It was why she'd agreed to do something this crazy in the first place. She'd wanted adventure, romance, to capture that feeling of being happy and carefree.

She had gotten so much more than that. She'd stopped living in the past, stopped looking backward, and started looking forward to the future that she was supposed to share with Camilla. She'd fallen in love for the first time.

And now she felt the crushing pain of heartbreak.

There was a knock on the door. Lindsey groaned. She didn't want to get up. She'd barely left the couch for the past few days, with the exception of this morning. Faith had forced her to take a shower, because, in Faith's words, Lindsey was 'getting stinky.' But Faith was out running errands, leaving Lindsey all alone in the house again.

There was another knock on the door, more insistent this time. Lindsey sighed and got up. Her muscles protested, but whoever this was wasn't going away.

Lindsey reached the front door and opened it wide. She froze.

It was Camilla.

Lindsey stared at her. She looked so different. This wasn't the warm, bright-eyed Camilla who had told Lindsey she loved her. It was the Camilla who had looked at her, stone-faced, that night Lindsey had sneaked into her rooms so long ago.

But this was so much worse.

Seconds passed, and neither of them said a word. Lindsey smoothed down her hair, self-conscious under Camilla's sharp gaze. Barefoot and in her sweats, Lindsey was sure she looked like a mess. Suddenly, she was grateful that Faith had made her take a shower.

Finally, Camilla held out an envelope. "Take it."

Lindsey stared at the envelope. It had already been opened, and it looked familiar. It was the check. The check that June had given her.

The check that Lindsey had left behind, sitting on the dresser in her old room, along with all the clothes and fancy things Camilla had bought her.

Camilla thrust the envelope at Lindsey. "Take it."

"I'm not taking it," Lindsey said.

"Why not?"

"Because I don't want it."

"This was the agreement." Camilla's voice was hard. "I'm just holding up my end of it."

"Our agreement?" Lindsey shook her head. "What are you talking about?"

"This is what you wanted, wasn't it? The money? That was the whole point of this."

"Well, yes, at first. But that obviously changed when I fell in love with you."

"Don't say that. Don't lie to me."

"It's not a lie," Lindsey said. "I love you, Mistress."

"Lindsey, stop. I know the truth. I heard you talking on the phone. You were never interested in women. You've been lying to me from the start. Why would you pretend you were in love with me if not for the money?"

Lindsey flinched. "All this time, that's what you thought? That I lied about being in love with you?" She thought back to her conversation with Faith. It would have been easy for Camilla to come to that conclusion if she'd overheard only part of it from the other side of a door. "That's why you kicked me out?"

"It's the truth," Camilla said.

"No, it's not. You need to let me explain. Just come in, so we can talk about this."

Camilla pressed her lips together. "There's nothing to talk about. Just take the damn check."

"You know what? Fine. I'll take it." Lindsey took the envelope from Camilla's hand. She pulled out the check and tore it in half.

Camilla gaped at her. "What are you doing?"

Lindsey tore the check in half again, and again, over and over until it was in a billion tiny pieces which she sprinkled on the floor at Camilla's feet.

"Why did you do that?"

"Why do you think?" Lindsey said. "I told you I don't care about the money. It's you that I want. Just hear me out. Give me five minutes to explain myself."

"Fine," Camilla said sharply. "Five minutes."

Lindsey opened the door and let Camilla in. Camilla followed her to the living room. Lindsey swept aside the candy bar wrappers and chip packets on the couch and gestured for her to sit down.

"Camilla. Mistress, I-" Lindsey took a breath, gathering her thoughts. "You're right. I lied to you. When we met, I pretended I was bisexual. That I liked women. That was a lie. I'd never been with a woman, never been attracted to one. Not until I met you."

Camilla said nothing. Her expression remained unchanged.

"From the moment I met you, I felt this incredible connection to you. I didn't understand what it was at the time because it was like nothing else I'd ever felt. I just wanted so badly to be near you, to be a part of your life, even though I couldn't explain it. That's why I agreed to your proposal. Sure, the money was part of it. But what I really wanted was to get to know you.

"And over those months we spent together, I got to know what an incredible woman you are," Lindsey said. "I got to know how strong you are. How kind and generous you are. How loyal and loving you are toward the people you care about. And in just a couple of short months, I fell in love with you. And even before I did, I stopped caring about the money. The moment you kissed me in the playroom that first night, I was yours."

Something flickered behind Camilla's eyes. A tiny spark of affection, a hint of longing. Camilla felt it too. Lindsey knew it.

"So yes, this started with a lie," she said. "But that was the only lie I ever told you. Every time I said I was yours, I meant it. Every time I said I miss you, I meant it. Every time I said I love you, I meant it. And I still do. That's the truth."

Lindsey folded her hands in her lap and waited for Camilla to do or say something. For what seemed like an eternity, all she did was stare back at Lindsey, an unreadable expression on her face.

"You really mean that," Camilla said.

"Of course I do, or I wouldn't have said it. I love you," Lindsey said. "I love you. I love you. I love-"

Camilla held up her hands. "Lindsey, stop."

Lindsey fell silent. There was nothing more for her to say. If Camilla wasn't convinced now, then all was lost.

"I love you too, Lindsey."

Relief flooded Lindsey's body. She threw her arms around Camilla's neck and kissed her as hard as she could. Camilla's hungry lips were as sweet and soft as ever, and her Mistress's strong embrace filled her with warmth.

Camilla drew back. "Come home, Lindsey."

Home. Lindsey looked around Faith's small apartment, at the couch littered with tissues and her suitcase in the corner. Although this place had been good to Lindsey, it was never going to be home.

But the manor? That was home. And it always would be, as long as Camilla was there.

"Yes, Mistress. I'll come home."

CHAPTER TWENTY-FIVE

That afternoon, Lindsey and Camilla returned to Robinson Estate. As soon as they passed through those wide gates, Lindsey was transported back to that little slice of paradise that belonged to Lindsey and her Mistress, and no one else.

When they reached the manor, Camilla went about making Lindsey's homecoming as perfect as their first night together. She called in a chef and gave Lindsey a new dress, a knee-length number made of delicate black chiffon which Camilla had bought to surprise Lindsey the night she'd returned early. They had dinner in the garden, complete with a dessert decadent enough to satisfy Camilla's sweet tooth. Then they relaxed in the courtyard under the soft lights and the stars.

Lindsey would have been happy to end the night simply falling asleep next to Camilla. But Camilla had bigger plans.

"I have one final gift to give you," Camilla said. "It's inside."

Lindsey followed Camilla back into the house and through the white double doors that led to Camilla's rooms. Camilla stopped at the playroom door and led Lindsey inside.

Despite the fact that last time Lindsey had been in here, she'd had a bad experience, the playroom still felt cozy and welcoming. As usual, the wooden chest was sitting on top of the table. Camilla opened it up, pulled out the cuffs, and fastened them around Lindsey's wrists and ankles.

"Now for the final piece." Camilla placed her hand on Lindsey's shoulder. "Kneel."

Lindsey kneeled down on the fluffy rug. Her Mistress's serious tone sent a thrill through her.

Camilla reached into the box again and produced a leather collar. It was made of the same embossed midnight blue leather as the cuffs around Lindsey's ankles and wrists. Hanging from a ring at the front was a little gold tag with Camilla's initials on it.

Camilla leaned down and swept Lindsey's hair to the side. Then, holding the collar as gingerly as if it were a precious diamond necklace, she fastened it around Lindsey's neck, securing it at the back with the gold buckle.

"Rise," Camilla said.

Lindsey stood up. The soft collar fit snugly around her neck, and the weight of the leather and gold was just hefty enough to remind her that it was there.

Camilla tipped Lindsey's chin up to inspect the collar. "You look radiant."

She hooked a finger into the ring at the front of the collar and pulled Lindsey toward her, kissing her feverishly. It took all Lindsey's strength not to crumble to pieces.

Still holding the collar, Camilla tugged her toward the bed. "Stand in front of the cross."

Lindsey did as she was told, anticipation welling inside her. Last time Camilla had tied her to the cross, the experience had been divine.

"Not that way," Camilla said. "Face it."

Lindsey turned around. Camilla fastened Lindsey to the cross by her wrists and ankles, leaving her spread-eagled, her back exposed. Lindsey's heart raced.

Camilla brushed her fingers down the back of Lindsey's

upstretched arm. "I'm not going to blindfold you. This time, you're going to keep your eyes closed. Can you do that for me?"

"Yes, Mistress." Lindsey shut her eyes.

Camilla planted a kiss on Lindsey's cheek. Her hands glided down Lindsey's sides, caressing her helpless body. "Let's get this dress out of the way."

Camilla's footsteps receded behind Lindsey. What was she doing? It was going to be impossible for Camilla to remove Lindsey's dress with her limbs bound as they were.

Her Mistress returned to her side. Suddenly, there was a metallic swish behind Lindsey's ear, then the bite of cold metal between her shoulder blades. *Scissors?* Lindsey's eyes tried to fly open, but she resisted the impulse. Then, she heard a sharp snip as the blade slid down the bare skin of her back.

Camilla was cutting off Lindsey's dress.

Heat suffused Lindsey's body. If she wasn't so turned on, she would have laughed at how outrageous it was. Her Mistress had gifted her this beautiful dress, just to ruin it a few hours later.

Camilla snipped all the way down to the hem at the bottom, cutting the dress in half completely, then snipped the straps at her shoulders. She yanked the dress out from between Lindsey's body and the cross, then cut away her bra and panties, piece by piece. The back of the scissors scraped Lindsey's skin, sending shivers down her neck.

Soon, Lindsey was left wearing nothing but the collar and cuffs.

"That's much better," Camilla said. "Now I can admire all of you."

Camilla turned Lindsey's head to one side and brought her lips to Lindsey's. Camilla's deep, yearning kiss flooded Lindsey with lust. And the way Camilla's body pressed against her back made Lindsey realize that Camilla was no longer wearing anything.

Suddenly, keeping her eyes closed was a much more difficult prospect.

"You're turned on already, aren't you?" Camilla said. "If I stuck my hand between your thighs, would I find you soaking wet?"

"Yes, Mistress," Lindsey replied.

"But I'm not going to do that yet. Not when I have you stretched out on display for me like this." Camilla spanked Lindsey across the ass cheek. "I'm going to have some fun with you instead."

Lindsey let out a shallow breath. She had a few guesses as to what Camilla had in mind. Lindsey was immobilized and naked, her bare ass right in the center of the X. It was the perfect target.

Lindsey felt something long and hard sweep along the back of her thigh. She stiffened.

"Remember this?" Camilla asked.

"Yes, Mistress." How could Lindsey forget the cane that Camilla had used on her that first night?

Camilla traced the cane up Lindsey's ass cheek. "This time, you're going to thank me for every strike. Do you understand?"

"Yes, Mistress."

Camilla stepped back. There were a few loud whooshes as Camilla swung the cane through the air. Lindsey waited for the impact, but none came. She wriggled impatiently.

"You're not trying to tempt me, are you?" Camilla asked.

"No, Mistress," Lindsey said.

"I think you are. Maybe some discipline will stop you being such a naughty little submissive."

There was a loud whoosh, then the white-hot strike of the cane against Lindsey's ass cheeks. She hissed.

"What do you say?" Camilla asked.

"Thank you, Mistress," Lindsey said.

Camilla swatted her again.

"Thank you, Mistress."

Again. This time, the searing sensation radiated through her whole body, to the tips of her fingers and toes, and into her core.

Thank you, Mistress. Thank you, Mistress. Over and over until every part of Lindsey ached with need. She moaned, her mind and body falling into a blissful trance. *Thank you, Mistress. Thank you, Mistress.*

Camilla ran a hand down the center of Lindsey's back. "Are you still with me?"

"Yes, Mistress," Lindsey said softly.

Camilla skimmed her hand downward, between Lindsey's ass cheeks and into her slit. Lindsey let out a hard breath.

"Do not come without asking for permission," Camilla said.

"Yes-" Lindsey gasped as Camilla's finger grazed the base of her clit. "Yes, Mistress."

Without hesitation, Camilla slipped her fingers inside Lindsey, plunging deep. Lindsey whimpered. She was so delightfully on edge that it was only seconds before she was ready.

"Please, Mistress. Can I come?"

"Not yet." Camilla slowed down slightly.

Lindsey's head fell back. There was no way she could last any longer. "I can't..."

"You can. For me." Camilla pushed Lindsey's hair aside and kissed and sucked behind her ear and down to the collar around her neck. Her free hand crept between Lindsey's body and the cross, all the way up to her chest.

Lindsey strained against her bonds, flexing her muscles. Somehow, despite Camilla's fingers thrusting inside her, and her lips on her skin, Lindsey held herself back from the edge. Somehow, despite being tormented with ecstasy, she kept her word to her Mistress. Lindsey was hers so completely that both her mind and body understood that it couldn't have true release without her Mistress's permission.

"Now." Camilla began moving her hand faster. "You may come."

Lindsey let out a primal cry as pleasure burst from within her, spreading through her like wildfire. Camilla kept her body pressed against Lindsey's as she worked her fingers inside, until Lindsey's body calmed.

"You can open your eyes now," Camilla said.

Lindsey opened her eyes, turning to watch her Mistress as she unfastened the restraints from the cross. Once Lindsey was free, her Mistress drew her to the bed and climbed onto it, lying back against the pillows.

Taking Lindsey by the ring of the collar again, she pulled Lindsey down to her. Wordlessly, their lips locked together, and their arms intertwined. Camilla's thigh brushed between Lindsey's legs. She rocked her hips on top of Camilla, burning with desire.

Camilla shifted out from under her, pulling Lindsey down so that they were side by side. She drew her hand up to the peak of Lindsey's thighs and strummed her aching bud. Lindsey pressed back against her Mistress. At the same time, she pushed her own fingers down to where Camilla's thighs met and slipped them gently up her folds. Camilla moaned and grabbed onto Lindsey's hand, guiding it to her entrance.

Lindsey got the message loud and clear. She eased a finger inside Camilla, delving it in and out slowly. A ripple went through Camilla's body. She arched toward Lindsey, a wordless command. *More.* Lindsey slid in another finger, eliciting a murmur of satisfaction from Camilla. Her walls seemed to swallow Lindsey's fingers. She pumped in and out again, getting into a rhythm, sinking into her Mistress's heat.

Camilla grabbed Lindsey's face and kissed her like a woman starved. Her other hand was still between Lindsey's lower lips, circling and stroking. Lindsey bucked against her. She was so close. She opened her mouth to beg for release.

But instead, it was her Mistress who was overcome. Camilla quaked against Lindsey, her head tipped back in a silent scream. Lindsey could feel every pulse that went through her Mistress's core, every shudder that went through her Mistress's body. It only made Lindsey ache even more.

Once Camilla's orgasm passed, Camilla began working her fingers on Lindsey's folds again. Lindsey bucked against her until she was right back at the edge.

"Mistress, please," she said. "May I come for you?"

"Yes," Camilla whispered.

This time when Lindsey came, it was like a slow tidal wave of bliss that stretched out endlessly until Lindsey was sure that she'd passed into some other plane.

She sank back onto the bed with a sigh. Camilla reached across the bed to shut the curtains around them, then lay back down and nestled in close to Lindsey.

Lindsey leaned over and kissed her. "Thank you, Mistress."

"No." Camilla drew her thumb down Lindsey's cheek. "Thank you."

"For what?"

Camilla planted a soft kiss on Lindsey's forehead. "For giving me the gift of your submission."

EPILOGUE

CAMILLA

Camilla held up the leather blindfold. "Put this on."

Lindsey's face turned a delightful shade of crimson. "Isn't it a little early for that? And, right here?" She glanced over at June, who was clearing their breakfast from the table.

Camilla placed her hands on her hips. "Are you questioning your Mistress?"

"No." Lindsey took the blindfold from Camilla and slipped it over her eyes.

"Don't get too excited. I want to show you something, that's all. A surprise." Camilla leaned in and whispered into Lindsey's ear. "Your mind always goes to the dirtiest of places."

The blush on Lindsey's face deepened.

Camilla stifled a chuckle. She just couldn't help herself. Not when Lindsey was so easy to tease. She took Lindsey's hand. "Come with me."

Camilla led Lindsey out of the dining room and up the stairs carefully. They turned and headed left.

"Are we going to the east wing?" Lindsey asked.

"You'll see," Camilla replied.

It was no surprise that Lindsey had figured it out. A couple of months after Lindsey had moved back in, permanently this time, Camilla began to have the east wing cleaned out and renovated. She told Lindsey not to go in there under any circumstances because it was unsafe due to all the work being done, which was partially true.

Lindsey had picked up on the fact that something else was going on. But, ever the obedient submissive, she played along anyway. And Camilla had promised her that it would be worth it in the end. Now, after six months, the wing wasn't yet complete. But that was the point.

Camilla led Lindsey into a vast, empty antechamber which several other rooms branched off. Just a few months ago, this room had been run down, with old, faded wallpaper and a decade of dust coating the floorboards. Now, it looked new and fresh, and more in line with the rest of the house. However, the walls were unpainted, the windows were bare, and there wasn't so much as a light fixture.

"We're here." Camilla removed Lindsey's blindfold.

Lindsey looked around. "Is this the east wing?"

"That's right. But this isn't just the east wing. These are our new rooms."

"Our new rooms?" Lindsey's forehead furrowed. "Why do you want us to move out of your rooms?"

"That's the problem. Those rooms have always been *my* rooms, not ours." Camilla took Lindsey's hands. "I don't want you to feel like you're living in my house. I want us to have a space that belongs to both of us."

"Camilla, I don't know what to say." Lindsey gazed around, wide-eyed. "Are you really okay with leaving your rooms behind? That's a big change."

Change. Once upon a time, that word terrified Camilla. But Lindsey had changed that. "It was a difficult decision. But I want to build something new with you."

"I want that too," Lindsey said. "This is perfect."

"Of course, it isn't finished. I want us to pick out all the details together. The decor, the furnishings, everything." Camilla pulled Lindsey to the center of the room. "We're going to decorate the entire wing together. Then we're going to finally throw that party we've been talking about for months. Not just a dinner party. A big housewarming celebration."

"That sounds wonderful."

"In fact, I've been thinking it's time we opened up the house more. I want to have more guests and throw more parties. I want to make the manor come alive again, like when I was a child. That is, if it's okay with you."

"I would love that," Lindsey said.

"Of course, we're going to need more staff. Some more help for June, perhaps a full-time chef. But I'm getting ahead of myself."

"No, it's great. I'm happy to see you this excited about something."

"I have some news that's going to make you even happier," Camilla said. "Remember that friend of mine you sent your portfolio to?"

"The one who owns a gallery?" Lindsey asked.

"The very same. She finally had a look at your work, and she was very impressed. She's opening another gallery in the city next year, and she wants your artwork to be in the opening exhibition."

Lindsey beamed. "Seriously?"

"Seriously. She'll get in touch with you soon, but I wanted to be the one to tell you."

"That's amazing." Lindsey slung her arms around Camilla's neck and pressed her lips to Camilla's. "I'm glad you pushed me to work on my art. I'm glad you made me put myself out there."

"This was all you, Lindsey," Camilla said. "It was always you. I gave you a little nudge, but you're the one who chose to take control of your life."

"Well, I couldn't have done it without you. Thank you for encouraging me."

"I did it because I believe in you. And I want the world to see how talented you are." Camilla kissed her again. "Now, why don't I give you a tour of our rooms?"

Camilla led Lindsey to the bedroom and opened the door, revealing a huge, light-filled space much brighter than Camilla's old bedroom. She showed Lindsey their sitting room, and the parlor, and the huge bathroom which made Lindsey squeal with excitement.

"Can we get a bath like the one in your rooms?" she asked.

"We can get an even bigger one." Camilla guided Lindsey back to the antechamber and out into a hallway. "Down this hall is my new study. Your new studio is right across from it." She pointed to the end of the hall. "And through that door is the most important room of all."

Lindsey's eyes lit up. "Do you mean the playroom?"

Camilla nodded.

"Can we go inside?"

"Of course." Camilla put her hand on the small of Lindsey's back and led her to the playroom. "I took the liberty of furnishing it already. I know I said we were going to do this together, but this is the one exception."

"I don't mind, Mistress," Lindsey said.

"I'm sure you'll love what I've done with it." Camilla opened the door and turned on the light.

Lindsey looked around the room. "It's the same?"

Camilla nodded. "I had everything moved in here when you were in the city last week."

And she meant everything. The four-poster canopy bed. All the cabinets and drawers filled with surprises. Even the dark wallpaper was identical.

"Do you like it?" Camilla asked.

"I love it," Lindsey said. "It's perfect."

Camilla walked over to the bed. Sitting on top of the table beside it was the large wooden chest with her initials etched into the lid. She placed the blindfold down next to the chest and opened it up.

Camilla pulled out the blue leather collar, letting it dangle from her finger. She fixed her eyes on Lindsey's. "Do you still think it's 'too early for that?'"

"No, Mistress," Lindsey said. "Not at all."

"Then come here."

A smile played on Lindsey's lips. She shut the door and joined her Mistress by the bed.

FREEING HER

CHAPTER ONE

Faith slipped the dress over her head and examined herself in her bedroom mirror. The shapeless shift dress was a dull shade of blue and went down past her knees. She frowned. She looked reliable. Responsible. That was what she was going for. But she didn't look like herself.

She pulled off the dress and tossed it onto her bed, then began flipping through her closet again. Surely she had something less frumpy that still looked professional. She needed to make a good first impression.

Faith glanced at the alarm clock on her nightstand. She only had five minutes until she had to leave for her job interview. She had a good feeling about this job. She'd been searching for a stable nanny position for months now. Over the past year, she'd had jobs on and off, but none of them had lasted. She'd had to deal with entitled brats, parents who treated her like a servant, or worse, parents who expected her to single-handedly raise their children.

However, this job sounded promising. A family she'd worked for in the past had recommended her to a friend of theirs, a divorcee named Eve. Faith didn't know much about her, other than the fact that she had twins, a boy and a girl. The address she'd been given was in an upper-class suburb so the family had to be outrageously rich. In Faith's experience that usually meant spoiled kids and detached parents, but Faith was staying positive.

She pulled a blouse from her closet and held it up before her. It was white with a contrasting black collar. She slipped it on, along with a black A-line skirt, and inspected herself in the mirror again.

It was an improvement on the dress, although it was a little drab for Faith's tastes. For most of her life, she'd been forced to dress conservatively. Now that she was free to experiment, her tastes were on the wilder side. From her clothes to her hair, her appearance was ever-changing. Over the years, she'd dyed her hair every color imaginable, from black to bright pink.

But for now she'd gone back to a natural-looking light brown. The kind of people wealthy enough to hire someone to take care of their kids full-time didn't want pink-haired nannies. They wanted only the most respectable, dependable people to watch over their little angels.

Her cell phone buzzed. She dug it out from under the pile of clothes on her bed. It was a message from her friend Lindsey.

Good luck with the interview! Let me know how it goes.

Faith shot Lindsey a reply and picked up her purse, tucking her phone away in it. It was time to get going. She paused by her dresser, then grabbed her favorite lipstick and swiped it across her lips, turning them a warm shade of red.

She smiled into the mirror. *That's better.*

Faith rang Eve's doorbell. She'd never been to this part of the city before. All the houses were multistory mansions, with photo-perfect gardens and expensive cars parked in the driveways. But the house she stood before, a three-story mansion at the end of a quiet cul-de-sac, was the grandest of them all.

The front door opened. A tall, blonde woman stood in the doorway, her deep hazel eyes hidden behind a pair of stylish tortoiseshell rimmed glasses. She looked to be in her early thirties.

The woman gave her a tight smile. "You must be Faith."

"Yes," Faith said. "Hi."

"Eve." The woman stepped to the side and gestured into the house. "Why don't you come in?"

Faith followed Eve inside, Eve's heels clicking on the marble floor with each step. Faith examined her as they walked. She was beautiful in an understated way. Despite her slender, willowy frame, her confident manner made it clear that she was anything but delicate. She wore a light-gray, structured knee-length dress that subtly enhanced her shape. Her hair was curly, but not like Faith's, which hung in loose, wild waves, no matter what she did with it. Eve's curls were neatly arranged in a short bob style that reminded Faith of a vintage pin-up model. Although the look could have used some color, Eve exuded a sense of style, which was something Faith had always found attractive in a person.

Not that Faith was thinking about her potential boss that way.

Faith peered around her as they walked down the hall. There were an endless number of rooms, all lavishly decorated. It wasn't surprising. Only the wealthiest of families could afford full-time nannies. But this house was like nothing Faith had ever seen. With its pristine white walls, marble floors, and elaborate decor, it was a palace in the middle of suburbia.

However, there was something off about it. Something missing. Faith realized what it was when Eve directed her into a lounge room. The house was too quiet. Too neat and organized. There were no signs that children lived here at all.

Eve gestured toward an armchair. "Take a seat."

Faith sat down. Eve sat in the couch across from her, folding her hands on her lap in a ladylike manner. She looked Faith up and down, appraising her. Her eyes narrowed at Faith's bright red lipstick.

Faith shifted in her seat.

"So, Faith," Eve said. "Tell me about yourself."

"Well, I've been babysitting my whole life," Faith began. "I had a huge family, and I used to take care of my younger brothers and sisters and all my cousins growing up. Then I did some babysitting in college, and when I graduated I started nannying full-time."

It wasn't what she'd planned to do after college. She'd attended art school, mostly because she'd had no idea what she wanted to do with her life, and when she'd finished she'd struggled to find a job. So, when one of the families she babysat for had offered her a nanny position, she'd snapped it up. She enjoyed it, after all. And she was good at it. "I've worked for a few families long-term. The Yangs were the last."

"They spoke highly of you. So did your references. And your qualifications all checked out. I also took the liberty of doing a thorough background check. It came up clean."

That was a relief. Faith was always worried that anyone who dug around in her background would find out about the brief period she went 'missing' eight years ago, but it hadn't come up yet. Perhaps it was because she'd been a minor at the time.

"I'm going to be frank," Eve said. "I'm in desperate need of a nanny. I returned to work recently for the first time since the twins were born. I was in marketing before I had the children so I decided to start my own small firm. But it's becoming impossible to keep up with work while looking after the twins' needs. For now, I share custody with their father, but most of the real work falls on me."

Eve crossed her stockinged legs and smoothed down her skirt. "I'm looking for someone to help out with the more practical parts of taking care of the twins. Taking them to lessons, chores, and so on. We have housekeepers for general household tasks, and I won't expect you to do anything that will get in the way of your duties with the children. But I may need you to do the odd personal errand for me. You'll be well compensated, of course."

"That's fine with me." The last family Faith had worked for briefly had had her scrubbing toilets, so this would be an improvement.

"Can you drive?" Eve asked.

"Yes."

"I'll supply you with a car to travel to and from work, and to drive the kids around. We used to use a car service, but I decided to cut down on some of our unnecessary expenses. Live more modestly."

Faith glanced around. This was living modestly? What had Eve been living like before?

"I'll need you to stay overnight on occasion," Eve said. "I'll have one of the spare rooms set aside for your use. And you're not to bring anyone else around the kids. Friends. Partners."

"I would never do anything like that."

"You'd be surprised how many babysitters I've had that think it's appropriate."

Faith studied Eve. For the past few minutes, she'd felt an air of discomfort coming from the other woman. Faith had just thought it was because Eve was uptight. But perhaps Eve was simply feeling uneasy about the idea of leaving her children in a stranger's hands.

"I'm no babysitter," Faith said. "I'm a professional. I might seem young, but I'm fully qualified, and I've been looking after children my entire life. I assure you, your kids will be in capable hands with me."

"And I expect nothing less." Almost imperceptibly, Eve seemed to relax. "Now, your hours will be erratic for now. Since my ex-husband and I don't have a custody agreement yet, the days I have the twins vary, but I'll make sure you get plenty of time off. Speaking of the twins, why don't I call them down so you can meet them? They're upstairs."

"Sure," Faith said.

Eve went out into the hall. "Leah? Ethan? Come down here, please."

Faith waited in silence. She heard the patter of feet coming down the stairs.

"No running, you two," Eve said.

The footsteps slowed. Moments later, Eve walked back into the room accompanied by two small children: a girl and a boy. They had their mother's blonde hair, carefully combed and styled, and the same hazel eyes, not to mention the same serious expressions. They were dressed as though they'd walked right out of an upmarket children's clothing catalog.

"Leah, Ethan, this is Faith." Eve sat them down on the couch and perched on the arm of it next to them. "Why don't you introduce yourselves?"

The children did as they were told. They were polite and well-spoken. Faith questioned them about school and their interests. They were both involved in half a dozen extracurricular activities.

"As you can see, Leah and Ethan have plenty on their plates," Eve said. "They're in first grade now, and they're getting extra tutoring. They both take Spanish and French lessons, as well as music classes. Piano for Ethan and violin for Leah. Leah does ballet, and Ethan plays baseball and soccer. That's on top of all their scheduled play dates and other social activities."

Scheduled play dates? Spanish *and* French? It was a lot for a pair of seven-year-olds. Faith had worked for parents like Eve before, who filled every moment of their children's days with activities and micromanaged their lives, but this seemed excessive.

"Now, house rules," Eve continued. "We keep screen time to a minimum unless necessary for schoolwork. There are no TVs in the house. And no junk food. Preparing breakfast and snacks will be your responsibility."

As Eve continued, Faith tried her best to keep her mind from wandering. Eve had a long list of rules. Faith glanced at the twins, sitting quietly beside Eve. They were extremely well-mannered for their age. Probably because of their mother.

Eve rested her hand on Leah's shoulder. "That's about everything. I have high expectations of anyone who works for me, but I'm offering a generous salary, plus benefits. Health insurance, dental, paid leave."

"Sounds great," Faith said.

"Then you can start tomorrow."

Faith blinked. That was it? "Sure." Everything about the job sounded perfect. The only thing she was uncertain of was how well she'd get along with Eve.

"The job is yours," Eve said. "All that's left to discuss is your salary."

"Right." Faith had been so thrown by the job offer that she hadn't thought about negotiating pay first.

But when Eve gave her a figure, it was far higher than anything Faith would have asked for. Eve wasn't kidding about offering a generous salary. Unease stirred within her.

Just how much did Eve expect from Faith in return?

After a brief discussion about Faith's duties, Eve sent Leah and Ethan back upstairs. "I have to get the twins to school. That will be your job from now on. I need you here at seven in the morning tomorrow to wake them up and get them ready."

Faith nodded. "I'll be here."

Eve ushered her to the door and said a polite farewell. Faith walked down the path cutting across the manicured lawn and onto the sidewalk. As soon as she was out of sight of the house, she skipped a couple of steps and pulled out her phone to call Lindsey.

Her friend answered after a couple of rings. "How did the interview go?"

Faith grinned. "I got the job."

"That's great! Let's hope it's better than the last one."

"I already know it's going to be. I have a good feeling about this."

But as she walked down the sidewalk, Faith remembered Eve's disapproving eyes on her red lips. The proper, buttoned-up woman was her complete opposite.

But Faith would make it work.

CHAPTER TWO

Faith shepherded the twins downstairs for breakfast. Both were dressed immaculately in tiny blazers and ties, the uniform of their exclusive private school. Faith had ironed them to Eve's specifications the evening before.

She'd been working for Eve for three days now. Her suspicions about her new boss had quickly been confirmed. She wasn't one of those rich parents who let 'the help' raise their kids. With Eve, Faith had the opposite problem. She could barely do anything without Eve looming over her, giving her instructions. Combined with the long workdays, the job was taxing. However, the twins were going to their father's in a few days, giving Faith three days off in a row. She was already looking forward to it.

She and the twins entered the dining room. Eve sat at the head of the table reading a newspaper, a cup of coffee in her hand. She was dressed for work in a pantsuit and cream-colored blouse.

"Good morning, sweethearts." Eve beckoned the twins over and planted a kiss on each of their foreheads. She looked at Leah and plucked the brightly colored butterfly barrette out of her hair, scowling. "You're not wearing that to school."

"Faith said I could wear it," Leah whined.

"Faith doesn't know the school's dress code." Eve looked pointedly at Faith. "I'll send you a copy. And no more pigtails. It looks childish."

"Okay," Faith replied. It wasn't like Leah was a child or anything.

Leah sat down at the table and pouted. "Everyone else wears stuff like this."

"That doesn't matter," Eve said. "Rules are rules."

Faith served the twins their breakfast, a perfectly balanced meal she'd prepared as per Eve's instructions, then sat down and drank her coffee while the family ate breakfast. They chatted animatedly as they did. Even Eve seemed to perk up. Despite her strictness, she wasn't an uncaring parent. And despite the kids being absurdly well behaved, they seemed happy and healthy.

It made Faith miss her own family. She wondered what they were all up to. It had been a while since she'd heard from her sister. She was getting worried.

When the twins finished their breakfast, Eve sent them upstairs to brush their teeth. Faith began clearing the dishes from the table.

"Make sure you get the kids to school on time," Eve said. "When they were with Harrison last week, they were late two days in a row."

"I will." School didn't start for another forty-five minutes. They had plenty of time.

"And don't forget, they have Spanish lessons this afternoon."

"Okay." Faith had already memorized their schedules, which Eve had given her on day one. But she still insisted on laying everything out every single morning. She managed Faith just as much as she managed her kids.

It was frustrating, but Faith tried not to hold it against Eve. Eve was working full-time and almost single-handedly raising two kids. Faith didn't know what the situation was with her ex-husband, but it didn't sound like he was much help in that department.

"Now, I need you to run some errands for me," Eve said.

As Eve continued to list off instructions, she took off her glasses and wiped down the lenses. With her glasses off, Faith could see all the colors in Eve's eyes, a mesmerizing swirl of greens and browns.

What lay behind those eyes of hers? Eve's face was the kind that gave nothing away. Faith found it equal parts frustrating and intriguing. She was like a puzzle to be solved. Was there more to Eve than the proper, boring facade she presented?

Eve replaced her glasses on her nose, breaking the spell. She stood up. "I need to get to work. Call me if you need anything. And make sure everything I asked of you gets done."

Faith nodded. It was going to be a long day.

Faith opened the trunk of her shiny new car and grabbed the bags of groceries inside. She'd finally finished the long list of errands Eve had given her. She still had a few hours before she had to pick up the twins, but she had plenty to do around the house.

As she carried the groceries to the door, her phone rang. She put her bags down and picked up the phone. It was Eve.

"I need a favor," Eve said. "My pen leaked on my blouse. I have a meeting in a couple of hours. Can you bring me a fresh one?"

"Sure," Faith replied.

"Just choose something from my closet. My work clothes are on the left."

Faith took the groceries inside, packed everything in the fridge, then headed toward Eve's bedroom. It was at the back of the house, along with a set of rooms that Eve reserved for her use only. The twins weren't allowed in this part of the house, so Faith hadn't seen it yet.

As she walked down the hall, she saw that Eve's rooms were off-limits to the twins for a good reason. They were even more pristine than the rest of the house and filled with all kinds of valuable, breakable furniture and decor. There were a few pieces of art on the walls by artists whose style Faith recognized from her art school days.

She walked further down the hall, spotting a sun-filled office, a huge bathroom, and a small lounge room. At the end of the hall, she came to a bedroom. Eve's bedroom. It was as luxurious as all the other rooms, and it was just as neat. The large bed looked like it had never been slept on, the crisp white sheets on it pulled tight. Eve's walk-in closet was on the other side of the bed.

Faith tiptoed into the room, afraid to disturb anything. She entered the closet and turned on the light.

Wow. The closet was the size of Faith's entire bedroom. All around her were endless racks of clothes and shelves of shoes. There was a full-length mirror surrounded by lights and a mannequin on which a simple black dress hung. A small dressing table held an array of jewelry.

Faith walked around the room, examining everything. For someone as fashion-mad as Faith, this was heaven. Although most of Eve's clothes weren't to Faith's taste, everything was stylish and finely made. She reached for a woolen pea coat, stroking it gently. It was delightfully soft. She wondered what it would feel like on.

No. Focus. She walked over to the rack on the left. Just as Eve had told her, it held all work-appropriate clothes. There were a dozen near-identical cream and white blouses, as well as pantsuits and skirts in various shades of black and gray. Judging by how well everything Eve wore fit her, each item in the closet was tailor-made for Eve's body.

Not that Faith had noticed her boss's body.

She pulled out a blouse at random. It would go well with the pantsuit Eve had been wearing. She found an empty garment bag and slipped the blouse into it.

Out of the corner of her eye, she spotted something tucked away at the other end of the wardrobe. It was a bright blue sequined cocktail dress. And it was scandalously short.

Faith flipped through the pieces next to it. There were a few more cocktail dresses, most of them more modest than the blue one, as well as some evening gowns. One of them was a stunning piece, a long black dress with a structured bodice. On the floor beneath the dresses, almost hidden by the long skirts, were two pairs of stiletto heels with red soles.

Did Eve ever wear such sexy clothing? Faith pictured it in her mind. Eve in sequins and stilettos, those long legs of hers bared, the low cut of the dress showing off the shoulders and chest that Eve kept under button-up work shirts.

Faith shook her head. Her imagination was getting out of hand. Besides, those stilettos were covered in dust. It was clear that they were rarely ever worn.

Faith hopped in the elevator and pressed the button for the floor of Eve's office. She looked around. She was the only person in the elevator who wasn't wearing a suit. These stuffy men and women made Eve seem eccentric.

She got out at Eve's floor and was faced with a wide-open reception area. A bored-looking woman sat behind the reception desk. Faith caught her eye.

"Can I help you?" the woman asked.

"I'm here to see Eve," Faith said. "She asked me to drop something off."

"You must be Faith. Ms. Lincoln is expecting you." The woman stood up. "I'll take you to her. Come with me."

Faith followed the receptionist into the office. She looked around, wide-eyed. The office was huge and abuzz with activity. This was Eve's definition of a 'small' firm? And all this belonged to her? Faith had underestimated Eve. Given the draconian way she ran her home, Faith shouldn't have been surprised that Eve commanded all of this.

They reached a door with Eve's name on the nameplate. The receptionist knocked.

"Come in," Eve said from inside.

The receptionist opened the door and gestured Faith inside. Eve sat behind a desk, her eyes fixed on her laptop. The room was very similar to Eve's office at home.

"Thank you, Andrea," Eve said. "Shut the door, please."

Andrea closed the door, leaving the two of them alone.

"Faith, thank you for this." Eve continued to type away. "You're a lifesaver."

"It's no trouble," Faith said.

"I usually keep a spare in my office, but the kids got their hands all over it when they were here with me last week." Eve shut her laptop, stood up and rounded the desk. "Andrea keeps telling me to hire a personal assistant for these things, but I can't bring myself to trust someone else with important duties."

So Eve's control issues weren't just to do with Faith? That was good to know.

Eve took the blouse from Faith and set it down on the desk behind her, then pulled off her jacket, revealing an ink stain near the top of her shirt. "Don't go anywhere. You can take this to the dry cleaner for me. With luck, they can get the stain out."

"Sure," Faith said.

Without hesitation, Eve began unbuttoning her shirt. The top of her bra peeked out of it. It was lacy, red, and cut low.

Did Eve always wear such racy underwear under her clothes?

Eve's hands stopped at the next button. "Faith?"

"Huh?" Faith looked up. Eve was staring back at her through her tortoiseshell glasses, her eyes piercing.

"I said, am I making you uncomfortable?"

"No." Heat crept up Faith's face. "I'll just turn around."

Faith spun around. Behind her, she could hear the swish of clothing. She willed herself to not imagine Eve undressing. What was wrong with her? Just this morning, Faith had been thinking about how much Eve got on her nerves, and now this?

"I'm done," Eve said. "Here."

Faith turned around to face Eve. Eve tucked the bottom of her blouse into her pants and handed Faith the ink-stained shirt.

"Before you go." Eve leaned back against the front of her desk. "How are you finding the job so far? Any issues?"

"No," Faith said. "Leah and Ethan are easy kids."

"And everything else? I know I can be"—Eve pressed her lips together, searching for a word—"*demanding* at times."

"It's fine. I can handle it."

"Good. Let me know if anything comes up." Eve slid her jacket back on and went to sit behind her desk. "Thanks again, Faith."

Faith left Eve's office. She needed to get a grip. Eve was her boss. And even if she wasn't, she was not Faith's type at all.

So why couldn't Faith stop thinking about her?

CHAPTER THREE

Faith sat on the floor in the lounge room with the twins, waiting for Harrison to pick them up. They were going to stay with their father for a few days, which meant Faith would finally get some time off.

In the meantime, Faith was helping the twins with their homework. For every question they got right, Faith gave them a sticker. At some point, the twins had started sticking the stickers on each other's arms and faces, laughing as they did. Eve definitely wouldn't approve, but it kept the twins motivated, so Faith didn't stop them.

She glanced out into the hall. Eve was in the other room working. It seemed like Eve disapproved of everything Faith did. Even when she didn't say so, the dark look in her eyes spoke volumes. At least, Faith thought it was disapproval that she sensed. It was hard to tell what was going on in Eve's head.

Leah stuck a sticker on Faith's cheek and giggled. The doorbell rang.

"Faith?" Eve's voice rang out across the hall. "Can you get that, please? It's probably Harrison."

"Sure." Faith ruffled Ethan's hair and got up. "I'll be right back."

She headed down the hall and opened the front door. A well-dressed woman around Faith's age stood before her.

"Hi," the woman said. "I'm Harrison's assistant. He sent me to pick up Ethan and Lily."

"You mean Leah?" Faith asked.

"Right. That's what I meant. Harrison, he's in a meeting, but he'll be out soon."

Faith looked her up and down. "Let me go get Eve."

She headed back inside, and found Eve in the lounge room, removing the stickers from the twins' arms, an irritated expression on her face.

"Eve?" Faith said. "There's a woman at the door. She says she's Harrison's assistant."

Eve let out a hard sigh. "Tall, red hair, looks like she's just out of high school?"

"Uh, yes. She says she's here to pick up the twins."

"Harrison is supposed to pick them up himself."

"She said he's in a meeting."

"Of course he is." Eve adjusted the collar of Ethan's shirt, her irritation held back. "You've packed the kids' bags?"

Faith nodded. "They're by the door."

Eve addressed the twins. "It's time to go to your father's. Let's go."

Obediently, the twins got up and said goodbye to Faith. Eve shepherded them to the door.

Faith packed up the books and toys strewn around the room. Three whole days off. She was looking forward to it. She'd made plans to catch up with friends, starting with dinner with Lindsey in a few hours. But mostly, she just wanted to put her feet up and relax.

Faith heard the front door slam shut, then the telltale click of Eve's heels on the floor in the hall.

"You sent your PA to pick up the kids again?" Eve's voice echoed through the empty house. "I don't care about your meeting. You knew you had to come get them this evening. You agreed to pick them up personally. You're lucky I let them go with her at all!"

Was Eve on the phone to Harrison? Faith tried her hardest not to eavesdrop, but it was impossible with Eve yelling as she was.

"You expect me to send my children off with some stranger?" There was a long pause. "That's different. A nanny is a professional, not someone who's barely qualified to get coffee, let alone work with children." Eve paused again. "Is that what your mother thinks? Last time I checked, she wasn't the one raising the twins."

Eve strolled past the lounge room and spotted Faith inside. Judging by the look on her face, she'd forgotten Faith was there.

"I have to go," Eve said. "Next time, pick them up yourself, or they're not going anywhere." She hung up the phone.

Faith made a show of busying herself putting away the kids' books.

"I suppose you heard all that?" Eve said.

"Er, just a little," Faith replied.

"I apologize for raising my voice. Things between Harrison and I can be strained at times."

"Sorry to hear that."

"Don't be. It's better than being married to him."

Silence hung over them. It was rare for the two of them to be alone in the house.

Eve looked at Faith's face. Her eyes slid down toward Faith's lips, her head tilting to the side. "Come here," she said.

Faith's heart began to race. She took a few steps forward, closer and closer to Eve. As soon as she was within reach, Eve lifted her hand toward Faith's face.

Faith's heart beat even faster. What was Eve doing?

Eve's fingertips brushed Faith's cheek. A shiver rolled down the back of Faith's neck. She'd never been this close to Eve before. She smelled faintly of flowers with a hint of spice, and her lips had a reddish tinge and an inviting fullness.

Eve pulled away and held up a little gold star. "You shouldn't let the kids treat you like a toy."

Faith blinked. *Right.* The sticker. Leah had put it there. "I… It's fine. I don't mind."

Eve gave her a slight smile. "They're lucky to have a nanny like you." She looked past Faith at the room beyond. "You've finished tidying up?"

"Yes," Faith stammered.

"You can go home now. I'll see you in a few days."

Faith mumbled a goodbye, grabbed her things, and left the room without looking back.

When Faith got home, she jumped straight into the shower. She had a couple of hours before she was due to meet Lindsey for dinner. Faith was hoping to convince her to have drinks afterward. She needed to unwind.

She was looking forward to catching up with Lindsey. She was the closest thing Faith had to family these days. The two of them had been inseparable since their first day of art school when they met. They'd lived together for most of their time at college, and they'd stayed close even after they'd graduated a couple of years ago. But last year, Lindsey had moved in with her girlfriend Camilla, who lived just outside the city. Since then, she and Faith didn't get to spend as much time together as they used to. Faith missed her.

As she got out of the shower and dried herself off, her phone rang. She darted into her bedroom. Her phone was on the dresser, Lindsey's name flashing on the screen.

Faith picked it up. "Hi, Lindsey."

"Faith," Lindsey said. "I know we're supposed to have dinner tonight, but I just remembered I have plans with Camilla. We made them a month ago. I completely forgot."

"Oh. That's okay."

"I'm really sorry. I can't get out of this. It's with a bunch of Camilla's friends, and it's really rare that everyone is free at the same time."

"It's all right." Faith tried her best to hide her disappointment. "We can reschedule."

"Maybe we don't have to," Lindsey said. "You could always join us. I should warn you, we're going to Lilith's Den."

Faith frowned. "Isn't that a sex club?" Lindsey had mentioned it to Faith before. She and Camilla went occasionally. They had some kind of kinky relationship that Faith didn't quite understand.

"It's *not* a sex club. It's a BDSM club. There's a difference. And we're going there to hang out and catch up, that's all."

"Right," Faith said.

"Really. To tell you the truth, it's probably going to be boring. Whenever Camilla's friends get together, everyone just sits around talking about investments and whiskey. I could use some company. Plus, it's 'ladies only' night."

That was a definite plus. Faith liked women, men, and everyone in between, but she rarely dated men these days. It seemed like every guy she dated ended up being too hung up on traditional gender roles. They wanted Faith to be this dutiful, subservient, utterly ladylike girlfriend. She'd had enough of that in her life. She rarely had to worry about that when she dated women.

"That doesn't matter," she said. "I'm not looking to meet anyone at a place like *that*."

"Since when are you such a prude?" Lindsey teased. "Usually, you're the one who has to convince me to do something wild."

It was true. Of the two of them, Faith was usually more adventurous. It was a side effect of having grown up sheltered. Nowadays, she liked to take full advantage of her freedom.

"I'm not a prude," Faith said. "I just don't get all that stuff."

"Come on. There'll be cocktails. Music. Maybe even dancing."

Faith drew her fingers through her hair with a sigh. Hadn't she just been thinking it would be fun to do something more exciting than dinner? "All right. I'll come."

"Great! I can't wait. Camilla will be happy to see you too." Lindsey told Faith the address and a time to meet. "Text me when you get there and I'll come out and get you. The club is members only, but I'll put you on the list as my guest."

"Okay. So, what exactly do I wear to a place like that?"

"You don't have to wear leather and chains if that's what you're wondering," Lindsey said. "Just dress like you're going to a high-end club. And if you want to look the part, wear something black."

CHAPTER FOUR

I'm out front.

Faith pressed send and waited for Lindsey in front of the club. From the outside, it was little more than a black door with a sign hanging above it that read 'Lilith's Den'. The secrecy of it all was exciting. Lindsey had mentioned that the club was exclusive, catering only to the uber-rich. What was it like inside?

A minute later, Lindsey emerged. Her auburn hair was loose, and she wore an expensive-looking black dress and heels, both of which her outrageously wealthy girlfriend had probably gifted her. Around her neck was an elaborate leather choker. Faith was sure that had been gifted to Lindsey by her girlfriend too. And she was pretty sure it wasn't just a choker.

"It's so good to see you." Lindsey pulled Faith into a hug. "Sorry again for the mix-up."

"It's okay," Faith said. "Honestly, I could use a night out. And a few drinks."

"The new job not going well, then?"

"It's just... taxing." That was one way to describe how working for Eve made Faith feel.

"Let's go in," Lindsey said.

Faith followed her through the black door into a small foyer. A large woman guarded the inner door, and another sat behind a desk beside it holding a tablet.

The woman addressed Lindsey. "A guest of yours?"

"Yep. She should be on the list. Faith Campbell."

The woman scanned her tablet and handed Faith a clipboard. "Sign these."

Faith flicked through the papers on the clipboard. There were several pages, all filled with threatening legalese. What kind of place was this that she needed to sign her life away just to step through the door?

Lindsey sensed Faith's hesitation. "Don't worry, it's just club rules, some waivers. An NDA. The people who go here just like to know their privacy is protected, for obvious reasons." She lowered her voice. "Don't be surprised if you see a famous face or two inside. Just remember, what happens at Lilith's stays at Lilith's."

Faith signed the papers and handed the clipboard back to the woman. The bouncer opened the inner door for them and nodded to Faith. "Welcome to Lilith's Den."

Faith walked through the door, staring around in awe. The dark club was packed with women, all of them drinking, chatting, and dancing. Most were dressed in all black, some in cocktail dresses and suits, others in leather, corsets, and sky-high stilettos. A few had collars and restraints on, wearing them as casually as jewelry.

The club itself was so lavish. It was like she'd entered another world, one of luxury beyond imagining. The people, the drinks, the decor—it all spoke of opulence and grandeur with a dash of sin.

A couple walked by, one in a latex bodysuit, the other wearing nothing but a thong and a thick leather collar with metal spikes. Faith gaped at her. All this kink and debauchery? It didn't bother Faith. It was kind of thrilling.

Clearly, she'd been spending too much time with Lindsey.

"We're over there." Lindsey pointed to a dimly lit corner where her girlfriend sat with another dark-haired woman Faith didn't know.

They headed over to the table. As soon as Camilla spotted them, she stood up and embraced Faith warmly.

"Lovely to see you," Camilla kissed the air next to Faith's cheek. "Has Lindsey told you about our party coming up?"

"Yep. I'll be there." Faith never turned down an invitation to go to Lindsey and Camilla's mansion, especially when there was a party involved.

Lindsey introduced Faith to the woman sitting next to Camilla. "This is Vanessa. She owns Lilith's Den."

"Nice to meet you." Vanessa folded her arms on the table in front of her. "I hear it's your first time here?"

"Yes," Faith said.

"And what do you think of my little club?"

"It's… interesting."

A smile played on Vanessa's lips. "Don't worry, no one in here bites. Not unless you want them to."

Faith's skin flushed. She sat down next to Lindsey. A few minutes later, they were joined by Vanessa's fiancée, along with a couple of other women. Lindsey introduced them to Faith, but she was so overwhelmed by everything around her that she forgot their names. Somehow, she ended up with a cocktail in her hand.

It wasn't long before the conversation turned to people and things Faith knew nothing about. Her eyes drifted around the room. In one corner, a tall, curvy woman stood beside a cage, inside which another woman kneeled. Nearby, a woman was tied to a cross, another woman pressed against her, her hand up the inside of the bound woman's top. The woman on the cross had a look of ecstasy on her face.

Suddenly, the room felt warm.

"See, I told you this was boring," Lindsey said.

Faith tore her eyes away. "Hm?"

"Oh?" Lindsey grinned. "I thought that distant look in your eyes was because you were bored, not because you were distracted. Something catch your interest?"

Faith crossed her arms. "No."

"It's nothing to be embarrassed about."

"I'm not embarrassed, because I'm not interested in any of this." She gestured across the room. "I don't want to be stuffed in a cage!"

Lindsey rolled her eyes. "Do you think Camilla stuffs *me* in a cage? Although that might just be because she hasn't thought of that yet." She glanced at her girlfriend. "Anyway, all this stuff, it isn't about whips and cages. It isn't even about sex, or anything physical. It's about so much more than that."

"I know." Faith and Lindsey had had this conversation a dozen times before. But it wasn't the sexual side of this kinky world that Faith was disturbed by. Although she'd been brought up to see desire of any kind as shameful, she'd gotten over it long ago. These days, she was pretty adventurous when it came to her sexuality.

No, Faith knew all too well what these kinds of relationships were about. Submission. Power. Control. And Faith hated being controlled. She hated being powerless.

A waitress wandered past. Faith caught her eye and ordered another drink, then changed the subject. She and Lindsey had plenty to catch up on.

But as the night wore on, Faith's eyes kept wandering around the club. At the far end, there was a small stage on which a near-naked woman was suspended from the ceiling, being tied up in all kinds of knots by another woman, all in front of the watching audience. Lindsey and the others were paying it all no mind, but Faith couldn't help but stare. It was so sensual. So erotic.

Something stirred inside her. What would that feel like? To be tied up and helpless, at the mercy of another woman? She examined the bound woman's face. It was so euphoric. What was it about all this that could make someone feel that way?

Beside her, Lindsey finished off her drink. Her eyes flicked to the dance floor. "Want to go dance?"

"Sure," Faith replied. The fact that there was a dance floor was just about the only normal thing about this club. And right now, Faith needed a dose of normal.

Lindsey leaned over to where Camilla sat nearby and spoke quietly to her. Camilla nodded, then kissed her passionately, as if she were leaving for another country rather than just the dance floor.

Faith rolled her eyes. Although she was happy that her friend had found love, Lindsey and Camilla had been together for a year now, and they still hadn't left that honeymoon period. It was sickeningly sweet. Faith couldn't help but envy them. Sometimes, she wondered if that kind of love would ever exist for her. After all, life had taught her that love always came with strings.

Lindsey pried herself away from Camilla and pulled Faith to the dance floor. They'd had a few drinks, and Faith was feeling the buzz. She let herself get carried away by the music and the crowd, the glamour and the flickering lights. It didn't take long before she was lost in this dark, twisted world.

Faith's eyes flicked over to the cage in the corner again. The woman inside hadn't left it all night. The other woman sat perched on top of the cage now.

Suddenly, the woman atop the cage met Faith's eye across the room and shot Faith a smile that reminded her of a large cat.

Faith looked away sharply, wiping her brow. She and Lindsey had been dancing for some time now, and she was starting to sweat. She leaned toward Lindsey and yelled over the music. "I'm going to grab a drink."

Lindsey nodded. Faith headed to the bar and asked for a glass of water. She'd had too many cocktails already. As she gulped her glass of water down, someone sidled up beside her.

"Hey."

Faith turned. Next to her stood the woman who had been sitting on the top of the cage. Now, standing before Faith in impractically high heels, she seemed positively Amazonian.

"First time here?" the woman asked.

Faith frowned. "What gave it away?"

"You just have that look." The woman smiled. "Like a kid in a candy store." She leaned down against the bar in a way that highlighted her generous chest. "I saw you dancing out there. You look like a woman who isn't afraid to take a walk on the wild side. Want someone to show you what this place is about?"

"Uh..." Faith had to admit, she was intrigued by everything around her. But she wasn't interested in this stranger.

She glanced toward the cage where the other woman waited.

"Don't worry about her," the woman said. "My girlfriend likes having another submissive to play with."

"What makes you think I'm a submissive?"

The woman raised an eyebrow. "So you prefer the other end of the whip?"

"No. I don't." Faith held up her hands. "I appreciate the offer, but I'm not interested. All this, it isn't for me."

"If you say so." The woman straightened up. "Come find me if you change your mind and I'll give you a taste. Of course, I might make you grovel first." The woman winked at her before walking away.

Faith shook herself and finished off her glass of water. She'd wanted an interesting night out, and she'd certainly gotten that. As she turned back toward the dance floor, something caught her eye. No, not something.

Someone.

Standing by the bar, half shrouded in darkness, was a woman. Her blonde hair was dead straight, the sharp ends of it grazing her bare shoulders. She was dressed in a black corset of silk and lace that cinched her waist tight, along with a short leather skirt, fishnet stockings, and heels.

Faith stared, unable to tear her eyes away. The woman gave off this unmistakable air of superiority that immediately told Faith that she was a Domme. The room was full of women like her, but this woman was different. She radiated this confidence that was so captivating.

But that wasn't all that drew Faith's eye. The woman?

She almost looked like Eve.

It was a crazy thought. Faith couldn't even see the woman's face. Was this mixed up attraction Faith felt toward Eve so bad that her mind was seeing Eve everywhere?

Suddenly, the woman turned Faith's way. Their eyes locked.

Faith's heart stopped. *It can't be.* The woman looked so much like

Eve. Her face was expressionless, but she had a dark, overpowering look in her eyes that set something deep inside Faith's body alight—

"Faith?"

She felt a hand on her arm. She spun around. Lindsey stood beside her.

"I saw that woman hitting on you. Thought you might need rescuing." She looked at Faith's face, her brows drawing together. "Everything okay?"

"Yeah. I'm fine." Faith glanced over her shoulder.

The woman in the corset was gone.

"Are you sure?" Lindsey asked.

"It's nothing. I thought I saw someone, that's all." Faith shook her head. She needed to sit down. "Come on. Let's go back to the others."

As they returned to the table, she looked back toward where the woman in the corset had been standing. There was no sign of her. Either she'd disappeared into the crowd, or she'd been no more than an apparition in the first place. Either way, one thing was certain.

The woman hadn't been Eve.

CHAPTER FIVE

A few days passed before Faith returned to work for Eve. And in those few days, Faith had thought about nothing but the woman in the corset from Lilith's Den. In her mind's eye, she couldn't stop seeing Eve's face on her.

It was almost like Faith was hoping the woman *was* Eve. But that didn't make any sense. Faith wasn't interested in Eve. She wasn't interested in that world of submission and power games that the woman in the corset was so clearly a part of either. So why was she obsessing about both of them?

And why did thinking about them make her hot all over?

Faith let herself into the house. She had a few minutes before she had to wake the twins up and get them ready for school. As she walked down the hall, she spotted Eve in the kitchen. Her hair was styled in her usual short curled bob, and she was dressed for work.

Eve turned and spotted her. "Good morning, Faith."

Faith entered the kitchen. "Hi."

Eve continued making her breakfast. Faith watched her as she did. Surely if she'd been at Lilith's Den that night she'd show Faith some kind of sign. It wasn't impossible that the woman had been Eve. If Eve swapped out her glasses for contact lenses and straightened her hair, she'd look just like her. And Eve hadn't had the twins that night. Would she have spent one of her rare free nights at Lilith's Den? And on a 'ladies only' night? Faith had no idea if Eve was interested in women. She'd been married to a man, but that didn't mean anything. Faith herself wasn't fussy about the gender of who she dated. Sexuality, attraction, love—it had never been one or the other to her. Perhaps Eve felt the same way.

Eve held up the pot of coffee. "Would you like some? I just made it."

"Sure," Faith replied.

Eve got out two mugs and filled them both with coffee. She handed one to Faith. Their fingers brushed. Faith nearly dropped the cup.

She muttered a thank you and took a sip, peering at Eve as she did so. Did Eve have a sister? An identical twin? One who was the opposite of her in every way? Well, not every way. Eve had the same domineering air. But while Eve was more likely to scold Faith for putting the milk in the wrong part of the fridge, she suspected the woman in the corset was a completely different kind of controlling.

Could they be one and the same? Could it be that behind this mother and businesswoman was a passionate Domme dying to come out?

Could Faith be the one to bring her out?

Why did she want that? She'd never had such desires before, not until that night at Lilith's Den. And seeing Eve, here and now, only made them stronger. She peered at Eve again. The resemblance was uncanny. What if they were the same person?

And if that were the case, which was the real Eve?

"Is something the matter?" Eve asked.

Faith shook her head. "No. It's fine."

The toaster popped. Eve plucked out her toast and began buttering it.

Faith steadied herself. It was time for her to start the morning routine. But something held her there in the kitchen.

She had to know.

She cleared her throat. "So, did you get up to anything while the twins were away?"

"What do you mean?" Eve asked.

"You know, did you do anything? Go anywhere?"

"I didn't do anything unusual." Eve narrowed her eyes. "Why?"

"No reason," Faith said quickly. "I'm just curious. I don't know much about you. Like, what you do in your spare time. For fun."

"I work full time, and until now I've been raising two kids by myself. It doesn't leave me with a lot of time for fun."

"Right." This was silly. Faith picked up her mug and headed out of the kitchen.

"What about you?"

"Huh?" Faith turned in the doorway to see Eve looking at her, her plate in one hand and coffee in another. Her eyes were dark behind her glasses.

"Did you do anything *fun* during your time off?"

"I… Yes." There was something suggestive in Eve's voice. Or was Faith imagining it?

Eve took a few steps toward her, cornering her by the doorway. Faith could feel the heat of her body. "And what did you get up to?"

Faith hesitated. "I went to a club. With a friend. On Tuesday." She didn't dare be any more specific. The way Eve was looking at her made Faith feel exposed.

"Did you enjoy yourself?" Eve asked.

Faith's voice caught in her throat. "Yes. I did."

Eve stepped closer. Faith froze. Her heart was beating so hard, she was sure Eve could hear it. Was Faith right after all? Had Eve been at Lilith's Den that night, dressed in a corset?

Did Eve know all about the sinful thoughts going through Faith's mind?

"Good," Eve said. "With me working you so hard, you should be making the most of your days off." She slipped past Faith, through the doorway and out into the hall. "I'll be in the dining room if you need me."

Faith let out a breath. As she watched Eve walk away, hips

swaying in her fitted skirt, she couldn't help but notice how much Eve's figure was like that of the woman in the corset.

Faith looked at her watch. It was time to pick up the twins from school. She grabbed her things and left her apartment. After finishing with the chores and errands Eve had given her in the morning, she'd gone home to have a lunch break. It was with Eve's permission, of course. She didn't do anything without Eve's permission.

She'd never had a job where she'd had to deal with this level of supervision, but she was getting used to it. The fact that she was being paid double her usual rate certainly helped. Plus, the twins were easy kids. As far as jobs went, this was a good one.

All Faith had to do was quash the inexplicable attraction she felt toward Eve, along with her obsession with Eve being the woman in the corset from Lilith's Den.

Faith headed down to her car. As she passed the mailboxes for the apartment, she noticed a letter sticking out of hers. Her heart leaped. Only one person ever wrote to Faith—her sister, Abigail. She and Faith had an arrangement. Abigail would write to her one month, and Faith would send her a letter in reply the next month. They'd been doing so for years, every month like clockwork. It was the only way they could communicate without the rest of their family catching on. But it had been more than two months since Faith had last heard from Abigail. She'd been waiting for a letter for weeks now.

She rushed over to her mailbox and yanked the letter out.

Her heart sank. It was a phone bill.

Faith stuffed the letter back into her mailbox, pushing her disappointment aside. She had to go pick up the twins. But as she sat in the car and drove to the twins' school, her mind wandered back to her sister. Why hadn't she written? There were so many possibilities, all of them awful. Was she sick? Injured? Did something terrible happen to her? Or worse—had someone else from her family found out that Abigail had been writing to Faith in secret? That would be bad news for her sister.

There was no point in speculating. Abigail was probably just busy. After all, she was married with a family of her own now, despite being even younger than Faith. That was perfectly normal in the community her family lived in.

Faith reached the elite private school the twins attended and went through the usual pickup procedure. It was routine now. As Eve had helpfully reminded her in the morning, Ethan had soccer practice in the afternoon, and Leah had a violin lesson.

Faith dropped Ethan off first. As she drove Leah to her violin tutor's house, she glanced at Leah in the rearview mirror. Leah hadn't said much the whole drive. She was a quiet kid, quieter than her brother, but this was unusual even for her.

"Leah?" Faith asked. "Is something the matter?"

Leah pouted. "We had a spelling test today. Ethan beat me."

"Well, how did you do in the test?"

"I got two words wrong."

"So you got all the rest right?" Faith asked. "You did amazingly. Just because Ethan did better doesn't mean you didn't do great too." Both the twins were practically geniuses, which wasn't surprising considering how hard their mother pushed them.

"But he's going to tell Mom, and Mom is going to be upset at me," Leah said.

"She's not going to be upset. I'm sure she'll be very proud of you."

Leah sighed. "She's never happy when I don't do as good as Ethan."

Faith frowned. Now that Leah mentioned it, Eve did seem a little more critical of Leah than she was of Ethan. It was just one of the many things about Eve that Faith didn't understand.

As they pulled out the front of Leah's tutor's house, Faith's phone buzzed on the seat next to her. She parked the car and grabbed the phone. She had a message from Eve.

Leah's tutor called to cancel. Take her home instead.

Faith sent Eve a reply and turned to Leah in the back seat. "No violin lesson for you today. Your tutor canceled."

"Oh." Leah's shoulders slumped. Playing the violin was one of the few activities Eve made Leah do that she actually seemed to enjoy.

"You can practice at home instead," Faith said. "I'll help. Or better yet, you can put on a concert for me. I'd love to hear you play."

"I guess," Leah mumbled. She looked out the window toward a park just down the road. Her eyes lit up. "Can we go to the park instead?"

Faith shook her head. "Not today. It's time to go home."

"Please? Just for a little bit?"

Faith sighed. Leah looked like she could use some cheering up. "Okay," she said. "Just ten minutes. Then we're going home."

Faith unlocked the front door and ushered Leah inside. "Let's go make a snack. Then you can put on that concert for me."

"Okay." Leah grinned and bounced down the hall.

Faith followed her into the kitchen. She opened the fridge. All the ingredients for Eve's pre-approved healthy snacks were right there on the shelves. Perhaps Faith could mix things up a bit, make something a little more interesting-

"Mom!" Leah said. "You're here!"

Faith turned. Eve was standing in the doorway, her eyes dark and her arms crossed.

She did not look happy.

"Eve," Faith said. "You're home."

"I finished up at work early." Eve looked down at Leah. "Why don't you go upstairs, sweetie? I need to talk to Faith."

"Okay." Leah skipped out of the kitchen, oblivious to the displeasure radiating from her mother.

"Faith," Eve said. "Come with me." She turned on her heel and started down the hall.

Faith followed Eve toward the back of the house and into her office. What did Eve want? Her voice had taken on the exact same tone she used when one of the twins was in trouble.

Eve shut the door and gestured to a chair in the middle of the room. "Have a seat."

Faith sat down.

Eve stood before her, looming over Faith's chair. "You were supposed to be home twenty minutes ago."

That was what this was about? "We were at the park," Faith said.

"Did I say you could take Leah to the park?"

"No. But it was just down the road from her tutor's house. We were already there when I got your message."

"And how was I supposed to know where you were?" Eve said coldly. "Where Leah was?"

"I'm sorry," Faith said. "I thought you were at wor—"

"That makes it okay for you to take Leah somewhere without my permission?"

"It was just for a little while. I didn't think you'd mind."

"I *do* mind. I've set out a schedule for them which I expect you to follow." Her face darkened. "Is this something you've been doing? Taking the twins places I haven't approved?"

"No, of course not," Faith said. "This was a one-off. I'll ask first next time."

"There won't be a next time." Eve put her hands on her hips. "You're not taking Leah or Ethan anywhere other than where I tell you to. You're not to do anything with them unless I've given you explicit permission. You're not to deviate from the instructions I've given you in any way."

Faith bit back her frustration. How was she supposed to do her job if she couldn't do anything without Eve's approval?

"Well?" Eve said. "Do you have something to say?"

"It's just—" Faith chose her words carefully. "I know I'm not their mother, but when the twins are with me it's my job to look after them. And it's hard to do that if I can't make judgment calls sometimes. Leah was upset. I was trying to cheer her up. I thought going to the park would help. It was only for twenty minutes. I brought her straight home after that."

Eve frowned. “Leah was upset? What about?”

“Just a test at school.” Faith didn’t elaborate. Telling Eve that Leah was upset because she didn’t want Eve to be disappointed in her wouldn’t go down well at the best of times.

“That’s no excuse,” Eve snapped. “I’m her mother, not you. I decide where she goes and what she does.” She leaned down over Faith’s chair. “You will do as I say, or I’ll find another nanny who can follow my instructions.”

“Okay.” Faith spoke through gritted teeth. “I won’t do it again.” She didn’t apologize. She’d just been doing her job, but Eve was behaving as though Faith had taken Leah to some seedy back alley, not the park.

Eve scowled. “Just go home. I can handle the kids for the rest of the night.” She walked over to the door and opened it wide.

Faith left the room in a huff. She’d thought this job had been going well, but Eve was more infuriating than anyone else she’d worked for. And to think, just hours before, Faith had been having all kinds of crazy thoughts about her. It was ridiculous. Eve was Eve, not this mysterious woman in a corset that Faith had been obsessing about.

And Faith wasn’t interested in either of them.

CHAPTER SIX

Faith arrived at the front of Lindsey and Camilla's house. It was evening and the grounds of the estate looked stunning in the fading light. She loved coming out here, to this little slice of paradise just outside the city. The huge estate was like its own little world.

She got out of the car and looked up at the mansion before her. She'd been here a dozen times now, but she still found it impressive. It made Eve's suburban palace look tiny in comparison.

Stop thinking about Eve. Faith had the whole weekend off. She was at her best friend's party. She was supposed to be letting her hair down.

So why couldn't she get Eve out of her mind?

The tension between the two of them had only risen since that afternoon in Eve's office. It was like Eve had been watching Faith's every move, her eyes dark and inscrutable behind her glasses. And every time Eve was around, it made Faith simmer inside with something that wasn't entirely annoyance.

A weekend away from Eve was exactly what she needed. Hopefully, it would help clear her head.

Faith headed into the house. Inside the entrance hall, Faith paused by a mirror to straighten out her outfit. The dress she wore, a knee-length blue number, had been borrowed from Lindsey. She didn't own many dresses that were fancy enough for an occasion like this. These parties Lindsey's girlfriend threw weren't Faith's usual scene, but she still loved attending them. They were so glamourous.

She fixed her hair, which she'd managed to style into loose waves instead of her usual messy curls, and followed a pair of guests to the ballroom. The party was in full swing, the room filled with dozens of people. She scanned the crowd until she found Lindsey. She was standing with her girlfriend by a table of canapés.

As Faith approached her friend, Lindsey spotted her. She rushed over to Faith and pulled her to the side, a sheepish look on her face.

"What's going on?" Faith asked.

"It's Eve," Lindsey said. "She's here."

Faith's stomach flipped. "What's she doing here?"

"Camilla invited her. I didn't realize she was *your* Eve until Camilla introduced us. We were all talking, and she mentioned some stuff that sounded familiar, like her job and that she had twins, and it clicked."

Great. That was just Faith's luck. She'd left the city, and she still couldn't escape Eve. "Where is she?"

Lindsey pointed to the other side of the room. Amid a group of people stood a stunning blonde woman holding a glass of champagne. Her back was turned, her hair straight and parted to one side. She wore a strapless black gown that went down to the floor. Faith wouldn't have been able to tell that the woman was Eve if she hadn't recognized the dress. She had seen it in Eve's closet, tucked away with all her other glamourous clothes.

Dressed like this, Eve looked even more like the woman in the corset.

"How does Camilla know her?" Faith asked.

Lindsey shrugged. "I haven't had a chance to ask. Camilla has never mentioned her before. I think they're just part of the same rich people social circle."

Faith glanced at Eve. "So they don't know each other from Lilith's Den?"

"Not that I know of. Why?"

"No reason," Faith said quickly.

"I hope this doesn't make things awkward," Lindsey said. "I know she's been giving you a hard time at work."

"It's fine." Faith had told Lindsey about how Eve had dressed her down in her office that afternoon. But that was only part of the reason Faith was frustrated with Eve.

Faith pulled herself together. She was not going to let Eve's presence ruin a good party. "So, where are the drinks?"

Lindsey led her over to the bar where Faith grabbed a glass of champagne. It was crisp and light, more delicious than any champagne Faith had ever tasted. She and Lindsey sat down in a quiet corner to talk. It wasn't long before Camilla found them and dragged them both off to meet people.

The evening wore on, the sky darkening to night outside the wide windows of the ballroom. After finishing off her second glass of champagne, Faith excused herself and went back to the bar for another drink. This time, she asked for a glass of rosé. It had just the right balance of sweetness.

She sighed contentedly. She was enjoying herself. Although she had little in common with most of the people in the room, there was delicious food, top-shelf drinks, and interesting conversation. It was enough to make her forget about Eve.

Almost.

Faith searched the room for her. Did Eve know she was here? The party was so big that Faith hadn't crossed paths with her yet.

Her eyes landed on Eve. She was nearby, deep in conversation with a pair of women, close enough that Faith could see her face. Without her glasses, the long, dark lashes that framed Eve's hazel eyes made their depths seem endless. Her cheeks had a faint flush, and her lips were a pale shade of pink that brought to mind the rosé Faith was drinking.

Would Eve's lips taste just as sweet?

As if overhearing Faith's thoughts, Eve turned toward her. There was a flash of surprise in Eve's eyes, followed by something else. A cool fire that made Faith burn inside. It was just like that night at Lilith's Den, that moment Faith had locked eyes with the woman in the corset.

Faith turned around sharply and took a deep breath. A minute passed, then two, then five, but Eve didn't approach her. And Faith didn't dare look for her again.

Faith finished off her glass of rosé and went off to mingle again. She didn't know why she was avoiding Eve. She had no reason to hide from her. But Eve hadn't sought her out either. Was she avoiding Faith too? Faith wasn't sure whether to be relieved or offended. She had no idea what she wanted from Eve.

She shook her head. She was being ridiculous. She couldn't avoid Eve all night. It was better to just speak to her, to get it out of the way.

And there was no time like the present.

She scanned the room for Eve again. This time, Faith found her sitting alone, her head down and her hair falling over her face, half hiding it from view. Faith steeled herself and headed over to her.

As Faith approached her, Eve didn't look up. Her eyes were fixed on the phone in her hand, a worried look on her face. Before Faith could reach her, Eve stood up and stormed out of the room.

Faith frowned. Was Eve upset? It took a lot to upset Eve. Faith hesitated, then followed her out the door.

The hall beyond led deeper into the mansion. Eve was already out of sight, but Faith could hear her voice faintly. As Faith followed her down the hall, the sounds of the party receded behind her, and Eve's voice grew louder. Eve was almost yelling, but Faith couldn't make out the words. Eve's voice became more agitated, then stopped abruptly.

Faith reached an open doorway and peered into the room beyond. It was a library of some kind, with books covering every inch of the walls. In the corner, Eve sat perched on the arm of an armchair, scowling at her phone.

Faith knocked on the door.

Eve looked up. "Faith."

"I saw you leave. You looked worried." Faith slipped into the room. "I just wanted to make sure everything's okay."

"You're not on the clock. You don't need to worry about me."

"I know I don't have to, but I do."

Eve let out a hard sigh. "I've been calling Harrison all evening so I could say goodnight to the twins, but he wouldn't pick up his phone. When I finally got through, his mother answered and said the twins were already asleep." Her grip on the phone tightened. "Of course they're asleep now. If someone had answered the phone an hour ago, I would have been able to talk to them before they went to bed." She shook her head. "I'm sure they're fine. I'm just sick to death of Eleanor's petty tricks. I have no doubt this was deliberate. She's been pulling this kind of thing for years."

Faith gave her a sympathetic look. "She sounds like a real piece of work."

"You don't know the half of it. I just wanted one night off, to not have to worry about the twins and all this custody business, yet here I am." Eve placed her phone down on the desk next to her. "What are you doing here, anyway?"

"I'm friends with Lindsey. We went to art school together. What about you?"

"Camilla invited me."

Faith hesitated. "How do you know each other?"

"I don't remember exactly. We have a mutual friend or two, so we run into each other a lot, but we don't know each other well."

Silence fell over them. Faith walked over to the window and looked out it. She had no reason to stay in this room anymore. But something held her there. Eve held her there.

Eve got up from the armchair and joined Faith by the window. "It's a lovely view, isn't it?"

Faith nodded. Outside, the moonlit estate grounds stretched on and on. Faith kept her eyes fixed on the view, not daring to look at Eve. Being alone with her, standing so close to her, set off the exact same feeling in Faith that the woman in the corset had.

"Look," Eve said. "About the other day, in my office. I'm sorry for the way I treated you. I shouldn't have yelled at you."

"It's okay," Faith replied. "You were just looking out for Leah's best interests."

"No, it wasn't about Leah. It was about me." Eve's eyes grew distant. "This is the first time I've ever let anyone else be responsible for my kids. I've been feeling so conflicted about it. I took it out on you."

"It's fine," Faith said. "Really, I understand."

"I know I can be controlling and critical, but you should know, I'm very happy about the job you're doing. I'd be lost without you. So thank you."

"No problem," Faith said. "I'm just doing my job."

"No, you're doing far more than that. You seem to really care about the twins. You have a way with them."

"They're great kids. Working with the twins is effortless. I enjoy it."

Eve turned to look at her. "And how do you find working with their mother?"

Faith smiled. "It's not bad either."

"Well, I appreciate everything you do for us." Eve touched Faith's arm. "And I appreciate having you around."

Faith's skin prickled. Suddenly, all those feelings of frustration Faith harbored for Eve were replaced with something else entirely.

"Is something the matter?" Eve asked.

"No," Faith replied. "It's just, you seem so different. You look different. The hair, the glasses, the dress. You look stunning."

Eve swept her eyes down Faith's body. "You don't look too bad yourself."

Suddenly, Faith felt very naked. "The dress isn't mine. I borrowed it from Lindsey."

"It looks like it was made for you." Eve took a step closer. "You seem different too, you know. You're much more relaxed outside work. More free. Wilder."

Faith's heart thumped hard against her chest. "Outside work?" Could she mean at Lilith's Den?

Eve didn't respond.

Faith drew in a breath. She couldn't stay silent any longer. She had to know the answer to the question etched on her mind or she'd never know peace again.

"Eve," she said. "Was it you?"

Eve tilted her head to the side, studying Faith. "Was what me?"

"Was it you, the other night at Lilith's Den? In the corset?" Faith searched Eve's eyes. They gave nothing away. Was she wrong? Had she imagined it all? "I have to know. Was it you?"

Eve didn't answer her at first. She just stared back at Faith, holding her in place with her gaze.

Finally, Eve spoke.

"Yes. It was me."

CHAPTER SEVEN

Faith stood frozen on the spot. She knew it. Eve and the woman in the corset were one and the same. "I haven't been able to stop thinking about her," she blurted out. "About you. About how much I wanted you to be her—"

Eve pressed her finger to Faith's lips. "Wait."

Faith nodded. Eve removed her finger. Faith's lips tingled.

Eve walked over to the door, shut it, and returned to Faith's side. "Tell me again. What were you saying?"

Faith spoke softly. "Ever since that night, I haven't been able to stop thinking about you." She looked into Eve's eyes. "I want you so badly, Eve."

Eve brought her hand up, her eyes smoldering, and drew it down Faith's cheek. "From the moment I laid eyes on you at Lilith's Den, all I've wanted to do was make you mine."

A tremor went through Faith's body. In the space of a heartbeat, Eve's lips were on Faith's, kissing her so furiously that she had to grab onto Eve's shoulder to steady herself. Eve's fingers curled in Faith's hair, her other hand around Faith's waist, pulling her close.

She closed her eyes, letting Eve's lips and arms engulf her. Eve's hunger and intensity took Faith back to that night at Lilith's Den the moment their eyes had met. This was the woman in the corset, the one who had made Faith breathless with just a glance. This was the woman who had filled her daydreams with all kinds of wicked images.

This was the woman who had made her realize she wanted something she never, ever thought she'd want.

Faith swept her hand up the side of Eve's neck, her other hand tightening around Eve's waist. Eve's body pressed against hers, pushing her back into the window. Faith trembled. The glass was cold against her bare shoulders, but the rest of her was on fire.

Eve slid her palm down Faith's chest, grazing it over her breast. Faith's nipples tightened under her dress. She slid her hand down the swell of Eve's hip, feeling the fullness of her curves. Eve grabbed hold of Faith's ass cheek, drawing her impossibly closer. A desperate murmur fell from Faith's lips.

Eve ran a hand down Faith's thigh, her fingertips seeking out the hem of Faith's dress. She dragged it up Faith's leg. Faith's pulse sped up. Was this really happening? Were they really doing this, here and now, just a few rooms away from a party full of people?

Eve broke away. Conflict and desire swirled behind her eyes, mixing with the greens and browns of her irises. "You want this?" It was as much a statement as it was a question.

"Yes," Faith said. "More than anything."

Eve kissed her again, hot and hard. Her lips still locked on Faith's, she slipped her hand between Faith's thighs. Faith's grip on Eve's hip tightened, heat flaring within her. She pushed back against Eve, spurring her on.

Breaking the kiss, Eve pulled Faith's dress all the way up to her waist and hooked her fingers into the sides of Faith's panties, pushing them down past her hips. They fell to the floor. Faith's whole body pulsed with need.

With painstaking slowness, Eve drew her hand up the inside of Faith's leg, all the way to the peak of her thighs. She slipped her fingers between Faith's swollen lips, sending a dart of pleasure through her.

Eve withdrew her hand and brought it up before her eyes. Her fingers were wet with Faith's arousal. "You really do want me." She drew her fingers down the center of Faith's chest, leaving a trail of her wetness down between Faith's breasts.

"Yes, I want you." After denying it for so long, Faith couldn't stop the words from spilling from her. "God, I want you."

Eve slid her hand down again. Faith's breath hitched, her head tipping back against the window. Eve ran her finger up and down Faith's slit, painting long slow strokes with her fingertips. Faith's hands scrabbled at the glass behind her. Eve's finger found Faith's hidden nub, strumming it gently.

Faith quivered. Here they were, in a darkened room at a party, with barely a few kisses for foreplay, yet Faith was already throbbing. She'd been craving Eve's touch for so long now. The hurried, forbidden nature of their tryst only made Faith hotter.

"Yes," she said. "Don't stop."

Eve pulled away, letting Faith's dress fall back down. "After all this time, you still haven't figured me out." Eve's voice was a whispered growl. "I like to take control. I like to do things my way. And I don't take orders.""

Eve took Faith's shoulders and spun her around so that she was facing the window. Faith gasped.

From behind her, Eve brought her hand up to Faith's chest, massaging her breast through her dress. "Was that an order, Faith?"

Faith shook her head, too off-balance to speak. Eve's body was pressed against hers, and with the low-backed dress Faith wore, all that separated their bare skin was the fabric of Eve's dress. Faith could feel Eve's peaked nipples through it.

"I wasn't planning to stop." Eve leaned in, her breath tickling Faith's neck. "I was going to tease you until you couldn't take it any longer. And then I was going to make you come undone."

A ripple went through Faith's body. Eve wasn't even touching her, yet her words made Faith just as hot as when Eve had had her hand between her legs.

"Is that what you want?" Eve asked.

"Yes," Faith said. "*Please.*"

Eve brushed a hand up to Faith's chin and tilted it to the side, pressing her lips against Faith's. "It seems we understand each other."

Once again, Eve drew up Faith's dress. She traced her hand up the back of Faith's leg, over her bare ass cheek, then back down to where her thighs met, seeking out her entrance. Faith bent at the waist, resisting the urge to push herself back toward the other woman. Eve seized hold of Faith's hip, holding her in place.

Faith closed her eyes, anticipation welling inside her. Slowly, Eve entered her, filling her completely. Faith let out a moan, her body threatening to collapse. Eve's fingers inside her felt so divine.

Eve thrust in and out, sending jolts of pleasure deep into Faith's body. Faith shuddered and moaned, delirious. Eve's stroking, curling fingers were unrelenting.

Eve quickened the pace. Faith rocked back against her, one of her breasts escaping from the top of her dress. Eve caressed it greedily. Far too late, Faith remembered they were standing by the window. Was anyone out there, wandering the grounds? She made a feeble attempt to pull the curtain next to her shut, but with Eve's fingers between her thighs and Eve's hand kneading her chest, she was so close—

Faith cried out as pleasure crashed through her. She pushed back into Eve, the other woman still surging inside her, and rode the waves of bliss rolling through her body.

Once Faith's orgasm receded, Eve whirled her back around and brought her lips to Faith's in a dizzying kiss. Her head spun, the world around her spinning with it. As her post-orgasm haze cleared, all the realizations from the past hour hit her. The woman in the corset was Eve. Faith's boss. And she'd just given Faith an earth-shattering orgasm up against the window at a party they both just happened to be at.

Eve drew back. "Here." She bent down, picked something up, and held it out to Faith.

Faith blinked at the bundle of fabric in Eve's hands. Her panties. "Um, thanks." She took them from Eve and slipped them back on.

"Is something wrong?" Eve asked.

"I just can't believe it, that's all," Faith said. "It was you all along.

I've been wondering ever since that night. Why didn't you say anything?"

Eve smoothed down her barely tousled dress. "What was I supposed to say?"

"But I asked you about it. That morning, in the kitchen."

"And I told you the truth. I said I didn't get up to anything unusual."

"You mean, you do that a lot?" Faith said. "Put on a corset and go to Lilith's Den?"

"Every now and then. Not so much lately. I've been busy. It's probably why I've never seen you there before."

"I'd never been there before. I only went there that night because I wanted to catch up with Lindsey."

Eve raised an eyebrow. "You went to Lilith's just to catch up with a friend?"

"Yes. I'm not interested in that stuff."

"You could have fooled me."

"I mean, I wasn't interested," Faith said. "Not at first. But going to that club made me realize how much it all appealed to me. And then I saw you, and I realized how much I wanted you. And god, how I've wanted you."

Faith looked into Eve's eyes. Eve turned away. The playfulness in her gaze had disappeared.

"We should get back," Eve said. "Before anyone notices we're gone."

Faith's stomach sank. "Shouldn't we talk about this?"

As Eve opened her mouth to speak, the door to the library swung open. In strolled Camilla, a glass of wine in her hand.

"Hello." Camilla walked over to a bookshelf, barely paying them any attention. "Don't mind me, I just need to grab something."

"Camilla," Eve said. "We were just talking."

Camilla's eyes fell on the two of them. A smirk crossed her lips. "No need to explain yourselves to me. This is a party, after all. You're supposed to be enjoying yourself." She looked from one woman to the other. "And it looks like the two of you are having fun."

Blood raced to Faith's cheeks. Eve was a terrible liar. Or maybe it was the fact that Eve's hair was in disarray and Faith's dress was askew. She straightened it up.

"Here it is." Camilla plucked a book from the shelf. "I'll leave you two alone."

Camilla sauntered out of the room. Faith turned to Eve. Gone was the passionate woman in the corset. The Eve that Faith knew was back.

"I'm going back to the party." Without a further word, Eve strode out the door, leaving Faith alone in the room.

When Faith returned to the party, Eve was nowhere to be found.

CHAPTER EIGHT

When Faith returned to work a few days later, her heart was in her throat. She hadn't seen or spoken to Eve since she'd walked out of the library that night at Lindsey's party. She had no idea how Eve was going to react.

Faith herself didn't know how to react. That night with Eve had turned her world upside down. Everything the woman in the corset had awakened in her that night at Lilith's Den had gone from a half-formed fantasy to an insatiable craving.

She unlocked the front door and entered the house. "Hello," she called. "It's Faith."

She was met with an eerie silence. At this time of the morning, the kids were still asleep, but Eve was usually up and about, getting ready for the day. Faith wandered through the house, peeking into rooms as she passed. Eve wasn't in any of the lounge rooms, or the kitchen, or the dining room.

Giving up, Faith went upstairs to wake up the twins. Once they were out of bed, she headed back downstairs to prepare their breakfast. At the base of the stairs, she almost ran into Eve.

"Good morning," Faith stammered.

"Faith," Eve said. "Are the twins up?"

Faith nodded.

"Good." Without another word, Eve walked off toward her bedroom.

Faith frowned. Was Eve avoiding her? Faith hadn't known what to expect from Eve, but this wasn't it. Just days ago, she'd had her hand up Faith's dress, whispering all kinds of dirty things in her ear, and now, this? Was Eve just going to pretend nothing had happened between them?

She went into the kitchen and began making the twins' breakfast. It was all routine now. Usually, Eve would be coming and going, giving Faith instructions. Not today.

A few minutes later, the twins came downstairs. Faith served them breakfast at the dining table and sat down across from them. Midway through the meal, Eve entered the room, greeting the kids and planting a kiss on each of their cheeks before sitting down to talk with them while they ate. Faith tried to catch her eye, but Eve avoided it. She barely acknowledged that Faith was even there.

Hurt welled up in Faith's chest. She couldn't believe Eve would be so cold. Faith had given in to all the feelings she'd been resisting for so long. Her longing for Eve. Her submissive desires. She'd exposed her deepest, darkest self to Eve.

And now, Eve was ignoring her.

Faith pushed her feelings aside. Getting upset at work was never a good idea. Then again, neither was hooking up with her boss at a party.

Once the twins finished their breakfast, Faith sent them upstairs to brush their teeth. Eve stood up to follow them out of the room.

"Eve," Faith said. "Do you have a minute?"

"I need to get ready for work." Before Faith could stop her, Eve slipped out the door.

Faith scowled. She wasn't upset anymore. She was mad. She wasn't going to let Eve brush her off. Eve wasn't going to make this easy, but Faith wasn't going to give up.

She helped the twins get ready for school. Today, they were carpooling with a friend who lived down the road, so Faith had to do little more than see them off at the street. Once they'd been picked up, she returned to the house. She had errands to run for the family. Grocery shopping, picking up school supplies. But they would have to wait.

Faith sat down at the bottom of the stairs. She didn't dare go barging into Eve's room. But sooner or later, Eve would have to walk past.

After a few minutes, Faith heard the distinctive click of heels on the marble floor. As Eve's footsteps grew closer, Faith stood up from her hiding place behind the banister, coming face-to-face with Eve.

Eve startled, almost dropping her briefcase. "Faith." She looked at her watch. "I need to get going."

"No." Faith crossed her arms. "You've been avoiding me all morning."

"I don't have time for this."

"I don't care." The intensity in Faith's voice surprised even Faith herself. "Why are you ignoring me?"

"I'm not ignoring you."

"Yes, you are."

"Fine," Eve said. "I am."

"Why?"

"Isn't it obvious?"

Faith flinched. "Do you regret what happened between us?"

"Believe me," Eve said. "That's not it."

"Then what is it?" This was like pulling teeth. "You won't talk to me, you'll barely look at me. You won't even be alone in a room with me! If you don't regret it, then why are you acting like this?"

Eve stiffened. Faith could see the battle going on in her mind. Still, Eve didn't speak.

"Eve, please! Just talk to me."

"You want to know why I've been avoiding you?" Eve said softly.

"Yes!"

Eve took a few steps toward Faith until they were almost touching. Her eyes blazed. "I've been avoiding you because I was afraid that if I was alone with you I wouldn't be able to hold myself back."

Faith's breath caught in her chest. Right there and then Faith realized that the difference between Eve and the woman in the corset had nothing to do with Eve's hair, or her clothes, or her glasses. It was this. This intensity that radiated from every part of her, from her gaze, to her stance, to her voice. That was what the woman in the corset possessed that Eve didn't. No, it was in Eve too, hiding behind that prim, proper woman.

All Eve had to do was let that side of her out.

"Then don't," Faith said. "Don't hold back."

Tentatively, Faith brought her hand up to Eve's cheek. Eve seized Faith's wrist in midair. Faith's heart began to race. They stood there, unmoving, searching each other's eyes. Eve's were filled with conflict and lust.

"Don't hold back," Faith whispered.

At once, Eve's lips crashed against Faith's in a firm, unyielding kiss. Faith crumbled. This was the woman from the other night, Eve and the woman in the corset all rolled into one. This was the woman who made Faith come undone.

She deepened the kiss, clutching at Eve's neck to anchor herself against the force of Eve's passion. The hard railing of the stairs pressed into her back, Eve's body pinning her to it. Her lips parted and their tongues swirled against each other. A soft purr rose from Faith's chest.

Eve jerked away. "We shouldn't."

Faith stifled a groan. "Why not?"

"You work for me. You're my nanny. And I just got divorced, and the twins… This is all so *wrong.*"

"What's wrong about this?"

"It's complicated. Believe me when I say this is just a bad idea." Eve's voice dropped low. "But I don't want to stop."

Eve let go of her briefcase. It fell to the floor with a thump. She pressed her lips to Faith's again and wrapped her hands up around Faith's waist, pulling her closer. Her lips traveled down Faith's cheek. Faith tipped her head back, baring her neck. Eve's kisses turned into gentle bites. One of Eve's hands roamed up to Faith's chest, groping her breast through her blouse. Faith let out a strangled whimper, her hands grabbing at Eve's curves.

Eve pulled back again. "We can't. Not now. I meant it when I said I need to go to work."

"No," Faith protested. "Stay."

Eve shot her a stern look. "What did I tell you that night in the library?"

Faith got even hotter at the thought. "That you don't like orders."

"Exactly."

"Stay, *please*?" Faith asked sweetly.

A faint chuckle rose from Eve's chest. "I would if I could." Eve took Faith's wrists and pried them from her waist. "But I have to go. I'll see you in the evening. We'll talk then." Eve kissed her again, then picked up the briefcase. "Don't forget to pick up milk while you're at the store. And remember, the twins have a dentist appointment after school."

Faith sighed. It seemed Eve still wasn't prepared to let go of control in that area of their relationship either.

CHAPTER NINE

So, when were you going to tell me about you and Eve?

Faith cursed to herself. The message was from Lindsey. She should have known that Camilla wouldn't have been able to keep something like that from her girlfriend.

It just kind of happened, Faith typed out. No, that was a lie. Everything between her and Eve had been brewing for so long. It had only been a matter of time before it boiled over. And now Faith's whole world had been turned upside down.

Faith placed her phone down on the coffee table without sending a reply and sat back to wait for Eve. It was 8 p.m., but Eve had been held up at the office.

The sound of the front door opening reached Faith's ears, followed by Eve's footsteps. A moment later, Eve entered the lounge room. She possessed her usual poise, but her face showed a hint of weariness. However, there was a spark of the woman Faith had glimpsed in the morning there.

"Thanks for taking care of everything for me," Eve said.

"No problem," Faith replied. "I just put the twins to bed if you want to say goodnight to them. Leah could use it."

"Is she all right?"

"She was upset all afternoon. She didn't want to do her homework. She's been struggling a little with it lately." Once again, Leah had expressed that she didn't want Eve to be disappointed in her, although not in as many words.

"I'll go talk to her. I'll be back down soon."

Eve disappeared upstairs. Faith busied herself tidying up the lounge room while she waited. She and Eve would have to have a conversation about Leah soon, but with Eve so clearly worn down from work, now wasn't a good time. Which also meant their other serious conversation, about the events of the morning, might have to wait too.

When Eve returned, she collapsed onto the couch next to Faith. "Christ, this has been a long day."

"Want to talk about it?" Faith asked.

"Well, aside from things at work getting busy, Harrison is being difficult. I'm taking the twins to see my parents in England next week, and he's up in arms about me leaving the country with them. He wants to get his lawyers involved." Eve threw her hands up. "He spent most of the twins' lives barely acknowledging their existence, and suddenly he wants to be a father to them. And now this with Leah. She's upset about something, but she refuses to tell me what. Did she say anything to you?"

Faith hesitated. "Not specifically."

"What is it?" Eve asked.

"I have an idea of why she's upset, but I don't know if it's my place to say anything."

"Go ahead. I won't hold it against you."

Faith chose her words carefully. "Leah, she feels like she's under a lot of pressure from you."

"I suspected as much," Eve said. "It's true, I push her. I want her and Ethan to make the most of their potential, that's all."

"I think she feels like you put more pressure on her than Ethan. That you compare her to him. That you're disappointed in her when she doesn't measure up to her brother."

Eve was silent for a moment. "That's not how I feel. Not at all. I didn't know Leah felt that way. She's never said anything to me."

"Well, she didn't say it to me in those words. But she sees that you push her harder than Ethan, and she's afraid of disappointing you."

"I never meant for this to happen." Eve rubbed her temples with her fingertips. "It's true. I've always put more pressure on Leah than Ethan. But it's for her own good. I want her to be able to choose her own future."

"And she'll be able to do that. You're giving Leah and Ethan every opportunity a child could possibly have."

"It's not just about opportunities. I need to make sure that Leah has all the tools she needs to do whatever she wants with her life. Ethan, his future is already secure. Harrison is grooming him to be the heir to his company and his family fortune. Even if Ethan doesn't want to follow in his father's footsteps, his status will open every door for him. But Leah? If Harrison and his family have their way, there's only one path for her, and it's a narrow one. They expect her to grow up, get married, pop out children, and be the perfect housewife, living only to serve her husband. Just like they expected of Harrison's sisters. Just like they expected of me."

Faith knew what that was like. Her own family had expected the same thing of her.

"If that's what Leah wants, that's fine," Eve said. "But I don't want her growing up thinking that's her only option. I want her to know that there are other paths she can take. I want to put her in a position where she can succeed in spite of her father and his family. I need Leah to know that she can build a fulfilling life for herself, one that doesn't revolve around her family. And I need her to know that she's not less than the men in her life."

A pained expression crossed Eve's face. "Everything I've done, all the pressure I've been putting on her, was so she wouldn't grow up thinking she's lesser. Instead, I've made her think she doesn't measure up to her brother. I need to fix this. I can't have her growing up believing she's a disappointment. I'll talk to her. Apologize. Lay off her a little, especially with the extra schoolwork. Clearly, it's making her miserable. Who knows what that will do to her grades?"

"Leah's already ahead of most kids her age. And she has lots of other talents too. Her violin teacher is impressed with her progress. He says she has a gift for music."

"Really? I haven't heard her play in a long time." Eve sighed. "I suppose it's because I'm never home these days. Juggling work and the kids, it isn't easy."

"Don't forget you have help," Faith said.

"I do. The best help I could ask for."

Eve gave Faith a small smile before folding her hands in her lap, her expression growing serious. Faith knew that face. It meant business.

"We should talk about this morning," Eve said.

"Right." Faith had been afraid to bring it up.

"Truthfully, I've been so busy today that I haven't had a chance to think everything through."

"Maybe it's better that way," Faith said. "Not thinking about it. Just doing what you feel."

"That's easy for you to say. My situation is complicated." Eve crossed her legs. "I've been separated from Harrison for a few years now, but our divorce was only finalized recently. We weren't on good terms when we separated, and we both brought lots of assets to the marriage, so it took a long time to untangle everything. We're still in the middle of this custody battle. I'm on the verge of convincing Harrison to give me primary custody of the twins, but he's unwilling to compromise on anything else. His lawyers are sharks. They won't hesitate to use any ammunition they can find to paint me as an unfit mother. And they already have plenty of that."

Eve, an unfit mother? The idea was crazy. What could Harrison possibly have on Eve to suggest that?

But Eve didn't elaborate. "So, I need to be on my best behavior. And my lawyers have advised me that it's in my best interests to avoid dating and relationships until the custody situation is resolved. And under no circumstances am I to bring a lover or partner around the children. I need to be able to show I can provide the twins with a stable home environment, and I need to demonstrate that my children are my priority, not my romantic life. Being involved with someone so soon after the divorce will really hurt my case. Having a relationship with my children's nanny, a woman who works for me, is not a good look."

"Oh." Faith stifled her disappointment. "I understand. I wouldn't want to make things any harder for you."

"On the other hand, I've spent most of my adult life being on my best behavior. Being that perfect wife and mother that everyone demanded I be. I'm tired of it." Something sparked behind Eve's eyes. "And I'm very good at being discreet."

Faith smiled. "So am I."

Eve leaned in closer and brought her hand up to Faith's cheek. Faith thought Eve was going to kiss her. Instead, she asked a simple question.

"What do you want from me, Faith?"

"I... don't know." Faith chewed her lip in thought. "When I saw you at Lilith's Den, it was like something inside me awakened. But I don't know what that something is."

"You said the other night that you hadn't been able to stop thinking about me. The 'woman in the corset.'"

"Yes." Now it seemed so silly to think of that side of Eve as a whole other person.

"When you thought about that woman, what did you want from her?" Eve asked. "What appealed to you about her?"

"I think it was about what she represented. An idea." Faith paused. She didn't know how to put it into words.

"Surrender?" Eve said.

Was that what it was? Was that what Faith wanted?

"I can show you what that's like," Eve said. "That surrender. But you'll have to show me that you can give me your submission in return."

Faith nodded. "I can do that."

A smile crossed Eve's lips. "We'll find out if that's true very soon."

CHAPTER TEN

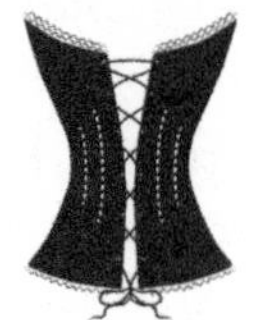

Can you go to the house? Eve's message read. *I need you to do something for me.*

Faith pried herself up from her couch and stretched out her arms. Eve and the twins were somewhere in the English countryside, visiting Eve's parents who had moved there years ago. Faith was taking full advantage of her time off. She'd spent the day at home doing absolutely nothing. But apparently Eve needed her, and she wouldn't ask if it wasn't important.

After replying to Eve's message, Faith got into her car and drove to the house. It was late evening, and the roads were clear. She arrived in record time.

As soon as she walked through the front door, her phone rang. *Eve.*

Faith picked it up. "I'm at the house."

"I know," Eve said. "The camera in the doorbell."

"Right." Faith had forgotten about it. "What do you need me to do?"

"First, I need you to go to my bedroom. I'll wait."

The other end of the line fell silent. Faith headed to Eve's bedroom. Even with Eve's permission, she felt an anxious thrill going into her boss's room.

"I'm in your bedroom," Faith said.

"I should let you know, there's a camera in the room," Eve said. "Hidden in the alarm clock."

Faith looked at the small clock on the nightstand. It looked like a regular alarm clock. She wouldn't have known it was a camera if Eve hadn't told her. Had it been in the room when Faith went into Eve's closet that day? Had Eve watched Faith snoop through her clothes?

Eve read Faith's mind. "I got it after an incident with a nosy babysitter, but I could never bring myself to use it. Spying on the help just seems wrong. But before I left for my trip I thought of a much more creative use for my nannycam."

Before Faith could ask what she meant, Eve gave her another command.

"Go into the closet and look to your left."

Faith entered Eve's walk-in closet. Hanging from a velvet coat hanger by the door was a baby doll chemise. It was made of sheer white fabric that was so fine and light it was almost transparent.

"Do you see it?" Eve asked.

"Yes," Faith said. "What do you want me to do?"

"Put it on."

"Now? Why?"

"Because my parents have taken the twins out for the evening. Right now, I'm all alone in the house, with nothing to do," Eve said. "I need some entertainment. You're going to put on a show for me."

It all clicked in Faith's mind. The camera. The lingerie. Warmth crept up her body. This was *not* the kind of task she expected to be doing for Eve this evening. Faith certainly wasn't complaining. Since the other night, when she and Eve had resolved to keep everything between them a secret, they'd barely had a moment alone. An illicit kiss here and there was all they'd been able to manage. Those fleeting kisses had only made Faith want Eve so much more.

She peered out at the room, her eyes falling on the hidden camera on the nightstand. "You're watching me?"

"Not yet," Eve said. "I want you to get ready first. Then the fun will begin."

Faith smiled. "What kind of fun?"

"So many questions." Faith could almost hear Eve shaking her head through the phone. "I told you you'd have to show me that you can submit to me. That you can obey my instructions. That you can surrender control. That is, if you still want that."

"Yes," Faith said. "I do."

"Then you're going to do exactly as I say. Now, put on the lingerie. And nothing else."

Faith put down the phone and slipped out of her jeans and t-shirt. When she was down to her panties, she took the chemise off the hanger. The delicate fabric was weightless in her hands. It was extremely short, and it didn't come with a pair of panties.

Heat rose through her. She stripped off her panties and slipped into the chemise, then turned to look at herself in the full-length mirror. The chemise only fell a few inches past her hipbones, barely enough to cover her. Through the sheer fabric, she could see the outlines of her nipples and the triangle of neatly trimmed hair at the apex of her thighs. Eve would be able to see everything.

Here goes nothing.

"I'm done," Faith said.

"Go back into the bedroom and put the camera at the end of the bed," Eve said. "Put your phone on speaker while you're at it."

Faith did as she was told. "Are you watching now?"

"Not yet. There are a few more things I need you to do first. Do you see the drawers under the bed?"

"Yes." The king-sized bed had several drawers built into the frame underneath the mattress for storage. Up close, Faith could see that they had locks on them.

"You'll need the key," Eve said. "It's in the bottom drawer of the dresser."

Faith went over to the dresser and retrieved the key. "Got it." She was starting to feel like she was on some kind of scavenger hunt.

"Open the first drawer on the right-hand side of the bed," Eve said. "Inside, you'll find a long box made of wood."

Faith unlocked the drawer and pulled it open. Sure enough, there was a long, thin box made of dark wood. And scattered in the velvet-lined drawer next to it were a dozen whips and canes, all of different lengths and sizes.

Faith stared. All of this had been in the house, right under her nose, the entire time she'd been working here?

How had she ever thought Eve was this boring, proper woman?

Faith glanced at the locked drawer next to it. There were even more drawers on the other side of the bed. Did they all contain kinky toys too?

"What's taking you so long?" Eve asked. "I hope you're not snooping."

"I'm not," Faith said. "I've found the box."

"Open it."

Faith placed the box on the bed. Inside was a long metal bar with a leather cuff attached to each end. "What's this?"

"You can't figure that out for yourself?"

It was obvious that it was some kind of restraint, but the cuffs were too big for Faith's wrists. Not that she'd be able to cuff her wrists by herself. And the bar was so long.

Oh. "These are for my ankles," Faith said.

"That's right," Eve said. "It's a spreader bar. Get onto the bed and put it on."

Faith climbed onto the bed and sat down in the center of it. The bed was so vast and soft that she felt like it was swallowing her up. She positioned her phone on the pillow and set about cuffing her ankles.

Once she had the first cuff on, she understood why it was called a 'spreader bar'. The long bar between the two cuffs would hold her legs wide apart. With nothing underneath the chemise Faith wore, Eve would have quite the view.

"Are you done?" Eve asked.

"Almost." Faith fastened the second cuff around her ankle. It wasn't easy. With her legs held apart, she had to stretch to her limits to reach her ankle.

When she was finished, she pulled the chemise down, covering as much of herself as she could. She wasn't shy. She simply wanted to draw things out, to reveal herself slowly to Eve. Eve wanted a show?

Faith would give her a show.

"I'm done," she said.

Eve's voice rang out from the phone next to her. "Then it's time to begin."

"Are you watching now?"

"I am. It's amazing how advanced technology is these days. I can see you as clearly as if I was in the room with you."

A thrill raced through Faith's body. "Do you like what you see?"

"I do." Eve's voice fell to a whisper. "That lingerie looks lovely on you. You have no idea how hot this makes me, seeing you in something I gave you, all laid out for me on my bed."

Faith bit her lip. Eve's sultry voice set off a thirst within her. "What do you need me to do for you, Eve? I'll do anything you want."

Eve chuckled softly. "Careful. You have no idea what goes on in the depths of my imagination. There are so many wicked things I'd love to do to you. For now, we're going to start with something simple."

Faith glanced at the phone, eagerly awaiting Eve's command.

"Do you ever touch yourself?" Eve asked. "Make yourself come?"

"You mean—" Faith's face grew hot. "Yes. Sometimes."

"Sometimes? When?"

"At night. Before I go to sleep."

"I want you to show me how you play with yourself when you're all alone. Show me what you do late at night, under the covers."

"Right now?" Although Faith had long gotten over the puritanical beliefs that came with her upbringing, she still had this visceral reaction to being told to do something so taboo. Was this why she found Eve and these twisted games so exhilarating?

"Yes," Eve said. "But start slow. I enjoy a bit of foreplay."

There hadn't been any foreplay between them that night in the library at the party. Just the memory of it was enough to spur Faith to begin.

Laying back against the pillows, Faith skimmed a hand up one thigh, trailing her fingers all the way up to her chest. The chemise was so thin it was like she was touching her skin. She drew her fingertips up her breast. The way the delicate fabric rubbed against her nipples made them threaten to harden. She slipped her hand into the top of the chemise.

"I want to see you," Eve said. "Pull the chemise down."

Faith took the straps of the chemise and slid them from her shoulders. The flimsy cups fell down, her breasts bared for Eve to see.

"That's better," Eve said. "Keep going."

Faith brushed her hair back and let her hand continue down her neck. Her other hand wandered over her breasts. She made sure to look straight into the camera, emphasizing the sensuality of her movements. She was putting on a show, after all. This was for Eve's benefit, not for hers.

But as Faith swept her hands over her body, she recalled how Eve's fingers had felt on her skin, how Eve's touch had been tender yet demanding at the same time. An ache grew deep in her core. Completely unbidden, her hand crept down her stomach, past her belly button.

"Yes," Eve said. "Make yourself come for me."

Faith took the hem of the chemise and drew it up to her waist. With the spreader bar holding her legs apart, Eve could surely see how obscenely wet Faith was.

Eve's voice rose from the bed beside Faith. "From now on, every part of you belongs to me, including that pretty pussy of yours."

Faith sucked in a breath. She never thought she'd hear the word 'pussy' come out of Eve's mouth. Then again, she never thought she'd be lying on Eve's bed with her legs strapped apart.

She slid her fingers down her slit. Her folds were so hot they seemed to burn.

"Show me what you like," Eve said. "How you like to be touched."

Faith drew a finger up to her clit and traced slow spirals around it. Her other hand stayed up at her chest, tweaking her nipples. Her eyes fell closed as she sank into Eve's bed. It usually took her a long time to get warmed up, but knowing that Eve was watching her had her throbbing in no time at all.

"Do you wish that was me touching you right now?" Eve asked. "Me in the room with you?"

"Yes," Faith said. "More than anything."

"Pretend, for a moment, that I'm there. Imagine those are my hands on you. Show me what you want me to do with you."

Faith slid her hand down and dipped a finger inside herself, then another, easing them back and forth.

"Are you imagining that's me inside you?" Eve asked. "Just like at the party that night?"

"Yes," Faith said. "It felt incredible." She shifted in the bed, raising her hips, letting the heel of her palm grind against her clit while her fingers curled inside her. Her legs trembled, fighting the spreader bar holding them apart.

"If I was really there with you, it wouldn't just be that spreader bar you'd be wearing," Eve said. "I'd tie your hands up too, so you'd have no choice but to let me have my fun with you."

An involuntary wave of heat rolled through her. Faith pumped her hand harder. Just minutes ago, she'd thought she was the one running the show, with her submissive words and sensual motions. There was no doubt now who commanded Faith's body. She was completely in Eve's thrall.

And it felt so good.

"You're close, aren't you?" Eve asked.

"Yes," Faith whispered. Could Eve really tell from the other side of the camera?

"Go on. Come for me."

Eve barely finished her sentence before Faith's pleasure peaked. She convulsed on the bed, Eve's name on her lips, her body overcome with an orgasm that stretched on and on until she came apart.

She fell back down to the pillows, breathing hard. Faintly, she could hear Eve's breaths through the phone.

After a moment, Eve cleared her throat. "Well, that certainly was entertaining. I asked for a show, and you delivered."

Faith murmured something senseless, her head full of fog.

"Sounds like you need to recover. Take all the time you want. And that lingerie? You can keep it."

"Really?" It had to be more expensive than any lingerie Faith owned. Or any other clothing she owned, for that matter.

"Consider it a gift. The matching panties too. They're in a bag in the closet. But since I didn't get to see them on you, I expect you to send me a photo of yourself wearing them later."

Faith grinned. "Okay. Thank you."

"I should go," Eve said. "Everyone will be back soon. And after the performance you just put on for me, I'm going to need a few more minutes of alone time."

Faith flushed all over. The thought of Eve pleasuring herself while thinking of her was almost enough to make Faith start touching herself again.

"I'll see you next week," Eve said. "Before you leave, make sure you put everything away and lock up the drawer."

Faith resisted the urge to roll her eyes in case Eve was still watching. Despite everything that had passed between them, Eve was still her usual bossy self.

Faith hung up the phone and took off the spreader bar, then carefully returned it to its drawer under the bed. Her eyes fell to the collection of whips. Now, they didn't look so intimidating. A picture of Eve wielding one sprung up in her mind. What would those whips feel like against her skin?

She shut the drawer, locked it up and got dressed. She was starting to see the appeal of giving up control. It was so addictive. Faith wanted more.

And she didn't know how to feel about that.

CHAPTER ELEVEN

Lindsey waved her hand in front of Faith's face. "Earth to Faith."

"Hm?" Faith shook herself out of her trance. She and Lindsey were sprawled out on the bed in one of the guest suites in Lindsey's mansion. Eve was still in England, and by coincidence, Lindsey's girlfriend was also out of town, so she'd invited Faith to stay overnight. Their days of sharing a college dorm were long gone, but every now and then they slept over at each other's houses like they were roommates again.

"Sorry," Faith said. "I have a lot on my mind right now."

Lindsey sat up. "Worried about your sister?"

"Yeah." That was one of the things that was troubling Faith. "I still haven't heard anything from her. I just hope nothing bad has happened."

"I'm sure she's fine." Lindsey gave her a sympathetic smile. "Maybe she's just busy. Or the letter got lost."

"Maybe." Her words did little to reassure Faith. Everything with Faith's family was far too complicated for Lindsey to understand. Although Faith had told her friend all about her past life, anyone who hadn't lived that life could never fully grasp the situation.

There was one person Faith could talk to who would understand. Her aunt. She was like Faith, having broken off from her family and their religion years before Faith did. When Faith had left home, it was her aunt Hannah who had taken her in. Other than her sister, Hannah was the only real family Faith still had a connection to. She made a mental note to call her later.

Faith's phone buzzed. It was a message from Eve. She opened it up.

I'm stuck at the world's dullest dinner party. To pass the time, I'm thinking about how you looked on my bed in that lingerie.

A rush went through her. She and Eve had been exchanging messages for days now, each racier than the last. Every one of them made Faith ache with desire.

But at the same time, doubt gnawed at her. It didn't make sense that she wanted this. To submit to Eve, to give Eve so much power over her. For most of Faith's life, she'd felt so powerless, trapped in a world where she didn't have any control or agency, where she was expected to be this dutiful, subservient woman. She'd chosen to leave that life behind years ago. How was she supposed to reconcile that with her newly discovered submissive desires?

"You're zoning out again," Lindsey said.

"Right. Sorry." Faith put her phone down. "I just got a message from Eve."

Lindsey grinned. "I'm guessing it wasn't about a nannying emergency?"

"Nope."

"So things are going well between the two of you?"

"Mostly." Faith had filled Lindsey in on what was going on between herself and Eve, with the caveat that she couldn't tell anyone, not even Camilla. "It's just that, I've never been with someone who's into the things Eve is. I have some reservations."

Lindsey frowned. "Do you feel pressured to do things you don't want to? Because I know you're new to all this, but consent is important in these kinds of relationships."

"No, that's not it. We've talked about that stuff." In between exchanging risqué messages, Faith and Eve had talked about their boundaries. Faith had told Eve in no uncertain terms was Eve to put her in a cage. "It's not the physical stuff. It's everything else."

"What do you mean?"

"It's about how all this makes me feel. How *she* makes me feel. I want her. I want to explore this submissive side of myself with her. And it bothers me that I want that." Faith sat up on the bed and crossed her legs underneath her. "I spent most of my life having everything about me controlled, from what I wore, to what I did with my life. And since I escaped that life, I've always been wary of people trying to control me. Friends, partners, anyone." She balled her fists in her lap. "I don't ever want to feel like I'm someone's property. Never again."

"Does Eve make you feel that way?" Lindsey asked.

"I don't think so. It's different with her. But maybe that's just because I'm blinded by everything I feel for her."

"Or maybe it's because, with Eve, it *is* different. What you're doing with her, it's not the same as being controlled. That's not to say it's not real, or it's just a game. The difference is that submission is a choice. You're not having power taken away from you. You're giving it to someone willingly. And there's nothing wrong with wanting to do that." Lindsey folded her arms on her chest. "Look at Camilla and me. Do you think there's anything unhealthy about our relationship?"

"No." Faith had to admit, she'd been skeptical of Lindsey and Camilla's relationship in the beginning. The two of them had jumped headfirst into this intense, 24/7 kinky relationship. But after witnessing the two of them together for a year now, it was clear to Faith that what they had was healthy and loving. It was all give and take, and they were equals where it really mattered.

"It still feels wrong for *me* to want that," Faith said. "I know it's silly, but I feel like it goes against all my principles. I fought to escape a life of submission and servitude, so I could become a modern woman, independent and strong."

"I get it. I've felt that way before too. Eventually, I realized that my desires don't reflect who I am as a person. Although they're a part of me, they don't define me. And they aren't a weakness."

"I guess that makes sense."

"Besides, that's what makes submission so appealing."

"What do you mean?" Faith asked

"Submission lets you explore a side of yourself you don't get to let out in the real world. That vulnerable side of yourself. It lets you feel things you're not supposed to feel, want things you're not supposed to want. But it's about more than just the thrill of the forbidden. It's about letting go of all the ideas you have about yourself and giving in to desire. And when you reach that point where you can let go of everything and just exist in the moment with that special person? It's so freeing." Lindsey brushed back her auburn hair. "Of course, it takes a long time to reach that place with someone. And it takes trust. But that's ultimately what it's all about. That surrender."

There it was again. That word. *Surrender.* The idea appealed to Faith. Was that what she wanted?

She groaned. "This is all too complicated."

"It doesn't have to be," Lindsey said. "Do you remember when Camilla and I first got together? Someone wise told me that I should stop worrying about what I thought I should and shouldn't feel and just let myself feel it. Maybe you should take her advice."

It was just like Lindsey to throw Faith's words back at her. "That was different."

"Was it?"

Faith sighed. "Maybe you're right."

"Of course, that same someone thought it was a good idea for us to go skinny dipping in the lake next to campus in the middle of the night, so maybe she isn't that wise."

Faith rolled her eyes. "That was years ago."

"God, it was, wasn't it? It still feels like yesterday."

Faith flopped back down on the bed. Lindsey was right. She had no reason to be ashamed of what she felt. She had to embrace it.

She was not powerless.

Submission was a choice.

And she chose to submit to Eve.

Faith picked up her phone and typed out a reply to Eve's

message. *I liked being bound on your bed for you. I just wish you'd been there to tie me up yourself.*

Eve's response was instantaneous.

When I get back, I'm going to tie you to my bed and do all those wicked things I've been dreaming about doing to you.

CHAPTER TWELVE

Faith unlocked the front door and strode into the house. "Eve? I'm back."

"In here," Eve replied.

Faith followed Eve's voice toward the living room, anticipation burning inside of her. Eve and the twins had returned from their vacation the day before, and Faith had returned to work this morning, but she and Eve hadn't had a moment alone.

Not until now.

Eve met Faith outside the living room. "You're back." She removed her glasses and slipped them into her pocket. "The twins are at school?"

"Just dropped them off," Faith replied.

"Good. We have the house to ourselves."

Without warning, Eve drew Faith in for an urgent, fiery kiss. A blissful hum rose from Faith's chest. The kiss drew out, Eve's lips growing hungrier and hungrier, filling Faith with a deep, aching need.

Eve broke away. "I have half an hour before I have to leave for work. That should give us enough time."

"For what?" Faith asked.

Eve pushed Faith hard against the wall and leaned close, speaking into her ear. "For me to make you come like you did for me on camera."

Faith's breath quickened. Who was this crazed woman who had taken over Eve's body? Faith wasn't complaining at all.

Eve pressed her lips against Faith's again, suffocating her. Faith grabbed onto the collar of Eve's blouse, holding herself up in the face of Eve's onslaught. Eve pulled the bottom of Faith's blouse out of her skirt, her hand creeping up underneath Faith's bra. At the same time, Faith began unbuttoning Eve's blouse. Eve had seen Faith in nothing but lingerie, but Faith hadn't seen so much as a bare patch of Eve's skin.

Eve drew away, shaking her head. "When are you going to learn that I'm the one running the show?" She took Faith's wrists and pinned them to the wall. "Keep your hands to yourself."

Faith nodded. She was so desperate for Eve's touch that she would have done anything Eve told her to do.

Eve released Faith's hands so she could lift up the hem of Faith's skirt. She yanked it up past Faith's hips, eliciting a gasp from Faith. Eve wasn't wasting any time. Faith flattened her palms against the wall to keep herself from touching Eve. It was sweet torture.

Eve drew back, her head cocked. "Do you hear that?"

"What?" Faith listened carefully. The faint sound of a key in the front door reached her ears.

Eve cursed. "Someone's here. Quick, go into the kitchen."

Faith pulled down her skirt and hurried into the kitchen. As she shut the door, she caught a glimpse of Eve hastily buttoning up her shirt and heard the sound of heavy footsteps in the hall.

"What are you doing here?" Eve's voice. "You can't barge in like this."

"Will you relax?" A man's voice this time. "I didn't think you'd be home."

"How did you get in here, Harrison?"

Harrison. Eve's ex-husband. Faith pressed her ear to the kitchen door, her curiosity getting the best of her. Eve rarely spoke of

Harrison, but when she did, it was with palpable disdain. What had happened between them to make Eve despise him so fiercely?

"I still have a key," Harrison said.

Eve huffed. "I'm changing the locks."

"No need. If it's such a big deal, you can have it back."

"It is a big deal!" Eve's voice rose. "You can't just let yourself into my house."

"Whose money do you think bought this house?"

"Don't start with that again."

"What?" Harrison said. "It's true."

"It's not like you don't have a dozen other houses. This house is the only thing I took in the divorce. Given all the sacrifices I made for the children, it's far less than I deserve."

"Those sacrifices were your choice."

Eve scoffed. "We both know I didn't really have a choice. Not with you and Eleanor constantly manipulating me."

Eve had mentioned Eleanor's name at the party that night. She was Harrison's mother.

"Settle down," Harrison said. "I'm not having this argument with you again."

Eve said something too quietly for Faith to make out, but she was certain it wasn't polite. She was beginning to understand why Eve felt so much contempt toward her ex-husband. He spoke to Eve like she was a child.

"Why did you come here?" Eve asked.

"I need Ethan's baseball gear," Harrison replied. "I have him this afternoon, remember? I'm taking him to the park after school."

"You should have called me."

"I thought you'd be at work. I didn't think you'd mind."

"I do mind," Eve said.

"Clearly. I said I was sorry."

"No, you didn't."

"Fine," Harrison said. "I'm sorry."

Faith's nose began to itch. *No. Not now.* She covered her face with her hands and screwed up her nose, just in time to muffle the sneeze. But it wasn't enough.

"What was that?" Harrison asked.

"The nanny," Eve replied. "She's doing some chores for me."

"I still don't see why you need a nanny."

"I have a job now. Looking after the kids is a lot of work. Not that you'd know anything about that."

"If someone else is going to be raising my kids, I want to meet her," Harrison said.

Eve's voice grew icy. "She's not raising our kids. *I* am. And you're one to talk. Whenever it's your time with them, it's Eleanor who looks after them."

"At least she's family and not some stranger."

"Faith isn't a stranger. And the children love her."

"Then let me meet her," Harrison said.

"Fine. Just don't be an ass. I know that's difficult for you, but at least try."

Eve's footsteps approached the kitchen. Faith hastily tucked in her blouse.

"Faith?" Eve opened the door. "Will you come out here, please? Harrison would like to meet you." She brought her hand up to smooth down Faith's hair and gave her an apologetic grimace.

Steeling herself, Faith followed Eve out into the hall.

"Faith, this is Harrison," Eve said through gritted teeth. "My ex-husband."

Harrison flashed Faith a smile. "Harrison Mathers."

He held out his hand for Faith to shake. His grip was firm and practiced, as if he spent all day shaking hands. From his suit to his stance, everything about him seemed meticulously crafted to project an image of the perfect man.

"Eve doesn't have you working too hard, does she?" Harrison asked. "I know the twins can be a handful."

"Don't pretend you actually know what parenting them is like," Eve muttered.

"The twins are great," Faith said. "They're easy kids."

Eve put her hands on her hips. "There, now you've met the nanny." She turned to Faith. "Would you bring Ethan's baseball gear down? It's in his room."

"Sure," Faith replied.

As Faith walked up the stairs, Eve and Harrison continued their conversation in hushed voices. Faith couldn't hear a word. By the time she returned with Ethan's baseball bag, they had fallen silent, tension hanging heavy in the air.

Faith handed Harrison the bag. He slung it over his shoulder.

"I need to get to work soon," Eve said.

"Hint taken. Here." Harrison dropped a key into Eve's hand. "I'll see you at the next pickup." With a nod of farewell, he sauntered back down the hall.

Eve glared at him until he was out the door. "That was close. The last thing I need is for Harrison to find us together."

"Right," Faith said. "The custody situation."

"Yes. I'm not supposed to be seeing anyone, especially not my nanny. I have no doubt his lawyers will crucify me if they find out. I don't want to make their job any easier than it already is."

What was that supposed to mean? It wasn't the first time Eve had implied Harrison's lawyers had some kind of dirt on her.

Eve pocketed the key. "Besides, these are two worlds that are never meant to collide."

"What do you mean?" Faith asked.

"I mean the 'me' who has two kids, an ex-husband, and goes to PTA meetings is a different person than the woman you saw at Lilith's Den. It's no coincidence you barely recognized me that night. It's deliberate, the way I express myself there. It's a way to keep those parts of myself separate."

"Why do you want to keep them separate?"

"It's simpler that way."

Faith thought back to her conversation with Lindsey. About how submission was about letting go, giving in to one's deepest desires. Was the same true in reverse? Was Eve seeking the same surrender that Faith was?

"And now I have a more practical reason to keep those worlds separate," Eve said. "I don't want anyone to catch wind of the two of us. We need to be more careful, especially with the twins in the picture. And we need to set some boundaries. No more of this in the house. We should have avoided that from the start. Whenever you're here, I'm your employer, and that's it."

"All right." Faith didn't want to put Eve's family at risk. But she didn't want things between them to end. "Can we still send each other messages? I like your messages."

"Sure." Eve's lips curled up into a smile. "I need some way to keep you on your toes until we get the chance to have some private time together."

Faith's cheeks flushed. "So, how are we going to do that? Have time together without anyone discovering us?"

"It won't be easy, but we'll manage. All this means is that we're going to have to get a lot more creative from now on."

CHAPTER THIRTEEN

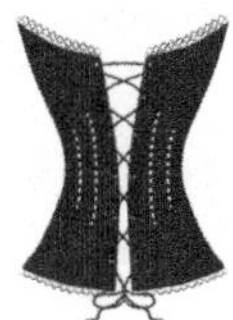

Faith got off the elevator at the floor of Eve's office. The twins were at their father's, so Eve had opted to work late. She'd called Faith an hour ago, asking her to drop off a flash drive she'd forgotten at home.

Faith was greeted at the reception desk by Andrea. The receptionist was packing up to leave.

"Go right in," she said. "Ms. Lincoln is expecting you."

Faith thanked her and headed into the office. It was late evening, but there were still a handful of people around. It seemed Eve worked her employees just as hard as she worked Faith.

She knocked on the door to Eve's office.

"Come in," Eve said.

Faith entered the room and shut the door behind her. Eve was sitting behind her desk again, focused intently on her laptop.

Eve looked up at Faith. "You have the drive?"

Faith nodded. "Here it is."

Eve took the drive and plugged it into her laptop, scanning the screen. "This is the one. Once again, you're a lifesaver. Thank you."

"No problem. Is there anything else I can do for you?"

Eve tilted her head to the side, a slight smile forming on her lips.

"Now that you mention it, there *is* something else I could use your help with."

"Sure," Faith said. "Whatever you need."

Eve leaned back in her leather chair and folded her arms across her chest. "There you go again with your unwavering obedience. Didn't I warn you about that? If you're not careful, I might take you at your word. Do all those dirty things I've been dreaming about doing to you."

Faith dropped her eyes to escape Eve's piercing gaze. "I wouldn't mind if you did."

Eve let out a soft laugh. "You're just insatiable, aren't you? For now, I have a simple task for you. I've been working all day. I need to relax. Unwind."

"What do you have in mind?"

Eve peered at Faith over her glasses. "I could really use a massage."

Oh. Faith glanced around. Suddenly, the room felt stuffy.

"Why don't you lock the door?" Eve said.

Faith went over to the door and twisted the lock shut.

Eve fiddled with her phone on the desk in front of her. Classical music began playing from a speaker on her desk. "That's better," she said. "Makes the outside world simply fade away."

Eve shrugged her jacket off her shoulders and folded it on the desk next to her. Then, she began unbuttoning her blouse, slowly exposing the smooth white skin of her chest and the lacy black bra she wore underneath. It was thin and low cut, her breasts appearing to spill out of them. Faith stared, her lips parting.

Eve slipped off her shirt and folded it on top of her jacket on the desk, then beckoned Faith with a finger. "Come stand behind my chair."

Faith rounded the desk to stand behind Eve. Eve drew the straps of her bra down her shoulders.

"Go on," she said. "Don't be afraid to use a little pressure."

Pushing aside her growing desire, Faith placed her hands on Eve's shoulders. Her skin was supple and warm. Faith began rubbing her thumbs in firm circles at the base of Eve's neck, working her way outward and over her shoulders. Her muscles loosened under Faith's fingertips.

Eve let out a satisfied groan. "God yes."

Faith kneaded Eve's shoulders even harder. Eve wasn't lying about being tense. But the sounds coming from Eve's mouth were so sensual. And touching her like this, skin to skin, was more than they'd touched in days. Was Eve trying to get Faith all hot and bothered?

Because it was working.

"Yes, right there," Eve said. "Harder."

Faith pushed harder into Eve's shoulders, eliciting even more pleasured murmurs from Eve. It was like music to Faith's ears. She had dreamed of making Eve come apart, but in an altogether different way...

"I didn't ask you to stop," Eve said.

"Right. Sorry." Faith resumed her massage, banishing all sexy thoughts from her mind. But Eve seemed determined to torment her. As she peered down over Eve's head, one of the cups of Eve's bra slipped down, exposing a rose-colored nipple.

God, how Faith ached to run her fingers over those soft, round breasts of Eve's. To feel Eve against her, just like at the party that night, but this time without any clothing between them—

Eve swiveled in her chair to face Faith. "Is something distracting you?"

"No," Faith said. "Well, yes. You are." She shook herself. She was having a hard time forming sentences. "But in a good way."

"Maybe I can do something about that." She drew a hand up Faith's arm, a wicked look in her eyes. "Relieve all that pressure."

Blood rushed to Faith's face. It wasn't hard to figure out what Eve was suggesting. "Here? Now?"

"Here and now." Eve stood up. Her face was barely an inch from Faith's. The scent of Eve's perfume enveloped her. She could practically taste those lips she so longed to kiss. "Unless you have any objections."

"No," Faith said. "No objections."

Eve stepped aside and pointed to the chair. "Sit."

Faith bit back a protest. She didn't want to sit down. She wanted to kiss Eve, to hold her, to drown in her. But the hard look in Eve's eyes told her Eve meant business.

Faith sat down in Eve's chair. It smelled like leather and Eve. It did nothing to quell the urge to bury herself in the other woman.

Eve opened the bottom drawer of her desk. "I did say I was going to tie you to my bed sometime, but since the house is off-limits we'll have to improvise." Eve pulled something out of the drawer. "This will work nicely."

Faith looked at the small package in Eve's hand. It was a two-pack of pantyhose.

"I always keep spares at work. It pays to be prepared." Eve tore the package open and pulled out both pairs of pantyhose, stretching them between her hands like a rope. "Do you have a safeword?"

"Uh..." Faith's mind went blank. She'd never needed a safeword before.

"Let's go with something simple? Red. Red means stop."

Faith nodded. "Okay."

"Arms on the armrests," Eve commanded.

Faith did as she was told. Using the pantyhose, Eve tied one of Faith's wrists to the arm of the chair, then the other, securing them with a series of knots. Faith's pulse raced. The bonds weren't tight, but the way they were looped around the armrests meant she had no chance of slipping out of them. She wasn't getting out of this chair. Not by herself.

Eve picked up her phone and turned the music up even louder. "I'm in the habit of playing music when I'm here after hours. It helps me concentrate. Anyone still in the office will just think I'm working late too." She leaned down over Faith's chair, resting a hand on the backrest above Faith's shoulder. "It'll help cover up all those delightful little sounds I'm going to coax out of you."

Faith squirmed in her chair. Suddenly, the ties around her wrists felt extremely tight.

Eve drew her hand up the front of Faith's thigh, continuing up her stomach. Even through the dress Faith wore, Eve's touch made her shiver. Eve traced the pads of her fingers between Faith's breasts and up to her collarbone, brushing them along it gently. Faith's skin sizzled under Eve's fingertips.

Eve tore down the top of Faith's dress and bra, exposing her breasts. The cool air made her nipples tighten. Eve pinched one lightly. Faith gasped, her head falling over the back of the chair.

Eve reached down, pulling Faith's loose dress up past her hips, then slipped her hand between Faith's legs, skimming her fingers down Faith's panties. They were getting wetter by the second. She ground the heel of her hand against the peak of Faith's thighs, stoking the fire between them.

"Eve." Faith lifted her hips out toward Eve's hand. "*Please.*"

"Oh, Faith," Eve purred. "How I love to hear you beg."

Eve grabbed the waistband of Faith's panties and ripped them down her legs, then tossed them onto the desk beside her. She planted her knee between Faith's thighs, forcing them apart again, then snaked her hand down, all the way to the top of Faith's slit.

Faith exhaled sharply. Eve pushed a finger between Faith's lips, rolling it over Faith's aching bud. Eve's touch was gentle and light, but Faith was already so turned on that Eve's teasing strokes sent ripples through her. Her arms twitched in her bonds. She longed to touch Eve, to pull her close, or even just to kiss her. With Eve leaning over her, her hot breath on Faith's cheek and her lips so close to Faith's, it was like she was dangling that kiss just out of reach.

Eve's eyes locked onto Faith's. "I've been waiting so long to do this again. Ever since I watched you on camera that night."

Eve ran her fingers down to Faith's entrance. Faith shifted forward to the edge of the chair, lifting her hips. The position strained her shoulders, but she was so drunk with desire that she barely noticed.

"I was watching very carefully," Eve said. "Watching what you like. Watching what makes you moan."

Eve slid into her slowly, easing in and out. Faith shuddered, pleasure lancing through her. Her fingers still inside Faith, Eve pushed her thumb up to graze Faith's clit. A cry fell from Faith's lips. She pressed them together. There were still people in the office, right outside Eve's door. Was the music loud enough to drown out all the noises Faith was making?

Eve picked up the pace, thrusting and stroking harder and faster. Faith bit the inside of her cheek, trying her hardest to keep silent, but the thrill of Eve taking her in an office full of people only pushed her closer to the edge.

"Eve," she whimpered.

"You're going to have to come quietly," Eve said. "Can you do that?"

Faith screwed her eyes shut. "Yes."

Eve sped up her fingers. "Then come."

At once, the pleasure inside her burst, flooding her entire body. The scream that escaped her was barely drowned out by the music. She gripped the arms of the chair until the tremors racking her body subsided.

As Faith caught her breath, Eve snipped through the pantyhose that bound her wrists, freeing her, then drew Faith up out of the chair and pulled her in close. Their lips met in a firm, insistent kiss.

A sigh rose from Faith's chest, her whole body singing. *Finally.* The deep kiss felt even better than an orgasm, and it was even more satisfying. Eve's lips were like honey to her starving body.

Eve pulled back. "I have one more job for you to do for me."

"Anything," Faith said.

Eve sat down in her chair and pushed it back from the desk. She pointed to the floor before her. "Get down on your knees."

Faith obeyed.

Eve reached down to tilt Faith's chin up toward her. "Now it's my turn to have a little fun." She dragged her free hand up her leg and slid her skirt up her thigh. "Do you want to taste me?"

"God, yes," Faith said.

Eve drew her skirt up around her waist and peeled down her pantyhose. Underneath, she wore a pair of black panties that matched her bra. She slipped out of her panties and placed them next to Faith's on the desk, before resting her arms on the armrests and sliding forward until her hips were at the edge of the chair.

Eve parted her legs. "Go on."

Faith let out a soft breath. Everything about Eve was so intoxicating. Her skin, her hair, her scent. What lay where her thighs met was no exception.

Slowly, Faith slid her hand up the inside of Eve's leg and up past her knee. The skin there was so soft. Eve spread her legs even further apart, her hand falling to where Faith's shoulder met her neck.

Faith leaned forward and parted Eve's lips with her fingertips, then pushed her tongue between them. She closed her eyes, savoring Eve's taste, exploring her folds with her mouth. The tip of her tongue found Eve's tiny pearl. She sucked it gently.

"Mm, god." Eve's grip on the side of Faith's neck tightened. "That feels incredible."

Faith reached up to anchor herself on the inside of Eve's thighs, licking and sucking fervently. A soft moan spilled from Eve's lips. Eve was holding back, keeping quiet so no one would hear them, but the way her body reacted to Faith's touch was uninhibited.

Faith let out a moan of her own. She couldn't help herself. She'd always found giving just as satisfying as receiving. She lost herself between Eve's legs, and in the sweet, muted sounds rising from her. The rest of the office faded away, along with the rest of the world. All that existed was the two of them. All that mattered was Eve.

Eve's thighs quivered around Faith's head. "Yes. I'm so close."

She rose up into Faith, her whole body shaking as she came hard and fast. Her mouth fell open, but she didn't make a sound. Faith didn't stop until Eve's hand slid limply from her neck.

Faith looked up at Eve. Her head was tipped over the back of her hair, her eyes glazed over.

"Get up here," she murmured.

Faith stood up, her knees aching and her legs tingling as blood rushed back into them. Eve grabbed Faith's arm and pulled her down onto her lap, planting a lazy, lingering kiss on her lips.

Faith smiled. "So, how did I do? Did that help you relax?"

"It certainly did." Eve then cupped Faith's cheek in her hand. "It makes me wish I didn't have to get back to work."

"Do you really have to?" Faith asked.

"I do. I didn't ask you to come here so I could get you out of your panties. That was a bonus. I really did forget that drive."

Reluctantly, Faith got up from Eve's lap. "And I'm glad you forgot it."

Eve planted a playful spank on Faith's ass cheek and handed over her panties. As Faith slipped into them, Eve put her blouse back on and straightened out the rest of her clothes.

She pulled Faith in for one last smoldering kiss, which drew on and on until Eve pushed Faith away. "I'll see you tomorrow," she said. "Don't be late."

Faith said goodbye and left Eve's office. There were still a few people around, so Faith tried her hardest not to betray the fact that she'd just had her mouth between their boss's thighs. Her head was still spinning from the thrill of it all.

And yet, it fell short of what Faith truly wanted from Eve. She was starting to understand what it was now, that elusive something she hadn't been able to articulate. She wanted more than these erotic games. She wanted to give Eve so much more, wanted Eve to take so much more of her.

She wanted true surrender, the kind that only Eve could give her.

CHAPTER FOURTEEN

Faith opened Leah's door a crack and peered through it. Just like Ethan, she was sound asleep. Eve had put them to bed ten minutes earlier before retiring to her office. She'd asked Faith to check on them before she left.

Faith shut Leah's door and headed downstairs. She was done for the day, but she didn't want to go home yet. She longed to steal a moment with Eve, even though they couldn't do anything but talk.

She sighed. That was how it was between them now. When they were in the house, they were strictly boss and employee. They had slipped a few times with a hurried kiss, or teasing touch, or whispered word. And every one of those moments filled Faith with an unquenchable thirst.

As she reached the bottom of the stairs, she heard a loud crash. It had come from the back of the house. Faith rushed down the hall, calling out Eve's name. Eve didn't answer her. But as she got closer, she heard Eve cursing from her office. Faith hurried toward the sound.

She found Eve standing in front of her desk. Faith breathed a sigh of relief. Eve was unhurt. However, everything that had been on top of the desk lay scattered across the floor, and Eve's face was clouded over with anger.

"Eve?" Faith entered the room tentatively. She'd never seen Eve like this before. "Is everything all right?"

"That bastard," Eve spat. "I can't believe he's doing this. He didn't even have the decency to tell me himself."

Faith didn't have to ask who 'he' was. There was only one man who Eve spoke of with such disdain. "What's happened?"

"I just got a phone call from my lawyer. Harrison's lawyer informed her that he's decided to petition for sole custody. He's trying to take the kids from me."

Faith's stomach dropped. "Eve, I'm so sorry."

"It's all because I went back to work and hired a nanny. He claims he's doing this because he doesn't want the twins to be raised by a stranger." The muscles in Eve's neck tightened. "He said I've abandoned my duties as a mother."

"That's not true at all." From the moment Faith had started working for her, it had been clear that Eve was dedicated to raising the twins herself. She had Faith take care of the practical things so she could take care of everything that mattered. Faith might be the one who took them to music lessons, but Eve made a point of going to all their recitals. It was Faith's job to get the twins ready for bed, but it was Eve who tucked them in and read them a bedtime story every single night. And since Eve and Faith's conversation about Leah, her attentiveness to the children's needs had only grown. Eve had followed through with her promise to stop pushing Leah so hard, and their relationship had only gotten stronger.

"The truth doesn't matter to him," Eve said. "And if he gets custody, it's not going to be him who raises them. They'll end up brought up by servants. Or worse, his mother, who will fill their heads with toxic ideas."

"You can fight this, can't you?" Faith asked.

"Of course. But this is going to be a dirty, drawn-out fight. He has the best lawyers money can buy. So do I, but my funds aren't infinite. Most of my money is in my firm. He has all his family supporting him, and you bet their ass they're going to help him."

Eve's jaw set. "It's always been me against them. And now they've made it their mission to take the twins away from me."

"It'll be okay," Faith said. "You'll get through this."

"I can't lose the twins," Eve said. "They're my everything. Harrison knows that. And he knows that cutting me out of their lives isn't what's best for them. I know he does."

Faith felt a pang of sympathy. Although it had always been clear there was no love lost between Eve and Harrison, it seemed that Eve hadn't expected Harrison to do something so extreme.

"He wasn't always like this." Eve's voice took on a bitter tone. "When we met, back in college, he was different. Kinder. I had no reason to believe he'd turn out to be the man he was. His family was the same. When I first met them, they all seemed lovely, if not a little old-fashioned and traditional. All old-money families are like that. Mine is too, although my parents aren't as extreme as his. They supported me going to college and making a career for myself, even if they did expect me to get married and have children one day. I wanted that for myself too. I always wanted to be a mother, and in this day and age I thought I'd never have to choose between having children and a career."

Eve leaned back against her desk and crossed one ankle over the other. "But Harrison's family felt differently. As soon as we got married, they started pressuring us to have children. I wasn't ready back then. I'd finished business school, and I was moving up the ladder at my job, and I didn't want to jeopardize that. He supported me at first. But as time passed, his family wore him down and he started pressuring me too." She shook her head. "I should have seen that as the red flag it was. But slowly, they all began to wear me down. Eventually, I agreed to start a family with Harrison, just as long as it didn't mean giving up my career. Harrison knew that. He understood that. Or at least, I thought he did at the time."

Faith thought back to the conversation between the two of them that she'd eavesdropped on. Harrison hadn't seemed like the supportive type at all.

"The truth became clear when I was pregnant," Eve said. "I ended up in the hospital for several months with serious complications. I almost lost the twins at one point." Her voice wavered. "It was then that Harrison suggested that for the twins' sakes, I needed to give up my career and dedicate my life to raising them. I was so emotional over almost losing the twins that I agreed. And I convinced myself that it would be enough. That the twins, my family, would be enough. But it wasn't."

She looked at Faith, a hint of guilt in her eyes. "Don't get me wrong. I find being a mother so fulfilling. But I needed something more in my life to feel whole. So when the twins were old enough, I told Harrison I wanted to go back to work. He said no. I tried to compromise. Said I'd work part-time, and we could have his mother look after the twins or hire a nanny. But he outright forbade it. It should have been a wake-up call for me, but with everything I was going through, I couldn't see what was right in front of my face."

Eve trailed off. Faith could hear the pain in her words. Was there something more there? Something Eve couldn't bring herself to speak about?

"It took a while, but in the end, I came to my senses," Eve said. "I separated from Harrison temporarily, and after only a few weeks, I knew that I couldn't stay with him any longer, so I ended things. That was years ago, but the divorce dragged out, and this custody battle has just dragged out even longer. I thought our negotiations were finally getting somewhere, but this nightmare never ends."

"Oh Eve." Faith took Eve's hand in both of hers. "I'm so sorry you went through all that. And I'm sorry things are still this hard."

"I'm not sorry. There was one good thing that came out of it. Two actually. Leah and Ethan. I'd do it all again for them." Her hand tightened in Faith's. "I won't let Harrison take them. His family is capable of terrible things, and I won't let them get their claws into the twins. If they think I'm going to roll over, they're wrong. I'm going to fight this."

"And I'll be right here if you need me," Faith said. "Even if you just want to talk. I'm here for anything."

"Thank you. I appreciate it." Eve pushed herself up to sit on the top of her desk. "This all seems like a bad dream. I don't know what

I'd do without the twins. For so long, my whole life, my whole identity, has been being a wife and mother."

"You're not going to lose the twins. And you're plenty of things besides a wife and a mother."

"I'm trying to be." Eve sighed. "I'm far too old to still be finding myself."

"I don't think finding yourself stops at a certain age." Faith sat on the desk next to her. "Isn't it just something we're all constantly trying to do?"

"Does that include you?" Eve asked.

"Of course."

Eve studied Faith. "You don't seem the type to worry about that kind of thing. Who you are. Your place in the world. Your purpose in life. You've always seemed so free-spirited. So carefree."

"I think about that stuff a lot. And I'm not carefree." If only Eve knew how much Faith had agonized over their secret relationship. "My identity is something I've struggled with my whole life. I grew up in a traditional, religious family. My parents, they expected me to be this devout, virtuous woman who followed all their rules, from what I wore, to who I'd marry one day." That was *who,* not *if.* Faith had never had a choice in the matter. "In the end, I just couldn't be this person they wanted me to be, so I left that life behind. I left my family behind." The reality was far more dramatic, but Faith didn't want to go into detail.

"That must have been difficult," Eve said.

"It was. But I got through it. And here I am." Faith looked at Eve. "I know what it's like, to be expected to live a life that isn't your own, to be shoved in a box you don't fit into. And I know how hard it is to try to move on from that, to figure out who you are when everything you know has been torn away from you. It's been almost eight years since then, and I'm still trying to figure myself out."

Eve gave her a soft smile. "We have more in common than I thought."

They sat in silence for a moment, shoulder to shoulder and hand in hand. It felt good to be able to support Eve in the tiniest way. For all their kinky games and dirty talk, Faith really cared about Eve.

And after working for the family for so long now, Faith had come to know the twins so well too. Eve losing the twins, the twins losing their mother, would be a terrible outcome. It pained her to think of the turmoil Eve was in.

Eve looked down at the floor where the contents of her desktop were scattered. "I need to clean this up."

"I'll help," Faith said.

"No. This mess is because of my tantrum. I'll deal with it. You should go home. You've been here since morning."

"Okay. Let me know if you need anything."

"There is one thing," Eve said. "What Harrison is doing, it changes things. The stakes are higher now. It makes it even more important that I be on my best behavior. We can't have anyone finding out about us now. What we did in my office was far too risky."

"You're right." Faith felt a tightness in her chest. "If things between us are causing problems for you, maybe we should stop."

Eve shook her head. "That's not what I want. We just need to be even more careful about keeping everything under wraps."

Faith felt a wave of relief. "Okay." Although she was glad to take a step back if it made things easier for Eve, the thought of giving up on what the two of them had made her heart ache.

"Fortunately, we still have options when it comes to seeing each other," Eve said. "There's a place we can go where no one will ever dare to out us."

"Where's that?" Faith asked.

Eve smiled. "How do you feel about a night at Lilith's Den?"

CHAPTER FIFTEEN

Faith held up a slinky black dress in front of herself in the mirror. She frowned. It was too plain. She needed something more daring. More risqué.

She tossed it onto her bed and started rifling through her closet again. In just a few hours, she and Eve were returning to Lilith's Den. They were finally going to get a chance to be together openly. Eve had told Faith that there was an unwritten rule in the BDSM community, that outing anyone was unforgivable. The rules of Lilith's Den added that extra layer of privacy. What happened at Lilith's stayed at Lilith's.

Faith let out a wistful sigh. They were going back to the place where it all began for her. The place that had awakened Faith to all kinds of unexpected pleasures. The place where Faith had discovered a side of her boss that she never expected.

But that wasn't all that made tonight special. Up until now, everything between her and Eve had felt like a game. So far, Faith had only dipped her toes into the world of submission.

Would she finally get that taste of surrender she yearned for tonight?

Faith wanted tonight to be perfect. Which meant she had to look perfect. She drew her fingers through her hair. Earlier in the day, she'd dyed it a darker brown to compliment her look for the night. She'd felt the need to do something different with her hair. She usually changed it whenever she was feeling restless. And she was definitely feeling restless today, mostly in a good way.

She pulled a short leather skirt out of her closet along with a dark red blouse with a neckline in the shape of a deep V. The low cut meant Faith couldn't wear a bra with it, but that wasn't a disadvantage. She held it up before herself in the mirror. *Yes.* This was it. With some fishnet stockings, a pair of heels, and lipstick in her favorite shade of red, it would be the perfect outfit. One look at her, and Eve wouldn't be able to resist doing all those dirty things she'd threatened Faith with.

Faith hung the outfit up on the door of her closet, then sat down on her bed. She still had an hour before she had to start getting ready. Perhaps it was time to deal with the problem that had been plaguing her for weeks now. She still hadn't heard from her sister. Had something happened to her? Had Abigail's letters with Faith been discovered? There were so many possibilities, each worse than the last.

As much as she worried about her sister, there was a selfishness behind Faith's concerns. She didn't want to lose the one connection she still had to her past. Despite what she'd told Eve, Faith hadn't entirely let go of her old life. It was hard for her to admit it, but she longed for what she'd left behind, what she'd given up. Purpose. Meaning. Family. Love. It didn't make sense. Her family had turned their back on her. They'd shown her that their love had strings. And yet, Faith still missed them.

She grabbed her phone and dialed her aunt's number. Faith's aunt Hannah had taken her in after she'd left her family home at sixteen. Hannah had sympathized with her young niece, having done the same thing herself. At ten years older than Faith, Hannah had been something of a big sister to her. Faith had needed one at the time. After her sheltered upbringing, the real world had been a shock. Without Hannah, Faith would have been lost.

Hannah answered the phone. "Faith. It's so good to hear your voice. It's been a while."

"Hi, Hannah." Faith felt a pang of guilt. Since moving to the city for college, Faith and Hannah only saw each other once or twice a year. They used to speak on the phone at least once a week, but over time, Faith had gotten lazy when it came to keeping in touch. "Sorry I haven't called in so long."

"It's fine. How are you?"

"I'm good. I found a job."

Faith told Hannah about her new job, leaving out the part about her and Eve having a secret relationship. Although Hannah was nowhere near as conservative as the rest of their family, Faith doubted she'd approve, mostly because Eve was Faith's boss.

"Sounds like things are going well for you," Hannah said. "So you're staying out of trouble?"

Faith rolled her eyes. "I'm not sixteen anymore." Back then, Faith had gotten into trouble constantly. She'd had a difficult time adjusting to her newfound freedom.

"How've you been?" Faith asked. "How are the kids?"

"They're great." Hannah filled Faith in on her life. Although she'd been single when Faith had lived with her, Hannah was married with kids now. Faith had no intention of ever getting married or living such a conventional life, but she envied the family Hannah had built for herself.

"So," Hannah said. "Is there a reason you called? I feel like you want to ask me something."

"That obvious, huh?" Faith said.

"I can tell there's something on your mind, that's all."

"You're right. It's my sister. I'm worried about her."

"The one you're still in touch with?" Hannah asked. "Abigail?"

"Yep. She writes to me every two months like clockwork, but her latest letter is overdue. I've written to her twice since then, and I've heard nothing back."

"You're worried something has happened to her?"

"Yeah," Faith said. "Or she got caught writing to me. That might be even worse. What if she's in trouble? And all because of me."

"It wouldn't be your fault, Faith. Your sister is an adult. She chose to keep in touch with you. Any trouble she gets in isn't your fault, or hers."

"I guess you're right."

"Look," Hannah said. "I'm still in touch with someone back home. A teacher at the high school. She's sympathetic to people like you and me. I'm sure she wouldn't mind finding out if anything has happened to your sister. Of course, if Abigail is fine, you won't know why the letters have stopped, but at least you'll know she's okay."

"That would be great, Hannah. Thanks for doing this."

"No problem," Hannah replied. "I'm always here if you need me."

They talked for a few more minutes until Hannah had to go. Faith hung up the phone, her gut churning with worry. There was one explanation for why her sister had stopped writing to her that Faith had refused to even consider until now. It was entirely possible that Abigail, like everyone else in her family, had started to believe that Faith's sin of betraying their religion was unforgivable. Maybe, like everyone else, Abigail had decided that Faith was dead to her.

It wouldn't surprise her. Her sister's letters had never been particularly warm or friendly. It was as if Abigail had been conflicted while writing them. They had this distant, factual tone, and they rarely contained any questions for Faith's life. Most of her letters were just superficial updates about their family. Her cousin had gotten engaged. Her oldest brother had a baby. The dogs had puppies. It wasn't much, but it was enough for Faith to know that her family was okay. And she still cared about them, despite everything. Despite the fact that they'd rejected her.

Faith had never really gotten over that rejection. She wanted so desperately to believe in people and the idea that love and acceptance were real. But it was hard to believe that when the people in her life who were supposed to love her unconditionally had turned their backs on her.

She pulled herself together. Now wasn't the time to dwell on the past. She had to get ready for tonight.

By the time Faith arrived at Lilith's Den, she was a jumble of nerves and excitement. She entered the foyer, where Eve had promised to wait for her, and scanned the room. It was 'ladies only' night again, and there were a few women milling about, but Faith couldn't find Eve.

Her eyes landed on a woman in a corset, with straight blonde hair and dark, smoky eyes. *Eve.* The corset she wore was different from the last time. This one was made of dark purple silk overlaid with black lace patterned with flowers. It was paired with a short black skirt, dark stockings, and those red-soled stiletto heels Faith had spotted in Eve's closet so long ago.

Faith's breath caught in her throat. For the first time, she felt like she was seeing Eve clearly. At first, she'd thought of Eve and the woman in the corset as two different people. As she and Eve had grown closer, and Eve had revealed more of herself, Faith had started to see Eve and the woman in the corset as two sides of the same coin. After all, Eve herself had said she thought of them as two different parts of her.

But that was wrong too. Eve and the woman in the corset were one. They were the same dominant, powerful, captivating woman who made Faith hunger for something she never thought she'd want. And Faith couldn't believe that this woman wanted her so badly that she was willing to risk everything.

Eve spotted Faith, her dark eyes lighting up. She beckoned Faith over. Faith's feet carried her to Eve's side.

Eve raked her eyes up Faith's body, her gaze brimming with lust. "You look so divine." She cupped Faith's cheek with her hand. "I'm going to enjoy showing you off tonight. Showing everyone you're mine."

Faith's pulse began to race. The idea of being possessed by anyone else would have unsettled her. But the idea of being possessed by Eve filled her with an undeniable heat.

"I have something for you," Eve said. "Something that will make sure every single person in this club knows that you belong to me."

Eve reached into her purse and produced a flat, square box. She opened it up and held it out to Faith, displaying its contents. Inside lay a wide choker-style necklace made up of rows and rows of sparkling diamonds.

Faith gasped. "Are those real?"

"Of course," Eve said.

Faith reached into the box and ran her fingers along the necklace. She'd never touched anything so precious. The choker wasn't the only thing in the box. Coiled beside the necklace was a chain as thick as a finger.

"The chain is platinum," Eve said. "Strong but beautiful. Only the best for my *pet*."

It all came together in Faith's mind. The necklace was a collar.

The chain was a leash.

Faith's skin began to tingle.

"I'll put it on for you." Eve took the choker out of the box. Brushing Faith's hair to the side, Eve fastened the collar around Faith's neck. It fit snugly. The silver felt cool against Faith's skin.

Eve stepped back, examining her. "It looks lovely on you. There's just one thing left to do."

Eve took the leash and clipped it to the small ring at the front of the collar. She gave it an experimental tug. The delicate-looking chain was surprisingly strong.

"Don't worry, I won't make you crawl around." Eve slid her hand up the leash to the base of the collar, reeling Faith in closer. "At least, not this time."

Faith's mouth opened then closed again. Eve wasn't serious, was she?

Eve laughed softly. "Come on. Let's go inside."

Faith followed her to the door. She didn't have much of a choice with Eve holding the other end of the leash. Mercifully, the leash was long enough for them to walk a few feet apart.

They entered the club. Just like the last time Faith had visited Lilith's Den, it was packed with all kinds of women, all dressed richly, whether in leather, lace, or suits.

"Let's find somewhere to sit," Eve said. "Have a drink. Relax. Just the two of us."

"Sure." Faith glanced around. No one was giving Faith and Eve a second look. A woman being led around on a leash was completely normal here. Faith liked that. And she liked having this tangible symbol of the relationship between her and Eve. Faith belonged to Eve. She was Eve's treasured pet. There was no doubt about it.

Eve tugged on Faith's collar, pulling her toward the other end of the room. Faith was so distracted by everything around them that she almost tipped over as she hurried to follow. She was still just as in awe of the glamour and spectacle of it all as she'd been that first night in Lilith's Den. But this time she didn't feel any conflict or unease.

This time, it excited her.

They sat down in a dimly lit corner. A server came by to take their drink orders. Eve draped an arm around Faith's shoulders, letting the leash hang loosely from her wrist. They lost themselves in each other's words, and touch, and the dark, kinky world of Lilith's Den.

Faith brought her hand up to the collar around her neck. She was starting to realize that what she felt for Eve was far more than just desire. Perhaps she was wrong to feel like she'd never again find that sense of belonging, that feeling like she had a place in the world. With Eve, she almost felt like she had that.

Eve reached out and drew her fingers through Faith's hair. "You look like you're enjoying yourself."

"I am," Faith replied. "Thanks for bringing me here tonight."

Eve smothered her with a kiss. Her lips were warm and soft.

Eve broke away. Her eyes wandered over to the far side of the room, where a crowd was gathered. There was a stage there, but Faith couldn't see it from their seat.

"Looks like there's a performance going on," Eve said. "Let's go take a closer look. I want you to see this."

Using the leash, Eve drew Faith up and led her toward the stage. They pushed through the crowd until they reached a spot from which they could both see clearly.

On stage were a pair of women. One was blindfolded and bound, her ankles tied together, her arms stretched up above her and tied to a hook hanging from the ceiling. She was on her tiptoes, dressed only in a bra and panties.

The other woman stood behind her, wearing leather from head to toe, a short whip with dozens of tails in her hand. Faith had seen one just like it in that drawer under Eve's bed. Beside her was a table with several items on it. A feather. A lit candle. More whips.

From behind her, Eve wrapped her arms around Faith's body, pulling her in close. "Watch her," Eve said. "See the way her Domme mixes all the different sensations, pain and pleasure."

On stage, the woman kissed her submissive's neck tenderly while trailing the tails of the whip up the other woman's bare back. She whispered something into her submissive's ear, then drew back and struck the other woman's thighs with the whip, over and over.

The bound woman twitched and quaked, her muscles tense. But slowly her body slackened in its bonds, and her face took on a euphoric expression. It was like she was under the influence of some incredible drug. And each time the other woman struck her, she let out a pleasured cry that could be heard even over the club's music. Faith felt heat growing deep within her.

"Tell me." Eve's breath caressed Faith's ear. "What's going through your mind when you look at her? The submissive."

"How amazing that must feel," Faith said. "How much I want to feel what she feels."

On stage, the woman put down the whip and kissed her bound submissive with unexpected tenderness. Her submissive trembled at her touch. Was this that sweet surrender Faith had heard so much about? Was this what she craved?

"Eve?" Faith's voice shook. "Can you show me? Show me what that's like?"

"I can," Eve said softly. "I can show you here and now if you want."

Here and now? Faith looked around. The club was set up with all kinds of equipment and restraints. No one was shy about using it all, but it hadn't occurred to Faith to try any of it out.

"Yes," she said. "I want that,"

"Even with everyone watching?"

Faith bit her lip in thought. There was something exhilarating about the idea, of having Eve toy with her while others looked on. Faith had never done anything like it before. But this was all new territory for her. And she wanted to explore it all.

She turned to face Eve. "Yes. Even with everyone watching."

Eve's lips twisted into a smile. "I knew from the day we met that you were the wild type. I underestimated just how wild you were." She wrapped the leash around her hand and gave it a tug, pulling Faith toward her. "Come with me."

CHAPTER SIXTEEN

Faith followed Eve away from the stage, the crowd thinning around them. They reached the back of the room where all kinds of equipment was set up. A big wooden cross. Something that looked like medieval stocks. A strange metal contraption that Faith couldn't even figure out how to use.

Eve wandered past it all, pulling Faith along behind her as she surveyed each piece of equipment. Faith's pulse thrummed in her ears. Had she really agreed to do this?

Eve waved her hand toward the cross. "All this is too showy." She stopped, her eyes fixing on the wall before her. "I prefer something simpler."

Faith followed the path of Eve's gaze. Bolted to the wall were four metal rings which formed the corners of a square. Two were near the ground and two were above head height. Attached to each ring was a short chain connected to a heavy metal cuff.

Something stirred deep in Faith's stomach. Cuffed spread-eagled to the wall, Faith would be even more helpless than the woman on the stage. Eve would be free to do whatever she wanted with her.

"We're going to do something a little different," Eve said. "Red is still your safeword. But if you want me to slow down, say yellow."

Faith nodded, unable to break her eyes away from the wall.

Eve drew her in, letting her lips sweep against Faith's cheek. "You're safe in my hands, pet."

Eve kissed her gently. At once, Faith's nerves transformed into anxious excitement. Eve pulled her over to the wall and let go of the leash. One by one, she shackled Faith's wrists to the wall, locking each cuff with a small metal pin.

"Feet apart." Eve pressed her knee between Faith's thighs, pushing them apart. She dropped to her knees and cuffed both Faith's ankles.

Faith pulled at her restraints, testing them. The cuffs were lighter than they looked, but they were solid and strong. Faith's heart hammered against her chest. She was unable to move. Unable to free herself. Unable to do anything but let Eve toy with her. And the Eve who stood before her was different from the woman who had tied Faith up in her office. This Eve was far more intense and far less playful.

Eve unclipped the leash from Faith's collar and coiled it around her hand before placing it to the side. "I wasn't planning to do this with you here tonight. But I like the idea of showing everyone how complete your submission to me is."

Faith looked around. Though the club was full, almost everyone was watching the stage or busy with their own play. But there were a few casual eyes on her and Eve, watching with mild interest. This was an everyday occurrence here. But for Faith, this was a first. The first time she let Eve fully take control over her. The first time she'd let anyone watch. And those watching eyes set her skin alight.

Eve drew her hand down the side of Faith's throat, her fingers brushing the collar. "It's a pity I didn't bring any of my toys," she said. "I'll have to improvise."

Eve waved over a wandering waitress and said something to her that Faith couldn't hear. The waitress disappeared. Faith didn't dare ask Eve what she was going to do with her. All she could do was squirm hopelessly in her chains.

Less than a minute later, the waitress returned. She placed a tray down on the table next to them. It held a single glass, filled to the brim with ice. Eve slipped the waitress a generous tip. Faith didn't know what Eve was playing at, but the waitress seemed unfazed by the unusual request.

Eve reached into the glass and pulled out two ice cubes. "Let's get started, pet."

Her eyes never leaving Faith's, Eve slipped one of the ice cubes between her lips. She leaned in and pressed her mouth to Faith's, the icy kiss sending a shock through Faith's body. It was so intense, so invigorating, that she almost forgot she was bound.

Something cool and hard slid down the side of Faith's neck. She gasped. It was the other ice cube. Her lips still on Faith's, Eve dragged the ice down the center of Faith's chest and between her breasts, leaving a trail of icy water behind. Faith drew in a sharp breath. The sting of the ice felt good against her warm skin. She'd been overheated all night, a combination of the stuffiness of the club and the desire that Eve ignited in her.

Eve glided the ice cube all over Faith's chest, letting it linger on the parts of her breasts uncovered by her blouse. The cube of ice melted down to nothing, leaving rivulets running over Faith's numb skin. Eve took another ice cube from the glass and drew it over the curve of Faith's breasts, right next to the neckline of her blouse. Faith sucked air through her teeth. She was dangerously close to Faith's nipples. Was Eve going to expose her there and then?

Eve read her mind. "I'm a selfish Mistress," she said. "What's underneath those clothes is for my eyes only. And my hands."

She slipped the ice cube into the front of Faith's blouse and dragged it over her nipple. Faith hissed. The burning sensation was so intense that her knees threatened to give out from under her. The word 'yellow' formed in her mind. But as the shock passed, her whole body flooded with the most intoxicating sensation. And when the ice was replaced by Eve's soft, warm fingers, Faith almost collapsed.

"You see how good that feels?" Eve said. "The way pain and pleasure blend together?"

"Yes, Mistress." The words tumbled from her lips unbidden. She was losing control of her own mind as well as her body.

A smile played on Eve's lips. Inside Faith's blouse, Eve wore the ice cube down to nothing, then took another and teased Faith's other nipple with it. Faith shivered feverishly, overcome by all the conflicting sensations. All the while, the eyes of those nearby looked on, watching as Eve toyed with her bound, powerless submissive. And all the while, the fire in Faith's core grew hotter and fiercer.

Eve reached around and unzipped the back of Faith's skirt, just enough to slide her hand inside Faith's waistband. Eve slid the ice cube down into Faith's panties, letting it graze over her outer lips.

Faith jerked against the wall. The kiss of the ice, the frigid water dribbling into her slit, only inflamed her even more. She whimpered.

"I've heard that sound before." Eve pulled the ice cube up out of Faith's panties and tossed it aside. "You want me to fuck you, don't you?"

Faith's face grew hot. She hadn't intended this when she asked Eve to show her what it felt like to be the woman on stage. But everything about this was turning her on.

She nodded furiously.

"I don't know about that." Eve drew her hand further down, cupping Faith's mound. Her fingers still felt cool from the ice. "You belong to me alone. Your pleasure belongs to me alone. Why should I share that with anyone else? Why should I let anyone see that?"

Faith let out a soft whine, the need within her becoming unbearable. She pushed her hips toward Eve in vain. She could barely move in her bonds.

"On the other hand, I like showing everyone just how obedient a pet you are," Eve said. "Do you think they'd enjoy watching me make you come?"

"Yes," Faith said. "*Please.*"

"Please, what? Tell me what you want me to do to you."

Faith looked around. There were a few more eyes on the two of them now. Although Faith was fully clothed, with Eve's hand down her skirt it was clear what was happening. But Faith wanted them to see. She wanted everyone to see how much Faith was Eve's, how masterfully Eve was able to command her body. She wanted everyone to know that Faith belonged to Eve completely.

She closed her eyes. "Please fuck me, Mistress."

At once, Eve slid her fingers into Faith's slit. There was no more teasing, no hesitation. Eve simply entered her with one shove. Faith shuddered, her eyes rolling into the back of her head. Something about being bound and teased for so long had set every nerve in Faith's body on edge.

Eve's ice-cooled fingers warmed inside her as they grew more frantic. Her lips crashed against Faith's again, her body pinning Faith against the wall. Faith writhed and tugged at her restraints. Eve's skin against hers, and her fingers inside, her warmth, her ravenous lips, her cool tongue, her taste—it was all too much.

Faith convulsed against Eve's body, straining against her chains as pleasure emanated out from her center, tearing through her like wildfire.

She gasped for air as she came back down from the pleasurable heights she'd reached, her body sagging in her bonds. Eve was right there with her, kissing her and holding her close.

"You're all right, pet." Eve stroked the back of her fingers down Faith's face. "I'm here. I'm going to release you now, okay?"

Faith nodded, her voice faltering.

"You did so well." Eve planted a gentle kiss on Faith's cheek. "Once I get you out of these cuffs, I'm taking you somewhere I can have you all to myself."

Faith and Eve got out of the cab at the front of a hotel. The drive had cleared the haze in Faith's head, but it did nothing to stem the longing within her.

"I booked us a room for the night," Eve said. "I thought you might need to go somewhere quiet after Lilith's Den. Somewhere less intense."

Faith followed Eve inside. Eve had removed the leash, but the collar still adorned Faith's neck. Eve glanced around before getting into the elevator. She'd chosen a hotel across town, presumably so they wouldn't run into anyone they knew. Still, Eve didn't relax until they reached their room.

"There." Eve shut the door behind them. "We're finally alone."

Faith barely had a chance to admire the lavish suite before Eve was upon her, drawing her into an urgent kiss and sweeping her toward the bed.

They crashed upon it, a tangle of arms, lips, and lust. Faith deepened the kiss, letting her hands roam Eve's body, from her soft hair down to the swell of her hips. After being restrained, unable to touch, Faith needed to feel Eve, to taste her, to immerse herself in Eve's presence. Faith's desire hadn't been satiated by their performance in the club. What she wanted from Eve went deeper than any physical craving.

Eve got up and removed her heels, then slipped out of her skirt. Underneath, her thigh-high stockings were topped with lace and held up by a garter belt. Faith stared, unable to tear her eyes away. Eve seemed so much freer in the corset and garters than in anything else. So much more real.

So much more mesmerizing.

Eve leaned down, one knee on the bed, and drew Faith's blouse up over her head. Faith lay back down and lifted her hips, allowing Eve to pull her skirt from her legs, then her fishnet stockings, then her panties, until Faith lay there wearing nothing at all.

Eve's eyes rolled along Faith's body. The possessive look in them made Faith's heart skip a beat. Eve fell upon her once more, devouring her with her hands and lips, the touch of her tongue against Faith's feather-light. Faith dissolved into Eve, drinking in her taste, and her scent, and her very essence.

Eve skimmed her hand up the inside of Faith's thigh. Faith drew back slightly, feeling torn. It was clear that Eve wanted nothing more than to ravish her until she couldn't take it anymore. But that wasn't what Faith needed from Eve. She'd given Eve a part of herself that night, a part she'd never shared with anyone. She had so much more to give. But at the same time, she wanted a part of Eve.

Faith ran her hand down to where Eve's thighs met, drawing it over the lace of her panties. "Let me serve you, Eve. Let me please you.

Eve's breath shuddered. Without hesitation, she lay back against the pillows, drew Faith to her, and gave her a look that could only mean *yes*.

Gingerly, Faith peeled back Eve's panties, drawing them from her legs, then crawled back up to kiss her Mistress on her lips, savoring her sweet softness. She kissed her way down Eve's neck and chest to where her breasts peeked out the top of her corset. She pulled the corset down further, uncovering the perfect buds of Eve's breasts, kissing them until they pebbled under her lips.

One hand bracing herself on the mattress, Faith slipped her other hand between Eve's legs again, feeling her silky heat. She grazed a finger over Eve's swollen nub, eliciting a soft hum from Eve's chest.

"Go on," Eve said.

A shiver went through Faith's body. Eve's velvet voice always made her commands impossible not to follow. But tonight, there was a yearning in it that made Faith's heart flutter. And the way Eve trembled at her touch was so electrifying.

Eve parted her legs further, her hips rising toward Faith, urging her on. Slowly, Faith slid her fingers down to Eve's entrance, feeling the pulsing within her. She pushed two fingers inside, deeper and deeper, until she hit a spot that made Eve shudder.

"God, Faith." Eve's eyes fell closed. "Yes."

Faith sank her fingers inside Eve, over and over. Eve moaned and shook, grinding back into Faith. She slung her arm over Faith's shoulder, pulling her in until they were pressed together, the lace of Eve's corset rubbing against Faith's bare skin. The hotel bed quaked around them as their bodies rocked in tandem, so in sync that they moved as one.

Eve tensed against Faith as her pleasure rose, until, at last, Eve tipped her head back and let out a wild cry. Faith felt every tremor that went through Eve's body, felt Eve pulse around her fingers, felt Eve lose herself, until finally, her body stilled.

Faith crumpled onto the bed next to Eve. The other woman let out a long breath. Her eyes were closed, satisfaction written all over her face. There was something gratifying about seeing Eve this way, disarmed and uninhibited. Not wanting to break the silence, Faith curled up against her, an arm over the other woman's stomach.

After a while, Eve returned to her body. Idly, she drew her hand along the collar around Faith's neck, tracing the diamonds on it. Faith had forgotten she was wearing it.

"Tonight was really something," Eve said.

Faith murmured in agreement.

"I mean it. This was… different."

"Different how?" Faith asked.

Eve seemed to think for a moment. "I first started exploring all this a few years ago, after the separation. It became a release of sorts. But I've never done this with anyone I've felt so connected to. Not until you." She looked into Faith's eyes. "This is more intimate. More complete. More real."

"I… I feel it too." Faith had felt that connection, that pull, since the moment they'd met. It had only grown stronger since. "I've never done anything like this before, but it feels more intimate than anything else."

Eve gathered Faith in her arms and drew her in closer. Faith closed her eyes, sighing contentedly. She felt so light and free. Earlier, at Lilith's Den, she'd felt something close to that complete and utter surrender, but it had been just out of her grasp.

What would it take to reach that? She'd resolved the conflict within her, embraced her submissive desires. But embracing everything she felt toward Eve? That was much harder. With so much standing in the way of Faith and Eve being together, she couldn't let herself believe this was real.

As long as everything between them had to remain a secret fantasy, she couldn't truly be Eve's.

CHAPTER SEVENTEEN

"Good morning," Eve said.

Faith entered the kitchen. "Hi."

She lingered by the doorway. She'd just arrived at work and the twins were still asleep. Eve herself looked like she'd just gotten out of bed. She was wrapped in a plush robe, her hair unbrushed and falling in loose, wavy curls. There was something endearing about seeing Eve in this wild state, at least compared to how she usually looked. She was still more put together than Faith was.

Eve held up her mug. "Would you like some coffee?"

"No thanks. I had some at home." Faith regretted it now. She wanted an excuse to stay here with Eve. "I'll go wake up the twins."

"Wait." Eve grabbed Faith's arm. "Don't. Not yet."

"I don't want them to be late."

"They won't be. And if they are, it's only one day." Eve pulled her close. "I want a few minutes alone with you."

"Okay." After all, Faith couldn't refuse Eve's commands.

Eve planted a soft, lust-filled kiss on Faith's lips before breaking away. "I know we shouldn't do this," she said. "But I won't be able to make it through the morning otherwise. This is agonizing, having you around and not being able to touch you."

A knot formed in Faith's chest. She felt the same way. After that incredible night she and Eve had spent together, pretending that they were just a nanny and her boss was becoming unbearable.

"I'm getting so tired of all this sneaking around. If only I could take you out on a date." Eve's eyes sparked. "If I'm going to tie you up and have you do my bidding, the least I could do is buy you dinner first."

A smile tugged at the corners of Faith's lips. "If you were to take me on a date, where would we go?" It was pointless to even think about such things. The two of them weren't going to be able to go on a real date any time soon. But she couldn't help but indulge her imagination.

"Where to begin? There's an amazing Moroccan restaurant downtown. It's one of the city's hidden treasures. It's this whole incredible experience. They only seat ten people a night. I'd take you there first."

"And then?"

"Then, we'd go to a quiet little rooftop cocktail bar nearby and drink champagne and watch the city go by." Eve's voice fell lower than a whisper. "Then, I'd bring you back here, and I'd open up all those drawers under my bed one by one and spend the rest of the night torturing you with pleasure."

Warmth spread through Faith's body. "That sounds like the perfect night."

The light in Eve's eyes dimmed. "But that's all a distant dream for now. This custody situation. Our relationship would complicate things."

"I know. It's okay. I understand."

Eve drew Faith to her again. "Whatever did I do to deserve you?"

She pressed her lips to Faith's once more. This time, the kiss drew out. Faith crumbled against the other woman's body, the scent and taste of Eve's coffee-tinged lips flooding her.

The sound of footsteps padding down the hall reached Faith's ears. Eve pulled away, groaning. Seconds later, Leah entered the kitchen, rubbing her eyes with her fists.

"Good morning, sweetie," Eve said.

She gave Leah an affectionate pat on the head. For all her sharp edges, Eve had a sweet, kind side. It showed at all the little moments she shared with Leah and Ethan.

"Why don't you go wake up your brother?" Eve said. "Breakfast will be ready soon."

Leah nodded sleepily and headed back out of the kitchen.

"She never wakes up by herself. God knows why she did today." Eve sighed. "I need to get ready for work. You should make sure Ethan wakes up."

"Okay," Faith said.

"I'll be in my room if you need me." Eve paused in the kitchen doorway. "How do you feel about me taking you back to Lilith's again?"

Faith's heart leaped. "I'd love that."

"Next week, then. When the twins are with Harrison." The softness in Eve's expression faded. "Don't forget, Leah's violin needs to be restrung. Drop it off in the afternoon. And Ethan has baseball practice."

Faith watched Eve disappear down the hall. So they were back to boss and employee.

It was going to be another long day.

That evening after work, Faith met Lindsey for dinner at a little Thai restaurant near her house. They sat down and ordered their food before getting into the important business of catching up. It seemed like an age since they'd last seen each other that weekend at Lindsey's house. So much had happened since then. So much had changed.

Faith had changed.

"So," Lindsey said. "How are things with Eve?"

"They're great," Faith replied. "Actually, we went back to Lilith's the other night. And we're going back again next week."

"Really?" Lindsey smirked. "And here I thought you weren't into 'that kind of thing.'"

"I wasn't. Not until her." Faith sighed. "There's just something about Eve that makes me want to be hers. She makes me feel things I've never felt before. She's brought out this whole new side of me."

"Maybe that side of you always existed. It just took someone special to bring it out."

"Maybe." Faith rested her chin on her hand. "Eve really is special. I have serious feelings for her."

"Have you told her that?"

"I don't want to make things harder than they already are. This whole situation she's in with the kids, it's complicated."

Lindsey gave Faith a sympathetic smile. "I'm sure it'll all work out in the end."

"Yeah." But Faith was trying her hardest not to get her hopes up.

"And when it does work out, and you and Eve can stop hiding, we're going on a double-date. I haven't told Camilla about the two of you, but I'm pretty sure she's figured it out. Either that, or she's trying to set you and Eve up. She keeps hinting we should have both of you over for dinner."

Faith shook her head. "How are things with Camilla, anyway?"

"They're good. We're thinking of going away soon. Taking a trip around Europe. Camilla has some distant relatives in France that she hasn't seen in years."

As Lindsey filled her in, Faith's mind drifted back to the morning with Eve. She'd been walking on air since, daydreaming about the two of them going back to Lilith's Den. Although Faith still found going to Lilith's Den exciting, she mostly just wanted to go somewhere she and Eve could really be together.

Lindsey looked around. "Our food is taking forever. I'm going to the ladies room. Be right back." She stood up and headed to the restrooms.

Faith dug her phone out of her purse while she waited for Lindsey to return. She had a message from her aunt Hannah.

I have some news about your sister. Call me when you get the chance.

Finally! Faith hesitated. She just couldn't wait until after dinner. She had to know what was going on with Abigail.

She dialed Hannah's number. Hannah picked up after a few rings.

"I got your message," Faith said. "What have you heard?"

"There's good news, and there's bad news," Hannah said.

"Yes?" Faith waited with bated breath.

"I talked to that friend of mine, and she asked around. The good news is that your sister is fine. So is the rest of your family."

Faith felt a surge of relief. "What's the bad news?"

"I know why she hasn't sent you a letter in a while." Hannah hesitated. "I don't know the details, just bits of gossip my friend heard. Apparently, Abigail was caught talking with someone who left the church."

Faith's heart stopped. It could only be her.

"Her husband found out and got your parents and the church elders involved. It caused a big scandal, so word got around."

This wasn't good. Abigail would be facing serious repercussions for committing what was a major sin in her family's eyes.

And Faith would never get to speak with her again.

"Faith?" Hannah said. "Are you there?"

Faith cleared the lump in her throat. "Yes."

"I'm so sorry. I know how hard it is to go through this, especially a second time."

It was little consolation. At least Hannah had a family of her own now. But Faith had no one. Her last connection to her family, even though it had been tenuous, was gone now. The only people in the world who were supposed to love her unconditionally had turned their backs on her.

Faith didn't blame her sister. She knew how hard it was to break free from a lifetime of brainwashing. Still, it stung. She should have seen it coming. She should have known Abigail would eventually get caught. Secrets don't stay secret forever.

Out the corner of her eye, Faith spotted Lindsey walking back to the table. "I should go. I'm at dinner. Thanks for looking into things for me."

"Are you going to be all right?" Hannah asked.

"Yeah, it's fine."

"If you need to talk, I'm here."

"I know. Thanks, Hannah." Faith hung up the phone.

Lindsey sat down. "Everything okay?"

"Yeah," Faith replied. "I was just talking to Hannah."

"Any news about your sister?"

"Not yet." Faith didn't like lying to Lindsey, but she didn't feel like talking about it.

"That's too bad. I'm sure you'll hear something soon. Hopefully good news."

Their dinner arrived and the conversation returned to Lindsey's travel plans with her girlfriend. Faith listened intently as she ate. She wasn't going to let everything with her sister upset her. In fact, this was a good thing. It meant Faith could finally leave her old life behind.

Right?

CHAPTER EIGHTEEN

Eve brushed Faith's hair over one shoulder and fastened the diamond collar around her neck. "No leash tonight," Eve said. "Think you can behave yourself without it?"

"I'll try my best," Faith replied.

They entered the crowded club. Eve drew Faith over to a quiet corner, hidden away from the rest of the club, and ordered them a bottle of champagne. Tonight, they weren't here to play. It wasn't one of the club's 'ladies only' nights. The last thing they wanted was to be fodder for the fantasies of gawking men. They were simply here to be with each other and immerse themselves in the atmosphere.

And yet, Faith felt none of the excitement she'd first felt when Eve first suggested they return to Lilith's Den. Being surrounded by all these people had Faith feeling empty. Ever since hearing the news about her sister she'd had this hollowness in her chest that wouldn't go away. All those feelings of rejection she'd thought she'd overcome years ago had come rushing back.

Faith refused to admit how much it upset her. She'd refused to let it show. She was good at that, at suppressing her feelings and pretending to be cheerful and happy. She'd spent most of her life pretending to be fine, when really, she'd felt trapped. She'd left that life behind long ago, but the way she was feeling now proved that she'd never truly escaped it.

As they waited for their drinks to arrive, Faith watched the club go by around her. Lilith's felt different this time. It had lost its luster. The whips, the chains, the excess—it all felt empty.

Faith pulled herself together. She wasn't going to let her feelings get in the way of enjoying herself with Eve. After all, wasn't that what mattered? That she was with Eve, and that they could be together freely?

Their drinks arrived. The champagne tasted flat.

Eve tucked a strand of Faith's hair behind her ear. "What's going on with you tonight?"

"Nothing." Faith plastered on a smile. "I'm not feeling this crowd, that's all."

"Neither am I." Eve leaned in closer. "How about we get out of here? Go somewhere I can have you all to myself?" Her lips brushed against Faith's cheek. "Or, if you're in the mood for something a little more interesting, there are private rooms upstairs that are well equipped with all kinds of naughty toys."

A shiver ran along Faith's skin. She couldn't deny how appealing that sounded. It would be a welcome distraction. But was that what she wanted right now?

Eve slipped a finger under Faith's collar, drawing her in for a hot, hard kiss. Faith melted into Eve's greedy lips. It was almost enough to make her forget about everything else.

"What do you say?" Eve asked. "I want to take you upstairs and do all kinds of wicked things to you."

Something twisted in Faith's gut. She wanted Eve, but not this. She shook her head, pulling away. "No."

"What's the matter?"

Faith didn't know how to answer her. She didn't know why everything suddenly felt so wrong. It was all just too much. She tugged at the diamond collar around her neck. It was too tight.

"Faith, what's going on?" Eve asked.

"I'm not your possession!" Faith crossed her arms between the two of them. "I'm not your pet. I'm not a thing. You don't own me."

Eve flinched. "I know that. Faith, I've never thought of you like that. I don't see you that way, I promise."

Faith's heart lurched. The hurt in Eve's eyes filled her with guilt. She wasn't mad at Eve. She was mad at herself. Everything was all messed up.

"I'm sorry." Eve reached out to touch Faith's arm, then pulled back. "I never meant to make you feel that way."

"I know. It's not you, I'm just—" Faith's voice quivered. "I can't do this right now. Be your submissive."

"Okay. That's fine. Let's just get out of here. Go somewhere just to talk."

"I just want to go home."

"At least let me take you." Eve held out her hand. "Please?"

Faith just wanted to be alone, but the softness in Eve's gaze swayed her. "Okay."

She slid her hand into Eve's, and Eve led her out of Lilith's Den.

The cab pulled up to Faith's apartment. Faith didn't get out of the car. She still didn't feel like talking, but she owed Eve an explanation for her behavior. She couldn't end the night with this hanging over them, especially since they might not have a chance to be alone again for a long time.

"Do you want me to come up with you?" Eve asked.

"Yeah," Faith said. "I'd like that."

They got out of the car, and Eve followed Faith up to her apartment.

"Come on in." Faith opened the door and turned on the light. She hadn't been expecting company. Fortunately, she'd tidied up in the morning.

Eve looked around Faith's living room. Her eyes fell on the old gray sofa. "This place is cozy."

Faith raised an eyebrow. For Eve, this was probably slumming it.

"I mean it. It reminds me of where I lived in college. I think I had the same couch." Eve sat down on it. "Come on. Sit. Let's talk."

Faith sat next to her. "I'm sorry about tonight."

"No, I'm sorry. I should have noticed you were feeling off."

"It's not your fault."

"It is," Eve said. "You're my submissive. You're new to all this. When emotions are running high, it's easy for things to go wrong. I need to be more vigilant."

"Still, it's on me to be responsible for my feelings," Faith said. "I guess I didn't realize I was so upset. Or maybe I just didn't want to admit I was upset."

Eve crossed her legs and shifted to face Faith. "What's been troubling you?"

"It's my little sister. We send each other letters. Well, we used to. I haven't heard from her for a while, and I just discovered why. She isn't supposed to be talking to me. No one in my family is. But she got caught, so she's stopped. She was my last connection to my family. Now I'm cut out from them entirely."

"Oh, Faith," Eve said. "I'm sorry."

"After everything I've been through with my family, this shouldn't upset me, but it does."

"What happened with them?" Eve asked. "Your family. You told me you left them because they wanted you to be something you're not?"

"Yeah. I mentioned that my family is religious. That's kind of an understatement. On the surface, the religion they follow seems like any other normal religion. But my family, the community they're part of, they take everything to extremes. There were all these rules and restrictions, most of them aimed at women. Men were the heads of everything. Women were expected to be nothing more than wives and mothers. There's a reason I'm good with kids. I'm the oldest of seven, so I grew up looking after all my siblings and cousins."

Faith folded her legs underneath herself on the couch. "The community, it was so insular. We were forbidden from associating with any nonbelievers on more than a superficial level. It was almost cult-like in that sense. And anyone who spoke out against the church? Or worse, anyone who left it? They were ostracized. Like my aunt Hannah. She left when I was nine. The way the adults all reacted to her leaving was so horrible. She just became this evil, toxic person to them. It was like she was less than human."

Faith's stomach knotted. Now Faith was that person to everyone in her family, even her sister. "I remember when Hannah disappeared. I asked my father what had happened to her. He grabbed my arms so hard and looked into my eyes with such raw hatred, and he told me never to ask about her again. Never to even speak her name again. It was the last time I ever brought it up. I had bruises on my arms for days."

Faith found Eve's hand on her arm. She'd been so lost in memory that she hadn't noticed how tense she'd gotten. It was comforting.

"But I never forgot about her, that aunt," Faith said. "And as I got older, I pieced together what happened to her, and I began to understand why she'd left. She was always a little eccentric. Different. That was why I liked her. I felt different too, growing up. No one else seemed to mind the constraints placed on them. Or if they did, they didn't show it. All the other girls seemed perfectly happy to one day get married, have kids, and live out their days serving their husbands, never leaving the town we grew up in.

"But that wasn't what I wanted for myself. I knew there was a whole world out there, beyond the confines of the cage that I lived in. I craved freedom. And things only got worse as I got older. My parents started talking about marrying me off as soon as I was old enough. They set up a meeting with one of our neighbors, a man who was ten years older than me, so we could start the courtship process. I was only sixteen."

"Sixteen?" Eve's face was marked with horror. "You were only a child. Your parents were going to force you to get married?"

"Not until I turned eighteen. And I don't know if they actually would have forced me to marry him. It was more like they simply expected me to do as they told me. I wasn't really a person, just property to be sold off, given away to a new owner like one of my family's puppies." Faith's stomach churned at the thought. "But I didn't want to get married. I was so confused about the idea. I had all these feelings, feelings I thought were wrong, for boys and for girls, and I didn't understand them. How was I supposed to? That kind of thing wasn't talked about. And we didn't even have a TV. All I knew were things I'd heard from kids from school, but none of it made sense. I just knew deep down that I'd never be able to figure myself out while living under the thumb of my family. I knew I had to get out.

"It wasn't as simple as that, of course. I had no money, nowhere to go. But I knew Hannah was out there somewhere. I started sneaking to the library to use the internet to track her down. It took a while, but I found her. We got in touch, and I told her about my situation. She was sympathetic, but I was a minor, so she couldn't do much. So I decided to take matters into my own hands." Faith's fists tightened in her lap. "I scraped together money for a bus ticket to the town Hannah lived in, and one day, instead of going to school, I got on the bus and left. I didn't leave a note in case my parents found it and tried to stop me. I planned to call them when I got to Hannah's house but the bus was delayed, so by the time I got there my parents had reported me to the police as missing. There was this huge search, and it was a big mess. I called my parents in the end, let them know I was safe, and where I was. They came to get me. But when I told them why I ran away, why I didn't want to go back with them, they just..."

Faith swallowed the lump in her throat.

"It was so stupid of me to think they'd react any way other than how they did," she said. "But I was their daughter. I thought it would be different with me. I prayed that they wouldn't be mad at me, but what happened was much worse. They didn't get angry at me. They didn't force me to go back with them or try to convince me to come home. They just left me there." Her voice cracked. "They gave up on me. To them, I was beyond saving. I was tainted. I could see it in the way they looked at me. I begged them not to cut me out of their lives. I told them I wanted to stay a part of the family. It was naive, but I still loved them. They were all I'd ever known. But they refused. They cut me off. I was dead to them."

"I can't imagine how awful that must have been," Eve said. "No one should ever have to go through that, especially as a teenager."

"It was hard, but I was lucky enough to have Hannah to help me through everything," Faith said. "I tried my best to move on, to start a new life. But I still missed my old life. My home. My family. That longing, it never really went away. Then one day, when I was in college, I got a message from my sister Abigail on social media. She'd made a profile just to find me and talk to me. She wanted to reconnect, but she didn't have a computer she could use without anyone getting suspicious, so we decided to send letters instead. She was married by then, and stayed home while her husband worked, so she was the one who got the mail. She could easily hide my letters. We came up with an arrangement. Abigail would send me a letter at the end of the month, and I'd write back to her next month, and so on. Any more often than that would be too risky. We took all these precautions, but in the end, she got caught. And now, my only connection to my family is gone."

Faith sighed. "I was the one who chose to leave. I should be happy that I'm free to live my life the way I want. And I am happy, most of the time. But sometimes, I miss that life. I miss my family. I shouldn't want their love. They rejected me. Why do I still care about them?"

"Oh, Faith," Eve said. "You're only human. It's not wrong to want all that. Love, family, a place to belong. And it's not wrong to be disappointed when people let you down, especially when those people are family. You can't be expected to stop caring about them despite everything."

"But they don't care about *me*. They're supposed to, aren't they? That's what family does."

"You're right. That's what family is supposed to do. But sometimes family lets you down. Sometimes, you have to find your own family in the people who make you feel like you have a place in the world." Eve put her hand on Faith's. "I know this probably doesn't help right now, but you're not alone, Faith. You have people who care about you. You have friends. You have your aunt."

Faith felt a pang of guilt. For all her talk of having no family, she'd forgotten all about Hannah, and Lindsey, and everyone who had acted as her family the past few years.

Eve squeezed Faith's hand. "And you have me."

"Thanks," Faith said. "It really means a lot."

Eve wrapped her arm around Faith's shoulders. "I know that no one can replace your family, but I'll be here for you all the same."

Faith felt a surge of warmth. Eve was right. Faith wasn't alone in the world. She had people who loved her.

But life had taught her that love always came with conditions.

CHAPTER NINETEEN

When Faith arrived at Eve's house, the sun was setting. She unlocked the front door and headed inside. The twins were due back from their father's that evening, and Eve had asked Faith to come by to help prepare them for the week ahead.

Faith walked down the hall, searching for Eve and the twins. The house was far too quiet. "Eve?" she called.

She heard a clatter in the kitchen. A moment later, Eve came out into the hall, drying her hands with a dish towel. She wore an elegant blue dress that made her hazel eyes look greener, especially without her glasses. She was dressed much too nicely for a night in with the twins.

"Eve. Wow." Faith stared. "Are you going somewhere?"

"Not exactly," Eve said. "I need a minute. Why don't you wait for me in the lounge room?"

"Are the twins back? Is there anything you need me to do?"

Eve put her hands on her hips. "What I *need* is for you to go wait in the lounge room."

Faith frowned. "Okay."

She went into the lounge room and sat down. Eve was behaving strangely. What was going on?

After a few minutes that seemed to stretch out forever, Eve appeared.

"Is everything okay?" Faith asked. "Where are the twins?"

"At their father's." Eve sat down next to her. "I asked him to keep them for one more night. I don't like asking Harrison for favors, but this is important."

"What's going on?" Faith was starting to worry.

Eve folded her hands in her lap. "I've been thinking about the other night. About you and me. About us. It made me realize something. You need more from me than what I've been giving you. More than to be my *possession*."

She held up her hand, cutting off Faith's protest. "There was truth to what you said. I've gotten so carried away with this game we've been playing, and it's made me careless. I need you to know that you're more to me than a plaything. I want to show you that when I say you're mine, it goes so much deeper than anything physical. I want you to feel just how much you mean to me. So tonight, I'm going to show that. I can't take you out on a date, but I'm going to give you the closest thing. We're going to have dinner together. Just the two of us, here." Her voice dropped low. "And after dinner, I'm going to show you the height of intimacy that comes with complete surrender."

"Eve." Faith's stomach fluttered. "That sounds perfect."

Eve clasped her hands together. "Now, I just finished making dinner. Why don't you have a seat in the dining room and I'll bring it out?"

Faith practically floated into the dining room, Eve's words playing in her mind, and sat down at the table. It was already set, not with the dinnerware they used every day, but with fine china, sparkling silver cutlery, and intricately folded white napkins. An arrangement of flowers sat in the center of the table.

Eve entered the room carrying two plates and set them down on the table. "I have a white that will pair well with this. I'll grab a bottle."

Faith stood up. "I'll get the glasses."

Eve gave her a sharp look. "Sit down. Tonight, you don't work for me."

Faith did as she was told. She stared at the dish before her while she waited for Eve to return. Arranged artfully on the plate was a tantalizing salmon dish that wouldn't have looked out of place at an expensive restaurant. It must have taken Eve hours to prepare. The idea of Eve slaving away in a kitchen was so at odds with the image Faith had of her.

It was funny how, over time, that image had changed. The prim and proper woman Faith had met on the day of the job interview had been replaced by the woman who wore corsets and took pleasure in chaining Faith to the wall.

Eve returned with the wine and poured them each a glass, then sat down across from Faith. "Dinner is served."

Faith took a bite of her salmon. It tasted as good as it looked. "This is incredible."

"It's an old family recipe, along with the salad," Eve said. "But dessert is my own creation."

Faith swallowed another mouthful. "What's for dessert?"

"The most decadent chocolate cream pie you've ever tasted. But we're going to save it for later. For afterward."

"After what?"

Eve sat back and narrowed her eyes at Faith. "You're full of questions this evening, aren't you? You'll have to wait and see. Right now, your only job is to relax and eat your dinner."

"You're the boss." A smile tugged at Faith's lips. "Thanks for all this. With everything that's been going on, I really needed it."

Eve's expression softened. "How've you been doing?"

"I'm okay. Honestly, more than anything else, I was upset with myself for being so upset. For not being able to let go of that old life. But maybe I don't have to let go of it altogether. There was some good stuff with the bad, after all. It was nice, being part of a big family. And there was this automatic sense of community, of belonging. Everyone was generous and kind." Faith sighed. "That was, as long as you did what was expected of you."

"It sounds like a lot of pressure," Eve said.

"It was. I was never very good at following the rules. There were just so many. Women weren't even allowed to wear pants or cut their hair. I can't even imagine what my life would have been like if I hadn't left. I guess I'd be just like my little sister. Married with three kids, living a life of domesticity. Not that there's anything wrong with that," Faith added.

"Believe me, I'm with you there. I was never suited for that life either."

"I'm just glad I have a choice now. That I have control over my own fate." Faith took a long sip of her wine. Freedom sure tasted sweet.

As dinner wore on, evening turned to night, and Faith found herself opening up more and more about her old life. She didn't usually talk about it much. Everything about her upbringing was so alien to most people. But Eve seemed to understand her in a way no one else did.

"It must have been difficult, leaving it all behind," Eve said. "Giving up everything you knew. Adjusting to a new life."

Faith nodded. "It was a big culture shock. I had to learn everything I thought I knew about the world all over again. It was hard, but not as hard as it could have been. Up until that point, for my life, I felt like the world I lived in didn't make sense. It was only after I left home that I was finally able to understand myself. Don't get me wrong, there was a long adjustment period. It took me months not to feel weird wearing jeans. And when I finally realized how much freedom I had, I went a little wild."

She thought back to her high school and college days. They'd been filled with drinking, partying, and fooling around. "But all that experimentation and exploration helped me figure a lot out. About myself, about my sexuality. And when I did figure it all out, I didn't have any negative feelings. It was a relief. It was like this whole world had opened up for me, one where I could be whatever I wanted to be, and love who I wanted to love, and experience all these things I never dreamed of. I eventually settled down, but there's still plenty I haven't figured out about myself."

"I've been thinking about it, and you're right," Eve said. "Life is just a constant quest to find ourselves. I've been doing a lot of that over the past few years too."

"I guess your world must have changed pretty drastically when you got divorced," Faith said.

"It did, and in a good way. It forced me to find out who I really was. I had to wrap my head around my attraction to women too. It was always something I suspected about myself, but I never got to explore it until the separation." Eve's lips curved up slightly, her eyes fixing on Faith's. "Since then, I've learned far more about myself and my tastes beyond just liking women."

"You mean, like how much you like having women tied up on your bed, so to speak?" Eve had mentioned her first foray into the world of BDSM had been after her separation.

"Exactly. But you should know, although there were women before you, you're the only one I've had bound up in my bed."

Faith bit back a smile. "Didn't you promise that you'd tie me up on your bed in person sometime?"

"I did. And I have every intention of keeping that promise." Eve picked up her glass of wine. "Just as soon as we finish dinner."

CHAPTER TWENTY

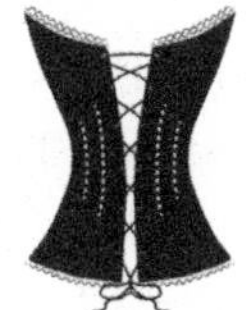

After dinner, Eve led Faith to her bedroom. Once they were inside, Eve went over to the dresser and retrieved a small, familiar key. It was the key to the drawers underneath her bed.

Faith waited in silence, anxiety swirling within her. From the moment she'd laid eyes on Eve at Lilith's Den all those nights ago, all she'd wanted was Eve to show her the depths of surrender. But now that she was faced with it, she felt wholly unprepared.

Eve unlocked a drawer and pulled it open. Inside was a selection of ropes in different colors and sizes, all neatly coiled, along with several pairs of handcuffs and restraints made of leather.

Eve withdrew two lengths of thick white rope and placed them on the bed. Wordlessly, she beckoned Faith to her. Piece by piece, she stripped off Faith's clothes. The soft brush of Eve's fingers made goosebumps sprout on her skin.

Eve unclipped Faith's bra and slid it from her shoulders, leaving her in just her panties. She raked her eyes down Faith's body. Faith resisted the impulse to shield herself with her arms. Something about the way Eve looked at her made her feel even more exposed than she was.

Without taking her eyes off Faith, Eve pulled off her dress, letting it fall to the floor, and removed her bra and panties. Faith drank Eve in with her eyes. It was the first time she'd seen Eve naked, and it was a sight to behold. The other night, Faith had thought there was nothing more irresistibly dominant than Eve in just a corset. She'd been so wrong. Here and now, before Eve's bare body, Faith was gripped with an urge to fall to her knees and to worship every part of Eve like she had the other night.

Instead, she stood by, her head bowed, awaiting Eve's command.

"Lie down on the bed for me," Eve said.

Faith climbed onto the bed and lay down. All the covers and cushions had been removed, leaving only a single pillow and dark silk sheets that felt smooth against her bare skin. The ropes lay on the bed next to her.

Eve joined Faith on the bed, straddling her body. Eve's weight atop her felt overpowering. But it was the sight of Eve, looking down at Faith with her breasts bared and her eyes ablaze, that took Faith's breath away.

Eve drew Faith's arms up toward the headboard, then picked up one of the coils of rope. She unwound it carefully. "Remember your safewords. Red. Yellow."

Faith nodded. Eve brought Faith's wrists together and looped the rope around and through them before tying a finishing knot. She took the tail of rope and pulled Faith's arms up, tying her wrists to the headboard.

Faith looked up. Her arms were stretched high above her. She wriggled her arms. The knots binding her wrists were strong and secure.

"Stop that." Eve looked down at Faith, her gaze hard. "Faith, what I need from you right now is for you to let go. To let all resistance fall away. To trust me. Can you do that for me?"

"Yes." In truth, Faith didn't know if she could give Eve what she demanded, but she wanted to with all her heart.

Still straddling Faith's body, Eve picked up the other coil of rope and turned herself around so she was sitting atop Faith's thighs, facing away from her. Faith stared at the other woman's smooth, hourglass-shaped back as she took Faith's ankles and bound them together.

Eve got up from her perch on Faith's thighs and looked down at her hungrily. With her wrists and ankles bound together, her body stretched out, Faith could barely move at all. She couldn't help but feel like she was a dish on a platter, served up for Eve.

Eve slid her hands down Faith's sides. "You look so lovely, laid out for me like that." She grabbed the waistband of Faith's panties and drew them all the way down to her bound ankles.

Faith let out a shuddering breath. She'd been tied up by Eve before, but not like this. Not naked and helpless, all alone with her. But Faith wasn't powerless. She had her words. *Red. Yellow.* She could control what happened next. She could choose to make everything stop. She could choose to take it slow.

Or, she could choose surrender.

Faith closed her eyes and let calm wash over her. It did nothing to still her racing heart. But her heart wasn't racing out of fear. Every part of her body was screaming for this.

Cradling Faith's cheek in her hand, Eve dipped down to speak into her ear. "That's it. Just relax. Give in to all those wonderful feelings."

Eve kissed her, long and slow. Faith dissolved into Eve's lips. Gently, Eve rolled Faith onto her stomach then got up from the bed. The bed shook beneath Faith as Eve opened and closed a drawer underneath it.

A moment later, Faith felt something soft and flat skimming across her back. She opened her eyes and twisted around to look. Eve stood by the bed, a long, thin riding crop in her hand. She drew it up the side of Faith's neck. A shiver went through her.

"Keep your eyes closed," Eve said.

Faith obeyed.

"Remember what we spoke about the other night? About mixing pain and pleasure?" Eve swept the riding crop down the curve of Faith's back, over her hipbones to the flesh of her ass cheeks. "I'm going to show you how a little pain makes the pleasure so much sweeter."

Silence fell over the room. Despite everything, all Faith felt was calm. When Eve began tapping Faith's ass cheek with the riding crop, that feeling only intensified. Each smack made Faith tingle all over. She pressed her cheek into the pillow, sinking into the bed as Eve slapped her harder and harder. The skin on her cheeks grew warm.

Suddenly, Faith felt a sharp sting on her ass, accompanied by a loud crack. She hissed. It should have shocked her out of her trance-like state. But as the heat dissipated through her, she found herself falling even deeper.

Eve ran the flat of the crop along Faith's ass cheek. "More?"

"Yes," Faith murmured. "Please."

Eve continued to strike her with the crop, one cheek after the other, the leather tip biting into her skin. Her whole body began to burn, her core flaring hot and bright, her veins flooding with adrenaline and desire.

She didn't know how long she lay there for, thrashing and squirming as Eve assailed her with the riding crop, loud cracks echoing through the room. The next thing she was aware of was a cooling hand on her ass. She peered over her shoulder, straining against the ropes binding her. Eve kneeled next to her, caressing her freshly spanked ass cheeks.

Faith lay back down with a sigh. Eve's touch felt exquisite. As the pain faded, she felt the warmth from her cheeks spreading deep into her. Eve's touch on her sensitized skin went from soothing to electrifying, sending sparks slithering between her lower lips. The fact that her legs were tied together only intensified the heat between them.

Faith ground against the bed, trying to put out the fire within. She let out a whimper.

Eve slid her hand down, forcing it between Faith's bound thighs, her fingers pushing into Faith's slit. "Do you see now? All that pain has primed your body for pleasure. And how I love seeing you so ready and eager." She drew her hand back up, tracing a wet finger over Faith's ass cheek. "Had enough of pain? Ready for some pleasure?"

"Yes," Faith whispered. She arched her back, urging Eve's fingers into where she wanted them.

Eve turned Faith onto her back and began untying her ankles. They were already trying to break free. Once her bonds were undone, Eve pulled Faith's panties from where they were tangled around her ankles, tossing them behind her, and pushed Faith's legs apart.

Anticipation flared inside her. Eve clawed her way up Faith's thighs, coming to rest with her head between them. Faith strained toward her, anticipation flaring inside. With her wrists still bound to the headboard, she couldn't move far.

"Eve," she whined.

Eve grabbed onto Faith's waist and drew her fingernails down Faith's sides, leaving long pink scratches behind. Still, she didn't give Faith what she so clearly wanted. Faith writhed and twisted about, but it was futile. Defeated, she settled back against the bed, lying still.

After what felt like an eternity, Eve parted Faith's lips with her tongue and ran it up Faith's slit. Faith shuddered. The way Eve swirled her tongue over Faith's folds and probed at her swollen nub set her whole body alight.

Faith bucked and writhed, overcome. Her ass still stung, a ghost of the earlier pain, but it was like the spanking had charged her body. Now, after only minutes, she was ready to explode.

"Eve. Oh, Eve—"

Faith cried out, ecstasy surging through her. Her muscles tightened, her thighs clenching around Eve's head and her arms pulling at the ropes. Eve continued, milking every last drop of pleasure from her until her body went slack, unable to take any more.

Faith let her head fall to the side. The silk pillow was cool against her warm cheek. Distantly, she felt Eve's hands at her wrists, untying the ropes that bound them. She was barely aware of her body, having been reduced to a puddle of lust.

Eve drew Faith's arms back down, pulling her close and kissing her. A soft murmur escaped her. Although Eve's kisses were gentle, there was a need in them, a possessiveness mixed with desire.

Faith's hands drifted lazily down Eve's body, feeling her curves. Eve quivered at her touch.

"Faith." She cupped Faith's cheeks in her hands. "Do you want to please me?"

"Yes," Faith replied. "Always."

Eve lay her hands on Faith's shoulders, pushing them downward in a wordless command. Faith crawled down Eve's body, exploring every part of her Mistress with her lips. Her neck, which smelled of perfume mixed with Eve's natural scent. Her collarbone, her shoulders, her breasts, round and full. Those delightful pink nipples that pebbled between her lips and under her tongue. Her stomach, soft and smooth, her hips and thighs. That soft hair between them.

Eve shifted against her, her hips pushing out. Faith drew her lips up to where Eve's thighs met and slid her tongue into Eve's slit. She snaked it up and down, relishing the sweetness of Eve's arousal, letting Eve's scent flood her. A purr rumbled through Eve's body, her hand falling to Faith's head. She threaded her fingers through Faith's hair, pulling her in harder.

Faith worked her mouth between Eve's legs, her tongue flickering and lips sucking. Eve let out a fevered moan, her hips rising up into Faith. Faith hooked her arms under Eve's thighs. Eve's legs settled on her shoulders.

"Yes," Eve said. "Worship me."

Faith worshiped the goddess before her with wild abandon. Faith needed to please her, to serve her, to take her to the same heights of pleasure Eve had brought her to. She lost herself, drunk on Eve, consumed by her. She was Eve's, body, mind, and soul.

This was the surrender she craved.

She felt the pressure building within Eve's body.

"Oh yes," Eve said. "Oh, Faith!"

A heartbeat later, Eve shattered around her, her cries of surrender filling the room. Faith didn't stop until Eve edged away, overcome.

They fell back down to the bed together, their bodies wrapped around each other. Faith could feel the rise and fall of Eve's chest against her own. Eve pressed her lips against Faith's with a tenderness that was so unlike the woman who had been raining blows down on her with a riding crop just minutes ago. Or had it been hours? Faith didn't know. She didn't care. All that mattered was Eve. Faith just wanted to drown in her skin.

But this delightful dream of theirs had to end. Slowly, the rest of the world came crawling back, reality setting in.

Faith's eyelids fluttered open. Eve was beside her, gazing back into her eyes.

"Welcome back to the land of the living," she said.

"What time is it?" Faith murmured. It had to be getting late. She couldn't stay here in Eve's bed forever. They'd broken so many rules tonight, crossed so many of the boundaries they'd set.

"Why? Do you have somewhere to be?"

Faith sat up slowly. "No, but—"

Eve pressed a finger to Faith's lips. "We have the house to ourselves until tomorrow evening. No one knows you're here. I wasn't planning on letting you leave this bed until at least midday."

Faith yawned and lay back down. "If you say so."

"And I'm not done with you yet. There's one more thing I want to do with you." Eve kissed Faith on the forehead and got up. "Stay right there."

As Eve left the room, Faith sprawled out across the bed. She wasn't going anywhere. She was so deep under Eve's spell that she was powerless to do anything but obey.

CHAPTER TWENTY-ONE

When Eve returned a minute later, she was carrying two bowls heaped with freshly whipped cream.

Faith sat up and dragged her fingers through her hair. "Is that dessert?"

"Chocolate cream pie, as promised." Eve handed her a bowl.

Suddenly, Faith was ravenous. She took a bite. It was sweet, rich, and tasted homemade in the best way. "Mm. This is just what I need right now."

"This is why I saved dessert." Eve slipped into bed next to her, her own bowl in her hand, and stretched her legs out. "Sweet things and aftercare go well together."

"What's aftercare?" Faith asked between mouthfuls.

"You're feeling really good right now, aren't you? Light. High."

Faith nodded.

"Eventually, you're going to come down from that high. Aftercare is a dominant's way of catching you when you do. It's me keeping all the good feelings flowing so you don't crash." Eve gestured toward the ropes still dangling from the headboard. "All this can be intense. Overwhelming. It can leave a person feeling vulnerable and raw, mentally and emotionally."

"I don't feel like that."

"Maybe not right now. But you still need this." Eve took a bite of pie and placed her bowl on the nightstand next to her. "Besides, this is as much for me as it is for you. I'll let you in on a little secret. It's not just the submissive that surrenders to her dominant. A Domme must surrender to her true desires, the kind that society considers perverse and twisted. She must trust her submissive to accept that dark side of her. It's a vulnerable state to be in."

"I never thought about it that way," Faith said. "This is all so much more complicated than I thought." She looked at Eve. "How did you get into this? Being a Domme, I mean?"

"Do you want the short answer or the long answer?"

"The long one." This was a big part of who Eve was. Faith wanted to know why.

Eve reached toward the foot of the bed and picked up the rope she'd used to bind Faith's ankles. "There was more to my marriage and divorce than I told you. More to what happened between me and Harrison and the rest of his family." She drew the rope through her hands, straightening out the kinks, then began tying it in a knot. "His parents, they were constantly trying to control our lives. Pressuring me to have children, to quit my job. At first, Harrison would stand up to them, but over time, he began to side with them. And when I became pregnant with the twins, it all became so much worse."

Eve finished her knot, then started on another one. "I ended up in the hospital because of complications from the pregnancy. I was drained of all my strength—physically, mentally, emotionally. I wasn't myself. And when I almost lost the twins, I was so afraid. I was vulnerable and weak, and Harrison, he took advantage of that to convince me to finally quit my job. He told me that I had to do what was best for the twins. That I was being selfish by continuing to work. That by putting my desires first, I'd be failing my children. There's so much pressure, as a mother, to make the right choices, and his words, they just ate at me."

This wasn't the first time Eve had spoken of Harrison's manipulative tendencies, but Faith hadn't expected anything so extreme.

How could anyone be so cruel toward someone they were supposed to love?

"His mother was even worse." Eve began tying another knot in the rope, this time looping it over and under in a complex pattern. "We were never close until I became pregnant, then suddenly, I was her beloved daughter. My parents had moved to England by then, and my mother was dealing with some serious health issues, so they weren't able to visit. Eleanor stepped into my mother's role, staying by my bedside while I was in the hospital. She pretended to be sympathetic, while really she was manipulating me. She convinced me that I'd be a bad mother if I didn't fully dedicate myself to the twins. This was while there was still a chance that I'd lose them. I spent the rest of my pregnancy in the hospital, terrified that the twins wouldn't make it. So when they were born happy and healthy, I was so relieved."

Eve looped the rope once more and pulled it tight, leaving an elaborate knot in the middle. "But still, I was unhappy. I loved the twins so much, but I just felt empty. As time went on, as they grew up, those feelings didn't go away. I needed something more to be fulfilled. Eventually, I decided something had to change. I told Harrison I was going back to work, but he forbade it. By then, I was so worn down from constantly being controlled by him and his family that I didn't fight him. And I was too depressed to see how messed up my situation was. Instead, I just became even more withdrawn. Harrison couldn't understand why I was so unhappy. I had the perfect life. I had everything a woman could possibly want. His mother told me the same thing. That my family should be enough for me."

Eve stared down at the knotted rope in her hands, guilt written all over her face. "I started to feel like there was something wrong with me. I started to believe that I was a bad mother. Eleanor certainly didn't help dispel that idea. She was so critical of everything I did. And she stopped me getting help for the way I was feeling. She threatened me, said that if I went to the doctor or spoke to anyone about my problems, she'd have me declared mentally unfit and have the twins taken away from me. She didn't have any real basis for it, of course. But at the time, I believed her."

Anger erupted deep inside Faith. Just the idea of someone trying to tear the twins from Eve filled her with rage.

"It was my own mother who saved me," Eve said. "My parents, they came to visit for the first time since the twins were born. As soon as my mother saw me, she knew something was seriously wrong. I ended up breaking down in her arms, sobbing, telling her everything. She was horrified by how bad things had gotten. She helped me see how toxic Harrison and his family's influence was and convinced me to seek help for my depression. She encouraged me to try a separation and helped me realize I could escape the life I was trapped in. When I started the divorce process, it was a weight off my shoulders. I knew it was the right decision. But still, I felt so hopeless. So powerless. I was lucky to have supportive and loving friends and family, but I'd been helpless for so long that I didn't know how to feel otherwise. Then one day, I crossed paths with an old friend of mine."

Eve pulled at one end of the rope. The last knot she'd tied vanished completely. "Her name is Vicki. We met in business school but fell out of touch because our lives went in vastly different directions. I got married and started a family, while she was living the life of a womanizing party girl. We ended up reconnecting, and when I told her about the separation, she made it her mission to help me make the most of my newfound freedom. She dragged me out to bars and parties, encouraged me to explore my sexuality. It was her way of being supportive. And it helped. I'd been living this restrictive, conventional life for so long, I'd forgotten how to have fun." She ran the rope through her hands, feeling each knot. "One day, Vicki invited me to go to Lilith's Den with her. She'd always been open about her tastes, but I'd never shown an interest in anything like that. I went along with her anyway. That night, it changed my life."

Faith thought back to the first time she'd gone to Lilith's Den. She'd felt the same way. Just walking through the door had awakened something in her.

"There was something so empowering about it," Eve continued. "Seeing all those strong, self-assured women who were completely in control. And the submissives. There was this power in them too, in vulnerability so freely given. It opened my eyes to a world where women could explore their sexuality, let out their true selves, discover their inner strength. I think that's why Vicki took me there. She must have sensed that it was something I needed. She was right. Lilith's Den helped me crawl out of the hole I was in, helped me take back control. It helped me rebuild my life and gave me the confidence to pursue what I wanted. It helped me live again.

"It's been a few years since then, and this?" Eve held up the rope. "It still makes me feel the way it did that very first night at Lilith's Den. And lately, those feelings have only gotten stronger." Her eyes met Faith's. "With you, those feelings have only gotten stronger."

Faith's heart sped up.

"That part of me," Eve said. "That woman in the corset. Until now, I've never let her be anything more than a persona. But being with you has made me realize she's as much a part of me as any other. Being with you makes me feel more complete and more alive than I have in years."

"Eve," Faith said softly. "I feel that too." She'd never felt freer than when Eve had her bound up in ropes. She'd never felt more content than when Eve had her arms around her. She'd never felt happier than when Eve said Faith was hers.

Eve tossed the rope aside and pulled Faith down to the bed, drawing her into an embrace. "As soon as we're free to be together, I'm going to treat you how you deserve to be treated. I'm going to take you out, and spoil you, and show the world you're mine. There are many more nights like this ahead."

"I can't wait." Faith melted into Eve's arms. She was starting to come down from that high, but with Eve by her side, it was impossible to feel anything but serene.

But at the back of her mind, Faith was still wary. It was too early to start dreaming about the future.

Too much was still up in the air.

CHAPTER TWENTY-TWO

It was nighttime when Faith received a phone call from Eve.

Faith was lounging around at home on one of her days off after having worked seven days in a row. That week had seemed tortuously long. Being around Eve, while keeping things strictly professional, was harder now than ever. And yet, being apart from Eve was even worse.

Faith had fallen hard.

She picked up the phone, eager to hear Eve's voice.

"I need you to come to the house," Eve said. "Now."

"Sure." Faith frowned. Eve's voice had a hard edge. "Is everything okay? Is it the twins?" They were supposed to be at their father's.

"I'll explain when you get here."

"I have to get dressed first, then I'll be right over."

"Just make it quick." Eve hung up the phone.

Dread rolled down Faith's back. Something was very wrong. She could hear it in Eve's voice.

She threw on some jeans and a jacket, grabbed her keys, and headed to Eve's house. It was late, and there was no traffic, so it wasn't long before she arrived.

She unlocked the door and let herself in. The house was eerily silent. "Eve?"

"In here," Eve called.

Faith followed Eve's voice to her office. Inside, Eve stood by her desk, her back to the door.

"Eve?" Faith said quietly. "Are you okay?"

Eve turned. Her face was deathly pale, and her lips were pressed into a thin line. She was staring down at the phone in her hand.

Faith approached her. "What's going on?"

"It's Harrison. He—" Eve swallowed. "It's easier if I just show you."

Eve handed her phone to Faith. A video was queued up on the screen, but it was too dark to see anything. Faith pressed play. The video looked like it had been taken inside a bar or club. As it played on, the crowd came into focus. Most of the people were dressed in skimpy, provocative clothing. In the background, all kinds of unusual fixtures and equipment could be seen.

Instantly, Faith knew where the video had been taken. "This is Lilith's Den."

Eve didn't respond. She didn't need to.

The video zoomed in on some seating in a corner, hidden away from the main floor of the club. Despite the dim lighting, the two figures in the seats could be seen clearly. Faith, with a collar around her neck, and Eve, dressed in a tight, revealing corset, her arm around Faith.

Faith's stomach churned. This was from the last night she and Eve had gone to Lilith's Den.

On the screen, Eve pushed Faith back against the chair before grabbing her by the collar and planting a forceful kiss on her lips, her hand straying down Faith's chest. A second later, Faith shook her head and cringed away, speaking angrily to Eve. The video had no sound, but Faith's gestures and expression made it clear that things were getting heated. After several seconds, Eve grabbed Faith's hand and dragged her out of frame. The video ended.

Faith cursed under her breath. This did *not* look good. The camera had captured the exact moment when Faith had gotten upset. While in reality, it had been nothing more than a minor quarrel, the distance and the angle of the camera meant that the video showed a very different scene. It looked like Eve was aggressively forcing herself on a somewhat unwilling woman in some kind of dark, perverted sex club. To the outside eye, the scene presented was scandalous. And Eve looked positively predatory.

Faith looked up at Eve. "What's this?"

"Harrison sent it to me," Eve said.

"I don't understand. How did he get this?"

"He took it himself. He was at Lilith's that night. Apparently, a friend of his who's a member let it slip that I go there too. Harrison wanted to see it for himself, so he convinced his friend to take him along as a guest. I don't know if he was trying to catch me in the act or if it was just a coincidence, but he was lucky enough to find me with you. My nanny."

It all clicked together in Faith's mind. Harrison had met her. He knew who Faith was. And now he knew Eve was having some kind of kinky relationship with her nanny.

"What do you think he's going to do with this?" Faith asked.

"I don't have to guess," Eve said. "He told me exactly what he's going to. He's going to use this video as evidence that I'm an unfit mother to bolster his case for custody and have the twins taken from me. That is, unless I comply with his demands."

"He's blackmailing you?"

"He wants me to drop my petition for custody. Let him have the twins full-time. If I do, he'll let me have visitation. If I don't cooperate, he and his lawyers will make sure I'll never get to see the twins again."

"But he can't do that. Not with just this video. It doesn't show you doing anything wrong or illegal."

"No, it doesn't." Eve folded her arms across her chest, holding them tightly to her. "But image matters in the eyes of family court. Good mothers don't go to BDSM clubs or have affairs with their nanny. He's going to use it to paint a picture of me as unstable."

"But that's a lie," Faith said. "And this is just one video. It isn't any evidence of anything."

"He has other evidence. From back when the twins were young. Doctors' reports about my mental state." Eve's voice wavered. "I was in bad shape by the time I went to see a doctor. He can use that."

"That's the ammunition Harrison has against you?" That was why, this entire time, Eve had been determined to be on her best behavior?

Eve nodded. "It's nothing damming, but his lawyers, they'll twist it, make it seem like a bigger deal than it was. Make me seem like a bad mother."

"But that was years ago. And all those problems you had, it was because of him and his messed-up family!"

"I can't blame his family for everything. I'm responsible for the state I was in. I'm responsible for the way I felt."

"No, you're not. Lots of women feel the way you did. It isn't unusual to get depressed after having kids. It doesn't make you a bad mother."

"Not everyone understands that," Eve said. "All a judge is going to see is a mother whose children drove her to despair. Harrison's lawyers will make sure of that. They're the best in the business. Pay them enough, and they can get anyone off for murder. All they have to do is spin me as some kind of mentally ill pervert, and that's it. I lose the twins."

"You have good lawyers too," Faith said. "You can fight this."

"The risks are just too great. If I fight this and I lose, I'll never see the twins again. I can't lose them, Faith."

"So what are you going to do? You can't just give up."

"I don't have a choice! Harrison, he's a powerful man. And he has a never-ending supply of money. I can't go up against him with so much at risk. I can't win against him."

"Yes, you can! You have to try, at least."

"You don't understand." Eve threw her hands up. "How could you? You're not a mother. You don't understand what's at risk here. You couldn't possibly comprehend what this is like."

It was true. Faith didn't know what this felt like. She couldn't imagine the depths of Eve's anguish. "You're right," Faith said. "I'm sorry. I'm sorry this is happening. If there's anything I can do to—"

"No," Eve said. "I called you here to let you know what was going on, but what I need right now is time and space to work this out. The twins will be staying with Harrison until everything is sorted, so they won't be needing a nanny. And I don't need you wrapped up in this mess any further."

"Oh." It was no surprise Eve wanted Faith gone. It was Eve's relationship with her that had caused this, after all. "You're right. It's for the best."

Eve didn't respond. She just continued to stare at nothing at all.

"I'll leave you alone, then." Faith hesitated. "And I'm sorry. I hope you can work things out."

Faith left the room. Eve didn't even look at her. She didn't say goodbye. And as Faith made her way home, Eve's haunted face was all she could see.

CHAPTER TWENTY-THREE

Faith was woken up by the sound of knocking on her front door.

She groaned and threw off her covers, squinting at the sun shining through her curtains. It was almost midday, but she'd spent most of the night a sleepless wreck. She'd only fallen asleep a few hours ago.

The knocking continued. Faith got out of bed and walked out to the door. She opened it up to find Lindsey standing in the hallway.

Crap. "We're supposed to go to lunch," Faith said. "I completely forgot."

"Did you just wake up?" Lindsey asked.

"Yeah. I didn't get much sleep last night."

Lindsey frowned. "Are you okay?"

"You should probably just come in."

Lindsey followed Faith inside. "What's going on?"

"It's Eve." Faith collapsed onto the couch. Lindsey joined her. "Everything is messed up, and it's all my fault." She'd stewed on it overnight. It had made her realize just how bad things were. Eve's family was at risk because of Faith. And now, Eve wanted nothing to do with her.

"What happened?" Lindsey asked.

"What happened is that I ruined everything for her."

"Just tell me what happened. Start from the beginning."

Faith told Lindsey everything, from that night at Lilith's when she'd exploded on Eve, to the moment Eve had shown her the video. Her explanation was all jumbled up, just like the feelings inside her.

"And then she said she needed space and told me not to come back." Faith slumped in her seat. "This is such a mess. Eve is going to lose her kids. All because of me."

"Faith, this isn't your fault," Lindsey said. "I'm sure Eve doesn't blame you for what happened."

"But it *is* my fault. We never should have gotten together in the first place. I was the one who kept pushing her. I had to find out if she was the woman in the corset. I had to confront her when she was being cold to me after the party. I convinced her to continue with this twisted fling of ours, even though we both knew it would put her family at risk. If I'd just let things lie, none of this would have happened."

"You know that's not true. You didn't force Eve into this relationship with you. She made a choice, just like you did."

"Well, clearly she regrets it now," Faith said.

"Are you sure? For starters, did Eve say things were over between you?"

"She didn't have to. She said she needed space. And considering what she's dealing with, that's understandable."

"I'm sure the two of you can work it out," Lindsey said. "Believe me, you don't want things between you to end over a misunderstanding."

"There's no point in trying to work things out. Even if she still wanted to be with me, I wouldn't want to mess things up with her family any further." Faith shook her head. "This is for the best."

"Faith—"

"Really, it is," Faith said. "This is hard. I want to be there for her. I care about her so much. But that's why I have to stay away. You should have seen the look in her eyes." Her shoulders shook in a silent sob. She steadied herself. "I can't risk tearing Eve's family apart. I can't be the reason the twins grow up without a mom."

"Oh, Faith." Lindsey put her hand on Faith's arm. "None of this is your fault. And you haven't torn her family apart. You still don't know how this custody situation is going to turn out."

"Eve doesn't even want to fight it. She's just given up. She thinks the video is the final nail in the coffin."

"Wait." Lindsey cocked her head to the side. "That video. It's from inside Lilith's Den?"

Faith nodded.

"And Eve's ex-husband took it?"

"Yeah."

"You can't take videos inside Lilith's. Didn't you read those agreements you signed the first time you went there?"

"Of course not," Faith said. "There were so many pages!"

"Well, if you'd read them, you'd know that filming inside the club isn't allowed. Even photos aren't allowed. Confidentiality is a big deal there."

"I don't think Harrison cares."

"Maybe he doesn't," Lindsey said. "But he signed those agreements too. Everyone who walks through the doors at Lilith's Den does. They're legally binding. There are serious penalties for breaching them."

"Penalties? Harrison can just pay his way out of them. Or lawyer his way out of them."

"I don't think so. You know the owner of Lilith's Den? Vanessa? You met her that night I invited you along, remember?"

Faith nodded.

"She'd want to know that this kind of thing happened at her club," Lindsey said. "She takes privacy really seriously. And she might be able to help."

"I doubt she can do anything. I don't think you understand how much money and power Harrison has."

"Vanessa has money and power too. You and Eve should talk to her."

"There's no 'me and Eve,'" Faith said. "Not anymore."

"Well at the very least, you can still tell Eve to talk to Vanessa. Let her know Vanessa might be willing to help." Lindsey frowned. "Now that I think about it, I'm surprised Eve isn't looking into that angle already. If she's a regular at the club, she knows what a big deal it is for someone to take a video inside Lilith's. And on top of that, there's an unwritten rule in the BDSM community that you don't out anyone. *Ever.*"

Eve had said the same thing to Faith once. "I guess she didn't think of that. This whole situation has her really shaken up."

"All the more reason you should talk to her about it," Lindsey said.

"She made it clear that she didn't want to see me." Eve was right to feel that way.

An exasperated look crossed Lindsey's face. "Just think about it, okay? Right now, you're hurting. Eve isn't the only one who isn't seeing things clearly. Promise me you'll take some time to think it over?"

"Fine," Faith muttered.

"Good." Lindsey placed her hands on Faith's shoulders. "You can't give up on her, Faith. What you have with her, it's something special. I don't even know her, but I can tell. You've been different lately. Happier. More like the Faith I met our first day of art school."

"Is that a good thing?" Back then, Faith had been newly eighteen and still adjusting to the real world after years of being caged. She'd gone a little wild.

Lindsey smiled. "I think it is."

Faith sighed. The years that had followed had been tumultuous, but she'd felt freer than ever before. And Eve had given her back that feeling.

But that was all over now. She'd screwed everything up for Eve. Eve was right to get rid of her. Right to ask for space.

It was better if she just stayed away.

CHAPTER TWENTY-FOUR

Faith lay on her old gray couch, staring up at the ceiling. She had nothing to do now that she was out of a job. Sure, Eve hadn't explicitly fired her. But she'd made it clear she didn't need Faith's services. And she'd made it clear she wanted nothing to do with Faith.

Faith hugged a cushion to her chest. Several days had passed since that night in Eve's office, and she'd been consumed by worry ever since. It wasn't just Eve she was worried about. What was going to happen to the twins if Eve gave up fighting for them?

Faith didn't know much about Harrison and his family other than what Eve had told her. They'd certainly made Eve's life hell. But that didn't mean they would treat the twins the same way. Leah and Ethan had never had anything bad to say about their father and grandparents. Maybe living with them full-time wouldn't be so bad for the twins.

Faith threw the cushion across the room. She was deluding herself. There was only one thing about the situation that Faith was certain of. Eve was a good mother. She was a good person.

She didn't deserve to lose her kids.

Lindsey's advice played in her head again. Faith had a potential solution to Eve's problem in her lap. Didn't she owe it to Eve to tell her? It was a solution Eve couldn't see for herself. She was too scared. She wasn't thinking straight. She was giving up when she could still fight.

Faith sighed. Wasn't she doing the exact same thing Eve was? Letting fear win? Wasn't that why she was so adamant that she had to stay away from Eve? She kept telling herself that Eve wanted her gone, but that wasn't what was truly keeping her away. She'd shut herself off from even the idea of ever seeing Eve again, not for Eve's sake, but for her own. She'd fled at the first sign of rejection, just to keep herself from feeling that same pain she'd felt so many times before.

Faith steeled herself. This wasn't about her, or her feelings. This was about Eve and keeping her family together. Faith owed it to Eve to help her in any way she could.

She just hoped Eve would listen.

Faith rang Eve's doorbell and waited. She didn't even know if Eve was home. She still had a key, but she wasn't about to waltz into the house after everything that had happened.

She glanced at the camera by the doorbell. Had Eve seen her already? Was she ignoring her, waiting for Faith to give up and leave? Faith wouldn't blame her. If she was in Eve's shoes, she wouldn't want to see Faith either.

She was about to leave when the door swung open.

"Hello, Faith," Eve said.

Faith's heart sank. Eve looked as put together as ever, but her face was a mask of worry. It hurt to see her like this. Faith longed to wrap her arms around her, tell her everything was going to be okay. But it wasn't her place. And that wasn't why she was here.

She pulled herself together. She had to focus on helping Eve.

Eve stepped to the side. "Why don't you come in?"

Faith followed Eve through the house and into the living room. There was no sign of the twins. Eve sat down stiffly on the couch. Faith joined her.

Eve looked at Faith, her eyes filled with emotion, and gave her a faint smile. "It's good to see you."

Why was Eve smiling at her? Why, when she was in the midst of this crisis, caused by Faith herself?

Faith's resolve crumbled under Eve's gaze. "I'm sorry," she blurted out. "I'm so sorry, and I know you don't want to see me again, but I want to help you. I want to fix this, and I think I know how."

"Faith." Eve held up her hands. "Slow down. What are you talking about?"

"I caused this whole mess, and you said you wanted space, but I need to tell you how you can fix all this."

"What? You didn't cause this. And when I said I needed space, I meant space to think." Realization dawned on Eve's face. "Did you think I meant I didn't want to see you again?"

"Well, yeah."

Eve flinched back. "I didn't mean that. I didn't mean to come across as so cold. I was distracted, worried about losing the twins, and I didn't think about what I was saying. I never meant for you to think this was your fault."

Had Faith really misread everything? For some reason, the knowledge didn't make her feel any better.

"I know I said some harsh things, and I'm sorry," Eve said. "I shouldn't have pushed you away. I shouldn't have said you wouldn't understand because you're not a mother. And I shouldn't have said I needed space. I regret saying that so much. Faith, this whole time, I've been beside myself with worry. I wanted so badly for you to be here with me. But I thought that you'd want space too." Her eyes wavered. "I dragged you into this family drama that you should never have been involved in. I didn't think you'd want to be a part of that."

"I thought that was what you wanted," Faith said. "Me, out of the way."

"I would never, ever want that. Faith, the other night I said that what we have has made me feel more alive than I ever have in years. More complete." She laid her hand on top of Faith's on the couch between them. "I didn't mean having you as my submissive. I meant how I feel about you in my heart. I care about you, Faith. I want to be with you."

Something flitted inside Faith's chest. Wasn't that what Faith wanted too?

But she had too many conflicting feelings swirling about inside her. Too many doubts, too many uncertainties. And she couldn't possibly be happy with Eve knowing that their relationship was destroying Eve's family.

She drew her hand away. None of that mattered right now. She had to tell Eve how she could fix things.

"That's not why I came here," Faith said. "I came to tell you that I have an idea of how to handle the situation with Harrison."

A pained expression crossed Eve's face, but it quickly disappeared. "All right. Tell me."

Faith took a breath and explained what Lindsey had told her. About Harrison breaching the club's agreement and how they could use it to fight him.

"So," Faith said. "What do you think?"

Eve sat forward, leaning toward Faith. "You're right. I hadn't thought about any of that. But I don't know if it will help. I don't know if there's anything we can do about it, even with Vanessa's help."

"I don't know either," Faith said. "But you have to try. Eve, I've gotten to know your family so well since I started working for you. I care about you, and I care about the twins. I know as well as you do that Harrison getting full custody isn't the best thing for them. I know that splitting your family apart like this isn't right. You have to fight this. If not for your sake, then for Leah and Ethan's."

"You're right," Eve said. "God, you're right. The more I think about it, the more I'm certain that I can't let this happen. I can't let the twins be taken in by the kind of people that would do something like this. By the kind of man who would blackmail the mother of his children." Her jaw set. "I can't let him do this."

"So you're going to fight this?"

Eve nodded. "Let's call Vanessa."

CHAPTER TWENTY-FIVE

Eve drummed her fingers on the tabletop. She and Faith were in the conference room at Eve's office, waiting for Harrison to arrive. The trap was set. However, one crucial piece of the plan was missing.

Faith looked at Eve. Her face was wrinkled with worry. She took Eve's hand under the table and squeezed it. "Don't worry," she said. "She'll be here. This is going to work." It had to. The fate of Eve's family all depended on it. "Everything will be okay."

Eve gave her a half-smile. "Thanks again for agreeing to come along. I really appreciate it."

"I meant it when I said that I'm here for you if you need me." Faith still hadn't made up her mind about the two of them, but she couldn't bear to see Eve like this.

The door swung open. A tall, raven-haired woman strode into the room. "Sorry I'm late," Vanessa said. "I got held up in traffic."

"It's fine," Eve said. "Harrison isn't here yet."

Eve had called her ex-husband the day before and asked him to meet her here to discuss the custody situation. She'd made it sound like she was ready to give in to his demands. He'd made her promise not to bring her lawyers.

He hadn't mentioned bringing anyone else along.

"Faith." Vanessa nodded at her. "Hello again."

"Hi." Faith was surprised that Vanessa remembered her. They'd only met once, at Lilith's Den that night. It seemed like so long ago. "Thanks for helping out with this."

"It's no trouble." Vanessa sat down at the end of the table. "Besides, it's in my best interests to resolve this. No one violates the privacy of my club and gets away with it. And I won't stand for this kind of disgusting blackmail."

Although Vanessa appeared calm and collected, the anger in her voice was palpable. That was reassuring. She really seemed to care about the situation. Faith sensed Eve relax a little too.

The door to the conference room opened again. In walked Harrison with that same confident swagger he'd shown the last time Faith had met him.

He looked around the room, his eyes clouding over. "I told you to meet me alone."

"You said no lawyers," Eve said. "You didn't say anything about anyone else."

Harrison's eyes landed on Faith. He snorted. "You brought your nanny? The one you're fucking?"

"She's not just my nanny," Eve said. "She's so much more to me than that. And I brought her along for support."

He looked between the two of them. "So this is the real reason you left me? Because you're a lesbian?"

"Oh, please. Leaving you had nothing to do with my sexuality."

Vanessa cleared her throat. "Are you two done? We have more important things to discuss."

Harrison looked at Vanessa, frowning. "I know you from somewhere."

"Vanessa Harper," she said.

Recognition dawned on his face. Apparently, on top of secretly owning Lilith's Den, Vanessa was some big-shot CEO. Her power and status were what their whole plan hinged on. It was clear from Harrison's reaction that her name held a lot of weight.

"What are you doing here?" Harrison asked.

Vanessa gestured toward a chair across from Eve and Faith. "Why don't you have a seat?"

Harrison sat down, a bemused expression on his face.

"Eve and I are acquaintances," Vanessa continued. "She told me all about you and your little blackmail plot. You see, you probably don't know this about me, but I own Lilith's Den."

Harrison's face twisted with disgust. "You own that fucked-up place?"

"I do. And that 'fucked-up place' is patronized by lots of powerful people. They all take their privacy very seriously, for obvious reasons. It's why the club has such strict confidentiality rules. By taking a video inside the club, you violated those rules."

Harrison crossed his arms. "So, I broke some rules. It's too late to do anything about it now. You can ban me if you like. I'm never going back there."

"Oh, I can do much more than ban you." Vanessa's voice grew icy. "Before you entered Lilith's Den, you signed a number of legally binding agreements. One of these was a confidentiality agreement, which included a clause prohibiting any photography or recording of videos inside the premises."

"What, you're going to sue me?" Harrison said. "You know as well as I do that we'll just end up in a drawn-out legal battle. Are you sure you'll come out on top?"

"I have no doubt I'd win such a case. My legal team created those agreements to be ironclad. But no, I'm not threatening to sue you. I could do that. But I could do much, much worse." Vanessa leaned back in her chair. "We have a lot of mutual friends, you and I. Colleagues. Business contacts. Given your distaste for what goes on in my club, you may be shocked to hear that many of our mutual contacts are regulars at Lilith's Den."

Harrison tensed. Could he see where this was going?

"All those regulars are very private about the fact that they go to my club. And for a good reason, when there are judgmental people like you out there who are willing to expose what they like to do behind closed doors. How do you think they'd react if they knew you'd entered their sanctuary and taken a video in order to blackmail someone?"

"I wouldn't do that to anyone else," Harrison said. "Eve is my ex-wife. The mother of my children. It's different."

"Is it? And how does anyone else know you wouldn't do the same thing to them? Why would anyone ever trust you again, knowing you violated such an important social contract? Knowing how little respect you have for their privacy? You know how the corporate world works. It's all about building relationships. Building trust. Why would anyone want to do business with someone who has proven they can't be trusted?"

"Are you saying you'll have me blacklisted?"

"I would never do anything as unsubtle as that," Vanessa said. "But the patrons of my club will want to know that their confidentiality has been violated, and by whom. When word gets around, you'll lose all your contracts, one by one. Do you think your company can survive that?"

Harrison looked at Vanessa, wide-eyed. "You're talking about sabotaging my company."

"I wouldn't be sabotaging anything. I'd simply be informing people of the facts and letting nature take its course. Of course, you have enough money that you'd be fine, even without your company. But what would that do to your reputation? You'll be ruined, just like you threatened to ruin Eve here."

"You're crazy." Harrison shook his head. "What do you want from me?"

"What do you think?" Vanessa narrowed her eyes. "I want you to wipe that video and any others you took inside Lilith's Den from the face of the earth. And I want you to give Eve whatever she asks for when it comes to this custody case."

"You don't know anything about that. About my family, about Eve."

"I know enough. I know that you're the kind of man who tries to blackmail his ex-wife, and that speaks volumes. My fiancée is a lawyer. She's informed me that judges don't look kindly upon people who blackmail their former spouses in custody cases. It's in your best interests to cooperate with Eve."

Harrison scoffed and turned to Eve. "Isn't this what you're doing to me? Blackmailing me, having *her* threaten me unless I agree to your demands?"

Eve shrugged. "You stopped playing by the rules a long time ago. I'm just leveling the playing field." She crossed her arms. "They're my children, Harrison. I'm willing to do anything for them. And I mean *anything*."

"If you cared about the kids you wouldn't be having an affair with their nanny and going to sex clubs. You're their mother for god's sake."

"Yes, I'm the twins' mother. But I'm a person too, with needs of my own, which is something you never understood. I'm allowed to have a life outside of my children. I'm allowed to find my own happiness."

"Happiness?" Harrison looked at Faith. "With their nanny? You're exposing the twins to this sick fetish of yours."

"I'm not exposing them to anything. They don't know about Faith and me, and I intend to keep things that way. What I do in my spare time is none of their business, or yours. Faith and I are both consenting adults. There is nothing sick about what's between us." Eve's jaw set. "What I have with Faith is more real than anything I've ever felt. I love her."

What? Faith looked at Eve. Her eyes were locked onto Harrison's, but the resolve on her face made it clear that she meant every word she'd said.

"This is crazy." Harrison threw his hands up. "If you think I'm going to roll over and give you whatever you want, you're out of your mind."

"I don't think you have a choice," Vanessa interrupted. "Not unless you want to lose your company." Vanessa's eyes bored into him. "This isn't an empty threat. Release that video and I will ruin you."

Faith stared at Vanessa in shock. She was serious, and Harrison knew it.

"Delete the video," Vanessa said. "Work things out with Eve. And if I hear of you doing anything less, I will let you and your company burn."

Harrison spoke through gritted teeth. "Fine."

"And I'm going to need the name of this friend of yours who invited you to Lilith's Den."

Harrison muttered a name.

"Good. I'm going to have a word with him about his choice of guests." Vanessa stood up. "We'll let the two of you talk. Faith?"

Faith got up. "Good luck," she said quietly to Eve.

Eve nodded. "Wait for me in my office. This won't take long."

Faith followed Vanessa out of the room and shut the door. She was dizzy with nerves.

Vanessa put her hand on Faith's shoulder. "Don't worry. Everything is going to be fine. I do my fair share of negotiating, and I can tell when someone is on their back. Harrison will give Eve whatever she wants."

"I hope so," Faith said. "Thanks for all your help."

"Once again, it's no trouble." Vanessa paused. "Eve told me about the two of you. How everything started when you ran into each other at Lilith's Den. I'm glad my club played a part in bringing two people together. That's what life's all about isn't it?"

"Yeah," Faith said. "Thanks again."

"I have to go. Let me know if Eve has any trouble, okay?"

"I will."

Vanessa strode off. Faith went to Eve's office and sat down in front of the desk. Several minutes passed. She got up. She was too nervous to sit still. She paced in front of the window. Eve was taking forever.

Faith hoped for Eve's sake that this worked. She cared so much for the beautiful family she'd spent so long getting to know. And she cared so much for Eve.

Eve's words echoed in her mind. *What I have with Faith is more real than anything I've ever felt.*

I love her.

"Faith."

She turned. She hadn't heard Eve walk in. "How did it go?"

Eve joined her by the window. "Harrison is going to delete the video. And we came to an agreement. He's giving me primary custody of Leah and Ethan."

Faith's heart swelled. "That's great!"

"We're still working out the finer details, and none of this is official until we get our lawyers to sign off on everything. But Harrison seems remorseful. He seems to genuinely want to work with me. I considered pushing for sole custody, but whether I like it or not, Harrison is the twins' father. Despite his many, many flaws, he deserves a hand in raising them. I'll just have to be extra careful that his family's values don't rub off on the twins. I'll have to set the best example I can and hope that it's enough."

"It will be," Faith said. "You're an incredible mother. Leah and Ethan are going to grow up just fine. I'm so happy for you all. I'm so glad you fought this."

"You were right all along. I should have listened to you. I was just scared."

"With so much at stake, you had a good reason to be scared. And once again, sorry for my part in this."

Eve gave her a hard look. "Faith, if you apologize one more time…"

"Sorry! I'll stop. I'm just glad everything is sorted out now."

"No. Everything isn't sorted out." Eve's eyes locked onto Faith's. "There's still the matter of us."

The air in the room grew still.

"There's nothing standing in our way anymore," Eve said. "Nothing stopping us from being together."

It was true. There were no more obstacles in their way. No reason for them to hide. Nothing stopping them from embracing what they felt.

Nothing stopping Faith from surrendering to what she truly felt for Eve.

Faith took a step toward Eve, and another, until they were barely a foot apart. "You said something in there. You said that you love me."

"Did I?" A slight smile crossed Eve's lips. "It must have slipped out. But it's the truth."

Eve took Faith's hand, closing the distance between them.

"I love you, Faith."

With those four words, all Faith's doubts melted away. "I love you too."

Eve swept Faith into her arms for a heady kiss that almost knocked Faith off her feet.

CHAPTER TWENTY-SIX

Faith stood in the living room door, watching Eve recline on the lounge with a book. Eve, spending the evening relaxing? That was a sight Faith never thought she'd see.

Eve looked up at Faith. "You're back. The kids are at Harrison's?"

Faith nodded. She'd just dropped them off. The new custody agreement had been in place for a few weeks now, and it was working well. Eve was much more relaxed these days. And Faith finally had a regular work schedule now that the twins had a set routine. However, she ended up spending most of her days off with Eve anyway.

It was a relief, to finally be able to be with Eve openly. However, they still hadn't told the twins about their relationship. They were taking things slow on that front. Whenever the twins were home, Faith and Eve continued to keep things strictly professional between them.

But right now, they had the house all to themselves.

"And you've tidied up the kids' rooms?" Eve asked. "Folded their laundry? Packed away their toys?"

"Everything is taken care of," Faith said.

"Good. I have one last task for you."

"What do you need me to do for you?"

Eve placed her book down carefully and stood up. "I need you to go wait for me in my bedroom." The look in her eyes made it abundantly clear that this task had nothing to do with Faith's job.

Faith chewed her lip, feigning hesitation. "I don't know. I'm supposed to be off the clock."

Eve grabbed Faith's arm and yanked her in close. Faith yelped in surprise.

Eve spoke into her ear in a sharp voice. "Consider this overtime." She released Faith from her grasp. "You have five minutes. When I come in, I expect to find you kneeling on the bed." She ran her eyes down Faith's body. "And take that dress off."

Faith gave her a cheeky grin. "You're the boss."

She headed to Eve's bedroom, closed the door, and stripped off her dress before climbing onto the vast bed, kneeling in the center of it. At least Eve had asked Faith to kneel on the bed and not on the floor like she had a few times before. Now that she and Eve were free of all the restrictions that came with a secret relationship, Eve had gotten far more creative with her games. She seemed to revel in coming up with delightful new ways to torment Faith. Just thinking about it made her ache.

After what seemed like an eternity, Eve entered the room. Faith's lips fell open. In that short space of time, Eve had undergone a transformation. Her hair was loose, and her lips were a dark crimson that made Faith want to taste them. And the rest of her? Faith didn't know where to look. The red-soled heels Eve wore elongated her smooth, bare legs, and the tiniest pair of black panties were on her hips. The only other piece of clothing Eve had on was a black corset. It was the same corset she'd worn to Lilith's the first night Faith had set foot inside.

Seeing Eve dressed in that outfit flooded every cell in Faith's body with need. And yet, the woman who stood before Faith was so far removed from the woman in the corset from that night. She wasn't the Eve that Faith had met the day of her job interview either. Although she was just as strict and domineering, the fire behind her eyes spoke of both passion and warmth. This Eve, Faith's Eve, was far more irresistible than the woman in the corset.

Eve's eyes wandered down Faith's near-naked kneeling form. She hadn't swapped her glasses out for contact lenses like she often did, and the way she gazed at Faith from over the top of them sent Faith's pulse racing.

Faith peered back up at her from under her eyelashes. "Do you like what you see?"

Eve grabbed Faith's chin, jerking it toward her. "You're being far too cheeky today. For the rest of the night, you're not to speak unless spoken to. Do you understand?"

Faith nodded. Pushing the limits of the woman who held Faith's pleasure in her hand was *not* a smart idea.

"For the record, I do like what I see," Eve said. "I always do."

Eve leaned down to kiss her, pressing herself against Faith so forcefully that they both tumbled onto the bed. Eve tore off Faith's bra and panties, her lips never leaving Faith's. Faith deepened the kiss, the fire within her flickering and flaring.

Eve drew back and reached over the side of the bed to open one of the drawers underneath it. It was already unlocked. Eve was prepared. What did she have planned?

Eve dug around in the drawer, then pulled out the spreader bar. She dropped it on the bed by Faith's feet. "I'll need your ankles."

Faith sat back, her legs stretched out before her, memories of that night on camera flooding her mind and body.

"Not like that," Eve said. "I want you on all fours. And turn around."

Heat rushed to Faith's skin. A position like that, combined with the spreader bar, would leave Faith vulnerable. But she trusted Eve. And that was what made it so delicious.

Faith got on her hands and knees, facing the headboard.

"That's better." Eve picked up the spreader bar and disappeared behind her.

Faith turned her head to watch. Eve pushed Faith's knees apart and fastened the cuffs of the bar around her ankles, leaving her legs spread out. Her thighs burned from the strain, but not in an unpleasant way.

"There." Eve's eyes met Faith's. "You just can't help but peek, can you? I'll have to do something about that." She leaned over, reached into the drawer under the bed again, and produced a long piece of black fabric. "Close your eyes."

Faith opened her mouth to protest. Eve hadn't told her not to look. It wasn't fair of her to make up the rules as she went along. But Eve had instructed Faith not to speak, so she clamped her mouth shut and closed her eyes.

Eve tied the blindfold around Faith's head. Here she was, her ass sticking out, unable to move her legs, unable to see a thing. This was going to be agonizing. Eve had a sadistic streak, but her tool of choice wasn't pain. It was pure, concentrated pleasure. She wielded it like a weapon, sometimes doling it out in agonizingly small slivers, sometimes assaulting Faith with it until she begged for release. Faith already knew that wouldn't take long. Just kneeling on the bed, waiting for Eve, had her hot all over. Not to mention, soaking wet.

The bed shifted under her as Eve got up from it and opened another drawer. Faith waited patiently, powerless to see or do anything. She rolled her shoulders just to remind herself that she could still move.

Finally, Eve returned to the bed, the unexpected motion of the mattress nearly throwing Faith off-balance. Without her sight, she had no frame of reference for anything. It was dizzying.

"All this, and you haven't spoken a single word?" Eve drew the back of her fingers down Faith's cheek and neck. "I thought you would have cracked by now."

Faith said nothing. Eve let her fingers skim between Faith's shoulder blades, along the concave curve of her back, all the way to her tailbone. Faith quivered with delight. The blindfold made all her other senses heightened.

Out of nowhere, Eve slid a finger between Faith's lower lips. Faith gasped. Eve's other hand crept up the back of Faith's thigh, then forward to cup her breasts.

Faith kneeled there, held in place by the spreader bar, as Eve worked her body with a familiarity unlike anything else. She traced the pads of her fingers over the sensitive spot on Faith's neck that made her shiver, teased her nipples with the lightest of touches until they hardened into peaks, scratched her fingernails along Faith's skin, leaving stinging trails behind. With her other hand, she painted swirls around Faith's nub and glided her fingers over Faith's entrance in a way that was equal parts pleasurable and maddening. Faith sank into the darkness, letting Eve and all the sweet sensations Eve lavished her with wash over her.

She let out a strangled breath, her pleasure rising.

"Already?" Eve's honeyed voice was right next to Faith's ear. "I'm nowhere near done with you yet. If I let you come now, you'll have to come for me again, okay?"

Faith whimpered. "Yes." She didn't even know if that was even possible for her, but she was so desperate for release.

"You don't sound convinced." Eve planted a sharp slap on Faith's ass cheek, inflaming her even more. "If I say you'll come, you'll come. Your body belongs to me. Your mind belongs to me. Your pleasure belongs to me."

Faith shuddered. "Yes, Eve. I'm yours."

Suddenly, she felt something warm and wet against her folds, trailing down to her clit. Eve's tongue. Faith let out a moan, her arms almost buckling.

Eve grabbed on to Faith's ass cheeks, devouring her. It took only seconds before Faith reached the edge. A soundless cry erupted in her chest, her fingers gripping the sheets as an earth-shattering orgasm rocked her.

Eve eased off, brushing her lips between Faith's legs with the gentlest of touches. Even so, it was too intense for her sensitized bud. She hissed through her teeth but resisted the urge to edge away. And as Eve caressed Faith's body, her touch began to feel good again.

A soft murmur spilled from Faith's lips. The ache at the peak of her thighs had gone from satisfied to hollow.

"You see?" Eve took hold of Faith's hips. "You should have a little more faith in your Mistress's talents. I'm going to unravel you again in no time."

The bed rocked again. A moment later, something pressed against Faith's lower lips. It wasn't Eve's fingers. Not only was it more solid, but Eve's hands were firmly clutching Faith's hips.

Anticipation welled up inside her. Eve was wearing a strap-on.

Eve drew the tip of the strap-on up and down Faith's slit, rolling it over her clit. Faintly, Faith could feel vibrations emanating from it. They ramped up, resonating deep into her. She bit the inside of her cheek, trying to distract herself from the throbbing inside, waiting for Eve to give her what she craved.

Instead, Eve pulled away and flipped Faith onto her back, propping her up against the pillows and pushing the spreader bar up so that Faith's feet were in the air. With the blindfold on, Eve's rough movements were disorienting.

Before Faith had a chance to regain her bearings, she felt the tip of the strap-on against her once more. With the spreader bar keeping her legs forced apart, all it would take was one push for Eve to be inside her.

Faith drew in a long breath. Slowly, Eve buried herself deep, filling Faith completely. A groan rose from her chest, her body loosening. She grabbed on to the pillow above her head with one hand, the other reaching up to pull Eve closer to her. Eve pierced her over and over to a steady rhythm, the vibrations shooting straight into her core. She rolled her hips back against Eve, her restrained legs trying vainly to clench around the other woman's waist.

In the darkness, Faith felt Eve's cheek press against hers. She clutched blindly at Eve's neck, holding on against the tide of sensations that threatened to sweep her away, chanting Eve's name as she came closer and closer to oblivion.

"Oh, Eve!" Ecstasy surged through her, overwhelming all her senses. She threw her head back, arching up into Eve. At the same time, Eve trembled atop her in an orgasm that mirrored Faith's. Despite the tremors going through her, Faith kept rocking in time with Eve, drawing out both their pleasure.

As they came back down to earth together, Eve smothered

Faith's lips with her own in an endless kiss. Faith had fallen into that heavenly trance that only Eve seemed to be able to bring about in her.

Eve crawled down the bed to remove the spreader bar from Faith's ankles before kissing her way back up Faith's body.

"Don't think for a second that I'm done with you," Eve said. "I plan to take full advantage of the fact that we have the house to ourselves for the night." She stroked a hand down Faith's hair, letting her fingers trail over the blindfold. "And don't think I missed your slip up just now. You said my name, didn't you?"

Faith nodded, remembering Eve's command for silence far too late.

"I'm feeling generous." Eve drew Faith in close. "I'll let you have a few minutes before dealing with your little lapse. My riding crop could use a workout."

Faith sank into the other woman's arms and let out a blissful sigh. She was in for a long night. She couldn't think of anything she'd rather be doing with Eve.

She understood it now, what everything between them was about. There was a kind of freedom in submission. A power in embracing her vulnerability. A sweetness that came with surrendering to Eve, and an intimacy unlike anything else.

Eve removed the blindfold from Faith's eyes, but Faith didn't open them. The stillness between her and Eve was too precious to disturb.

EPILOGUE

EVE

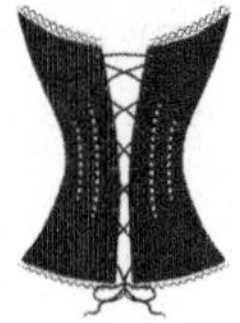

2 years later

Eve looked at the clock on the living room wall. Faith was due to arrive any minute now. The stage was set. The guests had arrived. All that was missing was the woman of the hour.

Down the hall, the front door opened. Faith and Lindsey's voices echoed through the house. The two of them had been out all day on a shopping trip to celebrate Faith's birthday. In reality, it was an excuse to get Faith out of the house so Eve could prepare for the night. As far as Faith knew, she and Eve were having a simple birthday dinner at home with Lindsey and Camilla. She had no idea that Eve had bigger plans.

"Eve?" Faith called down the hall. "I'm home."

"They're probably in the living room," Lindsey said innocently.

Faith and Lindsey's footsteps grew closer and closer, then stopped at the door.

"Let me get that for you," Lindsey said. A moment later, she slid the door to the living room open.

Two dozen voices rang out at once. "Happy Birthday!"

Faith's hand flew up to her chest. She stared wide-eyed around the room, scanning the faces looking back at her. Her eyes landed on Eve. "What's going on?"

"What do you think?" Eve said. "It's a surprise party."

Faith's mouth fell open. "How did you do everything without me noticing? How long have you been planning this?"

"Just a few months. Lindsey helped."

Faith glared at Lindsey, her hands on her hips. "So that's why you've been acting weird all day. I can't believe you kept this from me. Both of you."

"It wasn't easy," Eve said. "But it was worth it to see the look on your face just now."

"This is amazing." Faith looked around the room again. "There are so many people here."

Eve had sent out the invitations weeks earlier, and almost everyone she'd invited had shown up. There were a handful of Faith's classmates from college, and a few other people Lindsey had invited. Eve and Faith's mutual friends, including Lindsey and Camilla, Vanessa and her wife, and all the others they'd grown close to over the years. Vicki, the woman who had introduced Eve to Lilith's Den all these years ago, was here too, along with her girlfriend, although Vicki was no longer the womanizing playgirl she'd once been, having settled down long ago.

This was Faith's family now, all these people who loved her. It warmed Eve's heart that Faith had finally found that family she'd been so desperately searching for.

"Hannah?" Faith spotted her aunt, her eyes growing wide. "You're here."

Faith ran over to Hannah and threw her arms around her. It had been a long time since she and her aunt had last seen each other in person, so Eve had flown Hannah to the city just for the occasion. As for the rest of Faith's family, Faith never heard from her sister or anyone else again, but Hannah kept an eye on them and let Faith know they were okay now and then.

With the guest of honor in attendance, the party ramped up. As Faith greeted everyone, Eve helped herself to a drink and took a seat. It would take Faith a while to catch up with all her friends. Eve watched her bounce around the room. They'd both come a long way since that day Faith had turned up at Eve's house years ago.

It was Faith's house now too, although that was only a recent development. With the twins involved, she and Eve hadn't wanted to rush into anything. The fact that Eve kept Faith on as their nanny didn't make things easy. For the longest time, they'd hidden their relationship from the twins. It was the responsible thing to do. But as Leah and Ethan had grown older, it had become impossible for Eve and Faith to keep anything from them.

Fortunately, the twins were fully on board with the relationship. They loved Faith. Since Faith practically lived at the house anyway, it only made sense that she move in. It had been a bit of an adjustment, but Faith was a part of the family now. They hadn't made anything official. Faith was wary of marriage, given her history, and Eve wasn't in a rush to get married again. However, Eve fully intended to make Faith hers in her own way.

Lindsey and Camilla spotted Eve and came to sit down next to her.

"Thanks for your help today, Lindsey," Eve said. "I trust that keeping Faith occupied all day wasn't too difficult?"

"It was a breeze," Lindsey replied. "Although she did start to get suspicious in the afternoon. I had to distract her by asking her to be my maid of honor."

"I bet that worked like a charm," Eve said.

For someone who didn't want to get married, Faith sure liked weddings. When Lindsey and Camilla had announced their engagement a few months back, Faith had been giddy with excitement. But Faith had always been a contradiction of a woman, and Eve knew that, despite her experiences, Faith was a romantic at heart.

"Does that mean you've finally started planning the wedding?" Eve asked.

"Barely," Camilla said. "There's just so much to do."

Lindsey rolled her eyes. "Camilla is such a perfectionist. At this rate, the wedding is still years away."

"Now, everything worth doing is worth doing properly," Camilla said. “Speaking of weddings, I need to ask Vanessa who she used as her planner. They had such a lovely ceremony, don’t you think?”

Camilla spotted Vanessa nearby and waved to her. Vanessa grabbed her wife’s hand and drew her over to where Eve, Camilla, and Lindsey sat. Soon, they were deep in conversation about wedding planning. Eve excused herself and went to find Faith.

It was another hour before Faith and Eve were able to have a moment alone. Still brimming with excitement, Faith took Eve’s hand and pulled her out into the hall. The sounds of the party faded.

“Thanks for all this, Eve,” Faith said. “This is the best birthday present I could have ever asked for.”

“It’s my pleasure,” Eve said. “And the party isn’t the only present I have for you.” She held out a small box. “Here. Open it.”

Faith’s face lit up. She took the box from Eve, untied the ribbon, and opened it up. Inside was a silver eternity ring with rubies and emeralds all around the band. It was flashier than anything Eve would wear, but it suited Faith’s out-there style.

“It’s a ring,” Faith said.

“It’s not just a ring. It’s a promise.” Eve took Faith’s hand. “I know how you feel about marriage, but I wanted to give you something that says you’re mine. Something that says I’ll be here for you no matter what. Something that says forever.”

“Eve.” Faith eyes sparkled brighter than the ring. “It’s beautiful. I love it.” She wrapped her arms around Eve’s neck, drawing her into an embrace. “And just so you know, I’ve been reconsidering how I feel about marriage. With everyone around us getting married, all this wedding stuff, it’s kind of sweet. I still don’t know if I want to get married myself, but who knows? Maybe one day that will change.”

Eve smiled. “Either way, there’s one thing that will never change, and that’s the way I feel about you. I know I want to spend the rest of my life with you, and that’s all that matters.”

Eve kissed her softly, then took the ring out of the box and slipped it on Faith’s finger.

It was a perfect fit.

ABOUT THE AUTHOR

Anna Stone is the bestselling author of the Irresistibly Bound series. Her sizzling romance novels feature strong, complex, passionate women who love women. In every one of her books, you'll find off-the-charts heat and a guaranteed happily ever after.

Anna lives on the sunny east coast of Australia. When she isn't writing, she can usually be found with a coffee in one hand and a book in the other.

Visit annastoneauthor.com for information on her books and to sign up for her newsletter.

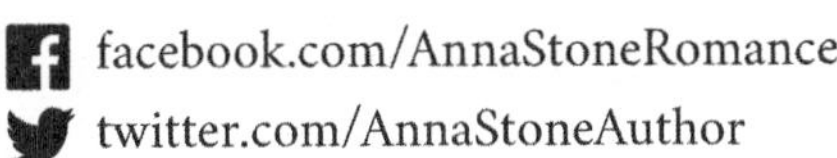